65

February 20 1679   Came Wm Reid of Dorchester County and proved his right to fifty acres of Land for transporting himself into this Province to inhabitt

eod die   Warrant then granted to Wm Reid of Dorchester County for fifty acres of Land due ut supra

eod die   Came James Colebourn Dorchester County and proved rights to five hundred Acres of Land for transporting himself Ann his wife, Elizabeth, Grace, Cohouro, Ann and Jane his Daughters, James his sonn, Thomas Brian and Dorothy Brian into this Province to inhabitt

eod die   Warrant then granted to James Colebourn of Dorchester County for five hundred acres of Land due ut supra

Elizabeth Harper —	Joseph Willson — —	Elizabeth Edwards —
Jasper Gooding — —	John Causon — —	Mary Edwards —
Ralph Hastings —	George Maddox —	Mary Edwards —
Roger Hambleton —	Jno. Hinton — — —	Charles Bulley —
David Hambleton —	Robert Roberson —	Wittn Hinton —
David Howes — —	James Mitchell —	Xbpher Watters —

eod die   Came John Edwards Merchant and proved rights to three hundred Acres of Land due ut supra

Shipt on board the Virginia ffactor by Mr Henry Rowlett Merchant five servants named Robert Browne Jur: Dorothy, Ann Ezard, Elizabeth Hentry, Elizabeth Slaby, which servants I doe hereby give my interest of their rights of Land unto John Edwards Maryland planter as witness my hand this one and thirtieth day of January 1679

eod die   Came Henry Rowlett Merchant and proved rights to two hundred and fifty Acres of Land due ut supra

I Henry Rowlett Merchant doe hereby assigne over unto John Edwards Merchant his heires and assignes all my right, title and interest of in and to ye above mentioned five rights to Land witness my hand february 2d 1679/80   Henry Rowlett

test
Nicholas Painter

eod die —   Warrant then granted to John Edwards of Ann arundell County for Eleven hundred and fifty acres of Land due ut supra

July 1st 1679   Warrant then granted to Lewis Blangy of Kent County for one hundred acres of Land due by renewing of a warrant for ye same quantity granted him ye 20th day of April anno 1677

Entries of proofs of rights to land and warrants granted to persons who transported themselves or other persons to settle in Maryland. Recorded in Patents Liber W.C. No. 2, folio 65.

THE
EARLY SETTLERS OF
MARYLAND

An Index to Names of Immigrants Compiled from
Records of Land Patents, 1633-1680, in the
Hall of Records, Annapolis, Maryland

Edited, With an Introduction

BY GUST SKORDAS
Assistant Archivist State of Maryland

and

A Foreword By

DR. MORRIS L. RADOFF
*Archivist and Records Administrator
State of Maryland*

INTRODUCTION

I. HISTORY OF THE RECORDS

The Charter of Maryland granted to Cecilius Calvert, the first Lord Baltimore, on June 20, 1632, established a proprietary form of government. This meant that Cecilius owned all of the land within the boundaries of the colony. The land was of little value without someone to live on it and work it, so as an incentive to settlement, he proclaimed in 1633, even before the first vessel had left for Maryland, the first of his several Conditions of Plantation. Under the terms of these Conditions, he offered certain amounts of land to those who furnished their own transportation or who provided for the passage of others to Maryland. New Conditions were issued from time to time, but except for a gradual reduction in the quantity of land offered, they remained basically the same.

The early officials of the Province were charged with a variety of responsibilities, so it is not surprising that they found it convenient to enter the records created in the performance of these duties in the same volume. Thus, in the volumes now designated as Patents Libers 1, 2 and 3, the searcher will find legislative, court and probate proceedings as well as entries relating to the granting of land. All the other volumes to which this index refers, are devoted exclusively to land matters.

For the first few years, the patenting of land was handled by the Governor and Council along with all the other business of the Colony. However, in 1637, John Lewger, a member of the Council, was appointed Secretary of the Province. His responsibility included the keeping and recording of the acts and proceedings of the Lieutenant General, as the Governor was then called, and his Council. This, of course, included proceedings relating to the granting of land.

Typically, the procedure for taking up land under the Conditions of Plantation was for the applicant to appear before the Secretary of the Province and claim a certain number of acres of land for transporting himself and other persons to Maryland. He was required to name each of the persons he had transported. The Secretary then issued a warrant to the Surveyor directing him to lay out and survey the specified quantity of land for the applicant and return the certificate of survey to the Secretary's office. The certificate named the person for whom the survey was made, described the boundaries of the land and gave the total acreage of the tract. If the certificate was made out in proper form and there were no conflicting claims, a patent was issued granting the land described in the certificate to the applicant. The patent was dated, sealed with the great seal of the Province and signed by the Governor, acting for Lord Baltimore in whose name the land was granted.

The Secretary retained this responsibility and the records associated with it until 1680 when the office of Register of the Land Office was established to perform this function. At the same time, the practice of granting free land under the Conditions of Plantation was discontinued. The records in the Secretary's office pertaining to lands were turned over to the custody of John Llewellin, the newly-appointed Register. A list of the records received by Llewellin is recorded in Warrants Liber 3, folio 0. This list is of more than casual interest as it includes, with the exception of Liber Z, all of the originals of the records covered by this index.

In 1716, the General Assembly appointed several commissioners to examine and have repaired the records of the Province (Bacon's Laws Ch. 1, 1716). The Patent records had been subjected to hard usage and so between 1717 and 1727 every volume dating in the period covered by this index was transcribed. The transcripts were certified and placed on the shelves as the official copies; the originals were stored away. Any index prepared thereafter referred to the transcripts and not to the originals.

These records remained in the official custody of the Land Office and accompanied the Land Office in its peregrinations from one location to another which eventually brought it to the Hall of Records building in 1935. There the Land Office remained until 1958 when the Office and its records were removed to the newly-erected State Office Building in Annapolis, where the records are at present writing. In 1966, the Land Office was abolished and its duties and records assigned to the Archivist and the Hall of Records Commission (Ch. 488 and 489, 1966). By the time this book appears in print, the records will have been returned to the Hall of Records Building.

Meanwhile the eighteenth century transcripts were beginning to show signs of deterioration. This time the laborious and tedius process of copying them by hand was rendered unnecessary by the development of the Photostat camera. About 1915, the Land Office acquired a camera and began producing bound photostat copies which were used to replace the worn transcripts. The only volumes not photocopied were Libers 15, Part 1 and 15, Part 2, which were transcripts made in 1836.

During the period when the Land Office was in the Hall of Records Building, Dr. Morris L. Radoff, the Archivist, became concerned about the condition of its records and offered the Commissioner of the Land Office the use of the repair equipment and facilities of the Hall of Records Commission, the only requirement being that the Office furnish its own labor and supplies. As a result, the transcripts were laminated, rebound and returned to the shelves in place of the photocopies. The only photocopy now in use is Liber 16, apparently because the transcript was considered too damaged to be reparable.

II. DESCRIPTION OF THE RECORDS

This book is an index to the names of the early settlers of Maryland that are found in the first twenty-four volumes of the Patent series. In the descriptive list of these records that follows, it will be observed that each volume has two reference numbers. The volume number is useful to the staff members in returning the books to their proper location on the shelves, but serves little purpose otherwise.

It is the liber number that identifies the volume for record purposes. Thus all references in this index are to the liber number. With one exception, the volumes listed are transcripts, so it was considered useful to give the date when the copy was made. The dates of the original records are given in parentheses immediately following the liber title.

Vol. 0   Patents Liber W. C. No. 2 (1679-81).   Original.
           A transcript of this volume was made in 1726. A photo-copy of the transcript is now designated as Warrants Liber 2.

Vol. 1   Patents Liber 1.   Transcript, completed 1724.
           Folios 1-161 copied from Liber F (1640-43) folios 1-176. Folios 162-640 copied from Liber B (1651-58) folios 4-48, 29-243.
           Original Libers F and B are now missing.

Vol. 2   Patents Liber 2.   Transcript, completed 1725.
           Folios 1-190 copied from Liber Z (1637-44) folios 1-164. Folios 191-626 copied from Liber A (1647-51) folios 57-340.

Vol. 3   Patents Liber 3.   Transcript, completed 1726.
           Folios 1-132 copied from Liber A (1647-51) folios 340-397. Folios 133-339 copied from Liber B (1651-58) folios 243-387. Folios 339-342 copied from Liber B (1651-58) folios 188-189. Folios 343-448 copied from Liber B (1651-58) no folio reference.

Vol. 4   Patents Liber AB&H.   Transcript, completed 1717.
           Folios 1-57 copied from Liber A (1647-51) folios 59-390 (land entries only). Folios 57-104 copied from Liber F (1640-43) folios 28-152 (land entries only). Folios 105-436 copied from Liber H (1650-55) no folio reference. Folio 437 copied from Liber L (1656-57) no folio reference. Original Libers H and L are now missing. Note that the proper liber designation should have been AF&H.

Vol. 5   Patents Liber Q.   Transcript, completed 1717.
           Folios 1-480 copied from Liber Q (1658) no marginal references. Folios 155-310 (equivalent to folios 216-480 of the transcript) of the original Liber Q have been preserved, but are in a badly damaged condition. The earlier folios are missing.

Vol. 6   Patents Liber 4.   Transcript, completed 1725.
           Folios 1-540 copied from Liber R (1659) folios 1-211. Folios 541-627 copied from Liber X (1661-63) folios 1-88. Liber R has double folios; the transcript contains no marginal references to the first thirteen folios. Original Liber X is now designated as Warrants Liber 1.

Vol. 7   Patents Liber 5.   Transcript, completed 1726.
           Folios 1-343 copied from Liber X (1661-63) folios 88-429. Folios 344-639 copied from Liber AA (1663-64) folios 1-302.

Vol. 8   Patents Liber 6.   Transcript, completed 1726. Folios 1-347 copied from Liber AA (1663-64) folios 302-532.

Vol. 9   Patents Liber 7.   Transcript, completed 1725. Folios 1-640 copied from Liber CC (1664-65) folios 1-720.

Vol. 10   Patents Liber 8.   Transcript, completed 1726. Folios 1-472 copied from Liber DD (1665) folios 1-520. Folios 475-518 copied from Liber CC (1664-65) folios 720-828.

Vol. 11   Patents Liber 9.   Transcript, completed 1726. Folios 1-516 copied from Liber EE (1665-66) folios 1-518.

Vol. 12   Patents Liber 10.   Transcript, completed 1725. Folios 1-541 copied from Liber FF (1666-67) folios 1-571. Folios 547-638 copied from Liber GG (1667-68) folios 1-70. Liber 10 was bound into two volumes after it was laminated.

Vol. 13   Patents Liber 11.   Transcript, completed 1725. Folios 1-586 copied from Liber GG (1667-68) folios 70-548.

Vol. 14   Patents Liber 12.   Transcript, completed 1725. Folios 1-417 copied from Liber HH (1668-69) folios 1-508. Folios 418-638 copied from Liber JJ (1668-71) folios 1-314.

Vol. 15   Patents Liber 13.   Transcript, completed 1726. Folios 1-133 copied from Liber JJ (1668-71) folios 315-540.

Vol. 16   Patents Liber 14.   Transcript, completed 1726. Folios 1-550 copied from Liber KK (1669-72) folios 1-501.

Vol. 17   Now vacant. It appears likely that this number was at one time assigned to the 1726 transcript of Liber LL, which has pasted at the top of its spine a small canvas tab with the number "17" stamped on it.

Vol. 18   Patents Liber 15 Part 1.   Transcript, completed 1836. From a transcript made in 1726 from original Liber LL (1673-79) folios 1-464 = 1726 copy, folios 1-344 = original Liber LL, folios 1-457. Note: References in the Index to Early Settlers refer to the page numbers of the 1726 copy. In the 1836 copy, these numbers are shown in the margin with the word "Folio" stamped in red ink above them.

Vol. 18A   Patents Liber 15 Part 2.   (See description above). Folios 465-909 = 1726 copy, folios 344-614 = original Liber LL, folios 458-913.

Vol. 19   Patents Liber 16.   Transcript, completed 1726. Folios 1-640 copied from Liber WT (1670-73) folios 1-673. A photocopy of the transcript is now on the shelf for reference purposes.

Vol. 20   Patents Liber 17.   Transcript, completed 1726.

Folios 1-240 copied from Liber WT (1670-73) folios 674-901. Folios 245-638 copied from Liber MM (1672-75) folios 1-536.

Vol. 21   Patents Liber 18.   Transcript, completed 1726. Folios 1-387 copied from Liber MM (1672-75) folios 537-893.

Vol. 22   Patents Liber 19.   Transcript, completed 1726. Folios 1-638 copied from Liber WC (1675-80) folios 1-500.

Vol. 23   Patents Liber 20.   Transcript, completed 1727. Folios 1-412 copied from Liber WC (1675-80) folios 500-899.

III. USING THE INDEX

As has been previously indicated, this is a selective index. It refers to the names of persons who came into Maryland with the intent of settling there, whether they furnished their own transportation or whether someone else provided it. There are a few instances, however, where the person indexed claimed the right to take up land by virtue of the fact that he had furnished the transportation of others to the Colony, but apparently did not intend to stay himself.

Liber and folio, of course, are the Latin words for book and page.

Certain words that recur frequently in the "Remarks" column have a special meaning as used in this index. "Immigrated," means the individual furnished his own transportation to Maryland, while "transported" means that someone other than the person indexed paid for his passage. Quite often a person "transported" is also described as a "servant," which means that he had contracted to repay the cost of his transportation by agreeing to act as a servant for a period of years. Under certain of the Conditions of Plantation, a servant was entitled to claim fifty acres of land upon completing his period of servitude satisfactorily. Such claims are indicated by the word "service."

Gust Skordas
Assistant Archivist
State of Maryland

Annapolis, Maryland
February, 1968

THE EARLY SETTLERS OF MARYLAND

NAME	Liber	Folio	REMARKS
Abbett, Edward	12	213	Transported 1668.
Abbett, Elizabeth	9	21	" 1665.
Abbett, Jane	8	89	" 1665.
Abbett, Samuel, Sr.	8	89	" 1665.
Abbett, Samuel, Jr.	8	89	" 1665.
Abbett, Thomas	2	511	" about 1649.
Abbot, Michael	12	386	Service 1669.
Abbot, Samuel	16	136	Transported 1671.
Abbott, Elizabeth	10	392	" 1666.
Abbott, Deborah	4	68	" 1651 – daughter of Simon.
Abbott, George	12	478	Transported 1670.
Abbott, John	18	137	" 1674.
Abbott, Mary	WC2	112	" 1679.
Abbott, Maudlin	4	68	" 1651 – wife of Simon.
Abbott, Richard	9	270	" 1665.
Abbott, Samuel	15	377	Of St. Mary's Co., Service, 1676.
Abbott, Simon	4	68	Transported 1651.
Abbott, Thomas	18	280	" 1675.
Abbotts, John	1	90	Petition to confirm title to land. Of Isle of Kent, 1640.
Abchurch, John	4	3	Transported 1657.
Abdee, John	16	17	Immigrated 1670.
Abell, Charles	13	1	Servant - Transported 1669.
Abell, Gartrick	11	105	Transported 1667 - child of Hendrick.
Abell, Hendrick	11	105	Of Somerset County - cordwainer. Immigrant 1667.
Abell, James	8	129	Of Baltimore County - Transported 1664.
Abell, Joseph	11	104	Servant. Transported 1667.
Abell, Macklett	11	105	Transported 1667 - child of Hendrick.
Abell, Robert	17	463	Transported 1673.
Abell, Sophia	11	105	" 1667 - wife of Hendrick.
Abery, William	12	472	Transported 1670.
Abington, Andrew	WC2	258	Immigrated 1678. Of St. Mary's County.
Abington, Andrew	21	207	Of the halfway house in St. Mary's Co., gent. - Commission from Vincent Love, Surveyor General, as Deputy Surveyor of part of St. Mary's Co., 1680.
Abington, John	WC2	406,407	Rights 1676-1680. Of London. Merchant.
Abington, Mr. John	ABH	199	Immigrated 1650.
Abington, John, Gent.	5	182	Warrant to keep an Indian and to hunt wild cattle, 1662.
Abington, Jone	17	463	Transported 1673.
Abington, Richard	7	79	" 1664 by Mr. John

NAME	Liber	Folio	REMARKS
			Abington.
Abington, Thomas	WC2	406	Transported 1677.
Abington, Thomas	15	454	" 1677.
Abott, Michael	Q	431	" 1658.
Abrahall, Richard	Q	323	" 1655-8.
Abraham, Charles	16	471	Of Talbot Co., Service, March, 1670.
Abraham, Corn.	21	139	Servant - Transported 1650.
			(Quaker ?)
Abraham, Eleanor	5	492	Transported 1659.
Abraham, Hugh	17	596	" 1673.
Abraham, Isaac	5	214	" 1658.
Abraham, Mary	17	596	" 1673.
Abraham, Nicholas	WC2	114	" 1680. Servant.
Abrahams, Elizabeth	10	500	" prior to 1667.
Abrahams, Henry	4	553	" 1661.
Abrahams, John	12	378	" 1669.
Abrahamson, Cornelius	ABH	140	" 1651 - on folio 141 of

Liber is described as an immigrant and designated as of "Patuxent River".

NAME	Liber	Folio	REMARKS
Abram, Morgan	9	216	Transported 1665.
Abrams, John	12	584	" 1670.
Abramson, Frances	Q	204	Service 1658.
Abridge, Jacob	17	567	Transported 1673.
Acan, Thomas	16	400	" 1671.
Acherly, Thomas	17	418	Immigrated 1672.
Acheson, Susan	6	123	Married Patrick Cannell in 1663.
Acheson, Thomasin	11	581	Transported 1668.
Ackrick, George & wife	ABH	14	" 1647.
Ackworth, Ann	15	398	Widow of Richard - married James
			Witherly prior to 1677.
Ackworth, Richard, Jr.	17	34	Transported in 1672 by Richard of
			Somerset Co.
Acreeke, George	2	248	Immigrated 1646 with wife.
Acreeke, George & wife	ABH	4	" 1646.
Acres, John	18	35	Transported 1672.
Acres, Margaret	4	204	" 1659.
Acres, William	3	173	" 1655.
Acroyd, William	15	376	" 1676.
Acton, Richard	5	415	Immigrated prior to 1658.
Acworth, Richard	5	125	" 1662.
Adames, William	WC2	406	Transported 1678.
Adams, Ann	15	432	" 1677 - daughter of
			Somer Adams.
Adams, Charity	Q	431	Transported 1653.
Adams, Charity	10	433	" 1666.
Adams, David	18	166	" 1674.
Adams, Edward	18	160	" 1674.
Adams, Eleanor	9	35	" 1664.
Adams, Elizabeth	15	432	" 1677. Wife of Somer
			Adams.
Adams, Francis	4	72	Transported 1658.

NAME	Liber	Folio	REMARKS
Adams, Francis	16	407	Of Charles Co. and Grace, his wife - Service 1671.
Adams, George	Q	29	Son of James - Immigrated 1677.
Adams, Hannah	15	432	Daughter of Somer - Transported 1677.
Adams, Henry	1	18	Transported 1638.
Adams, Henry	2	444	" 1639. Servant.
Adams, Henry	ABH	12	Servant, 1639.
Adams, Henry	ABH	377	Immigrated 1646.
Adams, Isabell	Q	29	" 1658. Daughter of James.
Adams, James	Q	29	Immigrated 1658.
Adams, Jane	16	469	Transported 1667.
Adams, Joane	10	637	" 1667. Wife of John, daughter of same name.
Adams, John	Q	29	Son of James, Immigrated 1658.
Adams, John	9	439	Transported 1664.
Adams, John	10	637	Of Talbot Co. Immigrated 1667.
Adams, John	16	469	Transported 1667.
Adams, John	16	78	" 1670.
Adams, John	15	540	" 1667.
Adams, Margaret	Q	29	Wife of James. Immigrated 1658.
Adams, Margaret	Q	29	Daughter of James. Immigrated 1658.
Adams, Margaret	16	115	Transported 1675.
Adams, Margaret	15	516	" 1678.
Adams, Margarett	WC2	320	" 1680.
Adams, Mary	5	262	" 1663.
Adams, Mary	15	446	" 1678.
Adams, Mary	15	517	" 1678.
Adams, Matthew	17	457	And Ann his wife, Service 1673.
Adams, Morgan	15	432	Son of Somer. Transported 1677.
Adams, Peter	15	432	Son of Somer. Transported 1677.
Adams, Philip	6	255	Transported 1663.
Adams, Philip	7	614	" 1665.
Adams, Philip	15	319	" 1675.
Adams, Richard	8	502	" 1665.
Adams, Richard	9	157	" 1665.
Adams, Richard	12	282	Service 1667.
Adams, Richard	12	270	" 1668.
Adams, Somer	15	432	Transported 1677.
Adams, Thomas	1	95	Rights 1640.
Adams, Thomas, Gent.	ABH	89	Immigrated 1635.
Adams, William	4	140	(Transported) Servant 1653. (Quaker ?)
Adamson, Evan	6	90	Transported 1663.
Adamson, John	15	442	" 1677.
Adcocke, Henry	WC2	21	" 1679.
Adcroft, Davy	3	17	" prior to 1650.
Adcroft, Davy	ABH	44	" many years prior to 1650.

NAME	Liber	Folio	REMARKS
Addams, Eleanor	17	408	Transported 1673.
Addens, Charles	6	10	" 1663.
Addens, Charles	7	461	" 1664.
Addeson, Katherine	9	269	" 1665.
Addick, Grace	5	516	" 1658.
Addick, James	5	516	" 1658.
Addick, Joane	5	516	" 1658.
Addick, William	5	516	" 1658.
Addinall, Philip	WC2	21, 22	" 1679.
Addison, Katherine	10	259	" 1665.
Adenbrooke, Edward	6	42	Of London, Merchant, Special Warrant for a "Mannor" of 100 Acres in Maryland, August 26, 1663.
Aderton, William	15	556	Immigrated 1675.
Adgett, Cicilly	5	64	Transported 1662.
Adgett, Margery	5	64	" 1662.
Adins, Charles	10	598	Immigrated 1667.
Adison, John	WC2	309	" 1680. Of St. Mary's County.
Adison, John	18	280	Transported 1675.
Adkins, Sampson	15	526	Immigrated 1678.
Adkison, Ellinor	WC2	13	Transported 1679.
Adkison, Sampson	WC2	13	Immigrated 1679. Of Somerset Co.
Adley, Hugh	18	160	Transported 1674.
Adrewes, Edward	16	109	" 1671. (See Andrewes).
Adrus, George	12	190	" 1668.
Agar, Thomas	4	551	" 1661.
Agent, John	17	610	" 1673.
Ager, Robert	18	335	" 1675.
Agley, Joane	17	452	" 1671.
Agnew, Aud.	18	152	" 1674.
Agus, Elizabeth	Q	204	" 1651.
Aharon, Derm'd	15	567	" 1679.
Ahagh, Catherine	20	184	" from Ireland 1678.
Aheygood, Thomas	Q	18	" 1655.
Aikenbocke, Alexander	11	441	" 1668.
Ainsworth, Hester	WC2	23	" 1679. Servant.
Ainsworth, Susanna	15	408	Wife of George. Service 1677.
Akell, Isabell	16	411	Transported 1671.
Akericke, George	2	457	Immigrated 1647 with wife.
Akers, John	17	448	Transported 1673.
Akeyne, Joseph	5	234	Cooper. Immigrated 1662.
Akith, George	9	69	Transported 1660-'5.
Akroid, Henry	WC2	21	" 1679.
Akyngs, Amy	18	166	" 1674.
Alanson, Thomas	4	217	Of London. Special Warrant for 1000 Acres, 1659, renewment of one dated 1658.
Alben, South	8	501	Transported 1665.
Albrims, Lucas	Q	63	Immigrated 1658.
Alchurch, Christian	16	532	Transported 1668-70.
Alcock, Elizabeth	12	403	" 1669.
Alcock, John	9	34	" 1665.

NAME	Liber	Folio	REMARKS
Alcock, John	16	507	Transported 1671.
Alcock, Isaac	8	503	" 1665.
Alcock, Isaac	12	457	Of St. Mary's Co. - Service 1669.
Alcock, Violet	9	488	Transported 1665.
Alcome, Mr. John	ABH	65	" 1633.
Alcorne, Andrew	15	525	Planter. Service 1678.
Alder, Henry	Q	219	Transported 1653.
Alder, James	6	128	" 1657.
Alder, Mary	16	411	" 1671.
Alderton, Isaac	11	294	Of Virginia. Cond. Warrant for
3000 Acres in Maryland, 1668.			
Aldeson, George	5	416	Immigrated 1663.
Aldred, Henry	15	520	Service 1664.
Aldred, Mary	15	520	Immigrated 1662 - now 1677. Wife of Henry.
Aldredge, Theophilus	5	56	Transported 1660.
Aldredge, Thomas	17	192	" 1662.
Aldren, Mary	WC2	402	" 1680.
Aldrich, Peter	17	567	Immigrated 1673.
Aldridge, Ja.	15	397	Transported 1676.
Aldridge, Jane	15	332	" 1675.
Aldridge, George	6	171	" 1663.
Aldsworth, John	10	605	" 1667.
Aldwell, John	10	277	" 1666.
Aldwell, Thomas	15	380	Of Calvert Co. Immigrated 1676.
Aldwell, Thomas	15	412	Service 1677.
Aldworth, William	15	454	Transported 1677.
Alibone, Thomas	9	156	Immigrated prior to 1660.
Alenby, Philip	Q	71	Transported 1657.
Alett, Elizabeth	5	125	" 1662.
Alewood, Will	15	516	" 1676.
Alexander, A---	6	218	Son in law of Lawrence Symond. Transported 1663.
Alexander, Charles	6	307	Transported 1664.
Alexander, Henry	Q	317	" 1658.
Alexander, James	15	553	" 1678.
Alexander, John	20	185	" 1679.
Alexander, Thomas	8	502	" 1665.
Alexander, Thomas	10	606,618	Immigrated 1667.
Alford, Ann	15	422	Transported 1665.
Alford, Anne	8	30	" 1665. Daughter of John.
Alford, Elizabeth	8	30	Transported 1665. Wife of John.
Alford, Elizabeth	8	30	" 1665. Daughter of John.
Alford, Elizabeth	15	422	Transported 1665.
Alford, Elizabeth	15	358	" 1676.
Alford, John	8	30	Immigrated 1665.
Alford, John, Jr.	15	422	Transported 1665.
Alford, John	15	350	Of Little Choptank River. Planter h--- in 1676.

NAME	Liber	Folio	REMARKS
Alford, Rachel	15	358	Transported 1676.
Alfred, Moses	15	356	" 1675.
Alicast, John	7	107	" 1660.
Alice, Edward	11	337	" 1668.
Alice, Mary	11	337	" 1668.
Alice, ----	5	268	A Welch Maid, transported 1663.
Aling, John	Q	430	Transported 1658.
Aling, Solomon	Q	430	" 1658.
Aliston, Elizabeth	5	88	" 1661.
Alkemore, John	4	553	" 1661.
Allanson, John	5	339	" 1663.
Allanson, Mary	5	240	Wife of Thomas. Transported 1662.
Allark, Elizabeth	15	454	Transported 1677.
Allbretton, Thomas	Q	443	" 1658.
Allcock, Samuel	5	514	" 1649.
Allcock, Violetta	5	514	Wife of Samuel. Transported 1657.
Allder, William	5	367	Transported 1663.
Alldridge, Henry	4	538	" 1659.
Aldridge, William	4	59	" 1649-52.
Allebone, Edward	WC2	412	" 1681.
Allebone, Thomas	Q	204	" 1651.
Allee, Elizabeth	17	396	" 1671.
Allen, Ann	12	393	" 1669.
Allen, Anne	WC2	309	" 1678.
Allen, Bar.	15	353	" 1676.
Allen, Edward	12	356	" 1669.
Allen, Edward	6	293	" 1664.
Allen, Elizabeth	4	5	" 1652-9.
Allen, Elizabeth	5	515	" 1660.
Allen, Florence	5	238	" 1662.
Allen, Giles	ABH	198	Immigrated 1651.
Allen, Henry	16	530	Transported 1672.
Allen, James	WC2	406	" 1677.
Allen, James	Q	199	" 1651.
Allen, James	ABH	310	" 1652.
Allen, James	6	62	" 1663.
Allen, James	16	482	" 1670-1.
Allen, James	15	318	" 1674. Of Virginia.
Allen, James	15	454	" 1677.
Allen, Jasper	5	268	" 1663.
Allen, Jasper	11	377	Of Calvert Co. Service 1668.
Allen, John	WC2	259,260	Immigrated 1667.
Allen, John	ABH	201	Transported 1650-1.
Allen, John	4	188	" 1659. Servant.
Allen, John	10	564	" 1667.
Allen, John	11	379	" 1668.
Allen, John	12	190	" 1668. Servant.
Allen, John	16	95	" 1670.
Allen, John	15	143	Of Maryland, Gent. Special War-

rant from Lord Baltimore for 2000 Acres, dated 1672, which John
Allen conveyed to Gov. Charles Calvert.

NAME	Liber	Folio	REMARKS
Allen, John	15	353	Transported 1676.
Allen, Joseph	WC2	352	" 1680.
Allen, Katherine	9	487	" 1665.
Allen, Mary	10	4	" 1665.
Allen, Mary	10	291	" 1666. Wife of Richard.
Allen, Mary	18	160	" 1674.
Allen, Patrick	4	212	" 1659.
Allen, Patrick	5	248	" 1663.
Allen, Richard	6	130	" 1656.
Allen, Richard	4	14	" 1658.
Allen, Richard	9	84	" 1663.
Allen, or Fitz Allen, Richard	9	191-2	Immigrated prior to 1665.
Allen, Richard	10	291	" 1666.
Allen, Richard	12	391	Transported 1669.
Allen, Robert	15	416	" 1677.
Allen, Thomas	1	121	" 1633.
Allen, Thomas	1	71-72	Gift of 50 Acres from Leonard Calvert 1640.
Allen, Thomas	1	92-93	Petition to confirm title to land granted by Capt. William Clayborne, 1640.
Allen, Thomas	ABH	98	Transported 1633. Servant.
Allen, Thomas	ABH	198	" 1651.
Allen, Thomas	Q	115	Son of Thomas, deceased prior to 1656.
Allen, Thomas	8	39	Transported 1662.
Allen, Thomas	8	128	" 1664. Servant, Baltimore Co.
Allen, Thomas	9	188	Transported 1665.
Allen, Thomas	15	438	" Oct. 1677.
Allen, Thomas	17	513	Of Baltimore Co. - Service 1673.
Allen, William	WC2	217	Transported 1680.
Allen, William	Q	115	Son of Thomas, died prior to 1656.
Allen, William	9	374	Service 1666.
Allen, William	18	38	" 1673.
Allenby, Jacob	5	417	Transported 1663.
Allenby, William	5	417	" 1663.
Allensby, Philip	5	489	Service 1662.
Alley, John	15	524	Transported 1678.
Alley, Sarah	17	395	" 1672.
Alleyne, Rebecca	10	558	" 1665. Servant.
Allford, Elizabeth	11	230	" 1667, by Walter Hall of St. Mary's Co., Gent.
Allibaster, Thomas	9	28	Transported 1664.
Allife, Joseph	WC2	320	" 1680.
Allin, Easter	15	454	" 1677.
Alline, John	15	453	" 1675-7.
Alling, William	15	360	" 1676.
Allison, Penelope	15	397	Of St. Mary's Co. Immigrated 1677.
Allison, Sarah	4	11	Transported 1659. Servant.
Allison, William	18	174	" 1674.

8

NAME	Liber	Folio	REMARKS
Allity, Edward	11	141	Transported 1668. Servant.
Allity, Edward, Jr.	11	141	" 1668.
Allkins, George	5	260	" 1662.
Allom, Nicholas	4	53	" 1659.
Allome, Nicholas	10	599	" 1667.
Allott, Elizabeth	WC2	73	" 1665.
Allsupp, George	Q	443	" 1658.
Allwood, Edward	5	86	Immigrated 1662.
Allwood, Sarah	16	507	Transported 1671.
Alman, Joseph	17	407	" 1673.
Alsop, Christopher	6	87	" 1649.
Altam, Jo.	1	166	" 1633. (See Althem, Altome).
Althem, Mr. John	1	19	Transported 1633. (See Altome, Altam).
Altome, Mr. John	1	37	Transported 1633. (See Althem, Altam).
Altrop, ---	18	137	Transported 1674.
Alvey, Joseph	Q	18	Servant 1657.
Alvey, Joseph	11	103	Of St. Mary's Co. and Elizabeth his wife, Service 1667.
Alvey, Pope	12	550	Of St. Mary's Co. Immigrated 1670.
Alworth, William	WC2	406	Transported 1677.
Alyworth, Sarah	15	413	" 1677.
Amark, Ellinor	WC2	406	" 1677.
Ambre, Thomas	7	567	" 1657. Servant.
Ambrosier, Anne	WC2	182	Service 1680.
Ameler, Humphrey	15	503	Transported 1678.
Amite, Elizabeth	15	514	" 1677.
Ammerson, Cornelius	Q	370	Immigrated (?) 1658.
Amore, Marrice	8	381	Transported 1665.
Amos, Michael	18	305	Of St. Mary's Co. Service 1675, or prior 15, 310.
Amsley, Elizabeth	11	581	Transported 1668.
Analy, Walter	4	585	Immigrated 1661.
Ancill, Robert	6	294	" 1664.
And, Thomas	18	167	Transported 1674.
Anderson, Amy	4	4	" 1659. Daughter of Nicholas Waddylove.
Anderson, Au.	5	530	Transported 1662.
Anderson, Christopher	6	89	" 1663.
Anderson, Cornelius	WC2	141-142	Immigrated 1679.
Anderson, Elizabeth	16	505	Transported 1665.
Anderson, Elizabeth	9	336	" 1666.
Anderson, Elizabeth	15	422	" 1669.
Anderson, Frederick	10	312	" 1666 (?).
Anderson, George	15	429	" 1674.
Anderson, Hane	10	312	" 1666 (?).
Anderson, Henry	5	530	" 1662.

NAME	Liber	Folio	REMARKS
Ball, Thomas	7	639	Immigrated 1665.
Ball, Thomas	12	189	Transported 1668.
Ball, William	WC2	38	Immigrated 1662. Of Baltimore Co.
Ball, William	4	54	" prior to July 1659.
Ball, William	6	124	" from Virginia 1663.
Ballard, Charles	7	601	" 1665.
Ballard, Charles	12	413	Transported 1669.
Ballard, Charles	14	374	Of Somerset Co. Gent. Married

Sarah, widow of Thomas Jordeyne prior to 1671.

NAME	Liber	Folio	REMARKS
Ballard, Christopher	6	128	Immigrated 1649.
Ballard, George	6	142	Transported 1656.
Ballard, Gerrard	12	406	" 1669.
Ballard, Thomas	15	376	" 1676.
Balldine, Mary	12	215	" 1668-9.
Balldine, Robert	12	215	" 1668-9.
Ballen, Elizabeth	15	564	" 1673.
Ballestone, Thomas	4	581	" 1661.
Balley, Alexander	17	635	" 1674.
Balley, John,	17	615	Of St. Mary's Co. Immigrated 1662.
Ballieff, Rose	15	565	Transported 1679.
Balmer, Ann	ABH	141	" 1651. Wife of Thomas.
Balmer, Thomas	ABH	141	Immigrated 1651. Of Patuxent River.
Balshaw, Susanna	18	137	Transported 1674.
Balson, John	18	291	" 1674.
Baltch, John	6	89	Immigrated 1658.
Baltestall, Yerick	7	135	Transported 1664.
Baltimore, Lord	7	559	A list of his Manors in the various

counties, 1665, ditto, 1660, 10, fol. 328. Lands reserved for his use 1673, 15, fol. 202, 203. List of his lands 1673, 15, fol. 293.

NAME	Liber	Folio	REMARKS
Balton, John	6	235	Transported 1663.
Baly, John	WC2	167,169, 230	" 1680.
Baly, Richard	15	422	Service 1677 (15, fol. 429).
Banck, George	3	24	Transported 1650. Servant.
Banckes, Charles	15	455	Of Kent Co. Service 1668.
Bancks, George & Eady	17	496	Service 1673.
Bancks, Nicholas	12	283	Transported 1668.
Bancks, Nicholas	18	25	Of Baltimore Co. Service 1674.
Bancks, William	16	532	Transported 1668-70.
Bancomb, Alice	11	372	" 1668. Wife of Peter.
Bancomb, Peter	11	372	Immigrated 1668. Of Talbot Co.
Bancraft, Thomas	18	144	Of St. Mary's Co. Service 1674.
Bancroft, Alice	ABH	273	Transported 1651. Daughter of

Elizabeth, wife of William Chaplin.

NAME	Liber	Folio	REMARKS
Bancroft, Alice	Q	211	Transported 1658.
Bancroft, J---	15	357	" 1676.
Band, Hatton	5	243	" 1662.
Bandall, Thomas	15	398	" 1676.
Banfield, Katherine	WC2	396	" 1680. Servant.
Banfield, Mary	15	300	" 1675.
Banford, John	16	394	" 1671.

NAME	Liber	Folio	REMARKS
Banford, Thomas	18	279	Immigrated 1675.
Bangall, Peter	16	393	Transported 1671.
Banis, Henry	8	502	Immigrated 1665.
Banister, Elizabeth	WC2	78	Transported 1679. Wife of Thomas.
Banister, Nicholas	3	22	Immigrated about 1648 with wife.
Banister, Richard	ABH	46	Immigrated 1648 with wife.
Banister, Thomas	15	559	Transported 1679.
Banister, Thomas, Jr.	WC2	78	" 1679. Son of Thomas.
Banister, Thomas, Sr.	WC2	78	Immigrated 1679 with wife and 7 children. Of Somerset Co.
Banjer, Robert	6	217	Transported 1663.
Banke, John	17	415	" Nov. 1669.
Bankes (als. Coudry), Elizabeth	15	347	" 1676.
Bankes, James	15	454	" Oct. 1677.
Bankes, Mary	15	530	" 1678.
Bankes, Robert	17	411	" 1673.
Bankroft, Thomas	16	43	" 1670.
Banks, George	10	523	Service 1667.
Banks, John	9	54	Transported 1665.
Banks, Peter	6	166	" 1658.
Banks, Richard	1	125	Immigrated 1641.
Banks, Richard	ABH	100	" 1641.
Banks, Lieut. Richard	2	458,480	" 1646.
Banks, Lieut. Richard	ABH	15	" 1646.
Banks, Thomas	4	18	Service 1659.
Bannam, Elizabeth	15	531	Transported 1678. Wife of John.
Bannam, John	15	531	Cooper. Immigrated 1678.
Banne, Peter	5	607	Transported 1663.
Bannister, John	13	122	" 1669.
Bannister, John	16	435	" 1671.
Banton, Samuel	18	37	" 1673.
Barant, Thomas	WC2	2	" 1679.
Barbage, Col. Thomas	ABH	213	Of Virginia, Merchant. Acquired land in Maryland 1652.
Barbar, Randall	5	411	Transported 1663.
Barbary, Susanna	20	45	Widow of Thomas of Calvert Co. Married John Webb prior to 1678. (See Barbery).
Barber, Conever	9	17	Transported 1665.
Barber, Elizabeth, the Younger	4	11	" 1659 by Luke Barber, Doctor in Physick.
Barber, Frances	WC2	168-169	Transported 1680.
Barber, Francis	6	88	" 1660.
Barber, George	6	132	" 1661.
Barber, George	16	428	" 1670-1.
Barber, James	16	135	" 1671.
Barber, John	5	80	" 1661.
Barber, John	5	256	" 1663.
Barber, John	16	40	Of St. Mary's Co. Service 1670.
Barber, Dr. Luke	5	76,77	Letter concerning, from Lord

NAME	Liber	Folio	REMARKS
			Baltimore, dated 1658.
Barber, Nathaniel	17	614	Of Calvert Co. Service 1673.
Barber, Newman	5	412	Transported 1663.
Barber, Peter	WC2	21-22, 122	" 1679.
Barber, Ursula	12	554	" 1670.
Barbery, Susanna	4	2	Wife of Thomas. Immigrated prior to 1658. (See Barbary).
Barbery, Thomas	4	1, 2	Immigrated prior to 1658.
Barbier, Edward	WC2	5	Brother to Luke Barbier.
Barbier, Robert	7	469	Transported 1664.
Barboe, Romain	10	556	" 1664-5.
Barbor, James	16	135	" 1671.
Barbor, Stephen	16	79	" 1670.
Barborn, Atwood als. Wm.	12	459	" 1669.
Barbour, Jacob	17	123	" 1672.
Barchall, Jane	17	451	" 1673.
Bardin, Charles	13	122	" 1668.
Barefool, Mary	15	382	" 1673.
Barefoot, William	17	411	" 1673.
Barfoot, John	17	490	" from "Southward of Virginia" 1665.
Barford, John	5	252	Mariner, 1663.
Barford, Joyce	5	252	Transported 1663. Wife of John.
Barie, Elizabeth	5	210	" 1662 by Philip Boriel.
Barington, William	12	342	Of Virginia. Immigrated 1669.
Barke, John	4	566	Transported 1661.
Barkeby, Alice	7	560	" 1665.
Barker, Ann	16	163	Wife of John. Service 1671.
Barker, J'n	15	354	Transported 1676.
Barker, John	5	89	" 1661.
Barker, John	6	211	" 1663.
Barker, John	7	471	" 1664.
Barker, John	9	25	" 1665.
Barker, John	18	337	Service 1668.
Barker, John	16	163	Of Talbot Co. Service 1669. Joyner 1671 (?). 13, fol.
Barker, John	15	344,354	Service 1675.
Barker, Martha	11	512	Transported 1668.
Barker, Michael	15	545	Immigrated 1676.
Barker, Rachel	16	394	Transported 1671.
Barker, Richard	15	397	" 1676.
Barker, Robert	7	507	" 1661.
Barker, Robert	5	488	" 1662.
Barker, Robert	12	472	" 1670. Service 1671. 16, fol. 418.
Barker, Thomas	WC2	211-212	Rights 1679. Of Liverpoole.
Barker, Thomas	7	87	Transported 1660. Service 1673. 17, fol. 611 of Calvert Co.
Barker, Thomas	WC2	201	Rights 1680. Of Liverpoole.

NAME	Liber	Folio	REMARKS
			Merchant.
Barker, William	10	395	Transported 1666.
Barker, William	17	407	" 1672.
Barkes, Elizabeth	10	503	" 1667.
Barkes, Sarah	10	395	" 1666.
Barkham, John	16	132	" 1671. (16, fol. 130).
Barkin, John	15	360	" 1676.
Barkley, Gabriel	5	188	" 1656. Servant. (5, fol. 191).
Barkum, Roger	16	40	Transported 1670.
Barley, Ann	8	498	" 1665.
Barley, Katherine	12	477	" 1670.
Barloe, Eleanor	15	438	" Oct. 1677.
Barloe, Joel	13	114	" 1671.
Barlow, Henry	6	142	" 1657.
Barlow, Robert	15	565	" 1679.
Barlow, Sarah	15	436	" 1677.
Barnaby, Elizabeth	8	19	" 1665.
Barnaby, James	8	19	" 1665.
Barnaby, James, Jr.	11	309	Of Somerset Co. Transported 1665.
Barnaby, John	12	393	Transported 1669.
Barnaby, Mary	8	19	" 1665.
Barnaby, Rebecca	8	19	" 1665.
Barnard, George	ABH	361	" prior to 1651. Servant.
Barnard, John	9	17	" 1665.
Barnard, John	12	380	Of Calvert Co. Immigrated 1669.
Barnard, Richard	12	403	Transported 1669.
Barnard, Richard	16	393	" 1671.
Barnard, Thomasin	12	380	" 1669. Wife of John.
Barnard, William	WC2	114	" 1680. Servant.
Barncrott, Sander	WC2	282	" 1680.
Barnes, Alice	10	116	" 1666. Daughter of Francis.
Barnes, Amy	15	359	Transported 1676.
Barnes, Ann	5	516	" 1661. (18, fol. 166).
Barnes, Ann	15	429	" 1677.
Barnes, Anthony	6	239	" 1663.
Barnes, Charles	12	194	" 1668. Servant.
Barnes, Christopher	10	392	And Elizabeth, his wife, Service 1666. (16, fol. 21).
Barnes, Clement	7	530	Transported 1664.
Barnes, Daniel	16	507	" 1671.
Barnes, Dorothy	10	117	" 1666. Daughter of Francis.
Barnes, Easter	17	451	Transported 1673.
Barnes (or Parnes), Fran.	4	22	" 1657 on the ship "Relief", Capt. Tulley, Com'r. Servant.
Barnes, Francis	10	116	Immigrated 1666.
Barnes, Francis	10	599	" 1667.
Barnes, Francis, Jr.	10	116	Transported 1666.

NAME	Liber	Folio	REMARKS
Barnes, Isabel	10	116	Transported 1666. Wife of Francis.
Barnes, James	15	369	" 1676.
Barnes, John	5	257	" 1659.
Barnes, John	5	79	" prior to 1662. Servant.
Barnes, John	6	82	" 1663.
Barnes, John	9	155	Of the Isle of Kent. Service 1663.
Barnes, John	7	530	Transported 1664.
Barnes, John	10	193	" 1666.
Barnes, John	12	554	Of St. Mary's Co. Service 1670.
Barnes, John	15	259	Transported 1675. (15, fol. 516).
Barnes, Joshua	17	449	Immigrated 1672.
Barnes, Margaret	WC2	120	Transported 1680.
Barnes, Mary	10	117	Daughter of Francis, Jr., Transported 1666.
Barnes, Richard	WC2	320	Transported 1680. Servant.
Barnes, Richard	18	35	And Susanna, his wife, Service 1672.
Barnes, Samuel	7	529	Transported 1664.
Barnes, Steven	16	319	Of Somerset Co. Immigrated from Accomack, Virginia 1671, with Mary, his wife.
Barnes, Thomas	10	116	Transported 1666. Son of Francis.
Barnes, Thomas	18	174	" 1674.
Barnes, Walter	6	85	" 1655.
Barnet, Henry	ABH	228	" 1651. Servant.
Barnet, John	15	533	" 1678.
Barnet, Julian	ABH	7	Servant 1639.
Barnet, Lawrence	12	478	Transported 1670.
Barnet, Mary	4	584	" 1660. Servant.
Barnett, Ellen	6	48	" 1662.
Barnett, John	WC2	152	" from Virginia 1680. Servant.
Barnett, John	15	358	Transported 1675.
Barnett, Jonathan	6	97	" 1654.
Barnett, Matthew	15	558	" 1679.
Barnett, Nicholas	9	297	" 1665.
Barnett, Richard	15	551	" 1679.
Barnett, Robert	6	90	" 1663.
Barnett, Thomas	WC2	167,169	" 1679.
Barnewall, Luke	10	140	Immigrated 1666.
Barnewell, Alee	15	565	Transported 1679.
Barnham, Frank	6	290	" 1663.
Barnington, Joane	9	54	" 1665.
Barnnett, William	9	38	" 1665.
Barns, James	7	150	" 1663.
Barns, William	13	1	" 1669. Servant.
Barnsby, Susan	15	40	" 1677.
Barnwell, Charles	16	413	" 1671.
Barnwell, Peter	16	413	" 1671.
Barom, John	11	307	" 1668.
Baron, Gertrayt	12	243	" 1669. Wife of Michael.
Baron, Michael	12	243	" 1669.
Barr, William	18	152	" 1674.

NAME	Liber	Folio	REMARKS
Barram, James	4	12	Transported 1659.
Barran, Thomas	5	63	" 1660. (18,fol.166).
Barrand, Giles	18	311	" 1675.
Barremore, John	Q	199	Immigrated 1653.
Barren, John	7	214	" 1666.
Barret, Alice	17	196	Transported 1673.
Barret, Diana	17	196	" 1673.
Barret, Elizabeth	17	196	" 1673.
Barret, John	17	543	Of Talbot Co. Service 1672.
Barret, Samuel	ABH	68	Transported 1638.
Barret, Sarah	12	270	" 1668.
Barret, Thomas	17	196	Immigrated 1673.
Barrett, Ann	18	279	Transported 1675.
Barrett, Christopher	9	449	" 1666.
Barrett, Darby	15	549	" 1678.
Barrett, Edward	Q	435	" 1658.
Barrett, Elizabeth	17	463	" 1673.
Barrett, George	6	85	Immigrated 1650.
Barrett, John	7	91	Transported 1666.
Barrett, John	WC2	211	" 1679. Servant.
Barrett, John	9	449	" 1666.
Barrett, John	11	337	" 1668. (11,fol.440).
Barrett, John	17	376	Service 1672.
Barrett, John	15	453	Transported 1675-7.
Barrett, John	15	598	" 1678-9.
Barrett, Joseph	10	523	" 1667.
Barrett, Margaret	6	170	" 1654.
Barrett, Margaret	5	129	" 1662.
Barrett, Samuel	1	27	" 1633-41.
Barrett, Samuel	1	43,128	" about 1638. Servant.
Barrett, Samuel	ABH	61	" 1633-41. (ABH,101).
Barrett, Sarah	7	78	" 1649. Servant.
Barrett, Thomas	18	331	" 1674.
Barrett, Walter	6	127	" 1659.
Barrett, William	WC2	110	Rights 1676.
Barrington, Joane	4	54	Transported 1659.
Barrom, John	11	469	" 1668.
Barron, Abraham	12	506	" 1668. Son of Michael.
Barron, Gertrude	12	506	" 1668. Wife of Michael.
Barron, Mary	15	366	" 1676.
Barron, Michael	12	506	Immigrated 1668.
Barron, Riners	12	506	Transported 1668. Son of Michael.
Barrow, Edward	WC2	380	" 1675-80. Servant.
Barrow, John	9	39	" 1656.
Barrow, John	15	560	" 1678.
Barrow, Paul	17	495	Of St. Mary's Co. Service 1673.
Barrow, Sarah	16	65	Transported 1670.
Barrowes, Thomas	16	83	" 1670.
Barry, Anne	WC2	128	" 1679.
Barry, Elizabeth	WC2	120	" 1680.
Barry, John	WC2	187	" 1678.

NAME	Liber	Folio	REMARKS
			11, fol. 527).
Bayly, George	16	507	Transported 1671.
Bayly, George	18	291	" 1674.
Bayly, Godfrey	4	53	Immigrated 1659.
Bayly, James	15	354	Transported 1676.
Bayly, James	18	174	" 1674.
Bayly, John	6	22	" 1663.
Bayly, John	10	475	Service prior to 1667.
Bayly, John	12	395	Son of John Bayly of St. Mary's Co.
"who lost his life in the late war in Anne Arundel County," 1669.			
Bayly, Mary	7	569	" 1663-4.
Bayly, Nicholas	17	475	" 1673.
Bayly, Richard	4	59	" 1658.
Bayly, Sarah	18	174	" 1674.
Bayly, Thomas	15	322	" 1674. (18, fol. 117).
Bayly, William	15	360	" 1676.
Baylye, Rachel	12	216	" 1668.
Baynam, James	12	269	Service 1668.
Baynard, John	15	340	Of Talbot Co. Immigrated 1676.
Bayne, Helena	5	305	Transported 1663. Wife of Walter.
Bayne, Joyce	5	89	" 1656.
Bayne, Judith	5	305	" 1663. Daughter of Walter.
Bayne, Walter	5	305	Immigrated 1663.
Baynton, Peirce	17	602	Transported 1667.
Bazell, Ralph	5	531	Of Anne Arundel Co., Service 1662.
Bazenoe, Mary	18	279	Transported 1675.
Bazill, Rice	5	530	" 1660.
Beach, Elias	1	62, 168	" 1637. Servant, aged 23 years.
Beach, Elias	2	581	Service 1649.
Beach, Elias	ABH	36	Immigrated 1638. Service 1649.
Beach, Mrs. Elias	2	581	" about 1640.
Beach, Thomas	7	553	Transported 1665.
Beach, Thomas	16	503	" 1671.
Beachey, William	11	344	" 1668. (11, fol. 465).
Beack, Isabell	Q	449	" 1658.
Beaford, Elizabeth	13	1	" 1669. Servant.
Beake, John	9	270	" 1665.
Beake, Thomas	18	331	" 1674.
Beal, John	Q	211	" 1658.
Beal, Capt. Ninian	WC2	60	Special Warrant for 500 Acres given by Lord Baltimore of Calvert County.
Beale, John	12	551	Transported 1670.
Beale, Susan	15	359	" 1676.
Beale, Thomas	9	436	" 1666.
Beale, Thomas	17	57	Of St. Mary's Co. Service 1672.
Beale, William	6	296	Transported 1664.
Beale, Winan	5	416	" 1658.
Bealey, Thomas	WC2	328, 357	Service 1680.

NAME	Liber	Folio	REMARKS
Beamon, John	WC2	33	Immigrated 1679 with wife. Of Anne Arundel Co.
Beamon, Sarah	WC2	33	Transported 1679. Wife of John.
Beamon, Thomas	5	59	" 1662.
Beamond, Elizabeth	11	436	" 1668.
Bean, Ralph	ABH	98	" 1633. Servant. (ABH, fol. 72).
Bean, Ralph	ABH	6	Immigrated 1640-8. Brother of Walter, living 1650. (ABH, fol. 49).
Bean, Walter	3	22	Rights 1650.
Bean, Walter	ABH	103	Immigrated 1641.
Bean, Mrs. Walter	3	22	Transported 1648.
Beane, John	16	482	" 1670-1.
Beane, Ralph	1	121	" 1633.
Beane, Ralphe	2	326-327, 507	Immigrated 1640-8 with 5 men. Brother of Walter.
Beane, Walter	2	327,507	Immigrated 1640-8 with wife. Brother of Ralphe.
Beane, Walter	1	131	Immigrated 1641.
Beane, Walter	ABH	6	Brother to Ralph. Immigrated with his wife between 1640-48. (ABH, fol. 46).
Beard, John	9	270	Transported 1665. Servant.
Beard, John	15	530	" 1678.
Beard, Lewis	17	495	" 1673.
Beard, Mary	16	507	" 1671.
Beard, Rachell	5	585	Immigrated 1650.
Beard, Richard	9	324	" prior to 1665.
Beard, Richard	5	585	" 1650.
Beard, Richard (son)	5	585	" 1650.
Beard, Robert	WC2	101	Transported 1679.
Beard, Robert	1	129	Transported 1641. Servant.
Beard, Robert	3	23	" before 1648.
Beard, Robert	ABH	102	" 1641. Servant. (ABH, fol. 47).
Beard, Robert	15	391	Transported 1676.
Beard, Thomas	18	166	" 1674.
Beard, Walter	8	501	" 1665. Service 1672. (17, fol. 354).
Beare, Elizabeth	9	156	Transported 1660. (17, fol. 463).
Beaske, Edward	Q	203	" 1658.
Beat, Nicholas	16	94	" 1670.
Beatsone, Frances	15	369	" 1676.
Beauchamp, Edward	9	116	Immigrated 1665.
Beaumont, David	Q	203	Transported 1658.
Beaumont, James	WC2	303	Immigrated 1680 with wife and Richard Beaumont. Of Charles County.
Beaumont, Mary	WC2	303	Transported 1680. Wife of Richard.
Beaumont, Richard	WC2	303	" 1680.
Beaumont, Thomas	5	307	" 1661.
Beavan, Alexander	5	411	" 1663.

NAME	Liber	Folio	REMARKS
Beaven, Charles	9	455	Immigrated prior to 1666.
Beaver, Francis	12	215	Transported 1668-9.
Beaver, Richard	18	95	" 1674.
Beavin, Alice	16	42	" 1670.
Beazley, Francis	17	619	Of Anne Arundel Co. Immigrated
1650 with Elizabeth, his wife, and John and Elizabeth, his children.			
Beazley, John	15	355	Son and heir of Francis living 1672.
Bebb, William	16	170	Transported 1671.
Bebford, Susan	15	535	" 1678.
Beck, Dorothy	WC2	309	" 1678.
Beck, Edward	WC2	160	Immigrated 1680. Of Cecil Co.
Beck, Francis	WC2	309	Transported 1678.
Beck, Henry	WC2	253,398	" 1680.
Beck, James	WC2	309	" 1678.
Beck, James	WC2	326	Service 1680. Of St. Mary's Co.
Beck, John	12	333	Transported 1668.
Beck, Richard	WC2	21	" 1679.
Beckell, Peter	6	121	" 1657.
Beckerstafe, Const.	15	359	" 1676.
Becket, Samuel	18	118	" 1674.
Beckford, Elizabeth	15	452	" 1678.
Beckham, Charles	12	343	" 1669.
Beckins, Humphrey	7	558	" 1665.
Beckless, Richard	ABH	336	Immigrated 1653.
Beckley, Richard	ABH	85	Transported 1636. Servant. (1, fol. 82).
Beckley, William	WC2	406	Transported 1677.
Beckly, Will	15	454	" 1677.
Beckwith, George	ABH	123	" 1648. Servant. (2, fol. 613).
Beckwith, George	7	82	Immigrated 1657. Married Fran-
ces, daughter and heir of Nicholas Harvey, dec'd. in 1658. (Q, fol. 416; 5, fol. 219).			
Beckwith, George	12	351	Immigrated 1669.
Beckwith, Henry	12	349	" 1669. Of Virginia.
Beckworth, Thomas	ABH	94	Transported 1633. Servant.
Beckworth, Thomas	1	110	" 1633.
Bedall, Robert	8	483	" 1665. From Virginia.
Bedell, Henry	8	483	" 1665.
Bedell, John	15	430	" 1677.
Bedford, Henry	16	83	Of Charles Co. Immigrated 1670.
Bedford, Henry	19	258	Transported 1675.
Bedford, Mary	5	531	" 1657.
Bedford, Miles	6	134	" 1652.
Bedford, Thomas	6	106	" 1663.
Bedford, William	11	344	" 1668.
Bedgood, Thomas	17	456	" 1671.
Bedingfeild, Lawrence	WC2	110	" 1676. Servant.
Bedle, Edward	4	576	" 1661.
Bedloe, Isaac	5	203	" 1662.
Bedmaine, Thomas	5	490	" 1662.

NAME	Liber	Folio	REMARKS
Bedson, Thomas	17	451	Transported 1673.
Bedur, William	15	449	Of Somerset Co. Immigrated 1677.
Bedwort, Richard	5	530	Transported 1662.
Bedworth, Isaac	11	441	" 1668.
Bedworth, Richard	11	167	Of Anne Arundel Co. Service 1667.
Bee, Sarah	15	442	Transported 1677.
Bee, Thomas	9	25	" 1665. Service 1674. (15, fol. 509).
Beech, Ann	4	19	Transported 1651. Wife of Elias. Married Thomas Jains prior to 1659.
Beech, Elias	4	19	" 1651.
Beech, James	17	417	" 1673.
Beech, Thomas	16	127	" 1671.
Beech, Thomas	6	217	" 1663.
Beech, Thomas	15	452	" 1678.
Beed, William	15	567	" 1678.
Beedall, Ann	WC2	22	" 1679. (See Beedle).
Beedall, John	WC2	22	" 1679. (See Beedle).
Beedell, Edward	9	489	Immigrated 1665.
Beedle, Anne	WC2	122	Transported 1679. Wife of John. (See Beedall).
Beedle, John	WC2	122	Transported 1679. (See Beedall).
Beedle, John	4	565	" 1661.
Beedle, Lawrence	17	551	" 1673.
Beel, Susanna	17	67	" 1672.
Beene, Jane	6	266	" 1663.
Beere, Cath.	4	59	" 1657.
Bees, Thomas	13	122	" 1670.
Beeston, William	7	61	Service 1664.
Beestons, George	12	584	Transported 1670. Servant.
Beeswing, John	5	411	" 1663.
Beetenson, Edmund	WC2	334-335	Married Lydia, widow of Thomas Watkins prior to 1680.
Beetenson, Lydia	WC2	334-335	Wife of Edmund and widow of Thomas Watkins 1680.
Beffen, Edward	15	544	Transported 1676.
Beffine, James	18	296	" 1674.
Beirs, Robert	12	492	" 1670.
Beist, Thomas	17	356	" 1672.
Belcher, Thomas	18	152	" 1674.
Belcher, William	11	344	" 1668.
Belcher, William	18	38	" 1673.
Belconsen (als. Godfrey), Mary	17	488	" 1668.
Belfield, Lydia	WC2	33	" 1679.
Belford, Alice	16	507	" 1671.
Bell, Andrew	6	117	" 1663.
Bell, And.	15	454	" 1677.
Bell, Daniel	17	608	" 1673.
Bell, Edward	12	205	" 1667. (12, fol. 216).
Bell, Elizabeth	5	485	" 1659. Wife of Thomas.

NAME	Liber	Folio	REMARKS
Bell, George	7	491	Transported 1664.
Bell, Henry	16	79	" 1670.
Bell, Isabella	13	66	" 1669. Servant.
Bell, James	15	340	Of Anne Arundel Co. Service 1675.
Bell, John	WC2	16	Service 1679.
Bell, John	WC2	101	Service 1679. Of Talbot Co.
Bell, Katherin	17	440	Transported 1673.
Bell, Mabel	17	396	" 1669.
Bell, Mary	10	286	" 1660. (10, fol. 417).
Bell, Nathaniel	15	376	" 1676.
Bell, Ninian	11	195	Of Calvert Co., Planter, Service 1667.
Bell, Ringing	5	416	Transported prior to 1663.
Bell, Sarah	18	306	" 1675.
Bell, Silvester	---	---	" 1667.
Bell, Thomas	WC2	16	Immigrated 1679.
Bell, Thomas	WC2	346-347	" 1680.
Bell, Thomas	9	92	Transported 1665.
Bell, Thomas	5	485	Immigrated 1659.
Bell, William	ABH	25	" 1648.
Bell, William	8	478	Transported 1665.
Bell, William	10	489	" 1667. Servant.
Bell, William	15	396	Immigrated 1667.
Bell, William	16	170	Transported 1671.
Bell, William	18	152	" 1674.
Bellacowson, Mary	5	485	" 1659. Wife of Michael.
Bellamy, Henry	1	75-6	Petition to confirm title to land, 1640.
Bellamy, Henry	3	17	Transported prior to 1650.
Bellamy, Henry	ABH	44	" many years prior to 1650.
Bellenle, Thomas	6	89	Transported 1660.
Bellett, Michael	7	78	" 1654. Servant.
Bellison, Benjamin	16	411	" 1671.
Bellman, Peter	18	15	" 1673.
Bellmayne, John	17	608	" 1673.
Bellosis, Francis	5	532	Immigrated 1657.
Belott, Michael	4	65	Service 1659.
Belt, Ann	5	373	Transported 1663.
Belt, Humphrey	5	373	" 1663.
Belt, John	5	373	" 1663.
Belt, Richard	15	505	" 1678.
Belt, Sarah	5	373	" 1663.
Beltam, John	1	25	" 1637.
Bemilson, Lass	12	473	" 1670.
Bemore, Francis	12	498	" 1670.
Benam, Anain	ABH	67	" 1633. Servant.
Benam, Anam	1	17, 41	" 1633. Servant.
Benam, Anam	2	346	" 1633. Servant.
Benbridge, Christopher	7	529	" 1664.
Bench, John	6	80	" 1656.
Bendall, Robert	12	471	Service 1670.

NAME	Liber	Folio	REMARKS
Benell, William	17	440	Transported 1668.
Benfield, Richard	WC2	363	" 1680.
Bengar, Robert	11	216	Of St. Mary's Co. Service 1667.
Bengo, Robert	7	553	Transported 1665.
Benhall, Edward	16	507	" 1671.
Benham, Anam	ABH	6	" 1633. (See Benam).
Benham, Temperance	5	305	" 1663.
Benian, John	20	185	" 1679.
Benington, Nicholas	15	454	" 1677.
Benitt, Mary	15	566	" 1678.
Benn, John	17	451	" 1673.
Benn, Thomas	15	370	" 1676.
Bennet, Andrew	12	506	Service 1669.
Bennet, Benjamin	12	505	" 1669.
Bennet, Eleanor	16	435	Transported 1671.
Bennet, John	18	167	" 1674. (18, fol. 174).
Bennet, Robert	Q	71	" 1658.
Bennet, Samuel	12	285	" 1667.
Bennet, Walter	WC2	112	" 1679.
Bennett, A.	15	565	" 1678.
Bennett, Ann	10	204	" 1666. Wife of Thomas.
Bennett, Benjamin	12	379	" 1669.
Bennett, Benjamin	17	599	Of Talbot Co. Immigrated 1673.
Bennett, Benjamin	15	455	Transported 1678.
Bennett, Charles	11	482	" 1668.
Bennett, Clodus	18	329	" 1675.
Bennett, Desbrough	4	565	" 1661.
Bennett, Dorothy	WC2	318	" 1680. Wife of Edward.
Bennett, Edward	WC2	318	Immigrated 1680 with wife and daughter.
Bennett, Eleanor	16	435	Transported 1671.
Bennett, Elizabeth	5	252	" 1648. Wife of Richard
Bennett, Elizabeth	8	486	" 1664.
Bennett, Elizabeth	10	204	" 1666. Daughter of Thomas.
Bennett, Elizabeth	17	454	" 1672.
Bennett, Francis	Q	317	" 1658.
Bennett, Francis	10	523	" 1667. Servant.
Bennett, George	10	204	" 1666.
Bennett, Grace	WC2	381	" 1675-80. Servant.
Bennett, Henry	11	500	Of New England. Immigrated 1664.
Bennett, Henry	17	454	Transported 1672.
Bennett, Jo.	WC2	112	" 1680.
Bennett, John	WC2	380	" 1675-80. Servant.
Bennett, John	WC2	112	" 1679.
Bennett, John	WC2	184	" 1680. Servant.
Bennett, John	WC2	289	Service 1680. Of Calvert Co.
Bennett, John	WC2	182	Service 1680. Of Talbot Co. (?).
Bennett, John	5	484	Transported 1662.
Bennett, John	5	248	" 1663.
Bennett, John	9	35	" 1664. (9, fol. 38).

NAME	Liber	Folio	REMARKS
Bennett, John	17	551	Transported 1673.
Bennett, John	15	455	" 1678.
Bennett, Mary	WC2	130	" 1679. Servant.
Bennett, Mary	WC2	318	" 1680. Daughter of Edward.
Bennett, Mary	5	252	Transported 1648. Daughter of Richard.
Bennett, Mary	17	608	Transported 1673.
Bennett, Mary	16	566	" 1678.
Bennett, Mechael	15	318	" 1675.
Bennett, Prudence	5	257	" 1663.
Bennett, Richard	2	220	Immigrated 1646 with wife and 5 children. Fol. 544 shows only 4 children.
Bennett, Richard	5	252	Transported 1648. (Immig. ?). Son of Thomas.
Bennett, Richard	9	489	Immigrated 1665.
Bennett, Richard	10	3	Of "Nansmum in Virginia" acquires land in Maryland from Hon. Phil. Calvert. Died prior to 1677, leaving a daughter, the wife of Chas. Scarborough of Accomack Co. (19, fol. 604).
Bennett, Richard	11	169	Immigrated 1667.
Bennett, Richard	15	443	Transported 1672.
Bennett, Richard	18	309	Immigrated from New England about 1675.
Bennett, Richard	15	448	Transported 1677.
Bennett, Robert	15	414	" 1677.
Bennett, Samuel	8	484	" 1665.
Bennett, Sarah	5	252	" 1648. Daughter of Richard.
Bennett, Sarah	15	322	Transported 1675.
Bennett, Susan	15	574	" 1678.
Bennett, Susanna	WC2	16	" 1677.
Bennett, Susanna Maria	15	393	Daughter of Richard, deceased, living 1676.
Bennett, Thomas	WC2	87	Transported 1679.
Bennett, Thomas	5	252	" 1648-63. Son of Richard.
Bennett, Thomas	5	262	Immigrated 1651.
Bennett, Thomas	4	16	" 1659.
Bennett, Thomas	6	26	Transported 1660-3. (6, fol. 268).
Bennett, William	5	488	" 1661.
Bennett, William	5	367	" 1663.
Bennett, William	12	215	" 1668-9.
Bennett, William	16	170	" 1671.
Bennett, William	17	608	" 1673.
Bennfield, John	4	531	Service 1658.
Bennie, Alexander	18	1	Immigrated from Barbadoes 1674.
Bennill, William	16	11	Transported 1670.
Bennington, Samuel	11	499	Of Virginia. Transported 1666. Servant.
Bennitt, John	7	154	Transported 1663.
Bennitt, Lawrence	7	154	" 1663.

NAME	Liber	Folio	REMARKS
Bennitt, Thomas	7	454	Transported 1664.
Benson, Elizabeth	5	2	" 1661.
Benson, Hugh	16	411	" 1671.
Benson, James	15	525	Immigrated 1674.
Benson, John	6	16	" prior to 1663.
Benson, John	12	382	Transported 1669.
Benson, John	17	424	" 1673.
Benson, Margaret	15	601	Wife of James. Service 1678.
Benson, Patrick	15	353	Transported 1676.
Benson, Richard	16	437	" 1671.
Benson, Richard	12	403	" 1669.
Benson, Robert	5	556	" 1663.
Benson, Robert	8	478	" 1665.
Benson, Sarah	Q	31	Immigrated 1651. Wife of Stephen. (8, fol. 86).
Benson, Stephen	8	86	Immigrated 1641. (Q, fol. 31).
Benson, Stephen	8	86	Transported 1641. Son of Stephen. (Q, fol. 31).
Benson, Stephen	9	39	Transported 1653.
Benson, William	16	639	" 1672.
Benster, James	16	394	" 1671.
Benston, Francis	18	37	Of Somerset Co. Immigrated 1673 with Mary, his wife, and William, Francis, John, James, and Mary, his children.
Benston, James	15	443	Transported 1674.
Benston, James	15	412	" 1675. Son of Francis.
Benston, John	15	412	" 1675. Son of Francis.
Benston, Mary	15	412	" 1675. Daughter of Francis.
Benstone, Alexander	15	549	Transported 1674. Son of William.
Benstone, Hester	15	549	" 1674. Daughter of William.
Benstone, Rebecca	15	549	Transported 1674. Wife of William.
Benstone, Rebecca	15	549	" 1674. Daughter of William.
Benstone, William	15	549	Of Virginia, Carpenter. Immigrated to Somerset Co. 1674.
Benstone, William	15	549	Transported 1674. Son of William.
Bentam, James	WC2	130	" 1679. Servant (26 years old).
Bentlett, John	6	117	Transported 1659.
Bentley, John	6	95	" 1659.
Bentley, Mathew	10	464	Immigrated 1666. (16, fol. 170).
Bentley, Samuel	6	133	Transported 1654.
Bently, Mark	ABH	175	" 1649. Servant.
Bently, Richard	Q	205	Immigrated 1657. (Q, fol. 30).
Benton, Mark	Q	75	" 1658.
Benton, Richard	15	369	Transported 1676.
Berdtege, Ann	12	498	" 1670.
Berkenhead, Rupert	16	305	Service 1672.
Berkett, Thomas & Ruth	11	569	Transported 1668.

NAME	Liber	Folio	REMARKS
Berkett, John	17	463	Transported 1673.
Berkley, Anthony	15	451	" 1678.
Bernard, John	4	70	" 1659.
Bernard, Peter	5	257	" 1663.
Bernett, Julian	2	347	" 1639. Servant.
Berow, Nathaniel	9	321	" 1666.
Berrer, Elizabeth	9	297	" 1665.
Berrer, Griffes	9	297	" 1665.
Berrer, Olive	9	297	" 1665.
Berrer, Phillip	9	297	Immigrated 1665.
Berret, Ralph	16	452	Transported 1671.
Berrow, Rice	11	378	" 1668.
Berry, Christopher	12	413	" 1669.
Berry, Edward	1	33, 171	" 1638. Servant.
Berry, Edward	2	605	" about 1638. Servant.
Berry, Edward	ABH	37	Servant 1638. (ABH, fol. 64).
Berry, Elizabeth	3	173	Transported 1655. Wife of James.
Berry, Elizabeth	Q	32	" 1652. Wife of James.
Berry, Elizabeth	5	220	" 1659.
Berry, Elizabeth	15	430	" 1677.
Berry, James	3	173	Immigrated 1655 with wife and 11 other persons.
Berry, James	Q	32	Immigrated Feb. 1652.
Berry, James	18	15	Transported 1673.
Berry, Jeremiah	15	356	" 1675.
Berry, John	15	433	" 1677.
Berry, Martha	3	173	" 1655.
Berry, Nicholas	15	453	" 1675-7.
Berry, Roder	Q	32	" Feb. 1652. Son of James.
Berry, Roger	3	173	Transported 1655.
Berry, Shelton	5	257	" 1663.
Berry, Thomas	15	397	" 1675.
Berry, William	3	173	" 1655.
Berry, William	Q	32	" Feb. 1652. Son of James. Living 1666, "heir and Ex'r. of my father James Berry". (10, fol. 203).
Berry, William	6	211	Transported 1663.
Berry, William	7	471	" 1664.
Berry, William	9	321	" 1666.
Berryman, Mary	16	297	" 1671.
Bersha, Andrew	5	128	" prior to 1662.
Bertleson, Hunning	12	473	" 1670.
Berwick, Richard	1	19	Service 1639.
Berwicke, William	18	15	Transported 1673.
Besford, Thomas	15	397	" 1676.
Beson, Daniel	13	116	" 1671.
Beson, Francis	10	272	" 1666.
Beson, Lydia	16	439	" 1671.
Besse, Elizabeth	5	320	" 1663.
Besse, Joseph	11	487	" 1668.

NAME	Liber	Folio	REMARKS
Bessing, Lewis	17	571	Transported 1673.
Besson, Hestor	4	66	" 1650. Wife of Capt. Thomas.
Besson, Stephen	18	317	Immigrated 1662. Of Dorchester County.
Besson, Thomas and family	Q	69	Immigrated 1649.
Bessoon, Mary	15	454	Transported 1677.
Best, Edward	17	486	" from Virginia 1667.
Best (or West), Henry	10	1, 2	" 1666.
Best, John	16	411	" 1671.
Best, Jonathan	17	330	" 1672.
Best, Judey	6	293	" 1664.
Best, Timothy	6	85	" 1662.
Bestenle, Thomas	6	36	" 1660.
Beston, George	15	405	Immigrated 1676.
Beston, Sarah	15	405	Transported 1676.
Beswick, James	17	396	" 1669.
Betenson, Edmond	12	206	Immigrated 1669.
Betham, Richard	3	21	Transported 1637. Servant.
Betham, Richard	ABH	45	" 1636. Servant.
Betoome, Ann	15	569	" 1678.
Betridge, Jonathan	15	396	" 1676.
Bettam (als. Smith), John	1	38-39	" 1637.
Bette, Judith	9	282	" 1665.
Bettle, Martha	6	127	" 1663.
Betton, James	8	131	" 1664.
Betts, George	10	569	" 1665, in the "Agreement of Bristol".
Betts, John	10	523	Transported 1667.
Betts, John	16	400	" 1671.
Betts, Margaret	10	541	" prior to 1666.
Betts, Mary	Q	208	" 1658. (4, fol. 555).
Betts, Robert	15	542	Of Talbot Co. Immigrated 1674.
Betts, Robert	15	542	Transported 1674. Son of Robert.
Betts, Ruth	15	542	" 1674. Wife of Robert.
Betts, William	15	542	" 1674. Son of Robert.
Betts, William	15	432	Immigrated 1677 with Alice, his wife.
Betty, Arthur	15	501	Transported 1678.
Beven, Elizabeth	WC2	112	" 1679.
Beven, John	11	337	" 1669. (11, fol. 440).
Bevens, Rowland	15	532	Of Somerset Co. Immigrated 1667.
Beverdly, John	4	216	Transported 1659.
Beverly, Nicholas	17	487	Immigrated from Virginia 1668.
Bevin, Andrew	12	460	Transported 1669.
Bevin, Ellis	16	452	" 1667.
Bevington, Obediah	15	317	" 1674.
Bevis, Robert	12	492	" 1670.
Bewin, David	9	437	" 1664.

NAME	Liber	Folio	REMARKS
Bey, Damascus	9	304	Transported 1665.
Bhickorne, John	Q	18	Immigrated 1652. Son of Robert.
Bhickorne, Mary	Q	18	" 1652. Wife of Robert.
Bhickorne, Mr. Robert	Q	18	" 1652.
Bhickorne, Robert	Q	18	" 1652. Son of Robert.
Biasent, Thomas	17	417	Transported 1673.
Biche, Judith	Q	431	" 1658.
Bicketton, Francis	9	327	" 1666.
Bicon, George	16	439	" 1671.
Bidder, John	19	258	" 1663.
Biford, Sarah	15	318	" 1674.
Bigg, John	15	380	" 1676.
Bigger, Ann	15	317	Wife of John. Service 1654. Living 1675. (15, fol. 347).
Bigger, Francis	4	549	Transported prior to 1661.
Bigger, John	ABH	312	" 1652. Servant. Service 1654. Of Calvert Co. (15, fol. 317).
Bigger, John	Q	239	Transported 1651-2.
Bigger, John	5	3	" 1661.
Biggs, Edward	4	140	" 1655. Servant. (Quaker ?)
Biggs, Thomas	15	416	Transported 1677.
Bill, John	9	336	" 1666.
Billacowson, Michael	5	485	Immigrated 1659.
Billett, Grace	8	499	Transported 1664.
Billingham, Alice	18	167	" 1674.
Billingham, Mary	18	167	" 1674.
Billingham, Thomas	18	167	" 1674.
Billingsly, Francis	Q	203	Immigrated 1652 with wife. Of Calvert Co. Planter. Brother to Thomas. 1669. (12, fol. 357).
Billingsly, James	5	73	Transported by Francis 1656.
Billingsly, Major John	ABH	213	Of Virginia, Merchant. Acquired land in Maryland in 1652.
Billingsly, John	Q	203	Immigrated 1652. Son of Francis.
Billingsly, Major	6	212	His Widow married William Burke prior to 1663.
Billingsly, Sarah	Q	73	Transported 1658.
Billingsly, Thomas	5	73	" by Francis 1656.
Billiter, Joseph	17	74	" 1671.
Bilson, Gulin	5	12	" 1662.
Binckloe, John	12	474	" 1670.
Bincks, Thomas	7	464	" 1656.
Bingam, William	12	190	" 1668. Servant.
Bingham, Ann	ABH	415	" 1653-4.
Bingham, Richard	Q	69	" 1658.
Bingham, Thomas	WC2	328,329, 357	Service 1680.
Bingham, Thomas	18	84	Transported 1674.
Bings, Robert	11	348	" 1668.
Binkes, Thomas	4	534	" prior to 1659. (Q, fol. 197).

NAME	Liber	Folio	REMARKS
Binkes, Thomas	5	243	Transported 1662.
Binnage, Joseph	16	308	Of Somerset Co. Service 1671.
Binningham, Jacob	12	385	Transported 1669.
Bins, Sarah	18	137	" 1674.
Binson, Margaret	17	440	" 1673.
Binson, William	4	5	" 1659. Servant.
Birch, Mary	12	190	" 1668.
Birch, Trustram	10	193	" 1666. Servant.
Birchfield, Samuel	11	170	Of Anne Arundel Co. Service 1667.
Birckett, Thomas	18	306	Transported 1675.
Birckhead, Richard	17	478	Of St. Mary's Co. 1673. Immigrated
1666 with Margaret, his wife.			
Bird, Charles	5	257	Transported 1663. Servant.
Bird, Elizabeth	4	61	" 1659. Wife of John.
Bird, Francis	12	391	" 1669.
Bird, Hannah	15	517	" 1678.
Bird, John	4	61	Immigrated 1659 with his wife and three children.
Bird, John	6	135	Transported 1663.
Bird, John	16	435	" 1671.
Bird, John	17	463	" 1673.
Bird, Judeth	16	435	" 1671.
Bird, Michael	18	174	" 1674.
Bird, Stephen	5	343	" 1663.
Bird, William	17	420	" 1673.
Birdwistle, Thomas	16	91	" 1670. (16, fol. 89).
Birk, Edmund	15	537	" 1679.
Birk, John	15	537	" 1679.
Birkby, Catherine	6	80	" 1654.
Birke, Thomas	15	440	" 1677.
Birkett, Richard	8	478	" 1665.
Birkley, Samuel	6	133	" 1657.
Birne, Ellin	WC2	87	" 1679.
Biron, Samuel	11	540	" 1668.
Bise, John	15	533	" 1678.
Bish, Ursula	1	148	License to marry Richard Thompson, June 24, 1641.
Bishop, Aaron	17	388	Transported from Virginia 1672. Son of Henry, Sr.
Bishop, Abraham	9	21	Of Talbot Co. Immigrated 1665.
Bishop, Ann	17	388	Transported from Virginia 1672.
Bishop, David	17	388	" from Virginia 1672. Son of Henry, Sr.
Bishop, Elizabeth	17	388	Transported from Virginia 1672.
Bishop, George	17	388	" from Virginia 1672. Son of Henry, Sr.
Bishop, Grace	WC2	78	Transported 1679. Wife of Joseph.
Bishop, Henry	1	20,37, 38,166	" 1633.
Bishop, Henry	ABH	36	" 1640.
Bishop, Henry	2	604	Immigrated about 1640.

NAME	Liber	Folio	REMARKS
Bishop, Henry, Jr.	17	388	Transported from Virginia 1672. Son of Henry, Sr.
Bishop, Henry, Sr.	17	388	Of Somerset Co. Immigrated from Virginia 1672 with Ann, his wife, and Mary Bowen, her daughter. Petition, 1775. (15, fol. 310).
Bishop, James	15	370	Transported 1676.
Bishop, Joane	WC2	253	" 1680.
Bishop, John	9	325	" 1666.
Bishop, John	16	358	" 1671.
Bishop, John	17	388	" from Virginia 1672. Son of Henry, Sr.
Bishop, Joseph	WC2	78	Immigrated from Virginia 1679 with wife and son. Of Somerset County.
Bishop, Margaret	9	21	Transported 1665. Wife of Abraham.
Bishop, Mary	17	37	Of Somerset Co. Service 1672.
Bishop, Nicholas	WC2	184	Transported 1680. Servant.
Bishop, Roger	15	517	" 1678.
Bishop, Sarah	17	388	" from Virginia 1672.
Bishop, Thomas	WC2	78	" 1679. Son of Joseph.
Bishop, William, Gent.	16	100	Of Talbot Co. Immigrated 1663.
Bishopp, William	WC2	112	Rights 1680. Of Talbot Co.
Bison, John	9	328	Transported 1665. Servant.
Bisse, William	4	56	Immigrated 1650.
Bissey, Richard	18	160	Transported 1674.
Biterby, Thomas	6	294	" 1664.
Bitts, Robert	15	454	" 1677.
Bizzick, John	Q	19	" 1658.
Blabe, Johanna	16	507	" 1671.
Blabone, Richard	WC2	73	" 1678.
Black, Albert	17	535	Of St. Mary's Co. Service 1673.
Black, Elizabeth	7	470	Transported 1664.
Black, Peter	6	19	" 1660-3. (17, fol. 531).
Black, Sarah	WC2	170	" 1679. Servant.
Black, Thomas	5	268	" 1663.
Black, William	Q	323	" or Service 1658.
Black, William	5	304	" 1662. Servant.
Blackard, Elizabeth	11	348	" 1668.
Blackboard, Peter	9	25	" 1665.
Blackborn, Thomas	ABH	150	" 1648. Servant.
Blackborne, Edward	WC2	49	Immigrated 1669. Of Calvert Co.
Blackborne, George	15	265	Transported 1674. (18, fol. 102).
Blackborne, Katherine	15	265	" 1674.
Blackborne, John	17	38	Of St. Mary's Co. Immigrated from Virginia 1672.
Blackborne, Thomas	15	354	Transported 1676.
Blackburn, Samuel	5	90	". 1660.
Blackburne, Robert	11	582	" 1668.
Blacke, Jeffrey	18	94	" 1674.
Blacke, Oner	16	435	" 1671.
Blacken, Judith	4	30	" prior to 1659. Servant.
Blackestone, Ann	15	544	" 1674.

NAME	Liber	Folio	REMARKS
Blackfield, Richard	15	446	Transported 1677.
Blackgrove, Martin	17	601	Immigrated 1671.
Blackhall, Ralph	16	469	Of Talbot Co. Immigrated Feb.

1668. Aged 28 years in 1672. (16, fol. 505).

NAME	Liber	Folio	REMARKS
Blackhurst, Roger	11	436	Transported 1668.
Blackiston, Nehemiah	18	126	Of St. Mary's Co. Immigrated 1674.
Blackiston, William	18	150	Of St. Mary's Co. Service 1674.
Blackliffe, Charles	WC2	16	Transported five persons in 1679.
Blackliffe, George	WC2	16	" 1679.
Blackman, Dorothy	5	124	" 1662.
Blackman, John	6	268	" 1663. Service 1667.

(11, fol. 229).

NAME	Liber	Folio	REMARKS
Blackman, William	15	565	Transported 1679.
Blackmore, Thomas	16	340	" 1671.
Blackstone, Barbary	16	70	" 1670.
Blackstone, Ebenezer	16	341	Of Baltimore Co. Immigrated 1671.
Blackstone, George	16	70	Transported 1670.
Blackstone, Hannah	16	70	" 1670.
Blackstone, John	4	549	" 1661. Servant.
Blackstone, John	16	70	Of St. Mary's Co. Immigrated

1670 with Sarah, George, Barbary, Robert, Hannah and Justice.

NAME	Liber	Folio	REMARKS
Blackstone, Justice	16	70	Transported 1670.
Blackstone, Robert	16	70	" 1670.
Blackstone, Sarah	16	70	" 1670.
Blackthorn, Thomas	12	333	" 1668.
Blackwell, Charles	15	359	" 1676.
Blackwell, Elizabeth	15	550	" 1659.
Blackwell, John	6	307	" 1664.
Blackwell, Josias	18	38	" 1673.
Blackwell, Mary	5	530	" 1661.
Blackwell, Samuel	16	432	" 1671.
Blackwell, Thomas	4	625	" 1661.
Blackwood, Phineas	15	519	Of Dorchester Co. Immigrated 1666.
Blades, Mary	15	531	Transported 1669. Daughter of Robert. (15, fol. 501).
Blades, Robert	15	531	Immigrated 1669. (15, fol. 501).
Blagg, Edward	WC2	132	Master of ship "James of Plymouth" 1680.
Blagge, Abraham	WC2	132-134	Rights 1680. Of Virginia.
Blairn, Alice	9	35	Transported 1665.
Blake, Deborah	15	311	" prior to 1675. Wife of Joseph.
Blake, Elizabeth	5	89	Transported 1661.
Blake, George	9	33	" 1660.
Blake, George	9	33	" 1660. Son of George.
Blake, Giles	ABH	316	Immigrated 1650.
Blake, Giles	ABH	249	Of the Isle of Kent. Immigrated 1652.
Blake, Henry	15	331	Of St. Mary's Co. Immigrated from Va. prior to 1675.

NAME	Liber	Folio	REMARKS
Blake, Henry	15	331	Transported 1675. Son of Henry.
Blake, Joel	6	210	Immigrated 1663.
Blake, Joseph	15	311	" prior to 1675. (19, fol. 38).
Blake, Joseph	15	311	Transported prior to 1675. Son of Joseph.
Blake, Katherine	15	331	Transported 1675. Wife of Henry.
Blake, Margaret	9	33	" 1660. Wife of George.
Blake, Mary	9	270	" 1665. Servant.
Blake, Obadiah	10	259	" 1666.
Blake, Peter	5	467	" 1662.
Blake, Richard	15	356	" 1675.
Blake, Robert	15	331	" 1675. Son of Henry.
Blake, Samuel	15	376	" 1676.
Blake, William	18	17	" 1669.
Blakeley, Benjamin	7	530	" 1664.
Blakely, Peter	12	576	" 1670.
Blaketer, George	6	62	Immigrated 1663.
Blaketer, Mary	6	62	Transported 1663. Wife of George.
Blan, Christopher	17	551	" 1673.
Blan, John	17	551	" 1673.
Blanch, John	15	601	Service 1679.
Blanch, Thomas	16	86	Transported 1670.
Blancher, Joseph	12	601	" 1669.
Blanck, John	15	397	" 1675.
Blanckett, Mary	15	530	" 1678.
Blancksteen, William	15	530	" 1678.
Bland,	5	529	1655.
Bland, Margaret	13	113	Transported 1670.
Bland, Susan	4	551	" 1661.
Bland, Thomas	17	56	Of Calvert Co. Gent. Immigrated 1672.
Bland, Thomas	WC2	310	Rights 1680. Of Anne Arundel Co.
Bland, Ursulah	18	291	Transported 1674.
Blandy, Adam	9	94	" 1665.
Blanford, Thomas	18	2	Of Calvert Co. Immigrated 1674.
Blangg, Lewis	17	167	Transported 1672.
Blankley, John	15	380	" 1676.
Blankroft, Thomas	12	601	" 1669.
Blanzy, Lewis	16	198	Of Kent Co. Immigrated 1671.
Blare, Elizabeth	17	572	Transported 1672.
Blashell, Robert	5	123	" 1662.
Blavin, Alice	9	35	" 1663.
Blay, Edward	9	456	Son and heir to William of Anne Arundel Co. 1666.
Blay, Mary	6	134	Transported 1658.
Blay, Samuel	7	567	" 1665.
Blayard, Thomas	6	290	" 1663.
Blayer, Susanna	15	429	" 1677.
Bleather, Rowland	5	411	" 1663.
Bleer, William	7	581	" 1665.

NAME	Liber	Folio	REMARKS
Blessed, Thomas	12	576	Transported 1670.
Bletsoe, Roger	2	524	" 1641. Servant.
Bletsoe, Roger	ABH	27	Servant 1641.
Bleven, Bartholomew	5	490	Immigrated 1661.
Bleway, Mary	18	291	Transported 1674.
Blince, James	16	170	" 1675.
Blinkhorne, John	4	216	" 1659. Son of Robert.
Blinkhorne, Mary	4	216	" 1659. Wife of Robert.
Blinkhorne, Robert	4	216	" 1659. Son of Robert.
Blinkhorne, Robert	4	216	Immigrated 1659.
Blinkorne, Hannah	4	68	Transported 1657.
Blisse, John	6	31	" Nov. 14, 1663.
Blisse, John	9	234	" 1665.
Blisswater, James	9	24	" 1665.
Blitght, Gedeon	15	322	" 1675.
Blith, John	WC2	282	" 1680.
Blomfield, John	12	308	Of St. Mary's Co. Immigrated 1669.
Blomley, Jane	15	567	Transported 1678.
Blomstead, John	6	290	" 1663. (16, fol. 40).
Blood, Mary	7	567	" 1665.
Bloom, Bartholomew	ABH	378	Immigrated 1653 with wife.
Bloom, John	16	428	Transported 1670-1.
Bloomfield, Nathaniel	15	565	" 1679.
Bloomley, Elizabeth	ABH	164	" 1651. Servant.
Blos, Stephen	WC2	73	" 1678.
Blouse, Thomas	6	125	" 1663.
Blower, John	9	333	" 1666.
Bloxon, Elizabeth	9	190	" 1665.
Bloyce, Frances	5	210	Immigrated 1662. Wife of Thomas.
Bloyce, Frances	5	210	Transported 1662. Daughter of Thomas. (8, fol. 486).
Bloyce, Judith	5	210	Transported 1662. Daughter of Thomas. (8, fol. 486).
Bloyce, Thomas	5	210	Immigrated 1662. (8, fol. 486).
Bloyd, Daniel	Q	202	Transported prior to 1658.
Bloyden, Ann	17	33	" 1672.
Blozeman, Eliza	10	306	" Jan. 1665. Servant.
Blumfield, Mark	ABH	9	" 1648.
Blund, Henry	8	203	" 1665.
Blundell, Ann	Q	316	Immigrated 1658. (5, fol. 64).
Blunfield, Marke	2	425	Transported 1648.
Blunt, Christopher	6	87	" 1660.
Blunt, Richard	5	214	" 1662.
Blunt, William	7	85	" 1661.
Blunton, Thomas	15	354	" 1676.
Bly, John	12	498	" 1670.
Boads, Lawrence	6	80	" 1660.
Boarman, Capt. William	5	56	" prior to 1650.
Boas, Henry	9	54	" 1665.
Boason, Elizabeth	4	2	" 1658.
Boat, William	ABH	87	" prior to 1640. Servant.

NAME	Liber	Folio	REMARKS
Boate, William	1	88	Transported prior to 1640.
Boates, Thomas	15	318	" 1675.
Boayard, John	20	185	" 1679.
Bocke, Thomas	8	495	" 1665.
Bockes, Charles	8	131	" 1664.
Boddy, Peter	16	629	" 1672.
Bodell, Atwell	5	243	Immigrated 1662. (2, fol. 70).
Bodell, Elizabeth	5	243	Transported 1662. Wife of Atwell.
Bodell, John	WC2	130	" 1679. Servant.
Bodell, John	15	566	" 1678.
Boden, James	WC2	73	" 1678.
Bodman, Edward	15	588	" 1679.
Bodwell, Andrew	5	358	" 1662.
Bodwell, James	7	465	" 1657.
Bodwell, William	16	166	Of Somerset Co. Immigrated 1670.
Boeth, Mary	16	85	Transported 1670.
Bogan, Cornelius	5	260	Immigrated prior to 1662.
Bogg, John	ABH	276	" Transported 1651.
Bogges, Benjamin	7	598	Transported 1664. Son of Philip.
Bogges, Mary	7	598	" 1664. Wife of Philip.
Bogges, Mary	7	598	" 1664. Daughter of Philip.
Bogges, Philip	7	598	Immigrated 1664. Of Calvert Co. (17, fol. 546).
Bognes, Patrick	17	571	Transported 1673.
Bogue, John	4	174	Service 1659. (4 fol. 630).
Bogue, Mary	5	185	Transported 1658. Wife of John.
Bohemend, Anne	8	129	" 1664.
Boice, Thomas	15	300	" 1675.
Bokin, Thomas	5	257	" 1663.
Boland, John	6	19	" 1662.
Boldin, Thomas	15	414	" 1677.
Boldin, William, Jr.	15	414	" 1677.
Boldin, William	15	414	" 1677.
Bole, Henry	15	566	" 1678.
Bolfield, Benjamin	15	347	Service 1673.
Bollard, Henry	15	535	Transported 1678.
Bollard, James	6	94	" 1663.
Bollen, John	16	342	Of Kent Co. Immigrated 1671.
Bolter, William	16	110	Of Calvert Co. Immigrated 1671.
Bolton, George	17	482	Of Dorchester Co. Immigrated 1673.
Bolton, Jane	15	376	Transported 1676.
Bolton, John	4	19	" 1652. Servant.
Bolton, John	6	268	" 1662.
Bolton, John	9	38	" 1665.
Bolton, John	16	125	Of Anne Arundel Co. Service 1671.
Bolton, Richard	4	56	Transported 1659.
Bolton, Thomas	7	496	" 1664.
Bolton, William	WC2	101	" 1679.
Bolton, William	15	391	" 1676.

NAME	Liber	Folio	REMARKS
Bolton, William	16	168	Transported 1671. Servant.
Bolus, Edward	5	529	" 1662.
Bomsgrove, John	11	579	" 1668 by George Mannering of London.
Bonan, Samuel	7	568	Immigrated about 1665.
Bond, Ann	15	379	Transported 1676. (15, fol. 391).
Bond, Anne	WC2	161	" 1680.
Bond, Benjamin	9	39	" 1651.
Bond, Elizabeth	7	520	" 1664.
Bond, Hatton	Q	28	Servant 1649-50.
Bond, Jane	18	37	Wife of Stephen. Immigrated 1673 with Mary Sewell, her daughter. (See Stephen).
Bond, Joseph	6	106	Transported 1663. (15, fol. 541).
Bond, Peter	5	467	" 1653.
Bond, Peter	9	448	Of Anne Arundel Co. Immigrated 1660.
Bond, Peter	15	567	Transported 1679.
Bond, Sarah	7	79	" 1663.
Bond, Stephen	18	35	" 1672. Married Jane Sewell, widow and died prior to 1678. (15, fol. 523).
Bond, William	12	242	Transported 1669. Servant.
Bonds, John	7	560	" 1665.
Bondwell, Abraham	15	402	Service 1676.
Bondwell, Amost	17	10, 40	Transported 1672. (See Boudwell).
Bone, Thomas	9	216	" 1665.
Bonefield, Christian	8	88	" 1665.
Bonefield, Mary	10	311	" Jan. 10, 1663.
Bonington, Edward	ABH	142	Of Patuxent River. Transported 1651.
Bonireck, Ann	5	307	Transported 1663.
Bonnefield, Elizabeth	6	210	" 1663.
Bonnefield, Mary	9	54	" 1665.
Bonner, Alice	9	400	" 1666.
Bonner, Elizabeth	18	334	" 1675.
Bonner, George	WC2	21	" 1679.
Bonner, Henry	12	393	Of Charles Co. Immigrated 1669.
Bonner, Richard	11	318	Transported 1668.
Bonner, William	15	390	" 1676.
Boni, Anne	WC2	411	" 1681.
Bonniday, William	ABH	242	Immigrated 1651.
Bonns, Hanna	9	33	Transported 1660-5.
Bonus, Hans	10	599	" 1667.
Bony, Richard	15	553	" 1678.
Boock, Hans	Q	63	Immigrated 1658.
Boocock, John	1	166	Transported 1650. Servant.
Boodin, Elianor	Q	208	" 1658.
Boodle, Sarah	9	26	" 1665. Wife of Thomas.
Boodle, Thomas	9	26	Immigrated 1665.
Booker, Jeremy	7	464	Transported 1657.
Booker, John	15	397	" 1676.
Booker, Mary	15	322	" 1674.

NAME	Liber	Folio	REMARKS
Booker, Richard	7	474	Of Virginia. Acquired title to land
in Maryland 1664. Immigrated 1665. (9, fol. 558). Certificate for land			
in Baltimore County. (9, fol. 75).			
Booker, Thomas	7	564	Of Virginia. Transported 1664.
Bool, Ann	15	222	Of Accomac Co., the Widow of
George Hock who died prior to 1665.			
Boolwell, Elizabeth	9	50	Transported 1665.
Boon, Elizabeth	17	573	Wife of John of Talbot Co. Service 1673.
Boon, John	5	247	Transported 1662.
Boon, John	6	10	" 1663.
Boone, John	12	350	Of Talbot Co. Service 1669.
Boone, Peter	16	414	Transported 1671.
Boone, Thomas	16	431	Service 1653.
Boone, William	17	417	Transported 1673.
Boone, William	16	293	" 1671.
Boote, Richard	15	569	" 1678.
Booth, George	9	222	" 1665.
Booth, John	WC2	201	" 1680. Servant.
Booth, John	WC2	310	" 1680.
Booth, John	7	507	" 1663.
Booth, John	8	502	" 1665.
Booth, John	13	65	" 1665. Servant.
Booth, John	16	135	Of St. Mary's Co. Transported
1671. Service 1671. (16, fol. 123).			
Booth, John	15	356	Transported 1675.
Booth, John	15	434	Immigrated 1677.
Booth, Robert	6	134	Transported 1663.
Booth, Robert	15	560	" 1678.
Booth, Thomas	17	382	Immigrated 1672 from Virginia.
Booth, Thomas	17	566	Transported 1673 with John and Joseph.
Booty, William	WC2	101	Transported 1679.
Booty, William	15	391	" 1676.
Boouth, John	9	104	Immigrated 1665.
Bord, John	15	567	Transported 1678.
Boreing, Ann	12	589	" 1670. Daughter of John.
Boreing, John	12	589	Of Baltimore Co. Immigrated 1670.
Borell, Peter	17	304	Transported 1672.
Boreman, Mary	4	609	" 1661.
Boreman, Richard	1	63,128	" 1640.
Boreman, Richard	ABH	101	" 1637-40. Servant.
Boreman, Robert	16	435	" 1671.
Boreman, Sarah	Q	33	" 1651. Wife of William.
Boreton, John	16	93	" 1670.
Borill, Olive	5	210	" 1662. Wife of Philip.
Borill, Philip	5	210	Immigrated 1662.
Bornd, Joseph	6	17	Transported 1663.
Borough, Ann	18	89	" 1674 by Joseph of St. Mary's County.

NAME	Liber	Folio	REMARKS
Boroughes, Paul	9	334	Transported 1666.
Boroughs, Sarah	13	114	" 1670.
Boroughs, Thomas	6	106	" 1655.
Borows, Elizabeth	WC2	71,242	" 1677.
Borsby, John	WC2	73	" 1678.
Borstall, John	15	501	" 1678.
Borwood, John	ABH	66	" 1635.
Boskes, Isaac	6	293	" 1664.
Bosman, Blandinia	16	302	Wife of John of Somerset County.
Transported from Virginia in 1671.			
Bosse, William	6	17	Transported 1663.
Bossell, John	11	374	" 1668.
Bostack, Thomas	6	49	Immigrated 1663.
Bosted, Thomas	15	416	Transported 1677.
Boston, Ann	6	125	" 1663. Wife of Henry. (9, fol. 282).
Boston, Henry	6	125	Immigrated 1663. (9, fol. 282).
Boston, Henry, Jr.	9	282	Transported 1663.
Boston, Isaac	6	125	" 1663. Son of Henry. (9, fol. 282).
Boston, John	13	122	Transported 1668.
Boston, Rebecca	6	125	" 1663. Daughter of Henry. (9, fol. 282).
Boston, Robert	15	436	Transported 1677.
Boswell, John	12	209	" 1668.
Boswell, John	15	600	Of Dorchester Co. Immigrated in 1679, with Ann, his wife, and John, his son.
Boswell, Mermaduke	7	569	Transported 1663-4. (16, fol. 437).
Boswell, Otewell	4	59	" 1657.
Boswell, Robert	15	500	" 1678.
Bosworth, Mary	20	185	" 1679.
Boteler, Ann	5	413	" 1663.
Boteler, Charles	15	327	Commission as Deputy Surveyor of Calvert Co., Dec. 27, 1675. Do. from Baker Brooke, Surveyor General 1676. (19, fol. 388).
Boteler, Edward	12	386	Transported 1669.
Boteler, George	16	482	" 1670-1.
Botham, Margaret	16	78	" 1670.
Bottell, Garrett	15	405	Service 1676.
Bottlo, Philip	12	472	Transported 1670.
Botts, Ann	15	507	" 1678.
Bouch, John	9	38	" 1665.
Bouch, Thomas	5	73	" 1660-1.
Boucher, Ab.	15	359	" 1676.
Boucher, Adam	11	307	" 1668. Servant. (11, fol. 469).
Boucher, George	6	129	Transported 1651.
Bouden, Elizabeth	16	428	" 1670-1.
Bouden, Jonathan	15	338	" 1676.
Bouden, Richard	18	173	" 1674.
Boudwell, Amos	17	40	" 1672.

NAME	Liber	Folio	REMARKS
Bouges, Thomas	Q	217	Transported 1652.
Boughely, Jullian	WC2	87	" 1679.
Boughely, Margaret	15	543	" 1678.
Boughton, David	12	190	" 1668. Servant.
Boulen, Ann	5	71	" 1659. Wife of James.
Boullay, James	WC2	160-161, 172,173	Commission as Deputy Surveyor Kent Co. 1680. Service 1680.
Boult, John	15	574	Transported 1678.
Boulter, Isaac	WC2	68	" 1679.
Boulton, Daniel	15	402	Service 1676.
Boulton, Elizabeth	9	336	Transported 1664.
Boulton, Philip	15	573	" 1678.
Boulton, Robert	12	403	" 1669.
Boulton, Sarah	Q	449	" 1658.
Boulton, William	Q	434	" 1658.
Bound, Anne	17	382	Immigrated 1672.
Bound, John	17	382	" from Virginia 1672, with his wife, Anne, and Son, William.
Bound, William	17	382	Immigrated 1672.
Boune, Thomas	Q	71	Transported 1652-3.
Bounsell, Andrew	9	436	Of Anne Arundel County. Immigrated 1666 on the Thomas & George.
Bounsell, George	9	436	Transported 1666. Son of Andrew.
Bounsell, Sarah	9	436	" 1666. Wife of Andrew.
Bounsell, Sarah	9	436	" 1666. Daughter of Andrew.
Bounsell, Walter	---	---	Of Talbot Co. Immigrated Oct. 1663.
Bounty, Will	15	443	Transported 1670.
Boures, John	6	62	" 1663.
Bourke, Edward	20	184	" from Ireland 1678.
Bourne, Will	15	397	" 1676.
Bourne, William	15	600	Of Dorchester Co. Immigrated 1679 with Mary, his wife, and Mary, his daughter.
Bouse, Thomas	WC2	111	Transported 1680.
Bouses, Margaret	5	85	" 1661.
Bousey, Robert	8	499	" 1664.
Bout, Charles	13	114	" 1671.
Boutell, William	7	462	" 1664.
Bouth, John	16	437	" 1671.
Boutwell, Elizabeth	4	14	" 1658. Servant.
Bow, Edward	13	122	" 1668.
Bowcock, John	9	105	" 1665.
Bowdell, George	10	469	" 1667.
Bowdell, Simon	10	469	" 1667.
Bowdell, Thomas	5	64	" 1662.
Bowden, Elizabeth	WC2	16,118	" 1679.
Bowden, George	WC2	16,118	" 1679.
Bowden, John	WC2	171	" 1679.
Bowden, John	15	598	" 1678-9.
Bowden, Thomas	5	188	" 1660.

NAME	Liber	Folio	REMARKS
Bowden, William	WC2	16,118	Transported 1679.
Bowder, Roger	18	160	" 1674.
Bowdle, Edward	17	567	" from Virginia 1673.
Bowdle, Elizabeth	17	551	" 1673.
Bowdle, John	12	201	Service 1669. (12, fol. 202).
Boweir, Githing	7	62	Transported 1664.
Bowen, David	1	166	" 1650. Servant.
Bowen, John	16	86	" 1670.
Bowen, Margaret	18	174	" 1674.
Bowen, Mary	17	388	" from Virginia 1672.

Daughter of Ann, wife of Henry Bishop, Sr.

NAME	Liber	Folio	REMARKS
Bowen, Richard	17	509	Service 1673. (15, fol. 344; 18, fol. 338).
Bowen, Susan	15	397	Transported 1676.
Bowen, Theorick	12	517	" 1670.
Bowen, William	16	405	" 1671.
Bower, Mary	20	184	" from Ireland 1678.
Bower, Richard	7	506	" prior to 1664.
Bower, Samuel	12	280	" 1668. (12, fol. 283).
Bowers, Giles	WC2	146,162	" 1680.
Bowers, Robert	WC2	146,162	" 1680.
Bowery, Mary	10	437	" 1667.
Bowes, Christopher	ABH	422	Immigrated 1655.
Bowes, Christopher	ABH	422	Transported 1655. Son of Christopher.
Bowes, Henry	10	600	Service 1667.
Bowes, Jane	ABH	422	Transported 1655. Wife of Christopher.
Bowgate, George	12	391	Transported 1669.
Bowker, Edward	ABH	198	Immigrated 1650.
Bowland, Elizabeth	8	203	Transported 1665.
Bowle, Thomas	12	341	" 1668.
Bowler, Henry	15	354	" 1676.
Bowles, Alice	4	54	" 1659. Wife of Christopher.
Bowles, David	WC2	10,17	Transported 1679.
Bowles, Edward	3	22	Immigrated 1650 with wife, two children and a servant.
Bowles, Edward	ABH	45	Immigrated 1650 with wife. (4, fol. 214).
Bowles, Elizabeth	4	214	Transported 1650.
Bowles, Joana	4	214	" 1650. (ABH, fol. 46).
Bowles, Joane	3	22	" 1650. Daughter of Edward.
Bowles, John	6	94	Immigrated 1661. Married Margery, widow of Wm. Batten, prior to 1666. (10, fol. 431).
Bowles, John	15	573	Transported 1668.
Bowles, Peter	12	584	" 1670.
Bowles, Sarah	10	342	" 1666.
Bowles, Simon	3	3	" 1650. Servant.
Bowles, Simon	ABH	42	Servant 1650.

NAME	Liber	Folio	REMARKS
Bowles, Thomas	15	307	Transported 1675.
Bowles, William	3	22	" 1650. Son of Edward.
Bowles, William	ABH	46	" 1650. Son of Edward.
Bowles, William	4	214	Immigrated 1650.
Bowleson, Thomas	8	3	Service 1665.
Bowley, James	15	428	Transported 1677.
Bowlin, Francis	8	202	" 1665.
Bowman, Edward	10	352	" 1666.
Bowman, Henry	17	67	" 1672.
Bowman, Mary	7	368	" 1660-4.
Bowman, Richard	ABH	78	" 1640.
Bowman, William	1	171	" about 1639.
Bowman, William	15	376	" 1676.
Bowrin, Edward	17	463	" 1673.
Bowring, Elizabeth	WC2	277	" 1680. Wife of John
and daughter of Edward Chester.			
Bowring, John	WC2	277	Transported 1680. Son-in-law of Edward Chester.
Bowry, Andrew	18	9	Of Talbot Co. Service 1673.
Bowry, Elizabeth	17	350	Transported 1671.
Bowry, William	17	350	" 1671.
Bowtle, Elizabeth	10	340	" 1666.
Bowtle, Thomas	8	427	Married the widow of Stephen Clifton prior to 1664.
Bowton, Thomas	ABH	307	Servant 1649.
Bowton, William	16	407	Transported 1671.
Bowyer, John	WC2	260	Service 1680. Of St. Mary's Co.
Bowyer, Richard	5	188	Transported 1662. Servant.
Boyce, Alexander	15	376	" 1676.
Boyce, James	15	443	" 1669.
Boyce, John	6	129	" 1658.
Boyce, John	10	259	" 1666.
Boyce, Joseph	15	318	" 1675.
Boyce, Mary	11	502	" 1668.
Boyce, Matthew	11	484	" 1668.
Boyce, William	15	167	" 1673.
Boyd, Alexander	18	167	" 1674.
Boyden, Ann	17	383	" 1672.
Boyden, John	17	533	Of Charles Co., and Eleanor, his wife. Service 1673.
Boyen, Henry	15	433	Transported 1677.
Boyen, John	15	431	" 1677.
Boyer, Alizabeth	10	600	Immigrated 1667.
Boyer, John	15	396	Transported 1675.
Boyer, Richard	10	600	" 1667.
Boyes, John	16	94	" 1670.
Boykin, Anne	Q	29	" 1657.
Boyne, John	Q	115	Service 1658.
Boynter, Robert	12	584	Transported 1670.
Boyre, Matthew	11	337	" 1668.
Boyst, Jeane	8	486	" 1665.

NAME	Liber	Folio	REMARKS
Boyst, Mary	5	211	Transported 1662. Wife of William. (8, fol. 486).
Boyst, William	5	211	Immigrated 1662. (8, fol. 486).
Bozman, Ann	6	171	Transported 1663.
Bozman, Bridgett	6	171	" 1663.
Bozman, Ellen	6	171	" 1663. Wife of William.
Bozman, George	6	171	" 1663.
Bozman, John	6	171	" 1663.
Bozman, Mary	6	171	" 1663.
Bozman, William	6	171	Immigrated 1663.
Bozman, William, Jr.	6	171	Transported 1663.
Brabant, George	WC2	310	" 1680.
Braborne, George	18	130	" 1674.
Brace, John	16	109	" 1670.
Brace, Thomas	15	527	" 1678.
Bradborne, Edward	17	363	" 1672.
Bradborne, John	16	92	And Ann, his wife. Service 1669.
Bradey, William	15	523	Of St. Mary's Co. Service 1678.
Bradford, Ann	12	283	Transported 1668. Wife of John.
Bradford, Bartholomew	6	87	" 1657.
Bradford, Dorothy	18	117	" 1674.
Bradford, Henry	15	504	" 1678.
Bradford, John	12	283	Immigrated 1668, with his wife, brother, George Reeves and one servant.
Bradford, William	5	484	Transported 1661. (5, fol. 315).
Bradford, William	18	144	Of St. Mary's Co. and Susannah, his wife. Service 1674.
Bradgall, Katharine	15	501	Transported 1678.
Bradgate, Alice	9	234	" 1665.
Bradham, Richard	17	486	Immigrated from Virginia 1668.
Bradkell, Nicholas	15	359	Transported 1676.
Bradle, Jane	18	306	" 1675.
Bradley, Andrew	15	259	" 1675.
Bradley, Ann	7	493	" 1659. Wife of William.
Bradley, Arthur	15	452	" 1677.
Bradley, James	15	369	" 1676.
Bradley, John	20	185	" 1679.
Bradley, Jone	4	585	" 1661.
Bradley, Mary	9	356	" 1666.
Bradley, Mary	15	332	" 1675.
Bradley, Nicholas	17	611	" 1673. Of St. Mary's Co.
Bradley, Rebecca	15	318	" 1674.
Bradley, Richard	1	121	" 1633.
Bradley, Richard	ABH	98	" 1633. Servant.
Bradley, Thomas	6	235	" 1635.
Bradley, Thomas	6	80	" 1654. Servant.
Bradley, Thomas	5	490	Immigrated 1660.
Bradley, Thomas	9	343	Transported 1666.
Bradley, Thomas	12	403	" 1669.
Bradley, William	ABH	339	" by Robert Brook, Esq. prior to June 1652. Servant.

NAME	Liber	Folio	REMARKS
Bradley, William	7	493	Immigrated 1650.
Bradly, Henry	18	90	Of Dorchester Co. Immigrated in

1674 with Mary, his wife, and Richard, Henry and William, his sons, and Samuel, his brother.

Bradney, William	1	166	Transported 1650. Servant.
Bradshaw, Alexander	16	393	" 1671.
Bradshaw, Alexander	17	601	Immigrated 1672 with Katherine,

his wife, and John and Richard, his children.

Bradshaw, Edward	15	598	Transported 1678-9.
Bradshaw, John	18	152	" 1674. (18, fol. 174, 291).
Bradshaw, Thomas	16	507	" 1671.
Bradshaw, William	17	382	Immigrated from Virginia 1672,

with his wife and Elizabeth, their daughter.

Bradshaw, William	15	530	Transported 1678.
Bradwell, John	Q	207	Servant 1658.
Brady, Henry	16	452	Transported 1671.
Brady, William	18	137	" 1674.
Brafeild, Amy	16	505	" 1672.
Brafeild, Edward	12	388	Of St. Mary's Co. Immigrated from Virginia 1669.
Brafitt, Elizabeth	15	378	Transported 1674.
Bragden, Edward	6	171	" 1663. Servant.
Bragg, Robert	15	376	" 1676.
Braham, William	12	386	Service 1669.
Braine, Henry	12	194	Transported 1668.
Brake, Elizabeth	Q	197	" 1658.
Brallett, Ann	6	131	" 1657.
Brallett, James	6	131	" 1657.
Brallett, Walter	6	131	" 1657.
Bramble, John	WC2	358	Service 1680. Of Dorchester Co.
Bramble, William	6	143	Transported 1663.
Brambles, Elizabeth	18	331	" 1674.
Brame, Christopher	11	235	" prior to 1667.
Bramley, Mary	18	84	" 1674.
Bramson (als. Cole), Mary	Q	183	Servant prior to 1658.
Bramwall, Luke	Q	217	Immigrated 1651. Son of William.
Bramwall, Mary	Q	217	" 1651. Wife of William.
Bramwall, William	Q	217	" 1651.
Branch, Christopher	6	126	Transported 1663.
Branch, Edward	10	600	Immigrated 1667.
Branch, Eliza	4	70	Transported 1659.
Branch, Elizabeth	4	549	" prior to 1661.
Branch, Marlett	10	600	" 1667. Wife of Edward.
Branch, Morrice	10	600	" 1667. Son of Edward.
Brancklin, William	16	394	" 1671.
Brand, Samuel	15	503	" 1678.
Brand, Thomas	15	530	" 1678.
Brandall, Moses	5	413	" 1662.
Branddreth, Mathew	6	216	" 1663.
Brandt, Judith	15	506	" 1674. Daughter of

NAME	Liber	Folio	REMARKS
			Randolph.
Brandt, Mary	15	506	Transported 1674. Daughter of Randolph.
Brandt, Mary	15	506	Transported 1674. Wife of Randolph.
Brandt, Mary	15	566	" 1678.
Brandt, Mr. Randolph	15	506	Immigrated 1674.
Brandt, Randolph	15	506	Transported 1674. Son of Randolph.
Branett, Mary	15	566	" 1678.
Brannough, Edward	17	76	Immigrated 1666 with Jane, his wife. Of Dorchester Co.
Branson, Thomas	ABH	157	Transported 1650. Servant.
Brant, Henry	6	129	" 1662.
Brasbie, Mary	15	454	" Oct. 1677.
Brashaw, Christopher	WC2	21	" 1679.
Brasheer, Thomas	15	414	" 1677. (15, fol. 403).
Brashier, Ann	6	63	" 1658.
Brashier, Benjamin, Jr.	6	63	" 1663.
Brashier, Benjamin, Sr.	6	63	" 1658.
Brashier, Elizabeth	6	63	" 1663.
Brashier, John	6	63	" 1663.
Brashier, Martha	6	63	" 1658.
Brashier, Mary, Sr.	6	63	" 1658.
Brashier, Robert, Jr.	6	63	" 1658.
Brashier, Robert, Sr.	6	63	" 1658-63.
Brashier, Susanna	6	63	" 1658.
Brashier, Thomas	15	430	" 1677.
Brasine, Eleanor	17	415	Immigrated Nov. 1669, with daughter Susanna.
Brasine, Susanna	17	415	Immigrated 1669.
Brasington, Robert	ABH	68	Transported 1638-9. (17, fol. 396; ABH, fol. 101; 15, fol. 502).
Brasinton, Robert	1	43,128	Transported about 1638. Servant.
Brass, Alice	7	86	" 1663.
Brass, Mary	ABH	47	" prior to 1648. Servant.
Brasse, James	17	440	" 1673.
Brasse, Mary	3	23	" before 1648.
Brassitt, Elizabeth	15	378	" 1674. (See Braffitt).
Braughton, Edward	WC2	406	" 1678.
Braun, Mary	WC2	85	Service 1679. Wife of Samuel.
Braun, Samuel	WC2	85	Granted Warrant in right of wife's service 1679. Of Baltimore Co.
Braune, Margaret	13	116	Transported 1671.
Bray, Christopher	6	86	" 1660.
Bray, Hannah	WC2	53	" 1677. Wife of William.
Bray, Hannah	15	445	Immigrated 1677. Wife of William.
Bray, Hannah	WC2	53	Transported 1677. Daughter of William. (15, fol. 445).
Bray, James	WC2	53-54	Transported 1677. Son of William. (15, fol. 445).
Bray, James	18	313	Transported 1675.
Bray, Marjory	12	357	" 1669.

NAME	Liber	Folio	REMARKS
Bray, Samuel	5	339	Transported 1663.
Bray, Walter	6	86	" 1657.
Bray, William	WC2	53-54	Immigrated 1677 with wife, three

children and eight other persons. (15, fol. 445).

Bray, William	15	445	Transported 1677. Son of William.
Bray, William, Jr.	WC2	53	" 1677.
Braydon, Margaret	16	79	" 1670.
Brayer, Edward	9	17	" 1665.
Brayfield, Susanna	9	17	" 1665.
Breadborne, Elinor	16	462	" 1671. Wife of John.
Breadbourne, John	16	462	Service 1666.
Bready, Thomas	17	451	Transported 1673.
Brearly, Thomas	16	122	" 1671.
Breden, Ann	16	43	" 1670.
Breem, Christopher	7	569	" 1663-4.
Breford, Jethro	15	322	" 1675.
Breme, Susanna	6	48	" 1661.
Bremer, James	15	536	" 1678.
Brenane, Eleanor	15	438	" Oct. 1677.
Brendevill, John	WC2	129	" 1679.
Brenson, Thomas	17	56	" 1672. Of St. Mary's Co.
Brent, Fulke	1	18	Immigrated 1638. Brother of Giles.
Brent, George, Gent.	6	26	Transported 1660-3, by James

Clifton, Gent. of Woodstock in Stafford Co., Va., brother to Ann, wife of
James Clifton, 1674. (19, fol. 382).

Brent, Giles	1	18,33-34	Immigrated 1638. Brother of Fulke.

Treasurer and member of Council.

Brent, Mr. Giles	ABH	64	Immigrated 1637-8.
Brent, Mrs. Margaret	ABH	63	" 1638. Location of her

house in St. Mary's 1639. (ABH, fol. 64). Conveys 2000 acres granted to
her and her sister to her nephew James Clifton, Oct. 12, 1663 (6, fol. 26).
Conveys lands to John Brooke of Calvert Co. (11, fol. 282). Sister to
Capt. Giles Brent. (ABH, fol. 37).

Brent, Mrs. Mary	ABH	37	Sister to Margaret and Giles. Im-

migrated prior to 1637. (ABH, fol. 63).

Brent, Mrs. Mary	1	18,24, 31	Immigrated 1638.
Brent, Mary	2	604-605	Special Grant from Lord Baltimore

for immigrating with her sister Margaret and 4 maid servants about
1637-8.

Brent, Mrs. Margaret	1	18,24, 31	Immigrated 1638.
Brent, Margaret	2	604-605	Special Grant from Lord Baltimore

for immigrating with her sister Mary and 4 maid servants about 1637-8.

Brentis, Nicholas	20	185	Transported 1679.
Brenton, John	16	41	" 1670.
Brerely, Thomas	15	517	Of Talbot Co. Service 1678.
Brereton, Sarah	15	318	Transported 1675. Wife of William.
Brereton, William	15	318	Immigrated 1675.
Brereton, William	15	318	Transported 1675. Son of William.

NAME	Liber	Folio	REMARKS
Brethwort, William	15	354	Transported 1676.
Brett, Ann	15	451	" 1678.
Brett, George	5	167	" 1660.
Brettam, John	ABH	60	" 1637. (ABH, fol. 66).
Brettam, William	6	294	" 1664.
Bretton, Ellen	8	501	" 1665.
Bretton, George	5	246	" 1657, by P. C. Esq.
Bretton, Lyonell	7	469	" from Virginia 1664.
Bretton, Oliver	16	505	" 1671.
Bretton, Richard	5	252	" 1663.
Bretton, Robert	12	575	" 1670.
Bretton, Seayone	5	71	Service 1654.
Bretton, Stephen	5	120	Transported 1661.
Bretton, Temperance	Q	58	Immigrated 1649. Wife of William.
Bretton, William	2	394	Immigrated 1637 with wife, child

and three servants. (See Britton).

Bretton, William	ABH	8	Lawful heir of Thomas Noble, who

came into Maryland in 1637.

Bretton, William	12	215	Transported 1668-9.
Brewer, Elizabeth	7	452-3	Widow of John. Acquired a tract

of land called "Widows Chance" in Talbot Co. 640 acres, 1664.

Brewer, George	10	500	Transported about 1658 by Lieut.

Col. Jarboe with Ann, his wife.

Brewer, Han'a.	15	397	Transported 1676.
Brewer, John	15	322	" 1674.
Brewer, John	19	615	Orphan of John, of Anne Arundel
			Co., died 1677.
Brewer, Nicholas	12	383	Of Dorchester County. Service
			1669.
Brewer, Susanna	17	395	Transported 1672.
Brewer, Thomas	9	269	" 1665. (9, fol. 155).
Brewer, Thomas	15	454	" Oct. 1677.
Brewer, William	18	84	" 1674.
Brewerton, Samuel	18	332	" 1674.
Brewerton, William	17	615	" 1673.
Brewest, Andrew	20	185	" 1679.
Brewington, Ellen	5	3	" 1661.
Breynton, John	13	112	Of Baltimore Co. Immigrated 1670.
Brian, Margaret	9	262	Transported 1665.
Brian, Walter	6	122	" 1655.
Brian, William	15	337	" 1676.
Briant, Darby	WC2	187	" 1678.
Briant, John	ABH	66	" 1634.
Briant, John	1	37-38	" 1634. (See Bryant).
Briant (Bryant), William	WC2	167,169	" 1679.
Briarly, Thomas	16	122	" 1671.
Brice, Eleanor	12	405	" 1669. Wife of William.
Brice, Elizabeth	12	591	" 1668.
Brice, John	WC2	171	" 1679.
Brice, Judith	12	405	" 1669. Daughter of

NAME	Liber	Folio	REMARKS
			William.
Brice, William	12	405	Immigrated 1669. Of Dorchester County.
Brice, William	12	405	Transported 1669. Son of William.
Bricker, Francis	7	463	" 1664.
Brider, Robert	6	171	" 1663. Servant.
Bridge, Ann	10	277	" 1666.
Bridge, Eleanor	15	511	" 1676.
Bridger, Joseph, Gent.	10	284	Of the Colony of Virginia, about
to acquire 10,000 acres in Maryland 1660. (10, fol. 438).
Bridges, Anthony	5	530	Transported 1660.
Bridges, Charles	9	433	Of New York. Immigrated 1666.
Bridges, Edward	15	500	Transported 1678. (15, fol. 501).
Bridges, James	4	434	" 1666.
Bridges, Richard	4	48	Immigrated about 1658.
Bridges, Stephen	11	374	Transported 1668.
Bridges, William	10	598	Immigrated 1667.
Bridges, William	16	41	Transported 1670. (16, fol. 43).
Bridgewater, Christopher	12	551	" 1670.
Brigg, John	15	442	" 1677.
Briggs, Ambrose	1	166	" 1650. Servant.
Briggs, Christopher	8	478	" 1665.
Briggs, John	7	502	" 1658.
Briggs, John	5	234	" 1662. Servant.
Briggs, John	17	538	" 1673.
Briggs, John	15	362	" 1676.
Briggs, Mary	8	203	" 1665.
Briggs, Mary	15	540	" 1677.
Briggs, William	18	84	" 1674.
Brigham, John	6	48	" prior to 1663.
Bright, Cecilie Evans	WC2	212	Service 1680. Second wife of Thomas Bright.
Bright, Elizabeth Crisp	WC2	212	Service 1662. First wife of Thomas Bright.
Bright, Francis	ABH	247	Immigrated 1651 with wife.
Bright, John	15	524	Of St. Mary's Co. Service 1678.
Bright, Priscilla	4	590	Transported 1660-1.
Bright, Thomas	WC2	212-213	Rights 1680. First wife Elizabeth
Crisp. Second wife Cecilie Evans. Of Kent Co.
Bright, Thomas	ABH	247	Transported 1651. Son of Francis.
Brightest, Lar.	15	454	" 1677.
Brightwell, Richard	5	560	" 1663. (6, fol. 63).
Brightwell, Richard	16	17	Immigrated 1670.
Brigwell, Ann	4	590	Transported 1660-1.
Brilson, John	12	190	" 1668. Servant.
Brimeridge, Jane	15	516	" 1676.
Brimerigg, Christopher	15	516	" 1676.
Brimington, Jacob	5	89	Immigrated 1659.
Brimstone, John	6	299	" 1664.
Brincks, John	12	190	Transported 1668. Servant.

NAME	Liber	Folio	REMARKS
Bring, John	5	488	Transported 1662.
Brinn, Edward	15	438	" Oct. 1677.
Brinscome, James	15	443	" 1677.
Brion, John	9	48	" 1665.
Brisben, Margaret	7	462	" 1664.
Briscoe, Arthur	6	123	" 1663.
Briscoe, Henry	ABH	65	" 1633.
Brispoe, Anthony	4	70	" 1659. (10, fol. 598).
Brispoe, Elizabeth	15	423	Immigrated 1677.
Brispoe, John	10	598	" 1667.
Briste, James	12	498	Transported 1670.
Brister, Edward	ABH	141	Of Patuxent River. Immigrated 1651.
Britchell, Edward	15	453	Transported 1675-7.
Brite, John	WC2	57	" 1678.
Britt, John	15	553	" 1678.
Brittain, John	4	551	" 1661.
Brittaina, Sarah	5	248	" 1663.
Brittaine, Richard	16	308	Service 1671. Of Somerset Co.
Brittan, William	17	388	Transported from Virginia 1672.
Brittingham, William	4	204	" 1659.
Brittingham, William	6	134	" 1663.
Britton, John	16	412	" 1671.
Britton, Margaret	8	202	" 1664.
Britton, Mary	1	18,68	" 1637. Wife of William, daughter of Thomas Nabbs. (ABH, fol. 81).
Britton, Thomas	12	208	Transported 1669.
Britton, William	1	18,68-69	Immigrated 1637 with wife, child and others. (See Bretton). (ABH, fol. 81).
Britton, William, Jr.	1	18,68-69	Transported 1637. Son of William. Aged 4 years.
Broad, Alice	17	396	Transported 1669.
Broad, John	12	554	" 1670.
Broad, Joseph	15	322	" 1675.
Broadband, John	8	42	" 1665.
Broadberry, Peter	18	115	" 1674.
Broade, Joane	11	537	" 1668.
Broade, Robert	5	203	" about 1662.
Broader, John	8	30	" 1665.
Broaderr, Peter	17	411	" 1673.
Broadhurst, Walter, Gent.	ABH	83	Immigrated 1638.
Broadhurst, Walter	1	18,75	" 1638 with two servants.
Broadrib, John	12	473	Of Talbot Co. Immigrated 1670.
Broadrib, Sibella	18	318	Transported by her husband, John, 1675.
Broadribb, John	7	154	Transported 1663.
Broadwater, Hugh	8	129	" 1664. Servant.
Broadwell, John	11	581	" 1668.

NAME	Liber	Folio	REMARKS
Broame, Lucretia	WC2	16	Transported 1679.
Brock, Elizabeth	17	440	" 1673.
Brock, Richard	1	26	" 1635-41.
Brock, Richard	1	124	" 1637. Servant.
Brock, Richard	ABH	60	" since 1635. Servant.
Brockas, Clare	10	434	" 1667.
Brockas, Elizabeth	10	434	" 1667.
Brockas, George	10	434	" 1667.
Brockas, Jane	10	434	" 1667.
Brockas, Mary	10	434	" 1667.
Brockas, Susanna	10	434	" 1667.
Brockas, William	10	434	" 1667.
Brockes, Christopher	7	91	" 1664.
Brockett, Bryan	12	243	" 1669.
Brockett, Edward	Q	32	Servant 1652.
Brockett, William	15	414	Service 1677.
Brocklebanke, Margery	WC2	21-22, 122	Transported 1679.
Brockman, Henry	18	13	Service 1674.
Brockwell, William	9	104	Transported 1665.
Brodgate, Else	9	156	" 1665.
Brodoway, Nicholas	Q	348	Receives a gift from Lord Baltimore 1658.
Brogden, Richard	13	1	Transported 1669. Servant.
Brokley, Mary	15	567	" 1678.
Bromfield, Margaret	8	128	Wife of John of Baltimore County.
Transported 1664. (John; 7, fol. 530; 15, fol. 501; 12, fol. 284).				
Bromfield, Richard	9	431	Of Virginia. Transported 1666.
Bromhall, Thomas	17	614	Of St. Mary's Co. Immigrated 1673.
Bromley, Andrew	9	39	Transported 1657.
Bromley, John	7	461	" 1664.
Brompton, Elizabeth	6	216	" 1663.
Bromsgrove, John	12	548	" 1670.
Bromwell, Richard	17	634	Son and heir of William of Calvert Co. died 1674.
Brongham, William	16	625	Transported 1663.
Bronk, Ann	Q	323	" 1650. (See Brouk).
Brood, Mary	Q	205	Married William MacDowell prior to 1658.
Brooder, Mary	Q	317	Transported 1658.
Brook, Ann	ABH	56	" 1650. Wife of Mr. Francis Brook.
Brook, Anna	Q	18	Servant 1651.
Brook, Elizabeth	ABH	37	Servant prior to 1637.
Brook, Frances	ABH	95	Transported 1641. Servant. (1, fol. 113). (See Brookes).
Brook, Francis	Q	66	Servant 1656. (See Brookes).
Brook, John	5	180	Transported 1661.
Brook, John	7	82	Immigrated 1662.
Brook, Richard	ABH	99	Transported 1637. Servant.
Brook, Thomas	Q	66	" 1656.

NAME	Liber	Folio	REMARKS
Brook, William	11	373	Transported 1668. Servant.
Brookbank, Abraham	15	598	" 1678-9.
Brooke, Alice	15	527	" 1678.
Brooke, Ann	15	384	" 1673. Grand-daughter of John Heamer.
Brooke, Anna	1	165	Transported 1650. Daughter of Robert.
Brooke, Anne	Q	17	Transported 1670.
Brooke, Baker	1	165	" 1650. Son of Robert.
Brooke, Baker	15	183	Surveyor General, Aug. 1, 1671.
Brooke, Charles	1	165	Transported 1650. Son of Robert.
Brooke, Charles	20	285	Of Calvert Co. By will dated 1671, devised land to his sisters Ann, wife of Christopher Baines, and Elizabeth, wife of Richard Smith.
Brooke, Dorothy	16	3	Wife of Roger, of Calvert Co. Gent., and daughter of James Neale of Calvert Co. Gent. 1670.
Brooke, Edward	16	402	Immigrated 1671. Of Calvert Co.
Brooke, Elizabeth	2	605	Transported about 1637-8. Servant.
Brooke, Elizabeth	11	540	" 1668 by Dr. John Brooke.
Brooke, Francis	1	165	Transported 1650. Son of Robert.
Brooke, Humphrey	9	336	" 1666.
Brooke, Joan	WC2	132	" 1680. Servant.
Brooke, John	1	165	" 1650. Son of Robert.
Brooke, John	5	516	" 1663.
Brooke, John	8	501	" 1665.
Brooke, Margery	11	540	" 1668 by Dr. John Brooke.
Brooke, Mary	1	165	Transported 1650. Wife of Robert.
Brooke, Mary	1	165	" 1650. Daughter of Robert.
Brooke, Michael	5	59	Enters a gift of 400 acres of land from the Governor and Council for public services. His widow marries Henry Trepp prior to 1665. (9, fol. 26).
Brooke, Robert	1	165	Immigrated 1650 with wife, ten children, 21 men servants and 7 maid servants.
Brooke, Robert	1	165	Transported 1650. Son of Robert.
Brooke, Robert, Esq.	Q	446	Agrees to immigrate with his wife, 8 sons and family in 1649.
Brooke, Roger	1	165	Transported 1650. Son of Robert.
Brooke, Sarah	10	541	Wife of Thomas. Transported by her husband, together with her three daughters named Jenkins 1667.
Brooke, Susan	15	397	Transported 1676.
Brooke, Mr. Thomas	6	42	Special Warrant for 1000 acres Aug. 14, 1663.
Brooke, Thomas	1	165	Transported 1650. Son of Robert.
Brooke, Thomas	15	540	" 1677.
Brooke, Major Thomas	15	561	His widow and Executrix married Col. Henry Darnall prior to 1678. (See Brookes, Maj. Thomas).
Brooke, William	1	165	Transported 1650. Son of Robert.
Brooke, William	12	206	Immigrated 1661.

NAME	Liber	Folio	REMARKS
Brookebank, Abraham	WC2	211	Transported 1679. Servant.
Brookefield, Mary	4	30	" prior to 1659. Servant.
Brookes, Ann	4	622	" 1661.
Brookes, Anne	3	116	" 1650. Wife of Francis.
Brookes, Elizabeth	15	442	" 1677.
Brookes, Francis	3	17	Immigrated 1636.
Brookes, Francis	3	116	Rights 1650.
Brookes, Francis	11	103	And Frances, his wife, Service 1667.
Brookes, Francis	15	442	Transported 1677.
Brookes, Henry	17	440	" 1673.
Brookes, James	4	556	And Mary, his wife. Service 1675.
Brookes, John	16	505	Transported 1671. (17, fol. 57).
Brookes, John	11	162	" 1667. Servant. (17, fol. 57).
Brookes, Joshua	15	530	Transported 1678.
Brookes, Matthew	5	207	" 1662.
Brookes, Sarah	10	498	" 1667.
Brookes, Major Thomas	5	125	Brother to Baker Brookes, Esq., living 1662.
Brookes, Thomas	11	316	Transported 1668. (City of Bristol ?).
Brookes, Thomas	17	608	Transported 1673. (18, fol. 293).
Brookes, Thomas	15	431	Immigrated 1677.
Brookes, William	7	135	Transported 1664. Service 1671. (16, fol. 537).
Brookes, William	WC2	89,92	Service 1679. Of Calvert County.
Brookeshaw, James and wife	18	39	Service 1674.
Brookewall, James	15	565	Transported 1679.
Brookland, Ann	12	217	" 1669.
Brookley, John	15	430	" 1677.
Brooks, Elizabeth	ABH	63	" 1638. Servant. (1, fol. 18, 31).
Brooks, Mr. Francis	ABH	44	Immigrated about 1636. Of the Isle of Kent, living 1651. (ABH, fol. 207).
Brooks, George	10	117	Transported 1666.
Brooks, Henry	2	425	" 1641.
Brooks, Henry	ABH	10	" 1641.
Brooks, Jane	3	62	Wife of Henry. Claims land due to her former husband, David Wickliffe. (ABH, fol. 49).
Brooks, Michael and wife	ABH	380	Immigrated 1654.
Brooks, Nath.	15	359	Transported 1676.
Brooks, Penelope	ABH	24	Servant 1646.
Brooks, Penelope	2	512	Transported about 1649. Servant.
Brooksby, Anthony	10	335	" 1660.
Broom, Margaret	ABH	213	" prior to 1652 by her kinsman, Robert Taylor.
Broomdon, Joane	11	167	Transported 1667. Wife of Thomas.
Broomdon, Thomas	11	167	Of Anne Arundel Co. Immigrated 1667.

NAME	Liber	Folio	REMARKS
Broome, Bartholomew	5	257	Transported 1663.
Broome, Edward	6	18	" 1658.
Broome, Rachel	18	109	" 1674.
Broome, Susanna	5	257	" 1663.
Broomfield, John	7	78	" 1651. Servant.
Broomfield, John	9	354	" 1662.
Broomfield, John	15	500	" 1678.
Brossey, John	11	337	" 1668.
Brotherhood, Thomas	5	87	" 1649-62.
Brothers, Dennis	20	184	" from Ireland 1678.
Brothers, John	10	429	" 1664.
Brotherton, Edward	WC2	309	" 1678.
Brothy, Dennis	15	553	" 1678.
Broucklin, William	17	456	" 1671.
Brough, Andrew	4	204	" prior to 1659. Servant.
Brough, William	ABH	99	Immigrated 1636.
Broughe, William	1	123	" 1636.
Broughton, Francis	9	304	Transported 1665.
Broughton, Samuel	5	85	" 1661.
Brouk, Ann	Q	323	" 1650.
Broune, William	16	79	" 1670.
Brouse, Samuel	17	333	" 1671. Of St. Mary's County.
Browen, George	Q	19	Servant 1656.
Browgham, William	16	137	Transported 1671.
Brown, Abigail	12	194	" 1668. Servant.
Brown, Adam	16	393	" 1671.
Brown, Alexander	18	296	" 1674.
Brown, Alice	7	371	" 1661. (7, fol. 577).
Brown, Andrew	ABH	372	" 1651. Servant.
Brown, Ann	8	499	" 1664.
Brown, Ann	WC2	73	" 1665.
Brown, Ann	17	597	Of Talbot Co. Service 1673.
Brown, Ann	15	318	Transported 1675.
Brown, Benjamin	18	137	" 1674.
Brown, Charles	17	551	" 1671.
Brown, Daniel	ABH	348	" prior to June 1652. Servant. (Q, fol. 17).
Brown, Daniel	17	444	Immigrated 1673.
Brown, Edward	5	489	Transported 1655.
Brown, Eleanor	12	215	" 1668.
Brown, Elizabeth	7	489	" 1664.
Brown, Elizabeth	17	463	" 1673.
Brown, Ellis	12	415	" 1669.
Brown, Gabriel	WC2	73	" 1665.
Brown, George	4	29	" 1659.
Brown, George	12	415	" 1669.
Brown, Henry	4	139	" 1657. Servant. (Quaker ?)
Brown, Henry	9	33	Transported 1660-5.
Brown, James	ABH	40	" 1649.

NAME	Liber	Folio	REMARKS
Brown, James	ABH	200	Transported 1659. Servant.
Brown, James	Q	49	Immigrated 1652.
Brown, James	7	506	Transported prior to 1664.
Brown, James	7	560	" 1665.
Brown, James	12	285	Immigrated 1668.
Brown, James	17	474	Transported 1672.
Brown, James	17	538	And Mary, his wife, of Dorchester County, Service.
Brown, James	18	137	Transported 1674.
Brown, Jane	18	279	" 1675.
Brown, Jean	11	374	" 1668.
Brown, Jeremy	ABH	374	" 1st cond. Servant. (Q, fol. 430).
Brown, Johanna	WC2	184	Transported 1680. Servant.
Brown, John	ABH	429	Late of St. Mary's Co. dec'd Aug. 22, 1655. Letters of Administration on his estate granted to Col. John Price and John Nevill.
Brown, John	5	248	Transported 1663.
Brown, John	9	44	" 1663.
Brown, John	10	558	" 1666.
Brown, John	17	348	" 1667.
Brown, John	11	378	" 1668.
Brown, John	12	203	" 1669.
Brown, John	16	95	" 1670.
Brown, John	13	127	Of St. Mary's County. Immigrated from Virginia 1671.
Brown, John	17	81	Service 1672.
Brown, John	17	352	Of Dorchester Co. Immigrated 1672 with Sarah, his wife, and William and Sarah, his children.
Brown, John	17	407	Transported 1672.
Brown, John	18	177	" 1674.
Brown, John	18	318	Of Anne Arundel Co. Service 1675.
Brown, John, Jr.	11	378	Transported 1668.
Brown, Jone	10	583	" 1667. Servant.
Brown, Margaret	ABH	429	Renounces administration on the estate of her husband, John Brown, Merchant, dec'd. 1655.
Brown, Margaret	Q	49	Immigrated 1658.
Brown, Margaret	11	339	Transported 1668.
Brown, Mary	4	140	" 1657. Servant.
Brown, Mary	9	330	" 1665.
Brown, Mary	17	407	" 1672.
Brown, Matthew	18	306	" 1675.
Brown, Michael	18	137	" 1674.
Brown, Nathaniel	5	484	" 1659.
Brown, Nicholas	11	344	" 1668. (11, fol. 465; 13, fol. 111; 18, fol. 13).
Brown, Rachel	ABH	60	Transported 1635. Servant.
Brown, Richard	ABH	10	Servant 1637.
Brown, Richard	1	18,26	Transported 1637.
Brown, Richard and wife	ABH	15	Immigrated 1648. (ABH, fol. 44).

NAME	Liber	Folio	REMARKS
Brown, Richard	12	591	Transported 1670.
Brown, Richard	17	538	" 1673. (17, fol. 414).
Brown, Robert	7	498	" 1660.
Brown, Rose	5	416	" prior to 1663.
Brown, Samuel	16	458	" 1672.
Brown, Sarah	17	411	" 1673.
Brown, Susan	7	454	" 1664.
Brown, Susan	16	480	" Jan. 1671.
Brown, Thomas	5	203	" 1662.
Brown, Thomas	17	486	" 1671.
Brown, Thomas	18	166	" 1674. (18, fol. 174, 288).
Brown, William	ABH	5	Transported 1633. Servant.
Brown, William	ABH	48	Service 1650.
Brown, William	16	447	Transported 1671.
Brown, William	17	407	" 1672.
Brown, William	17	557	Of Dorchester Co. Service 1673.
Brown, William	18	174	Transported 1674.
Browne, Alice	9	336	" 1665.
Browne, Andrew	4	140	" 1651. Servant.
Browne, Ann	15	567	" 1678. (15, fol. 560).
Browne, Barbery	10	398	" prior to 1668.
Browne, Charles	11	378	" 1668.
Browne, Cuthbert	6	255	Immigrated 1663.
Browne, Daniel	4	53	Transported 1659.
Browne, Daniel	6	14	" 1663.
Browne, David	16	167/169	Of Somerset Co. Immigrated 1670.
Browne, David	15	537	Transported 1678.
Browne, Edward	6	105	" 1655.
Browne, Edward	9	321	" 1666.
Browne, Edward	15	433	" 1677.
Browne, Eleanor	16	40	" 1670.
Browne, Elizabeth	9	25	" 1665.
Browne, Ellen	18	15	" 1673.
Browne, Francis	12	203	" 1669.
Browne, Gabriel and wife	8	129	Immigrated 1665.
Browne, Henry	16	40	Transported 1670.
Browne, Isabella	15	362	" 1676.
Browne, Isabella	15	442	" 1677.
Browne, James	5	488	" 1648.
Browne, James	4	216	" 1659.
Browne, James	2	615	" 1649.
Browne, James	9	37	Immigrated prior to 1665.
Browne, James	9	332	Transported 1666.
Browne, James	15	429	" 1674.
Browne, James	15	430	" 1677.
Browne, Jane	9	35	" 1664.
Browne, Joane	6	209	" 1663.
Browne, Joanna	4	216	" 1659.
Browne, John	WC2	88	Service 1679. Of Charles County.

NAME	Liber	Folio	REMARKS
Browne, John	WC2	199	Transported 1680.
Browne, John	WC2	253,398	" 1680.
Browne, John	5	467	" 1653.
Browne, John	4	216	Immigrated 1659.
Browne, John	4	585	Transported 1661.
Browne, John	5	228	Of New England. Demands land in Maryland 1662.
Browne, John	9	343	Transported 1666.
Browne, John	11	378	" 1668. (13, fol. 17).
Browne, John	14	343	Of Somerset Co. Immigrated 1671. (16, fol. 394).
Browne, John	16	437	Of Anne Arundel Co. Service 1671.
Browne, John	15	362	Transported 1676.
Browne, John	15	442	" 1677. (15, fol. 448).
Browne, John	15	566	" 1678.
Browne, Mr. John	15	520	Of Calvert Co. Immigrated 1677, per ship Rappahanock Merchant of London.
Browne, Jone	14	145	Transported 1665.
Browne, Margaret	15	348	" 1655. Servant.
Browne, Margaret	18	15	" 1673.
Browne, Mary	5	247	" 1658.
Browne, Mary	5	89	" 1661.
Browne, Mary	16	168,435	" 1671.
Browne, Mary	18	313	" 1675.
Browne, Mathew	5	218	" 1662.
Browne, Melchisedeck	6	264	Immigrated 1662.
Browne, Nan	6	159	Transported 1663.
Browne, Peter	5	267	" 1663.
Browne, Philip	5	306	Immigrated 1663.
Browne, Richard	2	426	Transported 1637. Servant.
Browne, Richard	2	458	Immigrated 1648 with wife.
Browne, Richard	4	79	Transported 1659.
Browne, Richard	9	54	" 1665.
Browne, Robert	WC2	65	" 1679. Servant.
Browne, Robert	4	140	" 1656. Servant.
Browne, Mr. Robert	4	207-8	Of Kent Co. Brother of Nicholas, dec'd. Immigrated 1658.
Browne, Sarah	17	395	Transported 1672.
Browne, Sarah	14	343	" 1671. Wife of William.
Browne, Sarah	14	343	" 1671. Daughter of John
Browne, Sarah	15	439	Transported 1677.
Browne, Stephen	5	467	" 1659.
Browne, Thomas	8	202	Immigrated 1665.
Browne, Thomas	13	113	Transported 1670. Service 1678. (15, fol. 545).
Browne, Thomas	WC2	130,145	Transported 1679. Servant.
Browne, Walter	4	625	" 1661.
Browne, Will.	15	332	" 1675.
Browne, Will.	15	540	" 1676.
Browne, William	1	110	" 1633.

NAME	Liber	Folio	REMARKS
Browne, William	WC2	16,21-22,122	Transported 1679.
Browne, William	2	254	Service 1641-6.
Browne, William	3	25	" prior to 1650.
Browne, William	8	129	Transported 1665. Son of Gabriel.
Browne, William	14	343	" 1671. Son of John.
Browne, William	16	79	" 1670.
Browne, Zach.	15	540	" 1677.
Brownhill, George	18	15	" 1673.
Browning, Elizabeth	WC2	73	" 1678.
Browning, Francis	12	584	" 1670.
Browning, George	WC2	73	" 1678.
Browning, Hester	WC2	73	" 1665.
Browning, John	9	490	" 1665. Son of Thomas.
Browning, Mr. John	15	574	Son of Mr. Thomas, dec'd 1679.
Browning, John, Jr.	WC2	73	Transported 1678. Son of Thomas.
Browning, Matthew	Q	201	" 1650. (ABH, fol. 22; 6, fol. 263).
Browning, Thomas	WC2	73	Immigrated 1665.
Browning, Mr. Thomas	9	490	Immigrated 1665 with wife. (6, fol. 17, 18).
Browning, Tobias	15	356	Transported 1675.
Brownless, William	9	54	" 1665.
Brownrigg, Christopher	ABH	140	" 1651.
Brownrigs, Eli	15	358	" 1675.
Browton, William	17	411	" 1673.
Broxhall, James	16	406	" 1671.
Bruce, John	16	109	" 1665.
Bruce, Robert	11	581	" 1668.
Bruer, Nicholas	7	582	" 1665.
Bruff, Henry	15	545	Service 1666.
Bruffe, Pusan	18	107	Immigrated 1665. Wife of Thomas, 1674.
Bruffe, Thomas	16	468	Immigrated July 1671. Of Talbot County.
Brumeridge, Joseph	8	486	Transported 1664.
Brumfield, Dorothy	13	65	" 1668. Servant.
Brumly, Andrew	5	90	" 1656-9.
Brummell, Robert	15	565	" 1679.
Brumton, Elizabeth	9	84	" 1663.
Brumwell, Robert	15	565	" 1679.
Brunellson, Foulke	11	537	" 1668.
Brunt, Edward	9	330	" 1665.
Brunt, Margaret	3	174	" 1656.
Brunt, Milka	9	330	" 1665.
Bruton, John	16	412	" 1669.
Bruton, Sarah	5	128	" 1662.
Brutonire, John	5	514	" 1656.
Bryan, Dennis	5	259	" 1657.
Bryan, Derby	11	378	" 1668.

NAME	Liber	Folio	REMARKS
Bryan, Elizabeth	15	446	Transported 1677.
Bryan, Honner	15	553	" 1678.
Bryan, Honor	WC2	57	" 1678.
Bryan, John	4	14	" 1656. Servant.
Bryan, Margaret	16	435	" 1671.
Bryan, Martin	15	446	" 1677.
Bryan, Mary	15	527,553	" 1678.
Bryan, Mathias	3	23	" before 1648.
Bryan, Mic.	15	446	" 1677.
Bryan, Moor	15	527	" 1678.
Bryan, Nicholas	ABH	47	" prior to 1648. Servant.
Bryan, Pat	15	553	" 1678.
Bryan, Patrick	WC2	57	" 1678.
Bryan, Thomas	9	49	Immigrated 1665.
Bryan, William	16	17	" 1670.
Bryant, Abigall	WC2	167,169	Transported 1679.
Bryant, Hugh	15	443	" 1667.
Bryant, John	1	20,166	" 1633-4. (See Briant).
Bryant, John	16	536	And Ursula, his wife. Service 1671.
Bryant, Robert	17	396	Immigrated 1672 with Honor, his wife.
Bryant, Thomas	17	44	Transported 1667.
Bryant, William	7	78	" 1663.
Bryay, Mary	18	137	" 1674.
Bryent, Martin	WC2	106	" 1679.
Bryent, Robert	17	417	" 1673.
Bryer, Ann	15	569	" 1678.
Bryne, Bridgett	WC2	82	" 1679.
Bryne, Derby	WC2	82	" 1679.
Bryne, Hanah	15	438	" Oct. 1677.
Bryne, John	WC2	91	Immigrated 1679 with wife and son.
Bryne, Mary	WC2	91	Transported 1679. Wife of John.
Bryne, Nicholas	WC2	91	" 1679. Son of John.
Bubb, Ann	15	560	" 1678.
Bucey, Paul	4	21	Service 1659.
Buchane, Mary	WC2	128	Transported 1679.
Buck, Elizabeth	4	576	" 1661.
Buck, John	6	94	" 1663. Service 1675. (15, fol. 301).
Buck, John	18	335	Transported 1675.
Buckes, Edward	14	443	" 1672.
Buckfield, Mary	5	128	" prior to 1662.
Buckingham, John	12	393	" 1669.
Buckingham, Peter	5	339	" 1663.
Buckingham, Thomas	9	28	" 1664.
Buckland, Richard	18	35	Immigrated 1672, with Elizabeth, his wife and Richard, his son.
Buckle, Samuel	17	411	Transported 1673.
Buckler, William	16	170	" 1671.
Buckley, Margaret	15	380	" 1676.
Buckley, Samuel	15	516	" 1678.

NAME	Liber	Folio	REMARKS
Buckman, Nathaniel	16	414	Transported 1671.
Bucknell, Isabel	6	83	" 1663.
Bucknell, Samuel	12	190	" 1668. Servant.
Bucknell, Thomas	6	79	" 1663.
Buckstone, George	18	31	" 1674.
Buckwood, Edward	11	374	" 1668.
Buckworth, Thomas	16	393	" 1671.
Bud, Giles	4	48	" 1659. Servant.
Budd, Peter	6	131	" 1661.
Budd, Richard	3	3	Immigrated 1650 with wife and two men servants.
Budd, Richard and wife	ABH	42	Immigrated 1650.
Buddell, William	10	117	Transported 1666.
Budden, Elizabeth	ABH	49	Daughter of Rev. Wm. Wilkenson's wife. Transported 1650.
Budden, Elizabeth	3	62	Transported 1650. Daughter of Mrs. William Wilkinson.
Budden, Sarah	6	117	Transported 1663.
Budgin, Thomas	17	608	" 1673.
Budworth, Isaac	11	337	" 1668.
Buelis, All Saints	9	334	" 1666.
Buer, Ann	17	396	" 1669.
Buffin, John	9	304	" 1665.
Buggonthistole, Alex.	11	1	" 1667.
Bugken, Daniel	15	527	" 1678.
Buker, Thomas	15	430	" 1677.
Bull, Eleanor	7	577	" about 1665.
Bull, Hannah	7	577	" about 1665.
Bull, John	7	577	" about 1665.
Bull, Mary	Q	204	" 1657.
Bull, Mary	6	166	" 1661.
Bull, Thomas	WC2	167,169	" 1679.
Bull, Thomas	15	300	" 1663.
Bull, Thomas	16	115	" 1671.
Bull, Thomas	17	440	" 1673.
Bull, Thomas	15	443	" 1674.
Bull, Tobias	16	302	" 1671.
Bull, William	15	566	" 1678.
Bullain, Ralph	6	85	" 1652.
Bullen, Eleanor	4	57	" 1659. Wife of Robert. (5, fol. 88).
Bullen, Henry	ABH	200	Immigrated 1650.
Bullen, Robert	4	57	" 1659. (5, fol. 88).
Bullen, Thomas	WC2	129	Transported 1679.
Bulles, John	9	313	" 1665.
Bullington, Thomas	15	566	" 1678.
Bullock, Francis	15	500	" 1678.
Bullock, Francis	WC2	395	" 1680. Servant.
Bullock, John	4	188	" about 1659. Servant.
Bullock, William	10	325	" prior to 1666.
Bullock, William	17	547	" 1673.

NAME	Liber	Folio	REMARKS
Bullpitt, John	8	483	Transported from Virginia 1665. (16, fol. 533).
Bullyshort, Mary	4	30	Transported prior to 1659. Servant.
Bulver, John and wife	6	264	Immigrated 1663.
Bulwark, Simon	7	506	Transported 1662.
Bulwick, Elizabeth	15	322	" 1674.
Bumpes, Thomas	Q	197	" 1658.
Bumpus, Thomas and wife	5	58	Immigrated 1662.
Bunce, Deborah	15	390	Transported 1675.
Bunckes, George	12	584	" 1670.
Bundick, Dorothy	9	17	" 1665.
Bunduck, Richard	4	5	" 1659. Servant.
Bunfield, Benjamin	16	112	" 1671.
Bungye, William	5	228	" 1662.
Bunn, Deborah	18	160	" 1674.
Bumne, John	6	19	" 1663.
Buntes, Ann	15	429	" 1677.
Buntlin, John	11	171	" 1667.
Bunts, Ann	18	166	" 1674.
Burbage, William	ABH	376	Lived in Kent Co. prior to 1654. Brother to Thomas of Virginia.
Burberry, Samuel	18	22	Of Talbot Co. Service 1673.
Burbridge, Alice	WC2	146,162	Transported 1680.
Burbridge, Ann	16	507	" 1671.
Burch, Thomas	8	3,503	Immigrated 1665.
Burch, William	18	174	Transported 1674.
Burch, William	WC2	120	" 1680.
Burchall, Robert	WC2	381	" 1675-80. Servant.
Burck, John	15	397	" 1675. (15, fol. 553).
Burd, Elizabeth	15	453	" 1675-7.
Burd, John	7	371	" 1663. Servant.
Burd, John	12	403	" 1669.
Burdett, Francis	5	307	" 1663 by Thomas Burdett.
Burdett, John	15	523	Of St. Mary's Co. Immigrated 1678.
Burdett, Peter	7	464	Transported 1660.
Burdett, Thomas	ABH	151	" 1649-50. Servant.
Burdett, Mr. Thomas	4	48	Immigrated 1659, and Violinda, his wife.
Burdges, Roger	5	93	Transported prior to 1661.
Burditt, Thomas	15	397	" 1676.
Burdon, Thomas	6	210	" 1663.
Burford, Elizabeth	WC2	380	" 1680. Daughter of Thomas.
Burford, Mary	16	414	Transported 1671.
Burford, Thomas	WC2	380	Immigrated 1680 with son and daughter. Of Charles Co.
Burford, Thomas, Jr.	WC2	380	Transported 1680.
Burgen, Philip	15	503	" 1678.
Burges, Edward	9	189	" 1665.

NAME	Liber	Folio	REMARKS
Burges, Elizabeth	WC2	415	Transported 1666-80. Servant.
Burges, John	17	396	" 1671. (16, fol. 635).
Burges, Jone	15	531	" 1678.
Burges, Joseph	12	591	" 1668.
Burges, Peter	WC2	303, 304, 307	Service 1680. Of Calvert Co.
Burges, Philip	4	551	Transported 1661. (6, fol. 10; 12, fol. 380).
Burges, Richard	16	507	Transported 1671.
Burges, Stephen	12	209	" 1668.
Burges, William	Q	403	Immigrated 1650.
Burges, William	16	20	Service 1667.
Burgess, Joane	1	18	Transported 1638. Servant.
Burgess, Philip	4	198	" 1659.
Burgesse, George	17	609	Of St. Mary's Co. Service 1673.
Burgin, Phil	15	454	Transported 1677.
Burgis, Richard	15	441	Service 1677.
Buring, Matthew	5	89	Transported 1661.
Burk, Eleanor	15	438	" Oct. 1677.
Burk, John	WC2	57	" 1678.
Burk, William	7	559	" 1663.
Burke, Jane	10	398	" 1666.
Burke, Patrick	WC2	120	" 1680.
Burke, William	6	212	Married the widow of Major Billingsley prior to 1663.
Burke, William	18	14	Of St. Mary's Co. Service 1674.
Burkes, Jeane	15	436	Transported 1677.
Burkesby, Alice	12	314	" 1669.
Burkitt, Jane	18	29	Wife of Thomas of Baltimore Co.
Transported from Virginia 1673.			
Burkitt, Thomas	18	29	Of Baltimore Co. Immigrated Oct. 1667.
Burl, Thomas	15	430	Transported 1677.
Burle, John	5	531	" 1656 by Thomas Burle.
Burle, Mary	2	608	" 1649. Wife of Robert.
Burle, Mary	ABH	39	Wife of Robert. Transported 1649. (5, fol. 12).
Burle, Robert	ABH	39	Immigrated 1649. (5, fol. 12).
Burle, Robert	9	336	Transported 1666 by Robert Burle.
Burle, Robert	5	12	Immigrated 1649. Of Severn River.
Burle, Robert	2	608	" 1649 with wife, two
sons and three other persons.			
Burle, Robert, Jr.	ABH	39	Transported 1649.
Burle, Robert, Jr.	2	608	" 1649. Son of Robert.
Burle, Sarah	5	12	" 1649. Wife of Robert.
Burle, Stephen	ABH	39	" 1649.
Burle, Stephen	2	608	" 1649. Son of Robert.
Burle, Thomas	5	12	" 1649. Son of Robert.
Burley, Henry	9	25	" 1665. (17, fol. 590).
Burley, James	9	321	" 1665.
Burley, John	13	112	" 1670.

NAME	Liber	Folio	REMARKS
Burley, John	17	567	Transported from Virginia 1673.
Burlin, Matthew	15	397	" 1676.
Burlingham, Deborah	12	415	" 1669.
Burnam, William	Q	47	Servant 1658.
Burne, James	15	446	Transported 1677.
Burne, John	18	137	" 1674.
Burne, Mary	15	446	" 1677.
Burne, Mary	WC2	108	" 1677.
Burne, William	WC2	87	" 1679.
Burnell, Thomas	6	49	Immigrated 1663.
Burnett, Roger	5	529	Transported 1662.
Burnett, Thomas	15	567	" 1679.
Burney, Anthony	17	424	" 1673.
Burnham, Ann	WC2	283	Service 1680. Wife of William.
Burnham, Gabriell	15	455	Transported 1678.
Burnham, William	12	498	" 1670.
Burnham, William	WC2	283,402	Service 1680. Of Charles Co.
Burr, William	3	173	Transported 1655.
Burrage, Elizabeth	4	625	" prior to 1658. Daughter of John.
Burrage, John	ABH	40	Transported 1649. (4, fol. 625).
Burrage, John	2	614	" 1649.
Burrage, Margaret	4	625	" prior to 1658. Wife of John.
Burrage, Margaret	4	625	Transported prior to 1658. Daughter of John.
Burraws, Mathew	ABH	94	Transported 1633. Servant.
Burrell, John	15	564	Immigrated 1673, with Ann, his wife and Ann, his daughter.
Burrell, Ralph	10	556	Transported 1664-5.
Burresse, John	6	63	" 1658-63.
Burridge, John	17	44	Of St. Mary's Co. Service 1672.
Burros, Michael	15	390	Transported 1676.
Burrough, George	4	534	" 1659. Son of Nathaniel. (ABH, fol. 347).
Burrough, Nathaniel	4	534	Immigrated 1659. (ABH, fol. 347).
Burrough, Rebecca	4	534	Transported 1659. Wife of Nathaniel.
Burrough, Thomas	10	603	Transported 1667.
Burroughes, John	12	516	Of Calvert Co. Service 1669.
Burroughs, George	ABH	347	Transported Oct. 1652. Son of Nathaniel.
Burroughs, Paul	9	448	Transported 1668. (11, fol. 230).
Burrowes, Matthew	1	110	" 1633.
Bursell, John	15	544	Service 1678.
Bursted, Jeremiah	Q	48	Servant 1658.
Burstone, Thomas	16	38	Transported 1670.
Burt, Elizabeth	15	566	" 1678.
Burt, Joane	15	566	" 1678.
Burt, Margaret	16	293	" 1671.
Burtbey, Alice	12	242	" 1669. Of Virginia.

NAME	Liber	Folio	REMARKS
Burtchfield, Samuel	7	491	Transported 1661-2.
Burton, Edmond	ABH	247	Immigrated 1651.
Burton, Edward	ABH	247	Transported 1657. Son of Edmond.
Burton, Francis	16	432	" 1671.
Burton, John	12	385	" 1669.
Burton, John	18	107	" 1674.
Burton, John	15	414	" 1677.
Burton, Rebecca	ABH	247	" 1651. Wife of Edmond.
Burton, Thomas	18	335	" 1675.
Burton, Thomas	15	433	" 1677.
Burton, William	12	359	Of Dorchester Co. Immigrated from Virginia 1669.
Burtonshire, Edward	WC2	395	Transported 1680. Servant.
Burty, John	15	422	Service 1677.
Bury, John	11	344	Transported 1668.
Bury, William	Q	32	Servant 1653.
Busbo, Robert	6	171	Transported 1663.
Busby, Henry	18	174	" 1674.
Busfield, Thomas	18	329	" 1675.
Bush, Ann	12	194	" 1668. Servant.
Bush, Daniel	6	134	" 1660.
Bush, John	16	86	" 1670. (16, fol. 393).
Bush, William	16	507	" 1671.
Bushell, Edward	10	598	" 1667.
Bushell, Elizabeth	5	87	" 1649-62.
Bushell, John	5	484	" 1661.
Bushell, Thomas	1	126	Immigrated 1640.
Bushell, Thomas and wife	ABH	100	" 1640. (ABH, fol. 162).
Bushell, Thomas	2	224	" 1642.
Bushell, Thomas	3	105	" 1640.
Bushell, William	5	320	" 1650.
Bushells, George	13	114	Transported 1671.
Bushnell, Christian	9	32	" 1664.
Bushy, George and wife	ABH	381	Immigrated Feb. 1653.
Bushy, George	ABH	381	Transported 1653. Son of George.
Bushy, Henry	ABH	381	" 1653. Son of George.
Buskee, Robert	15	455	" 1678.
Buskin, Thomas	12	576	" 1670.
Buskley, Samuel	WC2	309	" 1680.
Busse, Witten	17	395	" 1672.
Bussey, Hannah	16	482	" 1670-1.
Bustill, John	15	534	" 1678.
Bustle, Martha	WC2	410	Immigrated from Virginia 1681. Of St. Mary's County.
Bustoce, Mary	7	612	Transported 1665.
Buston, Matthew	4	56	" prior to 1659.
Busy, Paul	6	83	" 1655.
Butcher, Susanna	17	602	Service 1673.
Butcher, Thomas	12	403	Transported 1669.
Buther, John	18	329	" 1675.

NAME	Liber	Folio	REMARKS
Butler, Ann	15	436	Transported 1677.
Butler, Benjamin	12	403	" 1669.
Butler, Benjamin	17	608	" 1673.
Butler, Catherine	5	248	" 1663.
Butler, Christopher	WC2	395	" 1680. Servant.
Butler, Edward	ABH	142	" 1651.
Butler, Edward	12	496	" 1670.
Butler, Elizabeth	18	84	" 1674.
Butler, Henry	WC2	282	" 1680.
Butler, Henry	16	503	" 1671.
Butler, James	16	341	Of Dorchester Co. Immigrated
1671, with Mary, his wife, and James, William and John, his sons.
Butler, James	15	527	Transported 1678.
Butler, James	WC2	380	" 1675-80. Servant.
Butler, John	12	403	" 1669.
Butler, John	17	486	" from Virginia 1671.
Butler, John	18	137	" 1674.
Butler, John	15	360	" 1676.
Butler, John	15	436	" 1677.
Butler, John	15	553	" 1678.
Butler, Capt. John	1	92	Petition to confirm title to land
granted by Capt. William Clayborne, 1640.
Butler, John	WC2	120	Transported 1680.
Butler, Jone	15	553	" 1678.
Butler, Jone	WC2	380	" 1675-80. Servant.
Butler, Margaret	16	411	" 1671.
Butler, Richard	ABH	33	Immigrated 1646.
Butler, Richard	ABH	26	" 1646.
Butler, Richard	2	523,567	" 1646.
Butler, Richard	11	378	Transported 1668.
Butler, Robert	7	528	" 1664.
Butler, Thomas	ABH	86	Of the Isle of Kent. Planter. Im-
migrated with his wife and two children, prior to 1640.
Butler, Thomas	16	432	Transported 1671.
Butler, Thomas	15	400	Of Somerset Co. Immigrated 1676.
Butler, Thomas	1	87	Immigrated 1640 with wife, two
children and three servants. Of Isle of Kent.
Butler, Toby	15	553	Transported 1678.
Butler, Walter	11	571	" 1668.
Butler, William	12	343	" 1669.
Butter, Giles	6	31	" 1663. Service 1673.
			(17, fol. 412).
Butterfield, Eleanor	12	516	Wife of John. Service 1669.
Butterfield, John	12	516	Service 1669.
Butterfield, Samuel	16	482	Transported 1670-1.
Butterton, Edmond	8	203	" 1665.
Butterworth, Elizabeth	15	353	" 1674.
Buttexton, Edward	10	433	" 1667.
Buttler, Elizabeth	5	12	" 1662.
Buttler, George	6	95	" 1657.
Buttler, Hugh	6	295	" 1663.

NAME	Liber	Folio	REMARKS
Buttler, Robert	6	129	Transported 1660.
Buttler, Thomas	18	291	" 1674.
Button, Margaret	7	519	" 1664.
Button, Samuel	7	465	" 1656.
Buttrice, John	ABH	375	Immigrated 1650.
Buttwell, Richard	6	299	Transported 1664.
Butwell, Richard	17	573	Of Dorchester Co. Service 1673.
Buxon, Elizabeth	10	570	Transported 1666.
Buxston, Francis	5	536	" prior to 1663.
Buxton, James	15	383	" 1676.
Buxton, John	15	430	" 1677.
Buzart, Ann	4	57	Wife of John. Service 1659.
Buzart, John	4	57	Service 1659.
Bycoaff, Thomas	9	431	Transported 1666. Of Virginia.
Bymonds, Thomas	15	436	" 1677.
Bynon, David	WC2	288	" 1680.
Byshop, George	18	137	" 1674.
Byshop, Mary	18	174	" 1674.
Bysse, William, Gent.	12	348	Immigrated 1669.
Bysse, William	12	348	Transported 1669. Son of William.
Byssy, Richard	WC2	100	" 1679.
Bywater, Nathaniel	9	92	" 1665.
Cabbage, George	15	362	" 1676.
Cabbidge, John	WC2	259	" 1680.
Cabbin, John	15	565	" 1679.
Cabbiner, Charles	16	435	" 1671.
Cabell, John	5	249	" 1663.
Cabeller, George	9	33	" 1665.
Cabin, John	15	565	" 1679.
Cable, John	ABH	56	" 1648. Servant.
			(11, fol. 527; 3, fol. 106).
Cade, Robert	6	290	Transported 1663.
Cade, Thomas	Q	32	Servant 1653. (18, fol. 314).
Cadell, Joseph	5	245	Transported 1638-43. (ABH, fol. 47).
Cadell (Cadle), Zach-arias	WC2	328	" 1680.
Cader, John	12	194	" 1668. Servant.
Caderman, Samuel	6	267	" 1649.
Cadger, Thomas	17	578	Of St. Mary's Co. Immigrated 1649.
Cadger, Thomas	3	1	Immigrated 1650.
Cadle, Joseph	3	23	" about 1642 and again about 1646.
Cadman, John	10	4	Transported 1666.
Cadmore, Richard	17	416	Immigrated 1673. Of Talbot Co.
Cadock, Margaret	15	525	Transported 1678.
Cady, Eleanor	17	637	Service 1674. Wife of Robert.
Cady, Robert	17	637	" 1674.
Caeton, Garrett	18	137	Transported 1674.
Caffoe, Joane	WC2	87	" 1679.
Cage, John	ABH	244	" 1635. (20, fol. 2).
Cage, John	2	570	Service about 1649.

NAME	Liber	Folio	REMARKS
Cage, Noragh	Q	204	Servant 1658.
Cahane, Patrick	20	184	Transported from Ireland 1678.
Caine, Ann	5	488	" 1651-62.
Caine, Darby	16	371	" 1671.
Caine, Mary	11	348	" 1668.
Caines, James	5	235	Immigrated 1662.
Cakewood, Thomas	16	112	Transported 1671.
Calahone, Margaret	11	378	" 1668.
Calahone, Teag	11	378	" 1668.
Calcill, Cornelius	16	435	" 1671.
Cale, Susan	16	538	Service 1672. Wife of William.
Cale, William	16	538	Of Baltimore Co. Service 1672.
Calem, Robert	16	452	Transported 1671.
Callahan, Darby	WC2	287	" 1680.
Callahan, Dennis	WC2	287	" 1680.
Callanoa, Denis	15	438	" 1677.
Callaway, John	5	59	" 1662.
Callengood, Daniel	15	300	" 1675.
Calling, Alice	17	475	" 1673.
Callins, Thomas	15	446	" 1677.
Callis, Francis	12	373	" 1669.
Calloway, Anthony	11	294	Of Kent Co. Aged 39, Apr. 7, 1688.
Calloway, John	17	408	Service 1673.
Calloway, Mary	17	408	" 1673. Wife of John.
Calloway, Peter	18	35	" 1672.
Cally, John	15	430	Transported 1677.
Calthrope, Susan	5	80	" 1659.
Calvert, Anne	5	246	Immigrated 1656. Wife of Philip Calvert, Esq.

Calvert, Charles, Esq.   5   614   "Our dear son and heir", Special Warrant for 10,000 acres of land 1661.

Calvert, Gov. Charles   12   335   500 Acres "Marys Delight", in Anne Arundel Co. to his Godson Charles Calvert, son of Wm. Calvert, May 25, 1669.

Calvert, Charles, Lord Baltimore   19   294   Grants 500 acres called Fresh Pond Neck in St. Michaels Hundred, St. Marys Co. to his cousin, Col. Wm. Calvert, 1676.

Calvert, John   12   214   Of St. Mary's Co. Demands land for having served his time to the Hon. Philip Calvert, April 24, 1669.

Calvert, Leonard, Esq.   10   531-2   Deceased, His Mansion House leased to Lieut. Wm. Smith for 5 years by the Lord Prop. 1666.

Calvert, Philip, Esq.   5   246   Immigrated 1656.

Calvert, William, Esq.   5   183   Demands warrant for 3000 acres of land that remain upon record upon the account of Leonard Calvert, father of said Wm., etc. (4, fol. 614; 8, fol. 470; 11, fol. 434-5).

Cam, Godfree	5	79	Transported 1661. (12, fol. 376).
Cam, Thomas	5	88	" 1661.
Camamore, John	Q	32	" 1650.
Camawell, John	Q	32	" 1650.
Cambara, Elizabeth	9	18	" 1665. Wife of Domenico.

NAME	Liber	Folio	REMARKS
Cambden, Thomas	12	203	Transported 1669.
Camber, William	15	551	" 1679.
Camblington, Jane	178	440	" 1673.
Camell, Ester	17	469	" 1673.
Camell, John	Q	189	Service 1656. (4, fol. 19).
Camell, John	18	152	Transported 1674.
Camell, Patrick	6	123	Married Susan Acheson 1663.
Cammell, Patrick	15	322	Transported 1675.
Cammell, Rebecca	WC2	16,118	" 1679.
Camp, Gilbert	11	348	" 1668.
Camp, William	6	80	" 1657.
Camp, William	7	80	" 1664.
Campian, Richard	Q	70	" 1657.
Campire, Ann	5	73	" 1661. Wife of Thomas.
Campire, Mary	5	73	" 1661. Daughter of Thomas.
Campire, Thomas	5	73	Immigrated 1661. (10, fol. 613).
Canada, Cornelius	ABH	230	" Sept. 1652. (ABH, fol. 47).
Canada, James	ABH	230	Transported 1652. Son of Cornelius.
Canada, Susan	ABH	230	Transported 1652. Wife of Cornelius.
Canady, Jane	12	589	Transported 1670.
Canbarbe, Ann	15	507	Service prior to 1677.
Candlin, George	15	565	Transported 1679.
Cane, Edward	ABH	50	" prior to 1648. Servant. (3, fol. 63).
Cane, James	6	255	Transported 1663.
Cane, John	ABH	245	" 1652. Servant. (4, fol. 220).
Cane, John	5	260	Transported 1662.
Cane, Thomas	5	367	" 1649.
Cane, William	11	529	Service 1668.
Cane, William	15	329	Transported 1675.
Canellor, Thomas	5	90	" 1655.
Canenagh, Ellen	15	553	" 1678.
Canenagh, Mary	15	553	" 1678.
Caniday, Philip	12	282	Service 1668.
Canidie, James	15	499	Transported 1677.
Canker, Thomas	6	49	And wife. Service 1663.
Cann, Cate	15	553	Transported 1678.
Cann, Jane	9	21	" 1665.
Cannadie, John	6	121	" 1660.
Cannady, Cornelius	3	23	" before 1648.
Cannady, Dennis	4	623	" 1657-8.
Cannady, William	16	303	And Ann, his wife. Service 1671.
Canne, Thomas	15	429	Transported 1674.
Canneday, Edward	9	263	" 1665.
Canneday, Jeremiah	9	263	" 1665.
Canneday, Thomas	WC2	79,99	" 1679.

NAME	Liber	Folio	REMARKS
Canner, John	16	532	Transported 1668-70.
Canney, John	12	192	" 1668.
Cannon, Thomas	6	166	" 1663.
Cannon, Thomas	WC2	391-392	Service 1680. Of Baltimore Co.
Canny, Judith	15	167	Transported 1673.
Canny, Elizabeth	WC2	153	Service 1680.
Canon, Quintan	Q	199	Transported 1651.
Canstan, Samuel	15	440	Immigrated 1677.
Cantell, Mary	WC2	168-169	Transported 1680.
Canton, John	17	551	" 1673.
Canton, Will	15	359	" 1676.
Cantwell, Ann	15	553	" 1678.
Caoll, James	15	553	" 1678.
Cape, John	WC2	320	" 1680. Servant.
Capell, Peter	15	416	" 1677.
Capes, Edward	15	398	" 1676.
Capps, Edward	15	453	" 1676.
Capps, Elizabeth	Q	68	" 1657.
Capston, Susanna	11	436	" 1668.
Care, Peter	4	214	Immigrated 1659.
Carell, Will	15	446	Transported 1677.
Carelton, Edward	15	455	" 1678.
Carem, Mr. Thomas	4	20	Special Warrant from Lord Baltimore, 1658.
Carew, Henry	18	141	Of St. Mary's Co. Immigrated 1674.
Carew, James	15	553	Transported 1678.
Carew, Katherine	15	543	" 1678.
Carewood, Stephen	6	294	" 1664.
Carey, Henry	WC2	110	" 1676. Servant.
Carey, William	WC2	106	" 1679.
Caril, John	5	181	" 1661.
Carington, John	ABH	374	" 1st cond. Servant.
Carington, Thomas	15	376	" 1676.
Carkee, Edward	17	348	Of Anne Arundel Co. Service 1667.
Carkwood, James	18	152	Transported 1674.
Carleene, Dennis	11	573	" 1668.
Carles, John	WC2	206	" 1679. Servant.
Carleton, Arthur	11	571	" 1668.
Carleton, Elizabeth	11	571	" 1668. Wife of Thomas.
Carleton, John	12	190	" 1668. Servant.
Carleton, Thomas	11	571	Immigrated 1668, "and Eliz.
Carleton the child his wife now goes with."			
Carley, Samuel	8	478	Transported 1665.
Carlile, William	15	376	" 1676.
Carline, Andrew	15	403	Service 1676.
Carlisle, John	9	400	Immigrated 1666.
Carlisle, Jone	9	400	Transported 1666. Daughter of John.
Carlisle, Susan	9	400	Transported 1666. Wife of John.
Carlton, John	8	478	" 1665.
Carly, Thomas	WC2	380	" 1675-80. Servant.

NAME	Liber	Folio	REMARKS
Carmick, Christopher	15	553	Transported 1678.
Carmthall, Elizabeth	16	411	" 1671.
Carnall, Christopher	ABH	27	Immigrated 1646. (2, fol. 528).
Carnell, Daniel	15	22	" 1678.
Carney, Thomas	10	191	Of Manokin River. Immigrated 1666.
Carnil, Thomas	5	181	Transported 1661. (12, fol. 262).
Carnill, Mary	12	262	" 1668. Wife of Thomas.
Carnlau, Patrick	17	417	Immigrated 1673.
Carnock, Christopher	1	20	Transported 1633. (See Carnoll).
Carnol, Christopher	ABH	66	" 1633.
Carnoll, Christopher	1	37-38, 166	" 1634. (See Carnock).
Carol, Philip	WC2	128	" 1679.
Carpe, Simon	9	216	" 1665.
Carpenter, Charles	17	477	Of St. Mary's Co. Immigrated 1673, with his wife and three children.
Carpenter, Charles	17	477	Son of Charles. Immigrated 1673.
Carpenter, Edward	15	301	Transported 1675.
Carpenter, Elizabeth	17	477	Immigrated 1673. Daughter of Charles.
Carpenter, Elizabeth	8	501	Transported 1665.
Carpenter, Francis	7	470	Immigrated 1658. (4, fol. 69).
Carpenter, James	WC2	310	Transported 1680.
Carpenter, John	10	464	Immigrated Feb. 1666. (15, fol. 523).
Carpenter, Nicholas	12	391	Transported 1669.
Carpenter, Rebecca	17	477	Immigrated 1673. Wife of Charles.
Carpenter, Rebecca	17	477	" 1673. Daughter of Charles.
Carpenter, Richard	13	59	Transported 1670.
Carpenter, Robert	12	403	" 1669.
Carpenter, Symon	8	501	Immigrated 1665.
Carpenter, Thomas	ABH	204	Transported 1651. Servant. (ABH, fol. 338, 374).
Carpenter, Thomas	12	373	Transported 1669.
Carpenter, Thomas	5	257	" 1659-63. (5, fol. 267).
Carpenter, William	15	313	Of Anne Arundel Co. Service 1675.
Carr, Ann	12	317	Transported 1669.
Carr, Bryan	15	559	" 1679.
Carr, Elizabeth	8	40	Immigrated with her child 1665.
Carr, Elizabeth	15	318	" 1674. Wife of William.
Carr, Lionell	18	167	Transported 1674.
Carr, Mark	7	526	" 1664.
Carr, Mary	6	294	" 1664. (7, fol. 560).
Carr, William	15	318	Immigrated 1674. Of Virginia.
Carradive, Henry	17	451	Transported 1673.
Carre, Grace	10	523	" 1667.
Carre, John	Q	32	Servant 1653.
Carre, Capt. John	17	552	Immigrated from Delaware 1673, with Peteronella, his wife, and Richard, Elizabeth, Mary and Peteronella, his children. Of Baltimore County.
Carre, Susanna	10	598	Transported 1667. Servant.

NAME	Liber	Folio	REMARKS
Carre, Thomas	16	70	Transported 1668-70.
Carre, Walter	Q	201	Immigrated 1658.
Carre, William	17	475	Transported 1673.
Carrell, Mary	13	119	" 1670. Wife of Thomas, Sr.
Carrell, Teig.	15	527	Transported 1678.
Carrell, Thomas, Sr.	13	119	Of Somerset Co. Immigrated from Accomac in Virginia, 1670.
Carrell, Thomas, Jr.	13	119	Transported 1670. Son of Thomas, Sr.
Carrell, William	12	205	Transported 1667.
Carrew, Evan	16	168	" 1671.
Carridge, John	WC2	415	" 1666-80. Servant.
Carrier, John	5	482	" 1662.
Carrington, John	9	50	Immigrated 1665.
Carrington, Thomas	15	167	Transported 1673.
Carrman, Thomas	4	13	" 1653. (6, fol. 82).
Carroll, George	17	454	Service 1672.
Carry, Edward	11	307	Transported 1668. (16, fol. 537).
Carry, John	11	307	" 1668. (16, fol. 537).
Carry, Jane	11	307	" 1668. Wife of Thomas. (16, fol. 537).
Carry, Thomas	11	307	Immigrated from Virginia with Jane, his wife, 1668. (16, fol. 537; 17, fol. 636).
Carry, Thomas, Jr.	11	307	Transported 1668. (16, fol. 537).
Carryes, Walter	10	600	Immigrated 1667.
Carse, Katherine	16	435	Transported 1671.
Carter, Ann	15	516	" 1678.
Carter, Anne	WC2	213-214	" 1671-1673.
Carter, Barbara	15	322	" 1674.
Carter, Elizabeth	ABH	140	" about 1651.
Carter, Elizabeth	Q	18	" 1658.
Carter, Elizabeth	18	291	" 1674. (15, fol. 396, 416).
Carter, Elis	15	416	Transported 1677.
Carter, Erasmus	11	537	" 1668.
Carter, George	5	203	" 1662.
Carter, George	6	255	" 1663.
Carter, George	11	307	" 1668. Servant. (18, fol. 15; 15, fol. 301).
Carter, Henry	6	159	Transported 1652.
Carter, James	15	396	" 1676.
Carter, Jane	15	318	" 1675.
Carter, John	13	114	" 1669. (13, fol. 66).
Carter, John	WC2	78	Immigrated from New York 1679. Of Somerset County.
Carter, John	15	396	Immigrated 1676.
Carter, Maeyne	15	396	Transported 1676.
Carter, Margaret	12	475	" 1670.
Carter, Mary	WC2	16	" 1679. Wife of Philip.
Carter, Mary	15	396	" 1676.

NAME	Liber	Folio	REMARKS
Carter, Paul	8	130	Transported 1664.
Carter, Philip	WC2	16	Immigrated 1679.
Carter, Richard	11	581	Transported 1668. (16, fol. 532).
Carter, Sarah	6	134	" 1652.
Carter, Susan	15	436	" 1677.
Carter, Vertue	15	395	" 1677. (15, fol. 544).
Carter, Will	15	429	" 1677. (15, fol. 535).
Carter, William	15	397	" 1676.
Carter, William	WC2	152	" from Virginia 1680. Servant.
Carthey, Ellen	15	543	Transported 1678.
Carthey, William	15	600	" 1678.
Carthy, Dennis	WC2	380	" 1675-80. Servant.
Carthy, Eleanor	WC2	380	" 1675-80. Servant.
Cartlan, William	5	242	" 1662.
Carton, George	16	303	Service 1671.
Cartor, Richard	9	50	Immigrated 1665. Of Talbot Co.
Cartwright, Demetrius	6	295	" 1657. (5, fol. 89).
Cartwright, Elizabeth	6	295	Transported 1663. Wife of Demetrius.
Cartwright, Henry	3	17	Transported prior to 1650.
Cartwright, Henry	ABH	44	" many years prior to 1650.
Cartwright, James	11	344	Transported 1668.
Cartwright, Mary	15	380	" 1676.
Cartwright, Thomas	15	380	" 1676.
Carty, Charles	WC2	21	" 1679.
Carty, Dennis	15	553	" 1678.
Carty, Katherine	16	370	" 1671.
Carty, Owen	15	553	" 1678.
Carvell, Mary	5	305	" 1663.
Carvell, Thomas	12	372	" 1669.
Carver, Alice	6	128	" 1657.
Carver, Edward	18	329	" 1675.
Carver, Richard	5	411	" 1663.
Carvile, Johanna	WC2	200	" 1680. Wife of Robert.
Carvill, Robert	12	321	Immigrated 1669. Of St. Mary's Co.
Carvill, Thomas	12	416	Transported 1669.
Carwardine, Peter	16	12	Immigrated 1670. Of St. Mary's Co.
Carwell, Mary	17	572	Transported 1672.
Carwick, Christopher	WC2	57	" 1678.
Carwige, Hannah	8	3	" 1665. Servant.
Cary, Ann	10	286	" 1666. (10, fol. 417).
Cary, Charles	7	465	" 1658.
Cary, Christopher	7	560	" 1665.
Cary, James	15	553	" 1678.
Cary, John	15	375	Immigrated 1676.
Cary, Francis	7	85	Transported 1647.
Cary, Philemon	15	527	" 1678.
Cary, Richard	18	38	Immigrated 1673 with Mary, his wife.

NAME	Liber	Folio	REMARKS
Cary, Thomas	Q	475	Of London, Merchant. Signs to immigrate in 1657.
Cary, Thomas	4	53	Transported 1659.
Cary, Walter	9	45	" 1665.
Case, Henry	17	67	" 1668.
Case, Sarah	17	448	" 1673.
Case, William	9	309	" 1666. (9, fol. 343).
Casey, Ann	5	256	" 1663.
Casey, James	11	378	" 1668.
Casey, Thomas	12	502	" 1669.
Casey, Thomas	17	363	" 1672.
Cash, Richard	WC2	110	" 1676. Servant.
Cason, William	8	89	" 1665.
Cassaday, Mary	18	331	" 1674.
Cassaugh, John	8	495	" 1665.
Cassell, John	Q	217	" 1652.
Cassock, George	6	133	" 1651.
Caster, Elizabeth	6	122	" 1649.
Caster, Mary	5	538	" 1662. Servant. (10, fol. 541).
Castle, Jeremy	6	86	Transported 1661.
Castle, John	7	78	" 1663.
Castle, Ralph	5	488	" 1657.
Castleford, Robert	12	317	" 1669.
Castleton, Robert	17	463	" 1673.
Caston, James	12	190	" 1668.
Caswell, Ann	4	198	" 1659. (8, fol. 501).
Caswell, Edward	WC2	167,169	" 1679.
Caswell, Henry	19	258	" 1663.
Caswell, Mary	15	565	" 1679.
Catch, James	10	277	" 1666.
Catchpole, Judith	4	140	" 1655. Servant. (Quaker ?)
Cate, Elizabeth	8	478	Transported 1665.
Cate, John	ABH	103	" 1641. Servant.
Caten, Mary	15	353	" 1674.
Caterton, Margaret	16	393	Service 1671. Wife of Michael.
Catler, Elizabeth	15	454	Transported 1677.
Catlin, Henry	5	87	Immigrated 1649, with his wife

and his son (?) Richard Horner.

NAME	Liber	Folio	REMARKS
Catlin, Jeane	5	87	Transported 1649. Wife of Henry.
Catlin, John	12	217	" 1669.
Catlyne, Ann	10	342	" 1665.
Catlyne, Ann, Jr.	10	342	" 1665.
Catlyne, Joseph	10	342	" 1665.
Catlyne, Robert, Sr.	10	342	Immigrated 1665.
Catlyne, Robert, Jr.	10	342	Transported 1665.
Caton, William	18	177	. " 1674.
Catrup, Joane	18	162	" 1671. Wife of William.
Catrup, William	18	162	Immigrated 1671. Of Talbot Co.

With Joane, his wife, and William, his son.

NAME	Liber	Folio	REMARKS
Catrup, William, Jr.	18	162	Transported 1671. Son of William.
Catson, Charles	15	353	" 1676.
Cattell, Mary	16	393	" 1671.
Catterns, Edward	9	190	" 1665.
Catterton, Michael	4	137	" 1659.
Catterton, Thomas	WC2	122	" 1679. (See Chatterton).
Cattings, John	15	319	Immigrated 1675.
Cattling, Ann	6	255	Transported 1663. Wife of Robert.
Cattling, Ann, Jr.	6	255	" 1663. Daughter of Robert.
Cattling, Joseph	6	255	Transported 1663. Son of Robert.
Cattling, Robert, Jr.	6	255	" 1663.
Cattling, Robert, Sr.	6	255	Immigrated 1663.
Caufrey, Eleanor	5	93	Transported 1661.
Caufrey, James	5	93	" 1661.
Caufrey, Robert	5	93	" 1661.
Caules, Philip	5	516	" 1663.
Caules, Thomas	5	516	" 1663.
Causin, Nicholas	ABH	22	Married Jane Cockshott prior to 1648. (ABH, fol. 207). Living 1653. (4, fol. 27).
Causin, William	17	357	Immigrated 1672. Of Calvert Co.
Cave, George	12	190	Transported 1668.
Cave, Thomas	18	37	" 1673.
Cavenagh, Ellen	WC2	57	" 1678.
Cavenagh, Mary	WC2	57	" 1678.
Cavert, William	1	171	" about 1639.
Caviner, Hugh	16	115	Immigrated 1671. Of St. Mary's Co.
Cawood, George	4	590	Transported 1660-1.
Cawood, Stephen	16	81	Service 1670. Of Charles Co.
Cawsin, Nicholas	2	347	Immigrated 1639.
Cayner, William	6	293	Transported 1664.
Cayton, William	WC2	308	" 1678.
Ceaton, Alice	18	137	" 1674.
Ceely, Welthin	WC2	132	" 1680. Servant.
Cemball, Anne	WC2	167,169	" 1680.
Cennede, Darby	Q	431	" 1653.
Cennede, Sara	Q	431	" 1650.
Cennin, Edmund	4	63	" 1644.
Cerke, Jeage	15	397	" 1675. (See Clerke).
Chabmer, Jane	17	463	" 1673.
Chad, Sarah	5	606	" prior to 1663.
Chadborne, Sarah	18	177	" prior to 1674. (15, fol. 523).
Chadborne, Sarah	WC2	308	Transported 1678.
Chadborne, William	18	336	Of Cecil Co. Immigrated 1669. Deputy Surveyor of Baltimore and Cecil counties, November 1675. (15, fol. 308).
Chadley, Elizabeth	18	136	Transported 1674.
Chadwell, John	16	60	Of Baltimore Co. Service 1670.
Chaffe, Mary	16	166	Wife of John of Talbot Co. Service 1668.

NAME	Liber	Folio	REMARKS
Chaines, James	5	490	Transported 1662.
Chair, John	1	130	" 1641. Servant.
Chaire, John	ABH	102	" 1641. Servant.
Chaires, Hannah	WC2	182	Service 1680.
Chairs, John	9	234	Transported 1665.
Chalk, Francis	Q	316	Immigrated 1658.
Chalke, Gabriell	17	69	Transported 1672.
Challice, Francis	5	516	" 1663.
Chalnem, Jacob	16	167	Of Somerset Co. Service 1670.
Cham, Thomas	17	550	Transported 1673.
Chamberlayne, William	17	547	" 1673.
Chamberlin, Samuel	16	507	" 1671.
Chamberline, William	8	202	" 1665. (17, fol. 418).
Chambers, Ann	15	565	" 1679.
Chambers, Christopher	WC2	168-169	" 1680.
Chambers, Elizabeth	10	397	" 1666. Servant. (15, fol. 397).
Chambers, Francis	12	334	Transported 1668.
Chambers, John	17	547	" 1673.
Chambers, Michael	17	443	" 1662.
Chambers, Richard	16	40	" 1670.
Chambers, Thomas	15	397	" 1676.
Chambers, William	12	513	" 1669. (12, fol. 463).
Chambers, William	18	36	Immigrated 1673.
Champ, Robert	Q	70	Transported 1658.
Champ, Stephen	7	489	" 1664. (7, fol. 553).
Champ, William	4	16	Immigrated 1659.
Champ, William	10	429	Transported 1664.
Champe, William	17	475	" 1673.
Chanallie, Philip	13	57	" 1670.
Chance, Elizabeth	11	377	Immigrated 1668. Wife of William.
Chance, William	11	377	" 1668. Of Somerset Co.
Chancellor, Abigail	WC2	17,99	Transported 1679. Wife of John.
Chancellor, John	WC2	17,99	Immigrated 1679 with wife and daughter. Of Somerset Co.
Chancellor, Mary	WC2	17,99	Transported 1679. Daughter of John.
Chancellor, Philip	6	217	Transported 1663.
Chancey, Alexander	15	303	Of St. Mary's Co. Service 1675.
Chandler, Ann	ABH	269	Transported 1651. Wife of Mr. Job. Married --- Fowke 1673. (15, fol. 181).
Chandler, Ann	ABH	269	Transported 1651. Daughter of Job and Ann.
Chandler, Edward	5	307	Transported 1663. Service 1669. (12, fol. 389).
Chandler, Elizabeth	6	87	Transported 1657.
Chandler, Henry	5	208	" 1662.
Chandler, Mr. Joh	ABH	269	Immigrated 1651.
Chandler, John	8	87	Transported 1665.
Chandler, John	WC2	110	" 1676. Servant.
Chandler, Mary	6	94	" 1656.

NAME	Liber	Folio	REMARKS
Chandler, Mary	8	87	Transported prior to 1665. (11, fol. 170).
Chandler, Matthew	11	441	Transported 1668. (11, fol. 337).
Chandler, Richard	4	201-3	Of London. Merchant. About to immigrate in 1657. (He did not come over).
Chandler, Richard	9	48	Transported 1665.
Chandler, Richard	15	369	" 1676.
Chandler, Susanna	8	87	" prior to 1665.
Chandler, William	6	87	" 1651. Living 1673. (15, fol. 181). "Elder son and heir of Job".
Chanee, Mathew	15	322	Transported 1675.
Chanellour, Ralph	6	48	" prior to 1663. Servant.
Chapell, Moses	15	455	" 1678.
Chaplain, Annie	12	217	" 1669.
Chaplin, Elizabeth	ABH	273	" 1651. Wife of William. She married first, --- Bancroft.
Chaplin, Elizabeth	Q	211	Immigrated 1658. Wife of William.
Chaplin, Elizabeth	ABH	273	Daughter of Wm. and Eliz. Transported 1651.
Chaplin, Elizabeth	Q	211	Immigrated 1658. Daughter of William.
Chaplin, Humphrey	5	245	Transported 1638-43.
Chaplin, Humphrey	1	19	" 1637.
Chaplin, Mary	WC2	415	" 1680. Servant.
Chaplin, Stephen	4	140	" 1654. Servant. (Quaker ?)
Chaplin, William	ABH	273	Immigrated 1651.
Chaplin, William	Q	211	" 1658.
Chapling, Francis	12	459	Transported 1669.
Chapman, Charles	12	584	" 1670.
Chapman, Daniel	5	534	" 1662. Of Dorset Co. (12, fol. 342).
Chapman, George	16	411	Transported 1671.
Chapman, Hannah	7	471	" 1664.
Chapman, Humphrey	3	24	" 1650. Servant.
Chapman, John	12	548	" 1670.
Chapman, John	15	397	" 1676.
Chapman, John	WC2	21	" 1679.
Chapman, John	WC2	206	" 1680. Servant.
Chapman, Matthew	12	415	" 1669.
Chapman, Reacon	WC2	217	" 1680.
Chapman, Richard	8	130	" 1665.
Chapman, Richard	6	94	" 1661.
Chapman, Robert	6	80	" 1654. (17, fol. 554).
Chapman, Thomas	6	83	" 1653.
Chapman, Thomas	5	514	" 1659.
Chapman, Thomas	7	569	" 1663-4.
Chapman, Thomas	15	353	" 1676.
Chapman, William, Jr.	4	54	Immigrated prior to July 1659.
Chapman, Zachariah	15	551	Transported 1679.
Chappell, John	5	2	" 1661.

NAME	Liber	Folio	REMARKS
Chappell, William	ABH	12	Servant 1648.
Chappell, William	2	439	Transported 1648.
Chardge, Judith	15	569	" 1678.
Chares, John	9	516	" 1666.
Charinton, Thomas	ABH	66	" 1633. (ABH, fol. 90).
Charinton, Thomas	1	20,38	" 1633. (See Harington).
Charity, Alexander	13	116	" 1671.
Charles, Ann	15	452	" 1678.
Charles, Henry	6	183	" 1663.
Charles, John	9	17	Immigrated 1665. (9, fol. 100).
Charles, John	WC2	309	Transported 1680.
Charles, John	17	608	" 1673.
Charles, John, Jr.	15	452	" 1678.
Charles, John, Sr.	15	452	" 1678.
Charles, William	5	532	" 1662.
Charleston, Ann	4	434	" 1666. (New York ?)
Charlesworth, George	10	1	" 1666.
Charlesworth, George	17	60	Of St. Mary's Co. Service 1672.
Charlesworth, John	10	1, 2	Transported 1666. Son of George. (11, fol. 236).
Charleton, Ellen	6	105	Transported 1663.
Charleton, Mary	6	105	" 1663.
Charleton, Otwell	6	105	" 1663.
Charlett, Mr. Richard	15	550	Immigrated 1679.
Charley, Mary	15	318	Transported 1674.
Charlton, Sarah	8	477	" 1665.
Charlton, Susanna	8	477	" 1665.
Charlton, William	8	477	Immigrated 1665.
Charlton, William	8	477	Transported 1665.
Charman, John	ABH	12	Servant 1648.
Charman, John	2	439	Transported 1648.
Charnoe, Elizabeth	15	322	" 1675.
Charnutt, Elizabeth	15	386	" 1676.
Charon, John	Q	432	Immigrated prior to 1657 with wife.
Chartley, Alice	15	354	Transported 1676.
Charton, John	9	39	" 1654.
Chase, James	5	467	" 1667.
Chasmore, William	16	127	" 1671.
Chastoe, Cuthbert	10	600	" 1667.
Chaterly, John	15	369	" 1676.
Chatterton, Thomas	WC2	21-22	" 1679. (See Catterton).
Chattin, Thomas	7	371	Of Virginia. Acquires 800 acres in Maryland.
Chayres, John	17	514	Of Talbot Co. Service 1672.
Chearman, John	5	252	Kinsman of John Meeks, Chyrurgeon 1663.
Cheater, Francis	Q	70	Transported 1657.
Cheek, Thomas	12	213	Immigrated 1668. Of Charles Co.
Cheesman, William	18	9	And Wife, Service 1672.
Chelse, Gideon	6	171	Transported 1663.
Chelsey, John	Q	33	" 1653-8.

NAME	Liber	Folio	REMARKS
Chelsey, Mary	Q	33	Transported 1653-8.
Cheney, John	6	63	" 1658-63.
Cheny, Richard	18	176	" 1674.
Chery, David	12	262	Of Virginia. Immigrated to Dorchester Co. 1668.
Cheseldyn, Kenelem	12	346	Of St. Mary's Co. Immigrated 1669. (14, fol. 477).
Cheshire, William	8	131	Immigrated 1664 with wife.
Chesill, Francis	17	355	Service 1672.
Chessam, William	9	25	Transported 1665.
Chester, Edward	WC2	277	Immigrated 1680 with wife, daughter and son-in-law. Of St. Mary's County.
Chester, Ellinor	WC2	277	Transported 1680. Wife of Edward.
Chester, Francis	9	38	" 1665.
Chester, Hugh	10	306	" Oct. 1666. Brother to John.
Chester, John	10	306	Immigrated from Virginia to Talbot County 1666.
Chester, John	10	306	Transported Oct. 1666.
Chester, Mary	10	306	" 1666.
Chester, Sarah	10	306	" Oct. 1666. Daughter of John.
Chester, William	15	406	Immigrated 1676.
Chesterment, Mary	5	412	Transported 1663.
Cheston, John	5	242	" 1662. (5, fol. 606).
Cheswell, Joseph	9	489	Immigrated 1665.
Chetham, John	Q	428	Transported 1658.
Chevaler, Philip	12	281	Service 1668.
Cheverill, Clement	15	17	Of St. Mary's Co. Planter. Service 1670.
Cheverill, Clement	17	333	Transported 1672. Son of Clement.
Cheverill, Mary	17	333	Service 1672. Wife of Clement.
Cheverill, Theophilus	12	205	Transported 1667.
Cheverlier, John	7	80	" 1664.
Chew, Ann	12	584	" 1670. (12, fol. 378).
Chew, Ann	WC2	55	Service 1669.
Chew, John	10	352	Transported 1666.
Chew, Joseph	19	388	Commission from Baker Brooke, Esq., Surveyor Genl. as Deputy Surveyor of Cecil Co. 1676.
Chew, Leatita	10	598	Transported by Joseph Chew 1667.
Chew, Samuel	4	54	Immigrated 1659. Son-in-law of Wm. Ayres. (5, fol. 339).
Chewly, Samuel	15	540	Transported 1676.
Cheyney, Charity	Q	74	Immigrated 1650. Wife of Richard.
Cheyney, Nicholas	11	348	Transported 1668.
Cheyney, Richard	Q	74	Immigrated 1658.
Chezell, Joseph	5	413	Transported 1662.
Chicherly, Thomas	9	356	" 1666.
Chick, Thomas	WC2	319	Immigrated 1680.
Chick, Mrs. Thomas	WC2	319	Service 1680.
Chicke, Mary	9	35	Transported 1664.

NAME	Liber	Folio	REMARKS
Chickens, Edward	4	14	Transported 1659. Servant.
Chickes, John	4	14	" 1652. Servant.
Chickley, Thomas	17	67	Service 1672.
Chid, Ann	12	478	Transported 1670.
Chifford, John	1	166	" 1650. Servant.
Chil, Sarah	5	267	" 1663.
Child, John	5	253	" 1663.
Child, John	9	433	Immigrated 1666. Of New York.
Child, Lucy	4	59	Transported 1659. Married Wm.
Galloway who had also been a servant.			
Child, Magdalin	15	398	Transported 1676. (15, fol. 453).
Child, Mark	9	329	" 1663-4.
Child, Owen	15	553	" 1678.
Chilice, Francis	5	267	" 1663.
Chillam, Richard	17	363	" 1672.
Chillcott, Anne	WC2	352	" 1680.
Chilman, Richard	18	151	Of St. Mary's Co. Immigrated 1674. (18, fol. 301).
Chily, John	18	291	Transported 1674.
Chinenee, Nicholas	7	489	" 1664.
Chinesse, Elizabeth	9	33	" 1665. (See Cluneste).
Chinner, Rebecca	9	436	" 1666.
Chinner, Thomas	9	436	Joyner. Immigrated 1666 per ship "Constant Friendship".
Chipman, Dorothy	15	369	" 1676.
Chisell, Charles	15	454	" 1677.
Chisell, Francis	5	417	" 1663.
Chishollne, James	11	107	Of St. Mary's Co., Planter, Service 1667.
Chistrell, Elizabeth	15	318	Transported 1674.
Chittam, Ann	9	462	Service 1665.
Chittam, John	7	527	" 1664.
Chittcock, Ann	15	301	Transported 1675. Wife of James.
Chittcock, James	15	301	Immigrated 1675.
Chitterell, Elizabeth	18	24	Transported 1674.
Chiverall, Mary	16	393	" 1671.
Chivers, Michael	15	527	" 1678.
Chivers, Michael	WC2	111	" 1680.
Chives, Paternall	10	498	" 1667.
Chapman, Elizabeth	13	116	" 1671.
Chotle, Christopher	15	369	" 1676.
Choyce, Elizabeth	5	467	" 1661. (6, fol. 19).
Chriffrell, Cleme	8	503	" 1665.
Chrine, Alexander	17	604	Service 1673.
Chrisley, Mary	17	395	Transported 1672.
Christall, Robert	9	26	" 1665.
Christenson, William	12	473	" 1670.
Christian, Adam	4	13	Service 1659.
Christian, Alice	9	506	Transported 1666.
Christian, George	15	302	" prior to 1675.
Christian, Lawrence	9	489	Immigrated 1665.

NAME	Liber	Folio	REMARKS
Christian, Stephen	15	432	Transported 1677.
Christian, William	17	417	" 1673.
Christon, Thomas	15	517	" 1678.
Christopher, Christopher	5	247	" 1661.
Christopher, John	7	371	" 1662.
Christopher, John	WC2	320	Service 1680.
Christy, John	17	572	Transported 1672.
Chub, Edward	WC2	50,98	" 1679.
Chudson, Edmond	ABH	1	Immigrated 1646. (See Hudson).
Chuffe, John	7	530	" 1662.
Church, Elizabeth	15	567	Transported 1679.
Church, Katharine	15	567	" 1679.
Church, John	15	359	" 1676.
Church, Mary	15	430	" 1677.
Churchall, Samuel	15	357	" 1676.
Churchyard, Samuel	15	369	" 1676.
Cicil, John	4	29	Immigrated 1658.
Cillenell, Gillian	11	541	Transported 1665.
Cimbarbe, Ann	17	382	Service 1672.
Cincesse, Elizabeth	9	28	Transported 1664.
Clacer, John	5	373	" 1663.
Clachay, Arthur	Q	201	Immigrated 1649.
Clachay, Charles	Q	201	" 1649. Son of Arthur.
Clachay, Mary	Q	201	" 1649. Wife of Arthur.
Claine, Nathaniel	Q	70	Transported 1653.
Clamore, Henry	19	258	" 1663.
Clancy, John	WC2	128	" 1679.
Clapham, John	12	190	" 1668.
Clapham, Thomas	5	261	" 1662.
Clapham, William	WC2	21-22, 122	" 1679.
Clapp, Alexander	15	454	" 1677.
Clapp, John	15	516	" 1676.
Clarbore, Garford	WC2	33	" 1679.
Clare, Cor.	15	531	" 1678.
Clare, John George	WC2	21	" 1679.
Clare, Mark	Q	199	" 1651-8.
Clare, Mesabeth	6	160	" 1663.
Clare, Timothy	18	105	" 1674.
Clarey, Patrick	15	407	" 1676.
Clark, Abraham	6	85	" 1654. (15, fol. 548).
Clark, Alice	11	570	" 1668.
Clark, Charles	11	540	" 1668.
Clark, Daniel	9	399	" 1666.
Clark, Edward	8	482	Immigrated 1661.
Clark, Edward	8	502	Transported 1665. Married Ann, daughter of John Shirclif of St. Mary's Co. prior to 1667. (10, fol. 474).
Clark, Eleanor	ABH	59	Transported 1641.
Clark, Elizabeth	10	503	" 1667. Servant.
Clark, Francis	12	202	" 1669. Servant.

NAME	Liber	Folio	REMARKS
Clark, Grace	6	267	Transported 1660.
Clark, James	12	393	" 1669.
Clark, Joane	15	322	" 1675.
Clark, John	Q	239	" 1651-2.
Clark, John	Q	207	Service 1658.
Clark, John	4	217	Son of Robert Clark, Gen. "one of
our Councell". Special Warrant for 500 acres, 1659.			
Clark, John	7	83	Transported 1664. (7, fol. 498).
Clark, John	15	503	" 1678.
Clark, Mary	ABH	201	" 1650-1. Servant.
Clark, Neale	ABH	39	" 1649.
Clark, Phill.	15	359	" 1676.
Clark, Richard	15	332	Immigrated 1675. A "free passen-
ger" on the Ship Maryland, Merchant of London.			
Clark, Richard	15	499	Transported 1677.
Clark, Robert	ABH	81	Immigrated 1637.
Clark, Robert	ABH	9	" 1638.
Clark, Robert	8	409	Transported 1668. Son of Thomas.
Clark, Robert	12	213	" 1668.
Clark, Mr. Robert	ABH	403	Married Winifred, widow of
Thomas Green, Esq. prior to 1654.			
Clark, Sarah	8	409	Transported 1665. Wife of Thomas.
Clark, Sarah	8	409	" 1665. Daughter of
			Thomas.
Clark, Thomas	8	86	Immigrated 1665.
Clark, Thomas	8	409	" 1665.
Clark, Willi	15	505	Transported 1678.
Clark, William	7	550	" 1664. Servant.
Clarke, Abraham	5	2	" 1658-9.
Clarke, Ann	9	233	" 1665. Wife of John,
			of Port Tobacco.
Clarke, Ann	9	435	Transported 1664.
Clarke, Ann	17	37	" 1672.
Clarke, Arthur	20	185	" 1679.
Clarke, Benjamin	15	453	" 1657.
Clarke, Charles	11	319	" 1668.
Clarke, Daniel	6	299	" 1664.
Clarke, Daniel	9	429-30	Of Little Chaptank River in Md.,
a friend of John Pitt of Isle of Wight Co., Va., 1665.			
Clarke, Daniel	17	38	Of Somerset Co. Immigrated
			from Virginia 1672.
Clarke, Dorothy	17	37	Transported 1672.
Clarke, Edward	5	245	Immigrated 1653.
Clarke, Edward	12	472	Transported 1670.
Clarke, Elizabeth	5	2	" 1661. (6, fol. 90; 7
			fol. 467).
Clarke, Elizabeth	12	216	Transported 1668.
Clarke, George	5	211	" 1662.
Clarke, George	10	471	Immigrated 1667.
Clarke, Henry	15	353	Transported 1674.
Clarke, James	9	435	" 1664.

NAME	Liber	Folio	REMARKS
Clarke, James	17	554	Transported 1673.
Clarke, Jane	6	299	" 1664.
Clarke, Jeremiah	4	551	" 1661. (6, fol. 48).
Clarke, John	WC2	112	" 1679.
Clarke, John	9	435	Of Anne Arundel Co. Immigrated
1664, in the ship "Golden Wheat Sheaf".			
Clarke, John	9	270	Transported 1665. Servant.
Clarke, John	9	451	" 1666.
Clarke, John	12	333	" 1668.
Clarke, John	12	314	" 1669.
Clarke, John	17	411	" 1673. (17, fol. 566).
Clarke, Jonathan	12	211	" 1668.
Clarke, Katherine	6	299	" 1664.
Clarke, Margaret	5	244	" 1662.
Clarke, Mary	5	466	" 1659.
Clarke, Mary	5	261	" 1660. (5, fol. 2).
Clarke, Mary	5	128	" 1662.
Clarke, Mary	7	563	" 1665.
Clarke, Matthew	6	107	" 1651. (18, fol. 309).
Clarke, Nathaniel	4	69	" 1650.
Clarke, Nathaniel	20	185	" 1679.
Clarke, Neale	2	608	" 1649.
Clarke, Rebecca	17	38	Immigrated from Virginia 1672.
			Of Somerset County.
Clarke, Richard	4	551	Transported 1661.
Clarke, Richard	15	430	" 1677.
Clarke, Richard	15	432	" 1677.
Clarke, Robert	2	425	Immigrated 1638.
Clarke, Robert	WC2	114	Transported 1680. Servant.
Clarke, Robert	9	234	Immigrated 1665.
Clarke, Robert	12	205	Transported 1667. (17, fol. 81).
Clarke, Roger	12	333	" 1669.
Clarke, Rosamond	16	37	" 1670.
Clarke, Susanna	9	435	" 1664. Wife of John.
Clarke, Thomas	13	1	" 1669. Servant.
			(17, fol. 595).
Clarke, Thomas	15	397	Transported 1676.
Clarke, William	15	534	" 1667.
Clarke, William	15	534	" 1677.
Clarkson, Edward	ABH	246	" many years prior
			to 1652.
Clarkson, James	15	565	Transported 1679.
Claroe, George	15	369	" 1676.
Clarridge, Elizabeth	6	28	" 1663. Servant.
Clary, John	15	438	" 1677.
Clary, Sarah	15	369	" 1676.
Clash, Nicholas	16	293	" 1671.
Clast, James	18	144	Service 1674.
Claton, John	WC2	415	Transported 1666-80. Servant.
Claud, Nicholas	WC2	101	" 1676.
Clauson, Daniel	16	40	" 1670.

NAME	Liber	Folio	REMARKS
Claver, Thomas	6	47	Transported 1663. Servant.
Clavering, Peter	9	451	" 1666. (11, fol. 482).
Clawson, Derrick	17	567	" 1673.
Clawson, Jacob	4	72	" 1657-9.
Clawson, Tobias	6	48	Immigrated 1663.
Clawson, William	17	566	Of Worcester Co. Immigrated
1673, with Elizabeth and Mary, his daughters.			
Claxton, Bryan	15	451	Transported 1669.
Claxton, Edward	2	529	" 1639. Servant. Service 1649.
Claxton, Edward	ABH	27	Servant 1639.
Clay, John	20	185	Transported 1679.
Clay, Timothy	16	394	" 1671.
Clayland, James, Gent.	17	60	Immigrated 1672.
Clayton, Charles	9	436	Transported 1666.
Clayton, Ellen	16	505	" 1671.
Clayton, John	15	301	" 1675.
Clayton, Philip	12	489	Of Calvert Co. Service 1670.
Cleare, John	15	407	Immigrated 1676.
Cleare, Nathaniel	5	514	Transported 1642.
Cleave, Francis	6	105	" 1660.
Cleaveland, James	16	435	" 1671.
Cleavour, Thomas	10	598	Immigrated 1667.
Cleere, John	WC2	86	" 1679.
Cleeve, Nathaniel	4	533	Transported 1659.
Cleeveland, William	18	285	" 1674.
Cleft, James	12	496	" 1670.
Cleggat (Clagett), Thomas	WC2	53	Immigrated 1670.
Cleghorne, James	9	312	" 1666.
Clemen, Elizabeth	5	139	Transported 1662.
Clemence, Ambroze	9	34	" 1665.
Clemence, George	10	4	Immigrated 1666.
Clemens, Nicholas	17	516	Of St. Mary's Co. Service 1673.
Clemenson, Andrew	6	47	Transported 1663, with his two children.
Clements, Elizabeth	ABH	324	Transported 1652-3. Servant.
Clements, Hannah	5	489	" 1655.
Clements, Henry	5	248	" 1663.
Clements, John	15	536	" 1678.
Clements, Mary	12	498	" 1670.
Clements, Thomas	12	385	" 1669.
Clementson, Andreas	4	552	" 1663. Son of Andrew.
Clementson, Andrew	4	552	Immigrated 1661, with wife. (See Clemenson, Andrew).
Clementson, Clement	4	552	Transported 1661. Son of Andrew.
Clemson, Robert	15	452	" 1678.
Clenwellin, Dunken	4	140	" 1651. Servant.
Clerk, Dan.	15	376	" 1676.
Clerk, Daniel	17	331	" from Virginia 1672.
Clerk, Eleanor	1	24	" 1641.

NAME	Liber	Folio	REMARKS
Clerk, John	16	177	Transported 1672.
Clerk, John	17	407	" 1673.
Clerk, Robert	1	17,71, 74-75	Immigrated 1637.
Clerk, Teage	15	397	Transported 1675.
Clerke, Edward	18	132	Of St. Mary's Co. Service 1674.
Clerke, George	15	338	Transported 1676.
Clerke, Henry	12	604	" 1670.
Clerke, John	18	36	" 1673.
Clerke, Loghlin	17	363	" 1672.
Clerke, Margaret	17	407	" 1672.
Clerke, Robert	16	177	" 1672.
Clerke, William	9	216	" 1665.
Clerkson, William	15	354	" 1676.
Clerry, Latice	7	487	" 1663.
Clerry, Peter	7	487	Immigrated 1663.
Cleterbook, Elizabeth	15	550	Transported 1679.
Cleve, Daniel	9	105	Immigrated 1665.
Cleve, Jane	9	105	Transported 1665. Daughter of Daniel.
Cleve, John	9	105	Transported 1665. Brother to Daniel.
Cleve, Nathaniel	10	392	And Joyce, his wife. Service 1666.
Cleve, Thomas	17	375	Transported 1672.
Clever, Jane	4	551	" 1661.
Clever, John	15	404	Immigrated 1676.
Cleverly, Thomas	16	125	Of Anne Arundel Co. Service 1671.
Cleyson, James	16	412	Transported 1671.
Cleyton, James	17	356	" 1672.
Cleyton, Samuel	4	204	" 1659.
Cliff, John	12	205	" 1667. Servant.
Clifford, George	12	355	" 1669.
Clifford, John	12	194	" 1668. Servant.
Clifford, Mary	18	166	" 1674.
Cliffton, Ann	5	26	" 1660-3. Wife of James. Niece of Mrs. Margaret Brent. (19, fol. 382).
Cliffton, James, Gent.	6	26	Immigrated 1660-3.
Cliford, Samuel	15	376	Transported 1676.
Clifton, Martha	12	505	Service 1669.
Clifton, Sarah	Q	32	Transported 1650.
Clifton, Stephens	8	427	His widow married Thomas Bowtle prior to 1664.
Clifton, Thomas	5	248	Transported 1663.
Clifton, William	WC2	5	Gift of 300 acres from Lord Baltimore 1669.
Climate, Jane	WC2	381	Transported 1675-80. Servant.
Clinion, Symon	7	471	" 1664.
Clinton, Thomas	WC2	57	" 1678.
Clipsam, Thomas	WC2	263	Married widow of John Cage. Of Charles County.
Clipson, Alice	15	569	Transported 1678.

NAME	Liber	Folio	REMARKS
Clissell, Martha	6	16	Immigrated 1662.
Clites, James	6	293	Transported 1664.
Clitton, Ann	9	344	" 1665.
Clixton, James	15	445	" 1677.
Cloake, Frances	7	86	" 1656. Servant.
Cloater, William	15	369	Immigrated 1675.
Clockem, John	15	509	Transported 1677.
Clocker, Daniel	2	581	Service 1649.
Clocker, Daniel	ABH	36,244	Transported 1636.
Clocker, Mrs. Daniel	2	581	Service 1649. Formerly servant to Margaret Brent.
Clommin, George	15	560	Transported 1678.
Clother, Lues	9	157	" 1665.
Clothworth, Elizabeth	3	17	" prior to 1650.
Clothworthy, Elizabeth	ABH	44	" many years prior to 1650.
Clott, Symon	9	104	Transported 1665.
Clough, Thomas	16	411	" 1671.
Clough, William	15	354	" 1676.
Cloughnan, John	12	413	" 1669.
Cloughton, James	1	19	" 1638.
Cloughton, James	1	91	Petition to confirm title to land. Of Isle of Kent, 1640.
Cloughton, James, Jr.	3	18	Transported about 1640.
Cloughton, James, Jr.	ABH	45	" 1641-2. Son of James, Sr.
Cloughton, James, Sr.	ABH	45	Immigrated 1641-2.
Cloughton, James, Sr.	3	18	" about 1640 with wife, son and five men servants. Deceased by 1650.
Cloughton, Jane	3	18	Transported about 1640. Wife of James, Sr. Deceased by 1650.
Cloughton, Jane	ABH	45	Wife of James, Sr. Immigrated 1641-2.
Clower, Elizabeth	9	104	Transported 1665.
Cloyden, Samuel	18	314	Service 1668.
Cloyse, Jacob	9	216	Transported 1665.
Cloyster, Benjamin	12	465	Of Calvert Co. Service 1669.
Cluckson, William	15	354	Transported 1676.
Cluer, Stephen	15	397	" 1676.
Cluneste, Elizabeth	9	33	" 1665.
Cluxton, James	WC2	53	" 1677.
Clyant, Mark	WC2	179	" 1680.
Clyman, Symon	17	66	Service 1672.
Clymer, John	15	558	" 1669.
Clynton, Thomas	15	554	Transported 1678.
Coachy, William	7	84	" 1660.
Coale, William	16	482	" 1671.
Coane, Abraham	12	222	Of Brittans Bay. Immigrated from Virginia 1668.
Coane, Sarah	12	222	Transported 1668. Daughter of Abraham.

NAME	Liber	Folio	REMARKS
Coape, Edward	16	71	Transported 1670.
Coate, Leonard	17	440	" 1673.
Coateman, Robert	16	78	" 1670.
Coates, Alice	18	331	" 1674.
Coates, Bartholomew	4	614	Special Warrant for 500 acres 1661. (7, fol. 372).
Coates, George	8	478	Transported 1665.
Coates, Mary	15	181	Widow of Bartholomew. Living 1673.
Coates, Mary	17	531	Transported 1673.
Coates, Thomas	15	181	Son of Bartholomew. Living 1673.
Coates, Thomas	17	531	Transported 1673.
Coates, William	15	181	Son of Bartholomew. Living 1673.
Cobb, Elizabeth	6	623	Transported 1660. (4, fol. 560).
Cobb, Elizabeth	6	134	" 1663.
Cobb, James	12	271	" 1668. Servant.
Cobb, Walter	18	331	" 1674.
Cobbidge, John	15	359	" 1676.
Cobbington, John	ABH	140	" 1651.
Cobbs, Elizabeth	9	92	" 1665. (12, fol. 354).
Cobby, Benjamin	ABH	150	" 1637. Servant.
Cobby (Cobbie), Benjamine	1	17,19	" 1637.
Cobden, Mary	4	57	" 1659.
Cobden, Thomas	ABH	374	" under 1st conditions of plantations. Servant.
Cobham, Thomas	5	241	Immigrated 1662. (7, fol. 61).
Cobreth, John	Q	29	" 1658.
Cobsteed, Jane	5	84	Transported 1661.
Coburne, Ann	WC2	56	" 1679.
Coburne, Ann	15	553	" 1678.
Coburne, Charles	15	454	" 1677.
Cock, Anthony	16	507	" 1671.
Cock, John	6	266	" 1662.
Cock, Robert	17	457	" 1669.
Cockane, Mary	15	322	" 1674.
Cocke, Robert	9	33	" 1660-5.
Cocke, Thomas	10	433	" 1666.
Cocker, Thomas	18	161	Of St. Mary's Co. Service 1666.
Cockerall, John	15	440	And Mary, his wife. Service 1677.
Cockery, Alice	10	583	Of Virginia. Transported 1667. Servant.
Cockett, Lewis	15	354	Transported 1676.
Cockley, Philip	6	296	" 1664.
Cocks, George	5	125	" 1662.
Cocks, James	WC2	283,403	Service 1680. Of Charles Co.
Cocks, John	5	243	Transported 1662. (12, fol. 281).
Cockshot, Jane	ABH	59	Wife of John. Immigrated 1641.

In the next year she appears a widow, married Nicholas Causen prior to 1648. (ABH, fol. 22).

| Cockshot, Jane | 2 | 506-507 | Widow of John. Married Nicholas Cawsin. |

NAME	Liber	Folio	REMARKS
Cockshot, Jane	ABH	22, 59	Transported 1641. Probably daughter of John.
Cockshot, John	ABH	22, 59	Immigrated 1641. (ABH, fol. 207).
Cockshot, Mary	ABH	22, 59	Transported 1641. Daughter of John.
Cockshott, Jane	1	24	Transported 1641. Wife of John.
Cockshott, John	1	24	Immigrated 1641 with wife and others. Deceased 1642.
Cockshott, Mary	1	24	Transported 1641.
Cocner, John	WC2	277-278	" 1680.
Codd, Baltasar	1	19, 71	Immigrated 1638. Irishman.
Codd, Baltasar	ABH	81	" Aug. 1638.
Codd, Bartholomew	4	590	Transported 1660-1.
Codwell, Margaret	4	214	Immigrated 1659.
Codwell, William	4	214	" 1659.
Coe, Elizabeth	4	560	Transported 1661.
Coe, George	5	415	" 1663.
Coely, Mathe	15	455	" 1678.
Coffee, Rebecca	18	311	" 1675.
Coffee, Robert	WC2	140,142	Immigrated 1680. Of Somerset Co. Shoemaker.
Coffin, Robert	WC2	78	Immigrated from Virginia 1679. Of Somerset Co.
Coffin, Susan	9	459	Transported 1663.
Cofford, Thomas	12	352	Of St. Mary's Co. Service 1669.
Cogar, Jeremiah	6	129	Transported 1662.
Cogell, James	8	129	" 1664. Servant.
Coger, Richard	6	85	" 1658.
Coggin, George	8	19	" 1664.
Coghlan, Bartholomew	WC2	287	" 1680.
Coghland, Thomas	15	446	" 1677.
Coghlin, Horner	15	553	" 1678.
Cohell, Nicholas	15	524	" 1678.
Cohoon, John	15	433	" 1677.
Coke, Francis	4	14	" 1659. Servant.
Coke, Mary	8	130	" 1665. Child of Hugh Cornelius.
Coke, Solomon	12	375	Transported 1669. Of Virginia.
Cokeran, William	15	553	" 1678.
Cokes, Edward	9	38	" 1664.
Cokes, John	9	35	" 1664.
Colborne, Mary	5	254	" 1663 by Wm. Colborne of the Eastern Shore.
Cold, Robert	5	106	Transported 1654.
Coldfield, Christopher	11	337	" 1668.
Cole, Adam	5	409	" 1662.
Cole, Alice	17	490	" 1673.
Cole, Ann	ABH	35	Servant 1649.
Cole, Anne	2	575	Transported 1648-9. Servant.
Cole, Edward	16	79	" 1670.
Cole, Elizabeth	6	134	" 1663.

NAME	Liber	Folio	REMARKS
Cole, Flora	5	90	Transported 1653-61. (5, fol. 489).
Cole, George	15	573	" 1668. Son of Henry, of Calvert Co. (15, fol. 112).
Cole, Giles	17	635	Transported 1671.
Cole, Henry	7	569	" 1663-4.
Cole, James	8	501	" 1665.
Cole, James	10	503	" 1667. Servant.
Cole, John	2	327	" 1640-8.
Cole, John	1	131	" 1641. Servant.
Cole, John	2	425	" 1641.
Cole, John	WC2	110	" 1676. Servant.
Cole, John	WC2	50,98	" 1679.
Cole, John	WC2	352	" 1680.
Cole, John	WC2	412	" 1681.
Cole, John	ABH	6,10	" 1640-8.
Cole, John	6	83	" 1654.
Cole, John	7	567	" 1665. (8, fol. 410).
Cole, John	12	584	" 1670.
Cole, John	15	446	" 1678.
Cole, Margarett	WC2	254	" 1680.
Cole, Margery	5	416	" 1663.
Cole, Mary	WC2	50,98	" 1679.
Cole (als. Bramson), Mary	Q	183	Servant 1658.
Cole, Peter	17	548	Of Calvert Co. Service 1673.
Cole, Priscilla	2	614	Transported 1649. Wife of Thomas.
Cole, Priscilla	ABH	40	" 1649. Wife of Thomas.
Cole, Richard	ABH	65	" 1633.
Cole, Richard	ABH	60	" 1635. Servant.
Cole, Richard	ABH	102	" 1641.
Cole, Richard	1	20,38	" 1633.
Cole, Richard	1	26	" since 1635.
Cole, Richard	1	129	" 1641.
Cole, Robert	ABH	338	Immigrated 1652-3, with his wife and four children.
Cole, Robert	9	487	Immigrated 1664.
Cole, Samuel	15	353	Transported 1674.
Cole, Sarah	ABH	201	" 1650-1. Wife of William.
Cole, Susan	ABH	201	Transported 1650-1.
Cole, Susan (Susanna)	WC2	50	" 1679.
Cole, Thomas	ABH	40	Immigrated 1649. (Q, fol. 47).
Cole, Thomas	2	614	" 1649 with wife, Priscilla.
Cole, Thomas	15	433	Transported 1677.
Cole, William	ABH	201	Immigrated 1650-1.
Cole, William	9	34	Transported 1665.
Cole, William	17	585	" 1673.
Coleburne, Ann	4	581	" 1661. Wife of William.
Coleburne, William	11	337	" 1668.
Coleburne, William, Jr.	4	581	" 1661.

NAME	Liber	Folio	REMARKS
Coleby, William	18	31	Transported 1674.
Coleford, Richard	ABH	64	" 1638. Servant.
Coleman, Abigail	6	294	" 1664.
Coleman, Anthony	15	553	" 1678.
Coleman, Elias	9	325	Immigrated 1666.
Coleman, Elizabeth	WC2	415	Transported 1680. Servant.
Coleman, Mary	12	280	" 1668. Servant.
Coleman, Richard	6	134	" 1663.
Coleman, Samuel	16	77	" 1670.
Coleman, Thomas	15	553	" 1678. (WC2, fol. 56).
Coleman, Thomas	WC2	254	" 1680. (WC2, fol. 406).
Coleman, William	4	570	" 1661.
Colestone, Mary	12	477	" 1670. Wife of Robert.
Colestone, Robert	12	477	Immigrated 1670. Of Charles Co.
Colhoun, Jane	15	449,531	Wife of John, of Somerset Co. Service 1677.
Colhoun, John	15	534	Service 1675.
Coliston, Judith	15	569	Transported 1678.
Coll, Barnaby	15	454	" Oct. 1677.
Collahane, Dennis	WC2	380	" 1675-80. Servant.
Colled, Joan	13	116	" 1671.
Collefax, William	12	190	" 1668. Servant.
Colleott, Thomas	11	372	" 1668.
Coller, Jeremiah	7	87	" 1660.
Coller, John	6	83	" 1653.
Collerton, Edward	12	270	" 1668.
Collett, Alexandra	WC2	380	" 1675-80. Servant.
Collett, Ann	4	70,549	Immigrated 1659. Wife of John.
Collett, Elizabeth	5	607	Transported 1658.
Collett, Elizabeth	6	293	" 1664.
Collett, Emerentiana	Q	201	" 1651-8. Wife of Richard.
Collett, George	4	70,549	Transported 1659. Son of John.
Collett, John	4	14	" 1651. Servant.
Collett, John	4	70	Immigrated 1659. Of Baltimore Co.
Collett, John	4	70	Transported 1659. Son of John. (16, fol. 95).
Collett, John	4	549	Immigrated 1661.
Collett, John, Jr.	4	549	Transported 1661.
Collett, Richard	Q	201	Immigrated 1650.
Collett, Richard	ABH	322	" Nov. 1652.
Collett, Samuel	4	70	Transported 1650. Son of John. (16, fol. 327).
Collett, Samuel	4	549	Transported 1661.
Collick, James	15	443	" 1667.
Collier, Ann	8	89	" 1665.
Collier, Elizabeth	8	89	" 1665.
Collier, James	5	411	" 1663. (17, fol. 401).
Collier, Lieut. John	4	66	Service 1659.
Collier, Thurston	12	205	Transported 1667.
Collier, William	5	367	" 1649.

NAME	Liber	Folio	REMARKS
Collin, Samuel	15	531	Of Somerset Co. Bricklayer. Immigrated 1678.
Collingam, John	17	440	Transported 1673.
Collings, Bridgett	WC2	18	" 1679. Wife of John.
Collings, Elizabeth	WC2	18	" 1679.
Collings, Elizabeth	9	435	" 1666.
Collings, Frances	15	509	" 1674. Wife of Thomas.
Collings, John	WC2	18	Immigrated 1679 with wife and daughter.
Collings, Richard	9	435	Transported 1666.
Collings, Richard	15	509	Immigrated 1674.
Collings, Samuel	15	570	" 1679.
Collings, Thomas	10	560	Of Talbot Co. of Northumberland Co., Va. 1667.
Collings, Thomas	15	509	Immigrated 1664.
Collings, William	9	435	Transported 1666.
Collings, William	10	564	" 1667.
Collingsworth, John	10	523	" 1667.
Collington, George	6	134	" 1661.
Collingwood, Robert	16	411	" 1671.
Collingwood, William	18	15	Immigrated 1674. Of Calvert Co.
Collins, Anneky	10	557	Transported 1667. Daughter of Jonathan.
Collins, James	15	356	Transported 1675.
Collins, Jasper	ABH	58	" 1640. (1, fol. 22).
Collins, John	11	307	" 1667. Servant.
Collins, Jonathan	10	557	Of Baltimore Co. Immigrated from Delaware Bay 1667.
Collins, Frederick	10	557	Transported 1667. Son of Jonathan.
Collins, Francis	12	381,416	" 1669.
Collins, George	5	468	" 1661.
Collins, Mr. George	9	48	Immigrated 1665.
Collins, George	17	417	Transported 1673.
Collins, Herbert	6	130	" 1656.
Collins, Margaret	15	543	" 1678.
Collins, Thomas	17	304	" 1672.
Collins, Thomas	17	462	" 1673.
Collins, Thomas	WC2	182	Service 1680.
Collins, Veny	10	557	Transported 1667. Wife of Jonathan.
Collins, William	5	489	" 1655. (Q, fol. 73).
Collins, William	9	48	" 1665. Son of George.
Collins, William	15	318	Service 1674.
Collinson, Elizabeth	WC2	203	" 1680. Of Talbot Co.
Collinson, John	16	537	Transported 1671.
Collinson, Peter	WC2	326	Service 1680.
Collis, John	WC2	47,71	Immigrated 1679.
Collis, William	17	517	Transported 1673.
Collison, George	9	356	" 1666.
Collison, George	12	465	Of Talbot Co. Service 1669.
Collison, John	5	12	Transported 1662.
Collison, John	5	64	" 1662.

NAME	Liber	Folio	REMARKS
Collnell, Jane	15	527	Transported 1678.
Colloway, Anthony	4	66	Service 1659.
Collyer, Alice	17	331	Transported from Virginia by Robert, 1672.
Collyer, Ann	17	331	Transported from Virginia by Robert, 1672.
Collyer, Giles	12	604	Transported 1670.
Collyer, Robert	17	331	Immigrated from Virginia 1672.
Collyer, Robert	17	610	" 1673. Of Somerset Co.
Collyer, William	WC2	147	Transported 1680.
Colman, Philip	11	479	" 1668.
Colraine, George	16	115	" 1675.
Colson, James	9	233	" 1665.
Colson, John	16	302	" 1671.
Coltner, William	16	532	" 1668.
Coman, John	13	114	" 1671.
Comberton, Garrett	3	173	" 1655.
Combes, Elizabeth	7	484	" 1658. Wife of Philip.
Combes, George	9	45	" 1665.
Combes, Philip	7	484	"Formerly Mr. Gerranrd's over-seer". Immigrated 1664.
Combes, Richard	15	383	Transported 1676.
Combes, William	12	322	" 1669.
Combleson, Leonard	15	318	" 1675.
Combs, John	Q	18	" 1655.
Combs, Martha	16	293	" 1671.
Combs, Mary	5	89	" 1659. Servant.
Comegys, Cornelius	9	506	Immigrated 1666.
Comegys, Cornelius, Jr.	9	506	Transported 1666. Son of Cornelius.
Comegys, Willemyntye	9	506	" 1666. Wife of Cornelius.
Comes, Abraham	WC2	47	Immigrated 1679 with daughter. Of St. Mary's County.
Comes, Barbary	7	551	Transported 1664. Wife of Enoch.
Comes, Enoch	7	551	Immigrated 1664.
Comes, Enoch	7	551	Transported 1664. Son of Enoch.
Comes, Fenneky	10	307	" 1666. Wife of Walter.
Comes, James	10	564	" 1667.
Comes, Sarah	WC2	47	" 1679. Daughter of Abraham.
Comes, Walter	10	307	Immigrated from New York to Talbot Co. 1666.
Comine, Samuel	9	33	Transported 1665.
Comins, Edward	1	76-77	Petition to confirm title to land granted by Capt. William Clayborne, 1640.
Commerton, Garrett	5	244	Immigrated 1662.
Commins, Edward	2	529	" about 1639 with wife.
Commins, Edward	ABH	27	" 1639 with wife.
Commins, Elizabeth	ABH	105	Widow of Edward. Living 1650.
Companey, Catherine	WC2	87	Transported 1679.
Compton, Edward	11	337,441	" 1668.
Compton, Fitz Allen	17	424	" 1673.

NAME	Liber	Folio	REMARKS
Compton, James	ABH	60, 66	Transported 1637. (ABH, fol. 24; 1, fol. 20, 25, 38, 39).
Compton, James	2	512	Transported about 1649. Servant.
Compton, John	7	490	Immigrated prior to 1664. Of Charles County.
Compton, Jonathan	WC2	179	Transported 1680.
Compton, Mary	11	543	Service 1668.
Compton, Richard	15	416	Transported 1677.
Conant, Abigail	WC2	50, 98	" 1663. Wife of Robert.
Conant, Ann	WC2	50	" 1663. Daughter of Robert.
Conant, Margaret	WC2	50, 98	Transported 1663. Daughter of Robert.
Conant, Martha	WC2	50, 98	Transported 1663. Daughter of Robert.
Conant, Robert	WC2	50, 57, 89, 98	Immigrated 1663 with wife, three daughters and nine other persons. Of Anne Arundel County.
Conant, Robert	7	469	Transported 1664.
Conaway, Joseph	7	83	" 1663.
Conaway, William	6	62	" 1663.
Condict, Nath'l.	15	356	" 1675.
Condon, John	20	184	" from Ireland 1678.
Coneel, Sarah	10	325	" 1666.
Conell, Daniel	15	600	" 1678.
Coner, Richard	15	527	" 1678.
Conerie, John	5	486	Immigrated 1650. Transported his wife 1655.
Conery, Edward	11	333	Service 1668.
Conery, Mary	11	333	Wife of Edward. Service 1668.
Coney, Edward	Q	119	Transported 1655.
Coney, Francis	17	491	" 1667.
Conington, William	17	463	" 1673.
Conlane, Bryan	17	571	" 1673.
Conlane, Katherine	17	571	" 1673.
Conlane, Philip	17	571	" 1673.
Connar, Honor	WC2	57	" 1678.
Connaway, William	Q	71	" 1652-3.
Conne, Jane	8	478	" 1665.
Connell, Hugh	17	419	Service 1672.
Connell, James	17	548	Of Anne Arundel Co. Service 1673.
Connell, Morgan	20	184	Transported 1678 from Ireland.
Connell, Rebecah	WC2	16	" 1679.
Conner, Ann	9	211	" 1665.
Conner, Ann	15	353	" 1674.
Conner, Dorothy	WC2	12	Service 1679.
Conner, Hannah	WC2	24, 106	Transported 1678. Servant.
Conner, Howner	15	553	" 1678.
Conner, Hugh	9	156	" 1660.
Conner, Humphrey	18	12	Immigrated 1667. Of St. Mary's Co.
Conner, James	WC2	12	Service 1679. Of Somerset Co.

NAME	Liber	Folio	REMARKS
Conner, James	15	525	Tailor, and Dorothy, his wife. Service 1678.
Conner, John	WC2	18	Transported 1648.
Conner, Laurence	WC2	120	" 1680.
Conner, Mary	4	63	" 1648. Wife of Philip.
(11, fol. 170).	Married John	Wright prior to June 9, 1667. (11, fol. 265).	
Conner, Philip	ABH	84	Of the Isle of Kent. Immigrated prior to 1640. (12, fol. 572).
Conner, Philip	4	63	Immigrated 1648.
Conner, Philip, Jr.	9	211	Transported 1665.
Conner, Philip, Sr.	9	204	Immigrated 1665.
Conner, Phillip	1	79	" 1640. Of Isle of Kent.
Conner, Sarah	10	2	Daughter of Philip of Kent Co. Dec'd. 1666.
Conner, Sarah	9	211	Transported 1665.
Connery, Edward	4	533	" 1659.
Connery, Thomas	ABH	161	Immigrated 1650.
Connill, Sarah	5	246	Transported 1657.
Connor, Timothy	WC2	380	" 1675-80. Servant.
Connor, Timothy	WC2	129,380	" 1679.
Connough, John	15	409	" 1676 by Philip of Somerset County.
Conny, Elizabeth	WC2	247	Service 1680.
Conny, Francis	16	394	Transported 1671.
Connyworth, Robert	13	113	" 1670.
Constable, Henry	17	469	Of Anne Arundel Co. Merchant. Immigrated 1673.
Constable, John	7	469, 576-7	Transported 1664.
Constable, Nicholas	15	516	" 1676.
Constable, Richard	17	411	" 1673.
Constantine, Thomas	18	329	" 1675.
Contis, Raphael	9	333	" 1666.
Conty, William	WC2	108	" 1679.
Conway, Ann	15	454	" 1677.
Conway, Bryan	WC2	120	" 1680.
Conway, Coll.	15	454	" 1677.
Conway, James	15	454	" 1667.
Coode, Henry	15	439	" 1667.
Coohone, Daniel	5	63	" 1660.
Cook, Edward	ABH	151	" 1649-50. Servant.
Cook, George	Q	32	Servant 1653.
Cook, John	ABH	85	Transported 1636.
Cook, Miles	Q	459	Of London, Mariner. Immigrated 1658. (5, fol. 221).
Cook, Stephen	WC2	287	Transported 1680.
Cook, Susanna	7	87	" 1654.
Cook, William	Q	443	" 1658.
Cooke, Alice	5	12	" 1662.
Cooke, Andrew	7	524	" 1664.
Cooke, Ann	8	502	" 1665.

NAME	Liber	Folio	REMARKS
Cooke, Ann	15	383	Immigrated 1676. Wife of Edward.
Cooke, Anthony	5	211	Transported 1662.
Cooke, Arthur	15	530	" 1678.
Cooke, Benjamin	5	189,242	" 1658.
Cooke, Benjamin	12	393	" 1669.
Cooke, Benjamin	17	531	" 1673.
Cooke, Edward	11	546	Immigrated 1668.
Cooke, Edward	1	166	Transported 1650. Servant.
Cooke, Edward	WC2	66	" 1669.
Cooke, Edward	12	242	" 1669. Of Virginia.
Cooke, Eliza	13	65	" 1665. Servant.
Cooke, Elizabeth	5	489	" 1662.
Cooke, Elizabeth	12	209	" 1668. (16, fol. 71).
Cooke, Elizabeth	18	331	" 1674. (15, fol. 300).
Cooke, Elizabeth	15	435	" 1676 by Thomas.
Cooke, Francis	16	435	" 1671.
Cooke, George	8	381	" 1665 by Augustine Herman.
Cooke, Giles	5	85	Transported 1661.
Cooke, Joane	16	463	Wife of Rice. Service 1666.
Cooke, John	1	82	Transported 1636. Servant.
Cooke, John	9	249	" 1660. Son of John.
Cooke, John	9	249	Immigrated from London 1660 with his wife.
Cooke, John	5	244	Transported 1662.
Cooke, John	6	90	" 1663. (6, fol. 47).
Cooke, John	6	321	" 1664.
Cooke, John	12	333	" 1668.
Cooke, John	16	409	" from Virginia 1671.
Cooke, John	17	347	Of Dorchester Co. Immigrated 1672.
Cooke, John	15	544	Transported 1676.
Cooke, Joseph	15	430	" 1677.
Cooke, Joseph	9	334	" 1666.
Cooke, Margaret	9	249	" 1660. Daughter of John.
Cooke, Marmaduke	5	85	Transported 1661.
Cooke, Mary	17	531	" 1673.
Cooke, Mary	18	80	" 1674.
Cooke, Michael	16	133	" 1671.
Cooke, Rachel	8	494	" 1664.
Cooke, Ralph	11	282	" 1667.
Cooke, Rice	16	463	Of Talbot Co. Immigrated 1667.
Cooke, Richard	17	416	Transported 1673.
Cooke, Samuel	6	142	" 1658.
Cooke, Sarah	5	129,308	" 1662.
Cooke, Sarah	6	123	" 1663. (7, fol. 569).
Cooke, Thomas	9	249	" 1660. Son of John.
Cooke, Thomas	8	486	" 1664.
Cooke, Thomas	17	401	Immigrated from Virginia in 1671, with his wife, Eleanor.

NAME	Liber	Folio	REMARKS
Cooke, Thomas	17	417	Transported 1673.
Cooke, Thomas	WC2	86-87	" 1679.
Cooke, William	10	499	" 1667.
Cooke, William	12	403	" 1669.
Cooke, William	15	533	" 1678.
Cookerry, Sarah	WC2	380	" 1675-80. Servant.
Cookker, Samuel	12	601	" 1669.
Cooks, Elizabeth	11	374	" 1668.
Cooks, William	Q	431	" 1658.
Cooksey, Philip	4	198	" 1659.
Cooley, Richard	18	84	" 1674.
Coombes, Elizabeth	WC2	150	" 1680.
Coomes, Philip	Q	33	" 1653.
Coone, Mary	11	164	" 1667.
Coone, Robert	11	164	" 1667.
Coop, William	12	416	" 1669.
Cooper, Alice	15	601	Service 1679.
Cooper, Ann	ABH	173	Wife of Walter. Immigrated and died 1651.
Cooper, Ann	Q	430	Transported 1658.
Cooper, Ann	15	430	" 1677.
Cooper, Anna	7	577	" 1665.
Cooper, Catherine	Q	430	" 1658.
Cooper, Charles	WC2	76,212, 254	" 1679. Servant.
Cooper, Daniel	4	551	" 1661.
Cooper, Dorothy	Q	430	" 1658.
Cooper, Elizabeth	Q	430	" 1658.
Cooper, Elizabeth	17	440	" 1673.
Cooper, Elizabeth	15	531	" 1678.
Cooper, Henry	8	203	" 1665.
Cooper, James	5	73	" 1660-1.
Cooper, James	9	270	" 1665.
Cooper, Joane	16	72	" 1670.
Cooper, John	4	68,198	" 1659.
Cooper, John	5	343	" 1663. (6, fol. 347).
Cooper, John	7	567	" 1665.
Cooper, John	8	410	" 1665.
Cooper, John	9	155,269	" 1665.
Cooper, John	17	407	" 1672.
Cooper, John	17	532	Immigrated 1673. Of Calvert Co.
Cooper, John	15	353	Transported 1674.
Cooper, John	15	567	" 1678.
Cooper, Josias	7	581	" 1665.
Cooper, Margery	12	575	" 1670.
Cooper, Martha	WC2	396	" 1680. Servant.
Cooper, Mary	Q	69	" 1658.
Cooper, Mary	12	189	" 1668.
Cooper, Mary	12	575	" 1670.
Cooper, Nicholas	16	94	" 1670.
Cooper, Richard	15	452	" 1677.

NAME	Liber	Folio	REMARKS
Cooper, Richard	WC2	359,377	Transported 1680.
Cooper, Robert	1	91	Petition to confirm title to land Of Isle of Kent, 1640.
Cooper, Robert	Q	211	Transported 1658.
Cooper, Robert	17	571	" 1673.
Cooper, Robert	18	334	" 1675.
Cooper, Roger	15	560	" 1678.
Cooper, Samuel	5	128	" 1662.
Cooper, Samuel	15	531	Immigrated 1678. Of Somerset Co.
Cooper, Samuel	WC2	290	" 1679. Of Somerset Co.
Cooper, Sarah	18	130	Transported 1674.
Cooper, Sarah	WC2	310	" 1680.
Cooper, Simond	6	294	" 1664. (7, fol. 569).
Cooper, Stephen	8	97	" 1656.
Cooper, Susanna	Q	430	" 1658.
Cooper, Thomas	ABH	6, 67	" 1633. Servant. (1, fol. 17, 27, 41).
Cooper, Thomas	2	346	Transported 1633. Servant.
Cooper, Thomas	8	478	" 1665.
Cooper, Thomas	10	471,503	" 1667. Servant. (16, fol. 301).
Cooper, Thomas	15	300	Of Anne Arundel Co., and Margaret, his wife. Service 1675.
Cooper, Thomas	15	353	Transported 1675.
Cooper, Thomas	15	396	" 1677.
Cooper, Thomas	15	551	" 1679.
Cooper, Walter	Q	430	Immigrated 1658.
Cooper, Mr. Walter	ABH	173	" and died 1651. (Q, fol. 430).
Cooper, William	Q	430	Transported 1658.
Cooper, William	9	400	" 1666.
Cooper, William	12	381	" 1669.
Cooper, William	17	440	" 1673.
Coopey, Avis	WC2	105	" 1680.
Cooser, John	11	520	Of Charles Co. Immigrated 1668 with wife.
Coote, Hierom	ABH	10	Transported 1640. (2, fol. 425).
Coote, Jeremy	ABH	244	" 1639.
Cop, Henry	ABH	276	Immigrated 1651, and in the following year referred to his former wife, Elizabeth, widow of Bury.
Cope, George	17	517	Transported 1673.
Cope, James	ABH	35	Servant 1649.
Cope, James	2	575	Transported 1649. Servant.
Copely, Jeremiah	13	114	" 1668.
Copely, Thomas, Esq.	ABH	22,60	Immigrated 1637.
Coperworth, Jane	15	353	Transported 1674.
Copes, Henry	11	344	" 1668.
Copley, John	WC2	253	" 1680.
Copley, Savell	6	133	" 1653.
Copley, Thomas	1	17,20, 25	Immigrated 1637. (1, fol. 115-118).

NAME	Liber	Folio	REMARKS
Coplyn, Elizabeth	WC2	334	Daughter of Henry, deceased 1680.
Coppin, George	9	33	Transported 1665.
Copping, Edward	ABH	157	Immigrated 1650.
Copping, Henry	15	356	Transported 1675.
Copping, John	17	548	Immigrated 1671.
Copshire, Francis	18	167	Transported 1674.
Coram, William	18	31	Of Baltimore Co. Service 1673.
Corban, Margaret	15	553	Transported 1678.
Corbee, John	15	430	" 1677.
Corbell, Bridgett	16	65	" 1670.
Corbett, Ann	18	288	" 1674. Wife of Francis.
Corbett, Ann	WC2	51	Service 1679. Wife of Francis.
Corbett, Francis	18	288	Transported 1674.
Corbett, Francis	WC2	51	Service 1679.
Corbett, Henry	7	87	Transported 1656.
Corbett, John	9	54	" 1665.
Corbettle, Samuel	7	84	" 1658.
Corbin, Elizabeth	16	533	" 1671. Daughter of Nicholas.
Corbin, Elizabeth	16	533	Transported 1671. Wife of Nicholas.
Corbin, George	17	486	" 1667.
Corbin, Mary	16	533	" 1671. Daughter of Nicholas.
Corbin, Mary	WC2	396	Transported 1680. Servant.
Corbin, Nicholas	16	533	Immigrated Nov. 1671 with wife and two daughters.
Corbyn, Francis	13	114	Transported 1671. Servant.
Corcrane, Thomas	WC2	128	" 1679.
Cord, Ann	15	318	" 1675. Wife of William.
Cord, Sarah	15	318	" 1675. Daughter of William.
Cord, William	15	318	Immigrated 1675.
Corden, Jane	8	501	Transported 1665.
Corder, William	17	417	" 1673.
Cordery, Ann	11	545	Immigrated 1668.
Cordery, Elizabeth	11	545	Transported 1668. Daughter of Ann.
Cordin, Roger	11	235	" 1667.
Cording, Richard	4	585	Immigrated 1661.
Cording, Roger	7	569	Transported 1663-4.
Cordrop, Elizabeth	6	90	" 1661.
Cordwyn, Richard	15	452	" 1677.
Core, Toby	9	222	" 1665.
Coreleen, John	15	414	" 1677.
Corke, Robert	4	204	" 1659. (12, fol. 271).
Corker, Thomas	5	306	" 1663.
Corkeran, John	WC2	89	" 1676. Servant.
Corman, Hugh	6	37	" 1663.
Cormecke, Onera	15	565	" 1679.
Cormell, Eleanor	15	353	" 1674.
Cormote, John	15	452	" 1678.
Corne, Anthony	4	70	" 1659.

NAME	Liber	Folio	REMARKS
Cornelia, Hugh	17	26	Transported 1672.
Corneliason, Abraham	4	576	" 1661.
Corneliason, Cornelius	4	576	" 1661.
Cornelis, Gatry	5	89	" 1659.
Cornelis, Temes	5	89	" 1659.
Cornelison, Clan	9	24	" 1665.
Cornelison, Herman	17	567	Immigrated 1673. Of Worcester County.
Cornelius	4	64	(See Dawsonson).
Cornelius, Alicia	Q	63	Immigrated 1658. Daughter of Mathias.
Cornelius, Andrew	9	506	Transported 1666.
Cornelius, Ann	12	270	" 1668. Wife of John.
Cornelius, Ann	18	29	Wife of Henry of Baltimore Co. Service 1674.
Cornelius, Charles	8	30	Immigrated 1665.
Cornelius, Cornelius	12	270	Transported 1668. Son of John.
Cornelius, Eleanor	ABH	239	" 1651. Wife of John.
Cornelius, Frances	12	210	Wife of Cornelius. Service 1668.
Cornelius, Gartrid	5	88	Transported 1661.
Cornelius, Hendrick	5	485	Immigrated 1659.
Cornelius, Hendrick	12	270	Transported 1668. Son of John.
Cornelius, Hugh	8	130	Immigrated 1665 with his wife and her child, Mary Coke.
Cornelius, John	ABH	239	Immigrated prior to 1651.
Cornelius, John	12	243	Transported 1669.
Cornelius, John	12	270	Immigrated 1668.
Cornelius, Margaret	Q	63	" 1658. Wife of Mathias.
Cornelius, Margaret	4	70	Transported 1659.
Cornelius, Margaret	12	270	" 1668. Daughter of John.
Cornelius, Mary	8	130	Transported 1665. Wife of Hugh.
Cornelius, Mathias	Q	63	Immigrated 1658.
Cornelius, Miriam	9	216	Transported 1665.
Cornelius, Peter	7	466	" prior to 1655. Of Patuxent.
Cornelius, Rebecca	17	469	Transported 1673.
Cornelius, Rowland	15	433	" 1677.
Cornelius, Rowland	WC2	73	Service 1679.
Cornelius, Tenus	5	88	Transported 1661.
Cornell, Cornelius	12	210	Service 1668.
Cornell, John	WC2	340-341	" 1680. Of St. Mary's Co.
Corner, Gilbert	5	167	Transported 1659.
Corner, Margaret	5	167	" 1659.
Cornett, Eleanor	18	306	" 1674.
Cornier, Quinton	4	55	Service 1659.
Cornish, John	ABH	142	Immigrated 1651. Of Patuxent River.
Cornish, Robert	ABH	49	Transported 1650 by the Rev. Wm. Wilkinson. Servant.
Cornish, Robert	12	413	Transported 1669.

NAME	Liber	Folio	REMARKS
Cornish, Robert	3	62	Transported 1650. Servant.
Cornish, William	5	367	" 1663.
Cornor, Job	18	161	Of St. Mary's Co. Service 1667.
Cornwaleys, Thomas, Esq.	ABH	244	Came to Md. on the ship "Ark" in

1634, with his partner, Mr. John Saunders, who died during the voyage, and 12 servants.

NAME	Liber	Folio	REMARKS
Cornwall, Ann	17	551	Transported 1673.
Cornwall, John Hogben	18	333	" 1674.
Cornwall, Martha	WC2	112	" 1679.
Cornwalleys, Thomas	ABH	245	" 1651.
Cornwallis, Thomas	4	623	Immigrated 1633. Came again 1660. (4, fol. 623).
Cornwallis, William	20	147	Son and heir of Thomas, Esq. dec'd.1679.
Cornwell, John	18	283	Transported 1674.
Corobane, Mary	20	184	" from Ireland 1678.
Corrane, Margaret	20	184	" from Ireland 1678.
Corry, Mary	4	14	" 1659. Servant.
Corsey, John	WC2	319	Service 1680.
Corwyn, William	16	121	Immigrated 1671. Of St. Mary's Co.
Cosby, Mary	20	2	Transported 1678.
Cosby, Thomas	4	140	" 1656. Servant. (Quaker).
Cosden, Elizabeth	11	569	Transported 1668. Daughter of Thomas.
Cosden, Sarah	11	569	Transported 1668. Wife of Thomas.
Cosden, Sarah	11	569	" 1668. Daughter of Thomas.
Cosden, Stephen	15	433	Immigrated 1677.
Cosden, Thomas, Gent.	11	469	" 1668. Of St. Mary's County.
Cosi, Jane	15	501	Transported 1678.
Cosier, Mark	9	431	" 1666. Of Virginia.
Cosken, Elizabeth	WC2	167,169	" 1680.
Coslick, George	15	443	" 1670.
Cosly, Matthew	15	455	" 1678. (See Coely).
Coson, Charles	16	505	" 1671.
Cossam, Thomas	4	591	" 1661. (5, fol. 305).
Cossin, Nicholas	ABH	91	Immigrated prior to 1640. A Frenchman.
Costican, Denis	15	553	Transported 1678.
Costide, Ralph	5	90	" 1653-61.
Costin, Henry	Q	70	" 1657. (18, fol. 173).
Costord, Thomas	12	356	Service 1669.
Cosue, Philip	17	26	Transported 1672.
Coswell, Anne	WC2	253,398	" 1680.
Coterson, Hans	12	473	" 1670.
Cotesford, Richard	1	33,171	" 1638. Servant.
Cotsfort, Thomas	11	104	" 1667. Servant.
Cottalls, Walter	1	88	" prior to 1640.

NAME	Liber	Folio	REMARKS
Cottalls, Walter	ABH	87	Transported prior to 1640. Servant.
Cottam, Edward	1	20,25,38	" 1637.
Cottell, James	15	453	" 1675-7.
Cotten, Francis	15	531	" 1678.
Cotten, John	16	113	Immigrated 1671. Of Baltimore Co.
Cotten, Thomas	15	455	Transported 1678.
Cotterell, George	12	341	" 1668.
Cotterell, Walter	ABH	13,25	Immigrated 1640. (2, fol. 448).
Cotterell, Walter	2	517	" about 1645.
Cottirill, George	6	134	Transported 1661.
Cottman, Benjamin	15	338	Immigrated 1672 from Virginia,
with Mary, his wife. (16, fol. 303).			
Cottman, Mary	15	338	Transported 1672. Wife of Benjamin. (18, fol. 36).
Cotton, Edward	ABH	60	Transported 1637.
Cotton, Francis	15	598	" 1668.
Cotton, John	15	565	" 1679.
Cotton, Susanna	9	332	" in the "Golden Wheat Sheaf," 1664.
Cotton, Thomas	WC2	201	Transported 1680. Servant.
Cottworth, Henry	10	564	" 1667.
Couch, Ambrose	5	242	" 1662.
Coudry, Eliz. (als. Banks)	15	347	" 1676.
Couerie, John	5	486	Immigrated 1650. Transported his wife 1655. (See Conerie).
Coughlan, Honor	WC2	57	Transported 1678.
Coughlan, John	WC2	106	Rights 1679.
Coughlane, John	20	184	Transported from Ireland 1678.
Coughlin, Ann	15	565	" 1679.
Couircelli, Thomas	5	257	" 1663.
Couler, Ralph	20	185	" 1679.
Coulson, John	15	565	" 1679.
Coulson, John	WC2	120	" 1680.
Coulson, Maudlin	WC2	120	" 1680.
Coulson, Richard	18	331	" 1674.
Coulstone, John	WC2	321	Service 1680.
Coulton, Thomas	17	498	Of Dorchester Co. Immigrated
1673, with Mary, his wife, and Thomas and Ann, his children.			
Councellour, Thomas	6	15	Transported 1657.
Courgill, Joseph	18	137	" 1674.
Coursley, David	15	567	" 1679.
Coursey, Mr. Henry	ABH	313	Immigrated 1653.
Coursey, James	10	447	Of Lincolns Inn in the County of
Middlesex. Gent. sells to Dr. Richard Tilghman of Md. a tract of land on Chester River, 400 Acres, which he acquired by will of his brother, John C. Coursey, dec'd. July 20, 1663.			
Coursey, James	15	420	Of Talbot Co. Immigrated 1677.
Coursey, Jane	9	449	Transported 1666.
Coursey, John	Q	348	Brother to William. 1658.
Coursey, Mr. John	ABH	313	Transported 1653. Brother to

NAME	Liber	Folio	REMARKS
			Henry. (4, fol. 538, 204).
Coursey, Juliana	4	565	Transported 1661 by William.
Coursey, Katherine	ABH	313	" 1653. Sister of Henry.
Coursey, Mary	Q	183	" prior to 1658. Wife
			of Henry.
Coursey, Mr. William	ABH	313	Transported 1653. Brother to Henry.
Coursey, Mr. William	ABH	424	Immigrated 1651.
Court, John	ABH	23,95	Transported since 1635. Servant.
Court, John	2	509	" 1639. Servant.
Court, William	16	83	" 1670. (18, fol. 7).
Courte, John	1	112	" 1635. Servant.
Courtier, William	6	294	" 1664.
Courtney, ---	ABH	187	" years prior to 1651.
			Son of --- Courtney.
Courtney, George	6	293	Transported 1664.
Courtney, James	ABH	33	Servant 1638.
Courtney, James	2	567	Transported 1638. Servant.
Courtney, James	1	137	License to marry Mary Lawne,
			May 23, 1639.
Courtney, James	5	66	Immigrated 1661.
Courtney, Joane	18	166	Transported 1674.
Courtney, Jone	15	429	" 1677.
Courtney, William	15	443	" 1670.
Courts, John	2	217	Immigrated 1645.
Courts, John	3	14	Rights 1650.
Courts, Margaret	3	14	Transported 1649. Servant. Wife
			of John.
Courts, Margaret	ABH	44	Wife of John. Formerly a servant
			to Barnaby Jackson 1650.
Courts, Mary	4	556	Transported 1661.
Courtsey, William	16	411	" 1671.
Cousens, John	17	552	" from Delaware 1673.
Cousins, John	10	523	" 1667.
Cousins, Richard	12	190	" 1668.
Couthland, Margaret	11	378	" 1668.
Couzins, John	9	24	" 1665.
Covant, Ann	9	69	" 1660-5.
Covant, Mary	9	69	" 1660-5.
Covant, Thomas	9	69	" 1660-5.
Cove, Jane	8	40	" "in the good ship
		called the Adventure of Hull", prior to 1665. Servant.
Covell, George	6	122	Transported 1660.
Covell, Jane	5	71	" 1659.
Covell, Thomas	6	81	" 1681.
Coventan, Joane	5	210	" 1662. Daughter of
			Nehemiah. (7, fol. 562).
Coventan, John	5	210	Transported 1662. Son of Nehemiah.
			(7, fol. 562).
Coventan, Katherine	5	210	Transported 1662. Daughter of
			Nehemiah. (7, fol. 562).
Coventan, Margaret	5	210	Transported 1662. Daughter of

NAME	Liber	Folio	REMARKS
			Nehemiah. (7, fol. 562).
Coventan, Mary	5	210	Transported 1662. Wife of Nehemiah. (7, fol. 562).
Coventan, Nehemiah	5	210	Immigrated 1662. (7, fol. 562).
Coventan, Nehemiah	5	210	Transported 1662. Son of Nehemiah. (7, fol. 562).
Coventan, Sarah	5	210	Transported 1662. Daughter of Nehemiah. (7, fol. 562).
Coventon, John	4	139	Transported 1650. Servant.
Coventry, Jonathan	4	56	Immigrated 1659.
Coventry, Richard	15	530	Transported 1678.
Coventry, William	6	105	" 1661.
Coveny, Peter	15	353	" 1678.
Coverane, John	20	184	" from Ireland 1678.
Coverdale, Hannah	16	482	" 1670-1.
Coverdale, Thomas	12	391	" 1669.
Coverdale, Thomas	WC2	159	Service 1680. "Imported" 1669. Of St. Mary's Co.
Coverson, Henry	16	88	Transported 1670.
Covett, John	ABH	249	Immigrated May 1651.
Covett, Sarah	ABH	249	Transported 1651. Wife of John.
Covington, Ann	7	562	" 1665. (Probably wife of Thomas).
Covington, Thomas	7	562	Immigrated 1665.
Coward, Ann	15	499	Transported 1677.
Cowden, John	15	516	" 1678.
Cowdery, Edward	9	312	Immigrated from Virginia 1665 with wife.
Cowdrey, Edward	ABH	322	Transported Xmas 1662. Servant.
Cowdrey, William	16	83	" 1670.
Cowe, Francis	12	271	" 1668. Servant.
Cowell, Eleanor	17	490	" 1673.
Cowell, John	5	411	" 1663.
Cowell, William	15	539	Service 1678.
Cowland, John	4	55	Transported 1659.
Cowland, John	15	417,446	" 1677.
Cowler, James	10	390	" 1666.
Cowlers, Jam.	20	185	" 1679.
Cowley, George	9	38	Immigrated 1664.
Cownell, Patrick	15	353	Transported 1674.
Cowper, Philip	ABH	179	" 1650. Servant.
Cowper, Richard	WC2	395	" 1680. Servant.
Cowper, Robert	ABH	273	" 1650. Servant.
Cowsin, Nicholas	ABH	7	Immigrated 1639.
Cox, Ambrose	6	79	Transported 1663. (7, fol. 462).
Cox, Mrs. Ann	ABH	12	Immigrated 1633, and afterwards married Thos. Green, Esq.
Cox, Mrs. Anne	2	444	Special grant of 500 acres from Lord Baltimore 1633. First wife of Thomas Greene, Esq.
Cox, Anthony	8	89	Transported 1665.
Cox, Christopher	15	322	" 1675.

NAME	Liber	Folio	REMARKS
Cox, Daniel	15	318	Transported 1675.
Cox, Edwin	Q	72	Immigrated 1658.
Cox, Elizabeth	7	83	" 1657.
Cox, Elizabeth	9	54,344	Transported 1665.
Cox, Ellinor	WC2	48	" 1679.
Cox, James	2	614–615	Immigrated 1649.
Cox, Mr. James	ABH	40	" 1650.
Cox, James	11	374	Transported 1668. (12, fol. 209).
Cox, Jeremy	12	216	" 1668.
Cox, Joan	Q	72	Immigrated 1658. Wife of Edward.
Cox, Joane	10	558,569	Transported 1666. Servant.
Cox, John	7	502	" 1664.
Cox, John	9	34	" 1665.
Cox, John	11	374	" 1668. (12, fol. 209).
Cox, John	13	114	Immigrated 1670. Of St. Mary's Co. (14, fol. 349).
Cox, John	WC2	213–214	Transported 1671–1673.
Cox, John	15	370,500	" 1676.
Cox, John	15	558	" 1677. (WC2, fol. 399).
Cox, Joseph	15	454	" 1677.
Cox, Margaret	4	21	" 1659.
Cox, Marjory	13	114	" 1670. Wife of John. (14, fol. 349).
Cox, Martha	10	569	Transported 1665. Servant. (8, fol. 203).
Cox, Matthew	17	424	Transported 1673.
Cox, Rebecca	10	572	" 1667.
Cox, Richard	1	17,20, 25,38	" 1637.
Cox, Richard	2	458	Service about 1643–44. Deceased by 1649.
Cox, Richard	ABH	15	Service 1648.
Cox, Robert	7	154	Transported 1663.
Cox, Robert	15	516,530	" 1678.
Cox, Sarah	20	185	" 1679.
Cox, Stephen	7	135	" 1664.
Cox, Thomas	9	332	" in the "Golden Wheat Sheaf", 1664.
Cox, Thomas	7	556	Transported 1665.
Cox, Thomas	11	313	Of St. Mary's Co. Service 1667. (17, fol. 30).
Cox, Thomas	12	478,498	Transported 1670.
Cox, Thomas	WC2	281	Immigrated 1680. Of St. Mary's Co.
Cox, William	1	94	Petition to confirm title to land, 1640.
Cox, William	15	522	Of St. Mary's Co. Service 1678.
Coxall, William	7	530	Transported 1664.
Coxhead, Richard	17	36	" 1672.
Coxon, Anthony	18	306	" 1675.
Coxon, Francis	18	160	" 1674.
Cozen, James	WC2	86–87	" 1679.

NAME	Liber	Folio	REMARKS
Craage, John	12	343	Transported 1669. Of Charles Co.
Crab, Henry	9	21	" 1665.
Crab, Henry	17	354	Of Kent Co. Service 1672.
Crab, Martha	2	441	Transported 1648. Servant.
Crabb, Martha	ABH	12	Servant 1648.
Crabtree, John	18	291	Transported 1674.
Craefoot, William	4	214	Immigrated 1659.
Crafford, David	4	609	Transported 1661.
Crafford, George	6	127	" 1658.
Crafford, John	17	411	" 1673.
Craford, Ann	15	553	" 1678.
Craford, Ann	WC2	56	" 1679.
Craford, John	12	413	" 1669.
Craft, John	15	565	" 1679.
Craft, Thomas	16	341	" 1671.
Crafts, Elizabeth	4	591	" 1661. (17, fol. 457; 18, fol. 84).
Crafts, Peter	15	167	Transported 1673.
Crafty, William	9	54	" 1665.
Cragg, Henry	11	4	" 1667. Servant.
Cragg, Nehemiah	17	452	" 1673. (15, fol. 435).
Cragley, Ann	6	235	" 1663.
Crally, John	7	526	" 1664.
Cralon, Ann	4	622	" 1661. (See Crayton).
Cramfort, Nathaniel	WC2	167-169	" 1680.
Cramp, William	6	80,81	" 1657.
Cranane, John	13	66	" 1669. Servant.
Cranbrough, Nell	15	553	" 1678.
Crane, Henry	WC2	54	Service 1665. Of Anne Arundel Co.
Crane, Thomas	17	475	Transported 1673.
Cranford, James	15	515	" 1678.
Cranie, John	9	216	" 1665.
Crans, Robert	15	369	" 1676.
Crapper, Gilbert	11	525	Immigrated 1668.
Crapper, Katherine	11	525	Transported 1668. Wife of Gilbert.
Crasley, Peter	11	436	" 1668.
Crassell, Mary	5	203	" 1662.
Crauford, Richard	13	116	" 1671.
Crawford (Crawfoold), Thomas	4	5	" 1652-9.
Crawford, James	18	152	" 1674.
Crawford, Patrick	12	591	" 1668.
Crawford, William	10	352	" 1666.
Crawford, William	15	322	" 1675.
Crawle, Hannah	9	25	" 1665.
Crawley, John	17	50	Of Calvert Co. Service 1672.
Crayton, Ann	4	622	Transported 1661.
Creacroft, Ann	9	269	" 1665. Wife of John.
Creacroft, John	9	269	Immigrated 1665.
Creak, Hugh	ABH	150	Transported 1648. Servant.
Crediford, William	WC2	381	" 1675-80. Servant.

NAME	Liber	Folio	REMARKS
Creed, Edward	15	443	Transported 1670.
Creed, John	15	443	" 1670.
Creedess, Stephen	15	560	" 1678.
Creedwell, George	16	170	" 1671.
Creeke, Edward	16	507	" 1671.
Crescoe, James	6	166	" 1663.
Cresol, John	16	507	" 1671.
Cressey, Thomas	WC2	21	" 1679.
Creswell, Henry	8	501	" 1665. (10, fol. 541).
Cresy, Samuel	17	497	Immigrated 1671.
Crew, Daniel	15	353	Transported 1676.
Crew, Dorothy	9	156	" 1665.
Crew, Edward	WC2	133	" 1680.
Crew, Jonas	15	434	Of St. Mary's Co. Service 1677.
Crezall, Ann	15	436	Transported 1677.
Crimine, John	15	438	" Oct. 1677.
Cripps, Thomas	15	567	" 1678.
Crispe, Dorothy	5	188	" 1662.
Crispe, Elizabeth	WC2	212	Service 1662. First wife of Thomas Bright.
Crispe, Jane	10	390,608	Transported 1666.
Crispe, Nicholas	17	608	" 1673.
Critchell, Robert	9	104	" 1665.
Critwell, William	17	546	" 1664.
Crocker, Elizabeth	WC2	132	" 1680. Servant.
Crocker, Honor	WC2	380	" 1675-80. Servant.
Crockett, Richard	8	202	" 1664.
Crockford, Robert	15	448	" 1677.
Crockson, Elizabeth	18	291	" 1674.
Croft, Ann	12	406	" 1669.
Croft, Herbert	9	233	" 1665. (16, fol. 471; 12, fol. 592).
Croft, Robert	WC2	130	Transported 1679. Servant. (30 years old).
Crofton, William	15	167	Transported 1673.
Crofts, Nathaniel	8	502	" 1665. (9, fol. 310-11).
Crokford, Robert	WC2	107	" 1679.
Cromp, William	6	142	" 1658.
Cromwell, Ann	4	49	" 1653. Wife of Geessan.
Cromwell, Geessan	4	49	Immigrated 1653. Had surveyed for him a tract called "Cromwell on the Eastern Shore," Aug. 11, 1659. (4, fol. 239).
Cromwell, John	12	554	Transported 1670.
Cromwell, Rebecca	4	49	" 1653. (E. Shore). Daughter of Geessan.
Cromwell, William	WC2	18,38,79	Immigrated 1667. Of Baltimore Co.
Cromwell, William	12	554	Transported 1670.
Cromwell, William	16	439	" 1671. Servant.
Crone, George	15	544	" 1676.
Crooch, Richard	5	59	" 1662.
Crooke, Thomas	15	429	" 1677.

NAME	Liber	Folio	REMARKS
Crooked, Richard	17	33	Of Somerset Co. Service 1672.
Crookes, Robert	9	485	Transported 1665. Servant.
Crookshank, Elizabeth	7	462	" 1664.
Crookshanke, John	13	114	" 1671.
Croome, Edward	12	505	Service 1669.
Croper, Francis	5	532	Transported 1663.
Cropley, John	10	414	" 1665.
Cropper, John	WC2	320	Immigrated 1680.
Crosby, Constantine	6	81	Transported 1657 by Nathaniel.
Crosby, Cuthbert	7	111	" 1663.
Crosby, Jane	4	590	" 1661. Servant.
Crosby, John	7	498	" 1660.
Crosby, Jonathan	20	2	" prior to 1678.
Crosby, Mary	8	501	" 1665.
Crosby, Nathaniel	6	81	Immigrated 1657.
Crosby, Robert	15	442	Transported 1677.
Crose, William	10	541	" 1667.
Croslan, Walter	WC2	282	" 1680.
Crosle, William	8	501	" 1665.
Crosley, William	5	359	Immigrated 1663.
Cross, Abraham	7	464	Transported 1663.
Cross, Anne	Q	71	" 1657.
Cross, Edward	Q	75	" 1658.
Cross, John	Q	69	" 1658.
Cross, Philip	7	87	" 1661.
Cross, Richard	WC2	167,169	" 1680.
Cross, Richard	12	285	" 1668. Servant.
Cross, William	7	83	" 1663.
Cross, William	18	296	Of Calvert Co. 1675. Immigrated with his wife, Elizabeth, 1655.
Crosse, Edward	4	57	Service 1659.
Crosse, James	17	547	Transported 1673.
Crosse, John	5	531	Immigrated 1662.
Crosse, Thomas	15	356	Transported 1674.
Crosse, William	6	143	" 1663.
Crosse, William	17	537	Of Talbot Co. Service 1673.
Crossen, Phillis	17	469	Transported 1673.
Crossley, Mary	17	475	" 1673.
Croston, Elizabeth	17	451	" 1673.
Crouch, Barbara	Q	441	" prior to 1651.
Crouch, Edward	17	448	" 1673.
Crouch, George	3	19	Immigrated about 1640. Married servant of Richard Howbyn.
Crouch, George servant to Richard Hawlyn, 1650.	ABH	45	Immigrated 1640. His wife former
Crouch, George	12	341	Transported 1668.
Crouch, John	16	303	" from Virginia 1671. Son of Robert.
Crouch, Mary	ABH	45	Transported since 1640. Daughter of George.
Crouch, Mary	5	531	Transported 1661.

NAME	Liber	Folio	REMARKS
Crouch, Mary	3	19	Transported after 1640 by father, George Crouch.
Crouch, Mr. Ralph	ABH	161	Transported himself into this
Province from England. Service prior to 1648.			
Crouch, Richard	16	173	Of Talbot Co. Service March 21, 1671.
Crouch, Robert	4	54	Transported 1659.
Crouch, Robert	16	303	Of Somerset Co. Immigrated from
Virginia with Mary, his wife, and John and Rosamond, his children, 1671.			
Crouch, Rosamond	16	303	Transported from Virginia 1671. Daughter of Robert.
Crouch, William	6	80	Service 1663.
Crouch, William	12	463	Transported 1669.
Crouchley, Thomas	15	354	Service 1676.
Crow, Francis	17	532	Transported 1673.
Crow, Gournay	16	164	Of Dorchester Co. Immigrated 1671.
Crow, John	10	298	Transported 1666.
Crow, Ralph	15	356	" 1675.
Crowder, Alicia	Q	69	Servant 1649.
Crowder, Anthony	Q	189	Transported 1656.
Crowder, Daniel	12	282	Service 1668.
Crowder, Elizabeth	6	142	Transported 1655.
Crowder, Elizabeth	18	38	" 1673. Daughter of
Elizabeth, wife of Thomas Lampen. (15, fol. 549).			
Crowder, John	15	430	Transported 1677.
Crowder, Joseph	17	29	" 1672.
Crowder, Joshua	WC2	363	" 1680.
Crowder, Thomas	12	190	" 1668. Servant. (17, fol. 414).
Crowe, Ann	10	296	Transported 1666.
Crowere David	5	87	" 1649.
Crowley, Daniel	15	438	" 1677.
Crowley, John	9	17	" 1665.
Crown, David	Q	74	Service 1658.
Crowne, George	15	429	Transported 1677.
Cruff, Edmond	WC2	57	" 1678.
Crump, Elizabeth	6	136	" 1663.
Crump, Francis	6	136	" 1663.
Crump, Jarvis	16	115	" 1671.
Crump, John	6	136	" 1663.
Crump, William	6	135	Immigrated 1663.
Crump, William	6	136	Transported 1663. Son of William.
Crump, William	16	463	Of Talbot Co. Immigrated Feb. 1665, with Frances, his wife.
Crupps, Thomas	15	567	Transported 1678.
Cruse, Robert	WC2	114	" 1680. Servant.
Crutchill, Samuel	11	586	Immigrated 1667.
Crutchley, John	16	409	Transported from Virginia 1671.
Cryps, Mary	WC2	15	" 1679. Servant.
Cuarles, William	4	530	" 1659.
Cubbage, George	15	417	" 1677.

NAME	Liber	Folio	REMARKS
Cudberd, Leonard	6	133	Transported 1655.
Cuddon, John	12	588	Immigrated 1670.
Cufland, Francis	10	556	Transported 1664-5.
Culbert, James	9	262	" 1665.
Culhoun, John	15	319	Service 1675.
Culins, James	6	13	Immigrated 1659.
Cullamore, Thomas	1	17	Transported 1637.
Cullen, James	5	437	" 1660.
Cullen, Marcus	WC2	17	Service 1679.
Cullert, James	9	262	Transported 1665.
Cullhane, John	18	35	" 1672.
Cullier, John	16	507	" 1671.
Cullman, Thomas	WC2	106	" 1679.
Cullum, Mary	17	51	" 1672.
Cullums, James	11	518	Of Calvert Co. Immigrated 1668.
Cully, John	10	266	Transported prior to 1666. Of St. Mary's Co. Planter.
Culpepper, Elizabeth	6	209	Transported 1663 by Capt. Neale.
Culver, Henry	WC2	167,169	" 1679.
Culverhouse, William	WC2	326,357	Service 1680. Of St. Mary's Co.
Cumberford, Alexander	WC2	89	Transported 1676. Servant.
Cumberford, Gerrard	Q	32	Servant 1653.
Cummings, Samuel	5	256	Transported 1663.
Cumport, Katherine	12	456	" 1669.
Cuniell, Cornelius	4	623	" 1657-8.
Cunisby, William	11	378	" 1668.
Cuningham, James	17	469	" 1673.
Cunningham, Daniel	17	474	Of Calvert Co. Immigrated 1673.
Cunningham, Darby	5	251	Transported 1663.
Cunningham, Margaret	11	581	" 1668.
Cuper, John	6	122	" 1663.
Cupping, Joseph	18	329	" 1675.
Curby, George	11	104	" 1667.
Curby, Joseph	5	261	" 1663.
Curen, Martha	15	544	" 1676.
Curoe, Sarah	17	424	" 1673.
Currall, Daniel	WC2	120	" 1680.
Currell, Martha	5	267	" 1663.
Currer, John	18	149	Of Kent Co. Immigrated 1668.
Currey, Andrew	18	331	Transported 1674.
Currey, John	12	194	" 1668. Servant.
Currico, Peter	18	80	" 1674.
Curry, Alexander	WC2	18,125-126	Immigrated 1679. Of Calvert Co.
Curry, Barbery	4	625	Transported prior to 1661.
Curry, George	15	514	" 1677.
Curry, Thomas	7	502	" 1661.
Curtane, Mary	15	438	" Oct. 1677.
Curtis, Adam	15	359	" 1676.
Curtis, Ann	5	466	" 1658.
Curtis, Anne	WC2	214	" 1671-3.

NAME	Liber	Folio	REMARKS
Curtis, Daniel	10	541	Immigrated 1666.
Curtis, David	13	114	Transported 1671.
Curtis, Elizabeth	10	541	" 1667. Daughter of Daniel.
Curtis, John	9	270	Transported 1665.
Curtis, John	11	318	" 1668.
Curtis, John	18	115	" 1674.
Curtis, John	WC2	101	" 1679.
Curtis, Mary	7	462	" 1664. Wife of Robert.
Curtis, Mary	7	462	" 1664. Daughter of Robert.
Curtis, Mary	10	541	Transported 1666. Wife of Daniel.
Curtis, Richard	11	318	" 1668.
Curtis, Richard	15	413	Immigrated 1677.
Curtis, Robert	ABH	245	Transported 1651.
Curtis, Robert	5	90	Immigrated 1660.
Curtis, Robert	7	462	" 1664.
Curtis, Walter	6	106	Transported 1661.
Curtley, Thomas	17	451	" 1673.
Cusicke, Eleanor	15	565	" 1679.
Cusman, Martha	WC2	122	" 1679. (See Ouseman).
Cuss, Henry	15	404	Of Cecil Co. Service 1676.
Cussaus, Mary	15	353	Transported 1674.
Custan, William	15	452	" 1677.
Custins, Ann	WC2	58	" 1678.
Custis, John	WC2	112	" 1679.
Custone, Frances	WC2	415	" 1666-80. Servant.
Cutberd, Stephen	15	454	" 1677.
Cutberd, Thomas	15	430	" 1677.
Cuthberd, Jervis	7	469	" 1661. (10, fol. 264).
Cutler, Elizabeth	WC2	406	" 1677.
Cutler, Mary	WC2	77	Servant 1679.
Cuttbert, Thomas	WC2	260	Transported 1675.
Cutterson, Francis	15	523	Immigrated 1678. of St. Mary's Co.
Cuttinge, John	15	372	Late of Accomac Co., Virginia. Immigrated to Somerset Co., Md., prior to 1675.
Cuttingham, Thomas	15	438	Immigrated 1677.
Cuzens, Charles	17	440	Transported 1668.
Dab, John	Q	68	" 1649.
Dabb, Amy	9	216	" 1665.
Dabbe, John	Q	347	Of Isle of Kent. Demands 50 acres as a gift from Lord Baltimore, 1658.
Dabney, Henry	10	169	Immigrated 1666.
Daborne, Thomas	9	478	Transported 1659. Of Anne Arundle County.
Dabridgecourt, John	12	199,345	Transported 1668.
Dabwell, Henry	Q	71	" 1658.
Dackom, John	16	43	" 1670.
Dages, Joseph	16	407	" 1671.
Dagger, Elias	6	347	" 1663.
Dagger, Isaac	6	347	" 1663.

NAME	Liber	Folio	REMARKS
Dagger, Peter	9	33	Transported 1660-5.
Dakins, John (Thomas ?)	WC2	53	Service 1679. Of St. Mary's Co.
Dakins, John	2	253	Transported 1679.
Dalarne, Thomas	5	247	" 1662.
Dalby, Ann	15	322	" 1675.
Dale, David	16	168	" 1671. Son of David, of Somerset Co.
Dale, Elizabeth	9	269	Transported 1665.
Dale, John	12	391	" 1669.
Dale, John	13	64	" 1668.
Dale, Mary	6	183	" 1663.
Dale, Rachel	9	269	" 1665.
Dale, Thomas	17	605	Immigrated 1667, with Mary, his wife, and Thomas, his son.
Daley, Bryan	6	36	Immigrated 1663, and married the widow of Nicholas Keeling.
Dalle, Henry	8	43	Transported 1665.
Dalle, Thomas	WC2	199	" 1680.
Dalle, William	8	43	" 1665.
Dallen, William	WC2	73	" 1678.
Dalley, Bryan	4	14	" 1659. Servant.
Dalley, Daniel	20	184	" from Ireland 1678.
Dalley, David	9	269	Immigrated 1665.
Dallimore, Obediah	9	435	Transported 1666.
Dallimore, Peter	9	435	" 1666.
Dallimore, Robert	9	435	Immigrated 1664 in the ship, "Agreement", Christ. Borkett, Com. Of England.
Dallimore, Robert, Jr.	9	435	Transported 1666.
Dallimore, Sarah	9	435	" 1666. Wife of Robert.
Dally, Joane	WC2	128	" 1679.
Dallye, John	WC2	380	" 1675-80. Servant.
Dalton, Elan	15	553	" 1678.
Dalton, Elinor	WC2	56	" 1679.
Dalton, John	15	522	Immigrated 1678. Of St. Mary's Co.
Dalton, Nathaniel	10	498	Transported 1667.
Dalton, Richard	15	446	" 1677.
Dalton, Robert	15	566	" 1678.
Dalton, Stephen	15	553	" 1678.
Daly, Laughlin	15	553	" 1678.
Damarell, John (als. Demall).	Q	202	His widow and adm'x. married James Mulliken prior to 1658.
Dame, Thomas	7	135	Transported 1664.
Damer, Thomas	17	578	Of St. Mary's Co. Service 1673.
Damerill, John	12	506	Immigrated 1669.
Damghton, Mary	2	605	Transported about 1637-8. Servant.
Dammes, John	17	510	" 1673.
Damoras, Thomas	12	210	" 1665.
Dance, Abraham	11	552	" 1668.
Dancy, Thomas	16	168	" 1670.
Danderdell, William	9	50	" 1665.

NAME	Liber	Folio	REMARKS
Dands, Evan	18	84	Transported 1674.
Danell, James	WC2	112	" 1679.
Dangerfield, Edward	9	326	" 1666.
Dangerfield, John	7	464	" 1663.
Dangerfield, Rose	12	415	" 1669.
Daniel, Ann	18	331	" 1674.
Daniel, Clance	4	576	" 1661.
Daniel, Edward	15	553	" 1678.
Daniel, Isaac	6	217	" 1663. (12, fol. 515).
Daniel, Leonard	4	58	" 1659. (17, fol. 42).
Daniel, Margarett	WC2	333	Daughter and heiress of Morrice.
Daniel, Mariana	WC2	333	Widow of Morrice 1680.
Daniel, Morrice	12	504	Service 1669.
Daniel, Morrice	WC2	332,333	Order issuing warrant to heirs 1680.
Daniel, Nathaniel	15	503	Transported 1678.
Daniel, Owen	WC2	82	" 1679.
Daniel, Richard	15	418	" 1677.
Daniel, Rose	17	531	" 1673.
Daniel, Thomas	13	1	" 1669.
Daniel, Thomas	17	331	" from Virginia 1672.
Daniel, Thomas	15	533	" 1678.
Daniel, William	11	318	" 1668.
Daniel, William	5	254	" 1658-63.
Daniel, William	WC2	321	Service 1680.
Daniell, Constant	9	48	Transported 1665. (17, fol. 332; 11, fol. 202).
Daniell, Elizabeth	15	569	Transported 1678.
Daniell, John	9	44	" 1659.
Daniell, John	18	80	" 1674.
Daniell, Margaret	11	546	" 1668.
Daniell, Margery	15	446	" 1677.
Daniell, Mark	9	216	" 1665.
Daniells, Nicholas	8	131	" 1664.
Danielson, Daniel	11	537	" 1668.
Danielson, John	16	99	" 1670.
Danielson, William	WC2	406	" 1677.
Dannard, Katherine	12	270	Immigrated 1668.
Dansel, Phillis	15	322	Transported 1674.
Dansey, John	15	422	Service 1677.
Dansick, Charles	6	126	Transported 1659.
Dansicke, John	6	170	" 1657.
Dant, Thomas	18	131	Of St. Mary's Co. Service 1674.
Dant, Thomas	WC2	159	Of St. Mary's Co. Service 1680.
Dante, Thomas	12	391	Transported 1669.
Daphlet, Alice	16	94	" 1670.
Dapper, Lewis	10	272	" 1666.
Darbury, Edward	4	560	" 1661.
Darby, James	7	87	" 1654.
Darby, John	7	491	" 1664.
Darby, John	16	112	Of Talbot Co. Immigrated 1671.

NAME	Liber	Folio	REMARKS
Darby, Mary	9	190	Transported 1665. Servant.
Darby, Peter	15	565	" 1679.
Darby, Samuel	15	535	" 1678.
Darby, William	WC2	78	Immigrated from New York 1679. Carpenter. Of Somerset Co.
Darbyshire, John	15	598	Transported 1678-9.
Darcy, Richard	ABH	60	" 1637.
Darcy, Richard	1	38,39	" 1638. (See Darsy).
Darcy, Thomas	4	622	Immigrated 1661.
Dards, Benjamin	WC2	76	" from Virginia 1679. Of Somerset Co.
Dare, Ann	18	291	Transported 1674.
Dare, James	5	307	" 1662.
Dare, Margaret	17	571	" 1673.
Dare, William	15	530	Immigrated 1678. Of Cecil Co.
Darese, Henry	5	54	Transported 1660.
Darey, Sarah	10	499	" by Matthew Howard prior to 1667, when he styles her, his wife.
Darey, Thomas	18	14	Transported 1674.
Daring, Benjamin	18	174	" 1674.
Dark, William	11	582	" 1668.
Darling, Abigail	5	211	" 1662. Wife of Richard.
Darling, David	16	170	" 1671.
Darling, Elizabeth	5	211	" 1662. Daughter of Richard.
Darling, Richard	5	211	Immigrated 1662.
Darling, Richard	6	216	Transported 1663.
Darnall, Elizabeth	7	370	Received a Special Grant of 1500 acres from Lord Baltimore and died prior to 1664, bequeathing the same to her brother, Henry Darnall. (5, fol. 123).
Darnall, Col. Henry	15	561	Married the widow of Major Thomas Brooke, prior to 1679.
Darnall, Col. Henry	WC2	82	Special Warrant for 4000 acres from Lord Baltimore. Of Calvert Co.
Darnall, Philip, Esq.	5	418	Special Warrant from his kinsman, Lord Baltimore, 1662.
Darnell, Richard	18	291	Transported 1674.
Darson, Abraham	WC2	206	" 1679. Servant.
Darsy, Richard	1	25	" 1637. (See Darcy).
Dartford, John	7	86	" 1656. Servant.
Darwell, John	11	572	" 1668.
Darwell, John	WC2	206	" 1680. Servant.
Dary, Joane	6	117	" 1655.
Dary, William	17	452	" 1671.
Dasell, John	5	251	" 1663.
Dasey, Ralph	5	535	" 1660.
Dash, John	5	81	" 1661.
Dashbery, Thomas	11	104	" 1667.
Dashiell, Ann	9	99	" 1665.
Dashiell, Elizabeth	9	99	" 1665.
Dashiell, James	9	99	" 1665.

NAME	Liber	Folio	REMARKS
Dashiell, James, Jr.	9	99	Transported 1665.
Dauckley, Edward	4	588	" 1661. Servant.
Daughborne, Mary	4	554	" 1661.
Daughton, Mary	ABH	37	Servant 1637.
Daunce, Abraham	5	12	Transported 1662.
Dave, Roger	11	572	" 1668.
Davelling, Philip	Q	18	" 1655.
Davenish, Priscilla	18	174	" 1674.
Davenport, Elizabeth	15	302	Service 1675. Second wife of Humphrey.
Davenport, Humphrey	15	302	Immigrated prior to 1675. Of Talbot County.
Davenport, Katherine	15	302	Transported prior to 1675. Daughter of Humphrey.
Davenport, Margaret	15	302	Transported prior to 1675. Wife of Humphrey.
Davenport, Mark	6	85	Transported 1660.
Davenport, Rand	15	598	" 1678-9.
Davensh, Robert	18	84	" 1674.
Davey, William	12	403	" 1669.
Davice, John	15	501	" 1678.
David, Francis	17	417	" 1673.
David, Joane	17	355	Service 1672. Wife of John.
David, John	9	37,335	Transported 1664.
David, John	18	329	" 1675.
Davidge, Robert	12	471	Of Anne Arundel Co. Married Sarah Tanney prior to 1669. Carpenter. Immigrated 1670. (16, fol. 73).
Davids, John	12	385	Transported 1669.
Davidson, Elizabeth	11	298	" 1667. Wife of Robert.
Davidson, George	WC2	260	" 1675.
Davidson, Robert	11	298	Of Virginia. Immigrated to St. Mary's Co. 1667.
Davies, Ann	ABH	12	Servant 1648.
Davies, Elizabeth	6	19	Transported 1662. Wife of Hopkins.
Davies, Evan	Q	70	" 1657.
Davies, Francis	10	277,296	" 1666.
Davies, Hannah	6	170	" 1659.
Davies, Hopkins	6	19	Immigrated about 1662, with his wife and "His daughter, Elizabeth Lee".
Davies, James	6	255	Transported 1663. Eastern Shore.
Davies, John	6	210	Immigrated 1658.
Davies, John	4	198	Transported 1659.
Davies, John	6	134,171	" 1663.
Davies, John	10	414	" 1665. (7, fol. 639).
Davies, Jones	6	171	" 1663.
Davies, Joyce	4	198	" 1659.
Davies, Margaret	6	210	" 1663. Wife of John.
Davies, William	ABH	40	" 1649.
Davies, William	Q	66	" 1650.
Davies, William	8	501,502	" 1665.
Davies, Abraham	8	19	" 1664.

NAME	Liber	Folio	REMARKS
Davis, Alexander	5	252	Transported 1663.
Davis, Alice	12	382	" 1669.
Davis, Alice	18	334	" 1675.
Davis, Ann	6	293	" 1664.
Davis, Ann	9	488	" 1665.
Davis, Ann	16	410	" 1671.
Davis, Ann	15	359,540	" 1676.
Davis, Anne	2	439	" 1648. Servant.
Davis, Anthony	15	549	" 1678.
Davis, Catherine	7	86	" 1658.
Davis, Charles	5	529	" 1659.
Davis, Charles	5	73,243	" 1662.
Davis, Charles	15	505	" 1678.
Davis, Edward	9	21	" 1665.
Davis, Edward	16	167	Immigrated 1670. Of Somerset Co.
Davis, Edward	16	394	Transported 1671.
Davis, Edward	15	376	" 1676.
Davis, Edward	15	455,503	" 1678.
Davis, Edward	WC2	19	" 1679. Son of Walter.
Davis, Elizabeth	4	550	" 1661.
Davis, Elizabeth	15	527	" 1678.
Davis, Evan	16	130	" 1671. (15, fol. 549).
Davis, George	15	331	" 1675.
Davis, George	15	530	" 1678.
Davis, Griffith	15	354	" 1676.
Davis, Henry	15	318	" 1675.
Davis, Henry	WC2	16	" 1677.
Davis, Henry	15	574	" 1678.
Davis, Humphrey	16	537	Immigrated from Virginia 1671.
Davis, Izabell	WC2	309	Transported 1678.
Davis, James	8	486	Immigrated 1664.
Davis, James	12	472	Transported 1670.
Davis, James	16	394	" 1671.
Davis, James	15	362,417	" 1676.
Davis, Jane	WC2	19	" 1679. Wife of Walter.
Davis, Jeren	15	430	" 1677.
Davis, Joane	5	320	" 1663.
Davis, John	ABH	240	Immigrated 1653.
Davis, John	4	18	Transported 1659. Servant.
Davis, John	5	467	" 1660.
Davis, John	6	15,299	" 1660.
Davis, John	4	551	" 1661.
Davis, John	9	48	Immigrated 1665.
Davis, John	17	638	" 1666. Of Talbot Co.
Davis, John	12	381	Transported 1669 by Thomas Taylor of Anne Arundel County.
Davis, John	12	205	Transported 1667.
Davis, John	12	416	" 1669 by Joseph Taylor of Anne Arundel County.
Davis, John	12	575	Transported 1670.
Davis, John	13	114	" 1671.

NAME	Liber	Folio	REMARKS
Davis, John	17	395	Transported 1672.
Davis, John	17	511	Immigrated 1673. Of Somerset Co.
Davis, John	15	429	Transported 1674.
Davis, John	15	356	" 1675.
Davis, John	15	544	" 1676.
Davis, John	15	395	" 1677.
Davis, John	15	565	" 1679.
Davis, John	WC2	40-41, 90,382	Service 1679. Of Calvert Co.
Davis, John, Jr.	9	48	Transported 1665.
Davis, Jonas	17	63	Service 1672.
Davis, Joyce	4	551	Transported 1661.
Davis, Lewis	18	137	" 1674.
Davis, Lewis	15	369	" 1676.
Davis, Margaret	8	486	" 1664.
Davis, Mary	16	175	" 1671.
Davis, Mary	18	174	" 1674.
Davis, Mary	15	318	" 1675.
Davis, Mary	9	48	" 1665. Wife of John.
Davis, Mary	15	357,369	" 1676.
Davis, Mary	15	395	" 1677.
Davis, Mary	15	501	" 1678.
Davis, Morris	7	502	" 1661.
Davis, Nicholas	5	214	" 1661.
Davis, Nicholas	15	527	" 1678.
Davis, Rachel	15	319	" 1675 from Virginia by her father. Daughter of James.
Davis, Richard	5	319	Transported 1662.
Davis, Richard	8	486	Immigrated 1664.
Davis, Richard	15	354	Transported 1676.
Davis, Richard	WC2	89	" 1676. Servant.
Davis, Robert	4	5	" 1652-9. (5, fol. 90).
Davis, Robert	4	550	" 1661.
Davis, Robert	5	93	" prior to 1661.
Davis, Robert	12	190	" 1668. (11, fol. 487).
Davis, Robert	15	453	" 1676. (WC2, fol. 406).
Davis, Roger	6	293	" 1664. (18, fol. 90).
Davis, Rose	15	395	" 1677.
Davis, Samuel	12	415	" 1669.
Davis, Samuel	15	322	" 1674.
Davis, Samuel	15	319	" 1675.
Davis, Sarah	15	455	" 1678.
Davis, Sarah	WC2	395	" 1680. Servant.
Davis, Stephen	5	268	" 1663.
Davis, Thomas	15	307	" 1675.
Davis, Thomas	15	331,412	Of St. Mary's Co. Immigrated 1675.
Davis, Thomas	18	105	Transported 1674.
Davis, Thomas	18	38	Service 1673.
Davis, Thomas	17	479	Of Somerset Co. Immigrated 1673. (16, fol. 167).
Davis, Thomas	WC2	19,239	Transported 1679. Son of Walter.

NAME	Liber	Folio	REMARKS
Davis, Thomas	WC2	239	Son of Walter 1680.
Davis, Thomas and			
Thoe.	16	313	Sons of James of Somerset Co.
Transported from Virginia 1671. (16, fol. 540).			
Davis, Thomas	12	496	Transported 1670.
Davis, Thomas	11	318	" 1668.
Davis, Thomas	9	100	" 1665.
Davis, Thomas	4	616	Immigrated 1660.
Davis, Walter	5	245	Transported 1662. Servant.
Davis, Walter	11	344	" 1668. (12, fol. 190).
Davis, Walter, Sr.	WC2	19,115,	
		239	Immigrated 1679 with wife and 2 children. Of Dorchester Co.
Davis, Walter, Jr.	WC2	239	Son of Walter 1680.
Davis, Will	15	430	Transported 1677.
Davis, William	6	294	" 1664.
Davis, William	2	615	" 1649.
Davis, William	9	55	" 1665. (8, fol. 501).
Davis, William	17	490	Immigrated 1665.
Davis, William	16	37,86	Of Talbot Co. Service 1670. (16, fol. 91).
Davis, William	17	449	Immigrated prior to 1672. Of Somerset Co.
Davis, William	12	589	Transported 1670.
Davis, William	18	37	" 1673.
Davis, William	15	353,354	" 1676.
Davis, William	15	600	Of Baltimore Co. Service 1678.
Davis, William	15	504	Transported 1678.
Davis, William	WC2	2	" 1679.
Davis, William	20	158	Of Kent Co., died prior to 1679,
when his widow appears as the wife of Robert Neave.			
Davison, Ann	16	166	Transported 1670. Daughter of William.
Davison, David	16	166	Transported 1670. Son of William.
Davison, George	6	63	" 1658-63. (12, fol. 490).
Davison, Jane	16	166	" 1670. Daughter of William.
Davison, John	6	293	Transported 1664.
Davison, John	9	55	" 1665.
Davison, Margaret	18	166	" 1674.
Davison, Margaret	WC2	259,260	Service 1680.
Davison, Peter	WC2	77,80	Transported 1679. Servant.
Davison, Thomas	ABH	60,66	" 1637. (1, fol. 17, 20, 25, 38, 39).
Davison, Thomas	12	190	Transported 1668.
Davison, William	16	166	Immigrated 1670 with Elizabeth, his wife. Of Somerset Co.
Davison, William	6	118	Transported 1649.
Davisse, Edward	15	535	" 1678.
Davs, Henry	7	463	" 1659.
Davy, Elizabeth	ABH	40	" 1649. (2, fol. 615).

NAME	Liber	Folio	REMARKS
Davy, Jane	WC2	184	Transported 1680. Servant.
Davy, John	16	507	" 1671.
Davy, Thomas	12	472	" 1670.
Davys, John	15	452	" 1677.
Daw, John	9	450	" 1666.
Daw, Nathan	6	63	" 1658-63. (15, fol. 447).
Daw, Stephen	15	322	" 1675.
Dawe, Mary	12	489	Service 1670.
Dawes, John	10	5	Transported 1666.
Dawes, Mary	5	63	" 1660. (9, fol. 92).
Dawkins, Joseph	10	242	" 1656. Servant.
Dawlings, Margaret	15	390	Wife of Joseph of Calvert Co. Service 1667.
Dawly, Honora	WC2	87	Transported 1679.
Dawset, Elizabeth	17	448	" 1673.
Dawsey, Thomas	WC2	320	" 1680. Servant.
Dawsey, William	9	38	" 1659.
Dawson, Abraham	5	87,487	" 1649-62. Service 1663.
Dawson, Anthony	WC2	390,391	Married Rebecca Osbourne of Dorchester Co.
Dawson, Anthony	8	89	Transported 1665. Married Rebecca, one of the daughters and co-heirs of Henry Osborne of Calvert Co. dec'd prior to 1678. (20, fol. 46).
Dawson, Edmd.	15	530	Transported 1678.
Dawson, Edward	15	430	" 1677.
Dawson, Jeremiah	16	354	" 1671.
Dawson, Joan	Q	208	" 1658.
Dawson, Joane	4	555	" 1661.
Dawson, John	17	330	" 1672.
Dawson, Jone	8	89	" 1668.
Dawson, Mabel	5	235	" 1662. Wife of Ralph.
Dawson, Margaret	18	331	" 1674.
Dawson, Mary	6	18	" 1660.
Dawson, Mary	WC2	167,169	" 1679.
Dawson, Peter	5	240	" 1662.
Dawson, Ralph	Q	453	" 1658.
Dawson, Ralph	5	235	Immigrated 1662.
Dawson, Richard	11	265	Transported 1667.
Dawson, Richard	16	11	Immigrated from Virginia 1670. Of St. Mary's County.
Dawson, Richard	17	611	Service 1673. Of Calvert Co.
Dawson, Richard	WC2	113,165	Transported 1680.
Dawson, William	5	556	" 1660.
Dawson, William, Jr.	8	89	" 1665.
Dawson, William, Sr.	8	89	Immigrated 1665.
Dawsonson, Cornelius	4	64	" 1659.
Dawsonson, Cristine Cornelius	4	64	Transported 1659. Daughter of Cornelius.
Dawsonson, Eleanor	4	64	Immigrated 1659. Wife of Cornelius.

NAME	Liber	Folio	REMARKS
Dax, Thomas	15	318	Service 1674.
Day, Alice	15	560	Transported 1678.
Day, Charles	15	454	" 1677. (WC2, fol. 406).
Day, Edward	16	439	" 1671.
Day, George	7	471	Immigrated 1664.
Day, Grace	11	338	Transported 1668.
Day, Hana.	15	567	" 1678.
Day, Henry	10	475	" prior to 1667. Of
New Town Hundred, Service 1668.			
Day, Hum.	15	430	Transported 1677.
Day, James	7	84	" 1664.
Day, John	ABH	325	Immigrated with wife and daughter 1652-3.
Day, John	8	486	Transported 1664.
Day, John	WC2	363	" 1680.
Day, Jonas	15	376	" 1676.
Day, Katherine	WC2	363	" 1680.
Day, Margaret	15	553	" 1678. (WC2, fol. 57).
Day, Mary	16	439	" 1671.
Day, Nicholas	Q	70	" 1658. (20, fol. 2).
Day, Richard	12	584	" 1670.
Day, Roger	11	374	" 1668.
Day, Thomas	WC2	363,395	" 1680.
Day, Thomas	WC2	395	" 1680. Servant.
Day, the Widow	4	580	Married Thomas Markins prior to 1661.
Day, William	16	293	Transported 1671.
Day, William	WC2	114	" 1680. Servant.
Dayes, John	17	440	" 1668.
Dayle, Moses	12	280	" 1668. Servant.
Dayne, Joshua	16	85	" 1670.
Dayne, Robert	16	85	" 1670.
Dazwell, Elizabeth	16	507	" 1671.
Deacows, Thomas	12	199	" 1668.
Deadman, Thomas	18	84	" 1674.
Deag, Sarah	WC2	395	" 1680. Servant.
Deakes, Edward	15	525	Immigrated 1678. Turner.
Deakes, Robert	9	35	Transported 1665.
Deakins, Alice	12	209	" 1668.
Deale, James	12	341	" 1668.
Deale, Mary	12	270	" 1668.
Deale, Thomas	16	339	" 1671.
Deale, Thomas, Jr.	12	270	" 1668.
Dealy, Dorothy	17	395	" 1672.
Dean, Edward	Q	30	Immigrated 1652. Of Charles Co.
Deane, David	15	557	Service 1678. Of Kent Co.
Deane, John	11	524	Immigrated 1668.
Deane, Katherine	WC2	310	Transported 1680.
Deane, Mary	18	137	" 1674.
Deane, Sarah	17	395	" 1672.
Deane, Thomas	6	62	" 1663.

NAME	Liber	Folio	REMARKS
Deane, William	15	572	Service 1662. Of Kent Co.
Deane, William	15	446	Immigrated 1677. Of Charles Co.
Deane, Zachary	17	417	Transported 1673.
Deare, John	5	409	" 1663.
Dearing, John	9	52	Immigrated 1665.
Dearock, George	12	473	Transported 1668.
Dearsley, Nicholl	17	608	" 1673.
Dearth, Andrew	15	436	" 1677.
Deas, Manniwell	8	486	" 1665.
Death, George	8	131	" 1661. Servant.
Deaver, William	15	395	" 1677.
Debin, Henry	WC2	309	" 1678.
Decon, Charles	6	166	" 1655.
Decosta, Elizabeth	8	129	" 1664. Wife of Mathias.
Decosta, Mathias	8	129	Immigrated 1664. (9, fol. 489; 15, fol. 242.)
Decroft, Ann	12	315	Transported 1669.
Decroft, Anthony	12	209	" 1666.
Decroft, Robert	12	209	" 1666.
Decroft, Robert	12	315	" 1669.
DeCurtis, Philip	4	538	" 1659.
Dedicatt, Henry	11	338	Transported two persons into Md. 1668. Of Bristol. Merchant.
Dedley, Charles	17	424	Transported 1673.
Dee, Samuel	4	11	" 1659. Servant.
Deefs, Benonia	5	129	" about 1662.
Deekin, John	4	14	" 1659. Servant.
Deele, Edward	9	216	" 1665.
DeEllena, Andrew	4	61	Living on the Eastern Shore 1659.
Deepe, Gregory	5	515	Transported 1661. Servant.
Deere, Joane	WC2	112	" 1679.
Deere, John	4	60	" Elizabeth Hayling, whom he married prior to July, 1659. Widow married Thos. Hill. (10, fol. 272).
Deery, John	15	417	Immigrated 1677.
Defamue, Jane	8	486	Transported 1665.
Degrotte, Arian	12	269	Service 1668.
DeHattaway, Jacob	4	59	Transported 1649-52.
Dehay, Richard	17	552	Immigrated from New England 1662.
DeHirum, Derick Irenison	5	181	Transported 1661.
Dehyniosa, Christina Barbera	WC2	411	Immigrated 1681.
Deinar, Thomas	ABH	95	Servant 1635-41.
Deisbery, Thomas	9	24	Transported 1665.
Dekin, Elizabeth	7	349	Immigrated 1649.
Dekins, Thomas	12	345	Transported 1668.
Delahay, John	2	604	" about 1638. Servant.
Delahay, John	1	25	" 1641.
De la Hay, John	ABH	60	" 1641.
Delahay, Arthur	7	462	Immigrated 1637.

NAME	Liber	Folio	REMARKS
Delahay, Arthur	12	550	Immigrated from Virginia 1670. Of St. Mary's Co.
Delahay, Charles	7	462	Transported 1637. Son of Arthur. (12, fol. 550).
Delahay, Jane	4	623	Transported with her son, James Sisson, 1661. Wife of John.
Delahay, John	4	623	Immigrated 1661.
Delahay, Mary	12	550	Transported 1670. Wife of Arthur.
Delahay, William	12	475	" 1670.
Delany, Darby	15	553	" 1678.
Delany, John	15	446	" 1677.
Delany, John	15	553	" 1678.
Delany, Michael	15	553	" 1678.
Delany, Thomas	WC2	82	" 1679.
De Lapp, Thomas	ABH	201	" 1650-1. Servant.
Delaroach, Charles	11	519	Service 1668. Of Calvert Co.
Delaroach, Elizabeth	15	445	" 1677.
Delaroach, Peter	17	574	Transported 1664 by Charles of St. Mary's Co. (15, fol. 330).
Delastashies, Frances	15	449	Transporated 1677. Wife of Sevastian.
Delastashies, Sevastian	15	449	Immigrated 1677. Of Somerset Co.
Delastashies, Sevastian, Jr.	15	449	Transported 1677. Son of Sevastian.
Delavala, Bras	8	203	" 1665.
De la Valey, John	Q	204	" 1657.
De la Valey, Nicholas	Q	204	" 1657.
Delawood, Joseph	9	21	" 1665. (17, fol. 412).
Deline, Henry	15	452	" 1678.
Dell, John	6	106	" 1659.
Dell, Mary	5	513	" 1656. Wife of William.
Dell, William	5	513	Immigrated 1655.
Dell, William	12	281,514	Transported 1668.
Delvines, Joseph	Q	217	" 1652.
Demack, John	Q	323	" 1655-8.
Demeibilla, Simon	ABH	36	Immigrated 1640.
Demeibilla, Simon	2	604	" about 1640.
Demerry, Thomas	8	41	" prior to 1665.
Demondedier, Anthony	5	489,491	Transported 1656.
Demondedier, Hirkier	5	491	Service 1658. Daughter of Anthony.
Demondedier, Katherine	5	491	" 1658. Wife of Anthony.
Demounlede, Anthony	5	90	Transported 1653-6.
Dempsy, Joane	WC2	87	" 1679.
Demsey, Ann	15	558	" 1679.
Demson, Will	15	443	" 1677.
Denake, Daniel	15	318	Service 1674.
Denall, Peter	9	262	Transported 1665.
Denard, Levin	WC2	118	" 1679.
Denard, Lewen	WC2	118	Rights 1679. Of Somerset Co.
Denboe, John	19	258	Transported 1663.
Denby, Mary	7	88	" 1654.

NAME	Liber	Folio	REMARKS
Denby, Mary	15	430	Transported 1677.
Denham, Robert	WC2	394	" 1680. Servant.
Deniar, Thomas	1	112	" 1635. Servant.
Denier, Thomas	5	245	" 1638-43.
Dening, John	17	469	" 1668.
Denman, Thomas	WC2	328,357	Service 1680.
Denmarsh, Ann	7	214	Transported 1663.
Denn, Christopher, Sr.	8	203	Immigrated 1665.
Denn, Christopher, Jr.	8	203	Transported 1665. Son of Christopher, Sr.
Denn, Robert	8	203	Transported 1665. Son of Christopher.
Denner, John	17	608	Transported 1673.
Dennico, Margaret	11	541	" 1668.
Dennings, Lucia	15	416	" 1677.
Dennis, Arthur	7	471	" 1664.
Dennis, Barbara	11	526	" 1668. Daughter of Justinian.
Dennis, Dornick	11	514	Immigrated 1668.
Dennis, Edmond	WC2	23,54	" 1679. Of Charles Co.
Dennis, Elizabeth	11	514	Transported 1668. Daughter of Dornick.
Dennis, Ellis	11	514	Transported 1668. Wife of Dornick.
Dennis, Grace	15	537	" 1678.
Dennis, Jane	11	526	" 1668. Daughter of Justinian.
Dennis, Justinian	11	526	Immigrated 1668.
Dennis, Justinian, Jr.	11	526	Transported 1668. Son of Justinian.
Dennis, Katherine	11	526	" 1668. Wife of Justinian.
Dennis, Marmaduke	6	216	" 1663.
Dennis, Mary	11	526	" 1668. Daughter of Justinian.
Dennis, Mary	17	346	Immigrated 1668. Wife of Peter.
Dennis, Peter	17	346	" 1668.
Dennis, Rose	15	544	Transported 1676.
Dennis, William	11	514	" 1668. Son of Dornick.
Dennison, James	WC2	79,99	" 1679.
Denny, Christopher	15	505	Service 1678.
Denny, Thomas	15	347	" 1673.
Denovard, Jone	15	543	Transported 1678.
Denson, James	15	433	" 1677.
Dent, Abigail	15	430	" 1677.
Dent, Charles	7	464	" 1658.
Dent, Edward	Q	69	" 1658.
Dent, John	5	245	" 1662-3 by Thomas Dent, Gent.
Dent, John	17	448	Transported 1673 by Thomas Dent.
Dent, John	15	191	Immigrated prior to 1673. Of St. Mary's Co.
Dent, Rachel	18	331	Transported 1674.
Dent, Thomas, Gent.	5	245	Immigrated about 1662.

NAME	Liber	Folio	REMARKS
Dent, William	18	331	Transported 1674.
Dent, William	15	362,442	" 1676.
Dently, Sarah	17	635	" 1674.
Denton, Ann	15	437	" 1674.
Denton, James	4	585	" 1661.
Denton, James	8	129	Immigrated 1664 with wife.
Denum, Mary	WC2	112	Transported 1679.
Denwood, Elizabeth	11	229	" 1667.
Denwood, Elizabeth	12	359	" 1669.
Denwood, Leven	8	486	" 1664.
Denwood, Levin	16	302	" from Virginia 1671.
Son of Levin of Somerset County.			
Denwood, Mary	11	229	Transported 1667.
Denwood, Priscilla	16	13	" 1670. Wife of Liveing of Somerset Co.
Denwood, Rebecca	11	229	Transported 1667.
Denwood, Rebecca	12	359	" 1669.
Denwood, Sarah	8	486	" 1664.
Denwood, Thomas	11	229	" 1667.
Depoes, John	12	284	Service 1668.
de Qurinero, John	5	181	Transported 1661.
Derby, Ann	5	90	" 1656.
Derby, Thomas	12	379	" 1669.
Derime, Richard	17	417	" 1673.
Dermod, John	WC2	53	Service 1679.
Dermott, Edmond	15	417	Immigrated 1677.
Derrick, Mary	1	62,168	Transported 1637. Servant, aged 19 years.
Derrifield, Thomas	15	347	Transported 1676.
Derrimple, James	17	572	" 1672.
Derring, Hance	7	455	Immigrated 1664.
Derton, Ann	15	318	Transported 1674.
Derumpell, James	WC2	306	Service 1680. Of Talbot Co.
Desbrowe, Jane	15	530	Transported 1678.
Desbrowe, Thomas	15	436	" 1677.
Descote, Dermote	11	378	" 1668.
Detten, John	12	496	" 1670.
Deuar, John	16	309	Immigrated from Virginia 1671
with his wife, Elizabeth and her children, William and Mary Empson. (See Deverax). Of Somerset County.			
Deuch, Jonathan	20	185	Transported 1679.
Deuman, William	16	393	" 1671.
Deusly, Jerome	12	280	" 1668. Servant.
Devall, John	9	21	" 1665.
Devell, James	16	116	" 1671.
Devene, John	WC2	73	" 1665.
Dever, Grace	Q	72	Service 1658. Wife of Richard.
Dever, Richard	Q	72	" 1658.
Deverall, Thomas	12	584	Transported 1670.
Deverax, Elizabeth	15	501	Immigrated 1678. Wife of John.
Deverax, John	15	501	" prior to 1678 with

133

NAME	Liber	Folio	REMARKS
his wife, Elizabeth and her two children, named Empson. (See Deuar).			
Devereux, Joan	4	70	Transported 1659. Servant.
Devey, Peter	15	353	" 1676.
Devin, Symon	16	435	" 1671.
Devine, Daniel	6	38	Immigrated about 1663.
Devine, Dyman	16	435	Transported 1671.
Devine, Elizabeth	17	463	" 1673.
Devine, Francis	6	90	" 1660.
Devine, Lewis	17	463	" 1673.
Devine, Mary	6	90	" 1660.
Devine, Nelo	15	446	" 1677.
Devonish, Vertue	Q	32	Servant 1657.
Devorax, Elizabeth	WC2	94	Transported prior to 1679. Relict of John.
Devorax, Jane	4	549	Transported prior to 1661.
Devorax, John	WC2	94	Immigrated prior to 1679. Deceased husband of Elizabeth.
Devorin, Manus	WC2	380	Transported 1675-80. Servant.
Dew, Bridgett	5	416	" 1663.
Dew, Patrick	4	138	Immigrated prior to 1659.
Dewberry, Thomas	12	502	Service 1669.
Dewey, Elizabeth	WC2	381	Transported 1675-80. Servant.
Dewhadaway, Jacob			(See Hattaway).
Dewkennall, Margaret	4	610	Transported 1661.
Dews, Bennomee	10	325	" 1666.
Dewsberry, Robert	18	38	" 1673.
Dexter, Edward	Q	183	Servant 1668. (10, fol. 275).
De Young, Peter	18	174	Transported 1674.
Deziarden, Hester	16	39	" 1668. Wife of John.
Deziarden, John	16	39	Immigrated 1668. Of Baltimore Co.
Deziarden, John, Jr.	16	39	Transported 1668. Son of John.
Diamont, George	18	108	Immigrated 1674.
Diamont, Mary	18	108	Transported 1674. Wife of George.
Dibb, Ralph	15	449	" 1677.
Dickason, John	9	33	" 1660.
Dickason, Margaret	9	33	" 1660. Wife of John.
Dickenson, Ann	5	367	" 1649.
Dickenson, Charles	16	532	" 1668-70.
Dickenson, Eliza	12	190	" 1668.
Dickenson, George	Q	250	Immigrated 1656.
Dickenson, Marmaduke	7	464	Transported 1663.
Dickenson, Walter	4	54	Immigrated prior to July, 1659.
Dickenson, William	16	354	Transported 1671.
Dicker, William	12	601	" 1670.
Dickes, James	15	445	" 1677. WC2, fol. 53-54).
Dickes, Robert	13	64	Immigrated 1670. Of Dorchester County.
Dickeson, Ambrose	5	73	Immigrated 1661.
Dickeson, Ambrose, Jr.	5	73	Transported 1661. Son of Ambrose.
Dickeson, Edward	15	530	" 1678.
Dickeson, Elizabeth	5	73	" 1661.

NAME	Liber	Folio	REMARKS
Dickeson, Grace	5	73	Transported 1661.
Dickeson, John	5	124	" 1662.
Dickeson, John	6	305	" 1664.
Dickeson, John	9	25	" 1665. (11, fol. 312).
Dickeson, Mary	5	73	" 1661.
Dickeson, Mary	16	469	" 1667.
Dickeson, Robert	5	404	" 1659.
Dickeson, Samuel	11	293	Service 1668. Of St. Mary's Co.
Dickeson, Sarah	5	73	Transported 1661.
Dickeson, Thomas	5	73	" 1661.
Dickeson, Thomas	12	262	" 1669 by his father, Jeremiah Dickeson.
Dickeson, William	5	85	Transported 1661.
Dickinson, Henry	6	134	" 1661.
Dickinson, Jane	WC2	395	" 1680. Servant.
Dickinson, John	6	142	" 1659.
Dickinson, John	6	129	" 1661.
Dickinson, John	6	48	Immigrated prior to 1663.
Dickinson, Samuel	5	516	Transported 1663.
Dicks, Ann	15	539	" 1678.
Dicks, Augustine	6	16	Immigrated prior to 1662.
Dicks, Philip	15	539	Transported 1678. Son of Ann.
Dickson, Cate	18	137	" 1674.
Dickson, Mary	15	430	" 1677.
Dickson, Thomas	15	453	" 1676.
Didby, John	16	393	" 1671.
Didley, Will	10	605	" 1667.
Dier, Daniel	15	453	" 1675-7.
Digby, Henry	WC2	38	" 1679.
Digges, William	WC2	217	Rights 1680.
Digley, James	9	434	Transported 1661 (New York ?).
Diggin, Elin	18	137	" 1674.
Diggins, Roger	5	409	" 1662.
Dike, James	Q	199	" 1651.
Dike, John	12	548	" 1670.
Dike, Mathew	16	393	" 1671.
Dillewood, Joane	5	257	" 1659.
Dine, Grace	16	435	" 1671.
Dines, Rose	4	555	" 1661.
Dinger, James	5	484	" 1661.
Dingher, Jane	Q	70	" 1656.
Dirrickson, Dirrick	4	139	" 1650. Servant. (Quaker ?)
Disney, Will	15	430	Transported 1677.
Dissant, Timothy	WC2	380	" 1675-80. Servant.
Distant, Ralph	WC2	253	" 1679.
Diston, Ann	15	376	" 1676.
Ditcher, Robert	4	551	" 1661.
Ditchfield, Thomas	15	346	Immigrated 1673.
Diton, Clement	18	174	Transported 1674.
Ditton, Jane	17	463	" 1673.

NAME	Liber	Folio	REMARKS
Divine, Ann	15	441	Service 1677. Wife of Daniel.
Dix, Augustine	16	462	" Oct. 1671.
Dix, Robert	7	601	Transported 1665.
Dixon, Ambrose	5	255	Immigrated 1663. (See Dickeson).
Dixon, Edward	10	390	Transported 1666.
Dixon, Elizabeth	5	255	" 1663. Daughter of Ambrose.
Dixon, Grace	5	255	Transported 1663. Daughter of Ambrose.
Dixon, Jane	8	129	Transported 1664. Wife of Mr. John.
Dixon, John	13	17	" 1668.
Dixon, John	16	411	" 1671.
Dixon, John	15	317	" 1674.
Dixon, Mr. John	8	129	Immigrated 1664.
Dixon, Margaret	10	598	Transported 1667.
Dixon, Mary	5	255	" 1663. Wife of Ambrose.
Dixon, Mary	5	255	" 1663. Daughter of Ambrose.
Dixon, Richard	ABH	100	Immigrated 1640. (1, fol. 125).
Dixon, Richard	18	329	Transported 1675.
Dixon, Richard	17	67	Immigrated 1672.
Dixon, Samuel	7	464	Transported 1664.
Dixon, Sarah	5	255	" 1663. Daughter of Ambrose.
Dixon, Thomas	5	255	Transported 1663. Son of Ambrose.
Dixon, Thomas	WC2	406	" 1676.
Dixon, Timothy	17	67	" 1672.
Doalton, Robert	WC2	130,145	" 1679. Servant.
Doaty, Enoch	11	104	" 1667.
Doaty, Joy	11	104	" 1667 by Hugh O'Neall.
Doaty, Mary	11	104	" 1667. Wife of Enoch.
Dobbett, Samuel	7	463	" 1662.
Dobbins, Eleanor	5	90	" 1651. (4, fol. 65).
Dobbins, Ellen	6	159	" 1652.
Dobbs, Aninking	10	312	Relict of Mekin Mekenny of Kent Co. Planter 1666.
Dobbs, Gerrard	6	166	Transported 1659.
Dobbs, Henry	7	464	" 1659.
Dobbs, John	7	560	" 1665.
Dobbs, John	11	104	" 1667.
Dobbs, John	15	559	" 1679.
Dobbs, Thomas	5	411	" 1663.
Dobin, Margaret	WC2	57	" 1678.
Dobson, Bridgett	18	137	" 1674.
Dobson, Christopher	7	553	Immigrated 1665.
Dobson, Jane	15	353	Transported 1675.
Dobson, John	10	325	" prior to 1666.
Dobson, Lucy	4	589	" 1661. (11, fol. 525).
Dobson, Samuel	5	81	" 1659.
Dobson, Samuel	4	589	Immigrated 1661.
Dobson, Samuel	11	524	" 1668.

NAME	Liber	Folio	REMARKS
Docman, John	16	12	Transported 1670.
Dod, Jasper	10	526	" 1667.
Dod, John	6	120	" 1657.
Dodcaster, Peter	9	437	" 1666. Of Virginia.
Dodd, Peter	WC2	395	" 1680. Servant.
Doddew, Thomas	18	160	" 1674.
Dodds, Thomas	18	167	" 1674.
Dodson, John	4	5	" 1652-9.
Dodson, John	5	129	" about 1662.
Dodson, Katherine	10	434	" 1666.
Dodwell, Thomas	12	190	" 1668.
Dodworth, Anne	15	499	" 1677.
Doe, Christopher	17	608	" 1673.
Doe, Fran.	15	376	" 1676.
Doe, John	17	363	" 1672.
Doe, Michael	Q	431	" 1658.
Doe, Thomas	ABH	78,101	" 1640. (1, fol. 63, 128).
Dogger, Michael	5	305	" about 1663.
Dogget, Benjamin	17	469	" 1673.
Dolby, Edmund	11	307,469	" 1668. Servant.
Dolby, John	12	190	" 1668. Servant.
Doling, Patrick	15	527	" 1678.
Dollery, Anthony	18	20	Service 1674. Of Dorchester Co.
Dollett, Mary	6	85	Transported 1654.
Dollihid, Francis	WC2	363	" 1680.
Dolly, Teage	6	216	" 1663.
Dologhtey, James	15	527	" 1678.
Dolphin, Christopher	5	413,419	Immigrated 1657.
Dolphine, William	5	487	Service 1662.
Dolson, Martha	ABH	142	Transported 1651.
Dolte, George	ABH	355	Immigrated prior to 1653.
Dombell, Ellis	WC2	309	Transported 1678.
Dominer, Peter	---	---	" 1675.
Donahre, Easter	15	560	" 1678.
Donahre, Mary	15	560	" 1678.
Donahre, Patrick	15	560	" 1678.
Donane, Margaret	15	549	" 1678.
Donasill, William	15	454	" 1677.
Doncoms, Miles	9	333	" 1666.
Donderdell, William	6	294	" 1664.
Dondodell, William	10	480	Service 1667.
Donevan, John	15	530	" 1678.
Donevane, Daniel	15	549	Transported 1678.
Donnavan, Dennis	WC2	128	" 1679.
Donogh, Derby	15	553	" 1678.
Donor, Bridgett	15	433	" 1677.
Donoughan, Eleanor	Q	434	" 1658.
Donoughee, Michael	15	565	" 1679.
Donovane, Ellen	4	216	" about 1659.
Doolan, Robert	18	179	Service 1674. Of St. Mary's Co.
Doolin, Nicholas	17	451	Transported 1673.

NAME	Liber	Folio	REMARKS
Doone, George	9	99	Transported 1665.
Dopse, Thomas	15	540	" 1677.
Dordine, Peter	18	158	Service 1674. Of St. Mary's Co.
Dorell, Miles	7	85	Transported 1649. Servant.
Dorman, John	16	12	" 1670.
Dorman, John	16	536	Immigrated from Virginia 1671. Of Somerset Co. (17, fol. 36).
Dorman, John	WC2	77	Transported his daughter from Virginia 1679. Of Somerset County.
Dorman, Mathew	17	36	Immigrated from Virginia 1672. Of Somerset Co.
Dorman, Phillipa	15	319	Service 1675. Wife of Matthew.
Dorman, Robert	6	125	Transported 1663.
Dorman, Sarah	18	37	Service 1673. Wife of John.
Dorman, Sarah	WC2	77	Transported 1679. Daughter of John.
Dormar, Margaret	17	463	Transported 1673.
Dormedy, Michael	15	553	" 1678.
Dormer, Sarah	WC2	167,169	" 1679.
Dormisse, Frances	5	319	" prior to 1662.
Dormoore, Gabriel	6	131	" 1654.
Dornewell, Robert	9	282	" 1663.
Dornor, Dermott	Q	431	" 1658.
Dorrell, Ellen	15	356	" 1675.
Dorrell, Flora	Q	449	" 1658.
Dorrell, George	6	83	" 1653, and Elizabeth.
Dorrell, Martha	WC2	415	" 1666-80. Servant.
Dorrell, Nicholas	12	516	Service 1669.
Dorringer, Constance	7	464	Transported 1659.
Dorrington, Elizabeth	15	359,449	" 1676.
Dorrington, Francis	12	201,202	Immigrated 1669.
Dorrington, John	18	80	Transported 1674.
Dorrington, John	15	358	" 1675.
Dorrington, Mary	9	489	Widow. Immigrated prior to 1665. Married John Highland. (9, fol. 496).
Dorrington, Nicholas	4	553	Transported 1661.
Dorrington, Richard	18	94	" 1674.
Dorrington, William	3	172	Immigrated 1655.
Dorrington, William	Q	29	" 1658.
Dorsett, Mark	6	131	Transported 1657.
Dorsey, Edward	5	88	Came into Maryland in 1661, with Robert Bullen.
Dorsey, Edward	7	378	Aug. 25, 1664, Patent to him, John and Joshua for plantation in Anne Arundel Co. called "Hockley in the Hole", 400 acres on which the three lived. Boatwright living 1667. (10, fol. 498).
Dorsey, James	11	337	Transported 1668.
Dorton, Anne	WC2	380	" 1675-80. Servant.
Dortway, Ann	15	560	" 1678.
Dose, Voseley	10	598	Immigrated 1667.
Dosse, Ursula	5	492	Transported 1659.

NAME	Liber	Folio	REMARKS
Dossett, Stephen	12	403	Transported 1669.
Dosson, Christopher	9	304	Immigrated 1665.
Dossy, John	18	116	Service 1674. Of Dorchester Co.
Doubin, Margaret	15	553	Transported 1678.
Doudy, James	16	452	" 1667.
Dougharty, Nathaniel	WC2	319	Immigrated 1680.
Doughty, Edward	15	510	Transported 1676.
Doughty, Enoch	Q	184	Immigrated 1656.
Doughty, John	15	510	" 1676. Of Talbot Co.
Dougin, Priscilla	15	553	Transported 1678.
Douglass, Ann	WC2	17,35	" 1679. Wife of Reynald.
Douglass, Alexander	15	362,371	Service 1675. (15, fol. 417).
Douglass, Francis	Q	217	Transported 1652.
Douglass, Martha	WC2	17,35	" 1679. Daughter of Reynald.
Douglass, Mary	WC2	17,35	Transported 1679. Daughter of Reynald.
Douglass, Reynald	WC2	17, 35-36	Immigrated 1679 with wife, 2 children and two other persons. Of Somerset County.
Douglass, Will	15	565	Transported 1679.
Douguty, Robert	12	189	" 1668.
Doule, Ann	15	560	" 1678.
Doulster, Alice	16	94	" 1670.
Dousley, Ralph	11	582	" 1668.
Douty, Susan	11	465	" 1668.
Dove, John	15	454	" Oct. 1677.
Dove, William	12	392,403	" 1669.
Dovefield, Thomas	6	171	" 1663. Servant.
Dover, John	16	41,112	" 1670.
Dowd, James	16	42	" 1667.
Dowdale, James	18	10	Service 1673.
Dowell, John	9	313	Transported 1665.
Dowerson, Jane	16	452	" 1670.
Dowgane, Donogh	15	600	" 1678.
Dowglass, John	4	214	Immigrated 1659.
Dowglisse, John	18	152	Transported 1674.
Dowland, William	10	599	" 1667. Servant. (12, fol. 269; 16, fol. 534).
Dowlar, Mathew	WC2	253	Transported 1679.
Dowle, Richard	11	344	" 1668.
Dowles, John	7	569	" 1663-4.
Dowles, Mary	6	14	" 1663.
Dowlin, Barbar	6	122	" 1656.
Dowlin, John	6	82	" 1663.
Dowlin, Roger	15	553	" 1678.
Dowling, Joane	4	176	" 1659.
Dowman, William	15	440	" 1677.
Downe, Richard	5	106	Immigrated 1661.
Downe, Robert	15	449	Transported 1677.
Downes, Arthur	16	394	" 1671.

NAME	Liber	Folio	REMARKS
Downes, Arthur	17	545	Transported 1673.
Downes, George	12	613	Immigrated from Virginia 1670. Of Dorchester Co.
Downes, Henry & wife	8	130	Immigrated 1665.
Downes, Henry	10	566	" from York River, Va. 1667. Of Kent Co.
Downes, John	10	566	Transported 1667. Son of Henry.
Downes, Marjory	7	560	" 1665.
Downes, Mary	10	566	" 1667. Wife of Henry.
Downes, Mary	20	185	" 1679.
Downes, Richard	8	88	" 1665.
Downes, Robert	8	501	" 1665.
Downing, Mary	WC2	132	" 1680.
Downing, Robert	12	584	" 1670.
Downing, William	10	277	" 1666.
Downing, William	12	498	Immigrated 1670 with Mary, his wife. Of Somerset Co.
Downing, William	15	508	Service 1678. Of Calvert Co.
Dowringen, John	8	202	Transported 1664.
Dowse, Edward	17	411	" 1673.
Dowse, Elizabeth	17	411	" 1673.
Dowswaith, John	15	358	" 1675.
Dowty, Ann	17	30	Service 1672. Wife of Peter.
Dowty, Peter	17	30	Immigrated from Virginia 1672. Of Somerset County.
Dowty, Susan	11	344	Transported 1668.
Doxey, Thomas	12	267	Of St. Mary's Co. Married second-

ly, prior to 1669, Ann, widow of Robert Hooper of same county. He and
his first wife had performed their terms of service.

NAME	Liber	Folio	REMARKS
Doxey, Ursula	5	482	Transported 1662.
Doyan, William	WC2	309	" 1678.
Doyer, Samuel	10	499	" 1667.
Doyle, John	15	446	" 1677.
Doyley, Robert	Q	477	Of London. Merchant. Agrees to immigrate in 1657.
Doyne, Barbera	WC2	302	Transported 1680. Wife of Joshua.
Doyne, Joshua	16	85	" 1670.
Doyne, Joshua	WC2	302-303	Immigrated 1680 with wife. Of St. Mary's Co.
Doyne, Robert	16	85	Transported 1670.
Doyne, Robert	WC2	303	Immigrated 1680. Of Charles Co.
Doytes, Urian	10	599	Transported 1667.
Drackley, Mary	15	429	" 1674.
Drake, James	15	565	" 1679.
Drake, Mary	15	369	" 1676.
Drake, Richard	17	417	" 1673.
Drake, Susan	15	301	" 1675.
Drake, Thomas	WC2	378-379	Service 1680. Of St. Mary's Co.
Drake, William & wife	15	440	" 1677.
Drape, Alice	16	482	Transported 1670-1.
Drape, William	10	272	" 1666.

NAME	Liber	Folio	REMARKS
Draper, Esther	4	11	Transported 1659. Servant.
Draper, James	6	97	" 1657.
Draper, John	15	516	" 1676.
Draper, Lawrence	WC2	38	Immigrated 1679. Of Anne Arundel County.
Draper, Peter, Gent.	ABH	79	Immigrated 1633.
Draper, Peter	1	20,63, 121	" 1633. Deceased prior to 1644.
Draper, William	15	530	Transported 1678.
Draton, Florentine	6	86	" 1663.
Draton, Walter	6	96	" 1661.
Drax, Samuel	6	122	" 1657.
Drayer, Peter	ABH	98	" 1633. Servant.
Draylett, Edward	8	503	" 1665.
Drene (or Drere), Emanuel	Q	71	Married Elizabeth Maurice prior to 1658.
Dress, James	10	213	Transported 1665.
Drew, John	Q	201	" 1651-8.
Drewe, Ann	16	532	" 1668.
Drewman, John	ABH	273	" 1651. Servant.
Drewman, John	Q	211	" 1658.
Drewry, Isaac	18	160	" 1674.
Dridenn, James	12	215	" 1668-9.
Dridon, Elizabeth	18	15	" 1673.
Driffell, Nathaniel	WC2	368	" 1680.
Drigar, Deverax	15	433	" 1677.
Drimmell, William	18	166	" 1674.
Dring, John	5	367	" 1663.
Drings, Mathias	16	410	" 1671.
Drinker, Mary	15	313	" 1675.
Drinkwater, Sarah, Jr.	15	424	" 1677. (19, fol. 503).
Drinkwater, Sarah, Sr.	19	503	" prior to 1676. (15, fol. 424).
Driscall, Florence (Male)	17	417	Immigrated 1673.
Drisdale, Robert	WC2	110	Transported 1676. Servant.
Driskole, Cornelius	20	184	" from Ireland 1678.
Dritcheild, Nathaniel	15	504	" 1678.
Driven, Sarah	10	499	" 1667.
Driver, Ann	17	567	Immigrated 1673. Of Worcester County.
Driver, David	9	54	Transported 1665.
Driver, David	16	513	Immigrated 1672. Of St. Mary's Co.
Driver, Obediah	WC2	7	Service 1679.
Droper, Alexander	5	253	Immigrated 1663.
Droper, Catherine	5	253	Transported 1663. Wife of Alexander.
Druckle, John	16	170	Transported 1670.
Drudge, Mark	15	322	" 1674.

NAME	Liber	Folio	REMARKS
Druett, Robert	10	390	Transported 1666.
Drummer, Stephen	6	143	" 1659.
Drury, Richard	17	491	Immigrated from Virginia 1663.
Drury, Robert	12	571	" 1670.
Drury, William	5	607	Transported 1663.
Dry, Catharine	13	66	" 1669. Servant.
Drywood, John	Q	69	" 1654. (7, fol. 150).
Duanchall, Daniel	8	486	" 1665.
Duberry, Edward	12	210	Service 1664. (11, fol. 548).
Dublin, Jefry	15	567	Transported 1679.
Ducangall, Margaret	9	92	" 1665.
Duck, Susanna	9	476	" prior to 1666.
Duckan, John	12	517	" 1670.
Dudford, Daniel	7	465	" 1659.
Dudicke, John	WC2	50-51	" 1674.
Dudill, Thomas	18	310	" 1675.
Dudlesse, John	3	174	" 1656.
Dudley, Henry	18	35	" 1673.
Dudley, Richard	12	415	" 1669.
Dudly, Richard	16	435	" 1671.
Dudman, John	WC2	395	" 1680. Servant.
Dudridge, Elizabeth	17	417	" 1673.
Duffields, John	16	414	" 1671.
Duglass, Mary	7	463	" 1661.
Duglass, Robert	6	117	" 1658.
Duickley, Hannah	12	202	" 1669. Servant.
Duke, Henry	15	454	" 1677.
Duke, Richard	1	20,38	" 1633.
Duke, Richard	ABH	66	" 1663.
Duke, Richard	ABH	331	Immigrated 1653, with his wife and two children.
Duke, Richard	10	277	Transported 1666.
Duke, Thomas	10	520	" 1667.
Dukes, Francis	7	83	" 1660.
Dukes, Robert	9	332	" 1666.
Dukes, Robert	17	30	Immigrated from Virginia 1672. Of Somerset Co.
Dulen, Morish	20	184	Transported from Ireland 1678.
Dulin, Hugh	Q	29	" 1657.
Dullavon, Sille	9	448	" 1666.
Duly, John	6	81	" 1656.
Dummack, Elizabeth	18	174	" 1674.
Dummer, Martha	17	440	" 1668.
Dumsen, David	6	14	Immigrated 1662.
Dun, John	15	369	Service 1675.
Dunanan, Timothy	15	544	" 1674.
Dunavane, Eleanor	15	438	Transported Oct. 1667.
Dunavane, Teage	17	424	Immigrated 1673.
Duncaefe, Ralph	13	113	Transported 1670.
Dunce, Margaret	6	166	" 1657.
Dunch, Peter	7	86	" 1656.

NAME	Liber	Folio	REMARKS
Dunch, Samuel	6	85	Transported 1656.
Dunch, Walter	WC2	406	Master of Ship Charles.
Dunch, Walter	11	320	Of London. Mariner. Purchased 500 acres in Md. when he was living in 1668.
Dunckley, Edward	15	534	Transported 1677.
Dunckley, Moses	12	200	" 1668.
Duncks, William	7	471	" 1664. Servant.
Duncoms, Thomas	9	333	" 1666.
Dundas, Anthony George	6	290	" 1663.
Dundee, George	7	484	" 1664.
Duneld, Darby	17	635	" 1671.
Dunge, William	15	553	" 1678.
Dunill, Sarah	15	438	" Oct. 1667.
Duning, William	5	214	" 1662.
Dunington, James	15	362	" 1676.
Dunkan, Patrick	9	448	" prior to 1666.
Dunkerton, William	12	280,283	Immigrated 1668.
Dunn, Elizabeth	18	160	Transported 1674. (15, fol. 378).
Dunn, John	13	122	" 1668.
Dunn, John	15	370	" 1676.
Dunn, Obadiah	15	378	Immigrated prior to 1676.
Dunn, Pascho	6	159	" 1652.
Dunn, Robert	15	553	Transported 1678.
Dunnan, Eleanor	Q	18	" 1652-8.
Dunnavan, Darby	WC2	353	Service 1674.
Dunnavan, Mary	WC2	353	" 1674. Wife of Darby.
Dunne, Ann	17	395	Transported 1672.
Dunne, Isaac	17	608	" 1673.
Dunning, James	11	318	" 1668.
Dunnington, James	15	442	" 1677.
Dunnock, Joan	Q	32	Servant 1657.
Dunstaine, Ann	9	25	Transported 1665. Wife of John.
Dunstane, Anthony	10	259	" 1665.
Dunston, Francis	15	422	Service 1677.
Dunston, John	5	607	Immigrated 1663.
Dunston, Mary	8	202	Transported 1664.
Dunston, Peley	5	607	Immigrated 1663.
Dunston, Thomas	18	329	Transported 1675.
Dunstone, Thomas	16	319	" 1670. Of Accomacke in Virginia.
Dunt, Samuel	16	71	Transported 1670.
Dunton, Simon	WC2	217	" 1680.
Duohy, Margarett	WC2	128	" 1679.
Duparke, Elizabeth	5	211	" 1662. Wife of Thomas.
Duparke, Thomas	5	211	Immigrated 1662.
Durand, Elizabeth	ABH	35	" 1648-9. Daughter of William.
Durand, Elizabeth	2	575	Transported 1648. Daughter of William.
Durand, William	2	575	Immigrated 1648 with wife, daughter and six other persons.

NAME	Liber	Folio	REMARKS
Durand, Mr. William	ABH	25,35	Immigrated March 1648-9, with wife.
Durant, William	2	516	Immigrated 1648 with wife, four children and five other persons.
Durdell, Joseph	15	353	Transported 1674.
Durden, James	8	130	" 1665.
Durdenie, James	16	43	" 1670.
Durent, Eagell	15	356	" 1675.
Durford, Joseph	1	22	" 1640. Son of William.
Durford, Joseph	ABH	6	" 1640-8. (2, fol. 327).
Durford, William	1	22	Immigrated 1640 with son, Joseph.
Durford, William	ABH	10,244	Transported 1641. (2, fol. 425).
Durham, John	17	512	Service 1673. Of Baltimore Co.
Durham, Mary	Q	18	Transported 1658.
Durham, Richard	6	159	" 1659.
Durly, Bryan	WC2	82	" 1679.
Duroy, Richard	ABH	66	" 1637.
Durrell, John	WC2`	396-397	Rights 1680. Commander of the Ship Sea Flower. Of Poole Co., England.
Duston, Thomas	18	38	Transported 1673.
Duston, Thomas	15	412	" 1675.
Dusurd, Thomas	6	266	" 1662.
Dutton, Abraham	6	79	" 1663.
Dutton, Marthay	WC2	395	" 1680. Servant.
Dutton, Thomas	WC2	199	" 1680.
Duvall, John	15	553	" 1678.
Du Vall, Marin	4	60	Service 1659. Transported by Wm. Burgess, demands 50 acres of land having performed his term of service with John Cenell (Covell) and bought in by Wm. Burgess; (4, fol. 60). "Lavall", 100 acres. Surveyed. (4, fol. 259, 431; 7, fol. 450-1).
Duvane, Dennis	15	446	Transported 1677.
Dwane, Dennis	WC2	106	" 1679.
Dwayre, Edmond	15	446	" 1677.
Dwyer, Cate	15	553	" 1678. (WC2, fol. 57).
Dya, Warren	16	530	" 1672.
Dye, Martin	11	104	" 1667.
Dyer, Edward	13	114	" 1668.
Dyer, Malligo	15	438	" Oct. 1677.
Dyer, Margaret	15	438	" Oct. 1677.
Dyer, Mary	15	438	" Oct. 1677.
Dyer, Peter	9	48	" 1665. (11, fol. 139).
Dyer, Roger	WC2	380	" 1675-80. Servant.
Dykes, Thomas	Q	68	Service 1658.
Dynes, Rose	Q	208	Transported 1658.
Dynyard, Thomas	3	14	Service 1649.
Dyre, Thomas	8	129	Immigrated 1664.
Dyson, William	WC2	167,169	Transported 1679.
Eades, Susana	WC2	114	" 1680. Servant.
Eagell, Mary	16	407	" 1671.
Eagle, William	7	463	" 1663.
Eaglestone, Bernard	5	607	" prior to 1658.

NAME	Liber	Folio	REMARKS
Ealor, Elizabeth	WC2	100	Transported 1679.
Ealwood, John	15	344	" 1675.
Eard, Thomson	18	160	" 1674.
Eareckson, Benjamin	15	431	Service 1677.
Earickson, Mathew	WC2	212	Rights 1679. Of Kent County.
Earle, Thomas	7	463	Transported 1663.
Early, John	12	206	Service 1669. Of Dorchester Co.
Earnly, William	12	385	Transported 1669.
Easegate, Abraham	6	294	" 1664.
Easmore, Mary	15	331	" 1675.
Eason, John	5	415	" 1663.
Eason, John	15	567	" 1678.
East, Frances	12	597	Immigrated 1670. Wife of Simon.
East, Henry	8	42	Transported 1665.
East, Joane	18	291	" 1674. (6, fol. 209).
East, John	11	441	" 1668. (11, fol. 337).
East, Robert	18	160	" 1674.
East, Simon	11	294	Immigrated 1668. Of St. Mary's Co. Boatwright.
Eastereck, Susannah	6	321	Transported 1664. (6, fol. 90).
Eastwood, Henry	11	316	" from London 1668. Servant.
Eastwood, John	10	507	Transported 1667. Servant.
Eaton, Ann	12	393	" 1669.
Eaton, Elizabeth	15	504	" 1678.
Eaton, Grace	15	451	" 1678.
Eaton, Henry	WC2	342	Service 1680. Of St. Mary's Co.
Eaton, Jeremiah	16	534	Immigrated Feb. 1668.
Eaton, Joseph	WC2	146,162	Rights 1680.
Eaton, Miles	WC2	395	Transported 1680. Servant.
Eaton, Nathaniel	5	308	" 1663.
Eaton, Samuel	5	308	" 1663.
Eavens, Ann	WC2	65	" 1679.
Eaves, John	18	335	" 1675.
Ebb, Thomas	8	30	" 1665.
Ebbeus, Mary	5	260	" 1662.
Ebbons, John	17	330	" 1672.
Ebbs, Edward	ABH	61	" 1633-41. (4, fol. 63; 1, fol. 27).
Ebbs, Hannah	9	54	Transported 1665.
Ebbs, Matthew	7	150	" 1663.
Ebsworth, Mary	ABH	356	" 1650. Servant.
Ecrod, John	15	455	" 1678.
Ed---, Richard	7	520	" 1664.
Eddye, Nathaniel	9	233,269	" 1665.
Edee, Margaret	10	325	" prior to 1666.
Edelen, Elizabeth	7	508	" 1664. Wife of Richard. (12, fol. 210; 7, fol. 83).
Edelen, Philip	12	210	Transported 1669. Son of Richard.
Edelen, Richard	WC2	300-301	Commission as Deputy Surveyor of St. Mary's County.

NAME	Liber	Folio	REMARKS
Edelen, Richard	7	508	Immigrated 1664. Commission as Deputy Surveyor, from Baker Brooke, Surveyor General, 1670. (19, fol. 384; 7, fol. 83).
Edell, Richard	18	84	Transported 1674.
Eden, Thomas	11	319	" 1668. (15, fol. 385).
Edes, John	5	248	" 1663.
Edge, Daniel	17	55	Service 1672. Of Anne Arundel Co.
Edge, Elizabeth	15	301	" 1675. Wife of Daniel.
Edge, George	15	398	Transported 1676.
Edge, Richard	7	368	" 1660-4.
Edge, Thomas	17	608	" 1673.
Eding, William	7	499	" 1660.
Edis, William	ABH	4	Servant 1646.
Edley, Richard	17	444	Immigrated 1673.
Edloe, Jane	16	282	Service 1671. Wife of Joseph, of St. Mary's Co.
Edloe, Joseph	16	282	Service 1671. Of St. Mary's Co.
Edloe, Mary	4	570	Transported 1661.
Edloe, Michael	15	530	" 1678.
Edlow, Eleanor	ABH	349	" 1641. Wife of Joseph.
Edlow, Joseph	2	439	" 1648.
Edlow, Joseph	2	439-440	" 1648. Son of Joseph, under 16 years of age.
Edlow, Joseph	ABH	12,35	Servant 1648. Married Eleanor Forringham, 1641. (4, fol. 79).
Edlow, Joseph	ABH	12	A servant under 16 years of age, probably son of Joseph, above.
Edlow, Mrs. ---	2	440	Transported 1648. Wife of Joseph.
Edlowe, Joseph	2	579	Service about 1649. Servant of Lord Baltimore.
Edly, Richard	15	427	Immigrated 1672.
Edmison, Lewis	WC2	106	Transported 1679.
Edmonds, Edward	5	490	" 1662.
Edmonds, George	11	569	" 1668.
Edmonds, Hannah	15	186,435	" 1677.
Edmonds, Hannah	WC2	23	" 1679.
Edmonds, Isaac	15	186,435	Nephew of Randall Revell of Somerset Co., 1674.
Edmonds, Isaac	WC2	23	Transported 1679.
Edmonds, Joane	5	203	" 1662.
Edmonds, John	10	433	" 1666.
Edmonds, John, Jr.	15	319	" 1675.
Edmonds, John, Sr.	15	319	" 1675.
Edmonds, Lewis	15	446	" 1677.
Edmonds, Rebecca	15	319	" 1675.
Edmonds, Richard	17	401	Immigrated 1671 with Eleanor, his wife and Richard, his son.
Edmonds, Robert	15	384	Transported 1671.
Edmonds, Mr. Thomas	6	309	" 1663. Father-in-law of Gasper Gueren.
Edmonds, Thomas	4	553	Immigrated 1661.

Name	Liber	Folio	REMARKS
Edmonds, Thomas	16	532	Transported 1668-70.
Edmonds, William	16	37	" 1670.
Edmondson, John	4	4	" 1658. Servant.
Edmondson, John	8	203	" 1665.
Edmondson, Mary	11	582	" 1668.
Edmondson, William	11	582	" 1668.
Edmont, Edward	12	194	" 1668. Servant.
Edmunds, Bridgett	4	553	" 1661.
Edsworth, Mary	17	463	" 1673.
Edward, Symon	16	507	" 1671.
Edwards, Alice	4	204	" 1659.
Edwards, Ann	15	338,505	" 1678.
Edwards, Charles	15	401	Immigrated 1677. Of St. Mary's Co.
Edwards, Deborah	16	393	Transported 1671.
Edwards, Edward	17	451	" 1671.
Edwards, Eleanor	4	11	" 1659. Servant.
Edwards, Elizabeth	WC2	65	" 1679.
Edwards, Giles	15	443	" 1672.
Edwards, Henry	11	337,441	" 1668.
Edwards, Henry	WC2	65	" 1679.
Edwards, Hugh	15	530	" 1678.
Edwards, Hum.	15	380	" 1676.
Edwards, Isaac	ABH	93	Immigrated 1637. (1, fol. 107).
Edwards, James	10	390	Transported 1666.
Edwards, John	17	402	" 1652.
Edwards, John	5	416	" 1658.
Edwards, John	4	530	" 1659.
Edwards, John	4	553	" 1661.
Edwards, John	6	48	" 1663.
Edwards, John	7	429,536	Immigrated 1663.
Edwards, John	6	293	Transported 1664.
Edwards, John	12	202	" 1669. Servant.
Edwards, John	16	131	" 1671.
Edwards, John	16	522	" 1672.
Edwards, John	17	577	Immigrated 1673. Of Dorchester County.
Edwards, John	15	338,380	Transported 1676.
Edwards, John	15	535	" 1678.
Edwards, John	15	539	Immigrated 1678. Of Baltimore County.
Edwards, John	WC2	340-341	Service 1680. Of St. Mary's Co.
Edwards, Joseph	ABH	50,371	Transported 1649. Servant. (3, fol. 63).
Edwards, Joseph	WC2	146,162	Transported 1680.
Edwards, Margaret	15	398,453	" 1676. (15, fol. 428).
Edwards, Mary	15	443	" 1677.
Edwards, Mary	WC2	65	" 1679.
Edwards, Meredith	15	331	" 1675.
Edwards, Richard	16	37	" 1670.
Edwards, Robert	ABH	66	" 1633. (1, fol. 20, 38).
Edwards, Robert	16	85	" 1670.

NAME	Liber	Folio	REMARKS
Edwards, Sarah	WC2	167,169	Transported 1680.
Edwards, Stephen	15	443	" 1670.
Edwards, Thomas	7	80,639	" 1664.
Edwards, Thomas	9	104	" 1665. (11, fol. 216).
Edwards, Thomas	12	209,473	" 1668.
Edwards, William	7	154	Immigrated 1661.
Edwards, William	15	380	Transported 1676.
Edwards, William	20	185	" 1679.
Edwin, Andrew	16	165	" Oct. 1664.
Edwin, Margaret	6	16	" 1656. Wife of William.
Edwin, Thomas	WC2	16	" 1677.
Edwin (Edwyn), William	1	20,38	" 1633.
Edwin, William	6	16	Immigrated 1656 and died prior to 1663.
Edwin, William	6	266	Son of William and Margaret, living 1663.
Edwin, William	ABH	66	Transported 1633. Service 1646.
(ABH, fol. 5). Married Mary White prior to 1651.			
Edwin, William	2	272	Service 1648.
Edy, John	7	471	Transported 1664.
Edy, William	ABH	199	Immigrated 1651.
Edyar, George	15	453	Transported 1676.
Effin, William	5	82	" 1661.
Efford, Emanuel	8	89	" 1665.
Egan, John	15	553	" 1678.
Egan, Laughlan	15	553	" 1678.
Egane, Flowrance	WC2	381	" 1675-80. Servant.
Egell, Mary	16	407	" 1671.
Eger, James	15	565	" 1679.
Egerton, Mr. ---	1	18	Immigrated 1638.
Egg, Thomas	11	344	Transported 1668.
Eggell, Ann	15	359	" 1676.
Egius, Isabell	9	99	" 1665.
Eglesfield, Ann	1	19	" 1637.
Eglesfield, George	15	452	" 1678.
Egleson, William	18	152	" 1674.
Eglestone, Barnett	5	467	" 1657.
Eglestone, John	12	194	" 1668. Servant.
Egolden, Daniel	16	428	" 1670-1.
Eillen, Francis	10	600	Immigrated 1667.
Eillen, Mary	10	600	Transported 1667. Wife of Francis.
Einge, Richard	17	363	" 1672.
Ejeril, Chr.	15	553	" 1678.
Ekeson, als. Huson, Benj.	11	537	" 1668.
Ekloe, Ann	9	233	" 1665.
Ekon, Adam	8	131	" 1664. Son of Hugh.
Ekon, Hugh	8	131	Immigrated 1664 with his wife, son and two daughters.
Ekon, Mary	8	131	Transported 1664. Wife of Hugh.
Eldar, John	17	440	" 1673.

NAME	Liber	Folio	REMARKS
Elder, John	7	498	Transported 1660.
Eldesh, Thomas	15	443	" 1674.
Eldridge, William	15	436	" 1677.
Eldrige, Jerome	16	447	" 1671.
Eldrige, William	5	244	" 1662.
Elena, Andrew	ABH	27	Servant 1644.
Eley, William	11	338	Transported 1668.
Elford, John	18	160	" 1674.
Elgate, Hannah	6	207	" 1663. Wife of William.
Elgate, John	6	267	" 1663. Son of William.
Elgate, William	6	267	" 1663. Son of William.
Elina, Andrew	Q	365	Immigrated 1658. (See Elena).
Elinore, Thomas	16	482	Transported 1671.
Elison, Gosper	11	537	" 1668.
Eliston, Elizabeth	12	286	" 1668. Servant.
Elizabeth ---	Q	29	" 1658.
Elkin, John	ABH	65	" 1633. (1, fol. 20, 38).
Elkonhead, William	ABH	12	Immigrated 1648.
Ellcott, Arthur	6	81	Transported 1651.
Ellenden, Richard	12	189	" 1668.
Ellenor, Andrew	10	311-312	Of the Eastern Shore. Died prior

to 1666 leaving an heiress, Margaret Hanson, who married Alex. Waters.

Eller, Enoch	12	194	Transported 1668. Servant.
Ellery, Elizabeth	16	45	" 1668.
Ellery, Henry	ABH	396	" 1654 "from the Ter-

tudos". In 1663, demands 100 acres "for his services performed in Anarundall". (5, fol. 420).

Elleson, M.	6	105	Transported 1650.
Ellet, Francis	18	174	" 1674.
Ellet, Stephen	16	470	Service March 1661-2.
Ellet, Vincent	12	513	" 1668.
Ellett, Ann	15	516	Transported 1676.
Ellett, Rebecca	12	477	" 1670.
Ellett, Susanna	15	516	" 1676.
Ellgate, William	4	591	Immigrated 1661.
Ellin, James	WC2	254	Transported 1680.
Ellings, George	13	114	" 1671.
Ellingsworth, Richard	6	87	Immigrated 1658.
Ellinson, Barbara	18	331	Transported 1674.
Elliot, Christopher	5	339	" 1663.
Elliot, Henry	9	451	" 1666.
Elliot, John	ABH	15	Servant 1642.
Elliot, William	3	24	Transported 1640. Servant.
Elliott, Edward	9	47	" 1665.
Elliott, Edward	15	396	Immigrated 1667.
Elliott, Edward	15	297	Transported 1675.
Elliott, Elizabeth	5	238	" 1662.
Elliott, Henry	17	557	Service 1673. Of St. Mary's Co.
Elliott, John	6	212	Immigrated 1663.
Elliott, John	2	458	Transported 1642. Servant.
Elliott, John	18	331	" 1674.

NAME	Liber	Folio	REMARKS
Elliott, Mary	12	576	Transported 1670.
Elliott, Prosperos	15	397	" 1676.
Elliott, Rebeccah	WC2	398	" 1680.
Elliott, Stephen	6	171	" 1663.
Elliott, Thomas	12	209	" 1668. (11, fol. 374).
Elliott, William	ABH	48	" 1640. Servant.
Elliott, William	ABH	151	" 1614. Servant.
Elliott, William	ABH	247	Immigrated 1650. Of Isle of Kent.
Ellis, Andrew	15	353	Transported 1676.
Ellis, Benjamin	7	530	" 1664.
Ellis, Christopher	4	551	" 1661.
Ellis, Elizabeth	8	502	" 1665. Wife of John.
Ellis, Elizabeth	WC2	120	" 1680.
Ellis, Evan	16	71	" Nov. 1668.
Ellis, Gartwright	17	552	" from Delaware 1673.
Ellis, John	ABH	175	Immigrated Nov. 1649.
Ellis, John	5	367	Transported 1649.
Ellis, John	4	204	" 1659.
Ellis, John	8	502	Immigrated 1665.
Ellis, Lewis	6	37	Transported 1663.
Ellis, Mary	WC2	380	" 1675-80. Servant.
Ellis, Nicholas	7	507	" 1660. (11, fol. 105).
Ellis, Owen	9	189	" 1665. Service 1668. (15, fol. 390).
Ellis, Peter	4	472	Transported 1664.
Ellis, Peter	WC2	391-392	Service 1680. Of Baltimore Co.
Ellis, Sampson	15	380	Transported 1676.
Ellis, Thomas	10	277	" 1666.
Ellis, Thomas	12	209	" 1668.
Ellis, William	5	411	" 1663.
Ellis, William	17	416	" 1673.
Ellis, William	15	455	" 1678.
Ellison, John	17	395	" 1672.
Elliston, Elizabeth	5	89	" 1659. (See Alliston).
Ellit, Susanna	WC2	396	" 1680. Servant.
Ellit, Thomas	12	314	" 1669. Servant.
Ellitt, William	WC2	110	" 1676. Servant.
Ellmsworth, Christian	5	417	" 1663.
Ellott, Moses	12	216	" 1668.
Ellsford, Elizabeth	7	471	" 1664.
Ellsner, Gillian	12	496	" 1670.
Ellson, Ann	4	57	" prior to 1659. Wife of John.
Ellson, John	4	57	Service 1659.
Ellson, John	15	353	Transported 1676.
Ellstone, Eleanor	5	342	" March 1661-2. Wife of Ralph.
Ellstone, Ralph	5	342	Immigrated 1661-2. Of Talbot Co.
Ellstone, Ralph, Jr.	5	342	Transported 1661-2. Son of Ralph.
Ellton, James	5	65	Service 1662.
Elly, Capt. John	WC2	16	Transported 16 persons in 1679.

NAME	Liber	Folio	REMARKS
Elly, Capt. John	WC2	16	Rights 1679.
Ellyer, John	5	235	Immigrated 1662.
Ellys, Robert	16	112,540	Transported 1671. (15, fol. 262).
Elme, John	5	606	" prior to 1663.
Elmes, Joyce	8	3,503	" 1665.
Elmes, Thomas	8	3,503	Immigrated 1665.
Elmes, William	16	302	" from Virginia 1671, with Elizabeth, his wife.
Ellys, Thomas	WC2	382	Service 1680. Of Calvert Co.
Elmes, William	WC2	412	Transported 1681.
Elmore, Charles	16	112	" 1671.
Elmore, Thomas	16	409	" 1671.
Elsemore, Mary	18	84	" 1674.
Elsey, Peter	5	3	" 1661. (17, fol. 369).
Elsmore, Daniel	ABH	141	" 1651. (4, fol. 54).
Elson, William	ABH	411	" 1640. Servant.
Elstone, Thomas	1	166	" 1650. Servant.
Eltoffe, Mary	16	482	" 1670-1.
Elton, Ann	1	18	" 1638. Servant.
Elton, James	Q	317	" 1658.
Elton, James	15	454	" Oct. 1677.
Elton, John	5	73	" 1661.
Elton, Marcus	17	566	Immigrated 1673. Of Worcester County.
Elton, Margaret	12	479	Service 1670. Wife of James.
Eltonhead, Mr. William	ABH	165	Nephew of Edward Eltonhead, Esq., 1651.
Eltonhead, William	2	439-440	Immigrated 1648 with wife, son and others.
Elivin, John	12	566	Immigrated from Virginia 1670. Of St. Mary's Co.
Elward, William	16	452	Transported 1671.
Elwes, Thomas	11	436-7	Immigrated 1668. Of London. Merchant.
Ely, John	12	372	Transported 1669.
Elzey, Arnold	14	374	Son of John and Sarah, a minor in 1671.
Elzey, John	7	567	Transported 1665.
Elzey, John	14	374	Son of John and Sarah, died prior to 1671.
Elzey, Sarah	14	374	Relict of John, Sr. Married 2nd, Thos. Jordeyne, Merchant; and 3rd, Charles Ballard of Somerset Co. Gent. prior to 1671.
Elzley, Elizabeth	16	414	Transported 1671.
Ember, Jane	7	471	" 1664.
Emberson, Christopher	11	537	" 1668.
Emberson, Erick	11	537	" 1668.
Embury, Grisell	18	15	" 1673.
Emerson, Anthony	7	560	" 1665.
Emerson, Humphrey	6	237	" 1663.
Emerson, John	8	203	" 1665.

NAME	Liber	Folio	REMARKS
Evans, David	7	469	Transported 1664. (7, fol. 576).
Evans, David	18	137	" 1674.
Evans, David	15	544	" 1676.
Evans, David	WC2	395	" 1680. Servant.
Evans, Edward	15	505	" 1678.
Evans, Edward	9	24	" 1665. Service 1669. (12, fol. 502).
Evans, Edward	16	402	Transported 1671. Service 1675. (15, fol. 318).
Evans, Eleanor	17	416	Transported 1673.
Evans, Elizabeth	15	448	" 1677. Daughter of Thomas.
Evans, Elizabeth	15	557	Transported 1678.
Evans, Hannah	15	448	" 1677. Wife of Thomas.
Evans, Hugh	WC2	395	" 1680. Servant.
Evans, Humphry	WC2	395	" 1680. Servant.
Evans, John	5	124	" 1662.
Evans, John	8	484	" 1665.
Evans, John	16	402	" 1671.
Evans, John	16	303	Immigrated 1671 with Mary, his wife, to Somerset Co. Of Virginia. (17, fol. 33).
Evans, John	15	534	Transported 1677.
Evans, John	WC2	395	" 1680. Servant.
Evans, Jone	15	566	" 1678.
Evans, Lewis	17	417	" 1673.
Evans, Margaret	9	157	" 1665.
Evans, Margaret	12	477	" 1670.
Evans, Mary	7	605	" 1665.
Evans, Mary	16	402	" 1671.
Evans, Mary and John	15	448	" 1677. Children of Thomas.
Evans, Mary, Sr.	17	417	Transported 1673. (17, fol. 448).
Evans, Morgan	7	464	" 1661. Service 1667. (15, fol. 441, 446; 15, fol. 433; 12, fol. 472).
Evans, Obediah, Sr.	18	314	Transported 1667.
Evans, Obediah, Jr.	18	314	" 1667.
Evans, Rebecca	9	92	" 1665.
Evans, Rebecca	WC2	167,169	" 1679.
Evans, Rice	15	516	" 1675.
Evans, Richard	18	314	" 1667. Son of Obediah.
Evans, Richard	16	402	" 1671.
Evans, Richard	18	84	" 1674.
Evans, Sarah	6	268	" 1663. Wife of Thomas.
Evans, Sarah	15	443	" 1677.
Evans, Sarah	16	402	" 1671.
Evans, Sisily	17	417	" 1673.
Evans, Susannah	WC2	395	" 1680. Servant.
Evans, Thomas	6	18	" 1660.
Evans, Thomas	6	106,219	" 1661.
Evans, Thomas	18	150	Of St. Mary's Co., and Sarah, his wife. Service 1668. (9, fol. 432; 17, fol. 67).

NAME	Liber	Folio	REMARKS
Evans, Thomas	6	268	Transported 1663.
Evans, Thomas	15	379	Immigrated 1672. Of Kent Co.
Evans, Thomas	15	356	Transported 1674.
Evans, Thomas	18	38	Immigrated 1673 with Mary, his
wife and Mary, his daughter.			
Evans, Thomas	15	331	Transported 1675.
Evans, Thomas	15	448	Immigrated 1677.
Evans, Thomas	15	566	Transported 1678.
Evans, Thomas	WC2	254	" 1680.
Evans, Walter	18	313	" 1675.
Evans, Lieut. William	ABH	5,12	Immigrated 1646. (See Evins).
			(2, fol. 440).
Evans, William	Q	208	Immigrated 1647.
Evans, William	5	515	Transported 1661.
Evans, William	15	532	Service 1668.
Evans, William	12	475	Transported 1670.
Evans, William	18	121,160	" 1674.
Evans, William	16	402	" 1671.
Evans, William	15	448	" 1677. Son of Thomas.
Evans, William	15	446,523	" 1678.
Evell, Lucas	9	489	Immigrated 1665.
Evely, William	WC2	380	Transported 1675-80. Servant.
Evenden, Thomas	12	393	" 1669.
Evens, Franc	5	89	" 1661.
Evens, Magdalan	4	59	" 1649-52. (5, fol. 93).
Everard, Francis	6	268	" 1663.
Everard, Thomas	12	333	" 1668.
Everard, William	5	245	" 1638-43.
Everden, Edward	18	117	" 1674.
Everet, Henry	WC2	101	" 1679.
Everett, Philip	10	489	" 1667. Servant.
Everett, Susan	Q	68	" 1656.
Everson, Jacob	10	523	" 1667.
Everston, Alice	15	318	" 1674. Wife of Samuel.
Everston, Mary	15	318	" 1674. Daughter of
			Samuel.
Everston, Samuel	15	318	Immigrated 1674.
Everston, Samuel, Jr.	15	318	Transported 1674. Son of Samuel.
Everton, Samuel	8	41	Immigrated prior to 1665. (9,
			fol. 157).
Every, John	5	367	Transported 1649.
Every, William	5	607	" 1663.
Eves, Edward	9	356	" 1666.
Eves, Robert	WC2	395	" 1680. Servant.
Eveson, William	15	453	" 1675.
Evett, John	16	304	Immigrated from Virginia 1671.
			Of Somerset Co.
Evill, John	15	397	Transported 1675.
Evins, Ann	18	4	" 1674.
Evins, Lieut. William	2	255	Immigrated 1646. (See Evans).
Evitt, Arthur	8	486	Transported 1664.

NAME	Liber	Folio	REMARKS
Evitts, Ellen	9	21	Transported 1665. Wife of Nathaniel.
Evitts, Mary	9	21	Transported 1665. Daughter of Nathaniel.
Evitts, Nathaniel	9	21	Immigrated 1665. Of Talbot Co.
Ewen, Ann	ABH	40	Transported 1649.
Ewen, Ann	ABH	140	" 1651. Wife of William.
Ewen, Ann	2	615	" 1649. Daughter of Richard.
Ewen, John	ABH	40	Transported 1649.
Ewen, John	2	615	" 1649. Son of Richard.
Ewen, Richard	ABH	40	Immigrated 1649.
Ewen, Richard	2	615	" 1649 with his wife, four children and four other persons.
Ewen, Richard	4	66	Assigns land to his son-in-law, Richard Talbot, 1659.
Ewen, Richard	9	25	Transported 1665.
Ewen, Richard, Jr.	ABH	40	" 1649.
Ewen, Richard, Jr.	2	615	" 1649. Son of Richard.
Ewen, Sophia	ABH	40	" 1649. Wife of Richard.
Ewen, Suffa	2	615	" 1649. Wife of Richard.
Ewen, Susanna	ABH	40	" 1649.
Ewen, Susanna	2	615	" 1649. Daughter of Richard.
Ewen, William	ABH	140	Immigrated 1651. Of Patuxent River.
Ewens, Barbara	Q	449	Transported 1658.
Ewens, John	16	532	" 1668-70.
Ewens, Philip	11	139	Service 1667. Of St. Mary's Co.
Ewens, Mr. Richard	ABH	174	Immigrated 1650 with wife.
Ewens, Walter	9	304	Transported 1665.
Ewens, Capt. William	4	86	Immigrated prior to 1659.
Ewry, John	12	334	Transported 1668.
Ewstis, James	WC2	160,182	Immigrated 1680. Of Talbot Co.
Exelby, Jane	WC2	21	Transported 1679.
Exon, Elizabeth	16	591	Service 1672. Of Calvert Co.
Exon, Henry	12	355	" 1669.
Eyels, Mary	15	569	Transported 1678.
Ezard, Ann	WC2	65	" 1679. Servant.
Fable, Julian	6	132	" 1649.
Fadrie, Ann	16	91	" 1670.
Fadrie, John	16	91	" 1670.
Fadrie, Mary	16	91	" 1670.
Fagel, Susan	3	24	" 1650. Servant.
Faine, John	4	12	" about 1655. An Irish servant.
Fairefax, Nicolas	2	346	Immigrated 1633. (See Ferfex, Firfax).
Faireharson, Alexander	ABH	276	Transported 1651.
Fairfax, Mr. Nicholas	ABH	67	Immigrated 1633.
Fairfield, James	9	32	Transported 1664.
Faliner, Mathew	12	216	" 1669.

NAME	Liber	Folio	REMARKS
Falkner, Edward	17	608	Transported 1673.
Fall, Anthony, Jr.	17	76	" 1668.
Fall, Elizabeth	17	76	" 1668. Wife of Anthony.
Fall, Elizabeth	17	76	" 1668. Daughter of Anthony.
Famet, Nicholas	16	482	Transported 1670-1.
Fanin, Ellen	15	553	" 1678.
Faning, Elinor	WC2	57	" 1678.
Fanklin, Henry	15	560	" 1678.
Fanks, Pr. Sn.	Q	317	" 1658. (See Franks).
Fann, Henry	12	341	" 1668.
Fann, Thomas	WC2	110	" 1676. Servant.
Fannill, Jone	15	499	" 1677.
Fannin, Pat	15	553	" 1678.
Fanning, Edmond	12	348	Immigrated 1669. Of St. Mary's Co.
Fanning, John	12	189	Transported 1668.
Fanning, John	16	95	" 1670.
Faraer, Hannah	9	28	" 1664.
Farbott, Gabriel	WC2	396	" 1680. Servant.
Farbuson, William	11	265	" 1667.
Fardin, Jone	9	304	" 1665.
Fardinande, Peter	13	33	" 1668.
Farebank, Daniel	10	469	" 1667.
Farebrother, John	15	356,369	" 1676.
Farefax, Thomas	11	171	Dec. 18, 1667, Wm. Stanley of Calvert Co. demands land for transporting himself, Thos. Farefax and others.
Farell, Joane	11	442	Transported 1668.
Farent, William	18	141	" 1674 with Ann.
Fares, Roger	13	113	" 1670.
Fargason, Christian	4	552	" 1661. Daughter of Myles.
Fargason, Ellen	4	552	" 1661. Wife of Myles.
Fargason, Myles	4	552	Immigrated 1659.
Fargison, Grace	15	322	Transported 1674.
Faris, Peter	13	114	" 1670.
Farly, Arthur	15	565	" 1679.
Farman, Cottam	7	567	" 1657. Servant.
Farmadis, Eleanor	18	84	" 1674.
Farmer, Edward	15	433	" 1677.
Farmer, Elizabeth	4	570	" 1661.
Farmer, Grace	15	527	" 1678.
Farmer, Isaac	WC2	415	" 1666-80. Servant.
Farmer, Michael	Q	197	" 1658. Service 1666. (9, fol. 374).
Farmer, Richard	ABH	10,244	Transported 1639.
Farmer, Richard	2	425	" 1640.
Farmer, Richard	ABH	151	" 1649.
Farmer, Samuel	5	261	" 1660.
Farmer, Sarah	7	502	" 1659.
Farmer, Sarah	WC2	168-9	" 1680.
Farmer, William	12	403	" 1669.
Farmer, William	15	535	" 1678.

NAME	Liber	Folio	REMARKS
Farmor, Price	17	440	Transported 1673.
Farmur, Sarah	10	117	" 1666.
Farnandise, Pedroe	11	570	" 1668.
Farnando, Jeremiah	WC2	112	" 1679.
Farne, Robert	17	65	" 1669.
Farnely, Francis	16	85	" 1670.
Farr, George	ABH	323	" 1651. Servant.
Farr, John	9	451	" 1666.
Farr, John	15	433	" 1677.
Farre, Edward	17	330	" 1672.
Farrell, Alexander	16	308,537	Immigrated 1671. Of Virginia.
Farrell, Katherine	15	565	Transported 1679.
Farrell, James	WC2	287	" 1680.
Farren, John	16	439	" 1671.
Farrington, Ann	17	74	Immigrated 1671. Wife of Robert.
Farrington, Jane	17	74	" 1671. Daughter of Robert.
Farrington, Robert	17	74	Immigrated 1671.
Farrow, William	6	267	" 1653.
Farrs, James	17	607	Transported 1673.
Farthing, Joane	5	82	" 1661.
Farthing, John	15	416	" 1677.
Fatly, Arthur	15	565	" 1679.
Faulkener, Elizabeth	9	190	" 1665.
Faulkener, Francis	9	190	" 1665. (10, fol. 306).
Faulkener, John, Sr.	9	190	" 1665, of Hog Pen Neck, Kent Co. (10, fol. 306).
Faulkener, John, Jr.	9	190	Transported 1665. (10, fol. 306).
Faulkener, Thomas	9	190	" 1665. (10, fol. 306).
Faulkener, William	9	175	" 1665.
Faulkner, Elizabeth	10	306	" Jan. 1665. Wife of John.
Faulkner, Elizabeth	15	413	Transported 1677.
Favenell, Francis	15	357	" 1676.
Fawcett, John	6	211	" 1657.
Fawkes, John	15	548	Immigrated 1679. Of Calvert Co.
Fawkland, Richard	12	554	Transported 1670.
Fawsett, Charles	WC2	321	" 1680. Son of Rhodah.
Fawsett, Elizabeth	WC2	321	" 1680. Daughter of Rhodah.
Fawsett, John	WC2	320	Transported 1680.
Fawsett, Rhodah	WC2	321	Immigrated 1680 with 4 children.
Fawsett, Thomas	WC2	321	Transported 1680. Son of Rhodah.
Fawsett, William	WC2	321	" 1680. Son of Rhodah.
Fawskitt, Thomas	WC2	321	Immigrated 1680.
Fawson, William	15	450,507	Transported 1677.
Fayre, William	5	413	" 1661. Servant.
Feake, Mary	10	343	" 1665.
Feakes, Sarah	6	105	" 1663.
Feakine, John	20	184	" from Ireland 1678.
Feald, William	15	534	" 1678.

NAME	Liber	Folio	REMARKS
Fear, Richard	11	374	Transported 1668.
Featherstone, John	WC2	206	" 1679. Servant.
Featley, Sarah	Q	317	" 1658.
Fedgin, Francis	11	337	" 1668.
Fee, Reynold	11	374	" 1668.
Feear, John	15	531	" 1678.
Feebey, Edward	9	400	" 1666.
Feedes, Henry	10	568	" 1667, on a ship from Hull. Servant.
Feild, Edward	16	43	Transported 1670.
Feild, Elizabeth	9	334	" 1666.
Feild, John	15	573	Service 1664. Of Calvert Co.
Feild, John	6	118	Transported 1655.
Feild, John	16	10	" 1670.
Feild, Mary	15	573	Service 1664. Wife of John.
Feild, Sarah	17	486	Transported 1667.
Feild, Sarah	12	269	" 1668. Daughter of Elizabeth Williams.
Feild, Thomas	20	185	Transported 1679.
Feild, Walter	18	174	" 1674.
Feild, William	15	501	" 1678.
Feilder, William	16	67	" 1670.
Feilding, James	18	152	" 1674.
Feirix, George	6	87	" 1653.
Felgate, Joan	12	406	" 1669.
Fell, Anna	17	552	" from N.Y. 1672.
Fell, Edward	6	117	" 1659.
Fell, Margery	17	552	" from N.Y. 1672.
Fellett, Abell	5	514	" 1660.
Fellman, Ann	15	501	" 1678.
Fellman, John	15	343	Service 1675.
Felmore, William	15	567	Transported 1678.
Felp, Sarah	6	85	" 1657.
Felstead, Elizabeth	WC2	123	" about 1662. Widow. Of St. Mary's Co.
Felstead, William	7	638	Transported 1665.
Felsted, William	6	290	" 1663.
Felton, John	ABH	141	Immigrated 1651. Of Patuxent River.
Felton, Katherine	Q	28	Immigrated 1653-7. Wife of John. Married secondly, John Phillips prior to 1675. (15, fol. 290).
Felton, Philip	Q	28	Immigrated 1653-7.
Fencott, Ann	10	433	Transported 1667.
Fencott, John	9	431	" 1666. Of Virginia.
Fend, John	7	86	" 1659.
Fendall, Samuel	7	576	Immigrated 1665.
Fenley, David	11	581	Transported 1668.
Fenly, Mary	5	256	" 1663.
Fenn, Thomas	15	308	Service 1675. Of Dorchester Co.
Fennell, Mary	15	438	Transported Oct. 1677.
Fennell, Thomas	Q	18	" 1650.

NAME	Liber	Folio	REMARKS
Fennemore, Josias	4	204	Transported 1659.
Fennes, Thomas	12	472	" 1670.
Fennick, Mary	11	552	" 1668.
Fennie, Richard	5	245	" 1638-43.
Fennile, Katherine	15	499	" 1677.
Fennry, Derby	7	80	" 1664.
Fenwick, Cutberd	1	110	" 1633.
Fenwick, Cuthbert	ABH	94,244	" 1633 from Virginia.
Servant to Thos. Cornwalleys, Esq.			
Fenwick, Elisha	7	496	Transported 1664.
Fenwick, Mrs. Jane	Q	115	Immigrated 1649.
Fenwick, Thomas	13	1	Transported 1669. Servant.
Ferby, Henry	6	142	" 1657.
Fereley, James	9	216	" 1665.
Ferfex, Nicholas	1	17,42	Immigrated 1633. (See Fairefax, Firfax).
Feribee, Thomas	15	505	Transported 1678.
Ferings, Mary	Q	71	" 1652-3.
Fermer, Richard	1	26	" since 1635.
Fermor, Richard	ABH	60	" since 1635. Servant.
Fernandes, Anthonio	5	246	" 1660 by Philip Calvert, Esq.
Fernando, Peter	12	357	Transported 1669.
Ferne, Mary	15	301	" 1675.
Fernley, Henry	WC2	157-158, 247	Immigrated 1680. Of St. Mary's Co.
Fernty, Eleanor	13	1	Transported 1669. Servant.
Ferrar, Margaret	4	533	" 1659.
Ferrar, Sarah	4	533	" 1659.
Ferrell, Hannah	15	530	" 1678.
Ferriar, Thomas	8	478	" 1665.
Ferrill, Alexander	11	307	" 1668.
Ferris (Ferrys), Grace	WC2	253,398	" 1680.
Ferris, John	15	429	" 1674.
Ferris (Ferrys), John	WC2	253,398	" 1680.
Ferrissell, Alexander	5	207	" 1662.
Ferrys, Charles	15	525	" 1678.
Fersdon, Thomas	ABH	150	" about 1637. Servant.
Fesie, Ann	15	565	" 1679.
Fesly, John	4	551	" 1661.
Festus, Katherine	7	528	" 1664.
Fetcher, Samuel	6	137	" 1659.
Fetcherstone, Thomas	10	272	" 1666.
Fetherstone, Ann	17	448	" 1673.
Fettplace, Thomas	6	119	" 1653.
Fiddey, Alexander	12	202	" 1669. Servant.
Fiddler, George	18	177	" 1674. Service 1676. (15, fol. 377).
Fidell, Sara	3	24	Transported 1650. Servant.
Fidimore, Richard	15	322	" 1675.
Fidler, George	WC2	308	" 1678.

NAME	Liber	Folio	REMARKS
Fidler, George	WC2	23	Transported 1679. Servant.
Fidler, John the	5	339	" 1663.
Fidler, Thomas	1	171	" 1639.
Fidor, Richard	15	534	" 1677.
Field, Cornelius	WC2	128	" 1679.
Field, Edward	WC2	59-60	Service 1679.
Field, James	9	216	Transported 1665.
Field, Mary	ABH	12,33	Servant 1644. (ABH, fol. 246).
Filiale, William	12	552	Immigrated 1670. Of St. Mary's Co.
Filkins, Robert	18	37	Transported 1673.
Fillingham, Richard	17	355	Service 1672.
Fillmore, Elizabeth	15	430	Transported 1677.
Fillpot, William	9	55	" 1665.
Fillpott, Jerome	6	95	" 1659.
Finch, Constance	6	107	" 1663.
Finch, Francis	5	532	Immigrated 1659.
Finch, Guy	18	291	Transported 1674.
Finch, James	ABH	104	" 1641.
Finch, Joseph	12	333	" 1669.
Finch, Mary	16	465	" by Francis, Oct. 1664. Of Kent Co.
Finch, Peter	15	520	Transported 1677.
Finch, Roger	18	387	" 1668.
Finch, Samuel	16	507	" 1671.
Finch, Sibbell	10	277	" 1666.
Fingles, George	15	553	" 1678.
Finley, Elizabeth	11	581	" 1668.
Finley, John	WC2	65	" 1679.
Finney, Elizabeth	16	293	" 1671. Daughter of William.
Finney, Mary	16	293	Transported 1671. Wife of William.
Finney, Mary	16	293	" 1671. Daughter of William.
Finney, Susanna	16	293	Transported 1671. Daughter of William.
Finney, William	16	293	Immigrated 1671 with wife and three daughters. Of Talbot Co. Gent.
Finton, William	WC2	65	Transported 1679.
Firby, Cornelius	6	159	" 1658.
Firby, James	6	133	" 1654.
Firfax, Nicholas	1	41	Immigrated 1633. (See Fairefax, Ferfex).
Fiscariet, Thomas	11	546	Transported 1668.
Fish, Edmund	12	190	" 1668.
Fish, Geoffrey	5	59	" 1660.
Fish, James	15	454	" Oct. 1677.
Fish, John	13	17	" 1668.
Fish, Thomas	15	433	" 1677.
Fisher, Alice	7	491	" 1663.
Fisher, Ann	7	529	" 1664. (9, fol. 216).
Fisher, Benjamin	12	584	" 1670. Servant.

NAME	Liber	Folio	REMARKS
Fisher, Edward	15	318,437	Transported 1674. (15, fol. 552).
Fisher, Elizabeth	5	247	" 1661.
Fisher, Elizabeth	15	500	" 1675.
Fisher, James	4	14	" 1659. Servant.
Fisher, John	ABH	369	" 1651. Servant.
Fisher, John	6	85	" 1656.
Fisher, John	18	24	" 1674.
Fisher, Katherine	1	166	" 1650. Servant.
Fisher, Margaret	6	17	" 1663.
Fisher, Margaret	7	461	" 1664. Service 1668. (12, fol. 281).
Fisher, Mary	18	174	Transported 1674.
Fisher, Mary	15	454	" Oct. 1677.
Fisher, Nathaniel	4	568	" 1658. Service 1672. (17, fol. 44).
Fisher, Robert	15	359,370	Transported 1676. Of Calvert Co.
Fisher, Samuel	5	2	" 1661.
Fisher, Samuel	15	358	" 1675.
Fisher, Thomas	9	35	" 1664. Service 1672. (16, fol. 459).
Fisher, Thomas	15	369	Transported 1676.
Fisher, William	5	210	Immigrated prior to 1662.
Fisher, William	6	17	Transported 1663.
Fisher, William	9	35	" 1664.
Fisher, William	9	157	" 1665.
Fisher, William	18	274	Of Virginia, Chirurgeon, disposes of land in Maryland with consent of his wife, Frances, 1666.
Fisher, William	15	535	Transported 1678.
Fisher, Mr. William	7	427	Immigrated 1664 with 2 servants.
Fishwick, Edward	WC2	223-224	" from Virginia 1680. Of St. Mary's Co.
Fiswick, Edward	13	127	Immigrated from Virginia 1671. Of St. Mary's Co.
Fitch, Richard	6	216	Transported 1663.
Fitchen, Margaret	5	260	" 1662.
Fitter, William	ABH	94	" 1633. Servant.
Fitter, William	1	110	" 1633.
Fitzgaret, Garrt.	16	507	" 1671.
Fitzgaret, James	16	435	" 1671.
Fitz Gerald, Cate	15	553	" 1678.
Fitz Gerald, Luke	15	553	" 1678.
Fitz Gerald, Moriss	15	553	" 1678. (20, fol. 184). (from Ireland).
Fitz Gerald, Thomas	15	553	Transported 1678. (WC2, fol. 57).
Fitz Gerard, Richard	15	322	" 1675.
Fitz Gerrard, Gerrard	11	570	" prior to 1668. (17, fol. 357).
Fitzharbert, Dorothy	16	78	Transported 1670.
Fitzharbert, Edward, Esq.	16	78	Immigrated 1670 with Dorothy and John. Of St. Mary's County.

NAME	Liber	Folio	REMARKS
Fitzharbert, John	16	78	Transported 1670.
Fitzherbert, Mr. Francis	Q	416	Immigrated 1658.
Fitzherbert, Francis	16	112,403	Transported 1671 by Sir Wm. Talbot, Bart.
Fitzhugh, Henry	12	497	Immigrated 1670. Of Somerset Co.
Fitzpatrick, Griz'l	15	527	Transported 1678.
Fitzwalters, Garrett	1	171	" about 1639.
Fitz Williams, John	6	268	" 1663.
Fizzell, Thomas	Q	189	Immigrated 1658.
Flambeth, Abel	6	131	Transported 1654.
Flambrid, Jasper	12	360	Service 1667.
Flaming, Dor.	15	505	Transported 1678.
Flamingham, James	15	433	" 1677.
Fleck, Henry	15	428	" 1677.
Fleet, John	15	517	" 1678.
Fleet, Katherine	15	429	" 1674.
Fleete, Capt. Henry	1	97	Special Warrant from Lord Baltimore, 1640.
Fleete, Roger	16	86	Transported 1670.
Fleetwood, Edward	15	316	Immigrated 1675. Of St. Mary's Co.
Flegan, George	12	617	Transported 1670.
Fleming, Edward	15	446	" 1677.
Fleming, John	7	81	" 1662.
Flemings, John	15	452	" 1678.
Flemmin, Daniel	4	204	" 1659.
Flemming, John	5	319	" prior to 1663.
Flemming, John	WC2	309	" 1678.
Flenning, Patrick	11	309	" 1665.
Flestell, Elizabeth	18	285	" 1674.
Fletcher, Anne	Q	70	Servant 1658.
Fletcher, Curtis	13	34	Immigrated 1670. Of St. Mary's Co.
Fletcher, Edward	WC2	23	Transported 1679. Servant.
Fletcher, Elizabeth	Q	29	Servant 1657.
Fletcher, Francis	15	429	Transported 1674.
Fletcher, Henry	5	343	" 1663.
Fletcher, James	12	341	" 1668.
Fletcher, Joseph	WC2	310	" 1675. (15, fol. 322).
Fletcher, Richard	12	202	" 1669.
Fletcher, Sarah	9	356	" 1666.
Fletcher, Thomas	16	376	" 1676.
Fletcher, William	4	63	" 1645.
Fletcher, William	12	194	" 1668. Servant.
Flewelling, John	16	414	" 1671.
Flicke, James	18	293	" 1674.
Flid, Richard	15	369	" 1676.
Fling, Bryan	WC2	120	" 1680.
Fling, Philip	15	438	" Oct. 1677.
Flint, Richard	13	17	" 1668.
Flint, Tobias	6	81	" 1659.
Flints, Hannah	8	501	" 1665.
Floid, Jane	12	333	" 1668.

NAME	Liber	Folio	REMARKS
Flood, John	9	326	Immigrated 1666.
Flood, Katherine	6	171	Transported 1663.
Flood, Simon	15	396	" 1677.
Floode, John	5	73	" 1660-1.
Florey, Eleanor	15	430	" 1677.
Flowd, Elizabeth	15	413	" 1677.
Flower, Katherine	16	124	" 1671.
Flower, John	16	86	" 1670.
Flower, Sarah	17	571	" 1673.
Flower, Thomas	15	454	" 1677.
Flower, William	11	344	" 1668.
Flowers, Richard	18	94	" 1674.
Flowers, Richard	15	449	Service 1677. Of Somerset Co.
Flowers, Richard	WC2	346-347	Service 1680.
Flowers, Thomas	7	506	Transported prior to 1664.
Flowers, Thomas	10	503	Immigrated 1667.
Floy, William	WC2	394	Transported 1680. Servant.
Floyd, Elizabeth	9	353	" 1666.
Floyd, Elizabeth	WC2	16,170	" 1679. Servant.
Floyd, Francis	15	520	Service 1675.
Floyd, Hugh	15	453	Transported 1676.
Floyd, John	9	55	" 1665.
Floyd, Nicholas	9	49	Immigrated 1665.
Floyd, Richard	7	496	Transported 1664.
Floyd, Richard	15	534	" 1674.
Floyd, Robert	18	4	" 1674.
Floyd, Thomas	7	567	" 1665.
Floyd, Thomas	16	507	" 1671. Service 1677. (15, fol. 418).
Floyd, Winifred	6	293	Transported 1664. (9, fol. 505; 12, fol. 492).
Floyer, Thomas	5	203	Transported 1662.
Floyle, John	18	291	" 1674.
Fluelling, James	9	353	" 1666.
Fluelling, Samuel	WC2	318	Service 1680.
Flute, Alice	6	125	Transported 1656.
Flute, Jarvis	6	95	" 1657.
Flyharty, John	WC2	187	" 1678.
Flyharty, Margaret	WC2	187	" 1678.
Flynge, Margaret	WC2	128	" 1679.
Focroft, Isaac	15	295	Of Virginia, acquires land in Md.
Fogarth, John	WC2	158	Transported 1680.
Follam, John	15	554	" 1678.
Follett, Henry	11	344	" 1668.
Follom, John	WC2	57	" 1678.
Folly, John	17	475	" 1673.
Fonworth, John	Q	430	" 1658.
Fook, Col. Garrett	7	560	Immigrated 1665. (See Fowke).
Fook, Richard	7	569	Transported 1663-4.
Fook, Samuel	7	87	" 1661.
Fookes, Edward	15	445	" 1678.

NAME	Liber	Folio	REMARKS
Fookes, Henry	WC2	201	Transported 1680. Servant.
Fookes, Hester	18	4	" 1674.
Fookes, Jasper	6	85	" 1660.
Fookes, Richard	15	353	" 1674.
Fookett, Peter	5	238	" 1662.
Fooler, Peter	17	451	" 1673.
Foorte, Richard	6	85	" 1659.
Foot, James	9	488	Immigrated 1665 with wife.
Foot, Mary	Q	204	Servant 1658.
Foot, Richard	Q	470	Of London, Merchant. Undertakes to immigrate 1657.
Foote, Thomas	WC2	133	Transported 1680.
Footman, Henry	Q	18	" 1658.
Fope, Abraham	Q	430	" 1658.
Forbis, John	18	126	" 1674.
Forbis, Margaret	WC2	83	" 1679. Wife of William.
Forbis, William	WC2	83,241, 257,258	Immigrated 1679 with wife and son. Of Dorchester Co.
Forbis, William, Jr.	WC2	83	Transported 1679. Son of William.
Forbush, James	5	244	" 1662.
Forbush, John	16	70	" 1668-70.
Forbush, Margaret	5	244	" 1662. Wife of James.
Forcarson, Alexander	Q	202	Immigrated prior to 1658.
Forcey, Jeremy	4	212	Transported 1659. (5, fol. 2).
Ford, Alice	5	2	" 1661.
Ford, Amb.	15	390	" 1676.
Ford, Ann	15	437	" 1677.
Ford, Constance	6	122	" 1660.
Ford, David	16	79	" 1670.
Ford, Edward	11	482	" 1668.
Ford, Elizabeth	17	572	" 1672.
Ford, Elizabeth	18	166	" 1674.
Ford, Hannah	ABH	244	" 1640.
Ford, Joane	6	235	" 1663.
Ford, John	10	571	" 1667. Of Virginia.
Ford, John	17	572	" 1672.
Ford, Lydia	5	245	Service 1663. Wife of Robert. (10, fol. 499).
Ford, Margaret	15	527	Transported 1678.
Ford, Mary	ABH	95	" 1641. Servant. (1, fol. 113).
Ford, Mary	10	566	Transported 1667.
Ford, Peter	10	569	" 1665-6.
Ford, Rebecca	6	97	" 1659.
Ford, Robert	ABH	102	" 1641. A boy. (1, fol. 130).
Ford, Robert	10	499	Immigrated 1667.
Ford, Robert	15	443	Transported 1673.
Ford, Sarah	WC2	364	Widow of William 1680. Died 1674-1680.

NAME	Liber	Folio	REMARKS
Ford, Stephen	9	433	Transported 1663.
Ford, Thomas	ABH	348	" prior to 1652. Servant.
Ford, Thomas	WC2	67	Immigrated from Virginia 1673. Of Talbot Co.
Ford, Thomas	15	452	Transported 1678.
Ford, Tomison	WC2	120	" 1680.
Ford, William	WC2	364	Married Sarah, daughter of Richard Preston.
Ford, William	15	443	Transported 1670.
Forde, Ann	17	417	" 1673.
Fordum, Ann	Q	183	Servant 1658.
Foreland, Gillian	16	435	Transported 1671.
Foreman, Katherine	WC2	316	Service 1680.
Foreman, Robert	18	94	Transported 1674.
Forgason, William	15	525	Immigrated 1678.
Forgeson, Anne	WC2	318	Service 1680. Wife of William.
Forgeson, Henrick	8	483	Transported 1665. From Virginia.
Forgeson, William	WC2	318	Rights 1680.
Forgison, Barbara	15	544	Transported 1674.
Fork, Mary	5	610	" 1658.
Formaleer, Cornelius	WC2	21	" 1679.
Forman, Katherine	18	331	" 1674.
Forman, William	18	329	" 1675.
Forrell, Mary	2	510,613	" 1648. Servant.
Forrest, Patrick	2	613	" 1648. Servant.
Forrest, Henry	15	433	" 1677.
Forrest, John	15	565	" 1679.
Forrest, Michael	6	120	" 1657.
Forrest, Patrick	ABH	123,413	" 1648.
Forrester, John	12	242	" 1669. Servant.
Forrist, Jane	18	152	" 1674.
Forset, Heatry	17	350	Immigrated 1665. Wife of Thomas.
Forset, Thomas	17	350	" 1667.
Forsey, Jeremiah	18	24	Transported 1674.
Forstall, Catherine	WC2	82	" 1679.
Forster, Ann	ABH	370	" 1653. Wife of Richard.
Forster, Ann	ABH	370	" 1653. Daughter of Richard. (4, fol. 533).
Forster, Edward	4	554	Immigrated prior to 1661.
Forster, Jane	ABH	370	Transported 1653. Daughter of Richard.
Forster, John	4	554	Immigrated prior to 1661.
Forster, John	7	62	Transported 1662.
Forster, Mr. Michael	12	386	" 1669.
Forster, Richard	ABH	370	Immigrated 1653.
Forster, Richard, Jr.	ABH	370	Transported 1653. Son of Richard.
Forster, William	WC2	395	" 1680. Servant.
Fort, John	15	503	" 1678.
Fort, Marmaduke	6	129	" 1653.
Forth, Alice	17	351	" 1670.
Forth, Angell	17	351	" 1671.

NAME	Liber	Folio	REMARKS
Forth, Ann	17	351	Transported 1670.
Forth, Hugh	17	351	Immigrated 1670. Of Baltimore Co.
Forth, Joane	17	351	Transported 1670.
Forth, John	16	394	" 1671.
Forth, Joseph	7	507	" 1663.
Forth, Mary	17	351	" 1670.
Forth, Rosamond	17	351	" 1670. Wife of Hugh.
Forth, Rosamond	17	351	" 1670.
Fortin, Robert	15	381	Service 1675.
Fortington, Eliza	12	472	Transported 1670.
Fortry, George	15	501	" 1678.
Fortune, David	15	446	" 1672.
Fortune, David	WC2	106	" 1679.
Fortune, Eleanor	5	468	" 1662. (6, fol. 15).
Fortune, John	5	466	" 1662.
Fortune, Robert	12	415	" 1669.
Forwich, William	11	265	" 1667.
Foscue, Elizabeth	15	436	" 1677.
Foscue, George	6	120	Immigrated 1646.
Fosett, John	16	109	Transported 1665.
Foss, Richard	6	215	" prior to 1653.
Fossett, Julian	6	80	" 1659.
Fossett, Patrick	6	95	" 1657.
Fossitt, Anthony	7	508	" 1664.
Foster, Alice	17	551	" 1673.
Foster, Ann	4	533	" 1659. Wife of Richard.
Foster, Ann	6	81	" 1661.
Foster, Ann	9	489	Immigrated 1665.
Foster, Ann	WC2	16	Transported 1679.
Foster, Christopher	11	581	" 1668.
Foster, Christopher	15	378	" 1674.
Foster, Edward	5	491	" 1663.
Foster, Elizabeth	13	122	" 1670.
Foster, Elizabeth	16	354	" 1671.
Foster, Elizabeth	WC2	10,17	" 1679.
Foster, James	WC2	415	" 1666-80. Servant.
Foster, James	15	397	" 1676.
Foster, Jane	4	533	" 1659. Daughter of Richard.
Foster, John	7	107	Transported 1662.
Foster, John	6	255	" 1663.
Foster, John	7	150	" 1664.
Foster, John	9	270	" 1665.
Foster, John	11	104	" 1667. (12, fol. 357; 12, fol. 380).
Foster, John	11	524	Immigrated 1668.
Foster, John	15	380	Transported 1676. (15, fol. 402).
Foster, Joseph	9	45	" 1665.
Foster, Margaret	11	581	" 1668.
Foster, Mary	15	544	" 1674.
Foster, Nathaniel	15	565	" 1679.

NAME	Liber	Folio	REMARKS
Foster, Nicholas	7	81	Transported 1657.
Foster, Richard	5	339	" 1657. (11,fol.168).
Foster, Richard	16	71	" 1670.
Foster, Richard	4	533	Immigrated 1659. (9,fol.490).
Foster, Richard, Jr.	4	533	Transported 1659. Son of Richard.
Foster, Robert	13	119	Immigrated 1667. Of Calvert Co.
Foster, Robert	16	411	Transported 1671.
Foster, Sarah	12	334	" 1668.
Foster, Sarah	15	376	" 1676.
Foster, Thomas	Q	183	Servant 1658.
Foster, William	16	93	Transported 1670.
Foster, William	6	268	" 1662.
Foster, William	10	305	Immigrated Oct.1666. Of Anne Arundel Co.
Foster, William	16	93	Transported 1670.
Fostor, Edward	6	171	" 1663. Servant.
Fostor, Elizabeth	20	184	" from Ireland 1678.
Fostor, John	6	47	" 1661.
Fouke, Francis	16	94	Of Charles Co. and wife. Service 1670.
Foukes, Robert	17	605	Service 1673.
Foukhier, Henry	17	70	Transported 1671.
Foulcher, William	12	357	Immigrated 1669. Of Somerset Co.
Fouldingworth, Andrew	Q	430	Transported 1658.
Foule, Cornelius	10	433	" 1667.
Fouler, Alice	17	469	" 1673.
Fouler, Mary	17	469	" 1673.
Foulger, John	16	88	" 1670.
Foulkes, Robert	16	409	" from Virginia 1671.
Foulsheat, Margaret	18	314	Immigrated 1667.
Fountain, Nicholas	6	347	Transported 1663.
Fountain, Richard	5	73	" 1660-1. (16,fol.393).
Fountain, William	WC2	114-115	Rights 1680.
Fountaine, Allen	12	406	Transported 1669.
Fountaine, Aran	16	428	" 1670-1.
Fountaine, John	Q	70	Servant 1658.
Fountaine, Ralph	9	448	Transported 1666.
Fountane, Rebecca	15	397	" 1676.
Fourbush, John	5	125	" 1662.
Fourtane, Richard	15	362	" 1676.
Fowk, David	11	344	" 1668.
Fowke, Ann	15	181	Widow of Job Chandler, living 1673.
Fowke, Gerrard	15	160	Son of the late Col. Gerrard Fowke, by Anne, his wife, living 1673. (See Fook).
Fowke, Peter	8	484	Transported 1665.
Fowke, Thomas	10	463	Of "Pungatage", married Amy, widow of Nicholas Waddylove, prior to 1665.
Fowle, William	WC2	260	Service 1680. Of St. Mary's Co.
Fowler, Dorothy	4	610	Transported 1661.
Fowler, Edward	15	396	" 1676.
Fowler, Elizabeth	11	582	" 1668.

NAME	Liber	Folio	REMARKS
Fowler, John	Q	30	Transported 1658.
Fowler, John	4	610	" 1661. (5, fol. 515).
Fowler, John	9	92	" 1665.
Fowler, John	15	358	Of Talbot Co., and Sarah, his wife, Service 1675.
Fowler, John	15	397	Transported 1676.
Fowler, Nicholas	15	332	" 1675.
Fowler, Samuel	16	507	" 1671.
Fowler, Sarah	WC2	171	" 1679.
Fowler, Stephen	6	132	" 1652.
Fowler, Thomas	15	552	" 1679.
Fowler, William	6	299	" 1664.
Fowler, William	17	351	Service 1672. Of St. Mary's Co. (12, fol. 496).
Fox, Andrew	15	565	Transported 1679.
Fox, Daniel	WC2	21	" 1679.
Fox, Edward	16	85	" 1670.
Fox, Ellinor	WC2	45	" 1679.
Fox, Henry	ABH	413	" his wife about 1653-4.
Fox, James	6	133	" 1650.
Fox, James	6	294	" 1664.
Fox, John	5	245	" 1662. Servant.
Fox, John	17	596	" 1673.
Fox, John	18	4	" 1674. (15, fol. 395).
Fox, John	15	436	" 1677.
Fox, Mary	4	72	" 1658.
Fox, Mary	17	566	" 1673.
Fox, Mistress	4	136	Immigrated 1659.
Fox, Moses	15	455	Transported 1678.
Fox, Richard	7	640	" prior to 1665. Servant.
Fox, Richard	17	608	" 1673.
Fox, Robert	6	87	" 1649.
Fox, Susanna	WC2	167, 169	" 1679.
Fox, Thomas	5	211	" 1662.
Fox, Thomas	6	17	" 1663.
Fox, Thomas	16	319	" 1670, with Mary, of Virginia.
Fox, Timothy	WC2	120	Transported 1680.
Fox, William	5	218	Immigrated 1662.
Fox, William	12	190	Transported 1668. Servant.
Foxe, Ann	10	433	" 1666.
Foxe, Elizabeth	15	429	" 1674.
Foxhall, John	11	103	Of Westmoreland Co., Va., sells land in Md. 1667.
Foxhall, John	8	502	Immigrated 1665.
Foxhall, Martha	8	502	" 1665. Wife of John.
Foxhall, Mary	8	502	Transported 1665. Daughter of John
Foxon, Thomas	6	17	Transported 1663.
Foy, John	17	54	Service 1672.
Foy, Margaret	15	353	Transported 1674.

NAME	Liber	Folio	REMARKS
Frame, Arthur	12	350	Immigrated 1669. Of Virginia.
Frampton, Robert	WC2	89	Transported 1676. Servant.
Franar, Ann	4	48	" 1659. Servant.
Franar, Christian	4	48	" 1659. Servant.
Franar, Domingo	4	48	" 1659. Servant.
Franar, Edward	4	48	" 1659. Servant.
France, John	15	409	Service 1677. Of St. Mary's Co.
France, Thomas	WC2	406	Transported 1680.
Frances, John	15	540	" 1676.
Frances, Mary	9	328	" 1666. Servant.
Frances, Thomas	5	307	" 1663.
Francett, John	7	571	" 1664.
Franch, Mable	4	70	" 1659.
Franchman, Eliz.	17	463	" 1673.
Francis, Alexander	Q	430	" 1658.
Francis, Elizabeth	15	435	" 1676.
Francis, Henry	15	362	" 1676.
Francis, Jacob	6	299	" 1664.
Francis, John	17	516	" 1664.
Francis, Rachel	17	516	" 1664.
Francis, Thomas	5	221	" 1662. Servant.
Francis, Thomas	9	459	Of Anne Arundel Co. Son-in-law of William Toulson, 1666.
Francis, Walter	6	219	Transported 1663.
Francisco	ABH	66	"A Malato", 1635.
Francisco, Jo.	6	290	Transported 1663.
Franciscus, Francis	12	189	" 1668.
Franck, Michael	9	488	" 1665.
Franck, Robert	WC2	395	" 1680. Servant.
Franck, Thomas	12	341	" 1668.
Francklen, Margaret	5	73	" 1661.
Francklin, Jane	17	330	" 1672.
Francklin, John	17	351	" 1670 with Gennet, his wife.
Francklin, John	16	170	Transported 1671.
Francklin, Richard	17	351	" 1670.
Francklyn, Em	9	462	" 1665.
Francks, Isaac	17	330	" 1672.
Francks, Thomas	12	215	" 1668-9.
Franckum, John	12	209,501	" 1668.
Franers, John	15	353	" 1678.
Franke, Arnold	10	600	Immigrated 1667.
Franklin, Henry	15	560	Transported 1678.
Franklin, Joane	11	190	" 1667.
Franklin, John	5	339	" 1663.
Franklin, Margaret	5	255	" 1663.
Franklin, Richard	11	190	Immigrated 1667.
Franklin, Robert	11	168,188	" 1667.
Franklin, Thomas	11	190	Transported 1667.
Franklyn, Henry	ABH	373	" 1649. Servant.
Franks, Pr. Sr.	Q	317	" 1668.

NAME	Liber	Folio	REMARKS
Fraser, Zachariah	15	353	Transported 1675.
Frayner, Grief	5	308	" 1663.
Frayser, Alexander	15	356	" . 1675.
Freak, William	ABH	244	" 1639.
Fredd, John	1	27	" 1633-41. A boy bought of Thomas Keg of Virginia.
Frederick, Christian	Q	17	Transported 1650.
Freecklton, John	12	190	" 1668. Servant.
Freedes, Henry	10	394	" 1666. Servant.
Freek, Mary	7	529	" 1664.
Freeland, Isaac	15	454	" Oct. 1677.
Freeland, Robert	12	322	" 1669.
Freeman, Charles	7	82	" 1661. (5, fol. 319).
Freeman, Edward	15	413	Immigrated 1677.
Freeman, Elizabeth	6	27	Transported 1663.
Freeman, Elizabeth	7	581	" 1665.
Freeman, Elizabeth	9	488	" 1666.
Freeman, Francis	17	532	" 1673.
Freeman, George	17	469	" 1673.
Freeman, John	16	10,168	" 1670.
Freeman, John	17	34	And Rachel, his wife, of Somerset Co. Service 1672.
Freeman, Joseph	16	168	Transported 1670. Service 1672. (17, fol. 384).
Freeman, Mary	15	514	Transported 1677.
Freeman, Mary	15	501,514	" 1677.
Freeman, Morris	1	26	" 1635-41.
Freeman, Morris	ABH	10,244	" 1639.
Freeman, Nicholas	15	397	Immigrated 1677.
Freeman, Nathaniel	15	560	Transported 1678.
Freeman, Patrick	20	184	" from Ireland 1678.
Freeman, Rachel	17	34	Wife of John. Service 1672.
Freeman, Robert	11	319	Transported 1668. (17, fol. 491).
Freeman, Samuel	15	386	" 1676.
Freeman, Rosamond	15	396	" Dec. 1666. Wife of Timothy.
Freeman, Thomas	5	3	Transported 1661.
Freeman, Timothy	15	396	Immigrated Dec. 1666.
Freeman, William	ABH	150	Transported 1638. Servant.
Freemond, Lewis	ABH	65	" 1633.
Freemore, Joseph	11	525	Service 1668.
Freene, James	WC2	380	Transported 1675-80. Servant.
Freene, Mary	16	40	Service 1670. Wife of Thomas of St. Mary's Co.
Freere, John	WC2	21	Transported 1679.
Freman, Lewis	1	166	" 1633.
Fremond, Lewis	1	20,37,38	" 1633.
French, Hugh	5	256	" 1663. (17, fol. 185).
French, Hugh	WC2	378-379	Service 1680. Of Charles Co.
French, James	16	411	Transported 1671.
French, Margaret	WC2	120	" 1680.

NAME	Liber	Folio	REMARKS
French, Margaret	9	24	Transported 1665. Wife of Nathaniel.
French, Mary	15	505	" 1678.
French, Nathaniel	4	137	" 1659.
French, Nathaniel	9	24	Immigrated 1665.
French, William	WC2	132-134	Rights 1680. Of Plymouth.
Freshy, James	WC2	182	Transported 1680.
Fretwell, John	7	567	" 1657. Servant.
Fretwell, Roger	17	401	" 1671.
Friend, Constance	15	454	" 1677.
Frigg, Alice	8	503	Immigrated 1665.
Frippey, Margaret	12	379	Service 1669. Wife of Nicholas.
Frippey, Nicholas	12	379	Immigrated 1669. Of Dorchester Co.
Frisall, Robert	ABH	276	Transported 1651.
Frisar, Thomas	ABH	276	" 1651.
Frisby, Elizabeth	6	105	" 1649.
Frisby, Mr. James	8	130	Immigrated 1665. (7, fol. 427).
Frisby, James	8	130	Transported 1665. Son of James.
Frisby, Mary	8	130	" 1665. Wife of Mr. James.
Frisby, Mary	8	130	Transported 1665. Daughter of James.
Frisby, Thomas	8	130	Transported 1665. Son of James.
Frisby, Thomas	4	5	" 1652-9.
Frisby, William	8	130	" 1665. Son of James.
Frisell, John	ABH	230	" Sept. 1652. Servant. (See Frizell).
Frisell, Robert	15	560	Transported 1678.
Frisell, Susan	ABH	323	" 1652. Servant.
Frisell, Thomas	ABH	245	" 1651.
Frissells, Ferker	4	14	" 1659. (See Frissett).
Frissett, Farcher	4	13	Service 1659. (See Frissells).
Friswell, Thomas	12	285	Transported 1668. Servant.
Friswell, William	16	330	" 1671.
Friswith, James	12	281,514	" 1668.
Frith, Elizabeth	10	466	Service 1667. Wife of Henry.
Frith, Henry	Q	453	Transported 1658.
Frith, Henry	6	294	Immigrated 1664.
Frith, John	7	85	Transported 1661.
Frizell, Alexander	6	15	Immigrated 1657. (See Frisell).
Frizell, Duncombe	ABH	324	Transported prior to June 1652. Servant.
Frizell, James	5	489	Transported 1655.
Frizell, Mary	9	271	" 1665.
Frizell, Rebecca	6	15	" 1657. Daughter of Alexander.
Frizell, Sarah	6	15	Transported 1657. Wife of Alexander.
Frizell, William	5	491,607	Transported in 1649, Ann Porter, whom he subsequently married.
Froman, Morrice	2	425	Transported 1640.
Froman, Morris	ABH	60	" 1635. Servant.

NAME	Liber	Folio	REMARKS
Fronkom, Will	15	429	Transported 1674.
Frost, Alexander	6	133	" 1657.
Frost, Huerom	Q	18	" 1655.
Frost, Rachel	6	131	" 1655.
Frost, Rose	16	435	" 1671.
Frost, Thomas	6	63	" 1658-63.
Frost, Valentine	7	87	" 1657.
Frost, William	12	415	" 1669.
Froster, Evis	9	280	" 1665.
Froster, John	Q	316	Immigrated 1665.
Froth, John	16	393	Transported 1671.
Fruen, Braxton	15	353	Immigrated 1676.
Fruterer, Joana	15	429	Transported 1677.
Fry, David	12	203	Immigrated 1669. Of Anne Arundel County.
Fry, Edmund	12	203	Transported 1669.
Fry, Edward	15	525	Immigrated 1678. A Tailor.
Fry, Edward	WC2	30,90	" 1679. Of Somerset Co.
Fry, Joane	11	436	Transported 1668. (15, fol. 418).
Fry, Joane	WC2	41	" 1679.
Fry, William	15	433	" 1677.
Frye, Alice	WC2	381	" 1675-80. Servant.
Frye, Margaret	WC2	396	" 1680. Servant.
Fuiley, James	11	582	" 1668.
Fuish, Daniel	15	598	" 1678-9.
Fulcher, John	18	113	Service 1674. Of St. Mary's Co.
Fulford, Humphry	3	18	Transported about 1640. Servant.
Fuller, Edward	5	480	Immigrated prior to 1663. (8, fol. 41).
Fuller, Francis	6	293	Transported 1664.
Fuller, Francis	13	122	" 1669.
Fuller, George	12	317	" 1669.
Fuller, George	17	510	" 1673.
Fuller, Hugh	11	337,441	" 1668.
Fuller, John	9	93	" 1665.
Fuller, John	12	190	" 1668. Servant.
Fuller, John	15	369	" 1676.
Fuller, Martha	5	404	" 1659. (6, fol. 117).
Fuller, Mathew	12	205	" 1667.
Fuller, Nathaniel	10	541	" 1667.
Fuller, Phylida	5	248	" 1663.
Fuller, Richard	9	38	" 1665.
Fuller, Robert	8	202	" 1665.
Fuller, Samuel	10	541	" 1667.
Fuller, Sevate	9	17	" 1665.
Fuller, Thomas	6	347	" 1663.
Fuller, Thomas	17	330	" 1672.
Fuller, Thomas	WC2	278-279	Service 1680. Of St. Mary's Co.
Fullford, Humphrey	1	19,33, 171	Transported 1637. Servant.
Fulser, Edward	4	623	" 1661.
Funge, James	17	411	" 1673.

NAME	Liber	Folio	REMARKS
Furbie, Elizabeth	12	270	Immigrated 1668, with her five children. (See Furby).
Furbush, James	4	140	Transported 1656. Servant. (Quaker ?) (Q, fol. 75).
Furbush, John	17	411	Transported 1673.
Furby, Benjamin	12	280	" 1668. Son of Mrs. Elizabeth.
Furby, Elizabeth	12	280	Transported 1668. Daughter of Mrs. Elizabeth.
Furby, Mrs. Elizabeth	12	280	Immigrated 1668.
Furby, Felix	12	280	Transported 1668. Son of Mrs. Elizabeth.
Furby, George	12	280	Transported 1668. Son of Mrs. Elizabeth.
Furby, Mary	12	280	Transported 1668. Daughter of Mrs. Elizabeth.
Furker, Ann	12	496	Transported 1670.
Furley, James	18	15	" 1673.
Furlock, Abraham	5	267	" 1663.
Furlong, Edmond	5	253	" 1663. Servant.
Furmbro, Nath.	15	430	" 1667.
Furnace, Nicholas	16	113	Service 1671. Of Calvert Co.
Furnfield, John	6	216	Transported 1663.
Furnish, Olive	5	210	" 1662. Wife of William.
(6, fol. 216; 10, fol. 269; 8, fol. 495).			
Furnish, William	5	210	Immigrated 1662. (6, fol. 216; 8,
fol. 495; 10, fol. 269). Of Somerset Co.			
Furrell, Anne	WC2	339	Transported 1680. Wife of John.
Furrell, John	WC2	339-341	Immigrated 1680 with wife and son. Of Dorchester Co.
Furrell, Robert	WC2	339	Transported 1680. Son of John.
Furrill, George	15	354	" 1676.
Furrow, Benjamin	5	413	" 1657. A Youth. (5, fol. 419).
Fursden, Thomas	ABH	223	Immigrated 1650.
Furse, Henry	WC2	380	Transported 1675-80. Servant.
Furston (Fursdon), Thomas	1	17,19	" 1637.
Furth, John	6	217	" 1663.
Fusby, William	9	399	" 1666.
Futhy, Jane	WC2	120	" 1680.
Gab, Giles (Joyles)	WC2	253, 277-278	" 1680.
Gabby, William	16	507	" 1671.
Gabinett, John	8	460	" 1661.
Gad, James	16	165	Immigrated 1670. Of Somerset Co.
Gadd, Thomas	11	543	Service 1668. Of St. Mary's Co.
Gadner, Charles	5	63	Transported 1660.
Gaer, William	6	299	" 1664.
Gaffe, Ralph	16	334	Service 1667.
Gaford, Richard	15	433	Transported 1677.

174

NAME	Liber	Folio	REMARKS
Gage, Henry	15	433	Transported 1677.
Gage, John	15	452	" 1677.
Gagger, James	11	170	Service 1667. Of Anne Arundel Co.
Gaines, Richard	7	81	Married the widow of Andrew Wardner prior to 1664.
Gainey, William	17	411	Transported 1673.
Gakerlin, Mary	Q	107	Married James Veitch prior to 1658.
Gale, Ann	15	429	Transported 1677.
Gale, Catherine	5	246	" 1660.
Gale, Dorothy	11	338,344	" 1668.
Gale, Henry	17	396	" 1669.
Gale, John	6	15	" 1662.
Gale, John	15	376	" 1676.
Gale, John	15	500	" 1678.
Gale, Richard	18	335	" 1675.
Gale, Roger	15	430	" 1677.
Gale, Thomas	5	246	" 1660 by Philip Calvert, Esq.
Gale, William	6	125	Transported 1663.
Gale, William	17	469	" 1673.
Galey, John	18	313	" 1675.
Galey, Thomas	7	81	" 1663.
Gallahoe, Daniel	20	184	" from Ireland 1678.
Gallard, John	9	336	" 1661.
Gallavane, Edmund	WC2	381	" 1675-80. Servant.
Gallen, Alexander	16	512	Immigrated 1667. Of Charles Co.
Gallen, Alice	8	129	Transported 1664. Wife of Joseph.
Gallen, Joseph	8	129	Immigrated 1664.
Gallier, Martin	13	57	Transported 1670.
Gallop, Henry	17	475	" 1673.
Galloway, James	15	432	" 1677.
Galloway, Richard	4	204	" 1649.
Galloway, William	4	59	Service 1659. Married Lucy Child who had also been a servant.
Gamball, Thomas	11	496	Transported 1668.
Gamball, William	11	555	Service 1668.
Game, John	12	205	Transported 1667.
Gamer, Joane	5	467	" 1662. Wife of Thomas. (6, fol. 15).
Gamer, Thomas	5	467	Immigrated 1660. (6, fol. 15).
Gamer, William	6	84	Transported 1651.
Games, John	WC2	68	Service 1679.
Games, Mary	WC2	68	" 1679. Wife of John.
Games, Richard	4	4	" 1658.
Games, Thomas	18	338	" 1675. And Joan, his wife.
Gamlin, Margaret	18	15	Transported 1673.
Gamling, James	17	417	" 1673.
Gandey, William	11	552	" 1668.
Gandrell, John	WC2	406	" 1679.
Gandy, George	15	338	" 1676.
Gandy, William	16	418	Service 1671.

NAME	Liber	Folio	REMARKS
Ganly, John	9	216	Transported 1665.
Gannacke, William	9	321	" 1665.
Ganote, Jan.	15	397	" 1676.
Garaway, Nicholas	ABH	174	" 1649. Servant.
Garbird, Mathew	7	214	" 1661.
Garbitt, Martha	7	530	" 1664.
Gardan, Bridgett	9	328	" 1666.
Gardener, Susanna	18	279	" 1675.
Gardey, Adrian	15	318	" 1675.
Gardiner, Christopher	5	93	" prior to 1661.
Gardiner, (Elizabeth ?)	1	168	" 1637. Wife of Richard. Mother of Luke. (See Garnett).
Gardiner, Elizabeth	1	168	Transported 1637. Daughter of Richard.
Gardiner, Elizabeth	WC2	152	Transported 1680. Wife of Richard.
Gardiner, John	1	168	" 1637.
Gardiner, Julian	1	168	" 1637 and 1647. Daughter of Richard.
Gardiner, Luke	1	20	Transported 1637. (See Garnett).
Gardiner, Luke	1	167-168	" 1637 and 1647. Son of Richard.
Gardiner, Luke	3	65	Immigrated 1647 from Virginia.
Gardiner, Luke	ABH	206	Of St. Richards Manor, son and heir of Richard dec'd 1651. (See Gardner).
Gardiner, Richard	1	167-168	Immigrated 1637 with wife, children and others.
Gardiner, Richard	1	168	Transported 1637. Son of Richard.
Gardiner, Richard	WC2	152-153	Rights 1680.
Gardner, Edward	5	484	Transported 1662. Service 1668. (11, fol. 500).
Gardner, Elizabeth	15	397	Transported 1676.
Gardner, Hugh	16	83	" 1670.
Gardner, James	6	268	" 1661.
Gardner, John	10	471	" 1667.
Gardner, John	18	117	" 1674.
Gardner, John	15	359	" 1676.
Gardner, John	WC2	57,210-211,330	Service 1679. Of Talbot Co.
Gardner, Luke	ABH	50	Immigrated from Virginia 1647. Refers to a plantation in Maryland called "Sacawaxhit", which had belonged to his father (See Gardiner).
Gardner, Mary	5	188	Transported 1661. Servant.
Gardner, Mary	WC2	167,169	" 1679.
Gardner, Nathaniel	17	33	Immigrated from Virginia 1672. Of Somerset Co.
Gardner, Richard	Q	70	Transported 1649. (9, fol. 268).
Gardner, Richard	10	3	Immigrated 1665.
Gardner, Ursly	10	352	Transported 1666.
Gare, Eleanor	15	322	" 1675.
Gare, Richard	8	503	" 1665.
Gares, John	WC2	406	" 1678.

NAME	Liber	Folio	REMARKS
Garey, John	Q	28	Son-in-law (Stephen ?) of Peter Sharp, 1658.
Garford, George	15	531	Transported 1678.
Garland, Elizabeth	15	505	" 1678.
Garland, John	9	94	" 1665.
Garland, Mary	15	438	" Oct. 1677.
Garland, Samuel	5	90	" 1660.
Garland, William	WC2	24,106	" 1678. Servant.
Garlyn, Syman	16	91	" 1670.
Garnall, Richard	4	570	" 1661.
Garner, John	15	322	" 1674.
Garner, John	WC2	48	" 1679.
Garner, July	7	581	" 1665.
Garner, Stephen	17	454	" 1672.
Garner, William	7	560	" 1665.
Garnet, John	16	529	" 1672.
Garnett, Elizabeth	1	62	" 1637. Wife of Richard. (See Gardiner).
Garnett, Elizabeth	1	62	Transported 1637. Daughter of Richard. Aged 19 years.
Garnett, Hannah	10	443	Transported 1667.
Garnett, John	1	62	" 1637. Son of Richard, aged 4 years.
Garnett, Julian	1	62	Transported 1637. Daughter of Richard, aged 6 years.
Garnett, Luke	ABH	60,66	Transported 1637. (1, fol. 17, 25, 38, 39). (See Gardiner).
Garnett, Richard	ABH	77	Immigrated 1637 with his wife, four children and two servants. (1, fol. 17, 61-62).
Garnett, Richard, Jr.	1	17,62	Transported 1637. Son of Richard, aged 21 years.
Garnis, John	11	236	Service 1667. Of St. Mary's Co.
Garnish, Catharine	12	571,622	" 1670. Wife of John, of St. Mary's Co.
Garnish, Joane	10	499	Transported 1667.
Garnish, John	7	471	" 1664.
Garnish, Thomas	12	356	" 1669.
Garnish, Thomas	17	352	" 1672.
Garniss, Thomas	15	551	" 1679.
Garnisto, John	6	211	" 1660.
Garnsney, Edward	6	464	" 1658.
Garratt, John	5	339	" 1663.
Garratt, Thomas	9	433	Immigrated 1666. Of New York.
Garreson, Phillip	1	171	Transported about 1639.
Garret, John	12	201	Service 1669.
Garretson, Richard	11	309	Transported 1665.
Garrett, Ann	20	185	" 1679.
Garrett, Charles	18	310	" 1675.
Garrett, Hannah	10	410	" 1666.
Garrett, James	10	277	" 1666.
Garrett, James	18	137	" 1674.

NAME	Liber	Folio	REMARKS
Garrett, John	12	202	Service 1669.
Garrett, John	WC2	282	Transported 1680.
Garrett, Katherine	15	407	" 1676.
Garrett, Mary	10	1	" 1666.
Garrett, Nathaniel	16	117	Immigrated 1671. Of St. Mary's Co.
Garrett, Philip	6	128	Transported 1660.
Garrett, Richard	WC2	282	" 1680.
Garrett, Sarah	9	250	" 1665.
Garrish, George	15	369	" 1676.
Garrison, John	4	554	Immigrated 1661.
Garrison, John	9	216	Transported 1665.
Garry, Sarah	12	281,514	" 1668.
Garson, Martha	7	81	" 1660.
Gartar, John	7	464	" 1658.
Garter, Charles	7	464	" 1659.
Garter, James	11	581	" 1668.
Garter, William	18	334	" 1675.
Garvey, John	16·	414	" 1671.
Garvis, Thomas	4	214	Immigrated 1659.
Garway, Sarah	9	270	Transported 1665.
Gary, Clare	Q	204	Immigrated 1653. Wife of Stephen.
Gary, Daniel	10	575	Transported 1667.
Gary, Edward	WC2	99	" 1679. Son of Lawrence.
Gary, Elizabeth	7	509	" 1651.
Gary, Jane	7	509	" 1651.
Gary, John	6	90	" 1663.
Gary, John, Jr.	7	509	" 1651.
Gary, John, Sr.	7	509	Immigrated 1651.
Gary, Judith	7	509	Transported 1651.
Gary, Judith, Sr.	7	509	" 1651.
Gary, Lawrence	WC2	99	Immigrated 1679. Of Somerset Co.
Gary, Lawrence, Jr.	WC2	99	Transported 1679.
Gary, Mary	15	413	Service 1677. Wife of Lawrence. (See Gerry).
Gary, Mary	WC2	99	Service 1679. Wife of Lawrence. (See Gerry).
Gary, Richard	5	513	Immigrated 1650.
Gary, Sarah	5	513	" 1656. Wife of Richard.
Gary, Stephen, Gent.	Q	204	" 1650. Commission to Survey 1500 acres on the Eastern Shore.(7, fol. 581).
Gary, William	16	452	Transported 1671.
Garye, Sarah	9	488	" 1665.
Garye, Sarah	12	514	" 1668. Servant.
Gascoe, Philip	WC2	23	" 1679.
Gashee, Nicholas	7	553	Immigrated 1664.
Gaskey, Mark Antony	15	569	Transported 1678.
Gaskill, William, 1st	Q	453	" 1658.
Gaskill, William, 2nd	Q	453	" 1658.
Gaskin, Samuel	12	189	" 1668.
Gaskin, William	10	431	And Margaret, his wife. Service, 1666.

NAME	Liber	Folio	REMARKS
Gaskinn, Robert	18	160	Transported 1674.
Gasley, Edward	15	567	" 1678.
Gassaway, Nicholas	4	109	" 1649. Living 1663.
			(5, fol. 467).
Gassaway, Capt.			
Nicholas	WC2	363	Rights 1680. Of Anne Arundel Co.
Gastrell, Anthony	15	356	Transported 1675.
Gatan, Henry	9	157	" 1665.
Gate, John	5	245	" 1662. Servant.
Gate, Mary	17	463	" 1673.
Gater, Mathew	6	125	" 1661.
Gates, John	9	290	" 1665.
Gates, Robert	Q	18	Servant 1655.
Gates, Robert	11	524	Transported 1668.
Gates, Robert	17	475	" 1673.
Gath, Ralph	9	45	" 1665.
Gather, Bartholomew	4	621	Immigrated prior to 1661, when he was aged 30 years.
Gathewly, John	18	117	Transported 1674.
Gatonby, Luke	16	393	" 1671.
Gatson, Anthony	4	5	" 1659. Servant.
Gatts, James	6	118	" 1655.
Gauden, William	WC2	395	" 1680. Servant.
Gaunt, Jeoffrey	2	439	" 1648.
Gaunt, Thomas	6	126	" 1654.
Gaven, John	12	551	" 1670.
Gawnt, Jeffrey	ABH	12	Servant 1648.
Gay, John	1	26	Transported 1641. (Also spelled Guy).
Gay, John	ABH	60	Immigrated 1642.
Gayle, John	5	466	Transported 1662.
Gayler, Mary	WC2	402	" 1680.
Gaynes, Elizabeth	7	81	" 1662-3.
Gaynes, George	5	260	" 1660.
Gea, Richard	10	231	" 1666.
Geale, John	15	501	" 1678.
Geanes, Thomas	5	90	" 1660.
Gearle, Giard	16	435	" 1671.
Gedney, Elizabeth	5	87	" 1649-52.
Gee, George	18	84	" 1674.
Gee, John	Q	431	" 1658.
Gee, Thomas	15	344	" 1675.
Geekles, William	6	14	" 1663.
Geffen, Thomas	7	472	" 1664.
Gefferson, Richard	12	341	" 1668.
Gefs, John	5	181	" 1661.
Geist, Ann	15	454	" Oct. 1677.
Gelf, Henry	9	321	" 1665.
Gelfes, Edward	6	48	Immigrated prior to 1663.
Gell, Christian	13	65	Transported 1668. Servant.
Gelliburne, Thomas	WC2	129	" 1679.

NAME	Liber	Folio	REMARKS
Gellie, Helena	6	15	Transported 1657.
Gelstrop, James	7	561	Immigrated 1665.
Gemms, Elizabeth	9	333	Transported 1666.
Geniers, John	ABH	338	Immigrated 1652.
Genison, Robert	15	300	Transported 1675.
Gent, William	6	214	" 1663.
Geny, John	11	344	" 1668.
George, Amos John	7	135	" 1664.
George, Benjamin	11	344	" 1668.
George, Benjamin	12	478	" 1670. Service 1675. Kent Co. (15, fol. 311).
George, Gabriel	6	237	Transported 1663.
George, Griffin	6	154	" 1663.
George, John	9	156	" 1662.
George, John	5	343	" 1663.
George, John	WC2	73	" 1678.
George, Mary	Q	32	Servant 1653.
George, Richard	6	216	Transported 1663. Service 1670. (12, fol. 484).
George, Roger	15	439,534	Transported 1677.
George, Sampson	WC2	380	" 1675-80. Servant.
George, Sarah	6	36	" 1663.
George, Thomas	11	344	" 1668.
George, Thomas	12	478	" 1670. Service 1676. (15, fol. 371).
George, William	12	403	Transported 1669.
Gerald, Richard	Q	219	" 1652.
Geralld, Thomas	WC2	394	" 1680. Servant.
Gerard, Bridgett	Q	431	" 1658.
Gerard, John	5	242	" 1662.
Gerard, Robert	7	371	" 1664.
Gerard, Winifred	Q	431	" 1658. (See Gerrard).
German, Ann	9	216	" 1665.
Gernis, Hum.	15	500	" 1676-7.
Gero, John	11	107	Service 1667. Of St. Mary's Co.
Gerrald, Jane	WC2	395	Transported 1680. Servant.
Gerrald, Margaret	20	184	" from Ireland 1678.
Gerrald, Jone	15	543	" 1678.
Gerrard, Elizabeth	ABH	193	" 1650. Daughter of Thomas. (3, fol. 24).
Gerrard, Frances	ABH	193	Transported 1650. Daughter of Thomas. (3, fol. 24).
Gerrard, John	ABH	78,101	Transported 1637-40. Servant.
Gerrard, John	1	63,128	" 1640.
Gerrard, Justinian	ABH	193	" 1650. Son of Thomas. (3, fol. 24).
Gerrard, Katherine	15	150	Transported 1678.
Gerrard, Mr. Richard	ABH	66	Immigrated 1633.
Gerrard, Susan	3	24	Transported 1650. Daughter of Thomas.
Gerrard, Susanna	ABH	193	Transported 1650. Daughter of

NAME	Liber	Folio	REMARKS
			Thomas.
Gerrard, Temperance	ABH	193	Transported 1650. Daughter of Thomas. (3, fol. 24).
Gerrard, Thomas	1	19	Immigrated 1638. Surgeon.
Gerrard, Thomas	1	43	" 1638 with 5 men servants. Gent.
Gerrard, Thomas	3	24	Immigrated 1650 with wife, five children and others.
Gerrard, Thomas	ABH	47,193	Immigrated 1650 with wife and five children. Demands land. (ABH, fol. 198).
Gerrard, Mr. Thomas	ABH	68,78	Immigrated prior to 1635. (ABH, fol. 67; 4, fol. 549; see note ABH, fol. 6) Did not arrive until 1638.
Gerry, Edward	15	319	Transported 1675. Son of Lawrence.
Gerry, Lawrence	15	319	Immigrated 1675.
Gerry, Lawrence, Jr.	15	319	Transported 1675. Son of Lawrence.
Gervis, Humphry	WC2	399	" 1677.
Gery, Oliver	11	316	Of the City of London. Merchant in Maryland 1668.
Gess, John	15	376	Transported 1676.
Getings, Richard	20	185	" 1679.
Gibb, James	18	331	" 1674.
Gibbe, Richard	8	3	Service 1665.
Gibbons, Ann	4	188	Transported 1659. Servant.
Gibbons, Henry	17	408	" 1673.
Gibbons, Mary	4	188	" 1659. Daughter of Ann.
Gibbons, Mary	18	126	" 1674.
Gibbons, Oliver	ABH	78,101	" 1635-40. (ABH, fol. 83).
Gibbons, Oliver	1	62	" 1635-36 by Thomas Gerrard.
Gibbons, Oliver	1	128	Transported 1637-40 by Thomas Gerrard.
Gibbons, Oliver	1	75	Transported 1638 by Walter Broadhurst.
Gibbons, Symon	18	387	Transported 1668.
Gibbons, Thomasin	WC2	412	" 1681.
Gibbons, William	ABH	202	" 1650-1. Servant.
Gibbs, Ann	15	404	Service 1676.
Gibbs, Edward	5	467	Transported 1663. Son of Nath.
Gibbs, Ellen	15	397	" 1676.
Gibbs, Jonell	3	23	" before 1648.
Gibbs, Jonell	ABH	47	" prior to 1648. Servant.
Gibbs, John	5	247	" 1656.
Gibbs, John	17	67	" 1667. Son of John of Baltimore Co.
Gibbs, John	11	344	Transported 1668.
Gibbs, John	16	394	" 1671.
Gibbs, John	17	417	" 1673.
Gibbs, Martha	10	407	" in "The Providence" of Bristol, 1666.
Gibbs, Mary	5	467	Transported 1663. Wife of Nath.
Gibbs, Mary	6	19	" 1660-3.

NAME	Liber	Folio	REMARKS
Gibbs, Mary	16	88	Transported 1670.
Gibbs, Nath.	5	467	" 1663. (6, fol. 19).
Gibbs, Richard	6	216	" 1663.
Gibbs, Richard	9	92,268	" 1665.
Gibbs, Richard	10	3	Immigrated 1665.
Gibbs, Samuel	5	180	Transported 1661.
Gibbs, Thomas	4	140	" 1658. Servant.
Gibbs, Thomas	16	85	" 1670.
Gibbs, William	5	467	" 1663. Son of Nath.
Gibent, Ruth	7	526	" 1664.
Giblangton, Richard	8	410	" 1665.
Gibson, Ann	17	440	" 1673.
Gibson, Ann	18	328	" 1675.
Gibson, Batt.	17	463	" 1673.
Gibson, Henry	18	142	Immigrated 1674. Of St. Mary's Co. (15, fol. 335.)
Gibson, Isaac	15	414	Immigrated 1677 with Katharine, his wife.
Gibson, John	Q	374	Gift from Lord Baltimore to, 1658.
Gibson, John	15	436	Transported 1677.
Gibson, John	WC2	320	" 1680. Servant.
Gibson, Katharine	15	414	Immigrated 1677. Wife of Isaac.
Gibson, Lawrence	15	413	Transported 1677.
Gibson, Mark	15	533	" 1678.
Gibson, Miles	12	269,283	Service 1668.
Gibson, Ralph	15	565	Transported 1679.
Gibson, Robert	16	411	" 1671.
Gibson, Robert	18	152	" 1674.
Gibson, Thomas	10	498	Immigrated 1667. Of Virginia.
Gibson, William	16	393	Transported 1671.
Gidney, Diana	7	601	" 1665. (10, fol. 503).
Gids, William	7	524	" 1663.
Giett, John	17	417	" 1673.
Giffculd, Daniel	6	211	" 1662.
Gifford, Henry	18	136	Service 1674. Of St. Mary's Co.
Gifford, Ursula	1	133	License to marry William Lewis, Nov. 2, 1638.
Gifford, William	5	257	Transported 1659-63.
Giggins, Elizabeth	6	16	Immigrated prior to 1662.
Gilber, Rose	4	193	Widow of Richard, married Robert Smith prior to 1658. (See Gilbert).
Gilbert, Barbery	11	229	Transported 1667. (12, fol. 359).
Gilbert, Elizabeth	ABH	37	" prior to 1649. Daughter of Richard and Rose. (2, fol. 606).
Gilbert, George	7	577	Transported 1665.
Gilbert, Grace	ABH	37	" prior to 1649. Daughter of Richard and Rose. (2, fol. 606).
Gilbert, Henry	12	594	Transported 1670.
Gilbert, James	WC2	352	" 1680.
Gilbert, John	12	594	" 1670.
Gilbert, John	16	112	Immigrated 1671. Of Baltimore Co.

NAME	Liber	Folio	REMARKS
Gilbert, John	15	535	Transported 1678.
Gilbert, Joseph	15	446	" 1677.
Gilbert, Lancelott	7	464	" 1662.
Gilbert, Richard	1	121	" 1633.
Gilbert, Richard	2	606	" prior to 1649. Dec'd by 1649.
Gilbert, Richard	ABH	37	Immigrated prior to 1649.
Gilbert, Richard	ABH	98	Transported 1633. Servant.
Gilbert, Rose	1	133-134	License to marry Robert Smith, Nov. 23, 1638.
Gilbert, Rose	2	606	Transported prior to 1649. Widow of Richard. Married Robert Smith.
Gilbert, Rose	ABH	37	Wife of Richard. Immigrated prior to 1649, when she was the wife of Robert Smith.
Gilbert, Ruth	9	505	Transported 1666.
Gilbert, Thomas	14	347	Immigrated 1671. Of Dorchester County.
Gilbert, Thomas	15	405	Transported 1676 with Elizabeth, his wife.
Gilbey, Thomas	12	190	Transported 1668. Servant.
Gilbourne, Francis	5	305	" prior to 1663.
Gilby, Ann	17	469	" 1673.
Giles, Ann	20	2	" prior to 1678.
Giles, Dorcas	15	403	Service 1676. Wife of William.
Giles, John	9	477	Immigrated prior to 1666.
Giles, John	17	424	Transported 1673.
Giles, Jone	15	553	" 1678.
Giles, Rachel	12	314	" 1668.
Giles, Ralph	20	2	" prior to 1678.
Giles, William	4	72	" 1657-9.
Giles, William	17	38	Immigrated 1672 with Dorcas, his wife. Of Somerset Co.
Giles, William	15	403	Immigrated 1676.
Gilford, William	11	229	Service 1667.
Gill, Anne	14	145	Daughter and heir of Benjamin, married James Neale, Gent. prior to 1664.
Gill, Benjamin	ABH	27	Immigrated 1642. (4, fol. 543).
Gill, Benjamin	2	524-525	" 1642 with five persons.
Gill, David	18	137	Transported 1674.
Gill, Elizabeth	Q	73	Immigrated 1658. Wife of Thomas.
Gill, Francis	7	561	" about 1665.
Gill, Henry	4	533	Transported 1659.
Gill, Henry	5	243	" 1662.
Gill, John	5	188	" about 1662.
Gill, John	WC2	45	Service 1676.
Gill, John	15	408	" 1676. Of St. Mary's Co.
Gill, Mary	16	505	Transported 1671.
Gill, Mary	17	344	" 1672.
Gill, Randall	6	48	" prior to 1663. Servant.
Gill, Robert	13	66	" 1669. Servant.
Gill, Steven	7	461	" 1659-64. Servant.

NAME	Liber	Folio	REMARKS
Gill, Thomas	18	137	Transported 1674.
Gill, Thomas	Q	73	Immigrated 1658.
Gillam, John	17	363	Transported 1672.
Gillane, David	WC2	87	" 1679.
Gille, John	9	204	" 1665.
Gille, Mary	9	204	" 1665.
Gille, Thomas	9	204	" 1665.
Gillett, Henry	5	404	" 1659.
Gillett, Walter	15	338	" 1676.
Gillford, Margaret	5	93	" prior to 1661.
Gillford, Mary	4	181	" about 1651. Widow.
Gilliard, John	17	424	" 1673.
Gillin, Susanna	5	516	" 1663.
Gills, Henry	17	599	Service 1673. Of Talbot Co.
Gillum, John	11	139	Immigrated 1667.
Gillyett, German	5	481	" 1663.
Gillyett, Sarah	5	481	Transported 1663. Wife of German.
Gilman, Philip	16	532	" 1668-70.
Gilpen, Gilvanus	10	324	Immigrated 1666.
Gilsman, John	15	455	Transported 1678.
Gilson, Mary	16	77	" 1670.
Ginnce, Clause	9	489	" 1665.
Gipson, Ann	17	463	" 1673.
Girdler, Mary	8	409	" 1665.
Girlen, John	10	480	Immigrated 1667.
Girlings, Lionell	15	553	Transported 1678.
Girlings, Richard	18	107	Service 1672.
Gist, Christopher	WC2	66	Immigrated 1679 with wife and one other person. Of Baltimore County.
Gist, Edeth	WC2	66	Transported 1679, wife of Christopher.
Githin, Robert	WC2	120	Transported 1680.
Gitter, George	5	536	" 1663.
Gitting, John	7	640	Cousin to Wm. Perin.
Gittings, John	5	247	Transported 1659 by Philip Calvert, Esq.
Gittings, John	7	471	Immigrated 1664.
Gittings, Margaret	7	640	Transported 1664. Wife of John.
Gittings, Nicholas	17	416	Service 1673.
Gives, William	17	444	" 1673. Of Baltimore Co.
Givin, Michael	Q	197	Transported 1658.
Gladbone, Charles	7	85	" 1649. Servant.
Gladdus, Donsabell	ABH	85	A child --- 1636, massacred by the Indians on Poplars Island.
Gladdus, Donsbell	1	82	Transported 1636. Maidservant.
Gladin, John	18	141	" 1674.
Gladstone, John	WC2	318,400	Immigrated 1680. Of Somerset Co.
Gladwell, Sarah	11	436	Transported 1668.
Glanvill, William	11	351	Of the City of London. Mariner. Acquires land in Maryland 1668.
Glasbrooke, John	WC2	415	Transported 1666-80. Servant.

NAME	Liber	Folio	REMARKS
Glascock, Francis	9	354	Transported 1662.
Glascock, John	9	354	" 1662.
Glascock, Richard	9	354	" 1662.
Glascock, Richard	11	436	" 1668.
Glass, Elizabeth	15	531	" 1678. Daughter of John.
Glass, John	11	520	" 1668. Servant.
Glass, John	15	531	Immigrated 1678.
Glass, Joyce	15	531	Transported 1678. Wife of John.
Glasscock, Richard	17	469	" 1673.
Gleaw, Samuel	17	29	" from Virginia 1672.
Glendining, John	17	511	Service 1673. Of Talbot Co.
Glene, Thomas	10	499	Transported 1667.
Glent, Peter	15	565	" 1679.
Glerin (Glevin), Barthol'o.	5	89	" 1661. Of Kent Co.

His widow married Jno. Wright of same county prior to Mar. 9, 1667. (11, fol. 264).

NAME	Liber	Folio	REMARKS
Glifton, Francis	4	5	Transported 1652-9.
Gligg, Daniel	ABH	375	" 1653. Servant.
Glindining, John	8	483	" 1665.
Gloute, Isabel	6	268	" 1662.
Glover, Ann	15	369	" 1676.
Glover, Benjamin	Q	70	" 1658.
Glover, Elizabeth	11	176	Service 1667. Wife of John.
Glover, Elizabeth	18	174	Transported 1674.
Glover, Giles	5	307	" 1663.
Glover, Isaac	8	30	" 1665. Service 1670. (16, fol. 60).
Glover, John	7	78	Transported 1664. Servant.
Glover, John	11	176	Service 1667. Of Talbot Co.
Glover, John	13	57	Transported 1670.
Glover, Richard	11	104	" 1667.
Glover, Samuel	15	598	" 1678-9.
Glover, Samuel	WC2	211	" 1679. Servant.
Glover, Sarah	15	566	" 1678.
Glover, Sarah	WC2	130	" 1679. Servant.
Glover, Thomas	7	469	" from Virginia 1664.
Glover, William	18	136,137	" 1674.
Glover, William	15	452	" 1677.
Glynn, Morgan	16	510	" 1672.
Goad, William	18	177	" 1674.
Goade, William	WC2	308	" 1678.
Goaler, Jeremy	16	170	" 1671.
Goane, John	WC2	167,169	" 1679.
Gobert, John	6	124	Immigrated from Virginia 1663.
Godard, Joseph	12	356	Transported 1669.
Godard, Thomas	WC2	71	Chirurgion of the Crown Malago.
Godbey, Daniel	11	440	Transported 1668.
Goddard, Ann	WC2	84	" 1679. Wife of Thomas.
Goddard, Edward	18	174	" 1674.
Goddard, Elias	16	507	" 1671.

NAME	Liber	Folio	REMARKS
Goddard, George	18	36	Immigrated 1673.
Goddard, Langley	15	411	Transported 1677.
Goddard, Thomas	7	561,640	Immigrated 1665.
Goddard, Thomas	WC2	84,242	Transported wife, Ann, and other's
1679-1680. Of Talbot Co. (WC2, fol. 244, 332, 338).			
Godfrey, Charles	WC2	320	Transported 1680. Servant.
Godfrey, Elias	5	492	" 1662.
Godfrey, Elizabeth	16	507	" 1671. Married
Theodore Young, prior to 1677. (15, fol. 520).			
Godfrey, George	7	492	Transported 1664.
Godfrey, John	5	413	" 1662.
Godfrey, John	10	412	" 1665.
Godfrey, Robert	10	394	" 1666. Servant.
Godfrie, John	15	376	" 1676.
Godfry, John	10	4	" 1666.
Godfry, Mary Belcon-			
senats	17	488	" 1668.
Godgrass, John	9	400	" 1666.
Godlington, George	7	464	" 1657.
Godlington, Thomas	4	198	Of London. Merchant. About to
			immigrate 1659.
Godsall, John	12	358	Transported 1668.
Godsgrace, Hannah	ABH	312	" Feb. 1652. Wife of
			James.
Godsgrace, James	ABH	312	Immigrated Feb. 1652.
Godson, John	4	14	Transported 1659. Servant.
Godwin, Deveraux	ABH	64	" 1638. Servant.
Godwin, Devereux	1	33,171	" 1638. Servant.
Godwin, Edward	10	609	" from Virginia 1667.
			Servant.
Goeing, Ann	17	376	Service 1672. Wife of Esau.
Gofe, William	16	402	Transported 1671.
Goffe, Edward	16	428	" 1670-1.
Goffe, James	15	443	" 1673.
Goffe, Mary	7	498	" 1663.
Goffe, Samuel	6	117	" 1656.
Goffe, Stephen	10	556	" 1664-5.
Goffe, William	15	443	" 1670.
Goffe, William	16	536	" 1671.
Goffer, William	18	36	" 1673.
Gofford, Henry	11	374	" 1668.
Going, Thomas	16	135	" 1671.
Gold, Edward	15	442	" 1677.
Gold, John	16	122	Immigrated 1671. Of St. Mary's Co.
Gold, Jonathan	WC2	253	Transported 1680.
Gold, Margaret	4	208	" 1659.
Gold, Mary	15	560	" 1678.
Gold, Philip	15	565	" 1679.
Gold, Thomas	15	452	" 1678.
Goldborough, Nicholas	15	525	" 1678.
Golden, Gabriel	9	240	Dec'd prior to 1665, when his

NAME	Liber	Folio	REMARKS
widow appears as the wife of John Hollenworth.			
Golden, Henry	10	117	Transported 1666.
Golden, Nicholas	7	506	" prior to 1664.
Goldie, William	16	439	" 1671.
Golding, John	15	436	" 1677.
Golding, William	WC2	201	" 1680. Servant.
Goldsberry, James	10	390	" 1666.
Goldsborough, Ann	ABH	150	Wife of John Shircliffe in 1651.
Transported many years prior.			
Goldsborough, Judith	15	601	Service 1679. (18, fol. 4).
Goldsborough, Robert	15	538	Immigrated 1677.
Goldsby, Richard	15	572	Transported 1674.
Goldsmith, Blanche	Q	434	Immigrated 1658. Daughter of Samuel.
Goldsmith, George	Q	435	Immigrated 1658.
Goldsmith, Johnanna	Q	434	" 1658. Wife of Samuel.
Goldsmith, John	10	378	" 1665. Of Somerset Co.
Goldsmith, John	10	378	Transported 1665.
Goldsmith, Margaret	15	525	" 1678.
Goldsmith, Mary	10	378	" 1665.
Goldsmith, Matthew	Q	435	" 1658. (Q, fol. 250).
Goldsmith, Maj. Samuel	Q	434	Immigrated 1658.
Goldsmith, Susanna	Q	434	" 1658. Daughter of Samuel.
Goldsmith, Thomas	Q	435	Transported 1658.
Goldsnee, Joseph	18	311	" 1675.
Gole, Edward	12	459	" 1669.
Golledge, Joane	17	440	" 1668.
Golson, Daniel	ABH	142,322	Immigrated 1650, of Patuxent River.
Golson, Grisell	ABH	322	Transported 1650.
Golson, Matthew	ABH	322	" 1650. Son of Daniel.
Golson, Sarah	ABH	142,322	" 1650. Wife of Daniel.
Gonnie, Clement	6	268	" 1660.
Gonsay, Jonathan	7	526	" 1664.
Good, Edward	Q	204	Immigrated 1655.
Good, Joseph	5	411	Transported 1663.
Good, Lucy	7	569	" 1663-4.
Goodale, Ann	10	470	" 1666. Sister to Peter.
Goodale, Gilbert	17	635	" 1671.
Goodale, Humphry	10	470	" 1666. Brother to Peter.
Goodale, Isabell	17	635	" 1671.
Goodale, John	10	470	" 1666. Brother to Peter.
Goodale, Peter	10	470	Immigrated to Talbot Co. 1666. Of New York.
Goodale, William	15	376	Transported 1676.
Goodard, John	5	536	" 1663.
Gooday, Elizabeth	13	114	" 1671.
Goodby, Daniel	11	337	" 1668.
Goodchild, Robert	5	84	" 1661.

NAME	Liber	Folio	REMARKS
Goodchilde, William	8	381	Transported 1665.
Goodgroome, John	WC2	110	" 1676. Servant.
Goodhand, Christopher	17	67	Service 1672. (15, fol. 379).
Gooding, Jesper	WC2	65	Transported 1679.
Gooding, Judith	15	442	" 1677.
Gooding, Robert	5	87	" 1649-62.
Goodjeon, Robert	5	12	" 1649.
Goodman, Abegail	15	424	" 1677. Wife of Edward. (19, fol. 503).
Goodman, Benjamin	15	318	Transported 1674. (18, fol. 24).
Goodman, Daniel	7	530	" 1664.
Goodman, Edward	6	90	" 1656. Service 1662. (5, fol. 64).
Goodman, Edward	19	503	Of Baltimore Co. Immigrated prior to 1676 with Abegail, his wife, and Love and Sarah, his daughters.
Goodman, Gabriel	6	170	Transported 1657.
Goodman, George	WC2	100	" 1679.
Goodman, Henry	9	304	" 1665.
Goodman, Love	15	424	" 1677. Daughter of Edward. (19, fol. 503).
Goodman, Richard	6	134	Transported 1653.
Goodman, Sarah	15	424	" 1677. Daughter of Edward. (19, fol. 503).
Goodman, William	15	430	Transported 1677.
Goodner, Ann	5	218	" 1662.
Goodrick, Charles	6	294	" 1663.
Goodrick, Henry	5	203	" 1662.
Goodrick, Katherine	18	331	" 1674.
Goodrick, Margaret	4	22	Daughter of George. Transported prior to 1657 and married to Barnaby Jackson prior to 1659.
Goodrick, Mary	4	23	Immigrated 1659. Sister to William May.
Goodrick, Quinton	5	203	Transported 1662.
Goodrick, Robert	ABH	338	" 1652-3. Servant. (12, fol. 350).
Goodridge, Henry	8	203	Transported 1665. Service 1677. (15, fol. 400).
Goodridge, Thomas	12	204	Transported 1669. (15, fol. 451).
Goodson, Francis	16	393	" 1671.
Goodson, Jone	15	362	" 1676.
Goodson, Thomas	15	433	" 1677.
Goodwell, Paul	7	464	" 1661.
Goodwin, ---	1	18	" 1638. Blacksmith.
Goodwin, Devereux	ABH	37	Servant 1638.
Goodwin, George	6	210	Service 1663.
Goodwin, Jane	18	331	Transported 1674.
Goodwin, Susannah	WC2	415	" 1666-80. Servant.
Goodwyn, Devoreuxand	2	605	" about 1638. Servant.
Goodwyn, Susan	Q	31	" 1658.
Goody, Eliza	17	463	" 1673.
Goodyear, Thomas	6	89	" 1663.

NAME	Liber	Folio	REMARKS
Gookan, Richard	9	329	Transported 1663-64.
Gooks, Peter	9	44	" 1662.
Goold, Henry	6	130	" 1654.
Goold, John	6	130	" 1654.
Goold, Mary	6	130	" 1654.
Goore, John	3	23	" before 1648.
Goore, Mary	15	417	Immigrated 1677.
Goosey, Lawrence	12	517	Transported 1670.
Gopler, John	12	204	" 1669.
Gorda, St. Noby	18	150	" 1674.
Gorden, Ursula	5	63	" 1660.
Gorden, William	15	376	" 1676.
Gordin, Thomas	WC2	120	" 1680.
Gordon, Daniel	ABH	269	" 1651. Servant.
Gordon, John	15	525	Service 1678.
Gore, John	ABH	47	Transported prior to 1648. Servant.
Gore, Mary	WC2	51	" 1679.
Gore, Stephen	ABH	94	" 1633. Servant.
Gore, Stephen	1	110	" 1633.
Goremond, Edmund	WC2	129	" 1679.
Gorman, James	WC2	101	" 1679.
Gorsuch, Elizabeth	4	551	" 1661.
Gorsuch, Richard	4	54	Immigrated prior to 1659.
Gorsuch, Richard	4	551	Transported 1661.
Gorsuch, Robert	4	54	Immigrated prior to July 1659.
Gose, Thomas	15	510	Transported 1676 with Ann, his wife.
Goshaw, Nicholas	Q	204	Transported 1651.
Goslew, William	WC2	167,169	" 1679.
Goslin, Elizabeth	17	330	" 1672.
Gosling, Elizabeth	4	22	" 1658.
Gosling, Mathew	7	87	" 1655.
Gosling, Thomas	7	464	" 1654.
Gosling, William	9	54	" 1665. (15, fol. 450).
Goss, Henry	6	80	" 1658.
Goss, John	Q	189	His widow married John Waghot.
Goss, John	17	474	Transported 1672.
Gosse, Frances	ABH	396	" 1654. Daughter of John. (5, fol. 516).
Gosse, Joane	5	516	Transported 1654. Wife of John.
Gosse, John	ABH	396	Immigrated from the Tertudo's, 1654 with wife of St. George's hundred. (5, fol. 516).
Gosse, Margaret	6	132	Transported 1659.
Gosse, Samuel	5	404	" 1659.
Gossocke, Jerome	6	132	" 1657.
Gossom, Sarah	15	540	" 1677.
Gost, Jane	15	500	" 1678.
Gosten, Sarah	5	359	" 1663.
Gostwick, Joseph	15	540	" 1677.
Gosuch, Walter	15	530	" 1678.
Got, Richard	Q	32	Immigrated 1650.

NAME	Liber	Folio	REMARKS
Got, Juliallia	Q	32	Immigrated 1650. Daughter of Richard.
Got, Sarah	Q	32	Immigrated 1650. Daughter of Richard.
Got, Susan	Q	32	Immigrated 1650. Wife of Richard.
Gotee, John	WC2	84	Granted warrant in right of wife's Service, 1679. Of Dorchester County.
Gotee, Margaret	WC2	84	Service 1666. Wife of John.
Goteer, John	5	243	Transported 1662.
Goteley, Richard	12	194	" 1668. Servant.
Goter, William	15	567	" 1678.
Gott, Henry	6	81	" 1651.
Gott, Robert	13	1	" 1669.
Gottam, Edward	---	---	" 1637.
Goude, John	16	507	" 1671.
Gouge, Bridgett	17	25	" 1672.
Gouge, Mary	15	450,507	" 1677.
Gouge, Philip	6	106	" 1658.
Gough, Barnaby	6	107	Immigrated 1659.
Gough, Elizabeth	6	107	Transported 1659.
Gough, Mary	17	551	" 1673.
Gough, William	18	79	Service 1674. Of Charles Co.
Gough, William	19	597	Commission from Baker Brooke, Esq., Surveyor General, as Deputy Surveyor for Cecil Co., 1677.
Gould, Ann	Q	66	Transported 1655.
Gould, Ann	5	482	" 1662.
Gould, Katherine	4	213	" prior to 1659.
Gould, Mary	5	341	" 1656.
Gould, Richard	4	570	" 1661.
Gould, Richard	11	462	Immigrated 1668.
Gould, Robert	5	489	Transported 1662.
Gould, Ursula	11	462	" 1668.
Gouldberry, John	6	268	" 1662.
Gouldbush, ---	9	36	" 1665.
Goulden, John	6	294	" 1664.
Goulden, Philip	20	185	" 1679.
Gouldhawk, George	9	191	Immigrated 1665.
Gouldine, Gabriel	4	550	Transported 1661.
Gouldine, Mary	4	550	" 1661.
Goulding, James	16	85	" 1670.
Goulding, John	12	477	" 1670.
Gouldsmith, Elizabeth	5	238	Immigrated 1661.
Gouldsmith, George	5	238	" 1661.
Gouldsmith, John	3	24	Transported 1650. Servant.
Gouldsmith, John	6	347	" 1663.
Goulson, Daniel	9	92	His widow married Hugh Stanley prior to 1665.
Goun, William	15	300	Transported 1675.
Gourdon, Alexander	Q	70	Service 1658. Son-in-law of Richard Gott.
Gout, Thomas	20	185	Transported 1679.

NAME	Liber	Folio	REMARKS
Goute, George	15	430	Transported 1677.
Gouzell, Moses	15	565	" 1679.
Gove, Henry	5	610	" 1654.
Gove, Robert	15	322	" 1675.
Gover, Clement	17	344	" 1672.
Gower, Ann	4	551	" 1661.
Gower, George	18	288	" 1674.
Goyard, Franciscus - Fardinandos	17	411	Service 1673.
Goyer, Francis	5	211	Transported 1662. (9, fol. 34).
Grace, Ann	17	548	" 1666. Wife of John.
Grace, Henry	ABH	245	" 1652. Servant.
Grace, John	9	25	" 1665. Service 1666. (17, fol. 548).
Grace, Michael	8	501	Transported 1665. Service 1667. (16, fol. 166; 17, fol. 383).
Grace, Nathaniel	17	411	Transported 1673.
Grace, William	5	607	" 1658.
Grace, William	5	489	" 1660.
Grace, William	10	572	" 1667.
Grace, William	17	58	" 1672.
Gradwell, Elizabeth	11	229	" 1667.
Gradwell, Isabella	12	359	" 1669.
Grady, Edmund	17	424	Service 1673.
Grafford, Peter	12	372	Transported 1669.
Graham, Elizabeth	WC2	89	" 1676. Servant.
Graham, Jane	15	446	" 1677. Wife of John.
Graham, John	15	446	Immigrated 1677.
Graham, Robert	16	97	" 1666. Of St. Mary's County.
Graham, Robert	11	581	Transported 1668.
Grainger, Edward	4	551	" 1661.
Grainger, William	Q	357	Immigrated prior to 1651.
Grallett, John	6	137	Transported 1658.
Gramar, Peter	10	440	Service 1666.
Grame, James	16	411	Transported 1671.
Grammer, John	ABH	212	Immigrated 1650.
Grammer, John	3	173	Rights 1655.
Grammers, Edward	18	14	Transported 1674.
Gramon, Thomas	13	122	" 1668.
Grand, John	12	413	" 1669.
Grandee, Rachel	17	33	" from Virginia 1672.
Graner, James	6	90,321	" prior to 1663.
Grange, John	11	230	" 1667.
Granger, Ann	15	344	" 1675.
Granger, Benjamin	16	453	Service 1671. Of Dorchester Co.
Granger, Benjamin	WC2	1	Fled out of Province 1678.
Granger, Grace	17	63	Service 1672. Wife of William.
Granger, James	8	501	Transported 1665.
Granger, James	WC2	66	" 1669.
Granger, Richard	Q	202	Immigrated 1658.

NAME	Liber	Folio	REMARKS
Granger, Robert	15	501,559	Transported 1678.
Grant, Charles	6	120	" 1651.
Grant, Elizabeth	13	66	" 1669. Servant.
Grant, George	5	246	" 1657 by Philip Calvert, Esq.
Grant, John	15	544	Transported 1674.
Grant, Sarah	WC2	396	" 1680.
Grant, William	8	88	" 1664. Servant.
Grant, William	7	560	" 1665.
Grant, William	17	416	" 1673.
Grapes, John	Q	189	" 1654.
Grascum, Mary	5	129	" 1662.
Grasham, Margaret	7	467	" 1663.
Grasia, Hosea	15	429	" 1674.
Grathry, Thomas	Q	323	" 1658.
Graves, Daniel	9	332	" 1666.
Graves, Dorothy	5	254	" 1663. Wife of John.
Graves, Henry	17	615	" 1673.
Graves, John	5	254	Immigrated 1663.
Graves, John	15	567	Transported 1678.
Graves, Katherine	15	360,516	" 1676.
Graves, Katherine	WC2	135	" 1679. Servant.
Graves, Mary	17	510	" 1673.
Graves, Richard	6	172,264	Immigrated 1662.
Graves, Samuel	ABH	382	" Feb. 1653. Service 1670. (12, fol. 496).
Graves, William	4	534	Service, aged about 24 years, 1659.
Gravett, Ann	20	185	Transported 1679.
Gray, Andrew	15	316	Immigrated 1675. Of Talbot Co.
Gray, Ann	6	48	Transported prior to 1663.
Gray, Benjamin	15	452	" 1677.
Gray, Eleanor	6	130	" 1658.
Gray, Eleanor	16	428	" 1670-1.
Gray, Elizabeth	WC2	105	" 1680. Daughter of Jane Jones.
Gray, Francis	1	134	License to marry Alice Moreman, Nov. 26, 1638.
Gray, Francis	4	59	Transported 1654.
Gray, Francis	6	293	" 1664.
Gray, James	WC2	105	" 1680. Son of Jane Jones.
Gray, Jeffrey	16	437	Transported 1671.
Gray, John	2	429-430	Immigrated 1640. (Also spelled Gwy).
Gray, John	6	103	Transported 1663.
Gray, John	5	12	" 1662.
Gray, John	7	492	" 1664.
Gray, John	9	104	" 1665.
Gray, John	12	498	" · 1670. (16, fol. 333).
Gray, John	16	394	" 1671.
Gray, Joseph	7	569	" 1663-4.

NAME	Liber	Folio	REMARKS
Gray, Joseph	16	437	Transported 1671.
Gray, Joseph	WC2	105	" 1680. Son of Jane Jones.
Gray, Mary	Q	430	" 1658.
Gray, Mary	8	486	" 1664.
Gray, Mary	9	450	" 1666.
Gray, Mary	WC2	105	" 1680. Daughter of Jane Jones.
Gray, Miles	17	382	Immigrated from Virginia 1672.
Gray, Ralph	15	445	Transported 1677.
Gray, Richard	9	321	" 1666.
Gray, Richard	17	395	Service 1672. Of Kent Co.
Gray, Richard	17	444	Transported 1673.
Gray, Robert	5	247	" 1659 by Philip Calvert, Esq.
Gray, Robert	6	87	Transported 1660.
Gray, Stephen	ABH	60,244	" 1634-41. Servant.
Gray, Stephen	1	18,26	" 1637.
Gray, William	4	560	" 1661.
Gray, William	5	532	" 1663.
Gray, William	15	443	" 1667.
Gray, William	15	380	" 1676.
Graydon, Margaret	16	79	" 1670.
Grear, James	18	152	" 1674.
Greeke, Joane	5	516	" 1662.
Green, Alice	4	58	" prior to 1659.
Green, Alice	15	431	" 1677. (20, fol. 184).
Green, Andrew	12	209	" 1668.
Green, Clement	7	214	" 1662.
Green, Elizabeth	7	483	" 1661.
Green, Elizabeth	10	541	" 1667.
Green, Elizabeth	16	110	" 1671.
Green, Elizabeth	15	390,436	" 1676.
Green, Erasmus	12	215,341	" 1668-9.
Green, Francis	16	110	" 1671.
Green, Francis	WC2	19,88	Service 1679. Of Calvert Co.
Green, George	6	129	" 1653. (11, fol. 168).
Green, George	15	344	" 1675.
Green, Henry	4	555	" 1661.
Green, John	7	78	" 1654.
Green, John	6	71	" 1661, by a Quaker. (5, fol. 71).
Green, John	7	507	Transported 1662.
Green, John	6	90	" 1663.
Green, John	9	356	" 1666.
Green, John	11	374,571	" 1668. (12, fol. 209).
Green, John	17	412	Service 1673.
Green, Leonard	ABH	6	Transported 1644. (7, fol. 568). Living 1665.
Green, Luke	5	82	Transported 1662. Service 1668. (11, fol. 527).
Green, Margaret	6	211	Transported 1658.

NAME	Liber	Folio	REMARKS
Green, Margaret	15	530	Transported 1678.
Green, Margery	7	471	" 1664.
Green, Mary	15	560	" 1678.
Green, Mary	15	565	" 1679.
Green, Maudley	8	88	" 1665.
Green, Peter	16	482	" 1670-1.
Green, Ralph	5	306	" 1663.
Green, Robert, Esq.	ABH	11	Immigrated 1648.
Green, Roger	9	69	Transported 1660-5.
Green, Susan	Q	202	Servant 1658.
Green, Thomas, Esq.	ABH	6,67	Immigrated 1633. His sons, Leon-

ard, Robert, Henry and Francis were living in 1665. (7, fol. 568). He
married 1st, Mrs. Ann Cox, who came to Md. 1633. (ABH, fol. 12); 2nd,
Mrs. Winifred Seyborn. (ABH, fol. 6, 67; 7, fol. 427).

NAME	Liber	Folio	REMARKS
Green, Thomas	7	62	Married the widow of Nicholas Harvay prior to 1653.
Green, Thomas	Q	32	Servant 1653.
Green, Thomas	Q	430	Transported 1658.
Green, Thomas	11	309	" 1665.
Green, Thomas	10	469	" 1667.
Green, Thomas	12	576	" 1670.
Green, Thomas	15	567	" 1678.
Green, Gov. Thomas	12	560	Location of his house in St. Mary's 1639.
Green, Walter	12	348	Service 1669. Of St. Mary's Co., Carpenter, and wife.
Green, William	15	413	Immigrated 1676 with Susan, his wife.
Green, William	15	567	Transported 1678.
Green, Winifred	ABH	403	Widow of Thos. Green, Esq.,

married Mr. Robert Clarke, prior to 1654.

NAME	Liber	Folio	REMARKS
Greenaway, Allen	9	322	Transported 1666.
Greenaway, Richard	15	453	" 1675-7.
Greenaway, Thomas	5	220	" 1659.
Greenbury, Mrs. Ann	15	572	" 1674. Wife of Nicholas.
Greenbury, Charles	15	572	" 1674. Son of Nicholas.
Greenbury, Katherine	15	572	" 1674. Daughter of Nicholas.
Greenbury, Mary	15	300	Transported 1675.
Greenbury, Mr. Nicholas	15	572	Immigrated 1674 with his wife

and two children in the ship "Constant Friendship", Wm. Wheatly,
Master. (18, fol. 160).

NAME	Liber	Folio	REMARKS
Greene, Alice	WC2	282	Transported 1680.
Greene, Elizabeth	6	211	" 1658.
Greene, Elizabeth	16	78,110	" 1670.
Greene, Elizabeth	WC2	120	" 1680.
Greene, George	9	94	" 1665. Servant.
Greene, George	16	170	" 1671.
Greene, John	16	9	" 1670. Son of William.
Greene, John	18	94	" 1674.
Greene, Katherine	9	451	" 1666.

NAME	Liber	Folio	REMARKS
Greene, Leonard	2	346	Transported 1644.
Greene, Mary	18	167	" 1674.
Greene, Matthew	16	414	" 1671.
Greene, Richard	17	454	" 1672.
Greene, Richard	WC2	395	" 1680. Servant.
Greene, Robert	2	430	Immigrated 1648.
Greene, Samuel	16	70	Transported 1668.
Greene, Sarah	15	430	" 1677.
Greene, Thomas	16	507	" 1671.
Greene, Thomas	1	17,41-42	Immigrated 1633. (2, fol. 346).
Greene, Thomas	2	346	Transported 1644.
Greene, Thurston	WC2	201	" 1680. Servant.
Greene, William	16	8,9	Immigrated 1670 with his son, John. Of Calvert Co. Tailor.
Greene, William	17	381	Immigrated from Virginia to Somerset Co. 1672.
Greene, William	15	559	Transported 1679.
Greenefield, Peter	WC2	415	" 1666-80. Servant.
Greenehall, Francis	WC2	394	" 1680. Servant.
Greenehill, Thomas	WC2	406	" 1678.
Greenfield, Thomas	15	346	Immigrated 1666.
Greenfield, Thomas	12	372	Transported 1669 by Thomas Trueman, Esq.
Greenfield, Thomas	15	516	Immigrated 1678.
Greengoose, Mary	5	516	Transported prior to 1663.
Greenhill, Thomas	9	25	" 1665.
Greenoe, Katherine	10	498	" 1667. Servant.
Greenoway, James	9	489	" 1665. Servant.
Greenway, Edward	16	170	" 1671.
Greenway, John	ABH	420	" his wife 1650. Service 1654.
Greenway, John	15	525	Transported 1678.
Greenwell, James	Q	208	Son of John, 1654.
Greenwell, John	Q	208	Married 1st, Mary --; 2nd, Bridget Seaborne, 1654.
Greenwood, Armagill	5	488,531	Immigrated 1659.
Greenwood, Armiger	5	358	" 1663.
Greenwood, Christian	5	358,531	Transported 1659. Wife of Armagill.
Greenwood, Eliza	16	414	" 1671.
Greenwood, Samuel	16	77	" 1670.
Greere, John	5	79	Immigrated 1661.
Greere, Margaret	5	79	Transported 1661. Wife of John.
Gregory, Anne	15	451	" 1678. Wife of Edward.
Gregory, Charles	16	124	Immigrated 1671. Of Calvert Co.
Gregory, Edmond	6	62	Transported 1663.
Gregory, Edward	15	451	" 1678.
Gregory, James	ABH	202	" 1651. Servant.
Gregory, John	6	17	Immigrated 1663. Of Virginia.
Gregory, John	13	114	Transported 1671.
Gregory, Joseph	2	427	" 1640. Servant.

NAME	Liber	Folio	REMARKS
Gregory, Joseph	ABH	10	Transported 1646.
Gregory, Joseph	15	331	" 1675.
Gregory, Luke	15	397	" 1676.
Gregory, Mary	15	430	" 1677.
Gregory, Matthew	Q	388	Servant 1658. (4, fol. 140).
Gregory, Thomas	ABH	201	Immigrated 1651 with wife.
Gregory, Thomas	WC2	395	Transported 1680. Servant.
Gregory, William, Sr.	15	551	" 1678.
Gregson, Thomas	ABH	66	" 1633.
Grenah, Henry	12	355	" 1669.
Grendly, Margaret	17	635	" 1674.
Gres, Nicholas	ABH	200	" 1650. Servant.
Gresham, John	ABH	84	Immigrated prior to 1640. Of the Isle of Kent. (1, fol. 80).
Gresham, John	12	474	Transported 1670.
Gresham, Mary	5	532	" 1659.
Greske, Joane	5	516	" 1662.
Grey, Andrew	15	316	" 1675. Son of Andrew.
Grey, Elizabeth	15	316	" 1675. Wife of Andrew.
Grey, Elizabeth	15	503	" 1678. Daughter of John.
Grey, Hannah	15	319	Transported by her father 1675. Daughter of Michael.
Grey, Hannah	15	503	Transported 1678. Wife of John.
Grey, Hannah	WC2	290	" 1680. Daughter of Miles.
Grey, Hellen	15	527	Transported 1678.
Grey, James	8	30	" 1665.
Grey, James	15	356	" 1675.
Grey, John	4	59	" 1652-9.
Grey, John	18	152	" 1674.
Grey, John	15	503	" 1678. Son of John.
Grey, Margaret	15	439	" 1677.
Grey, Miles	WC2	290	Rights for daughter, Hannah, 1680. Of Somerset Co.
Grey, Ralph	WC2	53	Transported 1677.
Grey, Ruth	15	357	" 1676.
Grey, Samuel	15	430,431	" 1677.
Grey, Thomas	15	316	" 1675. Son of Andrew.
Grey, William	15	397	" 1676.
Grey, William	15	316	" 1675. Son of Andrew.
Greydon, Margaret	16	630	" 1670.
Gribell, Jos.	WC2	112	" 1680.
Grie, Margaret	6	17	" 1663.
Grifes, Bridgett	WC2	254	" 1680.
Griffen, Allice	7	469	" from Virginia 1664.
Griffen, Barnett	WC2	253	" 1679.
Griffen, John	5	185	" 1658.
Griffen, John	16	507	" 1671.
Griffen, John	18	160	" 1674.
Griffen, Katherine	5	185	" 1658.

NAME	Liber	Folio	REMARKS
Griffen, Mary	6	295	Transported 1664.
Griffen, Sarah	6	347	" 1663.
Griffen, Susan	6	295	" 1664.
Griffen, Walter	15	416	" 1677.
Griffeth, Alice	8	502	" 1665.
Griffeth, Bridgett	WC2	194	" 1680.
Griffeth, Elizabeth	Q	219	" 1652.
Griffeth, John	8	486	" 1664.
Griffeth, John	11	163	" 1667. Servant.
Griffeth, Rice	11	378	" 1668.
Griffeth, Richard	15	431	" 1677.
Griffeth, Thomas	7	507	Immigrated 1664. Of Virginia.
Griffey, Thomas	16	393	Transported 1671.
Griffeys, Mary	17	76	" 1668.
Griffin, Anthony	Q	66	Immigrated 1657.
Griffin, Frances	1	149-150	License to marry John Ormsby, Oct. 16, 1641.
Griffin, Japheth	15	407	Service 1676.
Griffin, John	4	140	Transported 1656. Servant.
Griffin, Katherine	12	217	" 1669.
Griffin, Michael	18	137	" 1674.
Griffin, Robert	WC2	346	Son of Lewis, deceased, 1680.
Griffin, Samuel	ABH	312	Immigrated prior to June 1651.
Griffin, Thomas	ABH	151	Transported 1649-50. Servant.
Griffing, John	17	571	" 1673.
Griffis, Margaret	15	319	" 1672.
Griffith, Bridgett	15	565	" 1679.
Griffith, Edward	12	459	" 1669.
Griffith, Edward	16	11	" 1670.
Griffith, John	WC2	288	" 1668. (12, fol. 473; 17, fol. 58).
Griffith, John Williams	WC2	288	Transported 1680.
Griffith, Jone	17	483	" 1667. (11, fol. 318).
Griffith, Lewis	9	188	" 1665. Of Dorchester Co. Service 1669. (12, fol. 379).
Griffith, Lucy	7	507	Transported 1664. Wife of Thomas.
Griffith, Margaret	17	381	" from Virginia 1672.
Griffith, Welth	15	370	" 1676.
Griffith, William	18	329	" 1675.
Grifith, David	15	380	" 1676.
Grifith, John	15	380	" 1676.
Grigg, George	15	376	" 1676.
Grigge, Mary	17	417	" 1673.
Griggs, John	16	592	Immigrated 1672. Of St. Mary's Co. Married the widow and Extx. of Rich'd Keen, 1676. (15, fol. 387).
Grigsta, Thomas	1	20	Transported 1633. (See Grigston).
Grigston, Thomas	1	38	" 1633. (See Grigsta).
Grills, Philip	17	462	" 1673.
Grime, Ann	18	331	" 1674.
Grimes, Daniel	9	48	" 1665.
Grimes, Daniel	15	452,516	" 1678.

NAME	Liber	Folio	REMARKS
Grimes, Francis	13	121	Transported 1667.
Grimes, John	11	167	Service 1667. Of Anne Arundel Co.
Grimes, Joyce	5	414	" 1663. Wife of William.
Grimes, Joyce	10	498	Transported 1667.
Grimes, Margaret	18	152	" 1674.
Grimes, Richard	WC2	320	" 1680. Servant.
Grimes, Robert	12	190	" 1668. Servant.
Grimes, William	5	414	Service 1663.
Grimes, William	10	498	Transported 1667.
Grimesditch, John	1	208	Immigrated 1644.
Grimeshey, John	15	525	Transported 1678.
Grimley, Hannah	4	207	" 1658. Servant.
Grimstead, Alse	15	443	" 1670.
Grimsted, John	9	356	" 1666.
Grippen, Jane	15	329	" 1675.
Grisle, John	16	168	" 1670.
Grist, Henry	18	12	Service 1667.
Grist, John	9	325	Immigrated 1666.
Gristoe, Anthony	10	556	Transported 1664-5 with wife.
Groce, Fratt	4	140	" 1653. Servant.
Grome, Mary	10	277	" 1666. Wife of William.
Gromes, James	15	406	Service 1676.
Grondge, Gabriell	8	477	" 1665.
Groome, Hannah	6	95	Transported 1657.
Groome, Samuel	20	185	Immigrated 1679 with 83 Trans-
ports in the ship "Globe",		(7, fol. 528-9) 1664.	
Groome, Samuel	WC2	130	Rights for 83 servants, 1679.
Groome, Samuel, Jr.	WC2	167-169	Rights 1679, 1680. Master of ship "Globe".
Groot, Richard	WC2	352	Transported 1680.
Grosee, Reynold	15	398	" 1676. (See Grosse).
Grosse, Anna	Q	68	" 1657.
Grosse, Baynold	15	453	" 1676.
Grosse, Nicholas	4	584	" 1651.
Grove, Alexander	6	97	" 1655.
Grove, Alice	7	87	" 1656.
Grove, Alice	6	120	" 1660.
Grove, Dorothy	5	87,514	" 1649-62.
Grove, Elizabeth	6	129	" 1660.
Grove, George	12	209	" 1668.
Grove, Joseph	6	81	" 1659.
Grove, Mary	9	100	" 1665.
Grove, Thomas	12	333	" 1668.
Groves, Edward	15	360	" 1676.
Groves, George	11	374	" 1668. Service 1673. (17, fol. 533).
Groves, John	15	368	Of Somerset Co. Service 1676.
Groves, Joseph	15	509	Transported 1677.
Groves, Will	15	369	" 1676.
Groves, William	18	174	" 1674.
Grubbs, Dorothy	9	48	" 1665.

NAME	Liber	Folio	REMARKS
Grumble, Richard	6	120	Transported 1660.
Grumell, William	7	491	" 1664.
Grundry, Gideon	8	130	" 1665.
Grundry, Mr. Joseph	8	130	Immigrated 1665.
Grymes, Thomas	6	130	Transported 1654.
Gubber, Henry	6	166	" 1655.
Gubbins, Simon	16	77	" 1670.
Gubbott, George	6	96	" 1659.
Gubins, Mary	WC2	100	" 1679.
Gubtill, Stephen	11	229	" 1667.
Gubtill, William	11	229	" 1667.
Gudgeon, Chris.	8	478	" 1665.
Gudgeon, Robert	18	316	Service 1675. Of Anne Arundel Co.
Gudridge, Thomas	11	229	Transported 1667.
Gudson, Joane	15	442	" 1677.
Guerin, Gasper	6	309	Son-in-law of Mr. Thomas Edmonds. 1663.
Guesst, Elizabeth	1	18,31	Transported 1638. Servant.
Guest, Eliza	ABH	37	Servant prior to 1637.
Guest, Elizabeth	2	605	Transported about 1637-8. Servant.
Guest, Elizabeth	ABH	24	" 1640. Wife of Walter.
Guest (Gweast), Elizabeth	2	512	" 1649. Wife of Walter.
Guest, Walter	ABH	24	Immigrated 1640.
Guest (Gweast), Walter	2	512	" 1646.
Gueste, Elizabeth	ABH	63	Transported 1638. Servant.
Guibert, Joshua	12	222	Service 1669.
Guift, Henry	6	290	Transported 1663.
Guither, Nicholas	1	26	" 1635-41.
Gullett, Dorothy	6	131	" 1661.
Gullick, Ann	15	318	Service 1674. Wife of William.
Gullinck, William	16	169	Immigrated 1671.
Gullock, Thomas	17	440	Transported 1673.
Gully, James	WC2	184	" 1680. Servant.
Gully, Joane	20	184	" from Ireland 1678.
Gumbe, Francis	11	284	Of Charles Co. Joyner, 1668.
Gumbleton, Obadiah	19	258	Transported 1663.
Gumms, Charity	15	499	" 1677.
Gun, John	4	533	" 1659.
Gunby, Henry	12	372	" 1669.
Gunby, William	12	416	" 1669.
Gunderput, James	7	371	" 1658.
Gundrey, Andrew	5	243	" 1662. Service.
Worcester County 1673. (17, fol. 444).			
Gundy, John	9	54	Transported 1665.
Gundy, William	12	372	" 1669.
Gunfield, James	Q	67	Servant 1658.
Gunn, John	5	555	Transported 1660.
Gunnell, Edward	17	334,485	Immigrated 1673.
Gunnell, George	17	334,485	" 1673. Married Jane,

NAME	Liber	Folio	REMARKS

widow and Admx. of Thos. Overton, of Baltimore County, prior to
1678. (20, fol. 49).

NAME	Liber	Folio	REMARKS
Gunnell, Moses	7	560	Transported 1665.
Gunnill, Elizabeth	4	551	" 1661.
Gunnill, James	4	551	" 1661.
Gunnill, Robert	4	551	" 1661.
Gunningham, George	16	411	" 1671.
Gunrey, Robert	6	133	" 1651.
Gunston, Ann	15	443	" 1677.
Gunter, John	7	87,88	" 1649. Servant.
Gunter, Philip	18	4	" 1674.
Gunter, Violetta	6	128	" 1655.
Guntley, Herbert	6	96	" 1656-9.
Gunto, Mathew	6	122	" 1658.
Gunton, Timothy	3	192	Immigrated 1656.
Gupler, John	10	561	Transported from Virginia 1667. Servant.
Guptile, Steven	12	204	Transported 1669.
Guptile, William	12	204	" 1669.
Gurley, Jane	WC2	329	Service 1680. Wife of John.
Gurley, John	WC2	329,358	" 1680.
Gurling, Judith	15	358	Transported 1675.
Gurnett, Thomas	5	82	" 1661.
Gutheridge, Henry	11	378	" 1668.
Gutheridge, Roger	12	217	" 1669.
Gutterage, John	16	132	" 1671.
Gutteridge, Henry	17	531	" 1673.
Gutteridge, Richard	15	329	" 1675.
Guy, John	ABH	11	Immigrated 1640.
Guy, John	1	26	Transported 1641. (Also spelled Gay).
Guy, John	ABH	370	Immigrated 1646.
Gwither, Nicholas	ABH	60,244	Transported 1639. Servant.
Gwy, John	2	429-430	Immigrated 1640. (Also spelled Gray).
Gwy, John	5	247	Transported 1659 by Philip Calvert.
Gwyn, Arthur	5	607	Immigrated 1663.
Gwyn, Evan	5	529	Service 1662.
Gwyn, John	5	307	Transported 1663.
Gwyn, John	15	331	" 1675.
Gwyn, Thomas	5	607	" 1658. Service 1670. (12, fol. 474).
Gwyne, Richard	9	25	Transported 1665.
Gwynn, Sarah	11	525	" 1668. Wife of John.
Gwyther, John	ABH	26	Son of Nicholas. Living 1649.
Gwyther, John	2	517	Son of Nicholas.
Gwyther, Lieut. Nicholas	ABH	10,26	Transported 1640 with wife. Service 1649.
Gwyther, Lt. Nicholas	2	425	Transported 1640.
Gwyther, Lt. Nicholas	2	517	Service 1649.

NAME	Liber	Folio	REMARKS
Gwyther, Mrs.			
Nicholas	2	517	Service 1649.
Gyele, Mary	15	569	Transported 1678. (See Eyels).
Gyles, Jonas	9	271	" 1665. Servant.
Gyles, William	5	533	Immigrated 1658.
Gyner, James	18	137	Transported 1674.
Haberdyne, John	17	411	" 1673.
Hack, George	4	17	Immigrated 1658. Died prior to
1665, leaving a widow, Ann, who married --- Bool of Virginia. Doctor			
in Physick.			
Hack, Sefryn	4	17	Transported 1658. Brother to
			Dr. George.
Hacker, Elizabeth	17	396	Transported 1671. (16, fol. 635).
Hacker, John	17	396	" 1671. (16, fol. 635).
Hacker, Mary	17	396	" 1671. (16, fol. 635).
Hacker, Michael	ABH	59	" 1641. (1, fol. 24).
Hacker, Rachel	17	396	" 1671. (16, fol. 635).
Hacker, Richard	17	396	Immigrated 1671 with Mary, his
			wife. (16, fol. 635).
Hacker, Samuel	17	40	Transported 1672.
Hackesby, George	8	478	" 1665.
Hackester, John	10	352	" 1666. Service 1674.
			(18, fol. 110).
Hacket, Katherine	WC2	67	Transported 1667. Servant. Wife
			of William.
Hacket, William	WC2	67	Transported 1667. Servant. Of
			Talbot Co.
Hackett, Mary	15	301	Transported 1675.
Hackett, Michael	15	314	Service 1675. Of Talbot Co.
Hackett, Theophilus	WC2	367	Immigrated 1675. Of Anne Arun-
			del County.
Hackett, Thomas	18	291	Transported 1674.
Hackett, Thomas	15	446	" 1677.
Hackling, John	17	64	Service 1672.
Hackman, Jefferry	16	400	Transported 1671.
Hackmillion, George	7	489	" 1664.
Haddell, William	5	89	" 1661.
Haddock (Huddock),			
Thomas	WC2	24,106	" 1678. Servant.
Haddoway, Richard	8	131	Immigrated 1664 with his wife
and three children and two servants.			
Hadelow, Edea	9	334	Transported 1666.
Hadloe, Thomas	10	499	" 1667.
Hadson, William	5	210	Immigrated prior to 1662.
Haemego, Roger	15	455	Transported 1678.
Haerford, Dan.	15	531	" 1678.
Hagan, Thomas	12	594	Service 1670.
Hagar, Robert	WC2	309	" 1680. Of St. Mary's Co.
Hage, Sarah	8	203	Transported 1665.
Hagelton, Thomas	15	391	Service 1676. Of Calvert Co.
Hages, Sarah	16	437	Transported 1671.

NAME	Liber	Folio	REMARKS
Haggamore, John	6	347	Transported 1663.
Haggett, Humphrey	5	201	Immigrated 1659.
Haghieren, John	WC2	128-129	Transported 1679.
Hagsley, Mary	15	527	" 1678.
Hague, John	6	305	" 1664.
Hague, Sarah	8	501	" 1665.
Hailes, John	7	483	" 1660. Service 1670. (12, fol. 554).
Hailes, Mary	16	132	Transported 1671.
Hailes, Mary	WC2	58	Service 1677.
Haine, Moses	7	484	Transported 1664.
Haines, George	WC2	171	" 1679.
Hainford, Richard	ABH	358	" 1640.
Hainsworth, George	7	506	" 1662.
Haire, Robert	9	33	" 1660-5.
Haker, Nicholas	9	38	" 1664.
Haland, Lar.	15	553	" 1678.
Halbard, Shilby	13	122	" 1668.
Halbert, Ann	9	189	" 1665.
Halbert, Richard	6	131	" 1657.
Halde, Barnet	15	430	" 1677.
Hale, Job	11	338	" 1668.
Hale, Joys	9	34	" 1665.
Hale, Robert	9	50	" 1665. Service 1667. (10, fol. 480).
Hale, Samuel	Q	29	Transported 1658.
Hales, Elizabeth	7	546	" 1663.
Hales, Elizabeth	12	477	" 1670.
Hales, Joyce	4	69	" 1659.
Hales, Robert	10	414	" 1665.
Hales, Spencer	17	545	Service 1673. Of Calvert Co.
Hales, Thomas	ABH	200	Immigrated 1631-6 with wife.
Hales, Thomas	1	85	Petition to confirm title of land granted by Capt. William Clayborne, 1640.
Halewell, John	16	437	Transported 1671.
Haley (Whaley), John	8	483	" from Virginia 1665.
Halfe, Abraham	18	80	Service 1674.
Halfeway, John	9	106	Transported 1665.
Halfhead, Anne	2	579	" 1649. First wife of John.
Halfhead, James	15	322	Transported 1675.
Halfhead, Jane	15	434	Service 1677. Wife of John.
Halfhead, John	1	121	Transported 1633.
Halfhead, John	2	579	Service to his Lordship, Lord Baltimore 1649.
Halfhead, John	ABH	35,98	Transported 1633. Servant 1649. Married 1st, a free woman; 2nd, Julian (See Jane), servant to Mr. White. (ABH, fol. 35; Q, fol. 208).
Halfhead, Julian	2	579	Transported 1649. Servant. Second wife of John.
Halfland, John	8	129	Transported 1665.

NAME	Liber	Folio	REMARKS
Halfoard, John	18	314	Service 1668.
Halfpenny, Thomas	15	446	Transported 1677.
Halfyeare (Halfyere),			
Thomas	WC2	253,398	" 1680.
Hall, Ann	11	168	" 1667.
Hall, Barbarry	17	440	" 1673.
Hall, Burges	12	406	" 1669.
Hall, Charles	10	343	Immigrated 1665.
Hall, Charles	12	206	Transported 1669.
Hall, Christopher	11	571	Service 1668. (12, fol. 207-314).
Hall, Cornelius	15	509	Transported 1673.
Hall, Edward	7	507	" from Virginia 1664.
Hall, Edward	15	535	" 1678.
Hall, Eleanor	17	469	" 1673.
Hall, Elisha	18	296	" 1674.
Hall, Elizabeth	Q	58	" 1651.
Hall, Elizabeth	ABH	162	" 1650. Servant.
Hall, Elizabeth	5	416	" 1663. Wife of Richard.
Hall, Elizabeth	8	484	" 1665. (16, fol. 505).
Hall, Elizabeth	10	469	" 1667.
Hall, Elizabeth	WC2	320	" 1680. Wife of Thomas.
Hall, Ellis	10	343	" 1665.
Hall, Francis	7	88	" 1652.
Hall, George	Q	71	" 1652-3. (6, fol. 83).
Hall, George	WC2	320	" 1680. Son of Thomas.
Hall, Hannah	20	185	" 1679.
Hall, Henry	12	584	Immigrated 1670. Of St. Mary's Co.
Hall, Henry	18	38	" 1673 with Grace, his
wife, and Ann and Mary, his daughters.			
Hall, Henry	15	543	Service 1677.
Hall, Isaac	6	22	Transported 1663.
Hall, Isaac	12	199,345	" 1668.
Hall, Isabell	16	411	" 1671.
Hall, James	4	59	" 1657.
Hall, James	17	608	" 1673.
Hall, James	20	185	" 1679.
Hall, Jane	13	65	" 1668. Servant.
Hall, John	5	2	" 1640.
Hall, John	11	527	Immigrated 1668.
Hall, John	17	395	" 1672. Of St. Mary's Co.
Hall, John	17	474	Transported 1672.
Hall, John	18	15,291	" 1673.
Hall, John	15	354,397	" 1676.
Hall, John	15	394,520	" 1677.
Hall, Joseph	12	379	" 1669.
Hall, Joseph	17	469	" 1671.
Hall, Joshua	18	15	" 1673.
Hall, Katherine	4	140	" 1657. Servant.
			(Quaker ?)
Hall, Katherine	11	282	Transported 1667. (12, fol. 584).
Hall, Margaret	9	488	" 1665.

NAME	Liber	Folio	REMARKS
Hall, Margaret	17	440	Transported 1673.
Hall, Margaret	18	167	" 1674.
Hall, Margaret	WC2	120	" 1680.
Hall, Margery	17	474	" 1672.
Hall, Martha	WC2	309	" 1678.
Hall, Mathew	17	615	" 1673.
Hall, Penelope	5	247	" 1659 by Philip Cal- vert, Esq.
Hall, Richard	5	416	Immigrated 1663. Before 1658. (5, fol. 416).
Hall, Richard	7	560	Transported 1665.
Hall, Roger	6	118	" 1657.
Hall, Samuel	12	194	" 1668. Servant.
Hall, Sarah	5	241	" 1662 by James Hall.
Hall, Steeven	6	86	" 1657.
Hall, Thomas	7	568	" 1665. Servant. (9, fol. 304).
Hall, Thomas	16	118,414	Transported 1671.
Hall, Thomas	17	54	" 1672.
Hall, Thomas	17	474	" 1672.
Hall, Thomas	15	356	" 1676.
Hall, Thomas	WC2	320	Immigrated 1680 with wife and son.
Hall, Thomas, Jr.	17	474	Transported 1672.
Hall, Mr. Walter	ABH	380	Immigrated prior to June, 1652.
Married the relict of John Lloyd, Gent., prior to 1663. (5, fol. 393-5).
Hall, Walter	17	475	Transported 1673.
Hall, Walter	15	450,507	" 1677.
Hall, William	1	22	" 1642.
Hall, William	7	605	Immigrated 1665.
Hall, William	8	495	Transported 1665.
Hall, William	16	432	" 1671.
Hall, William	17	416	" 1673.
Hall, William	18	167	" 1674.
Hall, William	15	360	" 1676.
Hallaway, Jane	WC2	167,169	" 1679.
Halliband, John	6	17	" 1663.
Hallican, Edward	15	553	" 1678.
Hallier, Ann	5	488	" 1651-62.
Hallock, Katherine	WC2	16	" 1677.
Halloway, Richard	9	55	" 1665.
Halloway, Thomas	12	416	" 1669.
Hallowell, James	10	434	" 1667.
Hallowes, John	1	26	" 1633. (See Hollis).
Halls, John	17	463	" 1673.
Halls, Margaret	17	56	Service 1672. Wife of Samuel.
Halls, Samuel	17	56	Immigrated 1662.
Hallyard, Ann	5	238	Transported 1662.
Halmes, Thomas	17	67	" 1668.
Halocke, Kat.	15	574	" 1678.
Haloorane, Catherine	20	184	" from Ireland 1678.
Halse, Abraham	16	100	" 1663.

NAME	Liber	Folio	REMARKS
Halse, Edward	WC2	107	Transported 1679.
Halsey, Edward	WC2	112	" 1679.
Halsey, Mary	10	430	" 1667.
Halson, Henry	15	172	" 1673.
Halson, Thomas	15	172	" 1673.
Halston, Ralph	ABH	24	" 1646. Servant.
Halway, Robert	15	370	" 1676.
Halyer, Thomas	17	545	" 1673.
Ham, Barbara	6	86	" 1650.
Ham, Emanuel	18	4	" 1674.
Ham, George	6	131	" 1660.
Ham, Joseph	17	352	" 1672.
Hambdin, Robert	5	56	Immigrated prior to 1661.
Hambleton, Amos	ABH	140	Transported 1651. (4, fol. 139).
Hambleton, David	WC2	65	" 1679.
Hambleton, Elizabeth	18	39	" 1674.
Hambleton, Francis	7	465	" 1657.
Hambleton, James	12	215	" 1668-9.
Hambleton, James	16	170	" 1671.
Hambleton, Jane	18	152	" 1674.
Hambleton, John	17	402	Immigrated 1652 with Temperance,
his wife. Of Calvert Co. (13, fol. 94).			
Hambleton, Peter	6	136	Transported 1656.
Hambleton, Ralph	15	566	" 1678.
Hambleton, Roger	WC2	65	" 1679.
Hambleton, Temperance	17	402	Immigrated 1652. Wife of John.
Hamby, Mary	Q	204	" 1658. Wife of Richard.
Hamby, Richard	Q	204	" 1658.
Hamby, William	Q	204	" 1658. Son of Richard.
Hamerston, Elizabeth	15	318	Transported 1675.
Hamerthy, Thomas	9	313	" 1665.
Hames, James	2	615	" 1649.
Hames, James	ABH	40	" 1650.
Hames, Ralph	WC2	395	" 1680. Servant.
Hamilton, And.	WC2	120	" 1680.
Hamilton, John	ABH	311	Immigrated Dec. 1652.
Hamilton, John	17	363	Transported 1672.
Hamilton, John	18	106	Immigrated 1674.
Hamilton, Judith	WC2	167,169	Transported 1679.
Hamilton, Margaret	WC2	120	" 1680.
Hamilton, William	Q	66	Immigrated 1657.
Hamilton, William	15	531	Transported 1678.
Hamlett, Dorothy	12	340	" 1668. (11, fol. 374).
Hamley, John	15	499	" 1677.
Hamlin, Elizabeth	18	37	" 1673. Wife of George.
Hamlin, George	18	37	Immigrated 1673.
Hamlin, Mary	18	37	Transported 1673. Daughter of George.
Hamlington, John	ABH	46	Transported 1650. Servant. (3, fol. 21).
Hamlyn, David	17	388	Transported from Virginia 1672.

NAME	Liber	Folio	REMARKS
Hammer, Pedro	9	399	Transported 1666.
Hammerslee, Ralph	18	329	" 1675.
Hammon, Ann	15	413	" 1677. Wife of Edward.
Hammon, Edward	15	413	Immigrated 1677. Of Somerset Co.
Hammon, Edward	15	413	Transported 1677. Son of Edward.
Hammon, Edward	WC2	318	Rights 1680.
Hammon, Jenkin	WC2	130	Transported 1679. Servant.
Hammon, John	15	413	" 1677. Son of Edward.
Hammon, Mark	15	413	" 1677. Son of Edward.
Hammon, Mary	15	413	" 1677. Daughter of Edward.
Hammon, Philip	15	499	Immigrated 1677. Of Somerset Co.
Hammond, Benjamin	1	166	Transported 1650. Servant.
Hammond, Daniel	9	271	Service 1665. (15, fol. 171).
Hammond, Edward	12	343	Transported 1669.
Hammond, Elizabeth	9	54	" 1665 by Cornelius Howard.
Hammond, Elizabeth	17	579	Service 1673. Wife of Daniel.
Hammond, Elizabeth	15	322	Transported 1674. Servant.
Hammond, Elizabeth	15	514	" 1677.
Hammond, John	6	90	" prior to 1663.
Hammond, Mary	9	354	" 1663.
Hammond, Moses	9	354	" 1663 on the ship "King Solomon".
Hamon, John	6	321	Transported 1664.
Hamon, John	13	59	" 1670.
Hamon, Robert	15	318,445	" 1675.
Hamond, Ann	ABH	338	" 1653. Wife of John.
Hamond, Ann	ABH	338	" 1653. Daughter of John and Ann.
Hamond, Benjamin	ABH	339	Transported by Robert Brook, June 1652. Servant.
Hamond, Bernard	ABH	338	Transported 1653. Son of John and Ann.
Hamond, Daniel	ABH	338	Transported 1653. Son of John and Ann.
Hamond, Garret	17	349	Immigrated 1672. Of Charles Co.
Hamond, Henry	15	430	Transported 1677.
Hamond, Jenkin	15	566	" 1678.
Hamond, Mr. John	ABH	338	Immigrated 1653.
Hamond, John	6	293	Transported 1664.
Hamond, John	15	436	" 1677.
Hamond, Mordecai	ABH	338	" 1653. Son of John and Ann.
Hamond, Mordecai	7	81	Immigrated 1661.
Hamond, Nicholas	12	317	Transported 1669, by Randall Revell of Somerset County.
Hamper, Christopher	9	399	Transported 1666.
Hamper, Thomas	ABH	104	Immigrated 1646. (ABH, fol. 157; 2, fol. 457).
Hamper, William	9	399	Transported 1666.

206

NAME	Liber	Folio	REMARKS
Hampson, Henry	12	270	Service 1668.
Hampson, James	15	530	Transported 1678.
Hampstead, William	ABH	421	Immigrated 1650, with wife.
Hampton, Hannah	16	339	Transported 1671. (17, fol. 601). Daughter of Wm.
Hampton, John	5	468	Transported 1661. (6, fol. 15).
Hampton, Philip	16	339	" 1671. Son of William. (17, fol. 601).
Hampton, Phillis	17	601	Transported 1668. Wife of William. Afterwards married --- Shackerly.
Hampton, William	17	601	Immigrated from Virginia 1673, with Phillis, his wife, and Philip and Hannah, his children. Died prior to 1673. Widow married --- Shackerly. (16, fol. 339).
Hamshaw, Robert	5	308	Transported 1663.
Hamson, Mark	6	87	" 1660.
Han, William	15	443	" 1673.
Hanagh, William	15	553	" 1678.
Hanaken, Mathias	7	135	" 1664.
Hanay, Daniel	16	354	" 1671.
Hance, Anakin	11	537	" 1668.
Hance, John	9	44	" 1659.
Hance, Robert	WC2	50,98	" 1669. (12, fol. 415).
Hancock, John	WC2	73	" 1678.
Hancock, Stephen	6	294	" 1664. (11, fol. 247).
Hancock, Thomas	9	38	" 1665.
Handbanch, William	6	214	" 1663.
Handborough, Richard	6	127	" 1657.
Handell, James	12	472	" 1670.
Handley, Deborah	6	87	" 1650.
Hands, Christopher	4	190	" 1659.
Handson, Henry	5	211	" 1662.
Handy, Daniel	16	354	" 1671.
Hanes, Darkiss	WC2	168-169	" 1680.
Haniford, Richard	1	22	" 1640.
Hanlegram, Ann	9	329	" 1665.
Hanley, Robert	ABH	41	Immigrated 1648. (2, fol. 625).
Hanlin, Patrick	17	57	Transported 1673.
Hanly, Robert	18	137	" 1674.
Hannagall, William	15	430	" 1677.
Hannah, William	7	560	" 1665.
Hannam, Ann	ABH	402	" 1650. Servant.
Hannes, Jane	WC2	73	" 1678.
Hans, Jacob	12	473	" 1670.
Hanscombe, Richard	16	130	" 1671.
Hanslap, Henry	WC2	171-172	Immigrated 1676. Of Anne Arundel County.
Hansmore, Jone	8	483	Transported 1665.
Hansmore, Stephen	8	483	" 1665.
Hanson, Andrew	Q	365	" 1658. (10, fol. 312).
Hanson, Anibeck	Q	365	" 1658.
Hanson, Anthony	17	566	Immigrated 1673. Of Worcester Co.

NAME	Liber	Folio	REMARKS
Hanson, Catherine	Q	365	Transported 1658.
Hanson, Cornelius	16	482	" 1670-1. (17,fol.567).
Hanson, Elizabeth	16	132	" 1671.
Hanson, Ellen	16	507	" 1671.
Hanson, Frederick	Q	365	" 1658.
Hanson, Hance	Q	365	" 1658. (16,fol.398).
Hanson, Hance	WC2	187-188,	
		414	Married Martha Wells, relict of John Wells. Of Kent Co.
Hanson, Margaret	Q	365	Transported 1658. Married Alex.
Waters, prior to 1666. (10,fol.311-12).			
Hanson, Martha	WC2	187-188	Wife of Hance and relict of John Wells.
Hanson, Mary	17	67	Transported 1672.
Hanson, Peter	17	567	" 1673.
Hanson, Randle	4	18	Service 1659.
Hapes, Jone	15	359	Transported 1676.
Hapre, Moses	9	34	" 1665.
Harber, John	15	501	" 1678.
Harbert, Charles	10	609	" 1667.
Harbert, George	16	482	" 1671.
Harbert, John	WC2	110	" 1676. Servant.
Harbert, William	15	356	" 1674.
Harbett, William	3	173	" 1655.
Harbinger, William	WC2	100	" 1679.
Harbord, Mary	15	531	" 1678.
Harbridge, John	18	174	" 1674.
Harburne, Will	8	478	" 1665.
Hard, John	10	272	" 1666.
Hardacre, Anthony	12	211	" 1668.
Hardell, William	9	233	" 1665.
Hardelston, John	11	265	" 1667.
Harden, Robert	9	157	" 1665.
Hardesty, Cecilia	9	54	" 1665. Wife of George of Patuxent River.
Hardesty, George	5	191	Immigrated 1662.
Hardgrave, Izabell	WC2	309	Transported 1678.
Hardidge, William	2	426	" 1636. Servant.
Hardie, Thomas	1	24	" 1641.
Hardige, John	9	17	" 1665.
Hardige, William	ABH	10	Servant 1636.
Hardiman, Dorothy	5	88	Transported 1662.
Hardin, John	16	393	" 1671.
Hardin, William	ABH	141	" 1651.
Harding, Ann	9	93	" 1665.
Harding, Ann, Sr.	12	203	" 1665.
Harding, Ann, Jr.	12	203	" 1669.
Harding, Henry	16	71	" Nov.1668.
Harding, John	12	498	" 1670.
Harding, Joseph	11	338	" 1668. Service 1674.
			(18,fol.12).

NAME	Liber	Folio	REMARKS
Harding, Mathew	5	203	Transported 1662.
Harding, Sarah	WC2	58	" 1678
Harding, Thomas	5	246	" by Philip Calvert, Esq., 1657.
Hardisse, Elizabeth	16	414	Transported 1671.
Hardman, Hendrick	9	488	" 1665.
Hardridge, John	16	86	" 1670.
Hardridge, William	16	86	" 1670.
Hardseaver, Peter	18	337	" 1675.
Hardy, Ann	11	499	" Oct. 1667. Wife of Robert.
Hardy, Barbara	4	198	Transported 1659.
Hardy, Charity	15	317	Immigrated 1674. Wife of John.
Hardy, Henry	9	308	Transported 1666. Service 1673. (17, fol. 533).
Hardy, John	15	317	Immigrated 1674. Of Virginia.
Hardy, John	15	500	" 1678 with Mary, his wife.
Hardy, Joseph	12	356	Transported 1669.
Hardy, Robert	11	499	Immigrated Oct. 1667.
Hardy, Robert	WC2	318	Transported 1680.
Hardy, William	13	66	" 1669. Servant.
Hardy, William	15	598	" 1678-9.
Hardy, William	WC2	211	" 1679. Servant.
Hare, Humphrey	7	83	" 1661.
Hare, James	2	458	Immigrated 1647.
Hare, James	ABH	15	" 1648.
Hare, Rebecca	15	322	Transported 1674.
Hare, Timothy	7	507	" 1659.
Hare, William	12	346	Service 1669. Of Patapsco.
Harett, Nicholas	9	37	Immigrated 1665.
Harff, Robert	12	340	Transported 1668.
Harford, William	ABH	403	" prior to June 1652. Servant.
Hargesse, Wm. & Ann	18	178	Service 1674.
Hargett, Margaret	4	216	Transported 1659.
Hargift, Thomas	4	198	" 1659.
Hargish, Thomas	6	296	" 1663.
Hargrave, William	5	56	" 1659. (11, fol. 139).
Hargraves, Edward	WC2	71,242	" 1678.
Hargraves, Elizabeth	15	553	" 1678.
Hargraves, John	15	553	" 1678.
Hargrove, Elizabeth	17	395	" 1672.
Hargroves, Elizabeth	WC2	57	" 1678.
Hargroves, John	WC2	57	" 1678.
Harington, Thomas	1	38	" 1633. (See Charington).
Haris, John	15	446	" 1677.
Harish, Thomas	WC2	82	" 1679.
Harison, Miles	15	507	Immigrated prior to 1677.
Harland, James	WC2	21	Transported 1679.
Harle, James	17	475	Service 1673. Of Dorchester Co.

NAME	Liber	Folio	REMARKS
Harley, Mary	WC2	112	Transported 1679.
Harley, Susana	17	424	" 1673.
Harlock, Edward	7	86	" 1653.
Harlock, George	10	609	Service 1667.
Harlock, William	15	500	Transported 1678.
Harloe, Anne	Q	33	" 1658.
Harloe, Stephen	Q	33	" 1658.
Harlow, Thomas	15	499	" 1677.
Harman, Abraham	8	88	" 1665.
Harman, Arian	9	506	" 1666.
Harman, Elias	7	81	" 1657.
Harman, George	4	139	" 1650. Servant.
Harman, George	15	422	" 1669.
Harman, Henry	18	37	Immigrated 1673.
Harman, Isabel	17	443	Transported 1662.
Harman, John	15	448	" 1678.
Harman, Mary	16	110	" 1671. Wife of Augustine of Baltimore Co.
Harman, Richard	8	484	Transported 1665.
Harman, William	8	502	" 1665.
Harmans, Hendrica	12	285	" 1667.
Harmer, Gothofrid	4	554	Immigrated prior to 1661. (Q, fol. 62).
Harmetage, William	Q	71	Transported 1654.
Harmon, Absolom	6	131	" 1653.
Harmon, George	ABH	140	" 1651.
Harmond, Randall	WC2	211	" 1679. Servant.
Harnborough, Martha	6	120	" 1654.
Harnes, William	6	48	" prior to 1663.
Harnesse, John	11	337	" 1668.
Harnett, Martha	15	313	" 1675.
Harpe, Henry	6	294	" 1664.
Harpen, Thomas	9	334	Immigrated 1661.
Harper, Edward	17	463	Transported 1673.
Harper, Edward	15	433	" 1677. Son of William.
Harper, Elizabeth	15	433	" 1677. Wife of William.
Harper, Elizabeth	WC2	65	" 1679.
Harper, Hellen	5	246	" 1656 by Philip Calvert.
Harper, James	15	422	Immigrated 1677.
Harper, James	15	452	Transported 1678.
Harper, John	7	87	" 1657.
Harper, John	15	500	" 1678.
Harper, Margaret	11	462	" 1668.
Harper, Robert	18	335	Service 1673. Of St. Mary's Co.
Harper, Stephen	6	47	Transported 1661. (7, fol. 86).
Harper, Stephen	11	184	" 1667.
Harper, William	ABH	42	Servant 1650. (10, fol. 440).
Harper, William	3	3	Transported 1650. Servant.
Harper, William	ABH	140	" 1651. (Q, fol. 323, 431).
Harper, William	15	433	Immigrated 1677.
Harrell, John	15	397	Transported 1676.

NAME	Liber	Folio	REMARKS
Harrice, John	10	558	Transported 1663.
Harridge, John	12	472	" 1670.
Harrington, Alice	5	367	" 1649.
Harrington, Humphrey	5	307	" 1658.
Harrington, Jeremy	4	533	Service 1659.
Harrington, Jo.	1	108	Immigrated 1635.
Harrington, John	ABH	93	" 1635.
Harrington, John	4	533	Service 1659.
Harrington, John	6	13	Immigrated 1659.
Harrington, John	5	485	Transported 1662.
Harrington, Richard	15	379	Immigrated 1675. Of Kent Co.
Harrington, William	1	27	Transported 1633-41. (ABH, fol. 61).
Harrington, William	17	67,497	Service 1671.
Harriott, Ambrose	17	596	Transported 1673.
Harris, Adam	WC2	120	" 1680.
Harris, Ales	13	122	" 1669.
Harris, Alice	15	527	" 1678.
Harris, Ann	10	557	" 1667. Daughter of Elizabeth.
Harris, Ann	17	411	Transported 1673.
Harris, Ann, Sr.	15	390	" 1676.
Harris, Ann, Jr.	15	390	" 1676.
Harris, Bridget	16	435	" 1671.
Harris, Charles	15	501	" 1678.
Harris, David	15	500	" 1676-7.
Harris, David	WC2	399	" 1677.
Harris, Edward	6	36	" 1663.
Harris, Edward	12	217	" 1669.
Harris, Edward	16	410,482	" 1671.
Harris, Eleanor	17	498	" 1673.
Harris, Elizabeth	10	557	Immigrated 1667. Of Long Creek Langford in Talbot Co.
Harris, Elizabeth	12	358	Transported 1668.
Harris, Elizabeth	17	474	" 1672.
Harris, Elizabeth	20	185	" 1679.
Harris, Elizabeth	WC2	381	" 1675-80. Servant.
Harris, Elizabeth	WC2	86-87, 381	" 1679.
Harris, Francis	17	56	Immigrated 1672.
Harris, Frederick	10	557	Transported 1667. Son of Elizabeth.
Harris, Gano'r.	15	560	" 1678.
Harris, George	Q	73	" 1658.
Harris, George	10	168	Immigrated 1660.
Harris, George	9	354	Transported 1662.
Harris, George	15	397	" 1676.
Harris, Henry	16	508	" 1670.
Harris, James	17	606	Service 1673. Of Calvert Co.
Harris, Jane	15	500	Transported 1676-7.
Harris, Jane	WC2	399	" 1677.
Harris, Jane	WC2	167,169, 246	" 1679.

NAME	Liber	Folio	REMARKS
Harris, John	1	71-72	Gift of 50 acres from Leonard Calvert, 1640.
Harris, John	Q	463	Of London, Merchant. Undertakes to immigrate 1657. (4, fol. 19, 198).
Harris, John	Q	434	Transported 1658.
Harris, John	6	237	" 1663.
Harris, John	9	332	" 1664, in the "Golden Wheat Sheaf".
Harris, John	11	348	Transported 1668. (12, fol. 190; 16, fol. 71).
Harris, Capt. John	WC2	130	Commander of ship "Dover", 1679.
Harris, John	WC2	411	Transported 1681.
Harris, Mary	10	557	" 1667. Daughter of Elizabeth.
Harris, Mary	13	59	Transported 1670.
Harris, Mary	17	610	" 1673.
Harris, Morris	17	573	Service 1673. Of St. Mary's Co.
Harris, Moses	6	124	Transported 1663. (17, fol. 412).
Harris, Richard	ABH	244	" 1641.
Harris, Richard	1	69	" 1637. Servant.
Harris, Richard	ABH	383	Immigrated Feb. 1653.
Harris, Richard	WC2	254	Service 1676. (15, fol. 354).
Harris, Mr. Richard	ABH	157	Immigrated 1650 with wife.
Harris, Robert	3	17	" 1650.
Harris, Robert	6	294	Transported 1664.
Harris, Robert	17	54	" 1672.
Harris, Roger	ABH	44,203	Immigrated 1650.
Harris, Samuel	4	621	" prior to 1661, when he was aged 22 years.
Harris, Samuel	5	415	Transported 1663.
Harris, Sarah	15	430	" 1677.
Harris, Susanna	16	293	" 1671.
Harris, Symon	9	269	" 1665.
Harris, Thomas	ABH	46	Immigrated 1650 with wife and one servant. (3, fol. 21).
Harris, Thomas	5	415	Transported 1661. (11, fol. 512; 17, fol. 634).
Harris, Thomas	18	84	Transported 1674.
Harris, Thomas	15	380,404	" 1676.
Harris, William	5	530	" 1662.
Harris, William	12	194	" 1668. Servant.
Harris, William	17	578	Immigrated Nov. 1669. Of St. Mary's County.
Harris, William	17	474	Transported 1672.
Harris, William	18	280	Immigrated 1675. Of St. Mary's Co. Carpenter.
Harris, William	15	559	Transported 1679.
Harris, William	WC2	130,145	" 1679. Servant.
Harrison, Ann	8	381,478	" 1665. (9, fol. 189; 8, fol. 204).
Harrison, Ann	18	167	Transported 1674.

NAME	Liber	Folio	REMARKS
Harrison, Ann	15	436	Transported 1677.
Harrison, Daniel	18	291	" 1674.
Harrison, Eleanor	18	15	" 1673.
Harrison, Elizabeth	Q	207	Immigrated prior to 1658. Wife of Joseph.
Harrison, Elizabeth	10	407	Transported on "The Providence" of Bristol, 1666.
Harrison, Elizabeth	18	174	Transported 1674.
Harrison, Francis	Q	207	" prior to 1658. Son of Joseph.
Harrison, Henry	9	229	Transported 1665.
Harrison, James	WC2	394	" 1680. Servant.
Harrison, Jane	17	396	" 1669.
Harrison, John	7	492	" 1664.
Harrison, John	10	231	" 1666.
Harrison, John	12	205	" 1667.
Harrison, John	16	43	" 1670.
Harrison, John	16	303,393	Immigrated 1671 with Judith, his wife. Of Virginia.
Harrison, John	15	362	Transported 1676.
Harrison, Jonas	16	132	" 1671.
Harrison, Joseph	ABH	415	Immigrated 1653.
Harrison, Joseph	7	601	Transported 1665. (9, fol. 48).
Harrison, Judith	16	303	" from Virginia 1671. Wife of John, of Somerset Co.
Harrison, Mary	17	416	Transported 1673.
Harrison, Peter	17	67	Immigrated 1668.
Harrison, Peter	17	54	Transported 1672.
Harrison, Richard	7	491	" 1663.
Harrison, Richard	7	577	Immigrated 1665 with wife.
Harrison, Robert	18	167	Transported 1674.
Harrison, Robert	WC2	112	" 1679.
Harrison, Rosemond	13	65	" 1668.
Harrison, Sarah	16	320	" 1670. Of "Accomacke" in Virginia. Daughter-in-law of Roger Patrick.
Harrison, Sarah	18	337	Transported 1675.
Harrison, Simon	12	190	" 1668. Servant.
Harrison, Stephen	4	590	" 1661.
Harrison, Thomas	ABH	244	" 1641.
Harrison, Thomas	5	534	" 1660.
Harrison, Thomas	14	341	" 1671.
Harrison, Thomas	15	514	" 1677.
Harsfurt, George	10	342	" 1665.
Harson, Robert	16	414	" 1671.
Harsone, William	9	69	" 1660-5.
Hart, Arthur	18	334	Service 1675. Of Dorchester Co.
Hart, Hannah	WC2	183	Transported 1680.
Hart, Henry	12	190	" 1668. Servant.
Hart, Hester	5	93	" 1661.
Hart, Margaret	6	126	" 1655.
Hart, Richard	10	407	" 1666 on "The Provi-

NAME	Liber	Folio	REMARKS
			dence" of Bristol.
Hart, Robert	6	24	Immigrated 1663 with his wife and child.
Hart, Sarah	6	170	Transported 1661.
Hart, Thomas	5	412	" 1661.
Hart, Walter	Q	435	" 1658.
Hart, William	13	65	" 1668. Servant.
Hart, William	15	433	" 1677.
Hartagane, Timothy	20	184	" from Ireland 1678.
Harte, George	12	413	" 1669.
Harte, John	12	413	" 1669.
Harte, John	16	394	" 1671.
Harthorp, Richard	15	344	Service 1675. (19, fol. 39). Of Calvert Co.
Hartley, Jane	13	65	Transported 1668. Servant.
Hartley, John	17	510	" 1673.
Hartly, Elizabeth	18	137	" 1674.
Hartly, Thomas	15	503	" 1678.
Hartnesse, John	17·	444	Service 1673.
Hartup, John	16	91	Transported 1670.
Hartwell, Ann	15	536	" 1678. Wife of John.
Hartwell, Ann	15	536	" 1678. Daughter of John.
Hartwell, John	15	536	Immigrated 1678. Of Charles Co.
Hartwell, Joseph	Q	66	" 1656. Son of Mary Wicks by a former husband.
Hartwell, Mary	Q	66	Immigrated 1656. Daughter of Mary Wicks by a former husband.
Hartwell, Mary	15	536	Transported 1678. Daughter of John.
Harver, Sarah	12	475	" 1668.
Harvey, Ellen	11	282	" 1667.
Harvey, Frances	ABH	102	" 1641. Daughter of Nicholas. Married George Beckwith, 1658. (Q, fol. 416).
Harvey, Henry	WC2	395	Transported 1680. Servant.
Harvey, Jane	7	62	Widow of Nicholas. Married Thomas Green prior to 1653.
Harvey, John	Q	33	Transported 1654.
Harvey, John	7	499	" 1660. (11, fol. 204).
Harvey, John	10	569	" 1665-6. (9, fol. 436, 437).
Harvey, John	12	548	Transported 1670.
Harvey, Nicholas	ABH	66	" 1634. (See Hervey). (1, fol. 38).
Harvey, Nicholas	ABH	102	Immigrated 1641 with wife.
Harvey, Richard	1	166	Transported 1634. (See Nicholas Harvey, fol. 38).
Harvey, Richard	ABH	244	Transported 1641.
Harvey, Richard	17	418	Immigrated Sept. 1670.
Harvey, Robert	17	551	Transported 1673.
Harvey, Thomas	10	558	" 1663.
Harvey, William	15	544	" 1676.
Harvey, William	15	395	" 1677.

NAME	Liber	Folio	REMARKS
Harvill, Edward	15	535	Transported 1678.
Harvis, William	15	353	" 1674.
Harvy, Alice	10	305	" 1666. Wife of John.
Harvy, Alice	10	305	" 1666. Daughter of John.
Harvy, James	10	305	Transported 1666. Son of John.
Harvy, John	10	305	Immigrated 1666.
Harvy, John, Jr.	10	305	Transported 1666. Son of John.
Harvy, Peter	10	305	" 1666.
Harvy, Thomas	17	454	" 1672.
Harwar, William	15	330	Service 1675. Of St. Mary's Co.
Harwes, William	17	330	Transported 1672.
Harwood, Edward	Q	33	" 1654.
Harwood, Elizabeth	7	565	" 1665. Daughter of Edward Williams.
Harwood, John	ABH	229	Service 1652.
Harwood, Phillip	1	166	Transported 1650. Servant.
Harwood, Philip	5	421	Of Battle, in Calvert Co. Immigrated prior to 1663.
Harwood, Ralph	15	508	Immigrated 1678 with Ann, his wife.
Harwood, Robert	5	236	Of Maryland, Planter, acquired by purchase 200 acres in Anne Arundel Co. in 1659, which he sold the following year.
Harwood, Capt. Thomas	12	140	Of London, Mariner, a grant of 600 acres on the Eastern Shore called Harwoods Lyon, 1663. Master of ship Thomas & Mary, transported several persons in 1667. (11, fol. 265).
Harwood, Thomas	17	33	Immigrated from Virginia 1672. Of Somerset Co.
Hary, Jeane	15	531	Transported 1678.
Hascar, James	15	416	" 1677.
Haseldowne, Joseph	10	598	Immigrated 1667. (5, fol. 91).
Hasell, Jane	20	185	Transported 1679.
Haselton, Ralph	ABH	411	" 1640. Servant.
Haselton, Robert	ABH	151	" 1641. Servant.
Hasker, Jane	15	535	" 1678.
Hasketts, James	18	311	" 1675.
Hasketts, Richard	18	311	" 1675.
Haskins, Anthony	15	359	" 1676.
Hasleton, Elizabeth	10	325	" prior to 1666.
Hasleton, Ralphe	2	512	" about 1649. Servant.
Hassald, Thomas	18	105	Immigrated 1674. Of Cecil Co.
Hassell, Alice	5	127	Transported 1660.
Hassell, Francis	15	537	" 1679.
Hassenson, Surill	12	473	" 1670.
Hast, Daniel	8	486	" 1664.
Hast, Giles	6	136	" 1659.
Hastings, James	18	291	" 1674.
Hastings, John	6	347	" 1663.
Hastings, John	12	190	" 1668.
Hastings, Richard	16	91	" 1670.
Hasulahat, Dennis	9	54	" 1665.

NAME	Liber	Folio	REMARKS
Hatch, David	Q	183	Servant 1658.
Hatch, George	9	433	Transported 1663.
Hatch, John	1	19	" 1637.
Hatch, John	ABH	101	" 1641. (1, fol. 127).
Hatch, John	ABH	23	" 1644 with wife.
Hatch, John	2	510-511	Immigrated about 1643-1644.
Hatch, Joseph	14	438	Service 1672. Of St. Mary's Co.
Hatch, Mrs.	2	511	Transported about 1647. Wife of John.
Hatchard, Sampson	WC2	309	Transported 1678.
Hatche, John	1	19	" 1638.
Hater, William	15	455	" 1678.
Hatfield, Elizabeth	WC2	331	" 1676. Wife of William.
Hatfield, Elizabeth	WC2	331	" 1676. Daughter of William.
Hatfield, John	18	334	Transported 1675.
Hatfield, William	WC2	331,358	Immigrated 1676 with wife, daughter and two other persons.
Hather, Warren	WC2	319	Immigrated 1680. "Sawyer".
Hathway, Rose	WC2	114	Transported 1680. Servant.
Hatinson, Benjamin	15	390	" 1676.
Hatso, William	6	171	" 1663.
Hatson, Elizabeth	WC2	406	" 1680.
Hattaway, Alice	4	58	Service 1659. Wife of Jacob Den.
Hattaway, Jacob Den	4	58	" 1659.
Hatter, Mary	15	443	Transported 1670.
Hattfield, Elizabeth	15	534	" 1677.
Hattfield, John	8	19	" 1664.
Hattfield, John	WC2	217	" 1680.
Hattle, William	9	262	" 1665.
Hatton, Ann	5	411	" 1663.
Hatton, Barbara	ABH	422	" 1649. Daughter of Margaret. (2, fol. 613).
Hatton, Constantine	6	96	Transported 1656.
Hatton, Eleanor	ABH	422	" 1649. Daughter of Margaret.
Hatton, Elinor	2	613	Transported 1649. Daughter of Margaret.
Hatton, Elizabeth	ABH	422	Transported 1649. Daughter of Margaret. (2, fol. 613).
Hatton, Elizabeth	15	353	Transported 1674.
Hatton, Henry	17	411	" 1673.
Hatton, Jasper	6	127	Immigrated 1649.
Hatton, John	5	106	" 1658.
Hatton, John	4	553	Transported 1661.
Hatton, John	15	543	Immigrated 1662.
Hatton, John	8	88	Transported 1665.
Hatton, John	17	27	Immigrated 1666 with Grace, his wife and John, his son.
Hatton, Margaret	ABH	422	Immigrated 1649. Widow of Richard,

the brother of Secretary Thomas. Appears as the wife of Lieut. Rich'd.

NAME	Liber	Folio	REMARKS
Banks, in Dec. 1652. (ABH, fol. 314).			
Hatton, Margarett	2	613	Transported 1649. Sister-in-law of Thomas Hatton, Widow.
Hatton, Mary	ABH	422	Transported 1649. Daughter of Margaret. (2, fol. 613).
Hatton, Mary	7	79	Transported 1664.
Hatton, Mary	12	549	" 1670.
Hatton, Richard	ABH	422	" 1649. Son of Margaret. Living in 1663. (2, fol. 613; 5, fol. 257; 19, fol. 375).
Hatton, Robert	16	115	Transported 1671.
Hatton, Robert	2	613	" 1648. Son of Thomas.
Hatton, Samuel	17	483	Immigrated 1667. Of Talbot Co.
Hatton, Sarah	11	374	Transported 1668.
Hatton, Sarah	16	115	" 1671.
Hatton, Thomas	ABH	431	Son of Thomas and Margaret. Born March 14, 1642.
Hatton, Thomas	ABH	123	Secretary of Maryland. Transported himself, his wife, Robert and Thomas, his sons, and Patrick Forest and George Beckwith, his servants, 1648. A Protestant. (ABH, 433). Gifts to his sons, Robert and Thomas, and his nephews, Wm. and Richard. (ABH, fol. 430; 7, fol. 608; 2, fol. 612-613).
Hatton, Thomas, Jr.	2	613	Transported 1648.
Hatton, William	ABH	422	" 1649. Son of Margaret. (2, fol. 613).
Haughlin, William	15	600	Transported 1678.
Haughton, Eleanor	18	14	" 1674.
Haughton, George	6	97	" 1660.
Haughton, Martha	18	84	" 1674.
Haughton, Thomas	WC2	199	" 1680.
Haukes, Richard	17	599	Service 1673. Of Kent Co.
Haukins, John	15	369	Transported 1676.
Haukshaw, Robert	15	369	Service 1675.
Haukson, Charles	15	531	Transported 1678.
Hauser, William	17	424	" 1673.
Hautschar, Thomas	4	533	" 1659.
Haver, Elizabeth	18	174	" 1674.
Haw, Abinadab	16	308	" from Virginia 1671. Child of Mary, wife of John Oakey, of Somerset Co.
Haward, Mathew	4	68	Transported prior to 1659.
Hawes, Joshua	15	568	" 1679.
Hawes, William	Q	430	" 1658.
Hawford, John	18	91	Immigrated 1674 with Elizabeth, his wife. Of St. Mary's County.
Hawker, Patience	6	31	Transported 1659. Widow of Henry Needham.
Hawker, Thomas	4	14	Transported 1659. Servant.
Hawkes, John	15	433	" 1677.
Hawkes, Thomas	8	484	" 1665.
Hawkins, Catherine	5	242	" 1662.
Hawkins, Daniel	6	98	Of New England. Mariner. Acquired land in Maryland 1663.

NAME	Liber	Folio	REMARKS
Hawkins, Eleanor	9	307	Transported 1666. Wife of Henry.
Hawkins, Henry	9	307	Immigrated 1666.
Hawkins, John	ABH	316	" 1651. Of New England. Mariner.
Hawkins, John	Q	435	Transported 1658.
Hawkins, John	9	307	" 1666. Son of Henry.
Hawkins, John	18	166	" 1674.
Hawkins, John	15	356	" 1676.
Hawkins, John	15	448,553	" 1677.
Hawkins, John	WC2	108	" 1679.
Hawkins, Katherine	4	622	" 1661.
Hawkins, Margaret	11	496	" 1668.
Hawkins, Mary	6	97	" 1660.
Hawkins, Philip	6	347	" 1663.
Hawkins, Richard	WC2	410	Service 1681. Of St. Mary's Co.
Hawkins, Robert	6	217	Transported 1663.
Hawkins, Robert	8	202	" 1664.
Hawkins, Robert	WC2	129	" 1679.
Hawkins, Thomas	12	584	" 1670.
Hawkins, William	ABH	100	" 1640 with wife.
Hawkins, William	1	124	Immigrated 1640 with wife.
Hawkins, William	ABH	150	Transported 1648. Servant.
Hawks, Richard	12	285	" 1668. Servant.
Hawle, Elizabeth	5	181	" 1661.
Hawley, Giles	WC2	50,57	" 1679.
Hawley, James	7	471	Of Virginia. Acquired land in Md. 1664.
Haws, Castine	10	598	Immigrated 1667.
Haws, Rowland	10	598	Transported 1667.
Hawsworth, John	18	84	" 1674.
Hawt, Ann	7	551	" 1664. Servant.
Hay, Andrew	Q	199	" 1651.
Hay, Arthur	ABH	60	Immigrated 1642.
Hay, Charles	17	411	Transported 1673. Service 1674. (18, fol. 109).
Hay, James	18	15,331	Transported 1673.
Hay, Thomas	6	299	" 1664.
Hay, Walter	12	190	" 1668.
Haydon, Thomas	12	282	Immigrated 1668.
Hayes, Alice	15	353	Transported 1674. (18, fol. 280).
Hayes, Bartholomew	16	135	" 1671. Service 1677. (15, fol. 563).
Hayes, Charles	18	279	Transported 1675.
Hayes, Dorothy	4	70,549	" 1659. Servant.
Hayes, George	18	295	" 1667. Of Talbot Co.
Hayes, George	13	114	" 1668.
Hayes, James	4	555	" 1661.
Hayes, John	4	53	" 1659.
Hayes, John	15	446,454	" 1677.
Hayes, Mary	15	514	" 1677.
Hayes, Richard	15	376	" 1676.

NAME	Liber	Folio	REMARKS
Hayes, Sarah	Q	323	Transported 1655-8.
Hayes, Teig	15	527	" 1678.
Hayes, Thomas	Q	250	" 1658.
Hayes, Thomas	15	455	" 1678.
Hayland, Lawrence	WC2	57	" 1678.
Hayler, Charity	7	483	" 1663.
Hayley, Jerome, Esq.	1	17	Immigrated 1637.
Hay, Arthur	1	26	Transported 1641.
Hayling, Elizabeth	4	60	" about 1659 and married to John Deen.
Haylings, Thomas	Q	19	Transported 1656. Service 1664. (16, fol. 462).
Haylocks, Will	15	501	Transported 1678.
Hayman, Eleanor	10	190	" 1666.
Hayman, Henry	10	190	Of Manokin River. Planter. Immigrated 1666.
Hayman, Henry, Jr.	10	190	Transported 1666.
Haynes, George	17	364	Immigrated 1672. Of St. Mary's Co.
Haynes, Mary	8	89	Transported 1665.
Haynes, John	11	313	" 1668.
Haynes, Margaret	15	553	" 1678.
Haynes, Thomas	8	89	" 1665.
Haynestreet, Thomas	5	307	" 1663. (See Staynestreet).
Hayre, Robert	4	204	" 1659.
Hays, Elizabeth	10	523	" 1667.
Hays, John	Q	29	Servant 1650.
Hayse, Richard	Q	435	Transported 1658.
Hayse, Thomas	Q	65	" 1650.
Hayse, William	Q	216	" 1665.
Hayton, Henry	WC2	77	Service 1679. Of Somerset Co.
Hayward, Edward	11	374	Transported 1668.
Hayward, Elizabeth	15	338	" 1676.
Hayward, Judith	15	338	" 1676.
Hayward, Nicholas	Q	470	Of London, Merchant. Undertakes to immigrated 1657. (See Samuel).
Hayward, Peter	ABH	68,101	Servant. Transported 1637-40.
Hayward, Samuel	4	544	Son of Nicholas, of London, Merchant, living 1659.
Hayward, Stephen	4	186-187	Of London, Merchant. About to immigrate 1657.
Hayward, Thomas	Q	427	Transported 1658.
Hayward, Thomas	6	90	" 1662.
Haywood, Raphael	9	336	Immigrated 1666.
Haywood, Susan	10	435	Transported 1665. (11, fol. 235).
Haywood, Thomas	10	435	Immigrated 1665. (11, fol. 235).
Hazard, Edward	8	486	Transported 1664.
Hazard, John	16	86	" 1670.
Haze, George	12	205	" 1667.
Hazelwood, Samuel	16	505	" 1671.
Head, Adam	4	198	" 1659.
Head, Edward	15	418	" 1677. (WC2, fol. 41).

NAME	Liber	Folio	REMARKS
Head, James	7	559	Transported 1663.
Head, Joseph	6	126	" 1654.
Head, Thomas	WC2	41	" 1677. (15, fol. 418).
Headley, Elizabeth	8	484	" 1665.
Headlock, Arion	9	33	" 1665.
Heafest, Cornelius	15	438	" 1677.
Heage, William	20	184	" from Ireland 1678.
Heager, Robert	12	209	" 1668.
Heal, Julian	Q	197	" 1658.
Healey, Samuel	16	79	" 1670.
Heaman, Joane	WC2	184	" 1680. Servant.
Heamer, Ann	15	384	" 1671. Wife of John.
Heamer, John	15	384	Immigrated 1671, with his wife, son and granddaughter, Ann Brooke.
Heamer, John	15	384	Transported 1671. Son of John.
Hearbotle, William	15	553	" 1678.
Hearch, Thomas	9	156	" 1663.
Heard, John	5	305	" 1663. (11, fol. 171).
Heard, Susan	10	584	" prior to 1667. Wife of John. Formerly servant to Col. Wm. Evans.
Heard, William	4	610	Immigrated 1661.
Heare, Richard	9	321	Transported 1665.
Hearn, Bednego	WC2	112	" 1680.
Hearon, William	15	320	Immigrated 1675.
Heart, Abraham	17	377	Transported 1668.
Heas, John	WC2	106	" 1679.
Heast, Daniel	9	450	" 1666.
Heath, Abraham	15	317,438	Immigrated 1674. Of Virginia.
Heath, Elizabeth	17	604	Service prior to 1673. Wife of Thomas.
Heath, Jane	WC2	380	Transported 1675-80. Servant.
Heath, John	9	44	" 1662.
Heath, Susanna	7	489	" 1664.
Heath, Susanna	15	317,438	" 1674. Daughter of Abraham.
Heath, Thomas	ABH	65	Transported 1633. (1, fol. 20, 37, 38, 166).
Heath, Thomas	9	44	Transported 1662.
Heath, Thomas	10	503	" 1667. Servant. (17, fol. 25).
Heath, Ursula	15	317,438	Transported 1674. Wife of Abraham.
Heath, William	13	114	Transported 1669.
Heath, William	12	498	" 1670.
Heath, William	15	317,438	" 1674. Son of Abraham.
Heath, William	WC2	380	" 1675-80. Servant.
Heathcot, Elizabeth	16	72	" 1670. Wife of Nathaniel.
Heathcot, Nathaniel	16	72	Transported 1670. Of Anne Arundel Co. (7, fol. 491).
Heathcote, Nathaniel	WC2	19	Transported six persons in 1670.

NAME	Liber	Folio	REMARKS
			Of Anne Arundel Co.
Heathcott, Hannah	5	533	Transported 1663. Wife of Thomas.
Heathcott, Thomas	5	533	Immigrated 1663.
Heathman, Ann	15	338	Transported 1676.
Hebbourn, Mary	6	121	" 1666.
Hebden, Thomas	1	19	" 1638.
Hebden, Thomas	1	105	Immigrated 1635. Transported wife 1640.
Hedge, George	15	376	Transported 1676.
Hedge, Henry	17	463	" 1673.
Hedge, Mary	17	463	" 1673.
Hedge, Samuel	15	300	Immigrated 1675. Of Anne Arundel Co. (16, fol. 133).
Hedge, Thomas	17	463	Transported 1673.
Hedger, Robert	ABH	45	" 1636. Servant. (ABH, fol. 60-66).
Hedger, Robert	1	17,20, 25,38	Transported 1637.
Hedges, Thomas	9	454	" 1666.
Heeling, Peter	16	409	" from Virginia 1671.
Heigh, Mary	5	248	" 1663. Wife of Robert.
Heigh, Robert	5	248	Immigrated 1663.
Heighington, Hannah	17	469	Transported 1668.
Height, Jacob	8	484	" 1665.
Heines, Darey	19	258	" 1663.
Heirs, Francis	9	229	" 1665.
Held, Charles	WC2	395	" 1680. Servant.
Helen, Nathaniel	16	396	" 1671.
Hell, Mary	15	501	" 1678.
Helly, Clement	15	311	" prior to 1675.
Helme, John	5	242	" 1662.
Helmet, Henry	5	247	" 1661 by Philip Calvert, Esq.
Hemback, Ann	8	478	Transported 1665.
Hemfford, Christopher	7	464	" 1660.
Hemlock, Ann	9	321	" 1666.
Hemmans, Edward	4	188	" 1659. Servant.
Hemper, Thomas	6	87	" 1660.
Hempstead, William	5	339	" 1663.
Hempsteed, Jone	18	36	" 1673.
Hempsteed, Mary	18	36	" 1673.
Hempsteed, William	18	36	" 1673.
Hempton, John	Q	115	" 1656.
Hemsley, Judith	4	14	" 1658. Wife of William.
Hemsley, Penelope	4	14	" 1658. Daughter of William.
Hemsley, William	4	14	Immigrated 1658.
Hemsley, William	13	127	Of Talbot Co. Aged 30 years in 1671.
Hemson, Nicholas	11	374	Transported 1668.
Hemson, Thomas	6	81	" 1658.
Hemsworth, John	6	137	" 1659.

NAME	Liber	Folio	REMARKS
Hemuel, Robert	16	137,437	Transported 1671.
Henall, Peter	15	565	" 1679.
Henchcliffe, Jeremy	16	532	" 1668-70.
Henchman, Edward	9	38	" 1665.
Henchman, Henry	9	304	" 1665.
Henchman, Jane	9	304	" 1665.
Henday, Thomas	11	374	" 1668.
Henderkin, David	15	553	" 1678.
Henderson, Davis	15	300	" 1675.
Henderson, Elizabeth	9	374	" 1666. Wife of Andrew.
Henderson, Flora	9	489	" 1665.
Henderson, George	20	185	" 1679.
Henderson, John	7	464	" 1655.
Henderson, John	16	88	" 1670.
Henderson, Patrick	5	257	" 1663. Servant.
Henderson, Sarah	15	395	Service 1676. Of St. Mary's Co.
Hendersontale, Martin	11	537	Transported 1668.
Hendley, Thomas	9	79	" 1665.
Hendrick, Francis	7	507	" from Virginia 1664.
Hendrick, John	15	322	" 1674.
Hendrick, Lidia	10	433	" 1667.
Hendricks, Cornelius	16	395	" 1671.
Hendricks, John	9	216	" 1665.
Hendricks, Katherine	17	516	" 1664.
Hendrickson, Bartlett	7	426	Immigrated 1664 with his wife
and her mother, Angueth Poulson.			
Hendrickson, Hendrick	5	176	Servant, living 1662.
Hendrickson, John	6	209	Transported 1663.
Hendrickson, John	9	89	Immigrated 1665. (12, fol. 271).
Hendrickson, Marg.			
Anguette	7	426	Transported 1664. Wife of Bartlett.
Heners, Magdalyne	19	506	" 1666.
Henesy, Catherine	20	184	" from Ireland 1678.
Henesy, Thomas	WC2	129	" 1679.
Henfree, Thomas	17	53	Service 1666. (18, fol. 149; 11, fol. 552).
Henley, Henry	15	378	Immigrated 1676.
Henley, Henry	10	498	Transported 1667.
Henley, John	12	206	" 1669. (15, fol. 396).
Henley, John	12	375	" 1669. Of Virginia.
Henlos, Mathew	7	508	" 1664.
Henly, Lawrence	16	308	Service 1671. Of Somerset Co. (17, fol. 123).
Henman, Will	ABH	175	Transported 1649. Servant.
Henmarr, William	11	440	" 1668.
Henning, Richard	17	416	" 1673.
Henricks, Floris	WC2	112	" 1679.
Henricks, John	WC2	112	" 1679.
Henrickson, John	5	88	" 1662.
Henry, Christian	6	293	" 1664.
Henry, Daniel	18	152	" 1674.

NAME	Liber	Folio	REMARKS
Henry, Mary	16	482	Transported 1671.
Henry, William	4	531	Immigrated 1659.
Henshall, Thomas	6	209	Transported 1663.
Henson, John	5	80	" 1661.
Henson, Robert	8	484	" 1665.
Hepborne, James	9	48	" 1665.
Hepord, John	15	565	" 1679.
Hepworth, Hester	15	536	Service 1678. Wife of John.
Hepworth, John	17	570	Immigrated 1673. Of St. Mary's Co.
Herbert, Ann	7	530	Transported 1664. Wife of William.
Herbert, Charles	10	390	" 1666.
Herbert, Clement	10	564	Immigrated 1667.
Herbert, Elizabeth	10	564	Transported 1667. Wife of Clement.
Herbert, Elizabeth	16	503	" 1671. (15, fol. 452).
Herbert, Rebecca	16	409	" from Virginia 1671.
Herbert, William	5	188	Immigrated prior to 1660.
Herbert, William	9	156	Transported 1661.
Herbert, William	WC2	24,106	" 1678. Servant.
Herd, James	10	204	" 1666.
Hereford, John	7	464	" 1660.
Herman, Ann	12	190	" 1668.
Herman, Augustine	8	381	Immigrated 1665. Letter to Lord
Baltimore dated "Bohemia Manor", 13 July 1674. (19, fol. 254). In relation to printing a map.			
Herman, Benjamin	12	474	Transported 1670.
Herman, Casper	8	381	" 1665. Son of Augustine.
Herman, Cornelius	17	567	" 1673.
Herman, Epherine Georgius	8	381	" 1665. Son of Augustine.
Herman, Frances	8	381	" 1665. Daughter of Augustine.
Herman, Francis	WC2	100	Transported 1679.
Herman, Henry	7	568	Immigrated about 1665.
Herman, Henry	WC2	100	Transported 1679.
Herman, Isabella	12	282	Service 1668.
Herman, Jane	8	381	Transported 1665. Wife of Augustine.
Herman, Judith	8	381	Transported 1665. Daughter of Augustine.
Herman, Margarita	8	381	Transported 1665. Daughter of Augustine.
Herman, Martha	10	325	Transported 1666.
Herman, Mary	16	110	" 1668. Wife of Augustine of Baltimore Co. (See Jane).
Herman, Robert	10	325	Transported 1666.
Hermison, Aaron	17	566	Immigrated 1673. Of Worcester Co.
Hermison, Martha	17	566	Service 1673. Wife of Aaron.
Herne, Bridgett	15	446	Transported 1677.
Herne, John	15	446	" 1677
Herne, Richard	Q	70	Servant 1658.
Herne, Thomas	16	409	Transported 1671. Of Virginia.

NAME	Liber	Folio	REMARKS
Hernes, William	15	319	Immigrated 1675.
Herreman (Harman), John	8	502	Transported 1665.
Herring, Ann	ABH	313	" 1650. First wife of Bartholomew.
Herring, Arthur	WC2	363	Transported 1680.
Herring, Bartholomew	ABH	175	" 1647. Servant.
Herring, Margaret	ABH	313	" 1651. Second wife of Bartholomew.
Herrington, George	18	329	Transported 1675.
Herrington, Humphrey	6	307	" 1664.
Herrison, Ann	12	548	" 1670.
Herrmon, John	15	397	" 1675.
Hervey, Frances	1	130	" 1641. Daughter of Nicholas.
Hervey, Nicholas	1	20,37	Transported 1633-1634. (See Harvey).
Hervey, Nicholas	1	129-130	Immigrated 1641 with wife, daughter and other persons.
Hervey, Nicholas	ABH	103	Special Warrant from Lord Baltimore for 1,000 acres, conditions on his emigrating with wife and five others. Dated London, 8 Sept. 1641.
Heth, Charles	10	312	Transported 1662.
Heumain, Ann	ABH	202	" 1651. Servant.
Hevermon, Thomas	15	567	" 1679.
Heward, Thomas	16	95	" 1670.
Hewes, Ann	18	27	Service 1673. Wife of Samuel of Baltimore Co.
Hewes, Avery	8	501	Transported 1665.
Hewes, Cornelius	9	216	" 1665.
Hewes, David	4	570	" 1661.
Hewes, Elias	5	305	" 1663.
Hewes, Francis	15	430	" 1677.
Hewes, George	16	409	" 1671.
Hewes, Jane	17	551	" 1673.
Hewes, John	ABH	140	" 1651.
Hewes, John	15	300,429	" 1674.
Hewes, Joseph	10	284	Immigrated 1666. Of Virginia.
Hewes, Richard	WC2	65	Transported 1679.
Hewes, Robert	5	239	Immigrated 1662. Planter.
Hewes, William	5	530	Transported 1660.
Hewes, William	17	596	" 1673.
Hewes, William	15	431	" 1677.
Hewett, Hannah	3	17	" prior to 1650. Widow of Robert Hewett. Married Hugh Lee.
Hewett, Hannah	ABH	44	Transported many years prior to 1650. Wife of Robert. Married secondly, Hugh Lee.
Hewett, Robert	ABH	44	Immigrated many years prior to 1650.
Hewett, Robert	3	17	Immigrated prior to 1650. Husband of Hannah.

NAME	Liber	Folio	REMARKS
Hewett, Susanna	18	280	Transported 1675.
Hewitt, Charles	17	411	" 1673.
Hewlton, Joseph	12	472	" 1670.
Hewson, John	17	415	" Nov. 1669.
Hewson, Ralph	10	507	" 1667. Servant.
Hewson, Richard	Q	66	" 1657.
Hewson, Thomas	18	306	" 1675.
Heyborn, Alexander	ABH	276	" 1651.
Heyborn, James	17	47	Immigrated 1668. Of Baltimore Co.
Heyden, Thomas	7	558	Transported 1665.
Heydon, Francis	15	452	Immigrated 1678.
Heydon, Mary	15	452	Transported 1678. Daughter of Francis.
Heydon, Penelope	15	452	Transported 1678. Daughter of Francis.
Heydon, Tomasin	15	452	Transported 1678. Wife of Francis.
Heylin, Henry	5	246	" 1658 by Philip Calvert.
Heylock, Walter	15	429	Transported 1674.
Heymens, Joseph	11	338	" 1668.
Heymond, Nicholas	5	259	" 1655.
Heynes, William	4	219	Immigrated 1651. (10, fol. 245).
Heyward, Peter	1	43,128	Transported about 1638. Servant.
Hiad, Mary	15	560	" 1678.
Hibbs, John	15	543	Service 1677.
Hickenson, James	ABH	33	Servant 1648. (See Atkinson).
Hicker, William	15	453	Transported 1675-7.
Hicker, William	16	115	" 1671.
Hickerry, Charity	WC2	380	" 1675-80. Servant.
Hickes, James	16	482	" 1670-1.
Hickes, John	5	85	" 1661. (See Hicks).
Hickes, William	15	530	" 1678.
Hickey, John	WC2	381	" 1675-80. Servant.
Hickford, Thomas	12	393	" 1669.
Hickinbotham, Henry	WC2	395	" 1680. Servant.
Hickins, Ann	12	280	" 1665. Servant.
Hickman, Ann	18	279	" 1675.
Hickman, Samuel	15	568	" 1679.
Hicks, Dorothy	12	189	" 1668. (See Hickes).
Hicks, Elizabeth	11	144-145	" 1667.
Hicks, George	4	570	" 1661.
Hicks, Henry	10	565	" 1667. Of Northumberland Co., Virginia.
Hicks, John	4	103	Transported 1667.
Hicks, John	10	565	" 1667. Of Northumberland Co., Virginia. (11, fol. 104).
Hicks, John	15	384	Transported 1671.
Hicks, John	15	440	" 1677.
Hicks, Joseph	WC2	89	" 1676. Servant.
Hicks, Philip	WC2	282	" 1680.
Hicks, Richard	WC2	16,170	" 1679. Servant.

NAME	Liber	Folio	REMARKS
Hicks, Robert	4	203	Immigrated 1659.
Hicks, Sarah	6	209	Transported 1663.
Hicks, Sarah	10	523	" 1667.
Hicks, Thomas	7	469	" 1664.
Hicks, Thomas	11	339	" 1668.
Hicks, Thomas	16	170	" 1671.
Hicks, William	6	105	" 1657.
Hicks, William	16	112	" 1671.
Hicks, William	17	417	" 1673.
Hickson, Henry	12	584	" 1670.
Hickson, Sarah	5	305	" 1663.
Hide, Christopher	8	130	" 1664.
Hide, Elizabeth	12	498	" 1670.
Hide, Henry	ABH	374	" under 1st Cond. of Plantation 1653. Servant.
Hide, Philip	ABH	371	Immigrated 1650.
Hide, Capt. Phineas	WC2	170	Rights 1678. Commander of the ship, "Hound". Of Middlesex Co., England.
Hide, Susan	12	465	Transported 1669. Of Va. Servant.
Hide, William	18	313	" 1675.
Higgate, William	9	269	" 1665.
Higgenbotham, George	12	507	Service 1668.
Higgens, Michael	4	140	Transported 1656. Servant.
Higgeson, Richard	6	134	" 1659.
Higgins, Richard	6	105	" 1649.
Higgins, Sarah	15	353	" 1674.
Higgins, Susan and Cath'n.	7	471	" 1664. Children of Christopher Thomas.
Higginson, George	ABH	348	Transported 1652. Servant.
Higgs, Henry	12	216	" 1668.
Higgs, Henry	15	422,452	" 1677.
Higgs, John	17	491	Immigrated from Virginia 1662.
Higgs, John	12	382	" 1669. Of Dorchester County.
Higgs, John	18	17	Immigrated 1674, with Mary, his wife, and John Thadlett, her son. Of Calvert Co. Chirurgeon.
High, Archibald	16	79	Transported 1670.
Higham, Lawrence	16	130	Service 1671. Of Calvert Co. Millright.
Highgate, Elizabeth	9	269	Transported 1665.
Highland, John	9	496	Of Baltimore Co. Married the widow Mary Dorrington prior to Dec. 1665.
Highlett, William	4	10	Transported 1658. Servant.
Highway, John	15	429	" 1674.
Highway, Thomas	WC2	18	Service 1679.
Higins, Honor	15	322	Transported 1675.
Hignett, Eliza	10	298	" 1666.
Hignett, James	10	298	" 1666.
Hignett, John	15	313	" 1675.
Hignett, Robert	10	298	Immigrated 1666.

NAME	Liber	Folio	REMARKS
Hignett, Robert, Jr.	10	298	Transported 1666.
Hiley, Julian	20	2	" prior to 1678.
Hill, Abell	13	1	" 1669. Servant.
Hill, Alice	12	314	" 1669. Wife of John.
Hill, Amos	ABH	348	" May 1652. Son of Thomas. (4, fol. 60).
Hill, Ann	15	422	Service 1677.
Hill, Mr. Austin	ABH	47	Transported 1650.
Hill, Azadiah	4	60	Son of Thomas. Living 1659.
Hill, Barbara	15	331,342	Freedom 1663.
Hill, Christian	ABH	348	Transported 1652. Wife of Thomas.
Hill, David	ABH	348	" May 1652. Son of Thomas.
Hill, Dorothy	8	478	Transported 1665. (9, fol. 333).
Hill, Elizabeth	8	484	" 1665 by William Hill.
Hill, Elizabeth	12	314,459	" 1669. Daughter of John.
Hill, Francis	4	5	Transported 1652-9.
Hill, Francis	9	229	" 1665. (8, fol. 503).
Hill, Hadasia	ABH	348	" May 1652. Daughter of Thomas.
Hill, Henry	ABH	174	Transported 1650. Servant.
Hill, Henry	8	202	" 1664.
Hill, Henry and Ann	16	406	" 1671 by Richard Hill, Gent. of Anne Arundel County.
Hill, Jacob	15	413	Immigrated 1677 with Mary, his wife.
Hill, Jane	5	411	Transported 1663.
Hill, Jane	16	307	" from Virginia 1671.
Hill, Joane	17	417	" 1673.
Hill, John	1	20, 37-38, 166	" 1633-4.
Hill, John	ABH	66	" 1634.
Hill, John	1	19	" 1638.
Hill, John	ABH	186	" 1651. Servant.
Hill, John	Q	453	Immigrated 1658.
Hill, John	7	62	Transported 1660.
Hill, John	5	82	" 1661. (5, fol. 208).
Hill, John	6	14	" 1663.
Hill, John	10	193	" 1666.
Hill, John	10	599	" 1667.
Hill, John	12	507	" 1668. Servant.
Hill, John	12	314	Immigrated to Charles Co. 1669. Of Virginia.
Hill, John	15	538	And Alice, his wife. Service 1678.
Hill, John	WC2	17,99	Transported 1679. Son of Richard.
Hill, Joseph	ABH	348	" May 1652. Son of Thomas.
Hill, Joseph	5	127	Transported 1662.
Hill, Joseph	15	446	" 1677.
Hill, Jude	12	314	" 1669. Daughter of John

NAME	Liber	Folio	REMARKS
Hill, Malken	4	139	Transported 1650. Servant.
Hill, Margaret	5	490	" 1654. Wife of William. (4, fol. 207).
Hill, Margaret	16	393	Transported 1671.
Hill, Martha	ABH	140	" 1651.
Hill, Mary	Q	453	Immigrated 1658. Sister of John.
Hill, Mary	7	469	Transported 1664.
Hill, Mathew	5	245	" 1662.
Hill, Mathew	20	185	" 1679.
Hill, Peter	WC2	108	" 1679.
Hill, Rebecca	16	623	Service 1672. Of Dorchester Co.
Hill, Rhodia	WC2	17,99	Transported 1679. Daughter of Richard.
Hill, Richard	ABH	244	Transported 1636.
Hill, Richard	5	484	" 1662.
Hill, Richard	9	25	" 1665. (17, fol. 67).
Hill, Richard	16	307	" from Virginia 1671.
Hill, Richard	WC2	17,99	Immigrated 1679 with wife, children and servant. Of Somerset County.
Hill, Richard, Jr.	WC2	17,19	Transported 1679. Son of Richard.
Hill, Robert	8	89,484	" 1665.
Hill, Robert et al	16	307	" 1671. Servants. Of Virginia.
Hill, Robert	15	533	Transported 1678.
Hill, Roger	12	500	Immigrated 1669.
Hill, Ruth	ABH	348	Transported May 1652. Daughter of Thomas.
Hill, Samuel	10	600	Immigrated 1667.
Hill, Samuel	17	635	Transported 1674.
Hill, Stephen	7	567	" 1665.
Hill, Thomas	ABH	348	Immigrated May 1652.
Hill, Thomas	Q	29	Service 1658. Servant 1654. (4, fol. 3).
Hill, Thomas	17	489	Immigrated from New England 1663.
Hill, Thomas	8	89	Transported by Wm. Hill 1665.
Hill, Thomas	11	462,571	" 1668. Servant.
Hill, Thomas	12	472	" 1670. (13, fol. 56; 16, fol. 72).
Hill, Thomas	20	185	Transported 1679.
Hill, Thomas, Jr.	ABH	348	" May 1652. Living 1659. Son of Thomas. (4, fol. 60).
Hill, Ursula	15	429	Transported 1674.
Hill, Ussilla	WC2	17,99	" 1679. Daughter of Richard.
Hill, Valentine	16	77	Transported 1674.
Hill, William	5	490	Immigrated 1658.
Hill, William	5	415	Transported 1662.
Hill, William	5	411	" 1663.
Hill, William	6	299	" 1664. (8, fol. 484).
Hill, William	9	334	" 1666. (12, fol. 516).
Hill, William	17	531	Service 1673. Of Dorchester Co.

NAME	Liber	Folio	REMARKS
Hill, William	17	636	Immigrated 1674. Of Calvert Co.
Hill, Wilmett	WC2	17,99	Transported 1679. Wife of Richard.
Hilland, Samuel	15	422	And Elizabeth, his wife. Service 1677.
Hillard, Rebecca	WC2	114	Transported 1680. Servant.
Hillary, Thomas	4	551	" 1661. (18, fol. 106).
Hilliard, Elizabeth	12	498	" 1670.
Hilliard, Isaac	WC2	319	Rights 1680.
Hilliard, Jace	16	308	Service 1671. Of Somerset Co.
Hilliard, Jane	9	304	Transported 1665.
Hilliard (Hillierd), John	1	20,166	" 1633.
Hilliard, John	ABH	157	" 1650. Servant.
Hilliard, John, Sr.	9	211	Immigrated 1665. (15, fol. 553).
Hilliard, John, Jr.	9	211	Transported 1665.
Hilliard, Joseph	15	429	" 1674.
Hilliard, Mary	9	211	" 1665.
Hilliard, Mary	WC2	319	Service 1680. Wife of Isaac.
Hilliard, Thomas	Q	403	Transported 1650.
Hilliard, Thomas	11	337,441	" 1668.
Hillman, Margaret	16	409	" from Virginia 1671.
Hills, Elizabeth	Q	29	Servant 1650.
Hills, Marke	9	38	Transported 1664.
Hills, Richard	ABH	98	" 1633. Servant. (1, fol. 121).
Hills, Richard	16	94	Transported 1670.
Hills, William	6	86	" 1655.
Hills, William	Q	18,69	" 1657.
Hilsey, James	11	344	" 1668.
Hilsey, Thomas	11	344	" 1668.
Hilson, John	16	358	Service 1671. Of St. Mary's Co.
Hilton, John	WC2	112,402	Transported 1679.
Hilton, John	WC2	402	" 1680.
Hilton, Mary	15	539	Service 1678.
Hilton, Robert	15	369	Transported 1676.
Hinberton, Anthony	12	477	" 1670.
Hinch, Daniel	WC2	211	" 1679. Servant.
Hinch, Mathew	16	79	" 1670.
Hinchloe, Sarah	6	209	" 1663.
Hinchman, Nathaniel	9	304	" 1665.
Hind, Edward	7	640	Immigrated prior to 1665.
Hinde, Thomas	18	293	Transported 1674 with Elizabeth, his wife and Mary, his daughter.
Hinde, William	5	218	Transported 1662.
Hinderson, Alexander	ABH	237	" 1651. Servant.
Hinderson, Alice	11	373	" 1668. Wife of James.
Hinderson, Andrew	4	590	Immigrated 1661.
Hinderson, Berett	4	552	" 1661.
Hinderson, Davis	18	160	Transported 1674.
Hinderson, James	11	373	Immigrated 1668. Of Somerset Co.
Hinderson, Jeane	11	373	Transported 1668. Daughter of James.

NAME	Liber	Folio	REMARKS
Hinderson, John	11	373	Transported 1668. Son of James.
Hinderson, Lancelot	9	399	" 1666.
Hinderson, Sendricke	4	552	" 1661.
Hinderson, William	11	373	" 1668. Son of James.
Hindes, John	11	501	Service 1666.
Hindes, Richard	11	499	Transported 1666. Of Virginia.
Hindes, William	17	449	" 1672.
Hine, Hester	9	26	" 1665.
Hingell, Jos.	WC2	110	" 1676. Servant.
Hinman, William	11	337	" 1668.
Hinnerstone, Timothy	16	513	" 1672.
Hinson, Ann	16	473	Service 1663. Wife of Thomas of Talbot Co., Gent.
Hinson, Ann	ABH	164	Transported 1651. Daughter of Thomas.
Hinson, Grace	5	488	Transported 1651-62 by her husband, Thos. Hinson.
Hinson, Grace	ABH	164	Transported 1651. Daughter of Thomas.
Hinson, John	ABH	164	Transported 1651. Son of Thomas.
Hinson, Philip	Q	211	" 1658.
Hinson, Thomas	ABH	164	Immigrated 1651 with wife. (10, fol. 193).
Hinson, Thomas, Jr.	12	393	Son and heir of Thomas, dec'd 1669.
Hinson, William	1	166	Transported 1650. Servant.
Hinton, Alice	WC2	410	Service 1681. Wife of Thomas. Of St. Mary's Co.
Hinton, Christopher	17	348	Service 1667.
Hinton, Thomas	5	516,536	Immigrated 1662 with wife.
Hinton, Thomas	12	614	" 1670. Of St. Mary's County. (16, fol. 537).
Hinxman, Ann	15	452	Transported 1678.
Hipord, John	15	565	" 1679.
Hippesly, Thomas	2	614	" 1649.
Hippkisse, Peter	11	524	Immigrated 1668.
Hipps, Thomas	5	530	Transported 1662.
Hipsley, Thomas	ABH	40	" 1649.
Hirift, William	9	35	" 1665.
Hisbet, Thomas	WC2	49	Service 1679. Of Calvert Co.
Hiscocke, Ann	4	551	Transported 1661.
Hiscocks, Hugh	9	20,24	" 1665.
Hishcock, Ralph	15	443	" 1670.
Hiskicke, Thomas	15	443	" 1673.
Hissle, Ralph	4	20	" 1658.
Hist, Elizabeth	WC2	167,169	" 1679.
Hitchcoake, Christopher	17	535	Service 1673.
Hitchcock, Thomas	12	415	Transported 1669.
Hitchcot, William	16	38	" 1670.
Hitchins, Ann	9	326	" 1666.
Hitchison, John	11	4	Immigrated 1667.
Hive, Mr. Isaac	ABH	35	" 1645.

NAME	Liber	Folio	REMARKS
Hix, Joane	16	435	Transported 1671.
Hoad, Morice	15	527	" 1678. (See Neat).
Hoane, John	WC2	60	" 1679. Servant.
Hoard, Thomas	18	331	" 1674.
Hoare, John	17	445	" 1673.
Hobart, Humphrey	17	67	Service 1672.
Hobart, Simon	WC2	409-410	" 1680.
Hobb, Thomas	17	547	" 1673. Of St. Mary's Co.
Hobbs, Elizabeth	15	432	Transported 1677. Wife of Thomas.
Hobbs, George	6	170	" 1663.
Hobbs, Gervis	6	96	" 1656.
Hobbs, John	8	495	" 1665.
Hobbs, John	10	352	" 1666.
Hobbs, Joyce	15	432	" 1677. Son of Thomas.
Hobbs, Robert	4	590	" 1661.
Hobbs, Thomas	15	432	Immigrated 1677.
Hobbs, Thomas	16	410	Transported 1671.
Hobdy, Mary	11	436	" 1668.
Hobdon, Thomas	ABH	92	Immigrated 1635 and transported his wife 1640.
Hobkins, William	5	87	Transported 1649.
Hobleton, James	7	464	" 1657.
Hoborne, Lidia	4	5	" 1652-9.
Hobs, Henry	7	84	" 1662.
Hobs, John	7	84	" 1662.
Hobson, Mary	5	489	" 1658.
Hobson, Roger	11	546	" 1668. Servant. (14, fol. 426).
Hobson, Ruth	7	506	Transported prior to 1664.
Hobson, Samuel	8	388	" 1665.
Hobson, Thomas	5	259	" 1655.
Hobson, Thomas	7	130	" 1656-63.
Hobson, Thomas	11	337	" 1668.
Hobson, Thomas	17	606	And Martha, his wife. Service 1673.
Hobson, William	17	331	Transported from Virginia 1672, with Mary.
Hockley, James	ABH	98	Transported 1633. Servant.
Hockley, James	1	63,121	" 1633.
Hockley, Michael, Gent.	16	431	Immigrated 1671.
Hoddell, Nathaniel	4	555	Transported 1661.
Hoddey, Mary	11	281	" 1667. Servant.
Hodge, Robert	16	537	Immigrated from Virginia 1671. (15, fol. 534).
Hodge, Robert	WC2	16	Transported his son Robert, 1679.
Hodge, Robert, Jr.	WC2	16	" 1679.
Hodge, Thomas	12	601	" 1670.
Hodge, William	18	31	" 1674.
Hodges, Anne	WC2	259	" 1680.
Hodges, Benjamin	ABH	65	" 1633. (1, fol. 38).
Hodges, Charles	5	607	" 1658-63.

NAME	Liber	Folio	REMARKS
Hodges, Charles	17	608	Transported 1673.
Hodges, Hugh	18	137	" 1674.
Hodges, Jane	12	217	" 1669.
Hodges, John	5	530	" 1657.
Hodges, John	10	407	Immigrated 1666.
Hodges, John	12	472	Transported 1670.
Hodges, John	WC2	24,106	" 1678. Servant.
Hodges, Katherine	WC2	120	" 1680.
Hodges, Nicholas	15	454	" Oct.1677.
Hodges, Robert	7	465	" 1661.
Hodges, Sander	8	88	" 1665.
Hodges, Thomas	1	20	" 1633.
Hodges, Thomas	18	291	" 1674.
Hodges, Thomas	15	354	" 1676.
Hodges, Uriah	20	185	" 1679.
Hodges, William	9	104	" 1665. (12,fol.378).
Hodgeson, Elizabeth	18	27	" 1671. Wife of John
			of Baltimore Co.
Hodgeson, Izabell	WC2	309	Transported 1678.
Hodgeson, Job	18	27	" 1671. Son of John.
Hodgeson, John	18	27	Immigrated 1668. Of Baltimore Co.
Hodgeson, John, Jr.	18	27	Transported 1669. Son of John.
Hodgeson, Joshua	18	27	" 1671. Son of John.
Hodghon, Jane	18	306	" 1675.
Hodgkin, John	ABH	141	Immigrated 1651. Of PatuxentRiver.
Hodgkin, Mary	ABH	141	Transported 1651.
Hodgkinson, John	15	390	" 1675.
Hodgshon, Milcah	18	167	" 1674.
Hodgson, Edward	17	396	Service 1671. (6,fol.17).
Hodgson, Edward	15	427	Immigrated 1673. (17,fol.566).
Hodgson, George	WC2	88	Service 1679. Chirurgeon of
			Charles Co.
Hodgson, William	WC2	18	Immigrated 1648. Of Calvert Co.
Hodgson, William	15	452	" 1678.
Hodkins, Thomas	15	386	Transported 1676.
Hodley, Elizabeth	16	43	" 1670.
Hodley, John	16	430	Immigrated Jan.1664 with Eliza-
beth, his wife. Of Talbot County.			
Hodskins, John	15	516	Transported 1676.
Hodskins, Richard	9	33	" 1660-5.
Hodson, George	15	357	" 1676.
Hodson, John	9	37	" 1664.
Hodson, John	9	37	" 1664. Son of John.
Hodson, Roger	12	589	" 1670.
Hodson, William	WC2	306	Rights 1680. Of Calvert Co.
Hodwell, Will	15	501	Transported 1678.
Hogan, Peirce	15	446	" 1677.
Hogan, Tary	15	553	" 1678.
Hogard, Richard	13	122	" 1668.
Hogben, als. Cornewall,			
John	18	331	" 1674.

NAME	Liber	Folio	REMARKS
Hogdes, Charles	10	398	Transported 1666.
Hogg, Christian	6	97	" 1657.
Hogg, George	12	209	Immigrated 1669.
Hogg, Samuell	WC2	21	Transported 1679.
Hogg, William	ABH	25	Transported 1648. Servant. (2, fol. 516, 575).
Hogg, William	ABH	35	Servant, March 1648-9.
Hoggins, William	9	45	Transported 1665.
Hoggon, William	18	10	Service 1673.
Hogstaffs, Samuel	5	307	Transported 1663.
Hoicks, John	15	453	" 1675-7.
Hoize, Thomas	6	107	" 1655.
Holand, Daniel	11	378	" 1668.
Holboard, John	10	398	" 1666.
Holbrooke, Elizabeth	5	2	" 1661.
Holbrooke, Mary	16	109	" 1665.
Holbrooke, Mary	12	602	" 1670.
Holdcraft, George	9	105	" 1665.
Holdcraft, Susanna	9	105	" 1665. Wife of George.
Holden, Henry	4	140	" 1658. Servant.
Holden, Margaret	11	581	" 1668.
Holden, Roger	6	47	" 1663. (10, fol. 599).
Holder, Hayah	18	166	" 1674.
Holder, John	6	36,89	" 1660.
Holder, Thomas	18	329	" 1675.
Holdern, John	1	26	" 1633.
Holdern, John	ABH	60	" 1635.
Holding, Samuel	17	349	" 1672.
Holding, Will	15	443	" 1670.
Holdsworth, Samuel	15	555	" 1678.
Holebrook, Margaret	12	602	" 1670.
Holefart, John	6	268	" 1662.
Holeman, Abraham	Q	68	Immigrated 1649.
Holeman, William	ABH	39	Transported 1649.
Holeman, William	Q	72	" 1658. Brother to Abraham.
Holin, Eli	16	507	Transported 1671.
Hollahane, Jane	WC2	380	" 1675-80. Servant.
Holland, Ann	15	370	" 1676.
Holland, Anthony	Q	403	" 1650.
Holland, Anthony	17	351	Service 1672. Of Anne Arundel Co.
Holland, Dennis	17	356	Transported 1672.
Holland, Elizabeth	18	137	" 1674.
Holland, Francis	5	530	Immigrated 1661.
Holland, Francis	5	530	Transported 1661. Son of Francis.
Holland, George	18	287	Service 1674. Of Anne Arundel Co.
Holland, George	19	293	Commission from Baker Brooke, Surveyor Genl. to act as Dep. Sur. for Anne Arundel Co. 1676. Do. 1678. (20, fol. 125). Do. 1679. (20, fol. 134). Do for Baltimore Co. 1679. (20, fol. 129).
Holland, George	WC2	197	Commission as Deputy Surveyor

NAME	Liber	Folio	REMARKS

of Baltimore and Cecil Counties, 1680.

NAME	Liber	Folio	REMARKS
Holland, John	15	430	Transported 1677.
Holland, John	WC2	321	Immigrated 1680.
Holland, Mary	5	530	Transported 1661. Wife of Francis.
Holland, Philip	16	39	Immigrated 1670 with Dorothy, his

wife, and children, Philip, John, Stephen, Martha and Joane.

Holland, Philip, Jr.	16	39	Transported 1670. Son of Philip.
Holland, Richard	18	17	Immigrated 1669, with Alice, his

wife, and Richard, his son. Of Dorchester Co.

Holland, Robert	17	330	Transported 1672.
Holland, Sarah	7	553	" 1665.
Holland, Stephen	16	39	" 1670. Son of Philip.
Holland, William	17	510	" 1673.
Holland, William	15	537	" 1679.
Holland, William	WC2	120	" 1680.
Hollard, George	WC2	122	Service 1674.
Hollawhane, Alice	WC2	380	Transported 1675-80. Servant.
Holleger, Philip	6	47	Immigrated 1663. (10, fol. 598).
Hollenworth, John	9	240	Of Calvert Co. Married the widow

of Gabrile Golden prior to 1665.

Hollett, Jacob	10	523	Transported 1667.
Hollett, William	6	63	" 1658-63.
Hollibone, Edward	16	170	" 1671.
Holliday, John	15	401	Of St. Mary's Co. Service 1677.
Holliday, Robert	9	55	Transported 1665.
Holliday, Samuel	15	516	" 1675.
Holliday, Thomas	15	574	" 1678.
Holliface, Lydia	15	362	" 1676.
Hollihane, John	WC2	380	" 1675-80. Servant.
Holling, Laughlin	6	117	" 1663.
Hollingsworth, George	15	397	" 1676.
Hollingsworth, John	ABH	276	" 1650.
Hollingsworth, Mr. John	9	326-327	Immigrated 1666. (9, fol. 269; 17, fol. 475).
Hollingsworth, William	15	353	Transported 1676.
Hollins, John	9	26	Immigrated 1665.
Hollins, William	4	24	Servant 1658.
Hollis, Ambrose	12	215	Transported 1668-9.
Hollis, Elizabeth	6	296	" 1664.
Hollis, Henry	5	248	" 1663.
Hollis, James	WC2	89	" 1676. Servant.
Hollis, John	1	20	" 1633.
Hollis (Hallowes), John	1	138	License to marry Restituta Tue,

June 1, 1639. Married June 2.

Hollis, John	2	251	Transported 5 servants 1640.
Hollis, John	ABH	48	Immigrated 1641. Of Virginia. (5, fol. 252).
Hollis, John	3	25	Immigrated aboute 1641. Deceased by 1650.
Hollis, William	4	68	Service 1659.
Hollister, Jacob	5	607	Transported 1663.

NAME	Liber	Folio	REMARKS
Holliwell, John	7	14	Transported 1663.
Hollman, Abraham	2	608	Immigrated 1650.
Hollman, John	WC2	406	Transported 1680.
Holloway, Hether	WC2	395	" 1680. Servant.
Holloway, Thomas	12	381	" 1669.
Hollowes, John	4	623	" 1633.
Hollowey, William	17	463	" 1673.
Hollows, John	ABH	60	" 1635.
Holly, Bernard	6	95	" 1658.
Hollyday, Henry	15	332	" 1667.
Hollyday, Thomas	WC2	16	" 1677.
Holman, Abraham	ABH	39	Immigrated 1650.
Holman, Elizabeth	12	576	Transported 1670.
Holman, William	2	608	" 1649.
Holmes, George	Q	197	" 1658.
Holmes, George	16	83	Immigrated 1670. Of Charles Co.
Holmes, Henry	16	95	Transported 1670.
Holmes, John	15	505	" 1678.
Holmes, Mary	17	610	" 1673.
Holmes, Michael	WC2	394	" 1680. Servant.
Holmes, Nicholas	ABH	9,150	" 1648. (2, fol. 425).
Holmes, Nicholas	15	530	" 1678.
Holmes, Robert	3	24	" 1650. Servant.
Holmes, Sarah	10	503	Service 1667. Wife of Nicholas.
Holmes, Thomas	6	210	Transported 1663.
Holmes, Thomas	9	79	" 1665.
Holmes, Thomas	10	117	" 1666.
Holmes, Thomas	16	437	" 1671. (17, fol. 575).
Holmes, Thomas	18	127	Immigrated 1674. Of St. Mary's Co. (15, fol. 307).
Holmes, Thomas	WC2	167,169	Transported 1679.
Holmet, Henry	6	48	" 1662.
Holmwood, Robert	15	537	" 1678.
Holso, Thomas	WC2	322,323	Service 1680. Of Somerset Co.
Holsteine, John	12	598	Immigrated from New England 1670. Of Talbot Co.
Holston, Elizabeth	Q	441	Transported prior to 1651.
Holt, Alice	9	271	" 1665.
Holt, Anne	9	32	" 1656.
Holt, Christian	6	210	Immigrated 1663.
Holt, David	5	74	Son of Robert. Living 1661.
Holt, David	12	313	Immigrated from Virginia 1669. Of St. Mary's Co.
Holt, Elizabeth	15	537	Transported 1678.
Holt, Francis	WC2	211	" 1679. Servant.
Holt, Henry	7	80	" 1664.
Holt, Henry	9	262	" 1665. (17, fol. 399).
Holt, John	15	507	" 1678.
Holt, Robert	ABH	3,32	Immigrated 1646 with wife and four children. (2, fol. 229, 550).
Holt, Susannah	WC2	211	Transported 1679. Servant.

NAME	Liber	Folio	REMARKS
Holt, William	WC2	395	Transported 1680. Servant.
Holtan, George	12	190	" 1668.
Holton, Robert	ABH	164	" 1651. Servant.
Holton, Thomas	7	472	" 1664. (12, fol. 270).
Holts, John	15	450	" 1677.
Homan, Harbert	16	123	Service 1671. Of St. Mary's Co.
Homan, John	15	531	Transported 1678.
Homer, Nicholas	16	477	" 1672.
Homer, Susanna	16	131	" 1671.
Homes, Elizabeth	13	114	" 1671.
Homes, Nicholas	Q	204	Service 1658.
Homes, Sarah	9	48	Transported 1665.
Homes, Silvester	Q	204	" 1657.
Homewood, Thomas	6	105	" 1650 with wife.
Hone, Charles	6	127	" 1659.
Honer, Mary	11	374	" 1668.
Honney, Thomas	12	498	" 1670.
Honon, Mathew	15	567	" 1679.
Honywell, Agnes	18	150	" 1674.
Hood, Elizabeth	WC2	406	" 1678.
Hood, George	10	305	Immigrated 1666. Of Anne Arundel County.
Hood, Robert	7	428,547	Orphan of John, of the Isle of Kent, 1664.
Hoodson, Henry	11	515	Immigrated 1668. Of Virginia.
Hoodson, Ledda	11	515	Transported 1668. Wife of Henry.
Hoodson, Ledda	11	515	" 1668. Daughter of Henry.
Hooke, Anne	WC2	319	Transported 1680. Wife of Jeremiah.
Hooke, Edward	5	238	" 1662. (17, fol. 350).
Hooke, Francis	17	397	" 1676.
Hooke, Jeremiah	12	559	Immigrated 1670. Of Somerset Co.
Hooke, Jeremiah	WC2	319,397	" 1680 with wife, three children and a servant.
Hooke, Jeremiah, Jr.	WC2	319	Transported 1680. Son of Jeremiah.
Hooke, Joseph	15	414,526	" 1677.
Hooke, Mary	WC2	319	" 1680. Daughter of Jeremiah.
Hooke, Roger	WC2	319	Transported 1680. Son of Jeremiah.
Hooke, Thomas	11	337	" 1668.
Hooke, William	12	403	" 1669.
Hooker, Martin	6	143	" 1660.
Hookin, Daniel	17	348	Service 1672. Of Dorchester Co.
Hooper, Abraham	Q	68	Transported 1657.
Hooper, Andrew	15	543	" 1678.
Hooper, Ann	9	399	" 1666. Daughter of Maximillian.
Hooper, Ann	12	267	Widow of Robert. Married Thos. Doxey prior to 1669.
Hooper, Elizabeth	ABH	140	Transported 1651. Daughter of Henry and Sarah.

NAME	Liber	Folio	REMARKS
Hooper, Elizabeth	Q	239	Immigrated 1651.
Hooper, Francis	6	136	Transported 1654.
Hooper, George	6	129	" 1662. (17, fol. 443).
Hooper, George	15	503	" 1678.
Hooper, George	15	599	Of Dorchester Co. Immigrated 1679, with his son, William.
Hooper, Henry	ABH	60,66	Transported 1637. (1, fol. 20, 25, 38, 39).
Hooper, Henry	ABH	140	Immigrated 1651. Of Patuxent River. (Q, fol. 239).
Hooper, Henry, Jr.	ABH	140	Transported 1651. Son of Henry and Sarah. (Q, fol. 239).
Hooper, Jane	Q	74	Immigrated 1658. Wife of Thomas.
Hooper, Jeane	15	543	Transported 1678.
Hooper, Jeane (Jane)	WC2	21	" 1679.
Hooper, Joseph	9	399	" 1666. Brother to Maximillian.
Hooper, Joseph	9	399	Transported 1666. Son of Maximillian.
Hooper, Mary	Q	239	Immigrated 1651.
Hooper, Maximillian	9	399	Transported his brother, several children and his daughter-in-law, Eleanor Wadsworth, 1666.
Hooper, Maximillian, Jr.	9	399	Transported 1666. Son of Maximillian.
Hooper, Richard	ABH	140	Son and Henry and Sarah. Transported 1651. (Q, fol. 239). Living 1664. (7, fol. 82).
Hooper, Robert	7	86	Transported 1663.
Hooper, Robert	1	166	" 1650. Servant.
Hooper, Sarah	ABH	140	" 1651. Wife of Henry. (Q, fol. 239).
Hooper, Sarah	ABH	140	Transported 1651. Daughter of Henry and Sarah.
Hooper, Suzan	9	399	Transported 1666. Daughter of Maximillian.
Hooper, Susanna	16	100	Transported 1667.
Hooper, Thomas	5	466	Immigrated 1653.
Hooper, Thomas	Q	74	" 1658.
Hooper, Ursula	16	170	Transported 1671.
Hooten, Matthew	16	82	Immigrated 1670. Of St. Mary's Co.
Hooten, Mary	10	229	Transported 1665. Wife of Thomas.
Hooton, Sarah	10	229	" 1665. Daughter of Thomas.
Hooton, Thomas	10	299	Immigrated 1665. Of Calvert Co. (11, fol. 44).
Hooton, William	16	306	Immigrated 1671. Of Virginia.
Hopcott, William	5	367	Transported 1663.
Hope, Abraham	ABH	173	" and dec'd. 1651.
Hope, George	11	581	" 1668.
Hope, George	18	117	" 1674.
Hope, Mary	15	452	" 1678.
Hope, Richard	7	560	" 1665.

NAME	Liber	Folio	REMARKS
Hope, Susanna	6	89	Transported prior to 1663.
Hope, William	6	86	" 1660.
Hopegood, Henry	6	293	" 1664.
Hopewell, Ann	WC2	100	Service 1663. Wife of Hugh.
Hopewell, Hugh	ABH	35	Immigrated 1641. His wife a ser-

vant. Receives a gift of 100 acres from the Lieut. Genl. (2, fol. 580; 5, fol. 212).

NAME	Liber	Folio	REMARKS
Hopewell, Mrs. Hugh	2	580	Service 1649.
Hopewell, Suzan	9	399	Transported 1666.
Hopkins, Ann	9	330	" 1665. Wife of William.

Of Anne Arundel Co.

NAME	Liber	Folio	REMARKS
Hopkins, Dennis	7	150	Transported 1663.
Hopkins, Elizabeth	12	283	" 1668.
Hopkins, Garrett	4	625	" 1658-61.
Hopkins, Hannah	WC2	321	" 1680. Wife of Samuel.
Hopkins, Hannah	WC2	321	" 1680. Daughter of

Samuel.

NAME	Liber	Folio	REMARKS
Hopkins, Henry	5	211	Transported 1662.
Hopkins, John	12	386	Service 1669. Of St. Mary's Co.
Hopkins, Mr. Joseph	8	128	Immigrated 1664. Of Baltimore

Co. (10, fol. 598).

NAME	Liber	Folio	REMARKS
Hopkins, Nathan	WC2	321	Transported 1680. Son of Samuel.
Hopkins, Peter	8	501	" 1665.
Hopkins, Prudence	4	616	" 1660.
Hopkins, Richard	17	417	" 1673.
Hopkins, Robert	Q	201	" 1650.
Hopkins, Robert	ABH	322	" 1652. Servant. (Q,

fol. 428).

NAME	Liber	Folio	REMARKS
Hopkins, Robert	18	36	Immigrated 1673 with Sarah, his wife and Robert, his son.
Hopkins, Robert	WC2	106	Immigrated 1679 with wife and son. Of Somerset Co.
Hopkins, Robert, Jr.	WC2	106	Transported 1679. Son of Robert.
Hopkins, Samuel	WC2	321	Immigrated 1680 with wife and four children.
Hopkins, Samuel, Jr.	WC2	321	Transported 1680. Son of Samuel.
Hopkins, Sarah	WC2	106	" 1679. Wife of Robert.
Hopkins, Temperance	WC2	321	" 1680. Daughter of

Samuel.

NAME	Liber	Folio	REMARKS
Hopkins, Thomas	Q	428	Immigrated 1652.
Hopkins, Thomas	4	176	Transported 1659. (6, fol. 85).
Hopkins, Thomas	5	59	" 1662.
Hopkins, Thomas	10	599	" 1667. Servant.
Hopkins, William	Q	72	Service 1658.
Hopkins, William	9	21	Transported 1665.
Hopkins, William	12	359	Immigrated 1669.
Hopkinson, Jonathan	10	392	And Elizabeth, his wife. Service 1666.
Hopper, Charles	15	322	Transported 1674.
Hopper, Dorothy	8	30	" 1665. Wife of John.
Hopper, John	8	30	Immigrated 1665.

NAME	Liber	Folio	REMARKS
Hopper, Marmaduke	13	66	Transported 1669. Servant.
Hoppon, George	WC2	150	" 1680.
Hopson, Mary	8	484	" 1665.
Horah, Jeremiah	15	537	" 1679.
Hore, George	15	322	" 1675.
Horesman, John	WC2	82	" 1679.
Horids, Mary	18	130	" 1674.
Horilbrooke, Samuel	16	307	" 1671. Servant. Of Va.
Horley, Dennis	11	479	" 1668.
Horn, Edward	7	398	Formerly a servant to Thos. Hatton,

Esq. and his wife, Winifred, formerly a servant to Capt. Cornwallis, 1664. (ABH, fol. 424).

NAME	Liber	Folio	REMARKS
Hornbee, William	18	329	Transported 1675.
Horne, Anthony	7	502	" 1661.
Horne, Dorothy	17	531	" 1673.
Horne, John	4	178-179	Of London, Merchant. Acquired land in Md., 1639.
Horne, John	4	4	Immigrated 1658.
Horne, Mary	15	451	Transported 1669. Daughter of William.
Horne, Thomas	15	451	Transported 1669.
Horne, Thomas	17	416	" 1673.
Horne, William	9	34	" 1665.
Horne, William	15	451	Immigrated 1669 and settled in Cecil Co.
Horne, William	18	136	Of Anne Arundel Co., and Margaret,

his wife. Service prior to 1674. (19, fol. 503).

NAME	Liber	Folio	REMARKS
Horne, William	15	424	Transported 1677.
Horner, Luke	5	87	" 1649-62.
Horner, Martha	13	122	" 1669.
Horner, Richard	5	87	" 1661.
Horner, Thomas	6	62	" 1663. (9, fol. 190).
Horner, Thomas	10	570	" 1666.
Horner, William	16	67	" 1670.
Horner, William	17	531	" 1673.
Horracks, Thomas	12	217	" 1669.
Horsan, Edward	4	565	" 1660.
Horsey, Abagain	4	580	" 1661.
Horsey, Isaac	8	19	" 1664.
Horsey, John	4	580	" 1661.
Horsey, Joseph	6	293	Immigrated 1664.
Horsey, Mary	4	580	Transported 1661.
Horsey, Nathaniel	8	19	" 1664.
Horsey, Philip	15	442	" 1677.
Horsey, Rose	6	293	" 1664.
Horsey, Samuel	4	580	" 1661.
Horsey, Sarah	4	580	" 1661. Wife of Stephen.
Horsey, Stephen	4	580	Immigrated 1661.
Horsey, Stephen, Jr.	4	580	Transported 1661.
Horsford, George	9	200	" 1665.
Horsley, Rebecca	6	255	" 1663.

NAME	Liber	Folio	REMARKS
Horsman, Thomas	15	499	Transported 1677.
Hort, George	17	440	" 1668.
Hort, Nicholas	17	440	" 1668.
Horte, Stephen	6	143	" 1660.
Horten, Eleanor	15	453	" 1675-7.
Horton, Edward	6	81	" 1660.
Horton, Edward	8	129	" 1664.
Horton, Edward	11	169	Immigrated 1667.
Horton, Joseph	5	180	Transported 1661.
Horton, Sarah	15	526	" 1678.
Horton, William	7	492	" 1664.
Horton, William	WC2	16	" 1679.
Horwood, John	1	37-38	" 1635.
Hose, John	9	304	" 1665.
Hosey, Bryan	15	537	" 1679.
Hosier, Henry	12	554	Immigrated 1670.
Hosier, Henry	17	547	" 1673 with Johanna,

his wife, and Henry, Johanna, Elizabeth and Mary, his children. Of Kent County.

Hosier, Nicholas	13	116	Transported 1671.
Hosier, Richard	WC2	171	" 1679.
Hoskins, Bennett, Esq.	Q	469	Agrees to settle a plantation in

1654. Special Grant of 2000 acres in Charles Co. "Manor of Friendship", of which he assigned 500 acres to Philip Hoskins. (16, fol. 546).

Hoskins, Dorothy	ABH	415	Transported 1653-4.
Hoskins, Edward	6	26	" 1660.
Hoskins, Elizabeth	6	22	" 1663.
Hoskins, Margaret	15	322	" 1675.
Hoskins, Thomas	6	263	" 1660.
Hoskins, William	15	362	" 1676.
Hosley, Derum	11	499	" Oct. 1677.
Hosley, Lewis	6	268	" 1662.
Hosman, Mary	15	558	" 1677.
Hossam, Richard	15	443	" 1671.
Hotham, Robert	17	487	Immigrated from Va. July 1662.
Hottspurr, Henry	7	464	Transported 1658.
Houg, John	5	208	" 1661.
Hough, John	WC2	23	" 1679. Servant.
Houghan, Pearce	WC2	106	" 1679.
Houghner, Mary	11	512	" 1668.
Houghton, Joyce	16	465	Service 1669. Wife of Mathew, of Talbot Co.
Houghton, Thomas	16	409	Transported from Virginia 1671.
Houghton, Thomas	18	177	" 1674.
Houkes, Elizabeth	12	403	" 1669.
Houlder, Christopher	5	257	" 1663.
Houlding, Joseph	15	428	Service 1677.
Houldsworth, Samuel	15	555	Immigrated 1678.
Houlshott, John	7	556	Transported 1665.
Houlshott, Mary	7	556	" 1665. Wife of John.
Houlston, Robert	18	38	Immigrated 1673.

NAME	Liber	Folio	REMARKS
Hoult, John	WC2	23	Transported 1679. Servant.
Hoult, Susanna	15	598	" 1678-9.
Houlte, Francis	15	598	" 1678-9.
Houlton, Robert	Q	75	Immigrated prior to 1658.
House, Joseph	17	508	Transported 1671.
Houseman, Charles	16	93	Immigrated 1670. Of Dorchester Co.
Housley, Edmond	17	608	Transported 1673.
Houstone, Grace	11	546	" 1668. Wife of Robert.
Houstone, Robert	11	546	Immigrated 1668. (14, fol. 420).
Hove, Dorothy	7	469	Transported 1664.
Hover, Blanch	6	85	" 1662.
How, Robert	7	553	" 1664.
How, Thomas	Q	206,211	" 1653.
How, William	ABH	376	" Xmas 1652. Servant.
How, William	18	331	" 1674.
Howard, Abraham	16	482	" 1670-1.
Howard, Ann	18	334	" 1675.
Howard, Charity	WC2	380	" 1675-80. Servant.
Howard, Charles	9	354	" 1662.
Howard, Cornelius	5	466	Immigrated 1659.
Howard, Edward	Q	71	Transported 1652-3.
Howard, Elizabeth	7	461	" 1659-64, and married
Henry Ridley. (This should be Ridgely.)			
Howard, Elizabeth	17	469	Transported 1673.
Howard, Elizabeth	15	454	" Oct. 1677.
Howard, Francis	12	465	" 1669. Son of Bartho-
			lomew Ennalls.
Howard, George	10	573	Transported 1667.
Howard, Henry	8	484	" 1665.
Howard, Henry	11	379	" 1668.
Howard, Henry	15	318	" 1674. (18, fol. 24).
Howard, Henry	15	388	" 1675. (18, fol. 334).
Howard, Hugh	1	19	" 1638.
Howard, Isaac	Q	197	" 1658. Service 1666.
			(10, fol. 573).
Howard, John	ABH	59,356	Transported 1641. (1, fol. 24).
Howard, John	5	208	" 1662. (9, fol. 448).
Howard, John	10	563	" 1667.
Howard, John	12	465	" 1669. Son of Bartho-
			lomew Ennalls.
Howard, John	10	571	Transported 1667 on the "Adventure"
			of Hull. Servant.
Howard, John	17	596	Transported 1673. (15, fol. 444).
Howard, John	WC2	23	" 1679. Servant.
Howard, Joseph	20	2	" prior to 1678.
Howard, Lidia	15	318	" 1674.
Howard, Marriott	15	318,388	" 1675.
Howard, Mary	15	428	" 1677.
Howard, Mathew	16	65	" 1670. (10, fol. 499).
Howard, Owen	17	416	Service 1673.
Howard, Peter	10	565	Transported 1667.

NAME	Liber	Folio	REMARKS
Howard, Philip	12	386	Immigrated 1669.
Howard, Richard	8	484	Transported 1665.
Howard, Richard	9	270	Immigrated 1665. Of Choptank.
Howard, Robert	8	484	Transported 1665.
Howard, Robert	12	205	" 1667.
Howard, Robert	15	429	" 1674.
Howard, Sarah	10	312	" 1662.
Howard, Solomon	5	209	" 1655. Servant.
Howard, Thomas	1	24	" 1641. (ABH, fol. 59,356).
Howard, Thomas	2	624	Immigrated about 1647.
Howard, Thomas	ABH	41	" 1647.
Howard, Thomas	6	160	Transported 1663.
Howard, Thomas	8	484	" 1665.
Howard, Thomas, Jr.	16	170	" 1671.
Howard, Thomas, Sr.	16	170	" 1671.
Howard, William	5	235,490	" 1662. Servant.
Howard, William	8	484	" 1665.
Howard, William	6	255	" 1663.
Howard, William	16	303	Service 1671. Of Somerset Co.
Howard, William	15	322	Transported 1675.
Howard, William	WC2	23	" 1679. Servant.
Howard, William, Jr.	15	428	" 1677.
Howard, William, Sr.	15	428	" 1677.
Howd, Anthony	5	248	" 1663.
Howder, Peter	6	95	" 1661.
Howe, Phill	15	396	" 1676.
Howe, Phillida	9	333	" 1666.
Howe, Thomas	9	333	Immigrated 1666.
Howell, Alexander	5	12	Transported 1662.
Howell, Ann	15	559	" 1679.
Howell, Charles	15	390	Immigrated 1675.
Howell, Daniel	16	507	Transported 1671.
Howell, Elizabeth	Q	32	" Feb. 1652. Servant.
Howell, Elizabeth	3	173	" 1655.
Howell, Elizabeth	15	390	" 1676.
Howell, George	11	378	" 1668.
Howell, George	12	601	" 1670.
Howell, Humfry	2	524	Immigrated 1647.
Howell, Humphrey	ABH	26	" 1647.
Howell, Humphrey	2	363	Husband of Blanch Oliver in 1648.
Howell, John	4	136	Immigrated 1659 with daughter.
Howell, John	10	1	Transported 1666.
Howell, John	11	164	" 1667. (18, fol. 11).
Howell, John	12	601	" 1670.
Howell, John	WC2	411	" 1681.
Howell, Lewis	17	552	" from Delaware 1673.
Howell, Morgan	8	130	" 1664.
Howell, Owen	12	551	Immigrated 1670. Of St. Mary's Co.
Howell, Robert	7	62	Transported 1664.
Howell, Roger	WC2	395	" 1680. Servant.
Howell, Thomas	16	503	" 1671.

NAME	Liber	Folio	REMARKS
Howell, Thomas	WC2	16	Transported 1677.
Howell, Thomas	15	574	" 1678.
Howell, Ursula	12	554	" 1670.
Howell, William	11	338	" 1668.
Howell, William	18	283	" 1674.
Howerd, William	15	559	" 1679.
Howerton, John	5	411	" 1663.
Howes, Ann	ABH	357	" Dec. 1653. Wife of William.
Howes, Francis	15	443	Transported 1672.
Howes, John	5	411	" 1663.
Howes, Mathew	5	359	" 1663.
Howes, Robert	10	286,417	" 1666. Servant.
Howes, Robert	12	403	" 1669.
Howes, Thomas	12	517	" 1670.
Howes, William	ABH	357	Immigrated 1653.
Howes, William	ABH	357	Transported Dec. 1653. Son of Wm. and Ann.
Howford, George	10	570	Immigrated from Virginia 1667. Of the Marrow Creek, Anne Arundel County.
Howford, Jane	10	571	Transported 1667. Daughter of George.
Howford, John	15	307	Immigrated prior to 1675.
Howford, Mary	15	307	Transported prior to 1675. Wife of John.
Howford, Sarah	10	571	Transported 1667. Wife of George.
Howgan, Thomas	5	242,606	" 1662.
Howgate, Sarah	7	484	" 1660. Servant.
Howgate, William	Q	33	" 1653-8.
Howker, Richard	15	443	" 1673.
Howker, Sarah	5	610	" 1660.
Howlands, Hugh	ABH	140	" 1651.
Howlditch, Joane	WC2	380	" 1675-80. Servant.
Howley, Jasper	15	598	Immigrated 1678. Of St. Mary's Co.
Howlt, Roger	15	516	Transported 1676.
Howse, John	Q	32	Servant 1653.
Howse, John	6	154	Transported 1663.
Howson, Samuel	12	617	" 1670.
Hoxton, Jane	5	489	" 1661.
Hoyle, Seth	13	66	" 1669. Servant.
Hubbard, Bridgett	15	452	" 1678.
Hubbard, Adley	7	368	" 1660-4.
Hubber, Isaac	6	136	" 1659.
Hubbert, John	4	625	" prior to 1661.
Hubbert, Robert	12	551	" 1670.
Hubberton, Miles	6	165	" 1651.
Hubbin, German	7	581	" 1665.
Huberlsley, Mary	17	531	" 1673.
Hubert, Abber	11	1	Servant to Barnaby Jackson. Free prior to 1667.
Hubert, Denis	13	57	Transported 1670.

NAME	Liber	Folio	REMARKS
Hubert, Simon	5	81	Transported 1661.
Hublethorne, Jone	9	434	" 1666.
Huck, Mary	6	154	" 1663.
Huck, Nath	15	370	" 1676.
Huckill, Daniel	9	505	" 1666.
Hudd, Elizabeth	8	486	" 1664.
Huddeson, Rebecca	18	335	" 1675.
Huddlestone, Valentine	5	416	" 1663. Service 1666. (10, fol. 209).
Hudle, Charles	9	435	Transported 1664.
Hudle, John	15	416	" 1677.
Hudleston, Mary	15	540	" 1676.
Hudson, Benjamin	13	122	" 1668.
Hudson, Christopher	16	482	" 1670-1.
Hudson, Edmund	2	194	Immigrated 1646.
Hudson, Elizabeth	15	422	Transported 1669.
Hudson, Francis	9	305	Immigrated 1665.
Hudson, Grisell	18	174	Transported 1674.
Hudson, Henry, Gent.	5	203	Immigrated prior to 1662.
Hudson, Isaac	15	410	Transported 1673. (18, fol. 37).
Hudson, John	ABH	56	" 1648. Servant.
Hudson, John	3	106	" about 1648. Servant.
Hudson, John	9	54	" 1665. (10, fol. 4).
Hudson, John	9	516	" 1666.
Hudson, John	15	358	" 1669. (15, fol. 422).
Hudson, John	18	106	Immigrated 1674. Of Dorchester Co.
Hudson, John, Jr.	15	422	Transported 1669.
Hudson, Juliana	5	203	" 1662.
Hudson, Mary	5	203	" 1662. Wife of Henry.
Hudson, Mary	15	514	" 1677.
Hudson, Mary	20	185	" 1679.
Hudson, Neptunia	5	203	" 1662.
Hudson, Nicholas	16	320	Of Somerset Co. Immigrated from Accomack in Virginia 1670, with Elizabeth, his wife, and Richard and Violetta, his children.
Hudson, Richard	16	464	Immigrated Dec. 1666. Of Talbot Co.
Hudson, Richard	16	320	Transported 1670. Son of Nicholas.
Hudson, Sarah	18	291	" 1674.
Hudson, Susanna	17	377	" 1669.
Hudson, Thomas	15	260	" 1674 with Joseph. Sons of John. (18, fol. 177).
Hudson, Thomas	WC2	308	Transported 1678.
Hudson, Violetta	16	320	" 1670. Daughter of Nicholas.
Hues, Charles	WC2	394	Transported 1680. Servant.
Hues, Frances	17	600	" 1662.
Hues, Griffin	16	169	" 1671.
Hues, James	13	111	" 1668.
Hues, Samuel	9	188	" 1665.
Hues, Thomas	15	534	" 1677.
Huett, Abraham	WC2	217	" 1680.

NAME	Liber	Folio	REMARKS
Huett, Robert	1	75-76	Petition to confirm title to land, 1640.
Huett, Susanna	WC2	58	Service 1677.
Hugate, Christopher	6	85	Transported 1660.
Hugate, Mary	6	142	" 1660.
Hugate, Michael	5	129	" 1662.
Huggins, John	5	2	" 1661.
Huggins, Peter	10	564	" 1667.
Hughes, Abraham	9	48	" 1665.
Hughes, Ann	15	403	Service 1676.
Hughes, Anne	4	20	Transported prior to 1659. Servant.
Hughes, David	4	53	" 1659.
Hughes, David	15	553	" 1678.
Hughes, Edward	5	411	" 1663.
Hughes, Elizabeth	18	137	" 1674.
Hughes, Elizabeth	15	453	" 1675-7.
Hughes, Evan	15	380	" 1676.
Hughes, John	4	73	" 1657-9.
Hughes, John	6	294	" 1664.
Hughes, John	12	194	" 1662. Servant. (15, fol. 573).
Hughes, John	15	354,452	Transported 1676. (15, fol. 573).
Hughes, Jone	9	26	" 1665. Wife of Thomas.
Hughes, Mary	9	270	" 1665. Servant.
Hughes, Mary	17	440	" 1673.
Hughes, Mary	15	353	" 1674.
Hughes, Mathias	12	360	Service 1667.
Hughes, Robert	18	30	" 1674. Of Baltimore Co.
Hughes, Samuel	12	242	" 1669. Of Dorchester Co.
Hughes, Sarah	9	250	Transported 1665. Wife of Thomas.
Hughes, Thomas	5	247	" 1659 by Philip Calvert, Esq.
Hughes, Thomas	5	411	Transported 1663.
Hughes, Thomas	9	26,250	Immigrated 1665.
Hughes, Thomas, Jr.	9	250	Transported 1665. Son of Thomas.
Hughes, William	12	477	" 1670.
Hughes, William	15	416,446	" 1677.
Hugeson, John	6	125	" 1663.
Hughs, Edward	15	354	" 1676.
Hughs, James	11	344	" 1668.
Huitt, Mary	15	569	" 1678.
Hulbert, John	10	433	" 1667.
Hulbert, Robert	15	369	" 1676.
Hulbert, William	6	290	" 1663.
Hull, Austen	3	24	" 1650.
Hull, Edward	6	212	Immigrated 1663.
Hull, Grace	15	353	Transported 1676.
Hull, John	7	461	" 1659-64. Servant.
Hull, John	6	212	" 1663. Son of Edward.
Hull, John	12	202	" 1669. Servant.
Hull, John	15	454	" 1677. (WC2, fol. 406).

NAME	Liber	Folio	REMARKS
Hull, Margaret	6	212	Transported 1663. Wife of Edward.
Hull, Margaret	6	212	" 1663. Daughter of Edward.
Hull, William	1	127	Immigrated 1641. Mariner.
Hull, William	ABH	101	Transported 1641. Mariner.
Hull, William	8	259	" 1665.
Hulling, James	18	37	" 1673.
Hulse, Meverrell	WC2	63	Service 1679.
Hulston, Ralp	ABH	24	Servant 1646. (See Halston).
Humber, Dorothy	6	106	Transported 1654. (7, fol. 561).
Humberston, John	4	580	" prior to 1661.
Humbert, Dennis	6	217	" 1663. (12, fol. 281, 286).
Humbes, James	Q	197	Immigrated 1658.
Humble, John	ABH	5	Service 1633-41.
Hume, James	Q	32	Transported 1653-8.
Humey, Barnard	9	451	" 1666. (11, fol. 482).
Humley, Francis	6	216	" 1663.
Humphrey, Alexander	5	248	" 1663.
Humphrey, Christopher	5	123	" 1662.
Humphrey, James	18	335	" 1675.
Humphrey, Robert	5	257	A soldier who assisted Gov. Calvert in regaining the province. Living in 1663, when he demanded land for transporting himself and others into the Province.
Humphrey, Thomas	4	54	Immigrated prior to July 1659.
Humphrey, Thomas	12	283	Transported 1668.
Humphreys, Ellis	15	379,391	Immigrated 1676.
Humphreys, Humphrey	7	154	Transported 1660.
Humphreys, Mary	4	565	" 1660.
Humphreys, Mary, Jr.	4	565	" 1660.
Humphreys, Peterr	8	129	Immigrated with his wife 1665.
Humphreys, Richard	16	124	Transported 1671.
Humphreys, Sarah	15	322	" 1675.
Humphreys, Sarah	15	379,391	" 1676. Wife of Ellis.
Humphreys, Stephen	6	80	" prior to 1663.
Humphries, Thomas	18	36	" 1673 with Katherine, his wife.
Humphry, Elizabeth	WC2	415	Transported 1680. Servant.
Humphry, Roger	WC2	395	" 1680. Servant.
Humphrys, Katherine	WC2	119	" 1676. Wife of Thomas.
Humphrys, Thomas	WC2	119	Immigrated 1676 with wife. Of Somerset County.
Hund, Edward	5	259	Transported 1656.
Hungerford, Eliz.	17	571	" 1673.
Hungerford, John	17	614	Immigrated 1673. Of Dorchester County.
Hungerford, Mary	17	571	Transported 1673.
Hungerford, William	ABH	6,14	Immigrated 1646. (2, fol. 345).
Hungerford, William	2	457,540	" 1647.
Hungerford, William	5	252	Transported 1648.
Hunking, Mary	12	505	" 1669. Wife of William.
Hunking, William	12	505	Immigrated 1669.

NAME	Liber	Folio	REMARKS
Hunsford, Stephen	7	88	Transported 1656.
Hunt, Ann	17	463	" 1673.
Hunt, Barbara	6	96	" 1659.
Hunt, Benjamin	WC2	370	Immigrated 1674. Of Dorchester Co.
Hunt, Mrs. Catherine	ABH	173	Transported and died 1651.
Hunt, Christopher	6	18	" 1661.
Hunt, Daniel	5	306	" 1663. Servant.
Hunt, Edward	16	72	" 1670.
Hunt, Edward	15	452	" 1677.
Hunt, Elizabeth	11	521	" 1668. Wife of John.
Hunt, Francis	Q	67	Immigrated prior to 1658. Dec'd.
Hunt, Henry	12	341	Transported 1668.
Hunt, Henry	16	115	" 1671.
Hunt, Isaac	4	21,140	" 1657. Service 1670. (12, fol. 613).
Hunt, John	4	204	Transported 1659.
Hunt, John	5	220	Immigrated 1662.
Hunt, John	11	521,540	" 1668. (12, fol. 209).
Hunt, John	15	322	Transported 1674.
Hunt, John	15	307	" 1675.
Hunt, Katherine	Q	430	" 1658.
Hunt, Margaret	Q	67	Widow of Francis Hunt. Married John Smith prior to 1658. (7, fol. 464).
Hunt, Nathaniel	ABH	41	Immigrated 1650.
Hunt, Nathaniell	2	624	" about 1650.
Hunt, Peter	6	117	Transported 1660.
Hunt, Samuel	15	516	" 1675.
Hunt, Sarah	17	615	" 1673.
Hunt, Sarah	18	94	" 1674.
Hunt, Susan	5	248,537	" 1660. Wife of William.
Hunt, Thomas	Q	74	" 1656.
Hunt, Thomas	6	87	" 1658.
Hunt, Thomas	5	89	" 1661.
Hunt, Thomas	6	154	" 1663.
Hunt, Thomas	11	540	" 1668.
Hunt, William	5	537	Immigrated 1655. (9, fol. 39).
Hunt, William	15	436	Transported 1677.
Hunt, William	15	530	" 1678.
Hunt, Woolfron	15	454	" 1677.
Hunter, Dorothy	16	394	" 1671.
Hunter, James	Q	75	" 1658.
Hunter, James	15	313	" 1675. (18, fol. 306).
Hunter, Jane	15	353	" 1676.
Hunter, John	13	1	" 1669. Servant.
Hunter, Richard	16	411	" 1671.
Hunter, Robert	4	72	" 1657-9.
Hunter, William	15	353	" 1676.
Huntey, Mary	16	394	" 1671.
Huntley, Christopher	6	95	" 1657.
Huntley, George	7	84	" 1650.
Huntley, Thomas	6	293	" 1664. (17, fol. 347).

NAME	Liber	Folio	REMARKS
Hunton, Benjamin	4	11	Transported 1659. Servant. (11, fol. 481).
Hunton, Edward	15	530	Transported 1678.
Hunton, John	15	530	" 1678.
Hunton, Robert	15	429	" 1674.
Hunton, Samuel	16	428	" 1670-1.
Huntred, Edward	WC2	206	" 1680. Servant.
Hurburt, William	Q	32	Servant, Feb. 1652.
Hurd, James	7	83	Transported 1657.
Hurd, John	15	322	" 1674.
Hurd, Robert	17	396	" 1671.
Hurdesse, Thomas	15	380	" 1676.
Hurdlston, Thomas	17	363	" 1672.
Hurham, Henry	6	239	" 1663.
Hurkeley, Sarah	14	145	" 1665.
Hurlestone, Thomas	6	266	" 1662.
Hurley, Daniel	15	544	" 1676.
Hurlock, Abraham	15	543	Immigrated 1676.
Hurlock, Joseph	WC2	213-214	Transported 1671-1673.
Hurlock, Richard	16	71	" Nov. 1668.
Hurly, Dennis	17	347	Service 1672. Of Dorchester Co.
Hurly, Eleanor	12	332	Immigrated 1669. Of Virginia.
Hurnby, Richard	16	435	Transported 1671.
Hurst, Alice	18	291	" 1674.
Hurst, Andrew	17	463	" 1673.
Hurst, Elizabeth	6	36,89	" 1660.
Hurst, Richard	11	582	" 1668.
Hurtter, Isaac	5	59	" 1662.
Husband, William	12	601	" 1670.
Husbands, Edward	15	445	Service 1677.
Husbands, Edward	WC2	50	Of Calvert Co. 1678. Chirurgion.
Husbands, Richard	Q	472	Of London, Mariner. Agrees to immigrate 1658.
Husbands, William	17	589	Of St. Mary's Co. Service 1673.
Husculan, Dennis	11	526	Service 1668.
Husculan, Jane	16	419	Immigrated 1671. Wife of Dennis of Charles Co.
Husey, John	11	551	Transported 1668. Servant.
Husey, Thomas	10	606	Servant to Col. Wm. Evans, 1667.
Husk, Elizabeth	9	34	Transported 1665.
Huson, Benjamin	11	537	" 1668. (Alias Erison).
Hussey, James	10	352	" 1666.
Hust, Daniel	15	357	" 1676.
Hust, John	7	567	" 1665.
Hust, John	16	71	" 1670. (16, fol. 304; 15, fol. 412).
Huston, William	15	565	" 1679.
Hut, William	12	393	" 1669.
Hutcheson, Alexander	9	69	" 1660-5.
Hutchin, Richard	16	276	Service 1671. Of Calvert Co.
Hutchin, Robert	18	152	Transported 1674.

NAME	Liber	Folio	REMARKS
Hutchings, Charles	16	67	Transported 1670.
Hutchings, Charles	16	629	Immigrated 1672. Of Dorchester Co.
Hutchins, Enoch	ABH	348	Transported prior to June 1652. Servant.
Hutchins, Francis	4	140	Transported 1652. Servant.
Hutchins, Humphrey	5	361	" 1663.
Hutchins, Henry	18	24	" 1674.
Hutchins, John	5	261	" 1658.
Hutchins, Matthew	15	337	" 1676.
Hutchins, Richard	Q	75	" 1659.
Hutchins, Richard	4	565	" 1661.
Hutchins, Richard	10	503	" 1667. Servant. (17, fol. 513).
Hutchins, Samuel	15	565	Transported 1679.
Hutchins, Thomas	16	393	" 1671.
Hutchins, Thomas	15	318	" 1674.
Hutchinson, Benj.	13	112	" 1670.
Hutchinson, Francis	15	526	" 1678.
Hutchinson, George	18	331	" 1674.
Hutchinson, John	WC2	21	" 1679.
Hutchinson, Thomas	WC2	130	Immigrated 1679.
Hutson, Elizabeth	WC2	363	Transported 1680.
Hutson, Isaac	18	36	" 1673.
Huttchinson, Eliz.	5	607	" 1658-63.
Hutten, Elizabeth	18	280	" 1674.
Hutton, Margery	16	411	" 1671.
Hutton, Mary	17	396	" 1671.
Hutton, Richard	9	229	" 1665.
Hutton, Robert	16	411	" 1671.
Huttson, Elizabeth	5	607	" 1658-63.
Hyam, Thomas	17	514	Service 1673. Of Talbot Co.
Hybard, William	15	443	Transported 1671.
Hyde, Daniel	6	79	" 1663.
Hyde, Edward	6	255	" 1663. (15, fol. 435).
Hyde, Elizabeth	13	114	" 1669.
Hyde, Elizabeth	17	531	" 1673.
Hyde, Henry	5	516	Immigrated 1656.
Hyde, Philip	ABH	142	" 1651. Of Patuxent River.
Hyett, Margaret	16	435	Transported 1671.
Hyllam, Thomas	WC2	57	" 1678.
Hylock, John	15	405	Service 1676.
Hynd, Edward	8	478	Transported 1665.
Hyoss, Lawrence	6	296	" 1664.
Hyse, Alexander	Q	68	" 1657.
Iabson, Eleanor	18	335	" 1675.
Ichcombe, William	11	484	" 1668.
Iego, Peter	17	552	" from N.Y. 1672.
Ielleson, Adam	7	83	" 1663.
Ielsop, Dorothy	Q	201	" 1651-8.
Ielves, William	WC2	395	" 1680. Servant.

NAME	Liber	Folio	REMARKS
Ilive, Isaac	2	581	Immigrated 1644.
Illing, Francis	6	105	Transported 1661.
Illingsworth, Richard	5	607	" 1658.
Illingsworth, Richard	11	110	Service 1667.
Illingsworth, William	5	607	Transported 1658.
Ince, Mary	15	540	" 1677.
Inch, John	9	325	Immigrated 1666.
Inchport, John	12	589	Transported 1670.
Ines, Richard	15	453	" 1675-7.
Inge, Jane	9	54	" 1665.
Ingerson, Daniel	17	454	" 1673.
Ingle, Henry	17	475	" 1673.
Ingle, William	18	37	Immigrated 1673. (15, fol. 557).
Inglis (Inglist), George	7	505	" 1664.
Inglis, George, Jr.	7	505	Transported 1664.
Inglis, Mary	7	505	" 1664.
Inglish, Katherine	15	438	" 1677.
Inglish, Richard	15	446	" 1677.
Ingobritson, Ann	17	478	" 1673. Wife of Bartholomew.
Ingobritson, Ann, Jr.	17	478	Transported 1673. Daughter of Bartholomew.
Ingobritson, Bartholomew	17	478	Immigrated 1673 with his wife and six children. Of Anne Arundel County.
Ingobritson, Bartholomew	17	478	Transported 1673. Son of Bartholomew.
Ingobritson, Dorcas	17	478	Transported 1673. Daughter of Bartholomew.
Ingobritson, Dorothy	17	478	Transported 1673. Daughter of Bartholomew.
Ingobritson, Hance	17	478	Transported 1673. Son of Bartholomew.
Ingobritson, Sarah	17	478	Transported 1673. Daughter of Bartholomew.
Ingram, Ann	8	486	Transported 1664.
Ingram, Ann	15	443	" 1677. Wife of James.
Ingram, Diana	WC2	146,162	" 1680.
Ingram, Elizabeth	WC2	146,162	" 1680.
Ingram, Ellen	4	30,188	" prior to 1659. Servant.
Ingram, James	8	486	" 1664. (15, fol. 449).
Ingram, James	15	443	" 1677.
Ingram, John	5	407	Immigrated 1663. (6, fol. 172).
Ingram, John	8	486	Transported 1664. (15, fol. 449).
Ingram, John	9	79	Immigrated 1665.
Ingram, John	12	216	Transported 1668.
Ingram, John	16	436	" 1671.
Ingram, John	15	443	" 1677.
Ingram, Robert	8	486	" 1664. (15, fol. 449).
Ingram, Robert	15	443	" 1677.

NAME	Liber	Folio	REMARKS
Ingram, Sarah	18	174	Transported 1674.
Ingram, Susanna	18	77	" 1674.
Ingram, Thomas	18	331	" 1674.
Ingram, Major Thomas	11	517	Immigrated 1668. Drowned 1669. (17, fol. 585; 16, fol. 36).
Inion, John	9	234	Transported 1665.
Inion, Mary	15	544	" 1676.
Inloe, Peter	12	504	" 1669.
Inlor, Elizabeth	15	525	" 1678.
Innis, Betheny	18	38	" 1674. Daughter of William.
Innis, Betheny	WC2	99	Transported 1679. Daughter of William.
Innis, Cornelius	18	38	Transported 1674. Son of William.
Innis, Cornelius	WC2	99	" 1679. Son of William.
Innis, Mary	18	38	" 1674. Daughter of William.
Innis, Mary	WC2	99	Transported 1679. Daughter of William.
Innis, Nathaniel	18	38	Transported 1674. Son of William.
Innis, Nathaniel	WC2	99	" 1679. Son of William.
Innis, Percy	18	38	" 1674. Wife of William.
Innis, Percy	WC2	99	" 1679. Wife of William.
Innis, Percy, Jr.	18	38	" 1674. Daughter of William.
Innis, Percy, Jr.	WC2	99	Transported 1679. Daughter of William.
Innis, Samuel	18	38	Transported 1674. Son of William.
Innis, Samuell	WC2	99	" 1679. Son of William.
Innis, William, Jr.	18	38	" 1674. Son of William.
Innis, William, Jr.	WC2	99	" 1679. Son of William.
Innis, William, Sr.	18	38	Immigrated 1674 with his wife and seven children. Of Somerset County.
Innis, William, Sr.	WC2	99	Immigrated 1679 with his wife and seven children. Of Somerset County.
Inon, John	9	156	Transported 1660.
Insley, Andrew	6	27	" 1663. Service 1667. Married Margaret Jones, whom he transported in 1668. (11, fol. 507).
Inson, Thomas	5	415	Transported 1663.
Insworth, George	11	512	Service 1668.
Ints, Jane	WC2	23	Transported 1679. Servant.
Iorins, Margaret	15	563	" 1678.
Iorton, Richard	16	482	" 1671.
Iowrns, Katherine	15	563	" 1678.
Iree, Isaac	5	393	" 1663.
Ireene, John	6	171	" 1663. Servant.
Ireland, Elizabeth	5	12	" 1662.
Ireland, John	15	535	" 1678.
Ireland, Joseph	12	459	" 1669. (15, fol. 431).
Ireland, Mary	18	174	" 1674.
Ireland, Mary	20	184	" from Ireland 1678.

NAME	Liber	Folio	REMARKS
Ireland, Stephen	20	185	Transported 1679.
Ireland, William	5	259	" 1655.
Ireland, William	18	84	" 1674.
Ireton, Thomas	5	244	" 1662.
Irish, Joan	Q	32,189	" 1657.
Irish, Sarah	17	33	" from Virginia 1672.
Irishman, Robert	Q	28	Servant 1649-50.
Ironmonger, William	18	291	Transported 1674.
Irons, Dorothy	WC2	68	" 1679.
Irons, Elizabeth	WC2	68	" 1679.
Irons, Frances	WC2	68	" 1679.
Irons, Susannah	WC2	68	" 1679.
Irons, Symon	WC2	68	Immigrated 1679.
Irons, William	15	530	Transported 1678.
Isaac, Rebecca	16	87	" 1670.
Isaac, Stephen	15	380	" 1676.
Isaacke, Mary	10	558	" 1665. Servant.
Isaacks, Ann	9	229	" 1665.
Isaacks, Edward	9	229	Immigrated 1665.
Isaacks, Mathew	10	571	Transported 1667. Servant.
Isgate, Katherine	10	390	" 1666.
Ishipp, Mary	18	84	" 1674.
Isnaith, Arthur	15	416	" 1677.
Isteed, Mary	8	87	" 1665.
Isum, Barbary	12	373	" 1669.
Ithell, Ann	15	354	" 1676.
Itigham, Ursula	10	305	" 1666. Servant.
Ivery, Margaret	9	297	" 1665.
Ives, James	17	486	" 1667.
Ives, James	15	455	" 1678.
Ivory, Margaret	5	210	" 1662.
Ivory, Mary	5	210	" 1662.
Ixon, David	15	353	" 1676.
Izard, John´	9	35	" 1665.
Jacebson, John	7	464	" 1661.
Jackaman, Thomas	18	15	" 1673.
Jackmore, Richard	12	205	" 1667. (13, fol. 114).
Jacks, Jone	10	565	" 1667.
Jackson, Ann	5	416	" 1651.
Jackson, Ann	5	537	" 1661.
Jackson, Ann	17	332	Service 1672. Wife of Samuel.
Jackson, Barnaby	1	18	Transported 1638.
Jackson, Barnaby	ABH	37	Service 1649. (2, fol. 604). Married Margaret, daughter of Geo. Goodrick, prior to 1659. (4, fol. 22).
Jackson, Diana	WC2	201	Transported 1680. Servant.
Jackson, Dina	WC2	199,201	" 1680.
Jackson, Edward	12	283	" 1668.
Jackson, Elizabeth	4	68	" 1659.
Jackson, Elizabeth	9	216	" 1665.
Jackson, Elizabeth	15	976	" 1676.
Jackson, Elizabeth	15	449	" 1677.

NAME	Liber	Folio	REMARKS
Jackson, Francis	5	64,65	Transported 1652. Service 1659. (ABH, fol. 312).
Jackson, Francis	5	204	"Of the Province of Md. Gent.",
			Special Warrant for 500 acres, Sept. 30, 1662.
Jackson, Francis	17	545	Transported 1673.
Jackson, George	15	530	" 1678.
Jackson, Humphrey	9	105	" 1665.
Jackson, Humphrey	15	318	" 1675.
Jackson, Humphrey	WC2	319	Service 1680.
Jackson, Jane	15	354	Transported 1676.
Jackson, John	5	529	" 1651.
Jackson, John	5	610	" 1659-63.
Jackson, John	15	322	" 1673. (17, fol. 513).
Jackson, John	18	84	" 1674.
Jackson, John	15	569	" 1678.
Jackson, John	WC2	19	" 1679.
Jackson, Jonathan	WC2	201	" 1680. Servant.
Jackson, Joseph	15	569	" 1678.
Jackson, Joseph	WC2	19	" 1679.
Jackson, Mallen	16	168	" 1671.
Jackson, Margaret	5	247	" 1652.
Jackson, Marmaduke	17	608	" 1673.
Jackson, Mary	5	246	" 1657 by Philip Calvert, Esq.
Jackson, Mary	17	351	Transported 1670. Wife of Richard.
Jackson, Nicholas	4	214	Of London, Merchant. About to immigrate 1657.
Jackson, Owen	WC2	320	Transported 1680.
Jackson, Peter	10	312	" 1662.
Jackson, Peter	16	411	" 1671.
Jackson, Peter	WC2	206	" 1679. Servant.
Jackson, Richard	6	82	" 1659.
Jackson, Richard	5	207	" 1662.
Jackson, Richard	8	478	" 1665.
Jackson, Richard	12	190	" 1668.
Jackson, Richard	17	351	" 1670. Son of Richard.
Jackson, Robert	13	66	" 1669. Servant.
Jackson, Samuel	4	581	" 1661.
Jackson, Samuel	16	536	Service 1671. (15, fol. 569).
Jackson, Samuel	15	569	Transported 1678.
Jackson, Samuel	WC2	19	" 1679.
Jackson, Sibella	5	73	" 1661.
Jackson, Simeon	WC2	19	" 1679.
Jackson, Simon	15	569	" 1678.
Jackson, Thomas	ABH	10	Servant 1636.
Jackson, Thomas	2	426	Transported 1636. Servant.
Jackson, Thomas	ABH	203	Immigrated 1651.
Jackson, Thomas	11	524	" 1668.
Jackson, Thomas	12	604	Transported 1670.
Jackson, Thomas	WC2	206	" 1680. Servant.
Jackson, Walbro	9	329	" 1665. Of Anne

NAME	Liber	Folio	REMARKS
			Arundel Co. (15, fol. 439).
Jackson, William	ABH	200	Transported 1636. Servant.
Jackson, William	ABH	212	Immigrated 1650.
Jackson, William	5	557	Transported 1659.
Jackson, William	16	436	" 1671.
Jacob, Eleanor	7	464	" 1656.
Jacob, Elizabeth	15	413	" 1677. Daughter of Isaac.
Jacob, Isaac	15	413	Immigrated 1677.
Jacob, John	18	128	Service 1665. Of Anne Arundel Co.
Jacob, Lawrence	17	503	Transported 1667.
Jacob, Margaret	15	553	" 1678. (WC2, fol. 57).
Jacob, Sarah	15	413	" 1677. Wife of Isaac.
Jacob, Sarah	15	413	" 1677. Daughter of Isaac.
Jacobley, James	WC2	415	Transported 1680. Servant.
Jacobs, Cornelius	12	505	" 1670. Servant.
Jacobs, Edward	15	443	" 1677.
Jacobson, Alicia	Q	63	Wife of Peter 1658.
Jacobson, Christian	11	537	Transported 1668.
Jacobson, Christopher	17	545	Service 1673. Of St. Mary's Co.
Jacobson, Hance	11	537	Transported 1668.
Jacobson, John	15	376	" 1676.
Jacobson, John	6	47	" 1663.
Jacobson, Peter	Q	63	Immigrated 1658.
Jacobson, Peter	16	95	Transported 1670.
Jacobson, Sifray	Q	63	Immigrated 1658. Son of Peter.
Jacques, Edmond	ABH	151,244	Transported 1640. Servant.
Jacus, Edm.	2	425	" 1640.
Jadwin, Bartholomew	9	304	" 1665.
Jadwynn, John	9	305	Immigrated 1665.
Jadwynn, John, Jr.	9	305	Transported 1665. Son of John.
Jagger, James	4	53	" 1659.
Jains, Thomas	4	19	Immigrated 1651 and married Ann Beech, prior to 1659.
James, ---	Q	28	A Servant, 1649-50.
James, Abel	16	88	Immigrated 1670 with Diana, his wife. Of St. Mary's Co.
James, Anthony	WC2	78	Transported 1679.
James, Charles	4	554	Immigrated 1661. Merchant. Married Eliz., daughter of Leonard Strong of A. A. Co., prior to 1670. (14, fol. 40). Deputy Surveyor under Baker Brooke for Baltimore and Anne Arundel Counties, July 28, 1674. (15, fol. 203).
James, Constantine	WC2	78	Transported 1679.
James, David	16	393	" 1671.
James, Diana	16	88	" 1670. Wife of Abel.
James, Edward	ABH	10	" 1640.
James, Edward	12	498	" 1670. (17, fol. 598).
James, Eleanor	9	21	" 1665. (12, fol. 505).
James, Elizabeth	WC2	78	" 1679.
James, Francis	18	167	" 1674.

NAME	Liber	Folio	REMARKS
James, George	15	505	Transported 1678.
James, Gilbert	15	449	Immigrated 1677. Of Somerset Co.
James, Henry	ABH	66	Transported 1633. (1, fol. 38).
James, Hugh	16	86	" 1670.
James, James	15	449	" 1677. Son of Gilbert.
James, Jeane	15	449	" 1677. Daughter of Gilbert.
James, John	6	85	Transported 1660.
James, John	4	654	" 1661.
James, John	9	399	Immigrated prior to 1666.
James, John	16	40	Transported 1670.
James, John	16	168	" 1671. Son of John.
James, John	16	168	Immigrated 1671, with Mary, his wife, John, his son, and Thos. Taylor, his son-in-law.
James, John	11	344	Transported 1668.
James, John	17	448	" 1673.
James, John	WC2	78	" 1679.
James, Jonathan	15	449	" 1677. Son of Gilbert.
James, Jone	17	452	" 1671.
James, Jone	15	449	" 1677. Wife of Gilbert.
James, Joseph	8	87	" 1665. Servant. Married the widow of Peter Underwood prior to 1676. (19, fol. 590).
James, Katherine	9	38	Transported 1665.
James, Lancelot	WC2	78	" 1679.
James, Lewis	15	449	" 1677. Son of Gilbert.
James, Owen	ABH	36	Immigrated 1645. (2, fol. 581).
James, Owen	15	331	Transported 1675.
James, Peter	15	551	" 1678.
James, Presilla	12	472	" 1670.
James, Rice	16	94	" 1670.
James, Richard	5	411	" 1663.
James, Richard	WC2	73	" 1665.
James, Richard	9	490	" 1665. Servant.
James, Richard	WC2	78	" 1679.
James, Robert	17	513	Immigrated 1673.
James, Rose	15	331	Transported 1675.
James, Samuel	11	338	" 1668.
James, Theophilus	6	130	" 1658.
James, Thomas	9	105	Immigrated 1665.
James, Thomas	11	319,344	Transported 1668.
James, Thomas	15	357,397	" 1676.
James, Will.	ABH	47	" prior to 1648. Servant.
James, William	6	86	" 1650.
James, William	5	305,413	" 1663.
James, William	7	563	" 1665.
James, William	10	434	" 1667.
James, Winifred	12	413	" 1669. (15, fol. 301).
Jameson, William	WC2	21	" 1679.
Janes, Mary	15	557	" 1675. Servant.
Janson, Jacob	9	489	" 1665.
Janson, Lambert	12	285	" 1667.

NAME	Liber	Folio	REMARKS
Jarbo, John	2	440	Immigrated 1646. (See Jerbo).
Jardy, Thomas	5	73	Transported 1660-1.
Jargurson, John	4	552	" 1661.
Jarret, Elizabeth	WC2	76	" 1679. Wife of Thomas.
Jarret, Mary	WC2	76	" 1679. Daughter of Thomas.
Jarret, John	WC2	76	Transported 1679. Son of Thomas.
Jarret, Thomas	WC2	76	Immigrated from Virginia 1679 with wife and 3 children.
Jarret, Thomas, Jr.	WC2	76	Transported 1679. Son of Thomas.
Jarvis, Eleanor	12	190	" 1668. Servant.
Jarvis, Henry	18	137	" 1674.
Jarvis, John	12	189	" 1668.
Jarvis, John	15	167	" 1673. (17, fol. 416).
Jarvis, Richard	18	311	" 1675.
Jarvis, Robert	6	63	" 1658-63.
Jasop, Joseph	16	412	" 1669. (13, fol. 114).
Jary, John	12	190	" 1668.
Jaxon, Thomas	5	81	" 1661.
Jay, Thomas	18	176	" 1674.
Jeames, Alice	15	531	" 1678.
Jeannison, Robert	18	160	" 1674.
Jefery, Richard	15	446	" 1677.
Jeffers, Eleanor	7	569	" 1663-4. (11, fol. 235).
Jeffers, Eliza. Jr.	7	569	" 1663-4.
Jeffers, John	15	527	" 1678.
Jefferson, James	16	411	" 1671.
Jefferson, John	11	581	" 1668. (15, fol. 431).
Of Dorchester County. Service 1677.			
Jefferson, Ralph	16	411	Transported 1671.
Jeffery, John	12	391	" 1669.
Jefferyes, John	11	374	" 1668.
Jefferyes, Thomas	9	304	" 1665.
Jefferys, Mary	7	372	" 1664.
Jefferys, Walter	12	382	" 1669. (15, fol. 343).
Jeffes, Henry	6	106	" 1657.
Jeffrey, Thomas	WC2	352	" 1680.
Jeffries, Mary	16	217	" 1671.
Jeffries, Mary	17	490	" 1673.
Jeffryes, Elizabeth	11	235	" 1667.
Jefry, Rachel	15	397	" 1676.
Jelfe, James	1	69	" 1637. Servant.
Jellell, Jery	8	130	" 1664.
Jelliard, John	11	546	" 1668.
Jelly, Alice	5	93	" 1661. Servant.
Jelly, Edward	7	483	" 1663.
Jemmeson, Alexander	9	101	" 1665.
Jenckins, Mathew	WC2	80	Service 1679. Of Somerset Co.
Jenckins, Morgan	17	408	Transported 1673.
Jenifer, Daniel, Gent.	20	48	Married, Mary, widow of Wm. Smith of E. (& Extric) (Consult record). Immigrated 1667. (10, fol. 489).

NAME	Liber	Folio	REMARKS
Jenifer, Jacob	17	615	Immigrated 1673 with Elizabeth, his wife. Of Dorchester Co. (18, fol. 118).
Jenifer, Margaret	5	253	Immigrated 1663. Sister to Daniel.
Jenifer, Sarah	12	576	Transported 1670.
Jenings, Eleanor	12	209	" 1668.
Jenison, Cuthbert	16	411	" 1671.
Jenkenson, William	7	135	" 1664.
Jenkin, William	12	460	" 1669.
Jenkindoe, Thomas	11	24	Service 1668.
Jenkins, Ann	Q	204	Transported 1651.
Jenkins, Ann	4	63	" 1654. Wife of John.
Jenkins, Ann	10	541	" 1667. Daughter of Sarah Brooke.
Jenkins, Ann	17	40	Transported 1672. Daughter of William.
Jenkins, Ann	15	531	Service 1678. Wife of William of Somerset Co.
Jenkins, Dorcas	17	40	Transported 1672. Daughter of William.
Jenkins, Eleanor	10	541	Transported 1667. Daughter of Sarah Brooke.
Jenkins, Elizabeth	10	4	Transported 1665.
Jenkins, Francis	5	236	" 1662. Servant.
Jenkins, Francis	11	465	" 1668.
Jenkins, Francis	16	297	Immigrated 1671. Of Somerset Co. Deputy Sur'r. (16, fol. 370). Do. Dorchester, Somerset and Worcester counties, 7th June 1676. (15, fol. 352; 20, fol. 129).
Jenkins, Griffen	7	469	Transported 1664.
Jenkins, Howell	15	530	" 1678.
Jenkins, Hugh	18	308	" 1675.
Jenkins, James	19	258	" 1663. (15, fol. 405).
Jenkins, Jane	15	543	" 1678.
Jenkins, John	ABH	381	" Feb. 1653. Servant.
Jenkins, John	4	63	Immigrated 1654. Married Joan, widow of Thos. Bachelor 1658. (Q, fol. 33).
Jenkins, John	10	575	Transported 1667. (15, fol. 319).
Jenkins, John	15	409	Immigrated 1675. Of Somerset Co.
Jenkins, John	WC2	253	Transported 1680.
Jenkins, Jone	17	40	" 1672. Wife of Wm. of Calvert Co.
Jenkins, Margaret	15	567	Transported 1679.
Jenkins, Mary	5	514	" 1658.
Jenkins, Mary	10	541	" 1667. Daughter of Sarah Brooke.
Jenkins, Mary	17	40	Transported 1672. Daughter of Wm. of Calvert Co.
Jenkins, Matthew	15	318	Transported 1675.
Jenkins, Richard	12	602	" 1670.
Jenkins, Richard	18	83	Service 1674. Of Calvert Co.
Jenkins, Robert	6	105	Transported 1657.
Jenkins, Stephen	15	167	" 1673.

NAME	Liber	Folio	REMARKS
Jenkins, Susanna	15	319,401	Transported 1675. Wife of John.
Jenkins, Thomas	Q	47	Servant 1658.
Jenkins, Thomas	5	240,253	Transported 1662.
Jenkins, Thomas	12	413,602	" 1669.
Jenkins, Thomas	16	12	Immigrated 1670 with Ann, his wife. Of Charles Co.
Jenkins, Thomas	15	565	Transported 1679.
Jenkins, William	4	190	" 1659.
Jenkins, William	12	594,602	" 1670. (18, fol. 39).
Jenkins, William	17	40	Immigrated 1672. Of Calvert Co.
Jenkins, William	15	319,409	Transported 1675. Son of John.
Jenkinson, Michael	7	79	" 1664.
Jenkinson, Robert	5	345	" 1662.
Jenner, Obedience	20	185	" 1679.
Jennings, Eleanor	12	501	" 1669.
Jennings, Humphrey	8	39	" 1665. (12, fol. 209).
Jennings, John	4	14	" 1659. Servant. Service 1677. (15, fol. 422).
Jennings, Mary	1	19,166	Transported 1633.
Jennings, Michael	Q	28	" 1656. Service 1662. (5, fol. 64; 64, fol. 139).
Jennings, Richard	4	190	Of London, Merchant. About to immigrate 1657.
Jennings, Richard	16	458	Transported 1672.
Jennings, Richard	17	440	" 1673.
Jennitt, Jane	5	415	" 1663.
Jenny, Ann	15	397	" 1676.
Jenny, John	16	394	" 1671.
Jerbo, John	2	255	Immigrated 1646. (See Jarbo).
Jermegan, Ellen	1	17	Transported 1637.
Jermegan, Mary	1	17	" 1637.
Jermegan, Thomas	1	17	" 1637.
Jermine, Robert	15	429	" 1677.
Jerrill, Henry	6	219	Immigrated 1663.
Jerrill, Henry	6	219	Transported 1663. Son of Henry.
Jerrill, Milven	6	219	" 1663. Wife of Henry.
Jerrill, Robert	6	219	" 1663. Son of Henry.
Jersey, James	11	170	Immigrated 1667. Of St. Mary's Co. (16, fol. 41).
Jervis, Peter	9	434	Transported 1664.
Jervis, Thomas	16	170	" 1671.
Jesop, Joseph	16	412	" 1669. (13, fol. 114).
Jessee, Thomas	16	170	" 1671.
Jessop, Dorothy	ABH	251	" Dec. 1652. Servant.
Jessop, Thomas	6	7	" 1663.
Jessop, William	15	434	Immigrated 1677. Of St. Mary's Co.
Jewell, John	WC2	206	Transported 1679. Servant.
Jinkes, Henry	WC2	415	" 1666-80. Servant.
Joane, Blake	12	202	" 1669. Servant.
Joanes, Abraham	Q	49	Immigrated 1658.
Joanes, Ann	18	329	Transported 1675.

NAME	Liber	Folio	REMARKS
Joanes, Elizabeth	5	367	Transported 1649.
Joanes, Isabella	5	73	" 1661.
Joanes, Jacob	5	203	" 1662.
Joanes, John	Q	73	Immigrated 1658.
Joanes, John	Q	203	Transported 1658.
Joanes, John	5	293	" 1661.
Joanes, John	5	249	" 1663.
Joanes, John	7	471	" 1664.
Joanes, Margaret	Q	18	" 1651.
Joanes, Margaret	15	500	" 1676-7.
Joanes, Mary	Q	73	Immigrated 1658. Wife of John.
Joanes, Mary	5	238	Transported 1662. Wife of Richard.
Joanes, Mary	18	329	" 1675.
Joanes, Meridith	5	234	Service 1662.
Joanes, Morgan	5	85	Transported 1661.
Joanes, Richard	5	238	" 1662.
Joanes, Richard, Jr.	5	238	" 1662.
Joanes, Thomas	5	260	" 1660.
Joanes, Walter	12	498	" 1670.
Joanes, William	Q	202	" 1658.
Joanes, William	5	253,257	Immigrated 1663.
Joanes, William	18	296	Transported 1674.
Joanes, Winifred	5	251	" 1663.
Joans, Margery	WC2	399	" 1677.
Jobson, Frances	16	409	" from Virginia 1671.
Joce, Thomas	WC2	184,207	Immigrated 1680. Of Talbot Co.
Joce, Thomas	WC2	184	Transported 1680. Servant.
Jackston, Margaret	7	464	" 1655.
John ---	8	381	"A boy". Transported 1665.
John, Edward	10	564-565	Transported 1667.
John, Edward	10	311	" Feb. 1665.
Johns, John	9	216	" 1665.
Johns, Katherine	15	358	" 1675.
Johns, Richard	12	554	" 1670.
Johns, Richard	16	93	Immigrated 1670. Of Calvert Co.
Johns, Richard	WC2	399	Transported 1677.
Johns, Robert	15	560	" 1678.
Johns, Roger	17	408	" 1673
Johns, William	7	581	" 1665.
Johns, William	WC2	309	" 1678.
Johnson, Aguetta	4	552	" 1661. Wife of Paul.
Johnson, Albert	10	307	Immigrated Mar. 10, 1665. Of Cowersey Creek in Chester River.
Johnson, Albert	10	567	Immigrated 1666 from the Meadows. Of Talbot Co.
Johnson, Albert	17	354	Immigrated 1672 with Bellia, his wife, and Anna Katherine, his daughter.
Johnson, Alice	18	314	Service 1668. Wife of William.
Johnson, Alice	15	544	Transported 1676.
Johnson, Amelia	Q	19	Relict of William Johnson 1658.
Johnson, Andreas	4	552	Transported 1661. Son of Paul.

NAME	Liber	Folio	REMARKS
Johnson, Ann	ABH	140	Transported 1651. Wife of Peter.
Johnson, Ann	10	168	" 1666. Wife of David.
Johnson, Ann	18	335	" 1675.
Johnson, Annakin	4	552	" 1661. Daughter of Paul.
Johnson, Anthony	8	495	Transported 1665.
Johnson, Barnes	4	181	" 1651. Servant.
Johnson, Bartle	8	381	" 1665.
Johnson, Cecilla	12	205	" 1667.
Johnson, Christian	4	552	" 1661. Daughter of Paul. (17, fol. 532).
Johnson, Christopher	9	435	Transported 1664.
Johnson, Christopher	10	566	" 1667. (11, fol. 374,527).
Johnson, Corn.	15	353	" 1676.
Johnson, Cornelius	3	169	Immigrated 1655.
Johnson, Cornelius	7	81	Transported 1662.
Johnson, Cornelius	16	592	Immigrated 1672 with Barbara, his wife, and Mary and Barbara, his daughters. Of Somerset Co.
Johnson, David	10	168	Immigrated 1666. Of Talbot Co.
Johnson, David, Jr.	10	168	Transported 1666. Son of David.
Johnson, Derrick	ABH	140	" 1651.
Johnson, Dorothy	WC2	415	" 1666-80. Servant.
Johnson, Dorothy	15	397	" 1676.
Johnson, Dorothy	WC2	306	" 1680.
Johnson, Edward	17	402,604	Service 1672.
Johnson, Eleanor	12	334	Transported 1668.
Johnson, Eleanor	16	395	" 1671. (17, fol. 356).
Johnson, Elizabeth	4	54	" 1659.
Johnson, Elizabeth	9	280	" 1665.
Johnson, Elizabeth	11	265	" 1667.
Johnson, Elizabeth	11	313	" 1668.
Johnson, Elizabeth	16	432,437	" 1671. (16, fol. 503).
Johnson, Elizabeth	16	595	Widow of Daniel of Charles Co., and wife of Francis Kilborne, 1672.
Johnson, Elizabeth	18	152	Transported 1674.
Johnson, Esther	WC2	201	" 1680. Servant.
Johnson, Fence	10	567	" 1666. Wife of Albert.
Johnson, Frances	16	39	" 1668.
Johnson, Francis	17	516	Immigrated 1664.
Johnson, Francis	WC2	158	Transported 1680.
Johnson, Garrett	10	600	Immigrated 1667.
Johnson, George	9	272	Transported 1665.
Johnson, George	15	501	" 1678.
Johnson, Gilbert	9	488	" 1665.
Johnson, Harmon	8	501	" 1665.
Johnson, Hendrick	10	567	" 1666. Son of Albert.
Johnson, Hendrick	4	552	" 1661. Son of Paul.
Johnson, Henry	7	465	" 1662. (10, fol. 609).
Johnson, Henry	17	552	Immigrated 1663. Of Calvert Co.
Johnson, Henry	10	466	" 1667.
Johnson, Honor	WC2	253	Transported 1679.

NAME	Liber	Folio	REMARKS
Johnson, Hugh	18	108	Transported 1674.
Johnson, Isaac	6	95	" 1661.
Johnson, Jacob	11	537	" 1668. (17, fol. 578).
Johnson, James	1	88	" prior to 1640.
Johnson, James	1	119	Immigrated 1641.
Johnson, James	2	458	" 1647.
Johnson, James	9	343	Transported 1666.
Johnson, James	ABH	87	" prior to 1640. Servant.
Johnson, James	ABH	1,97	Immigrated 1640.
Johnson, James	ABH	15	" 1646.
Johnson, James	ABH	140	Transported 1651.
Johnson, James	6	267	Immigrated 1667.
Johnson, James	Q	3	Second son of Peter, 1658.
Johnson, James	15	445	Transported 1678.
Johnson, James	WC2	319	Immigrated 1680 with wife and son.
Johnson, Jane	Q	17	Transported 1652-8.
Johnson, Jane	12	498	" 1670.
Johnson, Jane	15	453	" 1675-7.
Johnson, John	Q	449	" 1658. (4, fol. 29).
Johnson, John	Q	18	Servant 1657.
Johnson, John	6	268	Transported 1662.
Johnson, John	5	358	Immigrated 1663.
Johnson, John	7	372	Transported 1664.
Johnson, John	8	478,484	" 1665.
Johnson, John	9	280	" 1665 by Geo. Johnson.
Johnson, John	9	489	" 1665.
Johnson, John	10	307	" Mar. 1665. Son of Albert.
Johnson, John	16	415	Immigrated 1665 with Mary, his wife. Of Talbot Co.
Johnson, John	10	342	Transported 1666.
Johnson, John	15	422	" 1668. (18, fol. 387).
Johnson, John	12	357	Service 1669. Of St. Mary's Co. Shoemaker.
Johnson, John	16	110,437	Transported 1671.
Johnson, John	14	443	" 1672.
Johnson, John	17	452,463	" 1673.
Johnson, John	18	314	And Isabella, his wife. Service 1675.
Johnson, John	15	342	Service 1676. Shipwright.
Johnson, John	15	435	Transported 1677.
Johnson, John	WC2	23	" 1679.
Johnson, John	WC2	319	Service 1680.
Johnson, Joseph	WC2	306	Transported 1680.
Johnson, Katherine	10	307	" Mar. 1665. Daughter of Albert.
Johnson, Katherine	15	454	Transported Oct. 1677.
Johnson, Katherine, Jr.	6	154	" 1663.
Johnson, Katherine, Sr.	6	154	" 1663.
Johnson, Lambert	9	488	" 1665.
Johnson, Lewis	16	100	" 1668.
Johnson, Margarett	WC2	320	" 1680. Servant.

NAME	Liber	Folio	REMARKS
Johnson, Margaretta	4	552	Transported 1661. Daughter of Paul.
Johnson, Martha	15	446	Service 1677. Wife of Jacob. (20, fol. 2).
Johnson, Mary	ABH	140	Transported 1651.
Johnson, Mary	6	95	" 1658.
Johnson, Mary	15	422	" 1664.
Johnson, Mary	8	495	" 1665.
Johnson, Mary	10	567	" 1666. Daughter of Albert.
Johnson, Mary	15	452	Transported 1678.
Johnson, Michael	7	464	" 1659.
Johnson, Nicholas	15	500	" 1676-7.
Johnson, Nicholas	WC2	399	" 1677.
Johnson, Paul	4	552	Immigrated 1661.
Johnson, Paul	15	360	Transported 1676.
Johnson, Peter	ABH	140	Immigrated 1651. Of Patuxent River.
Johnson, Peter	Q	63	" 1658.
Johnson, Peter	7	80	" 1664.
Johnson, Peter	12	190	Transported 1668. Servant.
Johnson, Peter, Jr.	ABH	140	" 1651. Son of Peter.
Johnson, Priscilla	4	30	" prior to 1659. Servant.
Johnson, Rachel	9	335	" 1666. Wife of John of Talbot County.
Johnson, Rachel	WC2	319	Transported 1680. Wife of James.
Johnson, Richard	WC2	201	" 1680. Servant.
Johnson, Robert	16	131	" 1671.
Johnson, Robert	18	174	" 1674. (15, fol. 310).
Johnson, Robert	15	413	Immigrated 1677 with Izard, his wife.
Johnson, Robert	WC2	21,112	Transported 1679.
Johnson, Sarah	16	395	" 1671.
Johnson, Sarah	WC2	281	Service 1680.
Johnson, Thomas	5	123	Transported 1662.
Johnson, Thomas	7	461	" 1664.
Johnson, Thomas	18	137	" 1674.
Johnson, Thomas	15	353	" 1676.
Johnson, Thomas	15	558	" 1679.
Johnson, Tony	15	422	" 1664.
Johnson, Venemy	10	307	" March 1665. Wife of Albert.
Johnson, William	ABH	59	Transported 1641. (1, fol. 24).
Johnson, William	ABH	47	Immigrated 1646. (3, fol. 24).
Johnson, William	ABH	166	" 1646.
Johnson, William	4	551	Transported 1661.
Johnson, William	10	558	" 1663.
Johnson, William	7	606	" 1665. (8, fol. 484).
Johnson, William	9	54	" 1665. (10, fol. 5).
Johnson, William	10	4	" 1666.
Johnson, William	12	205	" 1667.
Johnson, William	18	314	Immigrated 1668.
Johnson, William	12	381	Transported 1669. Servant.

NAME	Liber	Folio	REMARKS
Johnson, William	15	443	Transported 1672.
Johnson, William	17	382	Service 1672. (17, fol. 457).
Johnson, William	WC2	255,340	Transported 1680.
Johnson, William	WC2	319	" 1680. Son of James.
Jolane, Francis	WC2	167,169	" 1680.
Jolif, John	15	566	" 1678.
Jolleff, John	WC2	130,145	" 1679. Servant.
Jolly, Edward	17	332	Immigrated 1662. Of St. Mary's Co.
Jolly, Elizabeth	ABH	424	Transported 1655. Wife of James.
Jolly, George	15	408	Immigrated 1673. Of Talbot Co.
Jolly, Isabella	15	408	Service 1676. Wife of George.
Jolly, James	ABH	425	Immigrated 1655.
Jolly, Margaret	17	333	Service 1672. Wife of Edward.
Jolly, Martin	12	285	Transported 1667.
Jolly, William	ABH	424	" 1655. Son of James.
Jollycomb, Robert	5	320	" 1662.
Jone, John	6	211	" 1659.
Jones, Abraham	16	86	" 1670.
Jones, Alice	7	82	" 1660.
Jones, Alice	19	40	Wife of William of A. A. Co. Transported 1675.
Jones, Ambrose	16	394	Transported 1671.
Jones, Andrew	18	36	" 1673.
Jones, Andrew	15	531	Immigrated 1678. Of Somerset Co. Planter.
Jones, Ann	7	502	Transported 1657.
Jones, Ann	7	487	" Nov. 1663.
Jones, Ann	10	558	" 1667. Servant.
Jones, Ann	17	417,475	" 1673.
Jones, Ann	15	429	" 1674.
Jones, Ann	15	437	" 1677.
Jones, Anne	WC2	217	" 1680.
Jones, Anthony	Q	323	" 1655-8.
Jones, Barbara	6	170	" 1658.
Jones, Barbara	7	464	" 1661.
Jones, Barbary	16	399	" 1667.
Jones, Barbary	11	338	" 1668.
Jones, Bridgett	11	378	" 1668.
Jones, Charles	5	185	" 1662. Son of John.
Jones, Charles	6	239	" 1663.
Jones, Charles	9	313	" 1665.
Jones, Charles	17	440	" 1673.
Jones, Charles	WC2	321	Immigrated 1680. Bricklayer.
Jones, Christopher	10	599	Transported 1667.
Jones, Clement	6	239	" 1663.
Jones, Cornelius	6	85	" 1650.
Jones, Cornelius	9	54	" 1665.
Jones, Daniel	11	496	Immigrated 1668. Of Talbot Co.
Jones, Daniel	WC2	171	Transported 1679.
Jones, Daniel	WC2	254	" 1680.
Jones, David	7	79	" 1664.

NAME	Liber	Folio	REMARKS
Jones, David	9	304	Transported 1665.
Jones, David	12	359,472	" 1669.
Jones, David	16	86	" 1670.
Jones, David	17	64,572	Immigrated 1672.
Jones, David	18	24,137	Transported 1674.
Jones, David	15	523	Service 1678. Of St. Mary's Co.
Jones, David	WC2	73	Transported 1679.
Jones, David	WC2	306	" 1680.
Jones, Dorothy	5	208	" 1661.
Jones, Edward	ABH	151	" 1641. Servant.
Jones, Edward	6	121	" 1660.
Jones, Edward	4	570	" 1661.
Jones, Edward	4	578	Immigrated prior to 1661. Of the Isle of Kent.
Jones, Edward	6	290	Transported 1663.
Jones, Edward	8	502	" 1665.
Jones, Edward	9	335	Immigrated 1666.
Jones, Edward	12	415	Transported 1669.
Jones, Edward	12	614–615	Service 1670. Of Kent Co.
Jones, Edward	16	86	Transported 1670.
Jones, Edward	16	129	" 1671.
Jones, Edward	17	56	" 1672.
Jones, Edward	17	608	" 1673.
Jones, Edward	18	116	Service 1674. Of St. Mary's Co. (15, fol. 402).
Jones, Edward	20	94	Chirurgeon. Commission from Baker Brooke, Surv. Genl. as Dep. Surv'r. of Cecil Co. 1678.
Jones, Elior	5	127	Transported 1660.
Jones, Elizabeth	5	530	" 1662.
Jones, Elizabeth	5	359	" 1663.
Jones, Elizabeth	18	387	" 1668.
Jones, Elizabeth	16	428	" 1670-1.
Jones, Elizabeth	17	407	" 1673.
Jones, Elizabeth	18	166	" 1674.
Jones, Elizabeth	15	319	" 1675.
Jones, Elizabeth	15	526	Service 1678. Wife of Rev. Morgan.
Jones, Ellen	2	569	Transported 1650. Servant.
Jones, Ellis	16	637	" 1665.
Jones, Esdras	9	157	" 1665.
Jones, Evan	16	78	" 1670. (15, fol. 380).
Jones, Francis	6	159	" 1661.
Jones, Francis	8	130	" 1665.
Jones, George	15	411	Immigrated 1677. Of Somerset Co.
Jones, Griffith	4	54	Transported 1659.
Jones, Henry	8	39	" 1657.
Jones, Henry	5	218	" 1662.
Jones, Henry	17	416,532	Service 1673. Of St. Mary's Co.
Jones, Henry	15	322	Transported 1675.
Jones, Henry	15	440	" 1677.
Jones, Hester	18	36	" 1673.
Jones, Howell	15	516	" 1675.

NAME	Liber	Folio	REMARKS
Jones, Hugh	12	192	Transported 1668.
Jones, Hugh	15	430	" 1677.
Jones, Hugh	WC2	309	" 1678.
Jones, Humphrey	7	581	" 1665.
Jones, Humphrey	9	400	" 1666.
Jones, Humphrey	12	190	" 1668.
Jones, Humphrey	15	445,505	" 1677.
Jones, Humphry	WC2	53	" 1677.
Jones, Jacob	7	567	" 1665.
Jones, James	9	332	" 1664 on the "Golden Wheat Sheaf".
Jones, James	9	99	Immigrated 1665.
Jones, James	10	561	Transported 1667.
Jones, James	11	227	" 1667.
Jones, James	12	282	Immigrated 1668.
Jones, James	15	319	" 1675. Mariner.
Jones, Jane	12	281	Service 1667.
Jones, Jane	16	431	Transported 1671. Servant.
Jones, Jane	15	362	" 1676.
Jones, Jane	15	430	" 1677.
Jones, Jane	WC2	23	" 1679. Servant.
Jones, Jane	WC2	105	Immigrated 1680 with 4 children and one servant. Wife of Thomas.
Jones, Jehovah	17	348	Transported 1667.
Jones, Jenkin	9	54	" 1665.
Jones, Jenkin	11	338	" 1668.
Jones, Jenkin	12	356	" 1669.
Jones, Jenkins	17	41	" 1672.
Jones, Joane	10	561	" 1667. Wife of Leonard.
Jones, Joane	17	407	" 1673.
Jones, John	1	19	" 1637.
Jones, John	1	50	" 1639. Servant. (ABH, fol. 72).
Jones, John	18	144	Service 1657. Of Anne Arundel Co.
Jones, John	4	10	Transported 1658. Servant.
Jones, John	5	185	Immigrated 1661.
Jones, John	5	211	Transported 1662. Son of Samuel.
Jones, John	9	313	Immigrated 1665. Of Talbot Co.
Jones, John	10	565	Transported 1666 from Northumberland County, Virginia by Edw. Jones.
Jones, John	16	86	Transported 1670.
Jones, John	16	507	" 1671.
Jones, John	17	503,572	" 1672.
Jones, John	17	417	" 1673. (17, fol. 424).
Jones, John	18	36	" 1673.
Jones, John	18	2	Immigrated 1674 with Elizabeth, his wife, and Elizabeth, his daughter. Of Dorchester Co.
Jones, John	WC2	370	Transported 1674. (18, fol. 166,174).
Jones, John	15	318	" 1675.
Jones, John	15	362	" 1676.
Jones, John	15	404	Immigrated 1676. Of Cecil Co.

NAME	Liber	Folio	REMARKS
Jones, John	20	184	Transported from Ireland 1678.
Jones, John	WC2	71	Immigrated 1679.
Jones, John	WC2	406	Transported 1679.
Jones, John	WC2	47,71	Immigrated 1679. Of Kent Co.
Jones, John	WC2	120	Transported 1680.
Jones, Johnson	9	99	" 1665.
Jones, Jonathan	6	81	" 1649. Servant.
Jones, Jonathan	5	514	" 1659.
Jones, Jonathan	6	79	" 1662. (11,fol. 500).
Jones, Jone	10	324,564	" 1666.
Jones, Jone	11	227	" 1667. Wife of Leonard.
Jones, Jone	15	428	Service 1677. Of Dorchester Co.
Jones, Jone	15	564	Transported 1679.
Jones, Katherine	5	484	" 1661.
Jones, Katherine	8	89	" 1665. Wife of Robert.
Jones, Katherine	17	407	" 1673.
Jones, Katherine	15	354	" 1676.
Jones, Leonard	10	561	Immigrated from Virginia 1667. (11,fol. 226-227).
Jones, Lerey	19	258	Transported 1663.
Jones, Lewis	15	318	Immigrated 1674. Of Va. (18,fol. 137).
Jones, Lewis	WC2	52,74	Service 1679.
Jones, Margaret	9	32	Transported 1657.
Jones, Margaret	5	489	" 1660.
Jones, Margaret	5	208	" 1662.
Jones, Margaret	6	123	" 1663.
Jones, Margaret	9	229	" 1665. Wife of William.
Jones, Margaret	10	565	" 1667. (10,fol. 561).
Jones, Margaret	11	227	" 1667. Wife of Leonard.
Jones, Margaret	11	507	" 1668 by Andrew Insley, whom she afterwards married.
Jones, Margaret	15	531	Transported 1678.
Jones, Margarett	WC2	288	" 1680.
Jones, Martha	15	380	" 1676.
Jones, Mary	ABH	276	" 1649. Servant.
Jones, Mary	5	516	" 1650.
Jones, Mary	6	81	" 1650.
Jones, Mary	5	211	" 1662. Wife of Samuel.
Jones, Mary	10	507	" 1667. Servant.
Jones, Mary	10	561	" 1667.
Jones, Mary	12	215	" 1668-9.
Jones, Mary	12	576	" 1670.
Jones, Mary	16	132	" 1671.
Jones, Mary	17	411	" 1673.
Jones, Mary	15	359	" 1676.
Jones, Mary	15	566	" 1678.
Jones, Mary	WC2	150	" 1680 by Francis Watkins.
Jones, Mary	WC2	259	Transported 1680 by Hugh Thomas.
Jones, Morgan	12	241	Immigrated 1669.
Jones, Morgan	18	121	Transported 1674. (15,fol. 431).

NAME	Liber	Folio	REMARKS
Jones, Rev. Morgan	15	526	Immigrated 1678. "Clerke".
Jones, Morrice	17	488	Service 1673. Of St. Mary's Co. (7, fol. 559).
Jones, Moses	18	313	Transported 1675.
Jones, Nathan	12	200	" 1668.
Jones, Nathaniel	ABH	47	" 1648. Servant.
Jones, Nathaniell	3	23	" before 1648.
Jones, Nicholas	15	318	" 1674.
Jones, Nicholas	WC2	10,17	" 1679.
Jones, Nicholas	WC2	411	" 1681.
Jones, Owen	8	30	" 1665.
Jones, Owen	11	348,520	" 1668.
Jones, Parnall	7	601	" 1665.
Jones, Patrick	16	393	" 1671.
Jones, Paul	15	397	" 1676.
Jones, Peter	6	48	" 1663.
Jones, Peter	15	422	" 1664.
Jones, Peter	9	489	Immigrated 1665.
Jones, Philip	4	551	Transported 1661.
Jones, Philip	5	256	" 1663.
Jones, Philip	9	505	" 1666.
Jones, Philip	12	492	" 1670. (18, fol. 115).
Jones, Philip	WC2	110	" 1676. Servant.
Jones, Rice	9	38	" 1665.
Jones, Rice	12	413	" 1669. (17, fol. 415).
Jones, Richard	6	37	" 1663.
Jones, Richard	9	313	" 1665.
Jones, Richard	11	316	" 1668. (12, fol. 270, 278).
Jones, Richard	12	592	Transported 1668.
Jones, Richard	18	137	" 1674. (15, fol. 405).
Jones, Richard	15	429	" 1677.
Jones, Richard Thomas	17	440	" 1668.
Jones, Robert	ABH	371	Service 1653.
Jones, Robert	Q	443	Transported 1658.
Jones, Robert	8	88,89	" 1665.
Jones, Robert	8	130	" 1665. Servant.
Jones, Robert	9	489	Immigrated 1665 with wife.
Jones, Robert	11	431	Of Va. Gent. acquires land on the Eastern Shore 1667. (12, fol. 352).
Jones, Robert	15	259	Transported 1675.
Jones, Robert	15	414	" 1677.
Jones, Robert	WC2	67	Service 1679. Of St. Mary's Co.
Jones, Rodwick	15	368	" 1676.
Jones, Rowland	11	378	Transported 1668.
Jones, Rowland	13	66	" 1670.
Jones, Samuel	5	211	Immigrated 1662.
Jones, Samuel	5	211	Transported 1662. Son of Samuel.
Jones, Samuel	6	239	" 1663.
Jones, Samuel	16	319	Immigrated from Accamac, Va. with his son. Transported his family 1674. Of Somerset Co. (18, fol. 39).

NAME	Liber	Folio	REMARKS
Jones, Sarah	5	482	Transported 1662. (7, fol. 107).
Jones, Sarah	6	293	" 1664.
Jones, Sarah	9	99	" 1665. Wife of James.
Jones, Sarah	9	325	" 1665.
Jones, Sarah	10	560	" from Va. 1667. Servant.
Jones, Sarah	16	435	Transported 1671.
Jones, Sarah	18	160	" 1674.
Jones, Solomon	12	584	" 1670. (15, fol. 523).
Jones, Stephen	15	313	" 1675.
Jones, Susanna	10	266	Immigrated prior to 1666.
Jones, Susanna	18	37	Transported 1673.
Jones, Thomas	ABH	7	" 1640-8. (Q, fol. 69; 4, fol. 41; 2, fol. 326).
Jones, Thomas	ABH	246	Transported prior to 1652.
Jones, Thomas	5	211	" 1662.
Jones, Thomas	6	210	" 1663. Servant.
Jones, Thomas	6	294	" 1664.
Jones, Thomas	7	469	" 1664.
Jones, Thomas	8	203,259	" 1665.
Jones, Thomas	9	48,304	" 1665.
Jones, Thomas	10	306	" 1665. Servant.
Jones, Thomas	11	537	Immigrated July 1665. Of Virginia.
Jones, Thomas	17	486	" from Virginia, 1667. Of Baltimore Co.
Jones, Thomas	11	318	Transported 1668.
Jones, Thomas	11	573	" 1668.
Jones, Thomas	12	215	" 1668-9.
Jones, Thomas	16	86	Immigrated 1670.
Jones, Thomas	16	110	Transported 1671.
Jones, Thomas	18	28	Immigrated from Virginia 1671.
Jones, Thomas	17	401	" 1672.
Jones, Thomas	17	543	Service 1672. Of Wye River.
Jones, Thomas	15	317	Immigrated 1674. Of Virginia. Tailor. (18, fol. 94, 285).
Jones, Thomas	15	389	Immigrated 1675.
Jones, Thomas	15	331	Transported 1675.
Jones, Thomas	15	403,405	" 1676.
Jones, Thomas	WC2	89	" 1676. Servant.
Jones, Thomas	15	446	" 1677.
Jones, Thomas	15	512	Immigrated 1678.
Jones, Thomas	WC2	308	Transported 1678.
Jones, Thomas	WC2	105	Granted Warrant in right of his wife, formerly Jane Gray.
Jones, Walter	17	605	Service 1673.
Jones, William	3	23	Transported before 1648.
Jones, William	1	166	" 1650. Servant.
Jones, William	5	341	" 1657.
Jones, William	4	58	" prior to 1659.
Jones, William	5	514	" 1658.
Jones, William	5	487,530	" 1660.

NAME	Liber	Folio	REMARKS
Jones, William	5	209	Immigrated 1662.
Jones, William	7	84	Transported 1663. Servant.
Jones, William	9	229	Immigrated 1665.
Jones, William	9	448	" 1666. Of Anne Arundel County.
Jones, William	10	561,609	Transported 1667.
Jones, William	11	227	" 1667.
Jones, William	12	282	" 1668.
Jones, William	12	202,243	" 1669.
Jones, William	12	475,602	" 1670. (12, fol. 624).
Jones, William	17	575	Service 1673. Of Calvert Co.
Jones, William	18	24,291	Transported 1674.
Jones, William	15	369,380	" 1676.
Jones, William	15	514	" 1677.
Jones, William	15	530	" 1678.
Jones, William	WC2	415	" 1666-80. Servant.
Jones, William	WC2	148	Deceased 1676-80. Of Anne Arundel Co. Physician.
Jones, Capt. William	WC2	187	Rights 1678.
Jones, William	WC2	84	Transported 1679.
Jones, William	WC2	325	Immigrated 1680. Of St. Mary's Co.
Jones, Winifred	5	212	Transported 1662.
Jones, Winifred	9	313	" 1665.
Jones, Winifred	12	554	" 1670.
Jonkin, Michael	11	265	" 1667.
Jonos, John	9	36	" 1665.
Jordaine, John	16	393	" 1671.
Jordaine, Jonas	12	241,354	Service 1669. (16, fol. 437).
Jordaine, Sarah	WC2	112	Transported 1679.
Jordaine, Thomas	17	363	" 1672. (See Jordwyne).
Jordan, Alexander	6	121	" 1656.
Jordan, Alexander	5	490	" 1662.
Jordan, Anne	5	416	" 1663.
Jordan, Margaret	7	576	" 1665.
Jordan, Samuel	WC2	16	" 1679.
Jordeine, Elizabeth	15	330	" 1675.
Jordeine, Joseph	17	40	" 1672.
Jordeine, Susana	15	430	" 1677.
Jorden, William	12	190	" 1668.
Jordeyne, Thomas	14	374	Merchant. Married Sarah, widow of John Elzey, 1671.
Jorenson, Andrew	8	130	Immigrated 1664 with wife.
Jorms, Margaret	15	563	Transported 1678.
Joslin, John	15	430,450	" 1677.
Jourdaine, Elizabeth	12	617	" 1670.
Jourdaine, John	12	617	" 1670.
Jourden, Hannah	5	307	" 1659.
Jowles, Col. Henry	WC2	144,164, 269	Immigrated 1680.
Joy, Ann	17	396	Transported 1669.
Joy, Peter	5	418	Service 1663.

NAME	Liber	Folio	REMARKS
Joy, Robert	WC2	59	Service 1666.
Joyce, Dorothy	11	316	Transported 1668.
Joyce, Edward	6	63	" 1658.
Joyce, Elizabeth	ABH	369	" April 1653. Wife of John.
Joyce, John	ABH	369	Immigrated April 1653.
Joyce, John	ABH	369	Transported April 1653. Son of John.
Joyce, John	15	376	Transported 1676.
Joyce, Mary	ABH	369	" April 1653. Daughter of John.
Joyce, Mary	11	378	Transported 1668.
Joyce, Rebecca	17	395	" 1672.
Joyce, Thomas	1	166	" 1650. Servant.
Joyce, Thomas	ABH	202	" 1651. Servant to Robert Brooke, Esq.
Joye, Margaret	ABH	40	Transported 1649. (2, fol. 614).
Joyly, William	7	559	" 1663.
Joyner, Elizabeth	6	48	" 1663.
Joyner, Mary	4	5	" 1659. Servant.
Joyner, Robert	Q	19	Servant 1651.
Joyner, Thomas	9	55	Transported 1665.
Joyner, William	17	414	Immigrated 1673.
Jub, Thomas	12	209	Transported 1668.
Jubb, Edward	15	540	" 1676.
Juckboard, John	13	1	" 1669. Servant.
Juckings, David	18	173	" 1674.
Judd, Michael	15	405	Immigrated 1676.
Judd, Michael	WC2	368	" 1680. Of Baltimore Co.
Judge, Richard	18	72	Service 1674. Of St. Mary's Co.
Juell, Jonn	18	166	Transported 1674.
Jugg, John	16	414	" 1671.
Julian, Elizabeth	1	24	" 1641. Servant.
Julian, Francis	10	434	" 1667.
Julors, Francis	4	553	Immigrated 1661 with wife.
Juman, Roger	15	565	Transported 1679.
Jump, William	15	422	" 1664.
Jump, William	8	30	" 1665. (9, fol. 216).
Junes, Thomas	ABH	201	" 1650.
Junis, James	4	338	" 1659. Servant.
Juppe, Thomas	7	559	" 1664.
Jux, John	17	395	" 1672.
Kab, Thomas	9	216	" 1665.
Kaible, Elizabeth	Q	70	" 1658.
Kalingee, Elizabeth	WC2	132	" 1680. Servant.
Kane, John	18	152	" 1674.
Karle, Thomas	11	318	" 1668.
Kartwright, Katherine	15	357	" 1676.
Kasey, Julian	15	527	" 1678.
Katch, Jane	18	121	" 1674.
Kate, Alice	18	151	" 1674.

NAME	Liber	Folio	REMARKS
Kater, William	17	363	Transported 1672.
Katey, Elizabeth	6	62	" 1663.
Kathernes, Edward	10	570	" 1666.
Katte, Robert	9	37	" 1664.
Keall, John	4	30	Service 1659.
Keally, Morrish	WC2	129	Transported 1679.
Keane, Thomas	1	19	" 1638.
Kearny, Robert	WC2	128	" 1679.
Keath, John	Q	18	" 1652-8.
Kedger, Robert	1	27	Immigrated 1640 with wife and servant.
Kedger, Robert	2	195,211	Immigrated 1641 with wife and servant. "Boatewright".
Kedger, Robert	ABH	1,61	Immigrated 1646 with wife.
Kee, John	12	403	Transported 1669.
Kee, John	WC2	406	" 1676.
Kee, Silvester	16	452	" 1671.
Keeble, John	17	381	Immigrated from Virginia 1672.
Keefe, Elizabeth	15	543	Transported 1678.
Keel, Isabell	15	307	" 1675.
Keele, Alice	17	363	" 1672.
Keele, Elizabeth	Q	66	" 1657.
Keelee, Elizabeth	17	304	" 1672.
Keelee, John, Jr.	17	304	" 1672.
Keelee, Mary	17	304	" 1672. Wife of John, of Anne Arundel Co.
Keelee, Thomas	17	304	Transported 1672.
Keeles, Robert	9	330	" 1665.
Keelin, Charles	17	475	" 1673.
Keeling, Henry	18	80	" 1674.
Keeling, Nicholas	6	36	Died prior to 1663, leaving a widow who married Brian Daly.
Keely, Jane	15	500	Transported 1678.
Keely, John	18	152	" 1674.
Keeme, Thomas	17	411	" 1673.
Keen, Darby	15	403	Service 1676.
Keen, Francis	15	432	Transported 1677.
Keen, Mary	11	499	" Oct. 1667. Wife of William.
Keen, Richard	15	387	Widow of, married John Greggs, 1676.
Keen, William	11	499	Immigrated 1667.
Keene, Ann	16	37	Service 1670. Wife of William of Calvert Co.
Keene, Edward	3	174	Immigrated 1653.
Keene, James	17	608	Transported 1673.
Keene, Katherine	15	567	" 1679.
Keene, Richard	11	337	" 1667.
Keene, Richard	11	440	" 1668.
Keene, Sarah	16	532	" 1668-70.
Keene, Susanna	WC2	108,163	Rights 1679. Relict of Edward.

NAME	Liber	Folio	REMARKS
			Of Calvert Co.
Keene, Timothy	20	185	Transported 1679.
Keep, Lancelot	ABH	5	Servant 1641.
Keep, William	15	537	Transported 1679.
Keeper, William	17	411	" 1673.
Keeping, William	18	115	" 1674.
Keeting, Katherine	18	174	" 1674.
Keeves, William	12	498	" 1670.
Keffe, Thomas	11	570	" 1668.
Keife, Arthur	17	417	" 1673. Son of Constant.
Keife, Constant	17	417	Immigrated 1673.
Keife, Eleanor	17	417	Transported 1673. Daughter of Constant.
Keife, Joan	17	417	Transported 1673. Wife of Constant.
Keighly, Katherine	15	549	" 1678.
Keith, Dorothy	18	175	Service 1674. Wife of George of Calvert Co.
Keith, George	12	594	Transported 1670.
Kelbie, Sarah	20	185	" 1679.
Keldy, Thomas	10	598	" 1667.
Kelee, John	12	343	" 1669. Of St. Mary's Co.
Kellam, Richard	5	412	Immigrated 1663.
Kellany, Peter	9	99	Transported 1665.
Kellaway, John	7	546	" 1662.
Kelley, Bryan	1	73	" 1635.
Kelley, David	8	42	" 1665.
Kelley, John	ABH	151	" 1641. Servant.
Kelley, John	16	17	Immigrated 1670.
Kellfull, William	Q	68	Transported 1657.
Kellman, Margery	8	485	" 1665. Daughter of William.
Kelly, Ann	15	499	Transported 1677.
Kelly, Bryan	ABH	82	" 1635. Servant.
Kelly, Giles	18	553	" 1678.
Kelly, John	ABH	58	" 1640. (1, fol. 22).
Kelly, John	4	2	" 1655. Son of John.
Kelly, John	4	2	" 1655.
Kelly, John	4	190	" 1659.
Kelly, John	16	17	Immigrated 1670.
Kelly, Mary	Q	428	Transported 1657.
Kelly, Patrick	15	565	" 1679.
Kelly, Roger	16	507	" 1671. (15, fol. 319).
Kelly, Sussanna	4	2	" 1655.
Kelly, Tobias	WC2	394	" 1680. Servant.
Kelsey, Francis	6	123	" 1663.
Kelson, Culb.	16	437	" 1671.
Kemball, Richard	15	338	Immigrated 1672. Of Worcester Co.
Kember, John	4	204	Transported 1659.
Keming, Jane	17	572	" 1672.
Kemmis, Elizabeth	4	138,203	" 1659. Servant.
Kemp, Ann	11	555	Immigrated 1668. Of St. Mary's Co.

NAME	Liber	Folio	REMARKS
Kemp, Henry	13	112	Transported 1670.
Kemp, John	11	555	" 1668. Son of Ann. (15, fol. 434).
Kemp, John	15	565	Transported 1679.
Kemp, Margery	15	332	" 1675 by Thos. Kemp of Calvert County.
Kemp, Mary	15	553	Transported 1678. (WC2, fol. 57).
Kemp, Michael	5	359	" 1663.
Kemp, Thomas	Q	18	" 1651.
Kemp, Thomas	9	49	Immigrated 1665. Of Patuxent River.
Kemp, Thomas	11	479	Transported 1668.
Kemp, William	6	88	" 1660.
Kemp, William	11	555	" 1668. Son of Ann. (15, fol. 434).
Kempe, Jone	16	94	Transported 1670.
Kempton, Robert	16	503	" 1671.
Kempton, Thomas	9	32	" 1656.
Kemsley, John	WC2	217	" 1680.
Kemster, William	18	84	" 1674.
Kenady, Margaret	17	572	" 1672.
Kenard, Richard	15	454	" Oct. 1677.
Kendall, Barbary	18	15	" 1673.
Kendall, Elizabeth	12	380	Immigrated 1669. Wife of Richard.
Kendall, George	15	449	Transported 1677.
Kendall, James	WC2	21	" 1679.
Kendall, Jone	9	449	" 1666.
Kendall, Mary	15	362,386	" 1676.
Kendall, Richard	6	171	" 1663. Servant.
Kendall, Richard	12	380	Service 1669. Of Dorchester Co.
Kendall, Robert	18	149	Transported 1669.
Kendall, Thomas	16	83	Immigrated 1670. Of Dorchester Co.
Kendar, Grace	15	397	Transported 1676.
Kendson, Thomas	12	459	" 1669.
Kenmore, John	7	461	" 1664.
Kenneday, William	9	200	" 1665.
Kennedy, Catherine	20	184	" from Ireland 1678.
Kennell, Henry	11	339	" 1668.
Kennemount, Ann	7	519	" 1664. Wife of John. (Q, fol. 62).
Kennemount, Hugh	7	487	Transported Nov. 1663. (Q, fol. 62).
Kennemount, John	7	519	Immigrated 1664. (Q, fol. 62).
Kennemount, John, Jr.	7	519	Transported 1664. Son of John. (Q, fol. 62).
Kennemount, Patrick	7	519	Transported 1664. Son of John. (Q, fol. 62).
Kennerve, Richard	6	59	Transported 1663.
Kenniston, Edward	7	463	" 1663.
Kenniston, Gabriel	7	463	" 1663.
Kenniston, William	12	403	" 1669.
Kennon, Sarah	18	152	" 1674.
Kennydy, Edmund	11	378	" 1668.

NAME	Liber	Folio	REMARKS
Kensye, Jonas	9	28	Transported 1664.
Kent, Ann	Q	199	" 1653. Wife of William.
Kent, Elizabeth	6	10	" 1663.
Kent, Francis	ABH	357	" 1653. Servant.
Kent, Francis	11	265	" 1667.
Kent, George	15	322	" 1675.
Kent, Henry	Q	200,203	Immigrated 1658.
Kent, Henry	7	563	" 1665. Of the Clifts.
Kent, John	7	563	Transported 1665.
Kent, Jone	12	332	" 1669. Wife of Robert.
Kent, Mary	15	560	" 1678.
Kent, Mary	WC2	171	" 1679.
Kent, Robert	9	343	" 1666.
Kent, Robert	12	189	" 1668.
Kent, Robert	12	332	Service 1669. Of Kent County.
Kent, Thomas	7	563	Transported 1663.
Kent, Thomas	10	558	" 1666.
Kent, Thomesin	7	563	" 1665.
Kent, Walter	5	411	" 1663.
Kent, William	Q	197	Immigrated 1658. (12, fol. 200).
Kentish, Richard	17	513	" 1673.
Keny, Rose	18	152	Transported 1674.
Keptly, Mary	15	530	" 1678.
Kerby, Edward	WC2	128	" 1679.
Kerby, George	4	591	" 1661.
Kerby, John	4	620	Immigrated 1661.
Kerby, Robert	15	390	Transported 1676.
Kerby, Thomas	17	570	Service 1673. Of St. Mary's Co.
Kerby, William	9	454	Transported 1666.
Kerbye, Peter	WC2	381	" 1675-80. Servant.
Kerckman, Melcher	5	181	" 1661.
Kere, Charles	9	39	" 1657.
Kerhern, William	7	462	" 1664.
Kerke, Alice	16	170	" 1671.
Kerksick, John	12	515	Immigrated 1669. Of Baltimore Co.
Kerksick Martha	12	515	Transported 1669. First wife of John.
Kerksick, Susan	12	515	Transported 1669. Second wife of John.
Kerly, Francis	15	567	Transported 1679.
Kersey, James	18	72	Service 1674. Of St. Mary's Co.
Kersey, Nicholas	8	131	Transported 1664.
Kerton, William	18	84	" 1674.
Kerwig, Thomas	15	527	" 1678.
Kesar, Mary	15	430	" 1677.
Kestian, Thomas	6	293	" 1664.
Kettleland, William	11	106	Service 1667.
Kettlewell, Henry	11	500	" 1665.
Kettlewell, Henry	5	466	Transported 1659.
Kettlewell, Mary	18	291	" 1674.
Key, Grace	11	247	" 1667.

NAME	Liber	Folio	REMARKS
Key, John	15	453	Transported 1676.
Key, Peter	11	247	Immigrated to St. Mary's Co. 1667. Of Virginia.
Key, William	18	79	Immigrated 1668. Of Kent Co.
Key, William	12	554	Transported 1670.
Keyes, Daniel	9	304	" 1665.
Keyes, Rachel	19	258	" 1663.
Keyle, Jane	Q	69	" 1658.
Keyler, Timothy	15	574	" 1678.
Keyn, Nicholas	ABH	102	Immigrated 1641. An Irishman.
Keyne, Edward	ABH	381	Transported Feb. 1653. Brother to Henry.
Keyne, Henry	ABH	381	Immigrated Feb. 1653.
Keyne, Richard	ABH	381	Transported Feb. 1653. Brother to Henry.
Keysar, Sarah	16	304	Immigrated 1671. Of Somerset Co.
Keysar, Timothy	WC2	16	" 1677 with 17 persons.
Keytin, Nicholas	1	129	" 1641. Irishman. (2, fol. 256).
Kibblethwait, Susan	5	489	Transported 1655. (Q, fol. 73).
Kibblewhite, Ann	Q	73	" 1658.
Kible, William	20	160	Orphan son and heir of John of Somerset Co., 1679.
Kid, Peter	18	331	Transported 1674.
Kidd, Henry	11	582	" 1668.
Kidde, Ann	Q	107	" 1658.
Kidde, Mary	9	272	" 1663. Wife of William.
Kidde, William	9	272	Immigrated March 1663. Of Va.
Kidmore, Nicholas	5	81	Transported 1661.
Kidson, Henry	---	---	Of Anne Arundel Co.
Kighley, William	13	66	Transported 1669. Servant.
Kilborne, Elizabeth	16	595	Wife of Francis, and widow of Daniel Johnson of Charles County, 1672.
Kilborne, Francis	4	591	Transported 1661.
Kile, John	11	378	" 1668.
Kilerbe, Hannah	18	280	" 1674. (15, fol. 353).
Kilerbe, Tabitha	18	280	" 1674. (15, fol. 353).
Kilgore, Robert	15	358	" 1675.
Kill, James	4	531	Service 1658.
Kille, Nicholas	15	537	Transported 1679.
Killen, John	8	130	" 1665.
Killman, Jane	9	25	" 1665.
Killman, Judith	8	485	" 1665. Wife of William.
Killman, Simon	6	211	" 1662.
Killman, Thomas	6	216	" 1663.
Killman, Thomas	15	553	" 1678.
Kilpin, Richard	12	353	Service 1669.
Kilshee, Edward	WC2	23	Transported 1679. Servant.
Kilson, Cuthbert	16	438	" 1671.
Kilvert, Mary	8	129	" 1664. Servant.
Kindon, Eleanor	12	209	" 1668.

NAME	Liber	Folio	REMARKS
Kindrick, Henry	5	529	Transported 1659.
Kindsey, Elizabeth	4	565	" 1660.
Kindsey, Hugh	4	565	" 1660.
Kindsey, Paul	4	565	" 1660.
King, Alexander	17	449	" 1672.
King, Arthur	WC2	57	" 1678. (15, fol. 554).
King, Catherine	17	33	" from Virginia 1672.
King, Eleanor	17	511	Service 1673. Wife of Samuel.
King, Eleanor	15	525	Transported 1678. Wife of John.
King, Elizabeth	17	557	Service 1673. Of Dorchester Co.
King, Francis	5	203	Transported 1662.
King, George	7	487	" 1663.
King, George	9	104	Immigrated 1665.
King, Jane	6	255	Transported 1663.
King, Jane	10	296	" 1666.
King, Johanna	WC2	282	" 1680.
King, John	ABH	44	" 1636. Servant. (3, fol. 17).
King, John	ABH	40	Transported 1649. (2, fol. 615).
King, John	ABH	303	Immigrated 1651.
King, John	5	412	Transported 1660.
King, John	6	255	" 1663.
King, John	10	296	Immigrated 1666.
King, John	16	303	" from Virginia 1671.
Of Somerset County. (16, fol. 342).			
King, John	15	553	Transported 1678.
King, Katherine	17	33	" from Virginia 1672.
King, Marke	1	166	" 1650. Servant.
King, Mary	6	255	" 1663.
King, Mary	10	296	" 1666.
King, Mary	11	348	" 1668.
King, Mary	15	411	Immigrated 1673. (18, fol. 37).
King, Mary	15	540	Transported 1677.
King, Obediah	15	417	" 1677.
King, Obediah	WC2	95,96,97	Service 1679.
King, Ralph	16	94	Transported 1670.
King, Ralph	WC2	120	" 1680.
King, Richard	ABH	186	" 1651. Servant.
King, Richard	6	293	" 1664.
King, Robert	ABH	151,244	" 1640. Servant.
King, Robert	4	140	" 1654. Servant.
King, Robert	9	311	Immigrated 1666.
King, Rose	18	291	Transported 1674.
King, Ruth	8	30	" 1665.
King, Samuel	17	511	Immigrated 1667. Of Kent Co. (16, fol. 125).
King, Samuel	18	313	Transported 1675.
King, Susanna	17	475	" 1673.
King, Susanna	9	311	" 1666. Wife of Robert.
King, Thomas	17	443	Immigrated 1664, married Joane Strand 1669-73. Of Baltimore County.

NAME	Liber	Folio	REMARKS
King, Thomas	9	56	Immigrated 1665.
King, Thomas	12	604	Transported 1670. (13, fol. 59).
King, Thomas	16	177	" 1672.
King, Thomas	18	33	" 1674.
King, Thomas, Jr.	16	170	" 1671.
King, Thomas, Sr.	16	170	" 1671.
King, Walter	ABH	60,66	" 1637. (1, fol. 17, 20, 25, 38).
King, William	1	112	Transported 1635. Servant.
King, William	ABH	95	" 1635-41. Servant.
King, William	10	169-170	Immigrated 1666. Of Calvert Co. Tailor.
King, William	15	359	Transported 1676.
King, William	15	446	" 1677.
King, William	WC2	108	" 1679.
Kinghall, Thomas	15	455	" 1678.
Kingham, Thomas	5	127	" 1662. Service 1671. (16, fol. 123).
Kingley, William	15	376	Transported 1676.
Kingould, Barbara	ABH	184	" 1649. Wife of Mr. Thomas K.
Kingould, James	ABH	184	Transported 1649. Son of Thomas.
Kingould, John	ABH	184	" 1649. Son of Thomas.
Kingould, Mr. Thomas	ABH	184	Immigrated 1649.
Kings, Thomas	ABH	203	" 1652.
Kingsberry, Mary	5	247,385	Transported 1651. Wife of Robert.
Kingsberry, Robert	5	247,385	Immigrated 1651, also Elizabeth
and Edward Wells, "his children".			
Kingskind, Anthony	9	505	Transported 1666.
Kingsland, Anthony	12	492	" 1670.
Kingstone, Elizabeth	16	297	" 1671.
Kinkhame, Rose	15	549	" 1678.
Kinline, Timothy	15	438	" 1677.
Kinnirson, Roger	12	415	" 1669.
Kinniston, Thomas	17	41	" 1672.
Kinsey, Catherine	5	320	" 1663.
Kinsey, Daniel	5	413	" 1662. Son of Hugh.
Kinsey, Hugh	4	54	Immigrated 1659.
Kinsey, Paul	5	92	Son of Margaret. Living 1661. (12, fol. 612).
Kinsey, Sarah	5	413	Transported 1662. Daughter of Hugh.
Kinsey, Welch	Q	28	" 1653.
Kinsley, William	WC2	96	Rights 1679.
Kinsman, William	16	411	Transported 1671.
Kipshaven, John	17	566	Immigrated 1673 with his wife and daughter. Of Worchester Co.
Kirby, George	5	305	Transported 1663.
Kirby, William	17	478	Service 1673. Of St. Mary's Co.
Kirk, Joan	12	392	Transported 1669. Wife of John.
Kirk, John	12	392	Immigrated 1669. Of Somerset Co.
Kirk, Sarah	12	392	Daughter of John. Transported 1669.

NAME	Liber	Folio	REMARKS
Kirk, Thomas	12	333	Transported 1668.
Kirke, John	9	333	" 1666.
Kirke, Mary	6	210	" 1663.
Kirkham, Francis	4	14,30	" 1659. Servant.
Kirkham, George	17	531	" 1673.
Kirkham, Henry	WC2	308	" 1678.
Kirkham, Roger	6	154	" 1663.
Kirkham, William	12	382	Immigrated 1669. Of Dorchester County.
Kirkley, Jane	Q	183	Servant 1658.
Kirkley, Francis	6	86	Transported 1659.
Kirkman, Melcar	17	347	Service 1672. Of Dorchester Co.
Kirkman, Roger	7	529	Transported 1664.
Kirkwood, Adam	18	152	" 1674.
Kirkwood, Elizabeth	18	152	" 1674.
Kirley, John	ABH	229	" 1650. Servant.
Kistom, Darvis	12	194	" 1668. Servant.
Kitchen, Dorothy	ABH	403	" 1652. Servant. (Q, fol. 431).
Kitchin, Anthony	1	166	Transported 1650. Servant.
Kitchin, John	15	565	" 1679.
Kitter, John	Q	28	" 1656.
Kitteredge, Rebecca	ABH	39	" 1649.
Kitteridge, Rebecca	2	608	" 1649.
Kitton, Theophilus	18	329	" 1675.
Knap, Aemilia	Q	67	Immigrated 1658. Wife of Robert.
Knap, Robert	Q	67	" 1658.
Knap, Susanna	Q	67	" 1658. Daughter of Robert.
Knapp, John	ABH	310	Immigrated Sept. 1651, with wife.
Knelewater, Judith	13	112	Transported 1670.
Knefemton, Matthew	8	131	" 1664. Servant.
Knight, Elizabeth	18	291	" 1674.
Knight, George	11	229	Service 1667.
Knight, Hannah	WC2	352	Transported 1680.
Knight, Jane	15	376	" 1676.
Knight, John	16	439	" 1671.
Knight, Margaret	7	84	" 1660.
Knight, Robert	ABH	35	Servant 1649.
Knight, Robert	2	575	Transported 1649. Servant.
Knight, Robert	Q	239	" 1651.
Knight, Robert	15	551	" 1679.
Knight, Thomas	ABH	68,101	" 1637-40. Servant.
Knight, Thomas	1	43,128	" about 1638. Servant.
Knight, Valentine	16	126	" 1671.
Knight, William	12	205	" 1667.
Knighton, Thomas	12	347	" 1669. Attorney of the Provincial Court. (12, fol. 491).
Knipe, William	ABH	64	Transported 1637. Servant. (1, fol. 33). (See Snipe, Snype).
Knivton, Mathew			

NAME	Liber	Folio	REMARKS
Knolls, John	1	17,20,38	Immigrated 1637.
Knot, Jane	16	411	Transported 1671.
Knott, Mr. James	ABH	237	Immigrated March 1651.
Knott, John	2	427	" 1643.
Knott, John	3	24	Transported 1650. Servant.
Knott, Nathaniel	ABH	237	" 1651. Son of Mr. James.
Knowl, John	ABH	10	Immigrated 1643.
Knowles, Ann	3	23	Transported before 1648.
Knowles, Ann	ABH	47	" 1648. Servant.
Knowles, Mr. John	ABH	66	" 1637.
Knowles, Lawrence	WC2	32,82, 111	Rights 1679.
Knowlman, Abigail	18	150	Transported 1674. Wife of Theophilus.
Knowlman, Anthony	18	150	Transported 1674.
Knowlman, Theophilus	18	150	" 1674.
Knowlman, Theophilus	18	150	" 1674. Son of Theophilus.
Koapland, Littis	18	152	Transported 1674.
Koe, Rich	15	439	" 1666.
Komp, Overton	15	390	" 1675.
Kreecher, John	15	424	" 1677. (19, fol. 503).
Kuinenten, Mathew	12	285	" 1667.
Ky, John	12	551	Immigrated 1670. Of St. Mary's Co.
L. --- Joane (A maid servant)	6	94	Transported 1663. Servant.
La Brittone, Peter	12	473	" 1670.
Labs, Elizabeth	10	609	" by Thomas Tarbie, whom she married 1667.
Lace, Francis	20	185	Transported 1679.
Lacey, Patrick	20	184	" from Ireland 1678.
Lachett, John	WC2	363	" 1680.
Lachvin, George	15	413	" 1677.
Lacy, Edward	16	507	" 1671.
Lacy, Francis	ABH	356	" May 1653. Servant. (4, fol. 140).
Lacy, John	15	454	Transported Oct. 1677.
Lacy, Margaret	15	446	" 1677.
Lacy, Richard	9	49	" 1665.
Lad, Richard	17	416	Immigrated 1668. Of Calvert Co.
Ladd, Richard	15	322	Transported 1674.
Ladderland, Robert	17	477	" 1673.
Ladderland, Sarah	17	477	" 1673. Wife of Robert.
Ladds, Jane	7	472	" 1664. Wife of William.
Ladds, William	7	471	" 1664.
Ladger, Thomas	ABH	41	Immigrated 1650.
Ladian, Stephen	9	38	Transported 1665.
Ladman, John	6	211	" 1663.
Ladmore, John	Q	29	" 1657.
La Feaver, John	7	556	" 1665.

NAME	Liber	Folio	REMARKS
La Hay, Arthur	2	347	Transported 1639.
La Haye, Arthur	ABH	7	" 1639.
Laister, Joane	15	446	" 1677.
Lake, George, Jr.	4	550	" 1661.
Lake, John	Q	208	" 1658.
Lake, John	4	555	" 1661.
Lalors, Clement	4	555	" 1661.
Lamare, Mary	9	312	" 1665. Wife of Thomas.
Lamare, Thomas	9	312	Immigrated 1665.
Lamb, Ann	15	358	Transported 1675.
Lamb, Elizabeth	15	425	Service 1677. Wife of Richard.
Lamb, Francis	11	374	Transported 1668. (12, fol. 209).
Lamb, Henry	16	469	" March 1667.
Lamb, James	20	185	" 1679.
Lamb, Nicholas	18	94	" 1674.
Lamb, Richard	15	376,441	Service 1676. Of St. Mary's Co.
Lamb, Richard	15	452	Transported 1678.
Lamb, Richard	WC2	158,159	Immigrated 1680. Of Talbot Co.
Lamb, Thomas	11	313	" 1668. Of St. Mary's Co.
Lamb, Penelope	16	432	Transported 1671.
Lambe, Pearcy	12	403	" 1669.
Lambe, Richard	9	489	Immigrated 1665.
Lamberd, John	15	453	Transported 1675-7.
Lambert, Amey	16	437	" 1671.
Lambert, Ann	6	294	" 1664. Wife of Josias.
Lambert, Eleanor	15	353	" 1674. (18, fol. 308).
Lambert, Josias	6	294	Immigrated 1664.
Lambert, Richard	17	470	Service 1673.
Lambert, Thomas	6	133	Transported 1654.
Lambeth, John	7	372	" 1664.
Lambeth, John	16	85	" 1670.
Lambeth, Samuel	7	372	" 1664.
Lambfeed, Francis	WC2	57	" 1678.
Lambier, Paul	18	2	Immigrated from Virginia 1674. Of Dorchester Co.
Lambseed, Francis	15	553	Transported 1678.
Lamden, Robert	5	516	" 1663.
Lame, John	6	290	" 1663.
Lamore, Mary	9	312	" 1665. Wife of Thomas.
Lamore, Peter	9	47	Immigrated 1665.
Lamore, Thomas	20	95	And Peter, late of Virginia., subjects of the King of France, Letters of Denization in Md. 1663.
Lampin, Anna Bella	15	549	Transported 1673. Daughter of Thomas. (17, fol. 38).
Lampin, Elizabeth	15	549	Transported 1673. Wife of Thomas. (17, fol. 38).
Lampin, Thomas	12	217	Transported 1669.
Lancashire, Edward	15	446	" 1677.
Lancaster, George	6	27	" 1660-3.
Lancaster, George	10	569	" 1665, in the "Agreement of Bristol". (17, fol. 514).

NAME	Liber	Folio	REMARKS
Lancaster, Richard	13	122	Transported 1669.
Lancaster, Richard	18	15	" 1673.
Lancellott, John	2	456	Immigrated 1647.
Lancelot, John	ABH	14	" 1647.
Lanchfield, Thomas	4	533	Transported 1659.
Land, Ann	ABH	385	" 1650. Second wife of Mr. Philip.
Land, John	16	293	Transported 1671.
Land, Martin	7	83	" 1659.
Land, Mr. Philip	ABH	40	Refers to his late wife, 1650.
Land, Phillip	2	346-347	Immigrated 1647.
Land, Phillip	2	615	Right for transportation of his deceased wife, 1650.
Land, Priscilla	ABH	385	Transported 1649. First wife of Mr. Philip.
Land, Susan	4	198	Transported 1659.
Lander, Samuel	15	397	" 1676.
Landing, Joyce	15	439	" 1667.
Landman, George	7	471	" 1664. Service 1670. (16, fol. 470).
Landsdell, James	15	397	Transported 1676.
Lane, Ann	5	236	" 1662. Servant.
Lane, Ann	7	553	" 1664.
Lane, Benjamin	10	498	" 1667.
Lane, Benjamin	12	505	" 1670. Servant.
Lane, Charles	17	54	" 1672.
Lane, Charles	15	447	" 1677.
Lane, Daniel	16	435	" 1671.
Lane, David	WC2	287	" 1680.
Lane, Dennis	16	435	" 1671.
Lane, Elizabeth	17	68	Service 1670. Wife of Philip.
Lane, George	5	210	Transported 1662.
Lane, James	12	517	" 1670.
Lane, James	15	553	" 1678.
Lane, Jasper	17	68	Immigrated from Virginia 1670. Of Somerset County.
Lane, John	8	498	Transported 1665.
Lane, John	16	435	" 1671.
Lane, John	15	397	" 1676.
Lane, John	15	413	" 1677.
Lane, John	WC2	80	Immigrated 1679. Of Somerset Co.
Lane, John	WC2	287	" 1680. Of Talbot Co.
Lane, Peter	15	537	Service 1679. Of St. Mary's Co.
Lane, Richard	WC2	86	Transported 1679. Servant.
Lane, Samuel	8	129	Immigrated 1664. (6, fol. 294).
Lane, Susan	15	553	Transported 1678.
Lane, Susan (Susanna)	WC2	56	" 1679.
Lane, Timothy	WC2	287	" 1680.
Lane, William	16	394	" 1671.
Lane, William	WC2	308	" 1678.
Langam, Mary	15	553	" 1678.

NAME	Liber	Folio	REMARKS
Langfield, Francis	ABH	370	Transported 1653.
Langford, Edward	Q	68	" 1644.
Langford, Edward	2	429	Immigrated 1648. (ABH, fol. 10, 11).
Langford, Elizabeth	Q	183	Servant prior to 1658.
Langford, Elizabeth	5	207	Transported 1662.
Langford, George	16	170	" 1671.
Langford, Vincent	18	117	" 1674.
Langfort, James	8	87	" 1665. Servant.
Langham, George	7	560	" 1665.
Langham, George	Q	17	" 1652-8.
Langhley, George	11	499	Service 1666.
Langley, Eleanor	5	56	Transported 1660.
Langley, George	5	484	" 1662. (16, fol. 130).
Langley, Henry	WC2	321	Service 1680.
Langley, John	6	89	Transported 1663.
Langley, John	15	569	" 1678.
Langley, Joseph	7	558	" 1665.
Langley, Joseph	17	457	Immigrated from Virginia with Lattice, his wife, 1671.
Langley, Lattice	17	457	Immigrated 1671. Wife of Joseph.
Langley, Mary	12	189	Transported 1668.
Langley, Philip	15	535	" 1678.
Langley, Rachel	10	1	" 1666.
Langley, Robert	16	458	" 1672.
Langley, Thomas	15	500	" 1678.
Langley, William	6	87	" 1657.
Langly, Henry	16	436	" 1671.
Langston, Thomas	15	422	Service 1677.
Langstone, James	15	423	Transported 1677.
Langthorne, John	Q	66	" 1657.
Langton, Edward	2	439	" 1648.
Langton, Edward	ABH	12	Servant 1648.
Langton, Edward	WC2	24,106	Transported 1678. Servant.
Langton, Jane	10	560	" 1667. Wife of Walter.
Langton, Jone	10	560	" 1667. Daughter of Walter.
Langton, Rebecca	15	331	Transported 1675.
Langton, Walter	10	560	Immigrated 1667. Of Anne Arundel County.
Langton, Walter, Jr.	10	560	Transported 1667. Son of Walter.
Langworth, James	1	112	" 1635. Servant.
Langworth, James	Q	19	Immigrated 1647. (4, fol. 530).
Langworth, John	ABH	101	Transported 1637-40. Servant. Living 1662 (brother to James, dec'd.) (5, fol. 125).
Langworth, Mary	6	347	Transported 1663.
Langworth, William	Q	19	Son of James 1658.
Lanham, John	15	566	Transported 1678.
Lanham, John	WC2	130	" 1679. Servant.
Lanham, Josias	16	71	" Nov. 1668.
Lanham, Josias	WC2	326	Service 1680. Of Kent County.
Lankashire, Richard	WC2	106	Transported 1679.

NAME	Liber	Folio	REMARKS
Lankford, John	15	396	Transported 1676.
Lannock, Martha	6	128	" 1653.
Lanshnane, Margaret	15	438	" Oct.1677.
Lanstell, Samuel	20	185	" 1679.
Lappington, Thomas	WC2	260	" 1675.
Lapray, Bartholomew	10	503	" 1667. Servant.
Larance, Ann	15	444	" 1675. Wife of Benjamin.
Larance, Benjamin	15	444	Of Somerset Co. 1675.
Larance, Benjamin, Jr.	15	444	Transported 1675. Son of Benjamin.
Larance, Eleanor	15	501	" 1678.
Larance, John	15	348	Immigrated January 1668.
Larance, Mary	10	272	Transported 1666.
Larance, Nehemiah	15	444	" 1675. Son of Benjamin.
Larance, Philip	15	437,565	" 1677.
Larance, William	8	501	" 1665.
Lard, Hester	7	87	" 1660.
Lard, Mary	15	376	" 1676.
Lardge, Elizabeth	16	165	" 1670. Servant.
Larding, Jasper	7	88	" 1651.
Laremore, Thomas	6	86	Immigrated 1650.
Larg, Curtis	15	386	Transported 1676. (See Long).
Large, Robert	4	560,623	" 1660.
Large, Robert	5	343	" 1663.
Large, Robert	12	376	Service 1669. Of St. Mary's Co.
Larkie, Nicholas	5	56	Immigrated 1661 with wife.
Larkin, John	14	44,253	Of Anne Arundel Co. Inn Holder - Patent for "Greenfield", Baltimore Co. 750 A. "Larkins Choice" 331 A. 12 Aug. 1670.
Laroach, Charles	8	501	Transported 1665.
Laroach, Peter	8	501	" 1665.
LaRoch, James	12	617	" 1670.
Laroe, John	17	475	" 1673.
Larramore, Edward	4	553	" 1661. Son of Roger.
Larramore, Rachel	4	553	" 1661. Wife of Roger.
Larramore, Roger	4	553	Immigrated 1661.
Larrance, Katherine	8	483	Transported 1665.
Larrance, Margaret	11	318	" 1668.
Larremore, Agnes	11	570	" 1668.
Larret, Robert	18	174	" 1674.
Lasey, Ann	15	516	" 1675.
Lashey, Robert	15	439	Immigrated 1666. Of Calvert Co.
Lashford, William	12	498	Transported 1670.
Lasker, William	ABH	352	Immigrated prior to June 1653.
Lasley, David	WC2	309	Transported 1678.
Lasse, John	5	254	" 1658-63.
Latemore, Annis	13	33	" 1668. (12, fol. 357).
Latham, John	16	313	Service 1671.
Latham, Richard	11	337	Transported 1668.
Latham, William	8	202	Service 1665.
Lather, William	5	73	Transported 1660-1.

NAME	Liber	Folio	REMARKS
Latherne, William	5	228	Transported 1662.
Lathum, Dorothy	18	15	Service 1674. Wife of Stephen.
Lathum, Stephen	18	15	" 1674. Of Calvert County.
Latimore, John	15	301	Transported 1675.
Latroyes, Elizabeth	12	507	" 1669. Wife of Peter.
Latroyes, Peter	12	507	Immigrated 1669.
Lattemore, John	9	105	Transported 1665.
Laughlin, William	15	565	" 1679.
Laurence, Daniel	15	429	" 1674.
Laurence, Thomas	12	285	" 1668. Servant.
Lavington, John	4	140	" 1658. Servant.
Law, Alexander	16	100	" 1663.
Law, Ann	WC2	15	" 1679. Wife of Richard.
Law, James	13	66	" 1669. Servant.
Law, Richard (Taylor)	WC2	15	Immigrated 1679. Of Somerset Co.
Lawder, Peter	15	601	Service 1678.
Lawens, John	9	333	Transported 1666.
Lawes, Nicholas	ABH	140	" 1651.
Lawes, William	15	301	Service 1675. Of Anne Arundel Co.
Lawfield, John	5	407	Immigrated 1663.
Lawforth, Richard	16	407	Transported 1671.
Lawlar, James	15	446	" 1677.
Lawn, Mary	ABH	63	" 1638. Servant.
Lawne, Mary	1	18,31	" 1638. Servant.
Lawne, Mary	1	137	License to marry James Courtney, May 23, 1639.
Lawrance, John	4	565	Transported 1661.
Lawrence, Ann	5	82	" 1661.
Lawrence, Ann	13	57	" 1670.
Lawrence, Ann	16	319	" 1670. Wife of Benjamin. (18, fol. 39).
Lawrence, Benjamin	16	319	Immigrated 1670 from Accomack, Virginia. (18, fol. 39).
Lawrence, Benjamin, Jr.	16	319	Transported 1670. Son of Benjamin. (18, fol. 39).
Lawrence, Daniel	6	266	Transported 1662.
Lawrence, Daniel	17	363,496	" 1672.
Lawrence, Elizabeth	5	93,341	" 1656.
Lawrence, Elizabeth	18	35	Service 1672. Wife of Henry of Somerset County.
Lawrence, Henry	18	35	Immigrated 1672. Of Somerset Co.
Lawrence, James	17	411	Transported 1673.
Lawrence, James	6	295	" 1664.
Lawrence, John	Q	316	Immigrated 1658.
Lawrence, John	5	80	Transported 1660.
Lawrence, John	12	202,243	" 1669.
Lawrence, Joseph	16	371	" 1671.
Lawrence, Margaret	17	483	" 1667.
Lawrence, Mary	Q	316	Immigrated 1658. Wife of John.
Lawrence, Nehemiah	16	319	Transported 1671. Son of Benjamin.
Lawrence, Richard	ABH	34	Immigrated 1642.

NAME	Liber	Folio	REMARKS
Lawrence, Richard	2	570	Immigrated about 1643.
Lawrence, Thomas	18	77	Transported 1674.
Lawrence, William	4	5	" 1659. Servant.
Lawrenson, Lawrence	12	271	Service 1668.
Lawrenson, Margaret	17	531	Transported 1673.
Lawrock, Peter	9	343	" 1666.
Lawson, Elizabeth	WC2	167	" 1680.
Lawson, Hans	12	473	" 1670.
Lawson, Hugh	4	190	" 1659.
Lawson, John	11	344	" 1668.
Lawson, John	12	478	" 1670.
Lawson, Mr. John	ABH	229	Immigrated 1650-1 with wife.
Lawson, Mary	15	380	Transported 1676.
Lawson, Paul	4	63	" 1652-9.
Lawson, Thomas	8	478	" 1665.
Lawson, Thomas	15	381,412	Service 1677.
Lawson, William	13	114	Transported 1671.
Lawter, James	WC2	24,106	" 1678. Servant.
Laycock, Mary	18	174	" 1674.
Layden, Thomas	6	171	" 1663.
Laydham, James	18	291	" 1674.
Laydonson, William	15	443	" 1672.
Layton, Katherine	16	533	Immigrated 1664.
Layton, Margaret	WC2	77,80	Transported 1679. Servant.
Layton, Ursula	15	319,557	Service 1675. Wife of William.
Layton, William	17	357	" 1672. Of Somerset Co.
Layton, William	13	66	Transported 1670.
Leach, Ann	15	454	" 1677.
Leach, Hannah	9	17	" 1665.
Leach, John	5	188	" 1662.
Leach, Josiah	9	26	" 1665.
Leads, Mary	11	581	" 1668.
Leaffe, Francis	WC2	60,134, 228	" his wife, 2 children

and servant in 1679. Of Anne Arundel County.

NAME	Liber	Folio	REMARKS
Leaffe, Francis, Jr.	WC2	60	Transported 1679.
Leaffe, Jane Eaton	WC2	60	" 1679.
Leaffe, Sarah	WC2	60	" 1679. Wife of Francis.
Leafslagh, Nathaniel	15	449	" 1677.
Leagar, William	16	170	" 1671.
League, William	WC2	147	Service 1680. Of Kent Co.
Leak, John	16	43	Transported 1670.
Leak, Edward	12	384	Immigrated 1669. Of Kent Co.
Leake, Nathaniel	12	551	Transported 1670.
Leake, Richard	6	47	" 1661.
Leake, Richard	9	489	Immigrated 1665.
Leake, Richard	11	104	Transported 1667.
Leakes, John	12	513	" 1669.
Leakey, John	15	600	" 1678.
Leaky, Robert	16	452	" 1671.
Lealy, John	15	553	" 1678.

NAME	Liber	Folio	REMARKS
Leane, Ann	15	322	Transported 1674.
Leanslip, Nathaniel	15	442	" 1677.
Leaphead, Thomas	16	407	" 1671.
Leapington, Daniel	13	1	" 1669.
Leapre, Bartholomew	15	545	Service 1668.
Leary, Katherine	WC2	128	Transported 1679.
Leary, Timothy	15	553	" 1678.
Leatherborow, Thomas	1	125	Immigrated 1638.
Leathett, Ann	18	306	Transported 1675.
Leavistone, George	WC2	58	" 1676.
Leavor, Dorothy	11	169	Service 1667. Wife of William.
Leavor, William	11	169	" 1667. Of Anne Arundel Co.
Lebbett, Samuel	WC2	381	Transported 1675-80. Servant.
Lebloy, Thomas	18	331	" 1674.
Lebrand, Ab.	15	554	" Oct. 1677.
Lecewer, William	4	59	" 1659.
Leckerish, Richard	5	66	" 1660.
Leckley, Thomas	16	170	" 1671.
Leckonby, William	15	442	" 1677.
LeCompt, Anthony	Q	440,441	Warrant for 700 acres on the

Eastern Shore, July 26, 1659. (4, fol. 61; 4, fol. 181; 4, fol. 244, 378; 5, fol. 243, 538; 7, fol. 125).

Ledeman, Mary	5	90	Transported 1656.
Ledget, Thomas	18	172	Immigrated 1674. Of Calvert Co.
Ledgett, Elizabeth	16	170	Transported 1671.
Ledgit, Julian	16	172	Service 1674. Wife of Thomas.
Ledgrave, Robert	ABH	60	Transported 1637.
LeDuke, Joseph	16	115	Immigrated 1671. Of St. Mary's Co.
Lee, Deborah	6	133	Transported 1653.
Lee, Edward	6	19,135	" 1663.
Lee, Edward	9	38	" 1665.
Lee, Edward	15	436	" 1677.
Lee, Elizabeth	5	188	" 1657. Servant.
Lee, Elizabeth	6	19,154	" 1662. Daughter of

Hopkin Davies.

Lee, Elizabeth	16	529	Transported 1672.
Lee, George	15	436	" 1677.
Lee, Grace	6	133	" 1653.
Lee, Hannah	3	17	" prior to 1650. Widow

of Robert Hewett, now wife of Hugh Lee.

Lee, Hannah	ABH	45	Transported prior to 1662. Wife

of Hugh. Mother-in-law to Matthew Rhodon. (ABH, fol. 44; 5, fol. 127).

Lee, Henry	ABH	92	Immigrated 1636. (1, fol. 104-105).
Lee, Henry	1	19	Transported 1638.
Lee, Henry	4	70	" 1659. Servant.
Lee, Henry	4	549	" 1661. (6, fol. 48).
Lee, Henry	10	600	" 1667.
Lee, Hugh	ABH	44	Of Checacone. Married Hannah,

widow of Robert Hewett, some time prior to 1650. His widow married Wm. Price prior to 1661. (6, fol. 215).

Lee, Humphrey	6	85	Transported 1657.

NAME	Liber	Folio	REMARKS
Lee, Jacob	6	121	Transported 1662.
Lee, James	17	574	Aged 50 years in 1673.
Lee, James	15	452	Transported 1678.
Lee, John	ABH	85	Transported 1636. Servant. (1, fol. 82).
Lee, John	5	413	Immigrated 1658.
Lee, John	5	240,253	Transported 1662.
Lee, John	15	504,530	" 1678. (WC2, fol. 309).
Lee, Mr. John	6	308	Of Westmoreland in Virginia.
			Acquired land in Maryland 1664. Do. in 1672. (17, fol. 98).
Lee, Katherine	15	381	Transported 1676.
Lee, Larance	15	544	" 1676.
Lee, Mary	5	413	" 1668. Wife of John.
Lee, Mary	6	36,89	" 1660.
Lee, Mary	9	216	" 1665.
Lee, Mary	15	540	" 1676.
Lee, Mary	WC2	352	" 1680.
Lee, Rebecca	4	20	" 1658.
Lee, Richard	1	110	" 1633.
Lee, Richard	1	18	Immigrated 1638 with wife.
Lee, Richard	ABH	97	" 1640.
Lee, Richard	Q	29	Transported 1657.
Lee, Richard	9	37-38	Immigrated 1658.
Lee, Richard	WC2	412	Transported 1681.
Lee, Robert	7	567	" 1657. Servant.
Lee, Robert	15	439	" 1677.
Lee, Samuel	17	356	" 1672.
Lee, Samuel	18	80	" 1674.
Lee, Thomas	16	89	" 1670.
Lee, Thomas	15	446	" 1678.
Lee, William	6	134	" 1663.
Lee, William	16	482	" 1670-1.
Lee, William	15	307,344	Immigrated 1675. Of Charles Co.
			Assignee of John Lee of Virginia 1675.
Lee, William	WC2	406	Transported 1680.
Leeacke, Jone	15	531	" 1678.
Leech, Jane	WC2	395	" 1680. Servant.
Leech, Thomas	18	84	" 1674.
Leeds, William	Q	68	Service 1658.
Leenne, Francis	9	55	Immigrated 1659.
Leenne, Mary	9	55	Transported 1659.
Lees, James	ABH	151	" 1649-50. Servant.
Lees, James	WC2	105	" 1679.
Lees, Thomas	WC2	105	" 1679.
Leese, James	WC2	24	" 1679. Servant.
Leese, Mary	1	18	" 1637.
Leese, Thomas	WC2	24	" 1679. Servant.
Leester, Dorothy	Q	199	" 1658. Wife of Henry Robinson.
Leet, Samuel	9	38	Transported 1664.
Leete, Humphrey	12	576	" 1670.

NAME	Liber	Folio	REMARKS
Leeze, Elizabeth	Q	32	Transported 1650.
Le Feirure, John	18	293	Service 1675.
Le Garroe, Jude	11	228	Immigrated 1667. Of Virginia.
Legate, John	ABH	322	" May 1652.
Legatt, Ann	15	386	Transported 1676.
Legett, Ann	15	322	" 1675.
Legge, John	WC2	129	" 1679.
Legre, Elizabeth	WC2	168,169	" 1680.
Lehagins, John	17	167	" 1672.
Leige, Peter	12	215	" 1668-9.
Leigh, Ann	15	569	" 1679.
Leigh, James	1	166	" 1650. Servant.
Leigh, Jared	18	169	Immigrated 1674.
Leikfield, John	16	115	Transported 1671.
Leister, James	Q	428	" 1658.
Leitch, Alicia	5	241	" 1662. Wife of John.
Leitch, James	6	16	Immigrated prior to 1662.
Leitch, James	18	334	Transported 1675.
Leitch, John	5	192	Service 1662.
Leitch, Susan	7	491	Transported 1664.
Leitch, William	5	530	" 1662.
Leith, James	8	388	" 1665.
Leman, Thomas	15	396	" 1676.
Lemaster, Abraham	11	545	Service 1668.
Lembry, Stephen	15	443	Transported 1670.
Lembry, Mary	4	214	" 1650-9.
Lembry, William	WC2	398	" 1680. (See Limbrick).
Lenard, John	12	280	" 1668. Servant.
Lent, Thomas	18	24	" 1674.
Lenthall, Richard	16	170	" 1671.
Leonards, Thomas	5	359	" 1663.
Lepo, John	9	216	" 1665.
Le Roche, Charles	10	560	" from Northumber-
land Co. , Virginia 1667. Servant.			
Le Roy, Etpnoy	15	454	Transported 1677.
Lesby, Robert	16	170	" 1670.
Le Sieur, Jeane	5	247	" 1661, by Philip Cal-
			vert, Esq.
Lesley, Thomas	7	371	Transported 1660.
Lested, Margaret	18	157	" 1674.
Lester, Hannah	6	347	" 1663.
Lestle, William	9	25	" 1665.
Lesuire, John	11	517	Service 1668. Of St. Mary's Co.
Letham, Richard	11	441	Transported 1668.
Letherborow, Francis	ABH	100	Immigrated 1640.
Lettimor, John	15	453	Transported 1675-7.
Letton, Joseph	3	14	" 1649. Servant.
Letton, Joseph	ABH	44	Servant 1649.
Levejay, Jane	9	21	Transported 1665.
Leverton, Martha	WC2	212	" 1679.
Levett, Ann	5	607	" 1658-63.

NAME	Liber	Folio	REMARKS
Levett, Arthur	17	354	Transported 1670.
Levick, John	11	552	Immigrated 1668.
Lewellin, John	WC2	124	" 1671. Of St. Mary's Co.
Lewen, Charles	12	217	Transported 1669.
Lewen, Robert	11	309	" 1665.
Lewes, Sarah	4	57	Service 1659. Wife of William.
Lewes, William	4	57	" 1659.
Lewger, Ann	1	17,19	Transported 1637. Wife of John.
Lewger, Ann	4	568	" 1658. (5, fol. 472).

Married Wm. Tattershall, and has Special Warrant from Lord Baltimore for 50 acres 1661. (4, fol. 618).

Lewger, John	1	17,19	Immigrated 1637 with wife, Ann,

son, John, and others. Member of Governor's Council and Secretary of Province. (1, fol. 13, 15).

Lewger, Mr. John	ABH	150	Living 1651.
Lewger, John, Jr.	1	17,19	Transported 1637. Aged 9 years.
Lewger, Martha	12	502	Widow of John. Living 1668.
Lewin, John	15	318	Transported 1674.
Lewin, Philip	4	14	" 1659. Servant.
Lewin, Robert	16	537	And Ann, his wife. Service 1671.
Lewin, Thomas	10	434	Transported 1667.
Lewis, Abigail	6	121	" 1659.
Lewis, Alexander	15	527	" 1678.
Lewis, Ann	9	233	" 1665.
Lewis, Anne	11	230	" 1667.
Lewis, Anne	WC2	146,162	" 1680.
Lewis, Charles	15	358	" 1675.
Lewis, Claude	WC2	71	Proved service of his wife, Sarah, 1679. Of Dorchester Co.
Lewis, Cload	16	532	Service 1672. Of Dorchester Co.
Lewis, Daniel	12	194	Transported 1668. Servant.
Lewis, David	17	416	Service 1673.
Lewis, David	15	357	Transported 1676.
Lewis, Edward	5	516	" 1661.
Lewis, Edward	6	305	" 1664.
Lewis, Edward	18	38	" 1673.
Lewis, George	6	85	" 1657.
Lewis, Griffin	15	565	" 1679.
Lewis, Henry	12	194	" 1668. Servant. (15, fol. 313; 17, fol. 416).
Lewis, Henry	15	322,506	Transported 1674. Servant.
Lewis, Hugh	15	353	" 1676.
Lewis, James	7	81	" 1658.
Lewis, James	4	11	" 1659. Servant.
Lewis, James	7	62	Immigrated 1664.
Lewis, James	17	424	Transported 1673.
Lewis, Jane	12	243	" 1669.
Lewis, John	5	367	" 1663.
Lewis, John	10	556	" 1664-5.
Lewis, John	16	461	Service 1664.
Lewis, John	8	203	Transported 1665.

NAME	Liber	Folio	REMARKS
Lewis, John	11	542	Transported 1668.
Lewis, John	12	413,478	" 1669.
Lewis, John	15	369	" 1676.
Lewis, John	15	430	" 1677.
Lewis, John	WC2	58	" 1678.
Lewis, Jonas	15	369	" 1676.
Lewis, Margaret	15	380	" 1676.
Lewis, Margaret	15	564	" 1679.
Lewis, Mary	17	440	" 1668.
Lewis, Mathew	16	393	" 1671.
Lewis, Morgan	15	433	" 1677.
Lewis, Nath.	12	194	" 1668. Servant.
Lewis, Patrick	18	144	Immigrated 1674. Of St. Mary's Co.
Lewis, Rebecca	9	505	Transported 1666.
Lewis, Robert	15	167	" 1673.
Lewis, Robert	WC2	406	" 1678.
Lewis, Rose	4	555	" 1661.
Lewis, Samuel	15	358	" 1675.
Lewis, Sarah	WC2	71	Service 1679. Wife of Claude.
Lewis, Sarah	WC2	71	Daughter of Claude 1679.
Lewis, Stephen	16	86	Transported 1670.
Lewis, Theodorus	18	311	" 1675.
Lewis, Theophilus	6	83	Immigrated 1659.
Lewis, Thomas	ABH	59	Transported 1641.
Lewis, Thomas	5	259	" 1655.
Lewis, Thomas	6	294	" 1664.
Lewis, Thomas	12	285	" 1668. Servant.
Lewis, Thomas	17	418	Service 1673. And Jane, his wife.
Lewis, Thomas	15	353	Transported 1676.
Lewis, Watkins	WC2	78	Service 1679. Of Somerset Co.
Lewis, William	1	133	License to marry Ursula Gifford, Nov. 2, 1638.
Lewis, William	1	24	Transported 1641.
Lewis, Lieut. William	2	512	Immigrated 1646 with wife. Service 1649. (ABH, fol. 23).
Lewis, William	12	190	Transported 1668.
Lewis, William	15	318	" 1675.
Lewis, William	15	530	" 1678.
Lewis, William	WC2	167,169	" 1680.
Lewkey, John	WC2	65	" 1679. Servant.
Lewreck, Darby	15	438	" Oct. 1677.
Ley, Edward	6	294	" 1664.
Leyoy, Col. Fant	6	41	Of Virginia. Grant from Lord Baltimore for 1000 acres, 14 August 1663.
Leyton, William	16	503	Transported 1671.
Lickfull, John	12	341	" 1668.
Liddle, William	Q	183	" 1658.
Ligh, Alice	5	268	" 1663.
Light, John	16	537	" 1671.
Light, Joseph	18	37	Immigrated 1673 with Winifred, his wife.

NAME	Liber	Folio	REMARKS
Light, Joseph	WC2	348	Immigrated 1680, with his wife.
Light, Winifred	18	37	" 1673. Wife of Joseph.
Light, Winnifred	WC2	348	Transported 1680. Wife of Joseph.
Lightwood, Mary	15	445	" 1678.
Ligings, John	12	589	" 1670.
Like, William	5	93	" 1661.
Lile, John	5	211	" 1662.
Lile, Priscilla	6	90	" 1656.
Lile, Thomas	17	510	" 1673.
Lile, William	6	90	" 1653.
Lille, Humphrey	5	211	" 1662.
Lillingston, John	WC2	107	Immigrated 1679.
Lilly, Mary	WC2	254	Transported 1680.
Lilly, Susan	5	66	" 1662.
Lilly, William	4	140	" 1658. Servant. (Q, fol. 388).
Limbrey, Humphrey	16	331	Immigrated 1668. Of St. Mary's Co.
Limbrick, William	WC2	253	Transported 1680. (See Lembry).
Lin, John	7	569	" 1663-4.
Linch, Hugh	15	446	" 1677.
Linch, Cornelius	WC2	287	" 1680.
Linch, James	1	132	" 1641. Servant.
Linch, John	16	435	" 1671.
Linch, Meryan	15	567	" 1679.
Linch, Vincent	10	1	" 1666.
Linck, Thomas	12	190	" 1668.
Lincolne, Ann	17	492	Service 1673. Wife of Jonathan.
Lincolne, Garret	WC2	57	Transported 1678.
Lincolne, Jonathan	17	492	" 1662.
Lindesey, Sergt. James	3	15	Immigrated 1647.
Lindle, Sarah	ABH	245	Transported 1651.
Lindsey, Alce	7	82	" 1661.
Lindsey, Edmond	Q	31	Immigrated 1656.
Lindsey, Edmond	5	307	" 1663.
Lindsey, Eleanor	5	307	Transported 1663.
Lindsey, Family	19	616	See Kenelm Macloreghton 1677.
Lindsey, Serjt. James	ABH	9,44	Immigrated 1647.
Lindsey, John	6	119	Transported 1650. (17, fol. 67).
Lindsey, Margaret	6	119	" 1652.
Lindsey, Marmaduke	11	525	Immigrated 1668.
Line, George	20	185	Transported 1679.
Line, Henry	12	415	" 1669.
Linen, Edmond	ABH	57	Immigrated Sept. 1643.
Lines, Philip	16	411	Transported 1671. And Margaret, his wife, Service 1674. (18, fol. 110).
Lines, Thomas	12	269	Transported 1669.
Ling, Francis	10	325	" prior to 1666.
Lingan, Ann	18	314	Service 1668.
Lingan, George	7	527	" 1664.
Lingger, Catherine	7	556	Transported 1665.
Linghorn, Katherine	11	265	" 1667.

NAME	Liber	Folio	REMARKS
Liniger, Darby	18	137	Transported 1674.
Liniger, Samuel	18	137	" 1674.
Linington, Mary	16	507	" 1671.
Lininston, John	WC2	86-87	" 1679.
Linkhorn, Robert	16	432	" 1671.
Linkhorne, Jonathan	6	93	" 1661.
Linle, Sarah	5	56	" 1650.
Linley, Ann	10	556	" 1664-5.
Linn (Luinn), Joseph	WC2	146,162	" 1680.
Linnen, Edmond	1	20	Immigrated 1643.
Linnex, William	17	424	Transported 1673.
Linnington, Elizabeth	Q	443	" 1658.
Linnis (Linnie), Phillip	1	17,19	" 1637.
Linscomb, Thomas	Q	71	" 1658.
Linsey, Daniel	15	422	Immigrated 1677 with Sarah, his wife.
Linsey, Daniel	WC2	17	Transported 1679.
Linsey, Darby	4	140	" 1656. Servant.
Linsey, David	WC2	17	Immigrated 1679.
Linsey, Eleanor	15	359	Transported 1676.
Linsey, James	15	454	" Oct. 1677.
Linsey, Sarah	15	422	" 1677. Wife of Daniel.
Linsey, Thomas	17	463	" 1673.
Linslie, Thomas	Q	71	" 1652-3.
Linsloe, Elizabeth	17	469	" 1673.
Linster, Thomas	Q	69	Service 1658.
Linthy, Daniel	WC2	10	Transported 1679.
Linton, John	ABH	200	" 1651. Servant.
Lion, John	15	172	Immigrated 1673. Of Somerset Co.
Lion, Margery	15	172	" 1673. Wife of John.
Liptrott, Charles	15	380	Transported 1676.
Liscom, William	15	395,454	" 1677. (15, fol. 503).
Lissell, Will	15	430	" 1677.
Lister, Capt. Edmond	16	83	Of Virginia, acquires land on the Eastern Shore, part of Devils Island, 1670.
Lister, Rebecca	17	29	Transported 1672.
Lister, Thomas	17	29	" 1672.
Liston, Morris	9	228,280	Immigrated 1665.
Litle, Arthur	WC2	82	Transported 1679.
Little, Christopher	17	33	" from Virginia 1672. Service with Jone, his wife, 1675.
Little, John	9	37	Transported 1664.
Little, John	9	304	" 1665.
Little, John	18	106	" 1674.
Little, John	WC2	206	" 1680. Servant.
Little, Jone	17	33	" from Virginia 1672.
Little, Lawrence	5	208	" 1662.
Little, Nehemiah	11	203	Service 1667. Of Charles Co.
Littler, John	5	415	Transported 1663.
Littler, Joseph	WC2	201	" 1680. Servant.
Littleton, Bowman	WC2	74	Son of Col. Southy Littleton.

NAME	Liber	Folio	REMARKS
Littleton, John	16	168	Transported 1670.
Littleton, Capt. Southy	15	321	Of Accomack Co., Va. acquires land in Maryland 1675.
Liveller, Alice	4	14	Transported 1651. Servant.
Livermore, Edward	15	356	" 1675.
Livesay, Gilbert	WC2	395	Rights 1680.
Livesey, Mark	ABH	151	Transported 1649-50. Servant.
Lloyd, David	18	174	" 1674.
Lloyd, Francis	16	135	" 1671.
Lloyd, George	17	51	" 1672.
Lloyd, Hugh	WC2	406	" 1676.
Lloyd, John, Gent.	5	393	His widow married Walter Hall, Gent., prior to 1663.
Lloyd, Morris	9	459	Transported 1665.
Lloyd, Richard	ABH	163	Immigrated 1648.
Lloyd, Richard	Q	11	" 1657.
Lloyd, Richard	9	488	Transported 1665. Servant.
Lloyd, Robert	5	484	Immigrated 1659.
Lloyd, Theodorick	12	189	Transported 1668.
Lloyd, William	17	440	" 1673.
Lloyde, Robert	4	538	Immigrated Sept. 1659. Chirurgeon.
Loader, William	2	567	Transported 1642. Servant.
Loades, William	ABH	33	Servant 1642.
Loading, William	15	396	Transported 1675.
Loathbruy, Bridgett	16	133	" 1671.
Lock, William	20	185	" 1679.
Locke, Mary	10	558	" 1667. Servant.
Lockelp, Elizabeth	Q	17	" 1657.
Locker, Annis	17	424	" 1673.
Locker, Christian	12	189	" 1668.
Locker, Elizabeth	8	502	" 1665.
Locker, John	12	416	" 1669.
Locker, John	15	433	" 1677.
Locker, Mary	9	343	" 1663.
Lockett, Martha	18	335	" 1675.
Lockey, Christopher	11	581	" 1668.
Lockey, Timothy	11	581	" 1668.
Lockman, Ann	16	546	" 1671.
Lockwood, Anthony	9	304	" 1665.
Lockwood, Robert	9	451	" 1666.
Lockwood, Robert	15	301	Immigrated 1675. Of Anne Arundel County.
Lodge, George	4	620	Immigrated from Virginia 1661.
Lodge, Henry	5	530	Transported 1661.
Lodge, Margaret	17	69	" 1672.
Lodge, Mary	WC2	33	" 1679.
Loe, Ann	13	56	" 1670. (18, fol. 84).
Loe, Elizabeth	6	623	" 1660.
Loe, Mary	15	429	" 1674.
Loe, Richard	ABH	94	" 1633. Servant.
Loes, Richard	12	513	Immigrated 1669.

NAME	Liber	Folio	REMARKS
Loffe, Thomas	12	406	Transported 1669.
Lofthouse, Margarett	WC2	308	"　　　　1678.
Loe, Richard	1	119	Immigrated 1640. Planter.
Loftus, Fabia	WC2	129	Transported 1679.
Loggett, Rose	6	305	"　　　　1664. (9, fol. 54).
Logings, Thomas	17	376	Service 1672.
Logsden, William	18	38	Transported 1673.
Loker, John	12	381	"　　　　1669.
Lolly, Gilbert	17	552	Service 1673.
Lomax, Blanch	15	358	Transported 1668. Wife of Cleborne.
Lomax, Cleborne	15	358	Immigrated 1668. Of Charles Co.
Lombard, Francis	ABH	246	Transported many years prior to 1652.
Londey, John	15	417	Immigrated 1677.
London, Abigall	9	200	Transported 1665.
London, Ambroze	9	200	Immigrated 1665.
London, Mary	9	200	Transported 1665.
London, Mary, Jr.	9	200	"　　　　1665.
London, Ruth	9	200	"　　　　1665.
Londry, Katherine	WC2	129	"　　　　1679.
Lone, Richard	7	560	"　　　　1665.
Long, Curtis	15	386	"　　　　1676.
Long, David	15	446	Immigrated 1677.
Long, David	WC2	113,165	Transported 1680.
Long, Elizabeth	15	446	"　　　　1677. Wife of David.
Long, Grace	17	424	"　　　　1673.
Long, John	9	334,448	"　　　　1666.
Long, John	17	635	"　　　　1674.
Long, Joseph	ABH	35	"　　　　March 1648-9.
Long, Joseph	2	575	"　　　　1648.
Long, Josias	17	611	Immigrated 1672. Of Baltimore Co.
Long, Josias	18	39	Transported 1674.
Long, Josias	15	397,504	"　　　　1677.
Long, Mary	3	173	"　　　　1655.
Long, Mary	17	608	"　　　　1673.
Long, Mary	15	452	"　　　　1677.
Long, Mary	15	446	"　　　　1677. Daughter of David.
Long, Richard	16	503	Transported 1671.
Long, Samuel	9	211	"　　　　1665.
Long, Thomas	ABH	361	"　　　　1652. Servant. (4, fol. 189).
Long, Thomas	16	170	Transported 1671.
Long, Thomas & John	15	446	"　　　　1677. Sons of David.
Long, Thomas, Gent.	17	64	Immigrated Nov. 1668.
Long, William	ABH	374	Transported under 1st Cond. of Plantations. Servant.
Long, William	12	589	Transported 1670.
Long, William	15	567	"　　　　1678.
Longbotham, Robin	15	432	"　　　　1677.
Longbottome, Robert	15	430	"　　　　1677.

NAME	Liber	Folio	REMARKS
Longburton, John	17	396	Transported 1669.
Longdale, Christopher	WC2	309	" 1678.
Longe, Edward	5	93	" 1662.
Longe, Mary	Q	431	" 1658.
Longg, Thomas	8	483	" from Virginia 1668.
Longhlin, Anthony	17	77	Immigrated 1672. Of St. Mary's Co.
Longland, Eliza.	7	559	Transported 1663.
Longman, Daniel	17	424	" 1673.
Longman, Elizabeth	17	463	" 1673.
Longman, John	17	424	" 1673.
Longworth, John	1	43,128	" about 1638. Servant.
Longworth, John	ABH	68	" 1638-9.
Lonton, James	16	432	" 1671.
Loockerman, Jacob	WC2	52	Immigrated 1679.
Loosemore, Henry	15	376	Transported 1676.
Loot, Samuel	9	35	" 1664.
Lope, Richard	ABH	66	" 1637.
Lord, Elizabeth	15	500	" 1678.
Lord, George	18	117	" 1674.
Lord, John	6	293	" 1664.
Lord, Thomas	17	363	" 1672.
Lorden, Cornelius	18	24	" 1674.
Lore, William	Q	430	" 1658.
Loren, John	WC2	78	Service 1679. Of Somerset Co.
Lorrimer, Alexander	ABH	276	Transported 1651. Servant.
Lossen, Elizabeth	WC2	170	" 1680. Servant.
Losthouse, Mary	18	177	" 1674.
Loterill, James	15	499	" 1677.
Lott, Mary	5	127	" 1662.
Lotts, Elizabeth	WC2	50,56	" 1679.
Loud, William	15	505	" 1678.
Louder, Richard	7	490	Immigrated prior to 1664.
Loule, John	WC2	16	Transported 1677.
Loury, Alexander	17	357	Service 1670. Of St. Mary's Co.
Lovander, Mary	WC2	352	Transported 1680.
Love, Andrew	WC2	320	" 1680. Servant.
Love, Charles	11	338	" 1668.
Love, Dorothy	7	576	" 1665.
Love, John	ABH	157	" 1650. Servant.
Love, John	4	590	" 1660-1. (12, fol. 201-2).
Love, Richard	15	438	" 1677.
Love, Robert	4	59	" 1649-52.
Love, Thomas	5	87	" 1660.
Love, Thomas	5	221	" 1662. Servant.
Love, Thomas	8	477	" 1665.
Loveall, Jane	8	258	" 1665.
Loveless, William	6	294	" 1664.
Lovell, Elizabeth	7	130	" 1650-63, and married Wm. Sears or Shears.
Lovell, Elizabeth	5	247	Transported 1662.
Lovely, Elizabeth	Q	359	Wife of Deliverance Lovely and

NAME	Liber	Folio	REMARKS
			widow of Thomas Ward, 1658.
Lovely, Thomas	Q	359	Transported 1651-8.
Loveridge, William	7	427	" 1664. Servant.
Lovesay, Marke	1	166	" 1650. Servant.
Lovet, William	18	84	" 1674.
Lovett, John	4	214	" 1659. (11, fol. 526).
Lovett, William	17	395	" 1672.
Low, John	7	546	" 1664.
Low, Margery	4	560	" 1661.
Low, Ralph	ABH	356	" 1651. Servant.
Low, Thomas	9	323	" 1666.
Low, William	16	396	" 1671.
Lowdell, Katherine	9	304	" 1665.
Lowden, James	11	569	" 1668.
Lowder, Edward	17	494	Of St. Mary's Co. Immigrated 1673
with Amos, his wife, and Edw. and Joan, his children.			
Lowder, George	WC2	167,169	Transported 1679.
Lowder, Mary	15	567	" 1679.
Lowder, Robert	12	584	" 1670.
Lowdon, Elizabeth	Q	49	Immigrated 1652.
Lowe, Barbara	18	174	Transported 1674.
Lowe, Christopher	18	291	" 1674.
Lowe, Francis	16	503	" 1671.
Lowe, Henry	18	169	Immigrated 1674.
Lowe, James	6	293	Transported 1664.
Lowe, Joseph	16	503	" 1671.
Lowe, Joseph	WC2	167,169	" 1680.
Lowe, Margery	6	623	" 1660.
Lowe, Ralph	ABH	46	" 1649. (3, fol. 22).
Lowe, Robert	18	137	" 1674.
Lowe, Thomas	17	440	" 1673.
Lowe, Vincent, Esq.	20	129	Commission as Surveyor Genl.
			April 3, 1677.
Lowe, Col. Vincent	WC2	100	Immigrated 1679. Of Talbot Co.
Lowe, William	Q	18	" 1658.
Loweber, Dermott	WC2	381	" 1675-80. Servant.
Lowell, Sarah	9	26	" 1665.
Lowers, Ralph	16	79	" 1670.
Lowes, David	13	111	" 1668.
Lowes, Henry	13	111	" 1668.
Lowrey, Elizabeth	5	252	" 1663. Wife of William.
Lowrey, William	5	252	Immigrated 1663.
Lowry, William	10	292	" prior to 1666.
Lowther, Margaret	16	505	Transported 1671.
Lowther, Peter	18	279	" 1675.
Loyce, Nicholas	18	174	" 1674.
Loyce, William	5	182	" 1662.
Loyd, Charles	15	397	" 1676.
Loyd, Edward	17	571	" 1673.
Loyd, Francis	16	135	" 1671.
Loyd, John	15	567	" 1678.

NAME	Liber	Folio	REMARKS
Loyd, Mary	17	52	Service 1672. Wife of Philip.
Loyd, Patrick	11	338	Transported 1668.
Loyd, Col. Philemon	15	567	Of Talbot Co. Atty. for Edward
Loyd of London, Merchant, 1678.			
Loyd, Philip	17	52	Immigrated 1666.
Loyd, Richard	8	482	Married the widow of Thos. Phillips prior to 1665.
Loyd, Richard	8	502	Immigrated 1665.
Loyd, Robert	17	395	Transported 1672.
Loyd, Thomas	15	380	" 1676.
Loyle, William	ABH	269	" from Virginia by
William Stone, 1650. Servant.			
Loynes, Philip	12	189	Transported 1668.
Lubey, Mary	12	471	" 1670.
Luby, John	15	553	" 1678.
Lucas, Ann	12	514	" 1668. Wife of Peter.
Lucas, John	15	443	" 1667.
Lucas, Peter	12	514	Immigrated 1668.
Lucas, Richard	WC2	86-87	Transported 1679.
Lucas, Thomas	16	411	" 1671.
Lucas, William	ABH	201	Immigrated 1650-1 with wife. (9, fol. 234).
Lucy, Diana	15	370	Transported 1676.
Luddington, Elizabeth	9	24	" 1665.
Luddington, William	15	167	" 1673.
Ludford, John	16	453	" 1671.
Ludman, Jone	9	431	" from Virginia 1666.
Ludman, Mary	10	313	" 1666. Wife of Thomas.
Ludman, Thomas	9	343	" 1663.
Ludman, Thomas	9	431	" 1666. Of Va. (10, fol. 313).
Luett, John	16	432	Transported 1671.
Luffe, John	15	454	" 1677.
Luffman, Daniel	9	54	" 1665.
Luffman, William	5	485	Immigrated 1658.
Luffman, William	8	86	Transported 1660.
Luke, Charles	16	407	" 1671.
Luke, Edward	7	567	" 1665.
Luke, Sarah	7	567	" 1665.
Lukeman, John	6	14	" 1663.
Lukith, Eleanor	9	34	" 1665.
Lumbar, Francis	15	530	" 1678.
Lumbard, Francis	4	62	His widow appears in 1659 as the wife of John Salter.
Lumbrey, Humphrey	16	331	Immigrated 1668. Of St. Mary's Co.
Lumbrozo, Elizabeth	5	557	Transported 1662. Wife of Jacob.
Lumbrozo, Jacob	5	557	Immigrated 1656. Alias John, of Charles County.
Lund, John	WC2	308	Transported 1678.
Lunn, George	WC2	112	" 1680.
Lunn, John	9	188	" 1665.

NAME	Liber	Folio	REMARKS
Lupton, William	12	190	Transported 1668. Servant.
Lurkey, Nicholas	Q	203	Service 1658.
Lusby, Dorothy	5	485	Transported 1662. Wife of Robert. (11, fol. 168).
Lusby, Elizabeth	5	485	Transported 1662. Daughter of Robert.
Lusby, Jacob	5	485	Transported 1662. Son of Robert. (11, fol. 168).
Lusby, Rebecca	5	485	Transported 1662. Daughter of Robert. (11, fol. 168).
Lusby, Robert	5	485	Immigrated 1662. (11, fol. 168).
Lusby, Sarah	5	485	Transported 1663. Daughter of Robert. (11, fol. 168).
Lush, John	15	443	Transported 1670.
Lushead, Richard	ABH	65	" 1633.
Lusthead, Richard	1	20,37, 38,166	" 1633.
Lustick, Richard	1	168	Married sister of Luke Gardiner. Deceased by 1650.
Lute, Charles	16	407	Transported 1671.
Luther, Grace	16	95	" 1670.
Lutt, Alice	ABH	241	" 1649. Servant.
Lycente, Jane	WC2	415	" 1666-80. Servant.
Lye, John	7	81	" 1660. (5, fol. 319).
Lyell, William	6	160	Immigrated 1663 with wife.
Lyhfy, John	18	152	Transported 1674.
Lyle, John	5	411	" 1663.
Lylley, John	6	237	" 1663.
Lynch, Cornelius	WC2	128	" 1679.
Lyne, Daniel	11	378	" 1668.
Lyne, Thomas	18	137	" 1674.
Lynes, Henry	18	6	Service 1674. Of Talbot Co.
Lynn, George	9	297	Transported 1665.
Lyon, Ann	Q	239	" 1652-3.
Lyon, Jane	18	152	" 1674.
Lyon, Jeremiah	WC2	395	" 1680. Servant.
Lyon, Mary	16	507	" 1671.
Lysey, Elizabeth	16	432	" 1671.
Lythkoe, John	18	152	" 1674.
Maais, Daniel	WC2	184	" 1680. Servant.
Mabbe, Thomas	17	440	" 1673.
Mabitt, Susanna	WC2	352	" 1680.
Macah, Oen	5	210	Immigrated 1662. (See Mackara).
Macall, George	16	97	And Ann, his wife, Service 1670.
Macall, James	15	343	Service 1675. Of Calvert Co.
Macalman, John	18	152	Transported 1674.
Macares, Angages	9	157	" 1665.
Macarty, Darby	17	44	" 1667.
Macarty, Moses	15	342	Immigrated 1675.
Macchoone, Jerman	11	378	Transported 1668.
Mac Coloth, John	5	248	" 1663.

NAME	Liber	Folio	REMARKS
Macconally, Jane	12	284	Service 1668.
Macconey, Patrick	9	434	Transported 1666.
Maccullough, John	4	212	" 1659.
Mac Donohue, Teague	Q	208	" 1658.
Mac Dowell, William	Q	205,317	Immigrated 1655,and married Mary Brood, 1658.
Mace, Rowland	ABH	5,48	Servant 1641.
Mace, Rowland	1	24	Transported 1641 by Francess White.
Mace, Rowland	3	24	Transported about 1643 by John Medley. Servant. (2,fol. 254).
Mace, Rowland	2	512	Transported about 1649 by William Lewis. Servant.
Mace, Samuel	11	441	Transported 1668.
Macelen, James	WC2	73	" 1678.
Mac Feinne, William	ABH	9	Immigrated prior to 1648.
Mac Ferlin, Daniel	ABH	202	Transported 1651. Servant.
Macglander, John	5	251	" 1663.
Macham, John	3	21	" 1637. Servant.
Machia, Daniel	17	511	Service 1673. Of Kent Co.
Machin, John	1	17,20, 25,38	Transported 1637. (ABH,fol. 37).
Machin, Ran.	15	454	" 1677.
Mack, William	Q	323	" 1652.
Mackahee, Robert	18	152	" 1674.
Mackanny, Joane	WC2	21	" 1679.
Mackara, Owen	8	484	" 1664. (See Macah).
Mackarell, Elizabeth	18	174	" 1674.
Mackary, Daniel	9	89	" 1665.
Mackay, Robert	Q	202	Immigrated 1658.
Mackcamon, James	15	537	Transported 1679.
Mack Charman, Patrick	18	152	" 1674.
Mack Choy, Daniel	18	152	" 1674.
Mackclarty, Daniel	18	152	" 1674.
Mack Daniel, Daniel	Q	431	" 1658.
Mack Daniell, Alex.	18	152	" 1674.
Mackdewell, Katherine	WC2	167,169	" 1680.
Mackdonell, Enis	18	137	" 1674.
Mackeele, Charles	WC2	233,312, 366	Son of John 1680. Of Dorchester Co.
Mackeiay, Patrick	17	572	Transported 1672.
Mackelling, Robert	WC2	217	" 1680.
Mackelly, John	Q	427	Service 1658.
Mackelroy, Patrick	18	137	Transported 1674.
Mackem, John	ABH	45	" 1636. Servant.
Mackenny, Margaret	5	306	" 1663. Wife of Martin.
Mackenny, Martin	5	306	Immigrated 1663.
Mackenzie, Collen	WC2	378-379	" from Virginia 1680. Of St. Mary's County.
Mackerell, Daniel	18	137	Transported 1674.
Mackerell, Giles	15	551	" 1679.

NAME	Liber	Folio	REMARKS
Mackerell, John	18	174	Transported 1674.
Mackerlderman, Murtan	16	85	" 1670.
Mackerlidge, James	12	190	" 1668. Servant.
Mackery, Nora	9	216	" 1665.
Mackery, Richard	9	216	" 1665.
Mackey, John	15	413	Immigrated 1677.
Mackey, Robert	15	574	Transported 1678. (WC2, fol. 16).
Mackfarer, Alexander	15	429	" 1677.
Mackfarnell, John	15	405	Service 1676.
Mackginnis, Edmund	18	137	Transported 1674.
Mackgowen, John	18	152	" 1674.
Mackgregor, James	7	510	Of Va. About to settle in Md. 1664.
Mackholister, Eleanor	18	152	Transported 1674.
Mackiele, John	17	567	" 1673.
Mackinney, Makyn	4	5	" 1659. Servant.
Mackkonna, Fenlow	ABH	202	" 1651. Servant.
Macklanan, James	17	571	" 1673.
Macklavee, James	15	537	" 1679.
Macklewd, Martha	9	54	" 1665.
Mackley, John	15	358	" 1675.
Macklin, Margaret	6	15	" 1661. Wife of Robert.
Macklin, Richard	WC2	112	" 1679.
Macklin, Robert	Q	61	Immigrated 1658.
Mackling, Mathew	5	517	" 1663.
Mackloughlin, Kenelm	19	616	Of Charles Co. Father-in-law of Eliz. Lindsey, 1677.
Mackmaikin, Cornelius	18	152	Transported 1674.
Mackmarow, Clement	16	435	" 1671.
Mackmorrish, Edmond	WC2	380	" 1675-80. Servant.
Mackmullen, James	18	152	" 1674.
Mackneele, Christopher	18	306	" 1675.
Mackneele, Daniell	18	152	" 1674.
Mackneele, James	18	152	" 1674.
Macknemara, Timothy	17	635	Service 1674. Of Calvert Co.
Macknemarrow, Cornelius	WC2	10,17	Transported 1679.
Mackneugh, Phillis	18	111	Service 1674. Wife of Jeremiah of Charles Co.
Macknew, Jeremiah	11	524	Immigrated 1668.
Macknomarrow, John	15	531	Transported 1678.
Mackmomorrough, Slane	WC2	380	" 1675-80. Servant.
Mackonina, John	Q	66	" 1650.
Mackonough, Dennis	5	361	" 1663.
Mackoy, Ann	17	571	" 1673.
Mackoy, James	8	502	" 1665.
Mackpeter, John	ABH	361	" 1652. Servant. (9, fol. 263).
Mackuaid, John	18	152	Transported 1674.
Mackramee, James	15	537	" 1679.
Mackrell, James	6	96	" 1660.
Mackshaan, Cornelius	5	188	" 1662.

NAME	Liber	Folio	REMARKS
Mackvey, Jeffery	18	152	Transported 1674.
Macky, John	16	406	And Eliz., his wife. Service 1671.
Mac Laughlin, William	ABH	9	Immigrated prior to 1648.
Macnamah, Eleanor	15	537	Transported 1679.
Macoby, Mor.	15	527	" 1678.
Macollingin, Dennis	7	519	" 1664.
Macom, Katherine	9	204	" 1665. Wife of Thomas.
Macom, Thomas	9	204	Immigrated 1665.
Macquier, Cornelius	Q	197	Transported 1656.
Macragh, Mary	15	537	" 1679.
Macrah, Dennis	16	435	" 1671.
Macrah, Mary	WC2	318	Service 1680. Wife of Owen.
Macrah, Owen	WC2	318	Rights 1680.
Madagon, Faulle	Q	71	Transported 1652-3.
Madbery, Elizabeth	17	66	Service 1672. Wife of John.
Maddock, Cornelius	WC2	199	Transported 1680.
Maddocks, Stephen	6	171	" 1663.
Maddon, Mary	18	15	" 1673.
Maddox, George	15	573	" 1668.
Maddox, George	WC2	65	" 1679.
Maddox, Henry	16	432	" 1671.
Maddox, Robert	13	114	Immigrated 1670. Of Charles Co.
Maddox, Thomas	Q	430	Transported 1658.
Maddy, Thomas	16	394	" 1671.
Madere, Denis	7	546	" 1657.
Maders, Thomas	4	54	" 1659.
Madgipe, Abraham	15	449	" 1677.
Madjeck, Jeane	15	530	" 1678.
Madrin, John	15	397	" 1676.
Madux, Samuel	9	24	" 1665.
Magareck, Hugh	4	585	" 1661.
Magason, John	9	356	" 1661.
Magaye, Anne	WC2	309	" 1678.
Magee, Edmond	18	152	" 1674.
Magee, Henry	18	152	" 1674.
Magee, Patrick	18	152	" 1674.
Magher, Teig	15	527	" 1678.
Magnaid, Hugh	18	152	" 1674.
Magniew, Tarlow	WC2	412	" 1681.
Magrath, Catherine	20	184	" from Va. 1678 with daughter.
Magrath, Morrish	20	184	Transported from Ireland 1678.
Magregory, Hugh	8	258	" 1665.
Magregory, James	8	258	" 1665.
Magroyer, Cornelius	Q	29	" 1658.
Magson, Margaret	13	66	" 1669. Servant.
Maguiare, Elizabeth	WC2	120	" 1680.
Maguire, John	WC2	120	" 1680.
Magumery, John	18	152	" 1674.
Magumery, Robert	15	358	" 1675.
Mahalton, Manns	18	152	" 1674.

NAME	Liber	Folio	REMARKS
Maher, Richard	15	553	Transported 1678.
Mahone, Jeane	11	570	" 1668.
Mahony, Ellen	15	549	" 1678.
Mahony, Teag	11	378	" 1668.
Mahoone, Dennis	WC2	113,165	" 1680.
Mahony, Mall	WC2	287	" 1680.
Mahopp, Archibald	ABH	269	" 1651. Servant.
Maicy, Henry	16	410	" 1671.
Maides, John	11	190	Immigrated 1667. Of St. Mary's Co.
Maine, Patrick	18	313	Transported 1675.
Maison, Ann	WC2	10	" 1679. Wife of John.
Maison, Hester	WC2	10	" 1679. Daughter of John.
Maison, John	WC2	10	Immigrated 1679 with wife and children. Of Somerset Co.
Maison, John, Jr.	WC2	10	Transported 1679. Son of John.
Maison, William	WC2	10	" 1679. Son of John.
Major, Robert	4	140	" 1658. Servant.
Major, Thomas	15	353	" 1674.
Major, William	4	2	" 1658.
Makall, James	9	505	" 1666.
Makall, James	12	492	" 1670.
Makelester, Dunken	ABH	164	" 1651. Servant.
Maken, William	WC2	73	" 1678.
Makepeace, Ann	17	30	" 1672.
Makepeace, William, Jr.	17	30	" 1672.
Makepeace, William, Sr.	17	29	" 1672.
Makey, William	4	434	" 1666.
Makoy, Daniel	9	35	" 1664.
Makpeace, George	7	372	" 1664.
Malakie, John	WC2	415	" 1666-80. Servant.
Malass, Mary	5	93	" 1661.
Malbie, John	5	489	" 1662.
Male, Anthony	11	462	" 1668.
Malin, Francis	Q	68	" 1653.
Mallershay, Geoffry	12	205	" 1667.
Mallett, Gregory	6	93	" 1661.
Mallett, Jenkin	6	129	" 1656.
Mallett, John	WC2	310	" 1680.
Mallett, Mathew	16	109	" 1665.
Mallett, Mathew	16	109	" 1671.
Malley, Matt.	15	533	" 1678.
Mallhone, Desmond	11	378	" 1668.
Mallond, Thomas	5	90	" 1653-61.
Mallott, Ellen	4	590	" 1660-1.
Mals, Mary	11	571	" 1668.
Malson, Samuel	WC2	206	" 1679. Servant.
Malt, John	WC2	309	" 1680.
Maltford, Susanna	18	335	" 1675.
Mami, Ezekiel	Q	430	" 1658.
Mamon, Thomas	17	396	" 1669. Service 1675.

NAME	Liber	Folio	REMARKS
			(15, fol. 382).
Man, Charles	15	516	Transported 1675.
Man, Edward	WC2	38,50	" his wife, daughter
and one other person 1679. Of Talbot County.			
Man, Elizabeth	WC2	38	Transported 1679. Daughter of Edward.
Man, James	4	59	Transported 1649-52
Man, John	10	312	" 1662.
Man, Luce	WC2	38	" 1679. Wife of Edward.
Man, Mary	4	66	" 1659.
Manawring, Margaret	Q	68	Servant 1653-8.
Manby, John	4	58	Transported 1659.
Mandson, Mary	5	118	" 1658.
Maneaster, John	19	41	Immigrated 1675. Of St. Mary's Co.
Manfield, Margaret	16	435	Transported 1671.
Manfield, William	17	417	" 1673.
Manford, Francis	17	424	" 1673.
Manghan, Timothy	11	479	" 1668.
Maning, Isaac	WC2	19	" 1679.
Maning, Jo.	WC2	112	" 1680.
Maninge, Isaac	15	569	" 1678.
Mankin, George	9	336	" 1666.
Manloe, Ann	6	31	" 1663.
Manloe, Jane	17	382	Service 1672. Wife of Thomas.
Manlove, Ann	9	204	Transported 1665.
Manlove, Christopher	9	204	" 1665.
Manlove, Elizabeth	9	204	" 1665.
Manlove, George	9	204	" 1665.
Manlove, Hannah	9	204	" 1665.
Manlove, Jane	WC2	36	Service 1679. Wife of Thomas.
Manlove, John	9	204	Transported 1665.
Manlove, John	17	38	Immigrated 1672, with Elizabeth, his wife. Of Somerset Co.
Manlove, Mark	9	204	Transported 1665.
Manlove, Mark, Jr.	9	204	" 1665.
Manlove, Perce	9	204	" 1665.
Manlove, Thomas	9	204	" 1665.
Manlove, William	9	204	" 1665.
Mann, Ann	9	433	" 1663.
Mann, John	15	370	Immigrated 1676. Of Talbot Co.
Mann, John, Jr.	15	370	Transported 1676. Son of John.
Mannaring, George	12	548	Immigrated 1670. Of St. Mary's Co.
Manne, Samuel	17	475	Transported 1673.
Mannering, George	11	568	Of London, Gent. Special Warrant
from Lord Baltimore for 600 acres, 9 Oct. 1688.			
Mannering, George	11	579	Immigrated 1668.
Manners, George	ABH	4,11	And Son. Immigrated 1646. His
wife formerly a servant of Mrs. Husbands, 1649. (ABH, fol. 36).			
Manners, George	2	249,439	Immigrated 1646 with son, William.
Manners, Mrs. George	2	581	Transported about 1649. Formerly
servant of Mr. Husband.			

NAME	Liber	Folio	REMARKS
Manners, John	4	14	Transported 1653. Servant.
Manners, Rebecca	4	19	" 1649. Servant.
Manners, William	ABH	11	" 1646. Son of George. (2, fol. 439).
Manning, Grace	Q	317	Transported 1658.
Manning, Hugh	6	38	Immigrated 1663. (18, fol. 164).
Manning, John	Q	317	Transported 1658.
Manning, Thomas, Jr.	Q	317	" 1658.
Manning, Thomas, Sr.	Q	317	Immigrated 1658.
Mannom, Elizabeth	18	160	Transported 1674.
Mannurey, John	WC2	380	" 1675-80. Servant.
Mansall, Sarah	15	332	" 1675.
Mansbridge, Ursula	7	81	" 1657.
Mansell, Ann	ABH	34	Service 1649. Wife of John.
Mansell, John	1	69	Transported 1637. Servant.
Mansell, John	ABH	150	Married Ann Peke, prior to 1651.
Mansell, Margaret	5	188	Transported 1659. Servant.
Mansell, Samuel	15	332	" 1675.
Mansell, Vincent	WC2	2	Demands land for transporting 3 persons, 1679. Of St. Mary's County.
Mansen, Peter	WC2	73	Transported 1678.
Manser, John	WC2	206	" 1680. Servant.
Mansfeild, John	WC2	89	" 1676. Servant.
Mansfield, Abraham	7	465	" 1661.
Mansfield, Philip	18	102	Service 1674. Of St. Mary's Co.
Mansfield, Richard	12	333	Transported 1669.
Mansfield, Richard	WC2	113,165	" 1680.
Manship, Eliz., Jr.	ABH	312,372	" 1652. (Q, fol. 428).
Manship, Elizabeth	Q	428	Widow of Richard, Sr. Married Matthew Smith 1658.
Manship, Mary	ABH	312,372	Transported 1652. (Q, fol. 428).
Manship, Rachel	ABH	312,372	" 1652. (Q, fol. 428).
Manship, Richard	ABH	372	Immigrated 1652-4 with wife. (Q, fol. 428).
Manship, Richard, Jr.	ABH	312,372	Transported 1652. (Q, fol. 428).
Manslow, Thomas	15	354	" 1676.
Manson, Peter	4	552	Immigrated 1661 with his wife and son.
Manton, Pricilla	6	239	Transported 1663. (8, fol. 89).
Manton, Sarah	6	239	" 1663. (8, fol. 89).
Mantone, Elizabeth	8	89	" 1665.
Mantone, Mary	8	89	" 1665.
Manwaring, Parsons	WC2	199	" 1680.
Manyord, Alce	WC2	9	Daughter of Samuel. Transported 1679.
Manyord, Elizabeth	WC2	9	Transported 1679. Wife of Samuel.
Manyord, Samuel	WC2	9	Immigrated 1679 with wife and daughter. Of Somerset Co.
Mapowder, Anthony	WC2	216	Service 1680. Of Baltimore Co.
Maquett, Charles	1	18	Transported 1637.
Marcam, John	5	210	Immigrated 1662 with son, John.

304

NAME	Liber	Folio	REMARKS
			(9, fol. 25).
Marcan, Philip	16	532	Transported 1668.
Marcarteilu, Timothy	15	499	" 1677.
Marchant, Thomazin	WC2	259	" 1680.
Marchegay, Bennett	8	460	Immigrated 1656.
Marchegay, Margaret	8	460	Transported 1659. Wife of Bennett.
Marcus, Charles	7	62	" 1661. (5, fol. 182).
Marcy, Henry	16	410	" 1671.
Marcy, John	12	194	" 1668. Servant.
Mard, Matthew, Gent.	16	356	One of the Attys. of the Provincial

Court. Commissioned to take the probate lands in Dorset, Talbot and
Baltimore Counties, 1671. (See Ward).

NAME	Liber	Folio	REMARKS
Mare, John	15	443	Transported 1677.
Mare, Rowland	ABH	59	" 1641.
Mare, Samuel	11	337	" 1668.
Mareen, Alexander	12	356	Service 1669.
Mareen, Millison	6	129	Transported 1655.
Maren, Bridgett	6	268	" 1662.
Marettrick, John	9	465	" 1666.
Marfield, Elizabeth	9	304	" 1665.
Margaret	Q	70	"A Welch Wench". Servant 1658.
Margyne, John	9	304	Transported 1665.
Mark, John	ABH	141	" 1651.
Mark, John	8	89	Immigrated 1661.
Mark, Margaret	8	89	Transported 1658 (?). Wife of John.
Marke, Anthony	5	2	" 1661.
Marke, Mary	18	291	" 1674.
Marke, Peter	5	2	" 1661.
Markehum, Elizabeth	10	118	" 1666. Wife of Jeremiah.
Markehum, Jeremiah	10	118	Immigrated 1666.
Markes, George	6	106	Transported 1657. (7, fol. 561).
Markes, John	15	531	" 1678. Of Somerset Co.
Markes, William	16	93	" 1670.
Markeyne, Thomas	Q	211	" 1658. (4, fol. 580).
Markmerland, George	6	216	" 1663.
Marks, John	5	242	Immigrated 1661.
Marlburgh, John	ABH	65	Transported 1633. (1, fol. 38).
Marler, Edward	11	555	Immigrated 1668.
Marler, Jonathan	11	108	" 1667.
Marleston, Charles	9	434	Transported 1666.
Marleston, Elizabeth	9	434	" 1666.
Marleston, John	9	434	Immigrated 1666. Of New York.
Marleston, John, Jr.	9	434	Transported 1666.
Marleston, Susan	9	434	" 1666.
Marleston, Thomas	9	434	" 1666.
Marlet, Matthew	20	185	" 1679.
Marley, Anthony	16	411	" 1671.
Marley, Katherine	16	129	" 1671.
Marley, Margaret	9	336	" 1666.
Marley, Thomas	16	129	" 1641.
Marling, Francis	9	155	" 1665.

NAME	Liber	Folio	REMARKS
Marloe, Ann	18	77,128	Transported 1674.
Marlow, Mary	Q	184	Immigrated 1656. Daughter of William.
Marlow, William	Q	184	Immigrated 1656.
Marlow, William	WC2	415	Transported 1666-80. Servant.
Marlowe, Mary	5	534	" 1661.
Marly, John	16	411	" 1671.
Marmacks, Elizabeth	15	532,570	" 1678. Daughter of Katherine Robins.
Marmacks, Hugh	15	532,570	Transported 1678. Son of Katherine Robins.
Marmacks, John	15	532,570	Transported 1678. Son of Katherine Robins.
Marmacks, Katherine	15	532,570	Transported 1678. Daughter of Katherine Robins.
Marmacks, Margaret	15	532,570	Transported 1678. Daughter of Katherine Robins.
Marmaduke, Robert	17	350	Transported 1671.
Marnith, Nathaniel	WC2	127	" 1679.
Maro, Rowland	ABH	24	Servant 1646.
Maroon, Gabriel	11	537	Transported 1668.
Marram, Charles	WC2	130	" 1679. Servant (20 years old).
Marrell, William	14	427	Transported 1668. (11, fol. 546; 12, fol. 584).
Marren, James	9	448	Transported 1666.
Marrett, Robert	5	373	" 1663.
Marriote, Elizabeth	17	395	" 1672.
Marrott, John	7	80	" 1664. Son of John Westlake.
Marsden, William	18	137	Transported 1674.
Marser, Sarah	17	463	" 1673.
Marsey, Nicholas	6	159	" 1652.
Marsh, David	9	400	" 1666.
Marsh, Elizabeth	9	94	" 1665. Servant.
Marsh, Hannah	15	358	" 1675.
Marsh, James	15	455	" 1678.
Marsh, John	9	459	" 1664.
Marsh, John	17	486	" 1667.
Marsh, Margaret	2	575	" 1648.
Marsh, Margaret	ABH	35	" 1648-9.
Marsh, Paul	8	202	Immigrated 1664.
Marsh, Thomas	2	575	Transported 1648.
Marsh, Thomas	ABH	35	" 1648-9.
Marsh, Thomas	11	107	Service 1667. Of Calvert Co. Carpenter.
Marsh, Thomas	20	185	Transported 1679.
Marsh, William	18	80	" 1674.
Marshall, Ann	1	166	" 1650. Servant.
Marshall, Ann	16	507	" 1671.
Marshall, Edward	15	455	" 1678. (als. Mildhall).

NAME	Liber	Folio	REMARKS
Marshall, George	6	37	Immigrated 1663.
Marshall, Isaac	5	305	Transported 1663. (16, fol. 638).
Marshall, Joane	17	76	" 1672.
Marshall, Margaret	10	605	" 1667.
Marshall, Marke	17	395	" 1672.
Marshall, Rebecca	17	475	" 1673.
Marshall, Richard	Q	30	" 1658.
Marshall, Richard	15	359	" 1676.
Marshall, Thomas	Q	62	" 1658.
Marshall, Thomas	WC2	31	Immigrated 1679 with 2 sons. Of Dorchester Co.
Marshall, Thomas, Jr.	WC2	31,32	Transported 1679.
Marshall, William	ABH	58	" 1640. (1, fol. 22).
Marshall, William	13	113	" 1670. (16, fol. 482).
Marshall, William	WC2	31	" 1679.
Marsham, Katherine	12	512	Service 1670. Wife of Richard of Calvert Co. (7, fol. 530).
Marsham, Richard	4	4	Transported 1658. Servant. (5, fol. 205).
Marshell, Joane	17	76	Transported 1672.
Marson, Ann	WC2	17	" 1679. Wife of John.
Marson, Hester	WC2	17	" 1679. Daughter of John.
Marson, John, Jr.	WC2	17	Transported 1679. Son of John.
Marson, John, Sr.	WC2	17	Immigrated 1679 with wife and 3 children. Of Somerset County. (See Maison).
Marson, William	WC2	17	Transported 1679. Son of John.
Marston, Richard	12	584	" 1670. (15, fol. 381).
Marston, Robert	7	605	" 1665.
Martage, John	15	380	" 1676.
Marten, Abraham	7	84	" 1661.
Marthers, Jone	15	443	" 1670.
Martin, Abdeloe	3	174	Immigrated 1656 with wife.
Martin, Ann	10	393	Transported 1648. Wife of James.
Martin, Ann	Q	115	" 1656.
Martin, Ann	12	554	" 1670.
Martin, Ann	16	11	" 1670. Wife of John.
Martin, Ann	11	378	" 1668.
Martin, Christopher	4	623	" 1633. (ABH, fol. 244).
Martin, Christopher	1	26	" since 1635.
Martin, Christopher	ABH	60	" since 1635. Servant.
Martin, Christopher	4	79	" 1659.
Martin, Eleanor	12	477	" 1670.
Martin, Elizabeth	7	567	" 1665.
Martin, Elizabeth	20	185	" 1679.
Martin, Frances	ABH	49	" 1649. Daughter of Francis. (3, fol. 62).
Martin, Francis	ABH	49	Immigrated 1650 with wife. (18, fol. 177). Of Nanticoke. (15, fol. 557).
Martin, Francis	3	62	Immigrated 1649 with wife, 3 children and two servants.

NAME	Liber	Folio	REMARKS
Martin, Francis	9	34	Transported 1665. (17, fol. 414).
Martin, Francis	15	431,446	" 1677.
Martin, George	6	122	" 1653.
Martin, George	7	487	" 1663.
Martin, George	17	36	" from Virginia 1672.
Martin, Henry	Q	208	" 1658.
Martin, Henry	4	555	" 1661.
Martin, James	7	546	Immigrated 1665.
Martin, James	6	142-143	Transported 1660.
Martin, James	16	37	" 1670.
Martin, John	ABH	339	Immigrated 1652.
Martin, John	5	93	" 1661 with wife.
Martin, John	6	268	Transported 1662.
Martin, John	5	268	" 1663.
Martin, John	10	395	" 1666.
Martin, John	12	217	" 1669.
Martin, John	16	11	Immigrated 1670, with Ann, his

wife, and John, Mary, Hannah and Elizabeth, his children. Of Baltimore County.

NAME	Liber	Folio	REMARKS
Martin, John	16	340	Transported 1671.
Martin, John	17	416	" 1673.
Martin, John	15	500,501	" 1678.
Martin, Joseph	4	14	" 1659. Servant.
Martin, Joseph	20	185	" 1679. (WC2, fol. 86-7).
Martin, Judith	16	431	" 1671. Servant.
Martin, Lodowicke	3	62	" 1649. Son of Francis.
Martin, Ludowick	ABH	49	" 1649. Son of Francis.
Martin, Mary	5	529	Service 1662. Wife of Thomas. (15, fol. 435).
Martin, Mary	WC2	89	Transported 1676. Servant.
Martin, Michael	WC2	217,253, 398	" 1680.
Martin, Owen	ABH	348	" 1652. Servant.
Martin, Richard	12	576	" 1670. (16, fol. 79).
Martin, Richard	20	185	" 1679. (WC2, fol. 21).
Martin, Robert	12	190	" 1668.
Martin, Robert	15	565	" 1679.
Martin, Sarah	17	469	" 1673.
Martin, Susanna	4	2	" 1655.
Martin, Thomas	ABH	273	" 1650. Servant.
Martin, Thomas	Q	197	" 1656.
Martin, Thomas	5	529	Service 1662. (15, fol. 435).
Martin, Thomas	5	268	Transported 1663.
Martin, Thomas	9	305	" 1665.
Martin, Thomas	12	217	" 1669.
Martin, William	ABH	49	" 1649. Son of Francis. (3, fol. 62).
Martin, William	WC2	415	Transported 1666-80. Servant.
Martin, William	15	427	Immigrated 1677. Of Calvert Co.
Martin, William	15	505	Transported 1678.
Martindale, Elizabeth	15	374,412	Service 1676. Of St. Mary's Co.

NAME	Liber	Folio	REMARKS
Martindale, John	18	113	Service 1674.
Marine, Mary	15	432	Transported 1677.
Martingale, John	12	497	" 1670.
Martoe, Jane	11	104	" 1667.
Martyn, John	9	343	" 1666.
Martyn, Marty	17	440	" 1673.
Martyn, Richard	9	44	Immigrated 1665.
Maruson, John	9	216	Transported 1665.
Marwood, Villers	4	533	" 1659. (5, fol. 556).
Maryan, Daniel	15	508	Service 1678.
Mascall, Jane	15	553	Transported 1678.
Mascall, Joane	WC2	57	" 1678.
Mascall, Richard	16	176	Immigrated 1671. Of Anne Arundel County.
Mascall, Stephen	17	285	Transported 1668. Servant.
Mascodd, Jane	15	332	" 1675.
Mascord, John	8	131	" 1664.
Mase, Nicholas	Q	449	" 1658.
Maser, Roger	5	267	" 1663.
Masey, Winifred	16	170	" 1671.
Mash, Edward	11	344	" 1668.
Mash, George	18	291	" 1674.
Masham, William	15	380	" 1676.
Mason, Elizabeth	Q	19	" 1656.
Mason, George	WC2	54	Service 1665. Of Calvert Co.
Mason, George	11	512	Transported 1668.
Mason, Henry	5	466	" 1662.
Mason, Hindrick	9	490	Immigrated 1665.
Mason, Hugh	18	166,293	Transported 1674.
Mason, Jane	WC2	120	" 1680.
Mason, John	7	467	" 1663. Servant.
Mason, John	11	582	" 1668.
Mason, John	WC2	199	" 1680.
Mason, Joseph	13	122	" 1668.
Mason, Katherine	17	421	" 1672. Daughter of Matthew.
Mason, Margaret	9	329	Transported 1663-4.
Mason, Margery	WC2	199	" 1680.
Mason, Matthew	10	310	Immigrated 1665. Of Chester River.
Mason, Michael	6	106	Transported 1659.
Mason, Miles	8	478	" 1668. Servant.
Mason, Rachel	17	421	" 1672. Daughter of Matthew. (18, fol. 38).
Mason, Rebecca	5	242	Transported 1662.
Mason, Robert	7	370	" 1663.
Mason, Robert	8	501,502	" 1665. (9, fol. 106).
Mason, Robert	16	437	" 1671.
Mason, Robert	14	443	" 1672.
Mason, Robert	15	433	Immigrated 1677. Of St. Mary's Co.
Mason, Susan	15	433	Transported 1677. Wife of Robert.
Mason, Thomas	13	17	" 1668.

NAME	Liber	Folio	REMARKS
Mason, Thomas	8	128	Transported 1664. Servant. Of Baltimore County.
Mason, Thomas	15	452	Transported 1677.
Mason, William	17	425	" 1673.
Mason, William	WC2	110	" 1676. Servant.
Mason, William	WC2	406	" 1679.
Masse, Philip	WC2	120	" 1680.
Masseter, Abraham	17	54	Service 1672.
Massey, Ralph	9	489	Transported 1665.
Massey, Winifred	12	215	" 1668-9.
Masson, John	4	590	" 1660-1.
Masson, Richard	15	516	" 1678.
Mast, Dorothy	6	125	" 1660.
Masten, William	16	414	" 1671.
Masterfield, John	7	464	" 1662.
Masterman, Ann	18	3	" 1674.
Masterman, Thomas	WC2	21,22	" persons in 1679-80.
Of Talbot County. (WC2, fol. 113, 114, 165).			
Masters, Alice	15	390	Transported 1676.
Masters, Charles	7	454	" 1664.
Masters, James	15	559	" 1679.
Masters, John	7	472	" 1664. (12, fol. 506).
Masters, John	15	353	" 1675.
Masters, Margaret	12	344	" 1669. Servant.
Masters, Robert	15	558	" 1679.
Masters, Thomas	15	455	" 1678.
Masters, William	15	567	" 1678.
Maston, Robert	6	16	Immigrated prior to 1663.
Mate, Ann	15	446	Transported 1677.
Matershaw, Jeffrey	17	354	Service 1672.
Mather, Thomas	5	339	Transported 1663.
Mathew, John	7	81	" 1663.
Mathewes, Thomas	3	21	Immigrated 1637 with 4 men servants.
Mathewes, Mrs. Thomas	3	21	Immigrated about 1643.
Mathewes, William	17	634	" 1674. Of St. Mary's Co.
Mathews, Amy	12	190	Transported 1668.
Mathews, Ann	7	454	" 1664.
Mathews, Edward	ABH	60	" 1635. Servant.
Mathews, Eleanor	17	531	" 1673.
Mathews, George	15	446	" 1677.
Mathews, Henry	6	90	" 1663.
Mathews, Henry	7	84	" 1666.
Mathews, Henry	18	130	" 1674.
Mathews, Henry	WC2	310	" 1680.
Mathews, James	18	84	" 1674.
Mathews, Love	16	115	Service 1671. Widow. Of St. Mary's County.
Mathews, Martha	ABH	396	Transported 1654 from the Tertudos.
Mathews, Mary	16	532	" 1668-70.
Mathews, Mary	17	64	Immigrated 1668. Wife of Henry.

NAME	Liber	Folio	REMARKS
Mathews, Mary	WC2	167-169	Transported 1679.
Mathews, Morrice	12	379	Immigrated 1669. Of Dorchester Co.
Mathews, Mr. Thomas	ABH	45	" 1636. (6, fol. 19).
Mathews, Thomas	ABH	60	Transported 1637.
Mathews, Thomas	ABH	66	" 1637.
Mathews, Thomas	ABH	186	" 1651. Servant.
Mathews, Thomas	4	565	" 1661.
Mathews, Thomas	18	84	" 1674.
Mathews, Thomas	WC2	253	" 1679.
Mathiason, Hendrick	4	137	Immigrated prior to 1658.
Mathin, John	ABH	60	Transported 1637. (5, fol. 358).
Matrah, Owen	16	304	Immigrated 1671. Of Somerset Co.
Matt, Mary	9	304	Transported 1665.
Mattershey, Thomas	13	114	" 1668.
Matteshaw, Jeoffry	WC2	183	Rights 1680.
Matthewes, Roger	WC2	16	Transported 1677.
Matthews, Edward	1	26	" since 1635.
Matthews, Eleanor	Q	71	Now wife of Edward Selby. Transported by him, 1658.
Matthews, Elizabeth	15	550	Transported 1679.
Matthews, Giles	Q	71	" 1654.
Matthews, Henry	11	162	Service 1667.
Matthews, John	WC2	276	Immigrated from Virginia 1678. Of St. Mary's Co.
Matthews, Mary	15	550,572	Service 1674. Of Somerset Co.
Matthews, Robert	11	344	Transported 1668.
Matthews, Roger	15	314,574	" 1675.
Matthews, Thomas	1	17,20	" 1637. (1, fol. 25, 38).
Matthews, Thomas Henry	10	391	And wife. Service 1666.
Matthiason, Anne	8	129	" 1664. Wife of Olive.
Matthiason, Olive	8	129	Immigrated with wife and three children 1664.
Matthyason, Elizabeth	Q	63	Immigrated 1658. Wife of Henry.
Matthyason, Henrick	Q	63	" 1658.
Mattingly, Cezar	8	88	Transported prior to 1665. Son of Thomas.
Mattingly, Elizabeth	8	88	Wife of Thos. Transported prior to 1665, when she appears as the wife of Walter Pakes.
Mattingly, Elizabeth	8	88	Transported prior to 1665. Daughter of Thomas.
Mattingly, Thomas	8	88	Immigrated prior to 1665 with wife and child, one of whom was Judith Turner.
Mattingly, Thomas	8	88	Transported prior to 1665. Son of Thomas.
Mattock, John	5	268	Transported 1663.
Mattock, Jonas	18	160	" 1674.
Mattocks, Benjamin	15	318	" 1675.
Mattocks, John	15	380	" 1676.
Mattox, Anne	12	513	Married. Service prior to 1669.
Mattson, Andrew	18	27	Service prior to 1673.

NAME	Liber	Folio	REMARKS
Mau, Elizabeth	5	417	Transported 1663.
Maude, Francis	6	216	" 1663.
Maude, Isaac	15	378	" 1674.
Mauke, Martha	12	515	" 1669. Servant.
Maultis, Katherine	16	169	" 1671. Servant.
Maunsell, John	2	568-569	Rights 1649.
Maunsell, Mrs. John	2	568-569	Service 1649.
Maurice, Elizabeth	Q	71	Transported 1654. Married 1658, Emanuel Drere.
Maurice, John	4	14	Transported 1650. Servant.
Mavy, James	16	406-407	" 1671.
Maw, Martin	6	209	" 1663.
Mawman, Thomas	12	378	" 1669.
Maxemilian, Christian	4	576	" 1661.
Maxemilian, Susanna	4	576	" 1661.
Maxfield, Richard	9	38	" 1665.
Maxwell, Alexander	7	150	Immigrated 1663.
Maxwell, James	5	530	" 1658. (17, fol. 571).
Maxwell, John	9	21	Transported 1665.
Maxwell, John	11	204	Immigrated 1667.
Maxwell, Mary	5	530	Transported 1659. Wife of James.
May, Christopher	WC2	415	" 1666-80. Servant.
May, Elizabeth	WC2	381	" 1675-80. Servant.
May, Isabell	6	290	" 1663.
May, John	8	381	" 1665.
May, Michael	15	332	" 1675.
May, Robert	7	371	" 1662. Servant.
May, Samuel	9	35	" 1664.
May, Thomas	9	355	His widow married Raymond Staplifort prior to 1666.
May, William	4	23,24	Immigrated 1654.
Maybanck, Elizabeth	17	608	Transported 1673.
Maycock, Thomas	17	412	Service 1673.
Mayden, Armill	18	36	Transported 1673.
Mayden, John	18	36	" 1673. (17, fol. 414).
Mayderund, Charles	WC2	120	" 1680.
Maye, Martin	14	145	" 1665.
Mayes, Thomas	9	105	" 1665.
Mayhew, Zachariah	17	513	Service 1673. Of Kent Co.
Mayhow, John	17	424	Transported 1673.
Mayland, Richard	16	522	" 1672.
Maylando, John	ABH	245	" 1651.
Maynard, Ann	11	582	" 1668.
Maynard, Charles	2	526	" about 1637. Servant.
Maynard, Charles	ABH	27,244	" 1637. Service 1649. (9, fol. 26).
Maynard, Charles	3	4	Service 1650.
Maynard, Margaret	12	498	Transported 1670.
Maynce, Katherine	7	469	" 1661.
Maynee, Katherine	10	264	" 1666.
Mayor, Herman	4	552	" 1661.

NAME	Liber	Folio	REMARKS
Mayor, Katherine	4	552	Transported 1661.
Mayor, Maudline	4	552	" 1661.
Mayor, Peter	4	552	Immigrated 1661.
Mayor, Thomas	11	344,463	Transported 1668.
Maypowder, Anthony	17	463	" 1673.
Mazand, John	15	454	" 1677.
Mazareene, Dorothy	5	514	" 1663.
McCarter, Robert	4	49	Gift from Lord Baltimore 1659.
McFinnye, Dermood	4	218	Service 1659.
McHenry, Mr. Murtagh	4	185	" 1659.
McMahony, Edward	15	553	Transported 1678.
Mead, Joseph	7	427	" 1664. Servant.
Mead, Margaret	15	540	" 1676.
Meade, Thomas	10	117	" 1666.
Meades, John	Q	323	" 1655-8.
Meades, John	11	540	" 1668.
Meades, Randall	11	348	" 1668.
Meades, Thomas	7	499	" 1660.
Meakes, Guy	5	489	" 1662.
Meakient, Richard	5	123	" 1662.
Meanely, Jeffery	5	2	" 1661.
Meares, Elizabeth	5	467	" 1657.
Meares, Elizabeth	9	229	" 1665. Wife of William.
Meares, William	5	188	" 1656. Servant.
Meares, William	9	229	Immigrated 1665.
Measur, Roger	12	281	Service 1667.
Mebrin, Hugh	17	571	Transported 1673.
Mecha, John	WC2	211	" 1679. Servant.
Meckane, James	ABH	239	" 1651. Servant.
Mecollin, Bryon	5	397	" 1675.
Medall, Roger	13	64	" 1668.
Medanell, Kadoe	17	571	" 1673.
Medanell, Patrick	17	571	" 1673.
Medcalf, George	15	354	" 1676.
Medcalf, James	7	464	" 1662.
Medcalf, John	17	496	" 1673.
Medcalf, William	1	19	" 1638.
Medcalf, William	1	80-82	Immigrated prior to 1640. Of Isle of Kent.
Medeare, Dennis	10	393	Transported 1657. Ward of Jas. Martin.
Medew, Daniel	WC2	127	Transported 1679.
Medgley, Samuel	15	446	" 1677.
Medler, John	18	166	" 1674.
Medley, Elizabeth	ABH	411	" 1638. Wife of John.
Medley, Henry	ABH	229	" 1650-1. Servant.
Medley, John	ABH	60	" 1635. Servant.
Medley, John	1	26	" 1635-41.
Medley, John	ABH	5	Immigrated 1641 with wife.
Medley, Mrs. John	3	24	Transported prior to 1650.
Medley, Roger	16	507	" 1671.

NAME	Liber	Folio	REMARKS
Medley, Thomas	7	464	Transported 1654.
Medone, John	15	524	" 1678.
Medston, John	6	127	" 1656.
Mee, Mr. George	ABH	173,201	Immigrated 1651 with wife.
Meeare, Felleme	Q	33	Transported 1655.
Meeco, William	17	463	" 1673.
Meed, Joseph	12	515	Service 1669.
Meek, John	7	426	Immigrated 1664.
Meek, Thomas	7	426	" 1663.
Meeke, Alice	18	137	Transported 1674.
Meeke, Guy	9	448	" 1666.
Meeke, John	18	291	" 1674.
Meeke, Sarah	18	28	Immigrated 1674. Wife of Walter.
Meeke, Walter	18	28	" from Virginia 1674 with wife and 3 children.
Meeke, William	18	313	Transported 1675.
Meekes, John	5	252,606	Immigrated prior to 1663. Chirurgeon.
Meekin, Andrew	16	79	Transported 1670.
Meekin, William	11	103	Service 1667.
Meekings, Richard	16	278	" 1671. Of Calvert Co.
Meekins, Johanna	12	381	" 1669.
Meeks, Moss	15	505	Transported 1678.
Meeres, Thomas	5	57	One of the settlers 1st year Severn River settled. Living 1662.
Meers, Ann	15	413	Transported 1677.
Meers, Hannah	Q	313	" 1658.
Meers, John	15	565	" 1679.
Meeton, Elizabeth	WC2	146,162	" 1680.
Meets, Thomas	4	21	" 1657.
Meggs, Francis	17	487	Immigrated from Virginia 1667.
Megloglsghean, Sarah	Q	28	Transported 1653. (See Neglogaghean).
Meher, Leavy	15	553	Transported 1678.
Meiston, William	WC2	53	" 1677.
Meka, John	15	598	" 1678.
Mekenny, Mekin	10	312	Died prior to 1666, leaving a widow "Aninking Dobbs".
Mekery, Daniel	8	130	Immigrated 1665.
Mekery, Homar	8	130	Transported 1665. Wife of Daniel.
Mekery, Richard	8	130	" 1665. Son of Daniel.
Melane, Jone	15	438	" 1677.
Melet, Indeeght	12	385	" 1669.
Mellahane, Durman	ABH	396	" 1654. "From the Tertudos".
Mellenix, John	15	354	Transported 1676.
Meller, John	20	195	" 1679.
Mellethorpe, Thomas	16	446	Service 1671. Of St. Mary's Co.
Mellington, Ruth	12	624	" 1670. Wife of Samuel.
Mellony, James	15	527	Transported 1678.
Mellor, John	7	505	" 1664.

NAME	Liber	Folio	REMARKS
Mells, Ann	7	80	Transported 1664.
Mellson, James	7	88	" 1650. Servant.
Melman, Michael	15	446	" 1677.
Meloy, James	15	527	" 1678.
Melson, John	16	530	" 1672 with Elizabeth.
Melton, John	5	181	" 1661. (12, fol. 284).
Melton, Thomas	10	575	Service 1667.
Melton, William	17	535	Immigrated 1673. Of Calvert Co.
Melvin, Elizabeth	6	89	Transported 1663.
Melvin, Richard	6	89	" 1663.
Mely, Pat.	15	553	" 1678.
Memox, Elizabeth	6	121	" 1661.
Mendum, Elizabeth	9	34	" 1665.
Menley, John	15	438	" Oct. 1677.
Menson, Elizabeth	7	83	" 1663.
Mercer, Thomas	18	152	" 1674.
Mercer, Thomas	15	433	" 1677.
Merchant, George	18	174	" 1674.
Merchant, Martha	7	474	" 1664.
Merchant, Samuel	15	437	" 1677.
Merchant, Thomas	15	501	" 1678.
Merchant, William	12	351	" from Virginia 1669. Servant. Of Dorchester Co.
Mercock, Thomas	15	540	Transported 1677.
Meredith, Elizabeth	9	99	" 1665.
Meredith, Elizabeth	18	94	" 1674.
Meredith, Lewis	18	149	" 1668.
Merian, Hester	15	430	" 1677.
Meribath, Mary	8	483	" from Virginia 1665.
Merichurch, Thomas	13	116	" 1671.
Meriday, Lewis	WC2	308	" 1678.
Meridith, John	7	524	" 1663.
Merkin, Richard	7	107	" 1662.
Merodit, Lewis	15	407	Service 1676.
Merrefield, Joane	15	322	Transported 1675.
Merrekin, Christian	6	82	Immigrated 1659.
Merrekin, Hugh	6	82	Transported 1659. (See Merrikin).
Merrekin, John, Jr.	6	82	" 1659.
Merrekin, John, Sr.	6	82	" 1659.
Merrekin, Joshua	6	82	" 1659.
Merrekin, Mary	6	82	" 1659.
Merrekin, William	6	82	" 1659.
Merrewether, John	9	434	Immigrated prior to 1666. Of Charles County.
Merrick, Julian	15	318	Immigrated 1674. Of Virginia.
Merriday, John	15	429	Transported 1674.
Merriday, Love	4	553	" 1661.
Merridith, Ab.	6	89	" prior to 1663.
Merridith, Richard	4	565	" 1660.
Merrikin, Hugh	10	217	Of Anne Arundel Co. Son of John by his wife, Christian, 1666. (See Merrekin).

NAME	Liber	Folio	REMARKS
Merrill, William	11	373	Transported 1668. Servant. (14, fol. 424).
Merritt, Mary	15	430	Transported 1677.
Merritt, Ruth	15	430	" 1677.
Merritt, William	15	402	Service 1676. And Jone, his wife.
Merry, Ann	6	37	Transported 1663.
Merry, John	18	4	" 1674.
Merrydeth, Lewis	WC2	67	Service 1679. Of St. Mary's Co.
Merryman, John	15	448	Transported 1677.
Merryman, John	WC2	108	" 1679.
Merryman, William	6	214	" 1663.
Merryweather, Thomas	11	307	" 1668. Servant.
Mersh, Thomas	4	63	" 1652-9.
Mertimore, Joice	7	84	" 1663.
Merty, Stephen	17	9	Immigrated 1672. Of St. Mary's Co.
Mery, Peter	WC2	57	Transported 1678. (15, fol. 554).
Mesenger, Elizabeth	15	535	" 1678.
Messar, Thomas	WC2	315,341	Service 1680. Of St. Mary's Co.
Messinger, Abraham	5	320	Transported 1663.
Metcalf, Alexander	15	442	" 1677.
Metcalf, Allen	WC2	183-184, 195	" 1680.
Metcalf, Gilbert	1	24	" 1641.
Metcalf, John	3	77	Immigrated 1635.
Metcalf, John, Gent.	ABH	206	Cousin to Antho. Metcalf, decd. 1651.
Metcalf, Rachel	4	207	Transported prior to 1659.
Metcalf, William	ABH	84	Immigrated 1640. Of Isle of Kent.
Metcalfe, Gilbert	ABH	59	Transported 1641.
Metcalfe, Mr. John	ABH	50	Immigrated July 1635. (claims land).
Metcalfe, Thomas	WC2	21	Transported 1679.
Metchell, Rachel	7	491	" 1664.
Metford, Bulmer	10	429	Immigrated 1664.
Metford, Fortune	10	429	Transported 1664. Wife of Bulmer.
Married Marmaduke Simm, 1669. (12, fol. 204).			
Metford, Thomas	10	429	Transported 1664. Son of Bulmer.
Metston, Will.	15	445	" 1677.
Mettcalfe, Robert	10	231	" 1666.
Mettin, Thomas	ABH	239	" 1651. Servant.
Mew, Ann	12	194	" 1668 with her child.
Mewell, Edward	15	380	" 1676.
Meycock, Seabright	16	418	Service 1671.
Meys, Lawrence	12	517	Transported 1670.
Mezzitt, Adam	WC2	129	" 1679.
Micale, Richard	Q	431	" 1658.
Michaell, Elizabeth	11	348	" 1668.
Michaell, William	11	500	Service 1667.
Michaellson, Chance	9	488	Transported 1665.
Michaellson, Clement	Q	63	Immigrated 1658.
Miche, William	17	601	" 1670.
Michelder, Alexander	16	304	" from Virginia 1671.

NAME	Liber	Folio	REMARKS
Michell, Humphrey	6	17	Transported 1663.
Michell, John	1	130	" 1641. Servant.
Michell, Thomas	ABH	48	Immigrated 1648 with wife and two children. (3, fol. 26).
Michemore, John	16	447	Transported 1671.
Mickam, James	7	467	" 1652.
Mickin, Richard	12	192	" 1668.
Mickson, William	12	269	" 1669.
Midcalfe, Margaret	18	306	" 1675.
Middingworth, Alice	15	353	" 1674.
Middleford, Thomas	6	48	" 1662.
Middleton, Alice	5	256	" 1663.
Middleton, Ann	18	291	" 1674.
Middleton, Charles	1	121	" 1633.
Middleton, Francis	16	78	" 1670.
Middleton, George	7	62	" 1661.
Middleton, John	16	537	" from Virginia 1671.
Middleton, Richard	5	529	" 1661.
Middleton, Robert	16	411	" 1671.
Middleton, Sarah	4	14	" 1655. Servant.
Middleton, Thomas	Q	441	" 1651.
Middleton, Thomas	9	468	" 1665.
Middleton, William	5	127	" 1662.
Middleton, William	8	482	" 1665.
Midford, Anthony	6	124	" 1663.
Midget, Richard	13	114	" 1670.
Midgley, Thomas	15	311	Service 1675. Of Calvert Co.
Midleton, Anne	WC2	167,169	Transported 1679.
Midleton, Elizabeth	7	80	" 1664.
Midleton, Francis	15	376	" 1676.
Midleton, John	15	516	" 1676.
Midlton, Charles	ABH	98	" 1633. Servant.
Midsley, Thomas	17	396	" 1669.
Mihiles, Roger	16	40	" 1670.
Miket, Alexander	16	79	" 1670.
Milborns, Leonard	18	306	" 1675.
Mildhall (als. Marshall), Edward	15	455	" 1678.
Mildmay, John	16	112	" 1671.
Miles, Andrew	6	134	" 1660.
Miles, Elizabeth	16	135	" 1671.
Miles, Francis	17	531	" 1673 with wife and children. (18, fol. 169).
Miles, George	16	507	Transported 1671.
Miles, Henry	17	123,382	" 1672.
Miles, Henry	WC2	79	" his wife, Winifred, from Virginia 1679. Of Somerset Co.
Miles, Humphrey	16	540	Transported 1671.
Miles, James	17	531	" 1673. Son of Francis.
Miles, Joane	12	554	" 1670.
Miles, John	17	489	" 1663.

NAME	Liber	Folio	REMARKS
Miles, John	ABH	232	Transported 1651. Son of Nicholas.
Miles, John	12	507	" 1668.
Miles, John	13	64	Immigrated 1670. Of Dorchester County.
Miles, John	16	402	Transported 1671.
Miles, John	17	531	" 1673. Son of Francis. (18, fol. 169).
Miles, John	WC2	352	Transported 1680.
Miles, Katherine	17	531	" 1673. Wife of Francis. (18, fol. 169).
Miles, Mary	15	405	Service 1676.
Miles, Morris	11	186	" 1667. Of St. Mary's Co.
Miles, Nicholas	ABH	232	Immigrated 1651.
Miles, Peter	ABH	232	Transported 1651. Son of Nicholas.
Miles, Priscilla	17	531	" 1673. Daughter of Francis. (18, fol. 169).
Miles, Sarah	16	402	Transported 1671.
Miles, Susanna	16	167,169	" 1671.
Miles, Thomas	6	121	" 1662. (17, fol. 595).
Miles, Winifred	WC2	79	" 1679. Wife of Henry.
Milikine, Joane	4	551	" 1661.
Mill, Samuel	15	449	Immigrated 1677. Of Somerset Co.
Mill, William	ABH	276	Transported 1651. Servant.
Mill, William	Q	202	Immigrated prior to 1658.
Millaine, Robert	16	400	Transported 1671.
Millan, John	13	113	" 1670.
Millard, Symond	9	27	" 1665.
Millborne, John	15	430	" 1677.
Millbourne, William	15	545	Service 1670.
Miller, Ann	15	353	Transported 1676.
Miller, Chris.	15	430	" 1677.
Miller, Dorothy	10	390	" 1666.
Miller, Dorothy	11	1	" 1667. Wife of John.
Miller, Edward	6	123	" 1663.
Miller, Edward	WC2	255,340	" 1680.
Miller, Elizabeth	WC2	11,16	" 1679. Wife of Robert.
Miller, Elizabeth	WC2	11,16	" 1679. Daughter of Robert.
Miller, Francis Bouser	WC2	11,16	Transported 1679. Son of Robert.
Miller, John	5	489	" 1661.
Miller, John	5	557	" 1661. "A youth".
Miller, John	6	27	" 1663.
Miller, John	11	1	Immigrated 1667. (18, fol. 7).
Miller, John	15	353	Transported 1674. (18, fol. 152).
Miller, John	17	497	And Grace, his wife. Service 1673.
Miller, Joseph	12	601	Transported 1669.
Miller, Martha	6	62	" 1663.
Miller, Mathew	5	247	" 1662.
Miller, Michael	16	41	Immigrated 1670. Of Kent County. Married widow of Robt. Hood, prior to 1678. (15, fol. 506).
Miller, Richard	WC2	167,169	Transported 1679.

NAME	Liber	Folio	REMARKS
Miller, Robert	7	78	Transported 1652.
Miller, Robert	4	68	" 1659.
Miller, Robert	WC2	11,12,16	Immigrated 1679 with wife and 2 children. Of Somerset Co.
Miller, Samuel	WC2	167,169	Transported 1679.
Miller, Sarah	10	352	" 1666.
Miller, Thomas	Q	48	Servant 1658.
Miller, Thomas	5	221	Transported 1662.
Miller, Thomas	5	307	" 1663.
Miller, Thomas	7	80	" 1664.
Miller, Thomas	12	513	" 1669. (18,fol.131).
Miller, Thomas	16	411	" 1671. (17,fol.34).
Miller, Thomas	15	445	" 1678.
Milles, Margaret	4	590	" 1661.
Milles, Thomas	4	590	" 1661.
Milles, William	9	191	Immigrated prior to 1665. Of Kent County.
Millet, Oliver	12	205	Transported 1667.
Millett, John	9	488	Immigrated 1665.
Milliner, Thomas	5	253	Transported 1663.
Millington, Samuel	5	3	" 1661. (8,fol.501).
Millington, Oliver	12	477	" 1670.
Millis, John	4	53	" 1659.
Millis, John	10	598	" 1667.
Millner, John	12	584	" 1670. Servant.
Millner, John	15	598	" 1678-9.
Mills, Chris.	15	530	" 1677.
Mills, Humphrey	15	445	" 1678.
Mills, James	12	588	Immigrated 1670. Of Somerset Co. (18,fol.39).
Mills, John	7	528	Transported 1664.
Mills, John	12	211	" 1668. (13,fol.34).
Mills, John	WC2	380	" 1675-80. Servant.
Mills, Mary	Q	18	Servant 1657.
Mills, Mary	7	429	Transported 1664. (9,fol.52).
Mills, Peter	10	477	Married Mary, daughter of Jno. Shirclif, of St. Mary's Co., prior to 1667.
Mills, Richard	6	239	Transported 1663.
Mills, Susan	16	83	" 1670.
Mills, Thomas	12	477,498	" 1670.
Mills, Thomas	9	476	" prior to 1666.
Mills, William	9	329	Immigrated 1665. Of Anne Arundel County.
Mills, William	12	190	Transported 1668. Servant. (17,fol.41).
Millward, John	15	319	Immigrated 1675. Of Va. Tailor.
Milner, Godfrey	32	61	His Executors.
Milnes, Thomas	5	167	Transported 1660.
Milsop, Thomas	4	70	" 1659.
Milton, John	18	335	" 1675.
Milton, Robert	18	174	" 1674.

NAME	Liber	Folio	REMARKS
Mimmock, Mary	7	491	Transported 1664.
Mimthorp, Thomas	10	352	" 1666.
Minchin, Susan	9	343	" 1666.
Minedob, John	15	422	" 1664.
Mines, Robert	15	430,440	" 1677.
Miniard, John	15	322	" 1675.
Minnett, John	5	412	" 1658-63.
Minnhane, John	20	184	" from Ireland 1678.
Minnikee, John	7	87	" 1659.
Minns, Elizabeth	15	505	" 1678.
Minns, Thomas	ABH	66	" 1633.
Minor, Charles	ABH	151	" 1649. Servant.
Minor, Robert	17	510	" 1673.
Minor, Samuel	4	568	" 1661.
Minshall, Richard	WC2	199	" 1680.
Minster, John	9	448	" 1666.
Minter, John	10	527	" 1667. Servant.
Minterns, Charles	4	5	" 1659. Servant.
Minthorn, Richard	12	194	" 1668. Servant.
Minton, Richard	7	536	" 1661. (See Mynton).
Mirick, Richard	Q	239	" 1651-2.
Mirtleby, John	15	353	" 1674.
Mishow, William	17	416	" 1673.
Mishue, William	WC2	41,116, 256	Immigrated 1679. Of Dorchester Co. Married Sarah Newton.
Miskin, Frye	16	168	Immigrated 1670.
Mison, John	15	356	Transported 1675.
Mitchel, John	ABH	10	" 1641.
Mitchell, Elizabeth	5	167	" 1661.
Mitchell, George	6	347	" 1663.
Mitchell, George	9	229	Immigrated 1665.
Mitchell, Henry	Q	317	" 1658.
Mitchell, James	WC2	65	Transported 1679.
Mitchell, John	ABH	103	" 1641. Servant. (10, fol. 480).
Mitchell, John	8	478	Transported 1668. (16, fol. 512).
Mitchell, John	15	568	" 1679.
Mitchell, Margaret	6	347	" 1663.
Mitchell, Margaret	16	482	" 1670.
Mitchell, Mark	7	553	" 1663.
Mitchell, Mary	12	317	" 1669.
Mitchell, Mathew	WC2	16	" 1679.
Mitchell, Rachel	5	610	" 1659-63.
Mitchell, Richard	WC2	371,372	Immigrated 1680 with wife and son.
Mitchell, Thomas	9	460	" 1662.
Mitchell, Thomas	9	335	" 1666.
Mitchell, Thomas	15	549	Transported 1674. Servant. Of Virginia. (18, fol. 94).
Mitchell, William	3	112	Rights 1650.
Mitchell, William	15	454	Transported 1677.

NAME	Liber	Folio	REMARKS
Mitchell, William	6	294	Transported 1664. (8, fol. 88; 18, fol. 166, 174).
Mitchemore, John	16	447	Transported 1671.
Mitchew, Silvester	17	41	" 1668.
Mites, Henry	Q	440	Servant 1651.
Mithell, John	2	425	Transported 1640.
Mitten, John	15	436	" 1677.
Mitten, Mary	8	478	" 1665.
Mitting, Ann	16	532	" 1668-70.
Mixture, John	16	405	" 1671.
Moag, Margarett	WC2	282	" 1680.
Moate, Peter	15	430	" 1677.
Mockernis, Daniel	15	455	" 1678.
Mockney, John	16	115	" 1671.
Mocobery, William	12	333	" 1668. (See Mowbery).
Moderman, John	17	448	" 1673.
Moffatt, John	6	160	" 1663.
Mogomery, William	15	574	" 1678.
Moiskens, Peter	15	453	" 1675-7.
Molder, Robert	17	449	Service 1672.
Molesworth, Mary	15	530	Transported 1678.
Molins, William	4	5	" 1659.
Mollet, Abraham	9	105	" 1665.
Moloane, John	18	137	" 1674.
Molson, Thomas	9	282	" 1663.
Momford, Stephen	6	128	" 1659.
Monck, Hannah	17	422	Service 1672. Wife of John.
Monck, John	17	422	" 1672.
Mondiford, Francis	17	482	Immigrated 1669. Of St. Mary's Co.
Moneley, Ann	15	598	Transported 1678-9.
Monely, Mary	15	598	" 1678-9.
Money, David	15	537	" 1679.
Monford, Ann	15	533	" 1678.
Monford, Katherine	15	533	" 1678.
Monford, Katherine, Jr.	15	533	" 1678.
Monford, James	15	533	" 1678.
Monford, Thomas, Jr.	15	533	" 1678.
Monford, Thomas, Sr.	15	533	" 1678.
Mongomery, Ann	4	70	" 1659.
Monk, Edward	6	268	" 1662.
Monk, Thomas	11	374,572	" 1668.
Monke, Ann	10	556	" 1664-5.
Monke, Elizabeth	5	240	" 1662.
Monke, John	4	549	" 1661. Servant.
Monke, William	7	81	" 1660. (5, fol. 319).
Monkey, John	10	5	" 1665.
Monniley, Anne	WC2	211	" 1679. Servant.
Monniley, Susannah	WC2	211	" 1679. Servant.
Monnshot, John	18	118	" 1674.
Monoughan, Brian	15	565	" 1679.
Monroe, Andrew	ABH	276	" 1651. Servant.

NAME	Liber	Folio	REMARKS
Montford, Elizabeth	17	440	Transported 1668.
Moods, John	9	32	" 1656.
Moody, Rachel	16	40	" 1670.
Moolson, Samuel	15	507	Of Somerset Co. Married Rachel
Mason, alias Williams, prior to 1677.			
Moone, Arthur	17	123	Transported 1672.
Moone, Owen	16	503	" 1671.
Moone, Siles	18	334	" 1675.
Moor, Ann	ABH	324	" 1652-3. Daughter of Richard.
Moor, Henry	ABH	44	Servant 1649.
Moor, James	7	86	Transported 1661.
Moor, Jane	ABH	324	" 1652-3. Wife of Richard.
Moor, Mary	ABH	324	" 1652-3. Daughter of Richard.
Moor, Richard	ABH	312	Immigrated 1652.
Moor, Richard	15	527	Transported 1678.
Moor, Richard, Jr.	ABH	324	" 1652-3. Son of Richard.
Moor, Roger	ABH	324	Transported 1652-3. Son of Richard.
Moor, Temperance	ABH	312	Immigrated 1652. Daughter of Richard.
Moore, Alice	5	214	Transported 1660.
Moore, Ann	5	139	" 1662.
Moore, Ann	6	37	" 1663. Daughter of William.
Moore, Ann	15	550	Transported 1678-9.
Moore, Chris.	13	66	" 1669. Servant.
Moore, Daniel	5	73	" 1661. (11, fol. 500).
Moore, Dorothy	4	140	" 1657. Servant.
Moore, Dorothy	18	84	" 1674.
Moore, Elizabeth	5	252,412	" 1658-63. (6, fol. 125).
Moore, Elizabeth	13	121	" 1667. Wife of Thomas.
Moore, Elizabeth	15	395	" 1677.
Moore, Elizabeth	15	530	" 1678. Wife of John.
Moore, Elizabeth	15	530	" 1678. Daughter of John.
Moore, Frances	15	530	Transported 1678. Daughter of John.
Moore, Francis	5	246	Transported 1656. (15, fol. 406).
Moore, Francis	15	534	" 1678.
Moore, Hannah	15	446	" 1677.
Moore, Henry	ABH	50	" 1649. Servant. (3, fol. 15, 77; 4, fol. 186).
Moore, Hester	15	530	Transported 1678. Daughter of John.
Moore, James	WC2	382	Immigrated 1680. Of Calvert Co.
Moore, Jane	5	139	Transported 1662.
Moore, John	12	332	Immigrated 1669. Of Charles Co.
Moore, John	12	498	Transported 1670.

NAME	Liber	Folio	REMARKS
Moore, John	16	532	Transported 1668-70.
Moore, John	17	451,463	" 1673.
Moore, John	18	174,291	" 1674.
Moore, John	15	433	" 1677.
Moore, John	15	530	Immigrated 1678.
Moore, John	WC2	321	Service 1680.
Moore, John, Jr.	12	332	Transported 1669. Son of John.
Moore, Martin	9	450	" 1666.
Moore, Mary	5	139	" 1662.
Moore, Mary	12	332	" 1669. Wife of John.
Moore, Mary	12	332	" 1669. Daughter of John.
Moore, Mary	6	37	Transported 1663. Wife of William.
Moore, Mary	15	530	" 1678. Daughter of John.
Moore, Mathew	15	526	Transported 1678.
Moore, Richard, Jr.	5	139	" 1662.
Moore, Richard	9	35	" 1663.
Moore, Richard	12	243	" 1669. Brother to Roger.
Moore, Roger	5	139	" 1662.
Moore, Samuel	6	125	" 1663. (9, fol. 282).
Moore, Thomas	6	89	" 1663 by Rev. Jas. Thompson. (15, fol. 402).
Moore, Thomas	13	121	Immigrated 1667. Of St. Mary's Co.
Moore, Thomas	WC2	331	Transported 1676.
Moore, Thomas	15	504	" 1678.
Moore, Thomas	15	559	" 1679.
Moore, Timothy	5	139	" 1662.
Moore, William	6	268	" 1662.
Moore, William	6	37	Immigrated 1663.
Moorehead, Samuel	6	97	Transported 1662.
Moortast, Mary	6	95	" 1662.
Moory, Elizabeth	5	89	" 1661.
Mooter, John	16	70	" 1668.
Mopted, Philip	4	63	" 1658.
Moraine, Dennis	WC2	184	" 1680. Servant.
Morbeck, Joyce	17	440	" 1673.
Morby, Stephen	12	386	" 1669.
Morcy, Thomas	15	446	" 1677.
Mordah, Robert	17	30	Service 1672.
Morecroft, John, Gent.	19	409	Uncle of Jonathan Squire, dec'd. 1676. (15, fol. 1).
More, Allen	17	503	Immigrated 1666.
More, Daniel	5	255	Transported 1663.
More, Edward	17	26,354	" 1672.
More, Elizabeth	15	544	" 1676.
More, Henry	16	437	" 1671.
More, James	7	463	" 1657.
More, John	17	553	" 1667.
More, John	16	20	Immigrated with Ann, his wife, 1670. Of Talbot Co. Shoemaker.

NAME	Liber	Folio	REMARKS
More, John	16	20	Transported 1670. Son of John.
More, John	17	356	Immigrated 1672 with wife and daughter. Of Somerset Co.
More, Martin	17	381	Immigrated 1672, with wife and daughter.
More, Robert	9	217	Transported 1665.
More, William	9	216	" 1665. (17, fol. 24).
Morebath, Mary	10	310	Immigrated Jan. 1665. Of Chester River.
Moreland, Christopher	1	19	Transported 1637.
Moreland, Christopher	ABH	72	" 1639. Servant. (1, fol. 50).
Morely, John	15	502	Service 1678.
Moreman, Alice	1	18	Transported 1637.
Moreman, Alice	1	134	License to marry Francis Gray, Nov. 26, 1638.
Mores, Thomas	Q	71	Transported 1652-3.
Morewint, John	15	428	Immigrated 1677 with Eliz., his wife.
Morewood, Ann	12	477	Transported 1670.
Morey, Nicholas	15	535	" 1678.
Morfey, Edmond	17	451	" 1673.
Morffet, William	WC2	101	" 1679.
Morfit, John	6	90	" 1663.
Morgan	1	18	" 1637.
Morgan, Abraham	4	17	" 1658. Servant.
Morgan, Abraham	4	554	Immigrated 1661 with wife, 2 children and 1 servant.
Morgan, Abraham	16	86	Transported 1670.
Morgan, Alice	10	469	" 1667. Wife of William.
Morgan, Alice	12	515	Service 1669. Wife of Jarvis.
Morgan, Andrew	15	455	Transported 1678.
Morgan, Ann	4	17	" 1658. Servant.
Morgan, Ann	10	5	" 1665.
Morgan, Barbara	19	603	Daughter and co-heir of Hy. Morgan, appears as wife of John Rousby, 1677.
Morgan, Bennitt	7	558	Transported 1665.
Morgan, Cicily	17	572	" 1672.
Morgan, David	7	554	" 1665.
Morgan, Edmund	15	565	" 1679.
Morgan, Elizabeth	4	198,533	" 1659. Servant.
Morgan, Elizabeth	11	344	" 1668. (18, fol. 27).
Morgan, Elizabeth	15	543	" 1678.
Morgan, Evan	15	322	" 1675.
Morgan, Even	5	87	" 1649-62.
Morgan, Frances	1	18	" 1637.
Morgan, Giles	15	443	" 1669.
Morgan, Henry	ABH	89	" 1635. Servant.
Morgan, Henry	1	95	" 1635-40.
Morgan, Henry	16	167	Immigrated 1670. Of Somerset Co.
Morgan, Hoell	1	19	Transported 1638.

NAME	Liber	Folio	REMARKS
Morgan, Humphrey	15	380	Transported 1676.
Morgan, James	5	228	" 1662.
Morgan, James	6	294	" 1664.
Morgan, James	8	259	" 1665.
Morgan, James	17	440	" 1673.
Morgan, James	WC2	108	" 1679.
Morgan, James	WC2	254,340-341	" 1680.
Morgan, Jarvis	5	367	" 1649. (11,fol.168).
Morgan, Jenkin	7	509	Immigrated 1661 with wife and five children.
Morgan, Jenkin	9	353	Transported 1666.
Morgan, John	4	63	" 1652-9.
Morgan, John	Q	66	" 1653.
Morgan, John	6	63,235	" 1658-63.
Morgan, John	8	501	Immigrated 1665.
Morgan, John	9	400	Transported 1666.
Morgan, John	17	34	" 1672.
Morgan, John	18	4	" 1674.
Morgan, John	15	431	" 1677.
Morgan, John	WC2	78	Service 1679.
Morgan, John, Jr.	Q	357	Gift from Lord Baltimore.
Morgan, Katherine	8	501	Transported 1665. Wife of John.
Morgan, Margaret	18	137	" 1674.
Morgan, Mary	4	17	" 1658. Servant.
Morgan, Mary	9	216	" 1665.
Morgan, Mary	16	435	" 1671.
Morgan, Mary	15	530	" 1678.
Morgan, Mathias	7	523	Of City of Bristol, Mer. Acquires 500 acres, "Morgans Reserve", on Choptank River.
Morgan, Philip	ABH	142	Immigrated 1651. Of Patuxent River.
Morgan, Rice	WC2	309	Transported 1678.
Morgan, Robert	5	411	" 1663.
Morgan, Robert	7	558	" 1665.
Morgan, Robert	15	505	" 1678.
Morgan, Robert	WC2	395	" 1680. Servant.
Morgan, Roger	1	26	" 1633.
Morgan, Roger	9	313	" 1665.
Morgan, Rowland	ABH	24	Servant 1646.
Morgan, Rowland	2	512	Transported about 1649. Servant.
Morgan, Rowland	5	359	" 1663.
Morgan, Samuel	5	238	" 1662.
Morgan, Samuel	18	166	" 1674.
Morgan, Thomas	6	63	" 1658-63.
Morgan, Thomas	7	491	" 1664. (9,fol.35).
Morgan, Thomas	16	86	" 1670.
Morgan, Thomas	16	297	" 1671.
Morgan, William	6	95	" 1655.
Morgan, William	10	168	" 1660.
Morgan, William	5	56	" 1661.
Morgan, William	9	115	Immigrated 1665.

NAME	Liber	Folio	REMARKS
Morgan, William	10	469	Transported 1667.
Morgan, William	12	478	" 1670. (17, fol. 63).
Morgan, William	15	531	" 1678.
Morgan, William	WC2	288	Rights 1680. Of Bristol.
Morgane, Blanch	9	330	Transported 1665.
Morganson, Daniel	WC2	253,398	" 1680.
Morgen, Jenken	15	516	" 1675.
Morgin, Edward	15	565	" 1679.
Morhed, And.	15	433	" 1677.
Morley, Anthony	13	113	" 1670.
Morley, Augustine	7	464	" 1662.
Morley, Francis	9	155	Immigrated 1663. Of Talbot Co.
Morley, Joseph	5	532	" 1661.
Morley, Thomas	5	416	Transported 1663.
Morley, Thomas	17	531	" 1673 with Ann, his wife.
Morley, Walter	ABH	66	Transported 1638. (1, fol. 38).
Morlidge, Robert	18	38	" 1673.
Morly, Mr. ---	1	18	Immigrated 1638.
Morne, Elizabeth	5	253	Transported 1663.
Morphew, James	2	425	" 1648.
Morra, Andrew	5	2	" 1658-9.
Morrell, Christopher	17	440	" 1673.
Morrell, George	5	536	" 1663.
Morrice, Ellen	9	356	" 1666. Wife of Richard.
Morrice, Jacob	16	637	Immigrated 1672. Of St. Mary's Co.
Morrice, James	15	335	Transported 1675. Servant.
Morrice, John	16	95	Immigrated 1665, with Elizabeth, his wife.
Morrice, John	12	415	Transported 1669.
Morrice, Philip	12	460	" 1669.
Morrice, Richard	9	356	" 1666.
Morrice, Richard	16	126	" 1671.
Morrice, Robert	Q	462	Immigrated 1658. Of London, Mariner.
Morrice, Thomas	5	557	Transported 1665.
Morris, Ann	7	553	Immigrated 1665. Wife of Richard.
Morris, Ann	9	400	Transported 1666.
Morris, Ann	11	338,378	" 1668. (11, fol. 569; 12, fol. 262).
Morris, Ann	12	356	Transported 1669.
Morris, Cornelius	16	165	Immigrated 1670 with Ann, his wife. Of Somerset Co.
Morris, Elizabeth	15	397	Transported 1676.
Morris, Elizabeth	WC2	77	" 1679. Daughter of William.
Morris, Francis	15	560	Transported 1678.
Morris, George	6	294	" 1664.
Morris, Griffin	18	166	" 1674.
Morris, Griffin	WC2	320	" 1680. Servant.
Morris, Hannah	12	284	Service 1668.

NAME	Liber	Folio	REMARKS
Morris, Henry	4	139	Transported 1651. Servant.
Morris, Jacob	12	472	" 1670.
Morris, Jane	15	499	" 1677.
Morris, Jenkin	7	520	" 1664.
Morris, Jenkin	16	535	" from Virginia 1671. (17, fol. 382).
Morris, John	4	1	Immigrated prior to 1658.
Morris, John	7	506	Transported 1662.
Morris, John	12	216	" 1668.
Morris, John	12	472	" 1670.
Morris, Katherine	15	549	" 1678.
Morris, Mary	15	362	" 1676.
Morris, Mary	WC2	77	" 1679. Daughter of William.
Morris, Mary	WC2	201	Transported 1680. Servant.
Morris, Philip	18	39	Service 1674. (15, fol. 422).
Morris, Rebecca	WC2	77	Transported 1679. Wife of William.
Morris, Rebecca	WC2	77	" 1679. Daughter of William.
Morris, Richard	2	516	Transported 1648. Servant.
Morris, Richard	ABH	25	Servant 1648.
Morris, Richard	4	214	Immigrated 1659.
Morris, Richard	7	553	" 1665.
Morris, Richard	12	209,262	Transported 1668.
Morris, Mr. Robert	4	19	Special Warrant from Lord Baltimore, 1658.
Morris, Ruthro	11	378	Transported 1668.
Morris, Samuel	8	502	" 1665.
Morris, Samuel	WC2	77	" 1679. Son of William.
Morris, Sarah	9	321	Service 1666.
Morris, Sarah	WC2	77	Transported 1679. Daughter of William.
Morris, Thomas	1	62	Transported 1635-36.
Morris, Thomas	1	128	" 1637-40.
Morris, Thomas	ABH	78	" 1635-40.
Morris, Thomas	ABH	101	" 1637-40. Servant.
Morris, Thomas	Q	17	" 1652.
Morris, Thomas	9	333	" 1666.
Morris, Thomas	15	553	" 1678.
Morris, William	17	451	" 1673.
Morris, William	WC2	77	Immigrated with wife, five children and two servants, 1679. Of Somerset County.
Morrise, Ann	ABH	12	Servant 1639.
Morrison, Robert	18	152	Transported 1674.
Morse, Henry	ABH	37	Servant 1643.
Morsell, Joseph	16	522	Transported 1672.
Morsey, William	15	438	" 1677.
Mortemore, George	6	80	" 1660.
Mortemore, Henry	6	133	" 1652.
Morth, John	3	173	" 1655.
Morthy, Teage	WC2	108	" 1679.

NAME	Liber	Folio	REMARKS
Morton, Gregory	16	79	Transported 1670.
Mose, Samuel	WC2	23	" 1679. Servant.
Mosely, Ann	6	171	" 1663.
Mosely, Thomas	11	379	" 1668. (13,fol.116).
Moser, Ann	15	524	" 1678.
Moser, William	12	216	" 1668.
Mosley, Francis	15	501	" 1678.
Mosley, James	12	355	" 1669.
Mosley, Thomas	17	556	Service 1673. Of St. Mary's Co.
Moss, John	WC2	198,200	" 1680.
Moss, Richard	6	105	Transported 1649.
Mosse, Elizabeth	9	488	" 1665.
Mosse, John	4	590	" 1660-1.
Mosse, John	7	526	" 1664.
Mosse, Margery	18	177	" 1674.
Mosse, Margery	WC2	308	" 1678.
Mosse, Mary	18	280	" 1675.
Mosse, Robert	Q	64	Immigrated 1658.
Mosse, Thomas	ABH	61	Transported 1633-41. (1,fol.27).
Mosse, William	15	370	" 1676.
Mossett, William	10	469	" 1667.
Mosten, Robert	12	314	" 1669.
Motley, Mary	15	505	" 1678.
Motley, Robert	18	174	" 1674.
Mott, Jenkin	6	159	" 1658.
Mott, Mary	7	462	" 1663.
Mott, Thomas	WC2	406	" 1677. (15,fol.454).
Mottee, Torlow	17	571	" 1673.
Mottershead, Zachary	ABH	244	" 1635.
Moudy, John	WC2	253	" 1679.
Mould, John	9	432	Immigrated 1660.
Mould, John	5	516	Transported 1663.
Mould, Martin	6	97	" 1657.
Mouldsey, Joseph	10	390	" 1666.
Moulins, James	ABH	99	" 1637. Servant. (1, fol. 124).
Moulins, James	1	18	Transported 1638.
Moulston, Thomas	17	567	And Ann, his wife. Service 1671.
Moulton, John	5	261	Transported 1660.
Mouman, Alice	ABH	244	" 1637.
Moumford, John	9	433	" 1660.
Moumsfor, Peter	8	130	Immigrated 1664, with wife.
Mounce, Christopher	15	405,434	" 1677.
Moundee, Alexander	9	313	Transported 1665.
Mount, Richard	8	486	" 1664.
Mountague, Abigael	1	166	" 1650. Servant.
Mountague, Cornelius	17	356	Service 1672.
Mountague, Henry	15	358	Transported 1675.
Mountague, Jane	8	499	" 1659.
Mountague, Jeane	6	212	" 1663.
Mountague, Katherine	15	358	" 1675.

NAME	Liber	Folio	REMARKS
Mountague, William	16	479	Immigrated Oct. 1667. Of Talbot Co.
Mountegne, Stephen	9	334	Transported 1666.
Mountgomery, Anne	Q	62	" 1658.
Mountgoomery, Edmond	WC2	16	" 1677.
Mountney, Alexander	17	67	Immigrated 1661.
Mounts, Hector	15	453	Transported 1675-7.
Mourice, Barborough	5	218	" 1662.
Mourton, Francis	20	185	" 1679.
Mouse, William	Q	17	" 1656.
Moustine, Thomas	16	536	And Ann, his wife. Service 1671.
Mouth, John	Q	32	Servant, Feb. 1652.
Mowbery, William	12	333	Transported 1668.
Mowedonahowe, Teage	4	555	" 1661.
Mowson, Charles	16	482	" 1670-1.
Moy, Daniel	WC2	282	Son of Richard.
Moy, Elizabeth	9	104	Transported 1665. Wife of Richard.
Moy, Elizabeth	9	104	" 1665. Daughter of Richard.
Moy, James	18	331	Transported 1675.
Moy, Richard	9	104	Immigrated 1665.
Moy, Richard	WC2	282	Deceased 1680.
Moy, Roger	1	134	License to marry Ann Phillipson, Nov. 24, 1638.
Moyer, Allen	10	5	Transported 1665.
Moykey, Thomas	WC2	114	" 1680. Servant.
Mubrony, Peter	20	184	" from Ireland 1678.
Muckell, Archibald	4	55	" 1659.
Muckellson, Warnell	9	216	" 1665.
Mudbury, John	Q	183	Servant prior to 1658.
Mudd, Thomas	WC2	402	Immigrated 1680. Of St. Mary's Co.
Muddeford, Maudlen	7	464	Transported 1662.
Muddihey, Daniel	WC2	287	" 1680.
Muduh, Dorothy	18	95	" 1674.
Muen, John	4	584	" 1661.
Muffet, William	Q	62	" 1654-7.
Muffett, William	5	87	" 1649.
Muffetts, John	18	314	Service 1668.
Mugenburgh, Martin	9	488	Transported 1665.
Mugg, Andrew	ABH	411	" 1651. Servant.
Muhelder, Alexander	16	304	Immigrated from Virginia 1671. Of Somerset County.
Mulhaw, John	16	370	Transported 1671.
Mullard, Thomas	5	89,488	" 1660.
Mullens, Francis	6	142	" 1655.
Mullens, Peter	7	87	" 1661.
Mullican, Jane	18	152	" 1674.
Mullick, Lawrence	7	470	" 1664.
Mullika, Andreas	4	552	" 1661.
Mullikin, James	7	498	" 1660. Married widow of Jno. Damaull, prior to 1658.
Mullikin, Patrick	4	551	Immigrated prior to 1661.

NAME	Liber	Folio	REMARKS
Mullin, Hugh	15	553	Transported 1678.
Mullins, Ann	5	516	" 1663.
Mullins, Eleanor	12	496	" 1670.
Mullrane, Alexander	8	204	" 1665. (7, fol. 553).
Mullreane, Cornelius	15	537	" 1665.
Mullreane, Mary	15	537	Service 1675. Wife of Cornelius.
Mulman, Thomas	15	443	Transported 1677.
Mulrean, Daniel	20	184	" from Virginia 1678.
Mulrean, Helena	20	184	" from Ireland 1678.
Mumby, William	8	478	" 1665.
Mumford, Edward	11	337,440	" 1667.
Muncee, Jeremiah	7	492	" 1664.
Mund, Martha	11	235	" 1667.
Munday, Elizabeth	12	189	" 1668.
Munday, Jane	11	571	" 1668.
Munday, Thomas	ABH	1	Immigrated 1646 with wife and child. (2, fol. 194).
Munford, Thomas	5	88	Transported 1662.
Munn, Mathew	7	569	" 1663.
Munns, Thomas	1	38	" 1633.
Munokin, John	15	430	" 1677.
Munrow, Alexander	5	367	" 1649.
Munrow, Andrew	6	63	" 1658-63.
Mun Tanych, John	8	381	" 1665.
Muphee, Owen	17	576	" 1673.
Murdake, Robert	9	99	" 1665.
Murfe, Daniel	17	635	" 1671.
Murfitt, Thomas	WC2	21	" 1679.
Murfy, Dennis	16	371	" 1671.
Murphew, James	ABH	9	" 1648.
Murphy, Abraham	18	152	" 1674.
Murphy, Bryan	15	565	" 1679.
Murphy, Daniel	15	527	" 1678.
Murphy, Daniel	WC2	128	" 1679.
Murphy, Daniel	WC2	287	" 1680.
Murphy, Dennis	WC2	128	" 1679.
Murphy, Edmund	15	527	" 1678.
Murphy, Henry	15	553	" 1678.
Murphy, Howard	15	549	" 1678.
Murphy, John	15	446	" 1677.
Murphy, John, Jr.	15	600	" 1678.
Murphy, John, Sr.	15	600	" 1678.
Murphy, Jone	15	553	" 1678.
Murphy, Margaret	15	527	" 1678.
Murphy, Mortagh	20	184	" from Ireland 1678.
Murphy, Sarah	18	137	" 1674.
Murphye, Timothy	WC2	106	" 1679.
Murray, Walte	15	416	" 1677.
Murre, John	Q	208	" 1658.
Murrell, George	Q	67	Demand for land on Severn 1658.
Murrell, Gregory	ABH	175	Immigrated 1650.

NAME	Liber	Folio	REMARKS
Murrey, John	4	555	Transported 1661.
Murrow, Angwith	16	629	" 1672.
Murrowe, William	5	123	" 1662.
Murry, Alice	WC2	213,214	" 1671-73.
Murry, James	15	540	" 1676.
Murtey, John	WC2	106	" 1679.
Murty, Stephen	12	496	" 1670.
Murty, Timothy	15	446	" 1677.
Muschamp, Edmond	9	321	" 1665.
Muschamp, John	14	145	" 1665. (17, fol. 349).
Muscoade, Jone	17	492	" 1662. Wife of John.
Musgrove, Anthony	15	322	" 1675.
Musgrove, Charles	18	160	" 1674.
Musgrove, Jane	9	104	" 1665.
Mustain, John	6	209	" 1663.
Musterd, John	18	152	" 1674.
Muthoda, Alexander	ABH	202	" 1650-1. Servant.
Mutton, Henry	15	454	" 1677.
Muxley, William	17	575	Service 1673. Of Calvert County.
Muxan, Ann	9	106	Transported 1665.
Myles, Tobias	5	2	Immigrated 1661.
Mynard, Alice	WC2	18,99	Transported 1679. Daughter of Samuel.
Mynard, Elizabeth	WC2	18,99	Transported 1679. Wife of Samuel.
Mynard, Samuel	WC2	18,99	Immigrated 1679 with wife and daughter.
Mynton, Richard	7	536	Transported 1661.
Mythee, John	ABH	237	" 1651. Servant.
N---, Ann	5	484	" 1661.
N---, Edmund	5	305	" 1663.
N---, Edward	5	484	" 1662.
N---, Katherine	5	484	" 1662.
N---, Martha	5	358	" 1663.
Nabbs, George	6	96	" 1657.
Nabbs, Thomas	1	68	Immigrated 1637 with wife. (2, fol. 394).
Nabbs, Mrs. Thomas	1	68	Transported 1637.
Nabbs, William	1	18	" 1637. Aged near 60 years.
Nabbs, Mrs. William	1	18	Transported 1637. Aged near 60 years.
Nabs, Johana	15	598	Transported 1678-9.
Nadgle, Nicholas	15	314	" 1675.
Naile, Jane	15	322	" 1674.
Naillor, George	15	573	" 1668.
Nale, Hugh	4	214	Immigrated 1659.
Nalour, Abraham	17	36	Transported 1672.
Nanfen, William	ABH	91,237	" 1637.
Napenis, John	9	17	" 1665.
Napier, Valentine	7	558	Special warrant for 100 acres, 1665.
Napkin, Ann	5	260	Transported 1660.

NAME	Liber	Folio	REMARKS
Napper, Lucy	6	209	Transported 1663.
Napper, Rowland	9	105	" 1665.
Narrison, Lancelot	12	415	" 1669.
Nary, Elizabeth	18	137	" 1674.
Nash, Alexander	9	270	" 1665.
Nash, Alice	7	560	" 1665.
Nash, Anne	WC2	215	Relict of Richard 1680.
Nash, Edward	13	111	Transported 1667.
Nash, Edward	11	482	" 1668. (17, fol. 609).
Nash, Francis	Q	74	" 1650.
Nash, Hugh	1	19	" 1637.
Nash, Hugh	4	623	" 1657-8.
Nash, Hugh	5	343	" 1663.
Nash, Hugh	9	489	" 1665.
Nash, Jeremy	16	170	" 1671.
Nash, John	18	150	" 1674.
Nash, Richard	17	26,68	" 1672.
Nash, Richard	WC2	215	Husband of Anne. Deceased 1677-80.
Natt, Richard	4	72	Transported 1658.
Natts, William	ABH	9	" 1648.
Naufin, William	1	102	Immigrated 1637.
Naunry, Thomas	20	184	Transported 1678 from Ireland.
Naylor, Christopher	6	129	" 1659.
Nayworth, Peter	10	558	" 1667.
Neady, George	12	513	" 1669.
Neagle, Peter	17	51	" 1672.
Neal, Charles	10	475	" 1667.
Neale, Agnes	1	166	" 1650. Servant.
Neale, Alexander	5	203	" 1662.
Neale, Alexander	6	62	" 1663.
Neale, Andrew	9	437	" 1664.
Neale, Ann Maria	6	209	" 1663 by Capt. Neale.
Neale, Anthony	6	209	" 1663.
Neale, Brian	15	353	" 1674.
Neale, Caleb	5	56	" 1660.
Neale, Coles	9	432	" 1660. Servant.
Neale, Dorothy	6	209	" 1663.
Neale, Eleanor	18	319	Immigrated 1674 with two children. Of Anne Arundel County.
Neale, Francis	7	371	Transported 1661. Servant. (17, fol. 537).
Neale, Helena	WC2	128	Transported 1679.
Neale, Henrietta Mary	6	209	" 1663.
Neale, Henry	5	181	" 1661. (10, fol. 477).
Neale, Honora	20	184	" 1678.
Neale, Jacob	17	411	" 1673.
Neale, Jacob	18	319	" 1674. Son of Eleanor.
Neale, James	1	112-114	Immigrated 1635.
Neale, James	6	84	Transported 1654.
Neale, James	5	181	" 1661.
Neale, James, Capt.	5	245	Immigrated 1638-43. Married

NAME	Liber	Folio	REMARKS

daughter and heiress of Benj. Gill prior to 1660. (4, fol. 543; 14, fol. 145).

NAME	Liber	Folio	REMARKS
Neale, James, Gent.	ABH	95	Immigrated 1635.
Neale, James, Gent.	16	3	Father of Dorothy, wife of Roger Brooke, 1670. Of Charles County.
Neale, James, Jr.	6	209	Transported 1663.
Neale, Jonathan	6	122	Immigrated 1650.
Neale, Judith	16	354	Transported 1671.
Neale, Mary	17	411	" 1673.
Neale, Mary	15	318	" 1675.
Neale, Susan	17	411	" 1673.
Neale, Susanna	18	319	" 1674. Daughter of Eleanor.
Neale, Thomas	18	94	Transported 1674.
Neale, William	6	159	" 1652.
Neale, William	6	105	" 1654.
Neales, William	5	90	" 1651.
Nealett, Margaret	6	97	" 1654.
Neares, William	5	529	" 1656.
Neat, Morrice	15	527	" 1678.
Neave, Fort	6	307	" 1664. (5, fol. 241).
Neave, Robert	5	55,467	" 1653. Servant.
Neave, Robert	20	158	Married widow of Wm. Davis of Kent Co. prior to 1679.
Nebbs, Johannah	WC2	211	Transported 1679. Servant.
Neckolin, Josias	5	367	" 1649.
Nedham, Elizabeth	15	452	" 1678.
Nedham, Robert	11	307	" 1668. Servant.
Neeare, Felleme	Q	33	" 1655.
Needan, Edmund	15	526	" 1678.
Needes, John	WC2	380	" 1675-80. Servant.
Needham, Christopher	ABH	186	Immigrated 1651. And Wife.
Needham, Dorothy	6	31	Transported 1659. Daughter of Henry.
Needham, Edward	ABH	186	Transported 1651. Son of Christopher.
Needham, Henry	6	31	Immigrated 1659, and died prior to 1663, leaving a widow, Patience, who married 2ndly --- Hawker.
Needham, Margaret	6	31	Transported 1659. Daughter of Henry.
Needham, Martha	6	31	Transported 1659. Daughter of Henry.
Needham, Thomas	ABH	186	Transported 1651. Son of Christopher.
Needham, William	7	79	Transported 1663.
Needham, William	12	498	" 1670.
Needs, William	18	35	" 1672.
Neels, Thomas	4	140	" 1657. Servant.
Neelso (?), John	WC2	381	" 1675-80. Servant.
Neeyes, Francis	9	38	" 1665.
Negloglaghean, Sarah	Q	28	" 1653.
Negro, Phillis	ABH	9	" 1648.

NAME	Liber	Folio	REMARKS
Negroe, Dina	11	235	Transported prior to 1637.
Negroes, Robt. Francis			
and Maria	6	299	Transported 1664.
Negw, Phillis	2	425	" 1648.
Nehart, Mary	4	17	" 1658. Servant.
Neife, Robert	6	48	Immigrated prior to 1663.
Neill, William	4	65	Transported 1652.
Nell, Ralph	16	372	Immigrated 1671. Of Baltimore Co.
Nelly, John	Q	29	Servant 1658.
Nelson, Alice	18	174	Transported 1674.
Nelson, Ambrose	15	439	Service 1677. Of Anne Arundel Co.
Nelson, Elizabeth	17	396	Transported 1671.
Nelson, Henry	17	395	" 1672.
Nelson, Jane	17	571	" 1673.
Nelson, John	9	25	Immigrated prior to 1665. Of Monokin, River.
Nelson, John	17	69	Transported 1672.
Nelson, Richard	WC2	135	" 1679. Servant.
Nelson, Thomas	16	625	" 1663.
Nelson, Thomas	7	527	" 1664.
Nelson, Thomas	16	437	" 1671.
Nerfolke, John	15	455	" 1678.
Nero, Peter	WC2	96	" 1679.
Nesbott, Ellen	10	11	" 1666.
Nesbott, Edward	10	11	" 1666.
Nesham, Benjamin	WC2	39,140, 141	Service 1679. Of St. Mary's Co.
Neterton, Richard	6	26	Transported 1660-3.
Netherington, Richard	9	50	Immigrated 1665.
Netherly, Robert	11	162	Transported 1667. Servant.
Netherton, John	7	88	" 1650.
Netherton, Richard	10	340	" 1666. (16,fol.27).
Netleship, Benjamin	15	544	Immigrated 1676.
Netleship, Elizabeth	15	510	Transported 1676.
Netleship, Roger, Jr.	15	510	Immigrated 1676. Of Talbot Co.
Netleton, John	15	505	Transported 1678.
Nettlingham, Thomas	10	305	" 1666. Servant.
Neutson, Henrique	12	473	" 1670.
Neve, Mary	5	238	" 1662. Servant.
Nevell, Joanna	4	13	Wife of John. Living 1656.
Nevell, John	ABH	98	Transported 1633. Servant.
Nevell, John	ABH	27	Immigrated 1646, with wife.
Nevell, John	4	186	Transported his former wife, Bridget Thorsby, about 1639.
Nevell, Mary	18	174	Transported 1674.
Nevill, Ann	ABH	150	" 1639. Wife of Richard.
Nevill, Benjamin	9	489	" 1665. Servant.
Nevill, Cornelius	WC2	128	" 1679.
Nevill, John	1	121	" 1633.
Nevill, John	2	528	Immigrated 1646 with wife.
Nevill, John	ABH	241	Married Joan Porter, whom he

NAME	Liber	Folio	REMARKS
			transported 1651.
Nevill, Richard	ABH	65	Transported 1633. (1, fol. 20, 38).
Nevill, Richard	---	---	" 1634-41.
Nevill, Richard	1	65	" 1641. Servant.
New, Mathew	9	216	" 1665.
New, Richard	WC2	308	" 1678.
New, Roger	9	322	Of Virginia. Immigrated to Choptank River, 1665.
New, Thomas	9	322	Of Virginia. Immigrated to Choptank River, 1665.
Newale, Jame	7	553	Transported 1664.
Newall, Lewis	15	370	" 1676.
Newbold, Adriana	15	526	" 1678. Wife of Thomas.
Newbold, Murphy	15	526	" 1678. Son of Thomas.
Newbold, Sarah	15	526	" 1678. Daughter of Thomas.
Newbold, Thomas	15	526	Immigrated 1678.
Newby, Eleanor	16	437	Transported 1671.
Newell, James	17	334,485	" 1663. Of St. Mary's Co.
Newfinger, William	Q	431	" 1658.
Newgent, William	3	15	Immigrated 1649.
Newgent, William, Gent.	ABH	44	" 1649.
Newhame, Christopher	12	473	Transported 1670.
Newing, Margaret	15	348	" 1655. Servant.
Newis, Robert	12	477	" 1670.
Newland, Henry	17	571	" 1673.
Newly, Mary	6	293	" 1664.
Newman, Abraham	5	240,393	" 1662. (17, fol. 554).
Newman, Ann	12	496	" 1670.
Newman, Elizabeth	12	496	" 1670.
Newman, George	ABH	102	" 1651. Servant.
Newman, Henry	15	356	" 1674.
Newman, James	10	572	" 1667.
Newman, John	6	295	" 1656.
Newman, John	5	63	" 1660.
Newman, John	5	268	" 1663.
Newman, John	10	391	Married 1st Jone ---, and 2ndly prior to 1666, Frances Richeson. All servants.
Newman, Joseph	10	569	Transported 1665-6.
Newman, Joseph	12	459	" 1669.
Newman, Nicholas	18	39	" 1674.
Newman, Ralph	17	602	Immigrated 1670, with Ann, his wife.
Newman, Richard	WC2	67	Service 1679. Of St. Mary's Co.
Newman, Sarah	7	527	Transported 1664.
Newman, Thomas	4	2	" 1658.
Newman, Thomas	5	120	" 1661.
Newman, Thomas	6	294	" 1663.
Newman, Thomas	9	269,376	" 1665.
Newman, Thomas	15	332	" 1666.
Newmarch, William	WC2	129	" 1679.
Newport, William	13	59	Immigrated 1670. Of St. Mary's Co.

NAME	Liber	Folio	REMARKS
News, Thomas	WC2	110	Transported 1676. Servant.
Newton, Edward	11	581	" 1668.
Newton, Elizabeth	9	216	" 1665.
Newton, Giles	15	443	" 1672.
Newton, James	20	185	" 1679.
Newton, John	5	411	" 1663. (17, fol. 533). Of Dorset Co.
Newton, John	18	24	Immigrated 1674. Of Baltimore Co.
Newton, Sarah	WC2	41	Married to Wm. Mishue 1679. Executrix of Samuell Pritchard.
Newtone, Henry	15	430	Transported 1677.
Newtown, Ann	5	125	" 1662.
Newwork, William	5	208	" 1662.
Neyo, John	6	263	" 1662.
Nibb, Edward	11	374	" 1668.
Nichaltson, Ralph	11	581	" 1668.
Nichell, Samuel	16	11	" 1670.
Nicholas, Constance	16	94	" 1670.
Nicholas, James	4	5	" 1659. Servant.
Nicholas, John	5	93	" 1661.
Nicholas, Susan	9	270	" 1665.
Nicholes, John	20	107	" 1678. Of St. Mary's Co.
Nicholes, John, Jr.	20	107	" 1678.
Nicholes, Margaret	12	190	" 1668. Servant.
Nicholes, Mary	20	107	" 1678. Wife of John.
Nicholes, Thomas	20	107	" 1678. Son of John.
Nicholls, Christobell	18	167	" 1674.
Nicholls, Edward	12	576	" 1670.
Nicholls, Francis	WC2	319	" 1680. Servant.
Nicholls, George	7	79	" 1664. (11, fol. 209).
Nicholls, Henry	Q	435	" 1658.
Nicholls, Humphrey	7	79	" 1664. (11, fol. 216; 15, fol. 405).
Nicholls, James	13	114	Transported 1671.
Nicholls, John	ABH	355	Immigrated 1648, with wife and children.
Nicholls, John	17	443	Transported 1662.
Nicholls, John	6	172,347	" 1663.
Nicholls, John	11	374	" 1668.
Nicholls, John	12	465	" 1669. Of Virginia. Servant. (17, fol. 532).
Nicholls, Luzanna	7	150	Transported 1664.
Nicholls, Martha	15	402	Service 1676.
Nicholls, Richard	5	203	Transported 1662.
Nicholls, Robert	ABH	244	" 1635.
Nicholls, Robert	8	482	" 1665.
Nicholls, Stephen	6	209	" 1663.
Nicholls, Stephen	14	145	" 1665.
Nicholls, Thomas	7	464	" 1655.
Nicholls, Thomas	WC2	380	" 1675-80. Servant.
Nicholls, William	12	415	" 1669.

NAME	Liber	Folio	REMARKS
Nichols, Henry	12	314	Transported 1669.
Nichols, James	18	84,174	" 1674.
Nichols, John	12	209	" 1668.
Nichols, Marina	15	402	Service 1676.
Nicholson, Alice	18	166	Transported 1674.
Nicholson, Helen	5	246	" 1657.
Nicholson, John	7	567	" 1657. Servant.
Nicholson, John	17	571	" 1673.
Nicholson, John	15	300	" 1675.
Nicholson, Mary	16	302	Service 1671. Wife of James.
Nicholson, Nich.	15	530	Transported 1678.
Nicholson, Nicholas	7	154	" 1660.
Nicholson, Ralph	11	581	" 1668. (See Nichaltson).
Nicholson, Richard	WC2	113,165	" 1680.
Nicholson, Thomas	17	571	" 1673.
Nicholson, Thomas	WC2	201	" 1680. Servant.
Nickelson, James	17	368	Aged 34 years in 1671.
Nicklas, Allen	17	463	Transported 1673.
Nickleson, Humphrey	15	440	And Sarah, his wife. Service 1677.
Nickolson, Alboth	10	600	Transported 1667.
Nicklus, Mathew	WC2	254,325	Rights 1680.
Nickslaugh, John	12	504	Transported 1669.
Nicoldes, Susanna	9	437	" 1664.
Nicolls, Frances	9	432-433	" 1666. Wife of William.
Nicolls, Nicholas	WC2	217	" 1680.
Nicolls, Sarah	12	496	" 1670.
Nicolls, William	9	432-433	Immigrated 1666. Of New England.
Nicolson, Elizabeth	WC2	201	Transported 1680. Servant.
Nicolson, James	4	140	" 1657. Servant.
Nicolson, John	WC2	201	" 1680. Servant.
Nicolson, Mary	WC2	201	" 1680. Servant.
Nicolson, Thomas, Jr.	WC2	201	" 1680. Servant.
Nimack, Jacob	4	21	Immigrated Palm Sunday, 1659.
Nimps, Edward	12	209	Transported 1668.
Ninivie, Thomas	5	489	" 1659.
Niott, Anthony	9	216	" 1665.
Nitingale, Rilingale	12	498	" 1670.
Niver, Katherine	16	116	" 1671.
Nixson, Ralph	17	377	" 1669.
Noabs, Thomas	Q	239	" 1651-2.
Noakes, George	12	383	Service 1669. Of Calvert Co.
Nobbs, Thomas	ABH	81	Immigrated 1637, with wife.
Daughter married Wm. Bretton.			
Nobbs, Thomas	17	469	Transported 1673.
Nobes, Thomas	4	23	Service 1659.
Noble, George	8	478	Transported 1665.
Noble, Isaac	8	205	" 1665. (17, fol. 381).
Noble, John	10	4	" 1665.
Noble, Sarah	18	291	" 1674.
Noble, Thomas	15	429	" 1674.
Nobson, John	WC2	110	" 1676. Servant.

NAME	Liber	Folio	REMARKS
Nock, William	16	40	Transported 1670.
Nodden, John	15	454	" 1677.
Nodmanson, Richard	17	424	" 1673.
Noell, James	17	347	Service 1672. Of Dorchester Co.
Noice, William	15	370	Transported 1676.
Noise, James	WC2	112	" 1679.
Nolan, Catherine	Q	119	" 1655. (4, fol. 533).
Noone, Owen	16	505	" 1672.
Norbank, Andrew	15	442	" 1677.
Norcott, William	18	313	" 1675.
Norfolk, Thomas	11	344	" 1668.
Norgraves, Samuel	15	505	" 1678.
Norish, Margaret	WC2	82	" 1679.
Nork, William	16	40	" 1670. (18, fol. 166).
Norly, Sarah	11	337,441	" 1668.
Norman, Daniel	15	557	" 1675.
Norman, Edward	6	171	" 1663. Servant.
Norman, Edward	17	412	" 1673.
Norman, George	6	15	" 1662. (5, fol. 68).
Norman, Joane	5	413	" 1663.
Norman, John	ABH	24,46	Service. Married widow of Jno. Smithson, Servant to Capt. Hawley, 1649. (2, fol. 514).
Norman, John	ABH	402	Transported 1650.
Norman, John	3	22	" 1650. Servant.
Norman, John	5	411	" 1663. (11, fol. 170).
Norman, Mrs. John	2	514	Service about 1649. Widow of John Smithson, now wife of John Norman.
Norman, Rebecca	15	374	Service 1676. Wife of Robert.
Norman, Robert	15	374	" 1663. Of Dorchester Co.
Norman, Robert	7	554	Immigrated 1665.
Norman, Thomas	16	115	Transported 1671.
Norman, Thomas	18	335	" 1675.
Norman, Walter	4	186	" 1656.
Norman, William	16	86	" 1670.
Normand, John	4	214	" 1650.
Norres, John	15	453	" 1675-7.
Norrice, Susanna	15	322	" 1675.
Norrice, Thomas	15	322	" 1674.
Norris, Ann	1	19	" 1637.
Norris, Ann	15	438	" 1677.
Norris, Thomas	18	176	" 1674.
Norris, William	15	566	" 1678.
Norrise, Anne	2	444	" 1639. Servant.
Norrish, Thomas	9	313	" 1665.
Norroway, Josiah	WC2	381	" 1675-80. Servant.
Norris, Henry	WC2	21	" 1679.
North, Alice	17	395	" 1672.
North, Daniel	17	475	" 1673.
North, Elizabeth	WC2	157	Service 1680. Wife of William.
North, John	5	89	Transported 1661.
North, John	15	439	" 1667.

NAME	Liber	Folio	REMARKS
North, John	17	416	Transported 1673.
North, Mary	16	452	" 1670.
North, Mary	15	454	" 1677.
North, Thomas	7	529	" 1664.
North, William	WC2	157	Immigrated 1680 with wife.
Northam, John	17	475	" 1673.
Northcrafte, Edward	15	429	" 1677.
Northend, John	4	549	" 1661.
Northington, John	16	133	" 1671.
Northis, Robert	15	353	" 1674.
Northover, Nicholas	WC2	253,398	" 1680.
Norton, Edmund	9	188	Immigrated 1665.
Norton, Hammond	18	110	Service 1674. Of Charles Co.
Norton, John, Elder	1	26	Transported 1635.
Norton, John, Younger	1	26	" 1635.
Norton, John	ABH	60	" 1635.
Norton, John, Jr.	4	623	" 1633. (ABH, fol. 244).
Norton, John, Sr.	4	623	" 1633. (ABH, fol. 244).
Norton, John	3	172-173	Immigrated 1655 with wife.
Norton, Mary	7	472	Transported 1664.
Norton, Richard	ABH	247	" 1649. Servant.
Norton, Mr. Tobias	ABH	357	Immigrated June 1653.
Norton, William	12	517	Transported 1670.
Norwood, Andrew	Q	29	Immigrated 1650. Son of John.
Norwood, Arthur	12	413	Transported 1669.
Norwood, Charles	13	113	" 1670.
Norwood, John	Q	29	Immigrated 1650 with wife.
Norwood, John	Q	29	" 1650. Son of John.
Norwood, John	9	54	Transported 1665.
Norwood, Robert	8	460	" 1662.
Norwood, William	Q	323	" 1655-8.
Noskes, George	6	293	" 1664.
Not, John	ABH	57	Immigrated 1643.
Notingham, Thomas	12	601	Transported 1669.
Notley, Mathew	12	601	" 1670 by Thos. Notley, Gent. of St. Mary's County.
Nott, John	1	21	Immigrated 1643.
Nottingham, Thomas	16	43	Transported 1670. (18, fol. 13).
Nottley, Thomas	9	24	Immigrated 1665.
Noun, Nich.	Q	385	In Anne Arundel Co. 1658.
Nour, Allen	17	356	Of Somerset Co. Service 1672.
Novell, James	6	305	Transported 1664.
Noew, Allen	10	4	" 1666.
Nowell, Ann	12	498	" 1670.
Nowell, Henry	18	141	" 1674.
Nowell, John	WC2	398	" 1680.
Nowell, William	18	152	" 1674.
Nowland, Henry	WC2	51,52	Immigrated 1679 with wife and two sons.
Nowland, Henry, Jr.	WC2	51	Transported 1679.
Nowland, Lettice	WC2	51	" 1679. Wife of Henry.

NAME	Liber	Folio	REMARKS
Nowland, Philip	15	446	Transported 1677.
Nowland, Richard	WC2	51	" 1679. Son of Henry.
Nowland, Shillam	WC2	57	" 1678.
Nowland, Shillman	15	554	" 1678.
Nowland, Thomas	15	553	" 1678.
Nowell, John	WC2	114,398	" 1680. Servant.
Nowles, Thomas	6	160	" 1663.
Noy, Denis	15	566	" 1678.
Nuell, John	9	34	" 1665.
Nuett, John	Q	431	" 1658.
Nugent, Robert	ABH	223	Immigrated 1650.
Numbers, John	9	489	" 1665.
Numpe, Alexander	6	89	Transported 1663.
Nunan, Thomas	WC2	10	" 1679.
Nunane, Dennis	WC2	129	" 1679.
Nune, Thomas	WC2	17	" 1679.
Nunn, John	17	510	Immigrated 1673.
Nunne, John	2	392	" 1640.
Nunne, John	ABH	187	Service 1651.
Nuport, William	16	11	Immigrated 1670. Of St. Mary's Co.
Nurcom, William	15	454	Transported 1677.
Nursery, Thomas	WC2	23	" 1679. Servant.
Nutbrown, Margaret	ABH	12	Servant 1640.
Nutbrowne, Margarett	2	444	Transported 1640. Servant.
Nuthall, Arthur	18	168	Service 1674. (5, fol. 223).
Nuthall, Nicholas	15	383	Transported 1676.
Nuton, Edward	9	36	" 1665.
Nuton, John	9	36	" 1665.
Nuton, Sarah	9	36	Immigrated 1665.
Nuton, Sarah	13	113	Transported 1670.
Nuton, Sarah, Jr.	9	36	" 1665.
Nuton, Thomas	9	36	Immigrated 1665.
Nuton, Thomas, Jr.	9	36	Transported 1665.
Nutt, Job	Q	473	Of London, Merchant. Agrees to immigrate, 1657.
Nutt, Thomas	11	572	Transported 1668.
Nuttan, Edward	15	422	" 1665.
Nuttan, Elizabeth	15	422	" 1665.
Nuttan, John	15	422	" 1665.
Nuttan, Nath.	15	422	" 1665.
Nuttan, Sara	15	422	" 1665.
Nuttan, Thomas	15	422	" 1665.
Nutter, Christopher	6	31	Immigrated 1663.
Nutter, Christopher	16	12	" 1670 (?). Of Somerset County.
Nutter, Mary	8	204	Transported 1665. Wife of Christopher.
Nutterfield, Ralph	17	602	Immigrated 1667.
Nutthall, Eleanor	12	576	Transported 1670.
Nutthall, James	5	343	" 1663. Son of John.
Nutthall, John	5	343	Immigrated 1663.

NAME	Liber	Folio	REMARKS
Nutthall, John	5	343	Transported 1663. Son of John.
Nutting, Thomas	10	595	" 1667. Servant.
Oak, Jeane	15	503	" 1678.
Oakely, George	17	375	Immigrated 1672.
Oakely, Thomas	WC2	21	Transported 1679.
Oakes, John	17	330	" 1672.
Oakey, John	16	308	Service 1671.
Oakey, Mary	16	308	Transported from Virginia 1671,
with her child, Abinadab Haw. Wife of Jno. of Somerset Co.			
Oakinton, William	8	130	Transported 1665.
Oakley, John	12	489	Service 1670. Of Calvert Co.
Oakley, John	20	185	Transported 1679.
Oakly, Edward	17	415	" Nov. 1669.
Oare, John	5	415	" 1663.
Obert, Barkram	2	523	Immigrated 1646. Son of Barkram. Under 16 years of age.
Obert, Barkram	2	523	Immigrated 1646.
Obert, Bartram	ABH	26	" 1646.
Obert, Bartram, Jr.	ABH	26	Son of Bartram, under 16 years of age 1646.
Oberton, Sarah	7	86	Transported 1661. Servant.
Oberton, William	Q	189	Service 1656.
O'Bryan, Bryan	15	446,599	Transported 1677.
Obryan, Mortimer	11	378	" 1668.
O'Bryent, Bryan	WC2	106	" 1679.
O'Cahett, James	15	553	" 1678.
O'Callahan, Dennis	Q	208	" 1658.
O'Cane, John	Q	18	Servant 1650.
Ocerlen, Peter	WC2	73	Transported 1678.
Ockford, Susan	16	307	Immigrated 1671. Wife of Thomas.
Ockford, Thomas	16	307	" 1671 from Virginia. Of Somerset Co.
O'Daly, Bryan	4	185	Service 1659.
O'Daniel, Thomas	6	49	Transported his wife 1663.
O'Daniel, Thomas	9	487	Immigrated 1664.
Odber, Capt. John	4	217,531	" prior to 1659. Special Warrant for 500 acres, 1659.
Odeere, Dennis	11	499	Immigrated 1666. Of Accomack, Va.
Odeere, Mary	15	319	Service 1675. Wife of Dennis.
Odger, William	17	600	Immigrated 1673 with wife and daughter.
Odian, Dorothy	WC2	65	Transported 1679.
Odian, Thomas	WC2	65	" 1679.
Odiliham, Mary	18	152	" 1674.
O'Dine, Nell	WC2	106	" 1679.
Odium, Andrew	10	117	" 1666.
Odorrant, Clore	WC2	75	Of Talbot Co. Deceased 1679.
Odorrant, Mary	WC2	75	Administratrix of Clore Odorrant, 1679.
Odrean, Richard	18	152	Transported 1674.
Oecley, Thomas	ABH	61	" 1633-41.

NAME	Liber	Folio	REMARKS
Offley, Barbara	17	462	Transported 1673. Daughter of John.
Offley, Edward	WC2	183	Transported 1680.
Offley, John	17	462	Immigrated 1673. Of Calvert Co.
Offley, John	WC2	183	Rights 1680. (WC2, fol. 232, 313, 330).
Offley, John, Jr.	17	462	Transported 1673. Son of John.
Offley, Mabel	17	462	" 1673. Wife of John.
Offley, Michael	9	478	" 1658. Of Anne Arundel Co. (5, fol. 247; 15, fol. 300).
Offley, Robert	WC2	183	Transported 1680.
Offstrong, Elizabeth	4	63	" 1652-9.
Offwood, James	9	28	" 1664.
Ofield, Henry	16	505	" 1671.
Often, Jane	5	125	" 1662.
Ogan, William	15	553	" 1678.
Ogborne, John	15	440	Service 1677.
Ogborne, William	19	258	Transported 1663.
Ogden, Jonathan	WC2	199	" 1680.
Ogham, Ann	5	241	Immigrated prior to 1662. Wife of Paul.
Ogle, Jane	15	517	Transported 1678.
Ogle, William	4	609	" 1661.
Oglethorpe, William	5	246	" 1658. (11, fol. 548; 12, fol. 210).
O'Hagan, Paul	Q	316	Service 1658.
Ohally, William	6	13	Immigrated 1659.
Ohy, John	8	486	Transported 1664.
O'Keene, Joseph	17	356	Service 1672. Of St. Mary's Co.
O'Keene, Roger	15	407	Immigrated 1676.
Okelson, Hans	16	411	Transported 1671.
Okely, Margaret	15	525	" 1678.
Oken, Thomas	16	394	" 1671.
Okey, John	9	450	" 1666.
Olandman, Denham	9	200	" 1665.
Olandman, Donnum	WC2	13	" 1679. Of Somerset Co.
Olandman, Donnum, Jr.	WC2	13	" 1679.
Olandman, Jane	WC2	13	" 1679. Wife of Donnum.
O'Lanman, Dunman	15	526	Immigrated 1678.
O'Lanman, Dunman, Jr.	15	526	Transported 1678.
O'Lanman, Jane	15	526	" 1678. Wife of Dunman.
Oldfield, George	17	474	Immigrated 1673. Of Calvert Co.
Olderidge, Ann	5	243	Transported 1662. Daughter of William.
Olderidge, Elizabeth	5	243	Transported 1662. Wife of William.
Olderidge, William	5	243	Immigrated 1662.
Oldis, Marmaduke	10	520	Transported 1667.
Oldridge, Nicholas	18	33	" 1674.
O'Lee, Hugh	Q	431	" 1658.
O'Lering, Ralph	12	209	" 1668.
Oliver, Dorothy	17	463	" 1673.

NAME	Liber	Folio	REMARKS
Oliver, Geoffrey	ABH	8	Immigrated 1646. (2, fol. 411).
Oliver, Humphrey	11	337,441	Transported 1668.
Oliver, James	17	74	Service 1663.
Oliver, Mary	15	300	Transported 1675.
Oliver, Mary	15	397	" 1676.
Oliver, Peter	8	131	" 1664.
Oliver, Thomas	ABH	61,150	" 1639. Servant.
Oliver, William	9	47	" 1665.
Oliver, William	15	359	" 1676.
Ollett, Elizabeth	5	12	" 1662.
Olliver, James	6	36	" 1663.
Olliver, Mary	18	160	" 1674.
Olliver, Roger	5	207	" 1662.
Olliver, Thomas	5	91	" prior to 1660.
Olliver, Thomas	6	218	" 1663.
Ollrick, ---	Q	71	" 1652-3. An Irish boy.
O'Lunge, Teige	4	5	" 1659. Servant.
Omealy, Bryan	WC2	206,224	Rights 1680. Of Talbot Co.
O'Mely, Bryan	4	17	Transported 1658. Servant.
Omley, Bryan	9	216	" 1665.
O'Neale, Charles	11	104	" 1667. Son of Hugh.
O'Neale, Daniel	11	104	" 1667. Son of Hugh.
O'Neale, Hugh	11	104	Immigrated 1667. Of Charles Co.
O'Neale, Hugh	18	152	Transported 1674.
O'Neale, Joy	11	104	" 1667. Child of Hugh.
O'Neale, Mary	11	104	" 1667. Wife of Hugh.
Oneale, Teage	12	379	" 1669.
Oneell, Hugh	WC2	89	" 1676. Servant.
Onenes, Cor---lander	9	249	Immigrated 1665.
Onesby, Stephen	15	565	Transported 1679.
Onger, John	9	35	" 1664.
Onion, Abell	15	530	" 1678.
Onley, Mary	12	243	" 1669.
Onley, Michael	12	243	" 1669.
Onley, Thomas	1	27	" 1633-41.
Ontemg, Samuel	9	269	" 1665.
Onyon, Susanna	17	531	" 1673.
Oolofson, Hana	4	138	Immigrated 1657.
Oraff, Dennis	15	553	Transported 1678.
Oram, John	WC2	53	" 1677. (15, fol. 445).
Oram, Val.	15	358	" 1675.
Oram, William	15	452	" 1677.
Orchard, Amy	12	517	" 1670.
Orchard, James	16	94	" 1670.
Orchard, Matthew	15	369	" 1676.
Orchard, Nathaniel	ABH	58	Immigrated 1640. (1, fol. 21).
Orchard, Richard	15	369	Transported 1676.
Orchard, Sarah	Q	428	" 1657.
Orchard, Susanna	9	489	Immigrated 1665. Wife of William.
Orchard, William	5	341	" 1644.
Orchard, William	5	93	Transported 1654. (4, fol. 69).

NAME	Liber	Folio	REMARKS
Orde, James	16	411	Transported 1671.
Orde, Peter	16	411	" 1671.
Oreed, Thomas	15	397	" 1676.
Oregan, Teage	17	44	" 1667.
Organ, John	WC2	306	" 1680.
Orgen, Lawrence	Q	28	Servant 1649-50.
Orke, Catherine	4	66	Transported 1658.
Orley, Thomas	1	19	" 1638.
Orme, Fabian	11	501	Immigrated 1668.
Orme, Robert	17	416	Transported 1673.
Ormond, Thomas	WC2	201	" 1680. Servant.
Ormsby, John	1	149-150	License to marry Frances Griffin, Oct. 16, 1641.
Oroneck, James	4	69	Immigrated 1650, and died prior to 1659, leaving an orphan.
Orough, James	15	553	Transported 1678.
Orr, Robert	18	152	" 1674.
Orwell, John	15	376	" 1676.
Osban, Thomas	9	156	" 1660.
Osband, William	10	394,395	" 1666.
Osberton, Hannah	8	478	" 1665.
Osborne, ---	5	203	" 1662.
Osborne, Edward	15	503	" 1678.
Osborne, Henry	ABH	273	Immigrated 1651.
Osborne, Henry	20	46	Of Calvert Co. Died intestate prior to 1678, leaving 2 daughters, Rebecca, wife of Ant. Dawson and Sarah, unmarried.
Osborne, James	15	390	Transported 1675.
Osborne (Osbourne), James	WC2	318,400	Immigrated 1675. Of Somerset Co. Schoolmaster.
Osborne, John	15	376	Transported 1676.
Osborne, John	15	452	" 1678.
Osborne, Jonas	5	373	" 1660.
Osborne, Richard	15	452	" 1678.
Osborne, Robert	15	517	" 1678.
Osborne, Samuel	6	217	" 1663.
Osborne, Thomas	4	70	Service 1659.
Osborne, Thomas	13	113	Transported 1676.
Osborne, Thomas	10	469	" 1667.
Osborne, William	9	487	Immigrated 1664.
Osbourn, Catherine	ABH	273	Transported 1651. Wife of Henry.
Osbourne, Charles	15	454	" 1677. (See Coburne).
Osbourne, James	WC2	318,400	Immigrated 1675. Of Somerset Co. Schoolmaster.
Osbourne, John	WC2	315,341	Service 1680. Of St. Mary's Co.
Osbourne, Rebecca	ABH	273	Transported 1651. Daughter of Henry.
Osbourne, Rebecca	WC2	391	Married Capt. Anthony Dawson. Daughter of Henry Osbourne.
Osbourne, Sarah	WC2	391	Married Thomas Walker. Daughter

NAME	Liber	Folio	REMARKS
			of Henry Osbourne.
Oseley, Mary	5	267	Transported 1663.
Osmand, Gillian	12	473	" 1670.
Osoulla, Donnock	ABH	421	" 1654. Servant.
Ostian, Thomas	WC2	71,242	" 1678.
O'Sullivan, Teage	Q	434	" 1658.
Oswald, Henry	15	369	" 1676.
Oteage, Fyning	17	348	" 1667.
Oton, Dorothy	4	70	" 1659.
O'Trasier, Trage	10	3	Immigrated 1665.
Otrasir, Trage	9	189,268	" 1667.
Otter, Thomasin	12	190	Transported 1668. Servant.
Oulde, Thomas	12	472	" 1670.
Ouldstoss, Margaret	6	47	" 1663.
Oureus, Thomas	15	553	" 1678.
Ouseman, Martha	WC2	21-22	" 1679.
Ously, Sarah	18	84	" 1674.
Ovall, Brian	4	585	" 1661.
Overman, Jacob	12	205	" 1667.
Oversee, Symon	16	595	Immigrated with one child, 1650.

Of Charles County. Died 1659. (Q, fol. 323).

Oversly, John	15	443	Transported 1670.
Overton, Francis	11	166	Immigrated prior to 1667, when

his widow appears as the wife of Thos. Phillips.

Overton, Jane	20	49	Widow and Admx. of Thos. O., of

Baltimore County; married George Gunnell, prior to 1678.

Overton, Mary	7	81	Transported 1661.
Overton, Mary	16	222	" 1668. Wife of Thos. of St. Mary's County.
Overton, Mary, Jr.	16	222	Transported 1668. Daughter of Thomas.
Overton, Sarah	16	222	Transported 1668. Daughter of Thomas.
Overton, Thomas	16	222	Immigrated 1668, with wife and

two daughters. Of St. Mary's County.

Overy, Mary	4	140	Transported 1656. Servant.
Ovington, Mary	9	309	" 1666.
Owen, Bartholomew	11	378	" 1668.
Owen, Elizabeth	18	288	" 1674.
Owen, George	17	608	" 1673.
Owen, Grace	5	304	" 1662. Servant.
Owen, Hugh	8	259	" 1665.
Owen, James	15	553	" 1678.
Owen, John	4	610	" 1661.
Owen, John	6	216	" 1663.
Owen, John	10	609	" from Va. 1667. Servant.
Owen, John	11	216	Immigrated 1667. Of Charles Co.
Owen, John	11	374	Transported 1668. (12, fol. 340).
Owen, John	16	86	" 1670. (17, fol. 399).
Owen, John	17	407	" 1673.
Owen, Joseph	6	63	" 1668.

NAME	Liber	Folio	REMARKS
Owen, Joseph	15	569	Transported 1678.
Owen, Joseph	WC2	19	" 1679.
Owen, Joshua	WC2	406	" 1677. (15, fol. 454).
Owen, Mary	10	598	" 1667.
Owen, Richard	7	63	" 1659.
Owen, Richard	5	203	" 1662. (7, fol. 82).
Owen, Richard	5	257	" 1663. (6, fol. 123).
Owen, Richard	10	193	Of London, Gent. Claiming land
in Anne Arundel County, 1666.			
Owen, Richard	18	174	Transported 1674.
Owen, Robert	Q	71	" 1651-3.
Owen, Thomas	Q	219	" 1653.
Owen, Timothy	Q	71	" 1652-3.
Owen, William	8	258	" 1665.
Owens, Ann	18	84	" 1674.
Owens, John	9	92	" 1665.
Owens, Richard	4	70	Immigrated prior to 1659.
Owens, Thomas	WC2	57	Transported 1678.
Owens, Timothy	5	238	" 1662. (8, fol. 131).
Owin, Evan	9	353	" 1666.
Owin, Parnall	9	353	" 1666.
Owin, Robert	8	131	" 1664.
Owins, John	8	88	" 1665.
Owins, John	WC2	309	" 1678.
Owins, Robert	15	369	" 1676.
Owldfield, Sarah	20	185	" 1679.
Owlison, Lawrence	16	411	" 1671.
Oxland, Francis	12	498	" 1670.
Oxmans, John	4	190	" 1659.
Oxnion, Francis	9	310	" 1664, aged 15 years.
Oxwell, Timothy	7	85	" 1660.
Ozier, Gabriel	ABH	14	Immigrated 1647.
Ozier, Gabriell	2	456	" 1647.
Ozye, Mary	6	305	Transported 1664.
Pace, John	WC2	112	" 1679.
Packer, Edward	3	105	Immigrated prior to 1648.
Packer, Mary	18	174	Transported 1674.
Packman, Sarah	17	463	" 1673.
Padering, Thomas	11	373	" 1668.
Padgett, John	17	463	" 1673.
Padon, Samuel	18	291	" 1674.
Page, Ann	9	188	" 1665.
Page, Anne	20	185	" 1679.
Page, Damaras	7	569	" 1663-4.
Page, Damaris	10	433	" 1666.
Page, Daniel	20	185	" 1679.
Page, Edward	17	469	" 1673.
Page, Elizabeth	17	424	" 1673.
Page, Hannah	11	502	" 1668. Wife of Robert.
			(17, fol. 512).
Page, Henry	9	69	Transported 1660-5.

NAME	Liber	Folio	REMARKS
Page, James	5	343	Transported 1663.
Page, Margery	9	334,448	" 1666.
Page, Mary	10	117	" 1666.
Page, Robert	7	560, 576-577	" 1665.
Page, Robert	10	502	Immigrated 1668. (17, fol. 512).
Page, Samuel	15	362	Transported 1676.
Page, Thomas	5	556	" 1660.
Page, Thomas	WC2	260	" 1675.
Page, Thomas	WC2	318	" 1680.
Pagell, Thomas	4	216	" 1659.
Paget, Eleanor	12	372	" 1669.
Paget, Thomas	Q	18	" 1652-8.
Paget, William	16	41	" 1670.
Pagett, Elizabeth	4	55	" 1659. Daughter of William.
Pagett, Noany	4	55	Transported 1659. Wife of William.
Pagett, Thomas	5	204	Immigrated 1654.
Pagett, William	4	55	" 1659.
Pagett, William	15	397	Transported 1676.
Paggett, Jacob	20	185	" 1679.
Pagler, Dorothy	Q	58	" 1646.
Pagrave, James	WC2	308	" 1678.
Paine, Edward	15	452	" 1677.
Paine, Elizabeth	7	483	" 1664. Daughter of Thomas.
Paine, Jane	7	483	Transported 1664. Wife of Thomas.
Paine, Jane	18	318	" 1675.
Paine, John	13	59	Immigrated 1670.
Paine, Joseph	12	381,416	Transported 1669.
Paine, Katherine	15	544	" 1676.
Paine, Margaret	4	174	" 1659.
Paine, Margery	9	48	" 1665.
Paine, Mary	7	483	" 1664. Daughter of Thomas.
Paine, Robert	WC2	11	Immigrated 1679. Of Somerset Co.
Paine, Sarah	7	483	Transported 1664. Daughter of Thomas.
Paine, Thomas	7	483	Immigrated 1664.
Paine, Thomas	ABH	7	Servant 1644.
Paine, William	12	194	Transported 1668. Servant.
Paine, William	16	170	" 1671.
Paine, William	WC2	109	Service 1679.
Painnter, Samuel	12	415	Transported 1669.
Painter, Alice	9	271	" Nov. 1662. Wife of John.
Painter, George	5	120	" 1661.
Painter, James	15	356	" 1675.
Painter, John	5	210	" 1662.
Painter, Nicholas	WC2	135	Service 1680.
Painter, Peter	15	369	Transported 1676.
Pakard, Ann	9	321	" 1665.

NAME	Liber	Folio	REMARKS
Pake, Robert	6	17	Transported 1663.
Pake, Walter	8	88	Married Eliz., widow of Thos. Mattingly, prior to 1665.
Pakes, Peter	ABH	26	Transported 1646. Son of Walter.
Under 16 years of age. (2, fol. 523).			
Pakes, Walter	2	523	Rights 1649.
Palin, Jane	13	65	Transported 1668. Servant.
Pall, Daniel	15	531	" 1678.
Pallanson, Hellen	11	581	" 1668.
Pallinson, Thomas	11	582	" 1668.
Pallmer, Thomas	15	432	" 1677.
Pallott, Thomas	15	397	" 1676.
Palmer, Anth.	ABH	150	" 1648. Servant.
Palmer, Elizabeth	9	326	" 1665.
Palmer, Frances	5	56	" 1661.
Palmer, Isabel	8	188,478	" 1665.
Palmer, Isabell	15	544	" 1674.
Palmer, John	17	469	" 1673.
Palmer, John	15	318	" 1674.
Palmer, John	WC2	21	" 1679.
Palmer, Joseph	18	285	" 1674.
Palmer, Margaret	10	412	" 1666.
Palmer, Margaret	20	185	" 1679.
Palmer, Rich.	15	443	" 1670.
Palmer, Richard	17	475	" 1673.
Palmer, Robert	16	100	" 1663.
Palmer, Samuel	Q	204	Immigrated 1658.
Palmer, Sarah	Q	197	Transported 1658.
Palmer, Thomas	17	567	" from Virginia 1673.
Palmer, Thomas	18	173	" 1674.
Palmer, Thomas	15	430	" 1677.
Palmer, William	ABH	58	" 1640. (1, fol. 22).
Palmer, William	8	478	" 1665.
Palmer, William	9	155	" 1665.
Palmer, William	9	321	" 1666.
Palmer, William	10	598	Immigrated 1667.
Palts, Elizabeth	11	581	Transported 1668.
Pander, John	WC2	328,329, 357	Service 1680.
Pander, Margarett	WC2	328,329	" 1680. Wife of John.
Pane, John	5	306	Immigrated 1663. (7, fol. 471).
Pane, Jo'n.	15	454	Transported 1677.
Pane, Mary	15	533	" 1678.
Pane, Richard	15	307	" 1675.
Pane, Robert	15	526	Immigrated 1678.
Pane, Thomas	7	639	Transported 1665. (15, fol. 362).
Pangrove, Job	15	353	" 1674.
Panil, Abigail	15	362	" 1676.
Panther, Dorothy	6	120	" 1657.
Panther, Mary	17	30	Wife of John of Somerset Co. Service 1672.

NAME	Liber	Folio	REMARKS
Panton, Olive	11	104	Transported 1667.
Papworth, Robert	4	68	" 1658.
Paradue, Stephen	8	4	Service 1665.
Paramore, Mary	15	318	Claims land for transporting her 1675. (Als. Robinson).
Paramour, John	18	36,38	Immigrated 1673, with wife, Mary,

sons, Thos., Richard, and John, and daughter, Mary. (15, fol. 310).

NAME	Liber	Folio	REMARKS
Pardis, Ann	15	598	Transported 1678.
Pardoe, Walter	18	285	" 1674.
Pardue, Edward	12	322	" 1669.
Paret, Peter	12	216	" 1668.
Parey, Richard	12	194	" 1668. Servant.
Parfett, William	5	245	" 1638-43.
Paris, Katherine	19	258	" 1675.
Parish, Edward	5	486	" 1662. Service.
Parish, Richard	WC2	167-169	" 1679.
Parish, Susanna	17	424	" 1673.
Park, Robert	15	380	" 1676.
Parke, Ann	18	166	" 1674.
Parke, Elizabeth	7	502	" 1664.
Parke, Robert	4	531	Immigrated prior to 1658.
Parker, Ann	12	576	Transported 1670.
Parker, Anne	WC2	395	" 1680. Servant.
Parker, Edith	9	106	" 1665. Wife of Noah.
Parker, Edward	ABH	91,237	Immigrated 1637. (1, fol. 102).
Parker, Edward	ABH	5	" 1648.
Parker, Edward	6	119	Transported 1658.
Parker, Edward	15	376	" 1676.
Parker, Eliza	16	394	" 1671.
Parker, Elizabeth	17	456	" 1671.
Parker, George	16	413	Immigrated 1671. Of Calvert Co.
Parker, George	17	397	" 1672. Of St. Mary's Co
Parker, Grace	5	418	Wife of William and Attorney 1663.
Parker, Grace	9	399	Transported 1666.
Parker, Hannah	15	515	" 1678 by Geo. Parker, Gent.
Parker, Henry	6	295	Transported 1664. (7, fol. 492-3).
Parker, Henry	WC2	202	Commission as Deputy Surveyor of Kent Co.
Parker, Henry, Gent.	16	129	Deputy Surveyor for Dorchester

Co. 1671. Do. Talbot Co. 1679. (20, fol. 134).

NAME	Liber	Folio	REMARKS
Parker, Honor	WC2	132	Transported 1680.
Parker, James	18	334	" 1675.
Parker, John	12	472,517	" 1670.
Parker, John	15	534	" 1677.
Parker, John	WC2	320	" 1680. Servant.
Parker, Katherine	10	216	" 1666. (16, fol. 304; 17, fol. 445).
Parker, Mary	15	412	Transported 1677.
Parker, Mary	15	515	" 1678.
Parker, Matthew	11	374	" 1668.

NAME	Liber	Folio	REMARKS
Parker, Noah	9	106	Immigrated 1665.
Parker, Peter	Q	355	Gift from Lord Baltimore, 1658.
Parker, Peter	18	94	Transported 1674.
Parker, Phillis	15	454	" Oct. 1677.
Parker, Quinteene	12	243	" 1669.
Parker, Richard	9	356	" 1666.
Parker, Richard	16	512	Immigrated 1672. Of Charles Co.
Parker, Richard	WC2	73	Transported 1678.
Parker, Robert	8	498	" 1665.
Parker, Robert	12	283	" 1668.
Parker, Samuel	ABH	186	Immigrated 1651. Brother-in-law of Thos. Bachelor.
Parker, Sarah	4	140	Transported 1658. Servant.
Parker, Sarah	5	2	" 1661.
Parker, Thomas	7	83	" 1663. (16, fol. 465).
Parker, Thomas	15	453	" 1676.
Parker, Thomas	15	552	" 1679.
Parker, William	4	1	Immigrated 1658.
Parker, William	11	348	Transported 1668.
Parker, William	17	463	" 1673.
Parker, William	158	544	" 1676.
Parker, William	20	185	" 1679. (WC2, fol. 86-7).
Parker, William, Jr.	9	38	" 1665.
Parker, William, Sr.	9	38	Immigrated 1665.
Parkes, Robert	ABH	203	" 1651.
Parkeson, Luke	16	530	Service 1672. Of Calvert Co.
Parkins, Richard	15	378	Transported 1674.
Parkinson, Dorothy	15	378	" 1674.
Parks, Edward	Q	68	" 1657.
Parks, John	18	296	" 1674.
Parkwood, John	9	104	" 1665.
Parmentary, Robert	WC2	68	" 1679.
Parmphe, Robert	5	89	" 1661.
Parne, John	16	85	" 1670.
Parnes, Francis	4	21	" 1657.
Parr, Robert	Q	203	" 1658.
Parradice, Thomas	5	341	" 1661.
Parramore, John	16	308	Immigrated from Virginia 1671, with Abia, his wife. Of Somerset County.
Parratt, Elizabeth	4	30	Transported 1659. Servant.
Parree, George	WC2	211	" 1679. Servant.
Parrett, Francis	6	132	" 1655.
Parrett, Henry	6	171	" 1663. Servant.
Parrett, John	9	325	" 1666.
Parrett, Richard	7	371	Of Virginia. Acquires 3000 acres in Maryland, 1664.
Parrett, Richard	8	388,484	Transported 1665.
Parrey, Bridgett	9	34	" 1665.
Parrie, Edmond	1	19	" 1638.
Parris, Isabell	17	635	" 1674.
Parris, James	9	54	" 1665.

NAME	Liber	Folio	REMARKS
Parrish, Edward	5	489	Transported 1655.
Parrish, Robert	12	242	" 1669. Servant.
Parrock, George	7	507	" 1660.
Parror, Thomas	15	360	" 1676.
Parrot, Rebecca	Q	30	" 1656.
Parrott, Francis	5	243	" 1662. (6, fol. 17, 18).
Parrott, Henry	11	436	" 1668.
Parrott, Lawrence	5	238	" 1662.
Parrott, Thomas	7	463	" 1658.
Parry, David	WC2	395	" 1680. Servant.
Parry, Elizabeth	ABH	151	" 1649-50. Servant.
Parry, Elizabeth	6	86	" 1658.
Parry, George	15	598	" 1678-9.
Parry, John	6	86	" 1658.
Parry, John	15	376	" 1676.
Parry, Margaret	9	356	" 1663.
Parsenall, Thomas	13	64	" 1668.
Parsley, Anthony	17	608	" 1673.
Parsley, Elizabeth	WC2	65	" 1679. Servant.
Parsley, John	17	635	" 1674.
Parson, Thomas	5	361	Immigrated 1663.
Parsons, Alice	WC2	181	Service 1680.
Parsons, Amos	16	536	" 1671.
Parsons, Andrew	17	566	Immigrated 1673. Of Worcester Co.
Parsons, Ann	17	608	Transported 1673.
Parsons, Ann	15	569	" 1678.
Parsons, Elizabeth	WC2	45	" 1679.
Parsons, Francis	8	483	" 1665.
Parsons, Francis	10	392	Service 1666.
Parsons, Francis	13	114	Transported 1671.
Parsons, Gillis	6	293	" 1664.
Parsons, Henry	15	369	" 1676.
Parsons, James	7	154	" 1663.
Parsons, James	11	462	" 1668. Servant.
Parsons, Jeremiah	7	464	" 1657.
Parsons, John	Q	28	" 1653.
Parsons, John	5	259	" 1659.
Parsons, John	17	417	" 1673.
Parsons, John	15	540	" 1676.
Parsons, John	15	558	" 1679.
Parsons, Margaret	Q	19	" 1656.
Parsons, Nath.	15	368	Immigrated 1676. Of Somerset Co.
Parsons, Peter	18	35	" 1672.
Parsons, Thomas	5	87	Transported 1649. (12, fol. 314).
Part, Thomas	9	328	" 1666.
Partington, Ellinor	WC2	199	" 1680.
Partis, Charles	WC2	352	Rights 1680. Commander of Ship Merchants Consent.
Partrick, William	12	403	Transported 1669.
Partridge, John	ABH	348	" 1652. Servant.
Parvey, Elizabeth	17	411	" 1673. (18, fol. 285).

NAME	Liber	Folio	REMARKS
Parvis, Richard	12	322	Transported 1669.
Parvy, John	18	285	" 1674.
Pascall, Elizabeth	4	65	" 1652. Wife of James. (6, fol. 159).
Pascall, George	4	65	Transported 1652. Son of James. Living 1659. (6, fol. 159).
Pascall, James	4	65	Immigrated 1652. Dec'd prior to 1659. (6, fol. 159).
Pascall, James	4	65	Transported 1652. Son of James.
Pascall, Mandely	5	486	Service 1662. Wife of George.
Paschall, Elizabeth	5	90	Transported 1651. Wife of James.
Paschall, George	5	90	" 1651.
Paschall, James	5	90	" 1651.
Pascho, John	2	581	" 1649. Servant.
Pase, Gregory	17	571	" 1673.
Pasmore, Martha	ABH	150	" 1637. Servant.
Pasmore, Thomas	ABH	13	Of Virginia. About to remove with his family to Maryland, 1634.
Pasmore, Thomas	1	18,25,72	Rights 1634-1640.
Pasmore, Thomas	2	453	Special grant of 1000 acres for immigrating from Virginia with family in 1634.
Pasmore, Thomas	4	61	Transported 1658.
Passiment, Ann	17	417	" 1673.
Pate, John	6	7	" 1663.
Pate, Nicholas	10	466	" 1667.
Pate, Roger	16	135	" 1671.
Pate, William	12	507	Service 1668.
Pateman, Priscilla	15	533	Transported 1678.
Pater, James	9	505	" 1666.
Paterfield, Adam	12	334	" 1668.
Paterson, Eleanor	ABH	202	" 1651. Wife of Robert.
Paterson, Elizabeth	11	164	" 1667.
Paterson, Robert	ABH	202	" 1651. Servant.
Patisson, William	9	448	" 1666.
Patrick, Ann	16	320	" from Accomack, Va. 1670. Wife of Roger.
Patrick, John	5	410	Transported 1663. (12, fol. 490; 16, fol. 303).
Patrick, John	16	320	Transported 1670. Son of Roger. (16, fol. 40).
Patrick, Roger	16	320	Immigrated from Accomack, Va. 1670, with wife, son and daughter-in-law. Of Somerset County.
Patricke, William	4	560	Transported 1661.
Patridge, Edmund	18	35	" 1672. Son of Richard.
Patridge, Margaret	18	35	" 1672. Wife of Richard.
Patridge, Richard	18	35	" 1665. Service 1672. (8, fol. 486).
Pattee, Elizabeth	15	338	Transported 1672. Wife of Richard. (16, fol. 304).
Pattee, Lydia	15	338	Transported 1672. Daughter of Richard. (16, fol. 304).

NAME	Liber	Folio	REMARKS
Pattee, Richard	15	338	Immigrated 1672. (16, fol. 304).
Patten, Darker	8	484	Transported 1665.
Patterson, John	16	414	" 1671.
Patterson, John	15	454	" Oct. 1677.
Patterson, Luke	6	293	" 1664.
Pattes, William	9	487	" 1665. Servant.
Patteson, Jane	6	48	" 1663. Servant.
Patthewes, Thomas	9	38	" 1665.
Pattison, James	4	568	" 1660.
Pattison, James	WC2	238	Son of Thomas, 1680.
Pattison, Joan	WC2	347	Daughter of Thomas, 1680.
Pattison, John	8	502	Transported 1665. Son of Wm. Richee.
Pattison, John	17	440	Transported 1673.
Pattyson, Ann	16	395	" 1671.
Pattyson, Ann, Jr.	16	395	" 1671.
Pattyson, Jacob	16	395	" 1671.
Pattyson, James	16	395	" 1671.
Pattyson, Priscilla	16	395	" 1671.
Pattyson, Thomas	16	395	Immigrated 1671 with wife and four children. Of Dorchester County.
Paul, Ann	6	31	Transported Nov. 14, 1663.
Paul, John	16	411	" 1671.
Paule, Stephen	15	560	" 1678.
Pauley, James	15	369	" 1676.
Paulhampton, Nicholas	ABH	32	Service 1649. (See Polhampton). (2, fol. 550).
Paull, Ann	7	476	Transported 1663.
Paulus, Deborah	1	150	License to marry Francis Stone, June 28, 1642.
Pavy, John	16	473	Service 1666. Of Talbot Co.
Paw, Michael	ABH	150	Transported 1648. Servant.
Pawell, Edward	15	391	" 1676.
Pawlett, Thomas	Q	449	" 1658.
Pawlett, Thomas	5	306	" 1663.
Pawley, John	ABH	140	" 1651.
Pawley, Lionell	16	38	Immigrated 1670. Of Anne Arundel County.
Pawling, John	9	92	Transported 1665.
Pawlyn, John	9	312	Immigrated 1666.
Pawson, John	13	65	Transported 1668. Servant.
Paxon, Hugh	13	122	" 1668. (15, fol. 574).
Pay, James	7	560	" 1665.
Payet, Henry	18	141	" 1674.
Payler, Jo.	6	290	" 1663.
Payne, George	6	126	" 1661.
Payne, Hugh	9	400	" 1666.
Payne, John	5	514	" 1660.
Payne, John	17	417	" 1673.
Payne, Margaret	Q	115	" 1649.
Payne, Richard	5	467	" 1657.

NAME	Liber	Folio	REMARKS
Payne, Thomas	2	390	Transported 1644. Servant.
Payne, Thomas	6	347	" 1663.
Payne, Thomas	17	463	" 1673.
Payne, William	4	11	" 1659. Servant.
Payne, William	WC2	95	Service 1679. Of Calvert Co.
Paynter, John	5	2	Transported 1658-9.
Paynter, Martha	Q	69	" 1658.
Paynter, Richard	18	83	Immigrated 1674 with wife and 3 children. Of Calvert County.
Payr, Francis	9	55	Transported 1659.
Peacake, John	16	169	Immigrated 1671 with 4 children.
Peace, Elizabeth	16	503	Transported 1671.
Peach, John	11	338	" 1668.
Peacock, Elizabeth	5	484,514	" 1660.
Peacock, Elizabeth	5	560	" 1663.
Peacock, Jacob	15	397	" 1676.
Peacock, John	4	63	Immigrated 1658. (See Poro).
Peacock, John	7	79	Transported 1664.
Peacock, John	13	114	" 1671. (16, fol. 170).
Peacock, Paul	16	432	" 1671.
Peacock, Richard	7	465	" 1662.
Peacock, Richard	5	254	" 1663.
Peacock, Richard	WC2	165-166	Commission as Deputy Surveyor of Talbot Co., 1680.
Peacock, Richard	WC2	183-184, 195	Immigrated 1680. Of Talbot Co.
Peacock, Sarah	WC2	415	Transported 1666-80. Servant.
Peacock, William	WC2	110	" 1676. Servant.
Pead, Elizabeth	WC2	17,99	Immigrated 1679. Wife of Timothy.
Pead, Jane	WC2	17,99	" 1679. Daughter of Timothy.
Pead, Timothy	WC2	17,99	Immigrated 1679 with wife and daughter.
Peage, William	12	403	Transported 1669.
Peake, Alice	15	353	" 1674.
Peake, Elizabeth	16	100	" 1667.
Peake, Edward	WC2	171	" 1679.
Peake, John	15	353	" 1674.
Peake, Thomas	17	416	" 1673.
Peake, William	WC2	113,165	" 1680.
Peakett, William	13	112	" 1670.
Peale, Elizabeth	7	82	" 1662.
Peale, Henry	5	127	" 1662.
Peame, Mary	WC2	23	" 1679. Servant.
Pearce, Andrew	4	70	" 1659.
Pearce, Henry	16	394	" 1671.
Pearce, Jane	5	3	" 1661.
Pearce, William	5	55	Service 1661.
Pearce, William	10	417	Transported prior to 1666.
Pearch, Mary	12	209	" 1668.
Pearch, Simon	7	469	" 1664. (9, fol. 336).

NAME	Liber	Folio	REMARKS
Pearcy, John	13	111	Transported 1667.
Peare, Nicholas	5	359	" 1663.
Pearle, Henry	16	510	Service 1672.
Pearle, William	15	391	Transported 1676.
Pearle, William	WC2	101	" 1679.
Pears, John	11	246	Service 1667. Of St. Mary's Co.
Pearsey, Thomas	Q	178	Immigrated prior to 1657.
Pearson, Andreas	11	537	Transported 1668.
Pearson, Canute	11	537	" 1668.
Pearson, Elizabeth	16	394	" 1671.
Pearson, Michael	18	160	" 1674.
Pearson, Wools	11	537	" 1668.
Pease, Thomas	13	66	" 1669. Servant.
Peasely, John	16	458	" 1672.
Peather, Mary	10	308	" 1663. Wife of Richard.
Peather, Mary	10	308	" 1663. Daughter of Richard.
Peather, Richard	10	308	Immigrated 1663. Of Talbot Co. Tailor.
Peck, John	16	393	Transported 1671.
Peck, William	ABH	179	" 1648.
Peck, William	11	571	" 1668.
Pecke, Humphrey	4	531	Immigrated 1659.
Pedder, Richard	18	9	" 1673 with wife and daughter.
Pederick, William	19	258	Transported 1663.
Peeke, Benjamin	15	358	" 1675.
Peeke, Edward	15	358	" 1675.
Peeke, Elizabeth	15	358	" 1675.
Peeke, Mary	15	505	" 1678.
Peele, Mary	18	38	" 1673. Wife of Robert. (15, fol. 412).
Peele, Robert	18	38	Immigrated 1673. (15, fol. 412).
Peerce, Aba	15	443	Transported 1671.
Peerce, Frances	12	602	" 1670.
Peerce, Dr. John	WC2	51	Immigrated 1678 with wife and one person. Of Calvert Co.
Peerce, Rachel	17	333	Service 1672. Wife of John.
Peerce, Sarah	WC2	51	Transported 1678. Wife of Dr. John.
Peerce, William	18	329	" 1675.
Peere, David	12	373	" 1669.
Peere, Henry	1	166	" 1650. Servant.
Peers, John	15	380	" 1676.
Peers, Richard	15	380	" 1676.
Pegg, Mary	15	397	" 1676.
Pegg, Stephen	17	510	" 1673.
Peirce, Frances	12	373	" 1669. Wife of Robert.
Peirce, John	Q	239	" 1651-2.
Peirce, John	Q	28	" 1656.
Peirce, John	17	554	Immigrated 1663. Of St. Mary's Co. Chirurgeon.

NAME	Liber	Folio	REMARKS
Peirce, John	15	338	Transported 1676.
Peirce, John	WC2	302,303	Immigrated 1680. Of Calvert Co.
Peirce, Mary	13	121	Transported 1667. Wife of Thomas.
Peirce, Richard	3	22	" 1649. Servant.
Peirce, Robert	12	273	Immigrated 1669.
Peirce, Robert, Gent.	ABH	77	" 1635 in the ship, "Merchant Adventure".
Peirce, Thomas	6	36,89	Transported 1660.
Peirce, Thomas	13	121	Immigrated 1667. Of St. Mary's Co.
Peirce, William	Q	62	Transported 1655.
Peirce, William	6	48	Immigrated prior to 1663.
Peirceson, Neale	Q	62	Transported 1658.
Peirchin, Thomas	12	498	" 1670.
Peire, John	10	499	" 1667.
Peirepoint, Elizabeth	16	393	" 1671.
Peirson, Isabella	18	280	" 1675.
Peirson, John	5	488	" 1657.
Peirson, John	17	457	" 1669.
Peirson, John	17	532	Immigrated 1673, with Mary, his wife. Of Dorset Co.
Peirson, Nathaniel	15	357	Transported 1676.
Peiy, Nicholas	13	111	" 1668.
Peizly, Ann	12	200	" 1668.
Peke, Robert	5	2	" 1661.
Pekett, John	16	122	" 1671.
Pelit, Thomas	1	26	Immigrated 1641 with wife.
Pelium, Peter	9	451	Transported 1666.
Pell, Mary	18	174	" 1674.
Pell, William	2	516	" 1648.
Pell, William	ABH	34	Immigrated 1648. (15, fol. 422, 428).
Pell, William	2	569	" 1649 with man servant.
Pelligan, Jane	16	507	Transported 1671.
Pelly, Richard	7	79	" 1663.
Pelsant, Thomas	18	144	Service 1674.
Pelson, Thomas	12	496	Transported 1670.
Pelton, John	17	33	" from Virginia 1672.
Pember, Charles	6	127	" 1656.
Pembers, Elizabeth	15	569	" 1678.
Pemberton, Thomas	WC2	120	Rights 1680. Of Liverpoole.
Peminton, Ellen	WC2	23	Transported 1679. Servant.
Pendaloe, Mary	15	436	" 1677.
Penderast, Robert	WC2	57	" 1678.
Pendergrasse, Thomas	16	435	" 1671. (15, fol. 537).
Pendergast, Robert	15	553	" 1678.
Penery, Morgan	16	532	" 1668-70.
Penett, Mabella	15	442	" 1677.
Penington, Henry	13	59	Service 1670. Of Baltimore Co.
Penington, Isabella	5	415	Transported 1659.
Penley, William	ABH	101	" 1637-40. Servant.
Penly, Arthur	8	484	" 1665.
Penn, John	17	36	" 1672.

NAME	Liber	Folio	REMARKS
Penn, James	15	452,531	Transported 1677.
Penn, Richard	17	27	Service 1672. (16, fol. 432).
Pennett, John	6	290	Transported 1663.
Penney, Joane	6	17	" 1663.
Pennington, Alice	17	635	" 1674.
Pennington, Mr. Francis	22	206	A priest, Cert. on behalf of Mr. Hy.
			Warrell (a priest for St. Thomas' Manor, 3337 acres in Calvert Co., 1685).
Pennington, Henry	ABH	201	Transported 1650-1. Servant.
Pennington, Henry	6	255	" 1663.
Pennington, Henry	7	614	" 1665.
Pennington, Rachel	15	422	Immigrated 1677.
Pennington, William	9	28	Transported 1664.
Pennistone, Nicholas	9	400	" 1666.
Pennistone, Sarah	9	400	" 1666.
Pennistone, William	9	400	Immigrated 1666.
Penniwell, Robert	12	552	Service 1670. Of St. Mary's Co.
Pennock, Obediah	11	570	Transported 1668.
Penny, Hugh	Q	449	" 1658.
Penny, Jone	7	79	" 1664.
Pennycoake, John	16	126	" 1671.
Penrice, Robert	18	278	Immigrated 1675, with wife and 2 children. Of Dorset Co.
Penrose, John	17	396	Transported 1669.
Penrose, Priscilla	17	396	" 1671.
Penry, Margaret	16	129	" 1671.
Penry, Mary	16	129	" 1671.
Penry, Morgan	17	444	" 1670.
Pent, Elizabeth	9	216	" 1665.
Pentcoate, James	12	386	" 1669.
Penticoate, James	12	199	" 1668.
Penyman, William	WC2	110	" 1676. Servant.
Peper, John	15	318,412	Immigrated 1676.
Peper, Margaret	15	318,412	Transported 1676. Wife of John.
Peper, Margaret	15	318,412	" 1676. Daughter of John.
Peper, Mary	15	318,412	" 1676. Daughter of John.
Peper, Richard	15	318,412	" 1676. Son of John.
Peper, Tobias	15	318,412	" 1676. Son of John.
Pepper, James	12	576	" 1670.
Pepper, John	17	551	" 1673.
Pepper, William	16	537	" 1671.
Pera, Peter	10	213	" 1665.
Perce, Richard	7	506	" 1664.
Perce, Sebilla	5	90	" 1656.
Perce, William	6	214	" 1663.
Perce, William	10	286	" 1666.
Percefield, John	9	333	" 1665.
Percen, Edward	15	414	" 1677.
Percer, Francis	15	411	" 1677.
Percie, Robert	1	60-61	Immigrated 1635.
Percivall, Elizabeth	15	452	Transported 1678.
Percivall, Thomas	18	114	Service 1674. Of Calvert Co.

NAME	Liber	Folio	REMARKS
Percwall, John	6	86	Transported 1659.
Percy, Joan	12	477	" 1670.
Percy, Robert	1	73-74	Immigrated 1635.
Perdue, Stephen	Q	29	Transported 1658.
Peres, Francisco	1	20,37, 38,166	" 1635-37. A Molato.
Perey, George	18	313	" 1675.
Perey, Peter	12	190	" 1668.
Perey, Thomas	12	203	Service 1669.
Perfett, William	1	171	Transported about 1639.
Perfitt, John	ABH	48	" 1643. Servant. (3, fol. 25).
Perfort, William	ABH	187	Service 1651.
Perin, William	7	640	Immigrated 1664. Cousin to John Gittings.
Perins, Mary	5	185	Transported 1661.
Perke, Robert	15	414	Service 1677.
Perkin, Edward	9	272	Transported 1665.
Perkins, Bridgett	7	469	" 1664.
Perkins, Edward	7	580	" 1665. (10, fol. 417).
Perkins, Edward	16	302	" 1671. Servant. Of Va.
Perkins, Emanuel	6	294	" 1664.
Perkins, Hannah	18	291	" 1674.
Perkins, James	ABH	44	" many years prior to 1650.
Perkins, James	7	454	Transported 1664.
Perkins, Jonas	3	17	" prior to 1650.
Perkinson, Elizabeth	18	152	" 1674.
Perkinson, John	13	1	" 1669. Servant.
Perle, Henry	8	501	" 1674.
Perpilion, Lues	5	489	" 1650.
Perriman, Ann	9	28	" 1664.
Perrin, Samuel	17	440	" 1673.
Perrott, Richard, Jr.	17	567	Immigrated from Virginia 1673. Of Worcester County.
Perry, Ann	12	333	Transported 1669.
Perry, Charles	15	319	Immigrated 1672. Of Somerset Co. (17, fol. 381).
Perry, Constant	10	503	Transported 1667. Servant.
Perry, Elizabeth	5	127	" 1662.
Perry, Elizabeth	15	559	" 1679.
Perry, Gilbert	15	366	" 1676.
Perry, Henry	Q	199	" 1651.
Perry, Jenkin	6	295	" 1663.
Perry, John	5	415	" 1663.
Perry, John	11	482	" 1668.
Perry, Sarah	Q	75	" 1651.
Perry, Sarah	20	185	" 1679.
Perry, Thomas	4	140	" 1652. Servant.
Perry, Thomas	12	472	" 1670.
Perry, Thomas	15	427	Immigrated 1672.

NAME	Liber	Folio	REMARKS
Perry, Thomas	15	418	Transported 1677.
Perry, Thomas	17	445	Immigrated 1673.
Perry, Thomas	WC2	41	Transported 1679.
Perry, William	16	358	" 1671.
Perry, William	15	362	" 1676.
Perryn, John	2	613	" 1649. Servant. (ABH, fol. 161, 422).
Person, John	15	353	Transported 1676.
Person, Michael	18	94	" 1674.
Person, Ralph	9	431	" 1666. (10, fol. 394-5).
Person, Sarah	16	302	" 1671.
Persons, James	11	571	" 1668.
Persons, James	16	452	" 1671.
Persons, Peter	17	395,407	" 1672.
Persons, Roger	17	452	" 1671.
Pert, James	7	507	" 1663. (15, fol. 524).
Pert, John	Q	199	" 1651.
Pert, John	7	507	" 1663.
Pertnier, John	7	563	" 1665.
Peruin, Michael	WC2	309	" 1678.
Pery, Margaret	17	451	" 1673.
Pery, Richard, Capt.	12	591	Immigrated 1668.
Pery, Sarah	10	503	Transported 1667. Servant.
Pestle, Richard	9	343	" 1666.
Peteet, Thomas	2	347	" 1639.
Peterkin, Abraham	17	567	" 1673.
Peterkin, Ann	WC2	65	" 1679. Wife of James.
Peterkin, Ann	WC2	65	" 1679. Daughter of James.
Peterkin, Elizabeth	WC2	65	Transported 1679. Daughter of James.
Peterkin, Grace	WC2	65	Transported 1679. Daughter of James.
Peterkin, James	WC2	65,279, 412	Immigrated with wife, 6 children and two other persons. Of Dorchester County.
Peterkin, James, Jr.	WC2	65	Transported 1679.
Peterkin, Jane	WC2	65	" 1679. Daughter of James.
Peterkin, Patience	WC2	65	Transported 1679. Daughter of James.
Peterkins, James	WC2	279	Immigrated 1680. Of Dorchester Co.
Peters, Ann	15	565	Transported 1679.
Peters, Augustine	11	482	" 1668.
Peters, Elizabeth	5	531	" 1662.
Peters, Elizabeth	15	422	" 1666.
Peters, Elizabeth	11	319	" 1668.
Peters, Hans	10	599	" 1667.
Peters, Henry	6	131	" 1649.
Peters, John	WC2	171	" 1679.
Peters, Joseph	4	72	" 1658.

NAME	Liber	Folio	REMARKS
Peters, Mary	10	573	Transported 1667.
Peters, Randall	15	339	Service 1672. Of Worcester Co. (17, fol. 445, 567).
Peters, Susanna	16	482	Transported 1671.
Petersfield, John	10	560	" from Va. 1667. Servant.
Peterson, Andrew	7	426-427	" 1664. Brother to Cornelius.
Peterson, Anthony	17	566	Immigrated 1673.
Peterson, Cornelius	7	426-427	" 1664.
Peterson, Court	4	576	Transported 1661.
Peterson, Derrick	9	327	" 1666.
Peterson, Edward	8	484	" 1665.
Peterson, Egbert	8	131	" 1664.
Peterson, Elizabeth	9	459	" 1662. Daughter of Jacob.
Peterson, "Ezer"	7	426-427	Transported 1664. Sister to Cornelius.
Peterson, Hance	17	489	Immigrated from Holland 1665. Of Baltimore County.
Peterson, Ingaber	17	489	Immigrated from New York, 1661. Wife of Hance.
Peterson, Jacob	9	459	Immigrated 1662, with Elizth., his daughter and Elizabeth Proter, whom he afterwards married. Of Charles County. (15, fol. 481).
Peterson, Jane	10	565	Transported from Virginia 1667.
Peterson, John	8	130	" 1664.
Peterson, Lawrence	8	130	" 1664.
Peterson, Margaret	17	418	" 1667. Wife of Mathias.
Peterson, Mathias	17	418	Immigrated 1665.
Peterson, Nelkey	9	327	Transported 1666.
Peterson, Peter	17	418	" 1667. Son of Mathias. (9, fol. 327).
Peterson, Samuel	7	464	Transported 1661.
Petit, Abraham Clement	12	271	" 1668.
Petit, Barbara	12	271	" 1668. Daughter of Abraham C.
Petit, Jertsnyt	12	271	Transported 1668. Wife of Abraham C.
Petit, Mary	15	430	Transported 1677.
Petit, Rachel	12	271	" 1668. Daughter of Abraham C.
Petit, Thomas	ABH	60	Immigrated 1642, with wife. (ABH, fol. 25).
Petite, Catherine	ABH	11	Transported 1645. A child.
Petite, Catherine (Katheren)	2	430,539	" 1645. Daughter of Thomas. Child.
Petite, Thomas	2	516	Immigrated about 1645 with wife.
Petite, Mrs. Thomas	2	430	Transported 1639. Wife of Thomas.
Petman, Francis	6	215	" 1663.
Petoe, Humphrey	18	168	Service 1674.

NAME	Liber	Folio	REMARKS
Petterson, Thomas	15	362	Transported 1676.
Pettichenz, Anthony	5	361	" 1663.
Petticoate, William	10	498	" 1667.
Pettipoole, Ann	9	50	" 1665. Wife of William.
Pettipoole, William	9	50	Immigrated 1665.
Pettipoole, William	9	50	Transported 1665. Son of William.
Pettman, Alice	5	373	" 1663.
Petts, Thomas	1	94-95	Petition to confirm title to land, 1640.
Petty, Elizabeth	15	322	Transported 1674.
Petty, Lawrence	12	284	" 1668.
Pettycoate, John	18	157	Service 1674.
Pettymon, Thomas	17	571	Transported 1673.
Pewell, George	7	569	" 1663-4.
Pewsey, William	WC2	320	" 1680. Servant.
Pexton, Hugh	15	574	Service 1673.
Pexton, Hugh	WC2	57	" 1679.
Pey, Nicholas	11	344	Transported 1668.
Peyton, Richard	15	397	" 1676.
Peyton, Thomas	7	553	" 1665.
Phares, Lydia	Q	58	" 1658.
Phelp, Cudbeard	4	49	Immigrated 1654, with wife.
Phelp, Cudbeard	4	49	Transported 1654. Son of Cudbeard.
Phelp, Derby	4	49	" 1654. Son of Cudbeard.
Phelp, Mary	4	49	" 1654. Wife of Cudbeard.
Phelps, Elizabeth	WC2	179	" 1680. Wife of Walter.
Phelps, Margaret	9	25	" 1665.
Phelps, Rebeccah	WC2	179	" 1680. Mother of Walter.
Phelps, Walter	WC2	178-179	Immigrated 1680 with wife, mother and three other persons. Of Anne Arundel Co.
Phelps, William	12	413	Transported 1669.
Phelps, William	15	300	" 1675.
Phenix, Edward	15	455	" 1678.
Phenix, George	16	74	Immigrated 1668. Of St. Mary's Co. Tailor.
Phenix, Patience	11	281	Transported 1667.
Pherry, John	15	376	" 1676.
Pheype (Pheypo), Marke	ABH	9,102	Immigrated 1641. Irishman. (1, fol. 129; 2, fol. 256, 425).
Philips, Alice	ABH	12	Servant 1648.
Philips, Anne	WC2	309	Transported 1680.
Philips, George	WC2	182	Service 1680.
Philips, Henry	WC2	318,400	" 1680. Of Somerset Co.
Philips, John	7	462	Transported 1663.
Philips, Joseph Thom.	ABH	151	" 1649-50. Servant.
Philips, Mary	WC2	182	Service 1680.
Philips, Samuel	WC2	406	Master of Ship, "Crowne Malago", 1678.
Philips, Thomas	ABH	14	Immigrated 1647.
Philips, Zachary	WC2	380	Transported 1675-80. Servant.

NAME	Liber	Folio	REMARKS
Phillingham, Richard	5	488	Transported 1651-62.
Phillips, Alice	2	444	" 1648. Servant.
Phillips, Alice	11	378	" 1668.
Phillips, Anthony	18	306	" 1675.
Phillips, Catherine	4	219	" 1659.
Phillips, David	4	136	Immigrated 1659 with family.
Phillips, Dorothy	4	219	Transported 1659.
Phillips, Dorothy	18	35	Service 1672. Wife of Roger of Somerset County.
Phillips, Edward	17	401	Transported 1669. Servant.
Phillips, Elizabeth	ABH	44	" many years prior to 1650.
Phillips, Elizabeth	3	17	Transported prior to 1650.
Phillips, Elizabeth	4	219	" 1659.
Phillips, Elizabeth	9	304	" 1665.
Phillips, Elizabeth	18	137	" 1674.
Phillips, Elizabeth	15	430	" 1677.
Phillips, Evan	11	378	" 1668.
Phillips, George	7	77	Immigrated 1664.
Phillips, Giles	9	313	Transported 1665.
Phillips, Henry	17	635	" 1674.
Phillips, Jacob	5	82	" 1661.
Phillips, James	5	488	" 1654.
Phillips, James	9	489	Immigrated 1665.
Phillips, James	16	100	Transported 1667. (17, fol. 4).
Phillips, John	ABH	89	" 1635. Servant.
Phillips, John	1	95	" 1635-40.
Phillips, John	4	219	" 1659.
Phillips, John	8	130	" 1664.
Phillips, John	16	465	" 1664. (12, fol. 379).
Phillips, John	16	358,507	" 1671. (17, fol. 63).
Phillips, John	17	408	" 1673.
Phillips, John	18	288	" 1674. (15, fol. 290).
Phillips, John	15	558	" 1677.
Phillips, John	15	565	" 1679.
Phillips, Jonas	5	411	" 1663.
Phillips, Loveday	10	305	" 1666. Servant.
Phillips, Margaret	12	498	" 1670.
Phillips, Martin	15	523	Immigrated 1678. Of St. Mary's Co.
Phillips, Mary	15	376	Transported 1676.
Phillips, Mary	ABH	244	" 1641.
Phillips, Mary	12	477	" 1670.
Phillips, Michael	11	436	" 1668. (17, fol. 538).
Phillips, Nicholas	5	129	" 1662.
Phillips, Nicholas	8	88	" 1665.
Phillips, Owen, Gent.	ABH	78	Immigrated 1638. (1, fol. 18, 63).
Phillips, Richard	12	216	Transported 1667.
Phillips, Richard	11	348	" 1668.
Phillips, Robert	7	86	" 1663.
Phillips, Roger	18	35	Immigrated 1672. Of Somerset Co.
Phillips, Symon	Q	68	Servant 1643.

NAME	Liber	Folio	REMARKS
Phillips, Thomas	2	456	Immigrated 1647.
Phillips, Thomas	5	513	Transported 1656. (4, fol. 30).
Phillips, Thomas	5	307	" 1663.
Phillips, Thomas	8	482	His widow married Rich. Lloyd, prior to 1665.
Phillips, Thomas	9	217	Transported 1665.
Phillips, Thomas	11	166	Of Talbot Co. Married Mary, widow of Francis Overton, prior to 1667.
Phillips, Thomas	16	507	Transported 1671.
Phillips, Thomas	15	353	" 1674. (18, fol. 30).
Phillips, Thomas	15	380	" 1676.
Phillips, Thomas, Jr.	4	219	" 1659.
Phillips, Thomas, Sr.	4	219	" 1659.
Phillips, William	ABH	140	" 1651.
Phillips, William	4	219	" 1659.
Phillips, William	6	17	" 1663.
Phillips, William	12	498	" 1670. (18, fol. 10).
Phillipson, Ann	1	134	License to marry Roger Moy, Nov. 24, 1638.
Phillpott, William	5	490	Transported 1662.
Philpot, Anthony	13	112	" 1670.
Philpot, Thomas	ABH	133	A minor, living 1650, and heir to Robert of the Isle of Kent, dec'd.
Philpott, Joan	7	470	Transported 1664.
Philpott, Robert	1	78-79	Immigrated prior to 1640. Of Isle of Kent.
Philpott, Robert	7	470	Transported 1664.
Philpott, Thomas	7	470	Immigrated 1664.
Philpott, William	Q	33	Transported 1658.
Phindell, Thomas	16	170	" 1671.
Phipes, Edward	15	380	" 1676.
Phipes, Elizabeth	15	514	" 1677.
Phipps, Henry	WC2	198-200	Immigrated 1680.
Phipps, Richard	WC2	16	Transported 1679.
Phirles, Arthur	9	437	" 1664.
Phisick, Julian	17	452	" 1671.
Phoebus, George	9	216	" 1665.
Phraser, Andrew	16	411	" 1671.
Phrayne, Joseph	5	411	" 1663.
Phron, John	16	432	" 1671.
Pias, Alice	15	430	" 1677.
Pickasgell, Thomas	15	369	" 1676.
Pickerell, Abigail	9	304	" 1665.
Pickerell, Mary	9	304	" 1665.
Pickerell, Michael	10	352	" 1666.
Pickering, Ann	16	414	" 1671.
Pickering, John	9	104	" 1665.
Pickering, John	18	313	Immigrated 1675, with Margaret, his wife, and Eliz., his daughter.
Pickett, Christopher	18	291	Transported 1674.
Pickett, Jone	4	30	" 1659. Servant.

NAME	Liber	Folio	REMARKS
Pickett, Susan	Q	435	Transported 1658.
Pierce, George	4	14	" 1659. Servant.
Pierce, Richard	ABH	46	" 1649. Servant.
Pierepoint, Elizabeth	WC2	198,200	Service 1680.
Pierpoint, Amis	9	34	Transported 1665. Eldest son of Henry.
Pierpoint, Elizabeth	9	34	Transported 1665. Wife of Henry.
Pierpoint, Elizabeth	9	34	" 1665. Daughter of Henry.
Pierpoint, Hannah	9	34	Transported 1665. Daughter of Henry.
Pierpoint, Henry	9	34	Immigrated 1665.
Pierpoint, Jabis	9	34	Transported 1665. Son of Henry.
Pierpoint, Moses	9	34	" 1665. Son of Henry.
Pigett, Walter	12	403	" 1669.
Pigg, Roger	18	15	" 1673.
Piggott, Richard	17	469	" 1673.
Pike, Ann	1	17,19	" 1637. Servant.
Pike, Ann	ABH	58,150	" 1637. Wife of John. Servant, 1642.
Pike, Bartho.	17	463	Transported 1673.
Pike, Humphrey	Q	47	Servant 1654.
Pike, John	1	21	Husband of Anne, 1642.
Pike, John	15	530	Transported 1678.
Pike, Mary	ABH	170	" 1650. Daughter of Mr. John.
Pike, Mary	6	166	Transported 1663.
Pike, Robert	1	121	" 1633.
Pike, Robert	ABH	98	" 1633. Servant.
Pike, Thomas	4	79	" 1659.
Pike, William	4	570	" 1661.
Pikes, Richard	8	486	" 1664.
Pilbet, Francis	15	501	" 1678.
Pilcher, Edward	4	581	" 1661.
Pile, John	4	543	And Benj. Gill, immigrated with
their families, 1642. (ABH, fol. 23).			
Pile, John	2	508	Immigrated prior to 1648 with wife.
Pile, Joseph	12	391	Transported 1669.
Pilgram, Walter	15	449	Service 1677. Of Somerset Co.
Pilherell, Thomas	12	283	Transported 1668. (See Pithorell).
Pillion, Peter	15	524	" 1678.
Pillion, Thomas	15	524	" 1678.
Pilo, Hastings	15	369	" 1676.
Pim, Alice	WC2	16	Service 1679. Wife of Richard.
Pim, Richard	WC2	16	" 1679.
Pimbleton, Solomon	12	243	Transported 1669.
Pimm, Richard	12	359	" 1669.
Pinato, Thomas	12	415	" 1669.
Pince, Edward	12	415	" 1669.
Pinchback, Jonah	15	455	" 1678.
Pindar, Jane	15	332	" 1675.

NAME	Liber	Folio	REMARKS
Pinder, Edward	12	192	Transported 1668.
Pinder, Thomas	WC2	17	Immigrated 1679.
Pindin, James	WC2	86-87	Transported 1679.
Pine, Elizabeth	ABH	151	" 1649-50. Servant.
Piner, Ann	7	569	" 1663-4.
Piner, Richard, Jr.	7	569	" 1663-4.
Piner, Richard, Sr.	7	569	" 1663-4.
Pingen, Robert	16	537	" 1671.
Pink, Francis	ABH	33	Servant 1646.
Pinke, Frances	2	567	Transported 1646. Servant.
Pinkney, Mary	15	560	" 1678.
Pinley, Dorothy	6	136	" 1663. (10, fol. 463).
Pinley, Thomas	6	136	" 1663. (10, fol. 463).
Pinley, Will.	1	27	" 1633-41.
Pinley, William	ABH	61,83	" 1633-41. (ABH, fol. 78).
Pinley, William	1	75,128	" 1638. Servant.
Pinly, William	1	62	" 1635-36.
Pinn, Charles	12	372	" 1669.
Pinner, Moses	12	203	" 1669.
Pinner, Richard	ABH	37,64	Servant 1638.
Pinner, Richard	1	33,171	Transported 1638. Servant. (2, fol. 605).
Pinner, Thomas	Q	19	Transported 1658. (18, fol. 284).
Pinnett, John	11	501	Service 1668.
Piper, Ann	5	489	Transported 1655 by Wm. Piper of Isle of Kent.
Piper, John	3	24	Transported 1650. Servant.
Pipes, David	9	105	" 1665.
Pippers, John	15	353	" 1675.
Pissell, William	9	399	" 1666.
Pitcorne, Lidy	4	22	" 1656.
Pitfield, Mary	7	464	" 1663.
Pithorell, Thomas	12	283	" 1668.
Pitstowe, Philip	15	332	" 1675.
Pitt, Elizabeth	15	300	" 1676-7.
Pitt, Elizabeth	WC2	399	" 1677.
Pitt, John	5	268	Immigrated 1663. (9, fol. 429-430).
Pitt, Mary	15	531	Transported 1678.
Pittison, Simon	12	190	" 1668. Servant.
Pittman, John	12	190	" 1668.
Pittman, William	WC2	253,398	" 1680.
Pitts, Mary	11	374	" 1668.
Pitts, Mary	16	115	" 1671.
Pitts, Susan	5	208	" 1662.
Pitts, Susanna	7	527	" 1664.
Pix, Daniel	16	115	" 1671.
Place, Henry	7	87	" 1659.
Place, Simon	7	87	" 1657.
Plane, Joane	16	89	" 1670.
Plane, William	ABH	164	" 1651. Servant.
Planer, William	5	211	Immigrated 1662.

NAME	Liber	Folio	REMARKS
Planner, Rebecca	16	307	Service 1671. Wife of Wm. of Somerset Co.
Planner, William	8	486	Immigrated 1665.
Plater, Richard	9	448	Transported 1666.
Platt, Ralph	8	478	" 1665.
Platt, Richard	17	635	" 1674.
Platt, Thomas	12	376	Immigrated 1669. Of Virginia.
Platters, William	4	553	Transported 1661.
Platts, Elizabeth	6	62	" 1663.
Platts, John	6	62	" 1663.
Playden, Robert	8	460	" 1661.
Playle, James	15	455	" 1678.
Pleasington, Barbara	9	25	" 1665.
Plenty, James	6	268	" 1662.
Pletso, Roger	ABH	9	Servant 1640.
Pletso, Roger	2	425	Transported 1640. Servant.
Pleydwell, Peter	4	585	" 1661.
Plomer, Henry	18	306	" 1675.
Plomer, John	15	520	Service 1677.
Plott, Thomas	ABH	312	Transported 1651-2. Servant.
Plovey, William	17	416	" 1673.
Plumcott, William	9	437	" 1664.
Plumer, Richard	6	95	" 1653.
Plummer, John	17	456	" 1673.
Plummer, Thomas	11	171	" 1667.
Ply, Robert	11	104	" 1667. Servant.
Plymott, Claudius	4	576	" 1661.
Pockwick, Elizabeth	6	63	" 1658-63.
Pococke, Phill	15	370	" 1676.
Podberry, Jane	16	100	" 1667.
Poe, Phil	15	516	" 1676.
Poell, Richard	7	560	" 1665.
Poesey, Mrs. Francis	3	3-4	" about 1643. Service 1650.
Poesey, Francis	2	427	Immigrated 1640.
Pointer, Elizabeth	18	329	Transported 1675.
Pointer, Francis	17	363	" 1672.
Pokely, Peter	8	42	" 1665.
Polax, Lawrence	4	64	" 1659. Servant.
Pole, Marina	WC2	415	" 1666-80. Servant.
Pole, Peter	4	616	" 1660.
Polhampton, Nicholas	ABH	61	" 1633-41. (1, fol. 27). (See Paulhampton).
Polland, John	15	455	Transported 1678.
Pollard, Anthony	WC2	124	" 1673. Servant.
Pollard, Christopher	7	463	" 1655.
Pollard, Hugh	16	17	Immigrated 1670.
Pollard, John	5	123	" 1662.
Pollard, John	17	451	Transported 1673. (15, fol. 564).
Pollard, John	WC2	1,311	" 1673. Of Dorchester County.

NAME	Liber	Folio	REMARKS
Pollard, Rebecca	9	454	Transported 1666.
Pollard, Richard	18	279	" 1675.
Pollen, William	7	88	" 1649.
Pollett, Elizabeth	4	30	" 1659. Servant.
Pollett, John	6	142	" 1656.
Pollitt, Francis	15	500	" 1678.
Pollitt, Richard	15	443	" 1672.
Polten, James	11	496	" 1668.
Poltson, John	11	581	" 1668.
Pomewood, Stephen	7	483	" 1664.
Pomfrey, Richard	17	547	Service 1673. Of Somerset Co.
Pomphrett, James	11	374	Transported 1668.
Pomphrey, Richard	6	36	" 1663.
Pomplin, Rebecca	15	414	" 1677.
Pond, Mary	4	5	" 1659. Servant.
Pond, Thomas	WC2	406	" 1676. (15, fol. 453).
Pond, William	WC2	327	Service 1680. Of Dorchester Co.
Ponder, John	18	84	Transported 1674.
Pondergra, Nich.	15	527	" 1678.
Poo, Magdelen	18	167	" 1674.
Pool, Thomas	ABH	348	" 1652. Servant.
Poole, Elizabeth	6	347	" 1663.
Poole, Elizabeth	13	114	" 1668.
Poole, Elizabeth	WC2	288	" 1680.
Poole, Mr. George	12	199	" 1668.
Poole, George	12	386	" 1669.
Poole, Hendrick	6	122	" 1650.
Poole, John	8	130	Immigrated 1668 with wife.
Poole, John	15	598	Transported 1668. Servant.
Poole, John	15	598	" 1679.
Poole, Launcelot	17	65	" Nov. 1669.
Poole, Marina	15	503	" 1678.
Poole, Martin	6	131	" 1660.
Poole, Rachel	17	449	" 1672.
Poole, Richard	15	314	" 1675.
Poole, Thomas	6	347	" 1663.
Pooler, Tho.	WC2	199	" 1680.
Pooley, John	17	419	And Mary, his wife. Service 1672.
Poolon, Katherine	7	474	Transported 1664.
Poor, Henry	Q	49	Service 1658.
Poor, John	4	5	Transported 1652-9.
Poor, Nicholas	15	527	" 1678.
Poor, Walter	15	527	" 1678.
Poore, Cesley	15	353	" 1674.
Poore, Elizabeth	15	446	" 1677.
Poore, George	10	600	" 1667.
Poore, George	11	546	" 1668.
Poore, George	15	362	" 1676.
Pooten, William	16	115	" 1671.
Pope, Andrew	4	11	" 1659. Servant.
Pope, Ann	15	317	" 1674. Wife of John.

NAME	Liber	Folio	REMARKS
Pope, Francis	1	112	Transported 1635. Servant.
Pope, Francis	ABH	23,95	" since 1635. Servant.
Transported his wife in 1649. (ABH, fol. 49).			
Pope, Francis	2	509	Transported 1639. Servant.
Pope, Francis	2	217	Immigrated 1645.
Pope, Mrs. Francis	3	26	Transported 1649.
Pope, Henry	15	370	" 1676.
Pope, John	11	318	" 1668.
Pope, John	17	572	" 1672. (15, fol. 407).
Pope, John	15	317	Immigrated 1674. Of Virginia.
Pope, Morgan	15	446	" 1677. Of Charles Co.
Pope, Nathaniel	1	53-55	" 1639. Of St. Mary's Hundred.
Pope, Nathaniel	ABH	50	Immigrated prior to 1648 with wife.
Pope, Nathaniel	2	610	" prior to 1650.
Pope, Nathaniell	3	63	" prior to 1648 with wife and five servants.
Pope, Oliver	4	11	Transported 1659. Servant.
Pope, Robert	WC2	415	" 1666-80. Servant.
Pope, Robert	12	203	" 1669.
Pope, Robert	15	318	" 1674. (18, fol. 24).
Pope, Robert	15	388	" 1675.
Pope, Robert	WC2	15	Immigrated 1679. Of Somerset Co.
Pope, Rose	4	14	Transported 1649. Servant.
Popham, Richard	5	180	" 1661. Service 1665. (9, fol. 312).
Popleton, Philip	WC2	128-129	Rights 1679.
Popley, Richard	12	415	Transported 1669.
Popley, William	5	257	" 1660.
Poppen, William	16	40	" 1670.
Poppitt, Thomas	7	504	" 1664.
Porescort, William	ABH	60	" 1635. Servant.
Porescourt, William	1	26	" since 1635.
Poro, John	4	63	Immigrated 1658.
Porringer, John	15	397	Transported 1676.
Port, John	7	83	" 1661.
Port, William	WC2	73	" 1678.
Porter, Ann	5	507	" 1649 and married Wm. Frezell prior to 1663.
Porter, Giles	6	48	Transported 1662.
Porter, Giles	11	104	" 1667.
Porter, James	12	403	" 1669.
Porter, Joan	ABH	241	" 1651, and married John Nevell prior to Jan. 29, 1652.
Porter, Joanna	12	351	Transported 1669.
Porter, Joseph	7	427	Immigrated 1664.
Porter, Joseph	11	337,441	Transported 1668.
Porter, Josias	17	602	" 1667.
Porter, Lawrence	5	93	Immigrated 1661.
Porter, Ma.	17	411	Transported 1673.
Porter, Mary	5	80	" 1661.

NAME	Liber	Folio	REMARKS
Porter, Nicholas	3	18	Transported about 1640. Servant.
Porter, Patience	9	216	" 1665. (18, fol. 22).
Porter, Priscilla	6	293	" 1664.
Porter, Raby	15	454	" 1677.
Porter, Robby	WC2	406	" 1677.
Porter, Stephen	11	167	" 1667.
Porter, Thomas	15	356	" 1675.
Porter, William	16	507	" 1671.
Portingall, Emanuel	5	210	" 1662.
Portland, Henry	4	616	" 1660.
Portles, Richard	WC2	73	" 1678.
Portry, Rebe	15	430	" 1677.
Portson, Edward	7	464	" 1658.
Portugall, Hugh	12	416	" 1669.
Portwood, Elizabeth	WC2	124	" 1679. Wife of John.
Portwood, John	WC2	124-125	Immigrated 1679 with wife and
her son, John Robinson. Of St. Mary's County.			
Posey, Francis	ABH	10,42	Immigrated 1640.
Posgate, Ann	17	469	Transported 1671.
Pott, Elizabeth	Q	33	Wife of John 1658.
Pott, Francis, Capt.	ABH	430	Of Virginia. Deed of gift to Thos.
and Margaret Hatton, 1648.			
Pott, Mr. John	Q	33	Immigrated 1658.
Pott, John	3	170	Rights 1655.
Pott, Rich.	15	540	Transported 1676.
Potten, William	12	341	" 1668.
Potter, Ann	5	556	" 1660.
Potter, Augent	11	374	" 1668.
Potter, Giles	13	56	" 1670.
Potter, John	10	466	Immigrated 1667.
Potter, Rebeccah	WC2	309	Transported 1678.
Potter, Samuel	15	317	Immigrated 1674. Of New England.
Potter, William	11	367	Transported 1668. Servant. (17, fol. 376).
Potter, William	18	160	Transported 1674.
Pottinger, John	8	42	" 1665.
Potts, Ann	15	450	" 1677.
Potts, Barbara	15	322	" 1674.
Potts, John	17	463	" 1673.
Potts, John	15	560	" 1678.
Potts, Robert	4	198	" 1659.
Potts, Thomas	8	502	" 1665.
Pouleson, Clare	4	555	" 1661.
Pouleson, Cosine	4	555	" 1661.
Pouleson, George	4	555	" 1661.
Pouleson, John	4	555	" 1661.
Pouleson, Mary	4	555	" 1661. Wife of Michael.
Pouleson, Mary	4	555	" 1661. Daughter of Michael.
Pouleson, Michael	4	555	Immigrated 1661.
Pouleson, Michael	4	555	Transported 1661. Son of Michael.

NAME	Liber	Folio	REMARKS
Pouleson, William	6	154	Transported 1662.
Poulson, Andrew	5	175	A Swede. Living 1662.
Poulson, Anguette	7	426	Transported 1664. Mother of Bartlett Hendrickson.
Poulson, Paul	4	555	Transported 1661.
Poultan, Thomas	WC2	66	" 1669.
Poulter, Charles	15	370	" 1676.
Poulter, Edward	5	259	" 1657. (17, fol. 382).
Poulter, Elizabeth	WC2	396	" 1680. Servant.
Poulter, Jane	15	445	" 1678.
Pountney, Henry	ABH	7	Immigrated 1644. (2, fol. 390).
Poure, John	18	111	Service 1674. Of St. Mary's Co.
Pourtree, John	3	173	Transported 1655.
Povenell, Thomas	4	10	" 1658. Servant.
Powell, Ann	4	551	" 1661.
Powell, Ann	6	90	" 1662.
Powell, Ann	6	71	" 1663, by a Quaker.
Powell, Ann	9	94,313	" 1665. Servant.
Powell, Ann	15	534	" 1674.
Powell, Bridgett	9	313	" 1665. Of Virginia.
Powell, Charles	9	313	" 1665. Of Virginia.
Powell, Daniel	10	390	" 1666.
Powell, David	16	100	" 1663.
Powell, Edward	5	106	" 1660.
Powell, Edward	4	560	" 1661.
Powell, Edward	15	379	" 1676.
Powell, Elizabeth	4	551	" 1661.
Powell, Elizabeth	16	168	" 1671. Daughter of Walter.
Powell, Elizabeth	18	280	Transported 1675.
Powell, George	5	63	" 1660. (17, fol. 422).
Powell, George	17	574	Immigrated 1673. Of St. Mary's County. (18, fol. 163; 15, fol. 310).
Powell, Howell	4	54,551	Immigrated 1659.
Powell, Isabell	15	569	Transported 1678.
Powell, James	16	307	" 1671 from Virginia.
Powell, James	17	416	" 1673.
Powell, Jane	16	40	" 1670.
Powell, Jane	WC2	282	" 1680.
Powell, John	3	18	" about 1640. Servant.
Powell, John	10	583	" 1667. Servant. Of Va.
Powell, John	11	344,463	" 1668. (12, fol. 282).
Powell, John	12	285	" 1668. Servant. (13, fol. 111).
Powell, John	16	60	Service 1670. Of St. Mary's Co. (17, fol. 57).
Powell, John	15	553	Transported 1678.
Powell, Mary	ABH	370	" 1653.
Powell, Mary	4	533	" 1659.
Powell, Mary	9	262,304	" 1665.
Powell, Mary	18	313	" 1675.

NAME	Liber	Folio	REMARKS
Powell, Mary	15	564	Transported 1679.
Powell, Ralph	8	128	" 1664. Servant. Of
Baltimore County. (11, fol. 500).			
Powell, Ralph	10	598	Immigrated 1667.
Powell, Richard	6	85	Transported 1651.
Powell, Richard	15	318	" 1675.
Powell, Richard	15	439	" 1677.
Powell, Robert	12	391	" 1669.
Powell, Roger	16	71	" 1668.
Powell, Rotherick	6	49	Immigrated 1663.
Powell, Samuel	WC2	73	Transported 1678.
Powell, Sarah	4	59	" 1649-52.
Powell, Sarah	8	87	" 1665. Servant. (9, fol. 310).
Powell, Thomas	4	54	Immigrated 1659.
Powell, Thomas	4	551	Transported 1661.
Powell, Thomas	16	428	" 1670-1.
Powell, Thomas	15	354	" 1676.
Powell, Thomas	15	433	" 1677.
Powell, Thomas	WC2	288	" 1680.
Powell, Ursula	16	503	" 1671.
Powell, Walter	ABH	276	" 1650.
Powell, Walter	16	168,304	Immigrated 1671 with wife and daughter, from Virginia. Of Somerset County.
Powell, Welthean	11	344	Transported 1668.
Powell, William	8	129	" 1664. Servant. (11, fol. 501).
Powell, William	9	313	Immigrated to Talbot Co. 1665. Of Virginia.
Powell, William	16	399	Transported Feb. 1667.
Powell, William	11	378	" 1668.
Powell, William	16	399	" 1671.
Powell, William	WC2	406	" 1679. (15, fol. 564; 20, fol. 185).
Powells, William	15	422	Transported 1664.
Power, John	15	517	Service 1663.
Power, John	15	553	Transported 1678.
Poweridge, Thomas	6	83	" 1663.
Powers, Elizabeth	15	567	" 1678.
Powes, Robert	17	304	" 1672.
Powford, John	10	573	" 1667.
Powle, Ann	15	443	" 1670.
Powley, Bryan	15	167	" 1673.
Powley, Elizabeth	6	62	" 1663.
Powney, Thomas	ABH	246	" years before 1652.
Powick, John	5	124-125	Immigrated 1662. Of London, Gent. Special Warrant for 300 acres 1661.
Poyell, Thomas	15	433	Transported 1677. (See Powell).
Poynes, Elizabeth	17	395	" 1672.
Poynter, Elizabeth	5	90	" 1653-61.
Poynter, Thomas	18	39	Immigrated 1674, with Frances,

NAME	Liber	Folio	REMARKS

his wife and Thomas, Wm. and Abegail, his children.

NAME	Liber	Folio	REMARKS
Poytley, James	6	63	Transported 1658-63.
Pranch, Morgan	12	241	" 1669.
Prane, Morgan.	15	563	" 1678.
Prat, Ann	12	492	" 1670.
Prate, Nicholas	7	567	" 1665.
Pratt, Elizabeth	5	339	" 1663.
Pratt, Elizabeth	18	306	" 1675.
Pratt, Henry	7	519	" 1664.
Pratt, Henry	WC2	106	" 1679.
Pratt, John	15	551	" 1679.
Pratt, Margaret	5	246	" 1656.
Pratt, Mary	6	106	" 1649.
Pratt, Mary	15	517	" 1678.
Pratt, Nicholas	5	203	" 1662.
Pratt, Ralph	15	442	" 1677.
Pratt, Thomas	4	212	Immigrated 1659.
Pratt, Tomlin	WC2	112	Transported 1679.
Prebins, Elizabeth	15	436	" 1677.
Prentice, John	5	409	" 1660.
Prentice, William	16	166	Immigrated 1670. Of Somerset Co.
Prescott, Walter	6	128	Transported 1653.
Presley, Fran.	20	185	" 1679.
Presley, Henry	6	126	" 1658.
Presley, William	15	300	" 1675.
Presse, William	9	325	" 1666.
Pressley, Margaret	15	516	" 1678.
Prest, Elizabeth	11	319	" 1668.
Prest, William	12	334	" 1668.
Prester, Thomas	ABH	89	" 1635. Servant.
Preston, Ann	15	553	" 1678.
Preston, James	ABH	140	" 1651.
Preston, John	8	130	" 1664.
Preston, John	11	582	" 1668.
Preston, John	15	369	" 1676.
Preston, Lydia	5	66	" 1662.
Preston, Margaret	18	280	" 1675.
Preston, Margaret, Jr.	ABH	140	" 1651.
Preston, Margaret, Sr.	ABH	140	" 1651.
Preston, Mary	6	27	" 1663.
Preston, Neomy	ABH	140	" 1651.
Preston, Rebeccah	WC2	363	Daughter of Richard.
Preston, Mr. Richard	ABH	139,140	Com'r. of the North side of Patux-ent River, 1650.
Preston, Richard	4	139	Immigrated 1650 with his 7 children.
Preston, Richard	3	172	Rights 1655.
Preston, Richard, Jr.	ABH	140	Transported 1651.
Preston, Samuel	ABH	140	" 1651.
Preston, Sarah	WC2	363-364	Daughter of Richard Preston. Married William Ford.
Preston, Thomas	11	337,484	Transported 1668.

NAME	Liber	Folio	REMARKS
Preston, Thomas	WC2	369,377, 392	Service 1680. Of Baltimore County.
Preston, Zachary	WC2	380	Transported 1675-80. Servant.
Prestwich, Samuel	WC2	199	" 1680.
Preswood, Thomas	15	359	" 1676.
Prether, Jonathan	Q	202	Immigrated 1658.
Pretious, John	17	444	" 1673, with Ann, his wife.
Pretty, Penelope	12	356	Transported 1669.
Price, Andrew	17	576	" 1673.
Price, Ann	19	375	Daughter of Jno. of St. Mary's. Married Rich'd. Hatton prior to 1674. Both dead prior to 1676.
Price, Ann	15	354	Transported 1676.
Price, Benjamin	7	560	" 1665.
Price, Caesar	ABH	199	" 1651. Son of John.
Price, Catherine	ABH	199	" 1651. Daughter of Jno. and Frances.
Price, Catherine	5	63	Transported 1660.
Price, Charles	11	378	" 1668.
Price, Daniel	15	530	" 1678. Son of John.
Price, David	12	513	" 1669.
Price, Edward	5	127	" 1662.
Price, Edward	12	203	" 1664. (11, fol. 128).
Price, Edward	16	535	Immigrated with Katherine, his wife, and James, his son, from Virginia 1671. Of Somerset County.
Price, Eleanor	WC2	399	Transported 1677.
Price, Elis	15	500	" 1676-7.
Price, Elizabeth	17	399	Service 1672. Of Calvert Co.
Price, Elizabeth	WC2	359,377	Transported 1680.
Price, Evan	15	354	" 1676.
Price, Frances	ABH	199	" 1651. Wife of John.
Price, Frances	5	516	" 1659. Wife of William.
Price, George	6	105	" 1654.
Price, Hester	15	544	" 1676.
Price, Hugh	12	333	" 1668.
Price, Isaac	15	452	" 1678.
Price, James	1	19,33, 171	" 1637. Servant.
Price, James	ABH	37,64	Servant 1637.
Price, James	5	412,514	Immigrated 1663.
Price, James	12	203	Transported 1664. Son of Edward.
Price, James	10	193	Immigrated 1666. (12, fol. 623).
Price, James	17	532	Transported 1673.
Price, James	15	530	" 1678. Son of John.
Price, James	WC2	320	Rights 1680.
Price, Jane	9	190,343	Transported 1665.
Price, Jane	10	570	" 1666.
Price, Jane	15	319	Service 1675. Wife of Edward.
Price, Jane	WC2	288	Transported 1680.
Price, Jenkin	12	203	" by Edward P. 1664. Servant.
Price, Jenkin	11	378	Transported 1668. (12, fol. 194).

NAME	Liber	Folio	REMARKS
Price, Joane	15	548	Immigrated 1669. Wife of Thomas, of St. Mary's Co.
Price, John (black)	ABH	66	Transported 1633.
Price, John (white)	ABH	66	" 1633.
Price, John, Capt.	ABH	10	Immigrated prior to 1636.
Price, John	ABH	199	" 1651.
Price, John	Q	48	" 1658.
Price, John	5	129	" 1662.
Price, John	5	536	Transported 1663.
Price, John	9	454	" 1666.
Price, John	12	243,514	" 1668. Servant.
Price, John	12	386	Immigrated 1669.
Price, John	17	396	" 1671.
Price, John	17	547	Service 1673. Of Talbot Co.
Price, John	18	134,167	" 1674. Of Anne Arundel Co. (18, fol. 291).
Price, John	18	313	Transported 1675.
Price, John	15	354,544	" 1676.
Price, John	15	430	" 1677.
Price, John	15	530	Immigrated 1678. Of Cecil Co.
Price, John	WC2	288	Transported 1680.
Price, John, Jr.	1	38	" 1633. (Als. White John Price).
Price, John, Jr.	Q	48	Transported 1658. Son of John.
Price, John, Sr.	1	38	" 1633. (Als. Black John Price).
Price, Capt. John	2	426	Immigrated about 1637.
Price, Capt. John	2	458	" about 1640-41.
Price, Judith	15	530	Transported 1678. Daughter of John.
Price, Katherine	12	203	Transported 1664. Wife of Edward.
Price, Katherine	9	454	Immigrated 1666.
Price, Lodowick	1	121	Transported 1633.
Price, Ludowick	ABH	98	" 1633. Servant.
Price, Margaret	12	576	" 1670.
Price, Margaret	Q	48	Immigrated 1658. Daughter of John.
Price, Margaret	9	332	Transported on the "Golden Wheat Sheaf", 1664.
Price, Margaret	15	530	Transported 1678. Wife of John.
Price, Martha	Q	48	Immigrated 1658. Wife of John.
Price, Mary	6	129	Transported 1652.
Price, Mary	4	140	" 1658. Servant. (Quaker ?)
Price, Mary	7	165	Transported 1665.
Price, Mary	12	386	Service 1669. Wife of John. (17, fol. 549).
Price, Mary	WC2	320	Transported 1680. Wife of James.
Price, Moses	WC2	120	" 1680.
Price, Peter	18	174	" 1674.
Price, Rese	16	482	" 1671.

NAME	Liber	Folio	REMARKS
Price, Richard	7	560	Transported 1665. (8, fol. 88).
Price, Richard	9	450	" 1666.
Price, Richard	WC2	320	" 1680.
Price, Robert	Q	183	" 1658. Servant.
Price, Robert	15	380	" 1676.
Price, Robert	WC2	259	" 1680.
Price, Roger	18	107	Immigrated 1669.
Price, Samuel	WC2	213-214	Transported 1671-1673.
Price, Sarah	5	254	" 1658-63. Daughter of John.
Price, Sarah	16	168	Transported 1671. Wife of John of Somerset Co.
Price, Sibill	8	88	Transported 1664. Servant.
Price, Susan	10	193	" 1666. Wife of James.
Price, Susanna	ABH	151	" 1641. Servant.
Price, Thomas	ABH	82	" 1634. Servant. (1, fol. 25, 73).
Price, Thomas	5	484	Transported 1661. (6, fol. 47).
Price, Thomas	5	252	Immigrated 1663.
Price, Thomas	7	80	Transported 1664.
Price, Thomas	11	104	" 1667. (12, fol. 270).
Price, Thomas	12	391	" 1669.
Price, Thomas	16	85	" 1670.
Price, Thomas	16	439	" 1671. (17, fol. 419).
Price, Thomas	18	166	" 1674.
Price, Thomas	15	439	" 1677.
Price, Thomas	15	568	" 1678.
Price, William	5	516	Immigrated 1653.
Price, William	6	215	" prior to 1661. Married the widow of Hugh Lee.
Price, William	5	127	Transported prior to 1662.
Price, William	7	823	" 1663.
Price, William	17	381	Immigrated from Virginia 1672.
Price, William	17	611	Service 1673. Of Calvert Co.
Price, William	18	24	Transported 1674.
Price, William	15	380	" 1676.
Prichard, David	ABH	25	Immigrated 1647.
Prichard, David	2	517	" 1649.
Prichard, Thomas	4	532	" 1659, with wife.
Prichards, Thomas	Q	431	Transported prior to 1658.
Prichatt, John	11	344	" 1668.
Prick, William	9	216	" 1665.
Prickett, Ann	4	550	" 1658.
Pricklove, Samuel	9	263	" 1665.
Pridd, John	ABH	61	" 1637.
Pride, Benjamin	16	469	Immigrated March 1667, with Ann, his wife, and two children, Benj. and Ann. Of Talbot Co.
Pridex, Thomas	17	382	Transported from Virginia 1672.
Pridg, Mary	15	557	" 1678.
Pridwell, Mary	15	359	" 1676.
Priest, Charles	9	269	" 1665.

NAME	Liber	Folio	REMARKS
Priest, Evan	13	56	Transported 1670.
Prigg, Richard	7	82	" 1661.
Prigge, Richard	5	319	" 1663.
Prigmere, Richard	12	415	" 1669.
Prime, Abigail	12	584	" 1670.
Primer, Ann	11	235	Wife of Richard. Transported
prior to 1667, when she appears as his widow and is styled als. Aitkins.			
Primer, Richard	11	235	Immigrated prior to 1667. Of Charles Co.
Primer, Richard, Jr.	11	235	Transported prior to 1667. Son of Richard.
Primer, William	11	235	Transported prior to 1667. Son of Richard.
Primms, John	WC2	86	Transported 1679. Servant.
Prince, David	18	296	" 1674.
Prince, Edward	15	318	" 1675.
Prince, John	15	505	" 1678.
Prince, Margaret	15	553	" 1678.
Prince, Penelope	ABH	33	Servant 1644.
Prince, Penelope	2	567	Transported 1644. Servant.
Prince, Penelope	10	503	" 1667. Servant.
Prince, Sarah	18	291	" 1674.
Prince, Sarah	WC2	319	Service 1680.
Prince, Stephen	5	87	Transported 1649-62.
Prince, Susanna	16	540	" 1671.
Prince, Thomas	18	331	" 1674.
Pringle, Eleanor	17	469	" 1673.
Prior, Daniel	12	594	" 1670.
Prior, Jone	9	490	" 1665. Wife of Thomas.
Prior, Mary	15	514	" 1677.
Prior, Thomas	9	490	Immigrated 1665.
Prior, William	9	334	Transported 1666.
Prirdom, Richard	11	229	" 1667.
Prirett, Andrew	WC2	86-87	" 1679.
Prison, Edmond	Q	18	" 1658.
Pristley, Richard	18	311	" 1675.
Pritchard, Abraham	5	530	" 1662.
Pritchard, David	ABH	339	Immigrated 1652.
Pritchard, Henry	17	475	Transported 1673.
Pritchard, John	17	440	" 1673.
Pritchard, Thomas	ABH	403	" 1652. Servant.
Pritchard, William	9	269	" 1665.
Pritchatt, Elizabeth	ABH	420	" 1654. Wife of Thomas.
Pritchatt, Jane	ABH	420	" 1654. Daughter of Thomas.
Pritchet, Daniel	16	503	Transported 1671.
Pritchet, Hester	17	333	" 1672.
Pritchet, Thomas	18	82	Service 1674. Of Calvert Co.
Pritchet, Weltherstone	16	124	Transported 1671.
Pritchett, Daniel	15	452	" 1678.
Pritchett, Henry	6	129	" 1653.

NAME	Liber	Folio	REMARKS
Pritchett, John	Q	68	Servant 1653-8.
Pritchett, John	12	592	Immigrated 1670. Of Talbot Co.
Pritchett, Samuel	6	299	Transported 1664.
Pritchett, Thomas	7	553	" 1665.
Pritchett, William	6	17	" 1663.
Pritchett, William	16	86	" 1670.
Pritchett, William	7	528	" 1664.
Pritt, Thomas	12	496	" 1670.
Probert, John	15	500	" 1678.
Proctor, Nathaniel	4	70,549	Immigrated 1659.
Proctor, Peter	9	54	Of Severn. Demands land in right of his deceased father.
Proctor, Robert	6	80	Immigrated 1660.
Proctor, Rosamond	6	80	Transported 1663.
Proctor, Samuel	17	475	" 1673.
Proffit, Elizabeth	Q	71	" 1652. Wife of Joseph.
Proffit, Mr. Joseph	Q	71	" 1652.
Proffit, Rachel	Q	71	" 1652. Daughter of Joseph.
Proley, Richard	6	129	Transported 1654.
Prosser, John	5	530	" 1662.
Prosser, Mathias	15	438	" 1677.
Prosser, Thomas	1	95	" 1635-40.
Proter, Elizabeth	9	459	" 1662 by Jacob Peterson, whom she afterwards married.
Prouce, George	9	48	Transported 1665.
Prount, John	7	62	" 1661.
Prouse, George	8	19	" 1664.
Prowse, Charles	17	566	Immigrated 1673 with wife and son. Of Worcester Co. (15, fol. 530).
Pruder, Mary	15	362	Transported 1676.
Prudum, Margery	15	442	" 1677.
Pruett, William	15	370	" 1676.
Pryor, Joane	14	446	" 1665. Wife of Thomas.
Pryor, Thomas	5	491	" 1663.
Pryor, Thomas	14	446	Immigrated 1665. Of Baltimore Co.
Pryor, Thomas	WC2	398	Transported 1680.
Puckley, John	15	534	" 1677.
Puddiford, Daniel	16	505	Service 1672. Of Dorchester Co.
Pudding, Joane	12	200	Transported 1668.
Puddington, Comfort	ABH	40	" 1649. (2, fol. 614).
Puddington, Mr. George	ABH	40	Immigrated 1649. (2, fol. 614).
Puddington, Jane	ABH	40	Transported 1649. (2, fol. 614).
Puddington, Mary	ABH	40	" 1649. (2, fol. 614).
Pudyfatt, Nathaniel	16	358	Immigrated 1671. Of St. Mary's Co.
Pue, Roger	WC2	395	Transported 1680. Servant.
Puiner, William	7	569	" 1663-4.
Pulison, Roger	18	174	" 1674.
Pullaine, Richard	5	467	" 1660.
Pullen, Anne	WC2	412	" 1681.
Pullen, John	15	324	" 1674.

NAME	Liber	Folio	REMARKS
Pullen, Mary	WC2	412	Transported 1681.
Pullen, Richard	WC2	412-413	Immigrated 1681.
Pullett, Margaret	9	373	Service 1666.
Pulley, Richard	6	7	Transported 1660.
Pullin, Margaret	9	374	" 1666. Servant.
Pullin, Richard	11	144	" 1667.
Pulton, Alexin	ABH	100	" 1641. Servant.
Pulton, Alexius	1	125	" 1641. Servant.
Pulton, Ferdinando	1	18,37-41	Immigrated 1638.
Pulton, Mr. Fernando	ABH	65-66	" 1638.
Pumfrey, Richard	12	385	Transported 1669.
Pumfry, Eliza	12	200	" 1668.
Pumphrey, Thomas	12	287	" 1668.
Puncke, Penelope	17	475	" 1673.
Puness, John	7	471	" 1664. Servant.
Punfield, James	5	251	" 1663.
Punfield, James	WC2	91	Service 1667. Of Calvert Co.
Punnett, Autin	15	362	Transported 1676.
Purchase, Nicholas	WC2	381	" 1675-80. Servant.
Purdon, John	9	28	" 1664.
Purdy, Nathaniel	16	358	Immigrated 1671 from Virginia. Of St. Mary's Co.
Purgear, George	WC2	23	Transported 1679.
Purlivant, Richard	1	84,89-90	Immigrated 1640. "Barber Chirurgeon". Of Isle of Kent.
Purlivant, Richard	ABH	87	Immigrated 1646. Barber and Chirurgeon.
Purnell, John	18	166	Transported 1674.
Purnell, Richard	WC2	20	Immigrated 1663. Of Talbot Co.
Purnell, Thomas	WC2	20	" 1663. Of Talbot Co.
Purnell, Thomas	18	37	Immigrated 1673 with Elizth, his wife. (15, fol. 310).
Pursall, Samuel	ABH	60,63	Transported 1638. Servant. (1, fol. 25, 31; 2, fol. 604).
Pursall, Thomas	1	132	Immigrated 1641.
Purse, Anthony	9	335	" 1666. Of Talbot Co.
Pursell, Edmond	WC2	21	Transported 1679.
Pursell, Thomas	ABH	104	Immigrated 1641.
Pursey, Francis	6	87	Transported 1657.
Purser, John	6	159	" 1652.
Purser, Thomas	12	413	" 1669.
Purveor, Henry	6	96	" 1657.
Purvis, John	18	167	" 1674.
Putteman, Charity	WC2	381	" 1675-80. Servant.
Puttyfer, Sarah	18	164	Service 1674.
Puver, Elizabeth	11	436	Transported 1668.
Py, John	16	639	" 1672.
Pye, George	ABH	90	Immigrated 1637. (1,fol.100).
Pye, John	16	393	Transported 1671.

NAME	Liber	Folio	REMARKS
Pye, Nicholas	16	538	Immigrated from Virginia 1672.
Pye, Timothy	7	454	Transported 1664.
Pye, Walter	9	321	" 1661.
Pygott, John	12	285	" 1667.
Pyke, Ann	ABH	12	Servant 1638.
Pyke, Ann	2	444	Transported 1638. Servant.
Pyman, William	15	574	" 1668.
Pyne, Charles	WC2	19	Service 1679. Of Calvert Co.
Pynes, Edward	5	89	Transported 1661.
Pynn, Edward	16	472	Service Feb.1671. Of Talbot Co.
Pynn, Edward	WC2	391-392	Immigrated 1679. Of St.Mary's Co.
Pynner, Richard	3	18	Transported about 1640. Servant.
Quaill, Alice	20	184	" from Virginia 1678.
Quarles, Anthony	17	417	" 1673.
Quarrell, Thomas	18	39	" 1674. (15,fol.397).
Quarterman, John	12	415	" 1669.
Quarterman, Thomas	17	383	" 1672.
Querk, Derby	WC2	128	" 1679.
Querk, John	15	567	" 1679.
Querke, William	WC2	120	" 1680.
Quigley, Austin	15	553	" 1678.
Quigley, Cane	15	553	" 1678.
Quigley, Cate	15	553	" 1678.
Quigley, Cate, Jr.	15	553	" 1678.
Quigley, Charles	15	553	" 1678.
Quigley, Daniel	15	553	" 1678.
Quigley, Jone	15	553	" 1678.
Quigley, Larance	15	553	" 1678.
Quigley, Margaret	15	553	" 1678, Ship St. George
of London, Capt. Jno. Quigley.			
Quigley, Matthew	15	553	Transported 1678.
Quigley, Terance	15	553	" 1678.
Quigley, Thomas	15	553	" 1678.
Quillane, Daniel	10	437	Immigrated 1667.
Quillane, Lidean	10	437	Transported 1667.
Quinney, Anne	WC2	412	" 1681.
Quinney, Rose	WC2	412	" 1681.
Quinney, Sutton	WC2	412	" 1681.
Quint, Edmond	18	137	" 1674.
Quintane, Walter	15	415	Service 1677.
Quinton, Walter	16	436	Transported 1671.
Quitt, William	12	496	" 1670.
Rabnet, Francis	ABH	66	" 1633.
Rabnett, Francis	1	38	" 1633.
Raby, John	4	69	Immigrated 1659.
Rackes, Edward	16	437	Transported 1671.
Radden, George	7	87	" 1654.
Raddon, Jone	15	566	" 1678.
Radford, Oliver	15	598	" 1678-9.
Radford, Oliver	WC2	211	" 1679. Servant.
Radford, Thomas	12	216	" 1668.

NAME	Liber	Folio	REMARKS
Radley, Henry	12	496	Transported 1670.
Radley, Mary	12	322	" 1669.
Radsey, Robert	10	410	" 1666.
Raethall, James	5	80	Immigrated from New England, 1661, with wife.
Rainbow, Edward	13	116	Transported 1671.
Rainbow, William	16	536	Immigrated from Virginia 1671.
Raine, Hannah	16	435	Transported 1671.
Raine, Thomas	15	443	" 1669.
Raineg, John	WC2	106	" 1679.
Raines, Francis	7	580	" 1665.
Rainford, Randall	15	454	" 1677. (See Ransford).
Rainnie, James	12	359	Immigrated 1669.
Rainsborough, Edmond	5	610	Transported 1656.
Raise, John	9	216	" 1665.
Raithwell, William	5	490	Service 1662.
Rakunhi, Daniel	12	459	Transported 1669.
Ralfe, Thomas	WC2	77	Service 1679. Of Somerset Co.
Rallenges, Ralph	WC2	65	Transported 1679.
Ralph, Margaret	16	115	" 1671.
Ralph, Mary	16	115	" 1671.
Ramford, Randall	WC2	406	" 1677.
Ramks, Sarah	9	321	" 1666.
Ramley, Samuel	8	478	" 1665.
Ramp, Mathew	6	15	" 1662.
Ramsell, William	17	416	" 1673.
Ramsey, Elizabeth	6	88	" 1654.
Ramsey, Elizabeth	9	323	" 1666.
Ramsey, Jane	17	363	" 1672.
Ramsey, John	9	250	" 1665. Mariner.
Ramsey, John	9	323	" 1666.
Ramsey, Margaret	9	250	" 1665. Wife of John.
Ramsey, Morgan	6	85	" 1653.
Ramsey, Stephen	6	119	" 1658.
Ramsey, William	5	257	" 1655.
Ramsey, William	6	88·	" 1650.
Ramsey, William	Q	74	Service 1658. (15, fol. 300).
Ramshaw, Elizabeth	WC2	395	Transported 1680. Servant.
Ran, Martha	6	82	" 1661.
Rand, Mathew	7	639	" 1665.
Randall, Benjamin	WC2	156,157	Immigrated 1680. Of Kent Co.
Randall, Christopher	6	125	Transported 1660.
Randall, Christopher	17	551	" 1673.
Randall, Elias	10	600	Service 1667.
Randall, George	15	442	Transported 1677.
Randall, Jacob	7	464	" 1654.
Randall, John	9	448	" 1666. Servant.
Randall, Joseph	6	48	" 1662.
Randall, Joseph	11	104	" 1667.
Randall, Mary	5	532	" 1662. (6, fol. 153).
Randall, Mary	15	442	" 1677.

NAME	Liber	Folio	REMARKS
Randall, Pascar	17	498	Immigrated 1673, with Eliz., his wife. Of Dorchester Co.
Randall, Philip	9	271	Transported 1665. Servant.
Randall, Richard	10	471	Immigrated 1667.
Randall, Samuel	12	205	Transported 1667.
Randall, Thomas	15	453	" 1676.
Randen, George	6	142	" 1657.
Rands, William	18	37	" 1673.
Rane, Darby	15	438	" 1677.
Ranenton, John	13	114	" 1671.
Range, Elizabeth	9	344	" 1665.
Rangfort, William	17	475	" 1673.
Ranish, Elizabeth	6	83	" 1654.
Ranken, William	16	79	" 1670.
Rann, Matthew	6	123	" 1663.
Ransford, Randall	6	129	" 1656. (See Rainford).
Ransford, William	6	105	" 1663.
Ranson, James	15	356	" 1675.
Ranson, William	16	482	" 1670-1.
Ransour, Jane	18	331	" 1674.
Rape, John	20	185	" 1679.
Raper, George	ABH	337	Immigrated 1651, with wife.
Rapier, George	Q	430	Transported 1658.
Rapier, John	7	321	Immigrated 1659.
Rapier, John	11	104	Transported 1667.
Raredon, Thomas	15	567	" 1679.
Raruth, Samuel	ABH	50	" 1648. Servant.
Rason, Richard	7	562	" 1665.
Rassick, John	5	516	" 1663.
Rastell, Thomas	5	218	" 1662.
Rastell, Thomas	8	501	" 1665.
Ratclife, Charles	15	413	Immigrated 1677. Of Somerset Co.
Ratclife, Elizabeth	15	413	Transported 1677. Wife of Charles.
Ratclife, Elizabeth	15	413	" 1677. Daughter of Charles.
Ratclife, John	15	539	Transported 1678.
Ratclife, Rachel	15	413	" 1677. Daughter of Charles.
Ratclife, Sarah	10	193	Transported 1666.
Ratcliff, Emanuel	12	262	Immigrated to St. Mary's Co. 1669. Of Virginia. (16, fol. 18).
Ratcliff, Mary	12	203	Transported 1664.
Ratcliffe, Abraham	16	482	" 1670-1.
Ratcliffe, Bridgett	16	165	" 1670.
Ratcliffe, Charles	5	412	Immigrated 1663.
Ratcliffe, Charles	15	413	Transported 1677. Son of Charles.
Ratcliffe, Charles	WC2	118	Rights 1679. (See Blackliffe, on fol. 16).
Ratcliffe, George	WC2	118	Transported 1679. (See Blackliffe on fol. 16).
Ratcliffe, Mary	16	165	Transported 1670.

NAME	Liber	Folio	REMARKS
Rate, William	7	483	Transported 1664.
Rater, Francis	15	455	" 1678.
Ratford, John	15	430	" 1677.
Ratlie, Mary	15	416	" 1677.
Ratliffe, Robert	Q	32	" 1657. Servant.
Ratlive, Robert	Q	431	" 1658.
Ratly, Robert	11	164	" 1667.
Raven, Elizabeth	17	376	" 1672. Daughter of John.
Raven, Jane	17	376	Transported 1672. Daughter of John.
Raven, John	17	376	Immigrated 1672 with wife, Jane, and children.
Raven, Luke	15	344	Transported from Virginia 1675.
Raven, Mary	17	376	" 1672. Daughter of John.
Raven, Sarah	15	344	Transported from Virginia 1675.
Raven, Susanna	17	376	" 1672. Daughter of John.
Raven, William	17	478	Immigrated 1673. Of Dorset Co.
Ravens, Richard	7	461	Transported 1659-64. Servant.
Rawden, Elizabeth	5	89	" 1661.
Rawles, William	WC2	47-48, 70-71	Immigrated 1679. Of Kent Co.
Rawley, Margaret	6	79	Transported 1663.
Rawley, Rachel	15	259	" 1675.
Rawlings, John	7	475	Of Stafford Freehold, Calvert Co. Son of Anthony, living 1664. (8, fol. 90).
Rawlings, John	16	164	Aged 30 years in 1671. Of Dorchester Co.
Rawlings, John	15	430,454	Transported 1677.
Rawlings, Nicholas	10	265	Immigrated 1666. Of St. Mary's Co. Cooper.
Rawlings, Rowland	Q	19	Servant 1651.
Rawlings, William	5	208	Transported 1661.
Rawlins, Anthony	ABH	15	Immigrated 1645 with wife and one child. Formerly servant to Justinian Snow. Deceased about 1652. (2, fol. 458, 479).
Rawlins, Elizabeth	WC2	113,165	Transported 1680.
Rawlins, Joan	ABH	19	Widow of Anthony 1652.
Rawlins, Joane	2	458,479	Transported 1645.
Rawlins, Philadelphia	5	410	" 1663. Wife of John.
Rawlinson, Charles	ABH	26,244	" 1641.
Rawlinson, Charles	2	517	Service 1649.
Rawlinson, John	WC2	16	Transported 1677.
Rawlinson, John	15	574	" 1678.
Rawson, Richard	15	598	" 1678-9.
Rawston, Richard	15	598	" 1678.
Raxell, Mary	8	30	" 1665.
Ray, Abraham	16	122	Immigrated 1671. Of St. Mary's Co.
Ray, Alexander	7	564	" 1664. Of Virginia.

NAME	Liber	Folio	REMARKS
Ray, Alexander	16	122	Immigrated 1671. Of St. Mary's Co.
Ray, Alexander, Jr.	7	564	Transported 1671. Son of Alexander.
Ray, Elizabeth	6	95	" 1653.
Ray, Hannah	7	564	" 1664. Daughter of Alexander.
Ray, Henry	9	34	Transported 1665.
Ray, Joane	7	564	" 1664. Daughter of Alexander.
Ray, Joane	7	564	Transported 1664. Wife of Alexander.
Ray, John	17	608	" 1673.
Ray, John	WC2	278-279	Service 1680. Of St. Mary's Co.
Ray, Marsh	7	564	Transported 1664. Daughter of Alexander.
Ray, Roger	17	535	Service 1673. Of Charles Co.
Ray, Sarah	7	564	Transported 1664. Daughter of Alexander.
Rayd, Anthony	5	73	Transported 1660-1.
Rayford, Emanuel	6	142	" 1659.
Rayman, Sarah	4	57	" 1659.
Raymond, Dorothy	12	551	" 1670.
Raymond, Peter	12	517	" 1670.
Raymond, Richard	16	164	Immigrated 1670, with wife and two children. Of Somerset County.
Raymond, Thomas	Q	441	Transported 1651.
Rayne, Isaack	WC2	213-214	" 1671-3.
Rayn'r. Barneby	6	97	" 1655.
Rayner, Elizabeth	9	104	" 1665.
Rayner, Richard	12	599	Immigrated 1670. Of St. Mary's Co.
Rayners, Elizabeth	9	190	Transported 1663.
Raynes, Cornelius	6	124	" 1663.
Rayney, Edmund	15	302	" 1675.
Rayston, Francis	6	107	" 1661.
Rayston, Robert	6	159	" 1661.
Reacham, William	13	111	" 1668.
Read, Amy	9	84	" 1663.
Read, Amy	7	567	" 1665.
Read, Ananias	ABH	82	" 1635. Servant.
Read, Andrew	9	354	" 1663.
Read, Andrew	10	572	Immigrated 1667 from York River in Virginia. Of Kent Co.
Read, Ashbell	5	220	Transported 1652.
Read, Call	16	507	" 1671.
Read, David	9	462	" 1665.
Read, George	Q	203	Immigrated 1658 with wife.
Read, George	10	558	Transported 1665. Servant.
Read, George	11	316,338	" 1668.
Read, James	12	190	" 1668.
Read, Jane	7	571	" 1663. Wife of Percival.
Read, Joab	7	464	" 1659.
Read, John	ABH	157	Immigrated 1651.
Read, John	7	464	Transported 1661.

NAME	Liber	Folio	REMARKS
Read, John	8	42,478	Transported 1665. (9, fol. 308).
Read, John	10	572	" 1667. Son of Andrew.
Read, John	16	411	" 1671.
Read, Katherine	18	313	" 1675.
Read, Mary	10	572	" 1667. Daughter of Andrew.
Read, Mary	16	435	Transported 1671.
Read, Mathew	ABH	247	Immigrated 1650.
Read, Mathew	7	559	Transported 1663.
Read, Richard	9	354	" 1663.
Read, Robert	12	190	" 1668.
Read, Thomas	ABH	322	Immigrated 1652 with wife and 3 children. Of North Patuxent. Gift from Lord B. 1658. (Q, fol. 347).
Read, Walter	ABH	89	Transported 1635. Servant.
Read, William	18	313	" 1675.
Read, William	15	436	" 1677.
Reade, Elizabeth	Q	29	First wife of Thomas 1658.
Reade, George	Q	29	Immigrated prior to 1658. Son of Thomas.
Reade, George	5	254	Transported 1663.
Reade, John	17	490	" 1673.
Reade, Thomas	Q	29	Immigrated prior to 1658.
Reade, William	Q	29	" prior to 1658. Son of Thomas.
Reader, Francis	17	463	Transported 1673.
Reader, Thomas	9	270	" 1665.
Readfoarne, Margaret	7	467	" 1663. (6, fol. 121).
Reading, Richard	8	502	" 1665.
Reading, Richard	15	541	" 1678.
Reading, Richard	WC2	15	" 1679.
Reading, William	12	190	" 1668. Servant.
Readman, Thomas	15	370	" 1676.
Ready, Richard	15	553	" 1678.
Reane, Joane	18	137	" 1674.
Reason, Elizabeth	5	307	" 1663.
Reaton, George	12	502	" 1669.
Reaves, Ann	17	486	" 1667. (17, fol. 491).
Reaves, Edward	17	486	" 1667. (17, fol. 491).
Reaves, Francis	17	486	" 1667. (17, fol. 491).
Reaves, John	17	486	" 1667.
Rebole, Edward	7	492	" 1664. Son of Mary.
Rebole, Mary	7	492	" 1664 by Andrew Skinner.
Redd, Asbell	ABH	200	Transported 1651. Servant.
Redd, George	ABH	276	" 1651. Servant.
Redding, Isabell	18	167	" 1674.
Redding, Mary	5	85	" 1661.
Redding, William	4	560	" 1661.
Reddington, Elizabeth	17	463	" 1673.
Redfort (als. Warren), Ellen	7	492	" 1664.

NAME	Liber	Folio	REMARKS
Redgell, Godfrey	15	442	Transported 1677.
Redich, John	WC2	199-200	Rights 1680.
Redich, Tabitha	WC2	199	Transported 1680.
Redin, Samuel	15	560	" 1678.
Reding, John	15	454	" Oct. 1677.
Reding, Richard	18	11	Service 1673.
Redley, Thomas	15	425	" 1677. Of St. Mary's Co.
Redman, Daniel	WC2	158	Transported 1680.
Redman, Richard	10	407	" in the "Providence" of Bristol, 1666.
Redman, Robert	12	382	Transported 1669.
Redman, Robert	15	433	" 1677.
Redman, Will.	15	499	" 1677.
Redman, William	17	552	" 1671.
Redmond, John	15	539	Immigrated 1678. Of St. Mary's Co.
Redmond, Katherine	15	539	Transported 1678. Wife of John.
Redmore, William	WC2	381	" 1675-80. Servant.
Redolphus, Thomas	3	174	Immigrated 1656.
Redoltus, Thomas	6	81	Transported 1653.
Rednap, Barbary	12	314	" 1668.
Ree, Sarah	15	449	" 1677.
Reece, Francis	16	409	" 1671.
Reed, Amey	6	216	" 1663.
Reed, Barbary	9	489	" 1665. Servant.
Reed, Ebenezar	15	553	" 1678.
Reed, James	6	122	" 1650.
Reed, John	4	609	Immigrated 1661. Mercer.
Reed, Nathaniel	16	470	Service 1670. Of Talbot Co.
Reed, Percivall	6	10	Immigrated 1663.
Reed, Ralph	15	416	Transported 1677.
Reed, Robert	WC2	16	" 1679.
Reed, William	15	567	" 1678.
Reedagh, Henry	9	304	" 1665.
Reede, Abraham	16	393	" 1671.
Reeffe, Ellin	WC2	87	" 1679.
Reeft, Jones	Q	323	" 1655-8.
Reeley, William	WC2	120	" 1680.
Reely, Michael	4	568	" 1660.
Reeres, Jone	15	443	" 1670.
Rees, John	11	378	" 1668.
Reese, John	12	505	" 1670. Servant.
Reese, William	9	489	" 1665. Servant.
Reese, William	15	558	" 1679.
Reeve, William	7	504	Immigrated 1664.
Reeves, George	12	283	Transported 1668. Brother to John Bradford.
Reeves, John	12	269	Transported 1668. Son of Elizabeth Williams.
Reeves, Rachel	18	285	Transported 1674.
Reeves, Sarah	15	519	" Sept. 1669.
Refew, Henry	16	130	Immigrated 1671. Of Calvert Co.

NAME	Liber	Folio	REMARKS
Regan, Cornelius	5	529	Service 1662.
Reger, William	12	190	Transported 1668. Servant.
Regells, James	WC2	167,169	" 1679.
Regly, Thomas	10	433	" 1667.
Reid, Abraham	15	445	Service 1678.
Reid, Elizabeth	18	331	Transported 1674.
Reid, George	15	530	" 1678.
Reid, Peter	18	331	" 1674.
Reid, Stephen	15	569	" 1678.
Reid, William	15	436	" 1677.
Reid, William	WC2	65	Immigrated 1679. Of Dorchester Co.
Reide, John	15	568	Transported 1679.
Reinger, Samuel	5	89	" 1661.
Rekin, Mary	WC2	309	" 1680.
Rele, John	ABH	242	" Jan. 1652. Servant.
Relfe, John	17	567	" 1673 from Virginia.
Relfe, Thomas	17	383	" 1672.
Relfe, Thomas	WC2	140,142	Service 1679. Of Somerset Co.
Remamore, Clanson	8	130	Transported 1664.
Rematt, Walter	WC2	380	" 1675-80. Servant.
Reme, William	12	190	" 1668.
Remmore, Sulle	8	130	" 1664.
Remnant, Elizabeth	15	413	" 1677.
Remnant, Isaac	15	413	" 1677.
Remolds, John	16	393	" 1671.
Renalds, William	15	565	" 1679.
Renalls, Thomas	5	127	" 1662.
Rend, Mathew	5	466	" 1662.
Rennedy, Cate	18	137	" 1674.
Rennick, Ann	18	167	" 1674.
Rennolds, Henry	16	414	" 1671.
Rennolds, Mary	12	415	" 1669.
Rennolds, Mary	17	469	" 1673.
Rennolds, William	15	565	" 1679.
Renolds, John	16	393	" 1671.
Renolds, Samuel	17	551	" 1673.
Renolds, William	5	79	" prior to 1662.
Rensha, John	4	588	" 1661. (16,fol.536).
Reny, John	16	530	Immigrated 1672. Of Somerset Co.
Reny, Mary	16	530	Transported 1672. Wife of John.
Resim, Christopher	9	216	" 1665.
Restall, Elizabeth	Q	203	" 1658.
Revell, Ann	6	347	" 1663.
Revell, Hannah	6	347	" 1663.
Revell, John	ABH	79	" 1634-5. Son of Randall.
Revell, John	1	65	Transported since 1634. Son of Randall.
Revell, Katherine	6	347	Transported 1663.
Revell, Katherine, Jr.	6	347	" 1663.
Revell, Randall	ABH	79	Immigrated 1636. (1,fol. 64-65).

NAME	Liber	Folio	REMARKS
Revell, Randall	1	19	Transported 1638.
Revell, Randall	6	347	Immigrated 1663. (17, fol. 368; 15, fol. 186).
Revell, Randall, Jr.	6	347	Transported 1663.
Revell, Rebecca	1	65	" since 1634. Wife of Randall.
Revell, Rebecca	ABH	79	Transported 1634-41. Wife of Randall.
Reves, Jane	16	507	Transported 1671.
Rexon, John	15	410	Service 1673.
Reyley, John	15	302	" 1675. Of St. Mary's Co.
Reylings, John	WC2	23	Transported 1679. Servant.
Reynalls, Ellen	WC2	206	" 1679. Servant.
Reynold, Edward	17	419	Service 1672.
Reynolds, Ann	1	19	Transported 1637.
Reynolds, Anthony	11	338	" 1668.
Reynolds, Cha.	15	376	" 1676.
Reynolds, Elizabeth	5	81	" 1659.
Reynolds, Elizabeth	6	290	" 1663.
Reynolds, Hannah	9	270	" 1665.
Reynolds, Henry	5	256	" 1663.
Reynolds, John	6	268	" 1662.
Reynolds, John	7	80	" 1664.
Reynolds, John	9	270	" 1665.
Reynolds, John	17	396	" 1672.
Reynolds, Joshua	6	165-166	" 1653.
Reynolds, Merreby	9	270	" 1665.
Reynolds, Rose	18	291	" 1674.
Reynolds, Rowland	4	56	Immigrated 1649.
Reynolds, Thomas	5	482	Transported 1662.
Reynolds, Thomas	9	270	" 1665.
Reynolds, Thomas	18	130	Of St. Mary's Co. And Ann, his wife. Service 1674.
Reynolds, William	15	318	Transported 1675.
Reynor, Timothy	18	334	" 1674.
Rhany, Thomas	18	152	" 1674.
Rhode, Robert	11	541	" 1668.
Rhodes, Abraham	18	313	Service 1673. Of St. Mary's Co.
Rhodes, Elizabeth	ABH	312	Transported 1651-2. Servant.
Rhodes, John	ABH	239	" June 1651. Servant.
Rhodon, Mathew	3	18	Immigrated about 1643.
Rhodon, Matthew	ABH	45	" 1643. Son-in-law of Hannah Lee, wife of Hugh, of Chicacone, in Virginia.
Riall, Thomas	6	293	Transported 1664.
Rice, Evan	15	430	" 1677.
Rice, James	16	393	" 1671.
Rice, John	5	417	" 1663.
Rice, John	9	322	" 1666.
Rice, John	18	151	Immigrated 1674. Of Dorset Co.
Rice, John	15	383	Transported 1676.
Rice, Nicholas	9	100	Immigrated 1665.

NAME	Liber	Folio	REMARKS
Rice, Richard	18	164	Service 1674.
Rice, Roger	5	319	Transported 1662.
Rice, Walter	15	500	" 1678.
Rice, William	32	65	
Rich, John	15	360	" 1676.
Rich, Susan	6	159	" 1652.
Richard, ---	Q	28	" 1658.
Richard, John	9	216	" 1665.
Richard, Sarah	7	464	" 1660.
Richards, Benjamin	15	438	" 1677.
Richards, Eleanor	15	443	" 1677.
Richards, Elizabeth	18	39	" 1674.
Richards, Elizabeth	15	413	" 1677. Daughter of John.
Richards, George	12	194	Transported 1668. Servant.
Richards, John	6	19,135	" 1663.
Richards, John	11	166	" 1667.
Richards, John	12	194	" 1668. Servant.
Richards, John	17	40	" 1672.
Richards, John	15	413	Immigrated 1677.
Richards, John	15	598	Transported 1678-9.
Richards, John	WC2	77	Proved rights for wife's service, 1679. Of Somerset Co.
Richards, John	WC2	211	Transported 1679. Servant.
Richards, John, Jr.	15	413	" 1677. Son of John.
Richards, Jonathan	8	478	" 1665.
Richards, Mary	11	166	" 1667.
Richards, Mary	15	413	" 1677. Daughter of John.
Richards, Miles	2	195	Transported 1641. Servant. (See Ricketts).
Richards, Oliver	18	174	Transported 1674.
Richards, Rebeccah	WC2	167,169	" 1679.
Richards, Will	15	530	" 1678.
Richards, William	12	554	" 1670.
Richardson, Amy	15	332	" 1675.
Richardson, Angell	15	432	Service 1677.
Richardson, Angell	WC2	10,11,17	" 1679.
Richardson, Bard.	15	380	Transported 1676.
Richardson, George	6	90	" 1661.
Richardson, Francis	11	139	Immigrated 1667.
Richardson, Francis	15	530	Transported 1678.
Richardson, James	15	454	" Oct. 1677.
Richardson, Joane	WC2	11	" 1679.
Richardson, Joane	WC2	11,17	Service 1679.
Richardson, John	1	19	Transported 1638.
Richardson, John	5	87	" 1649-62.
Richardson, John	6	17	Immigrated 1663.
Richardson, John	8	503	" 1665.
Richardson, John	11	265	Transported 1667.
Richardson, John	16	115	" 1671.

NAME	Liber	Folio	REMARKS
Richardson, John	16	513	Transported 1672.
Richardson, John	18	38	" 1673.
Richardson, John	18	160	" 1674.
Richardson, John	15	319	Immigrated 1675.
Richardson, John	15	537	Transported 1679.
Richardson, Jone	9	327	" 1666.
Richardson, Joseph	18	166	" 1674.
Richardson, Judith	17	396	" 1672.
Richardson, Margaret	7	576	" 1665.
Richardson, Mark	15	376	" 1676.
Richardson, Mary	6	264	Service 1662. Wife of John.
Richardson, Mary	6	36,90	Transported 1663.
Richardson, Mary	8	503	" 1665.
Richardson, Mary	12	498	" 1670.
Richardson, Nicholas	17	482	Immigrated 1664. Of St. Mary's Co.
Richardson, Nicholas	8	203	Transported 1665.
Richardson, Richard	6	90	" 1663.
Richardson, Robert	16	302	Immigrated 1671, with Susan, his

wife, and Wm., Eliz., Susanna and Tobia, his children. Of Somerset Co.

Richardson, Robert	15	310	Petition 1675.
Richardson, Sarah	10	433	Transported 1666.
Richardson, Simon	ABH	61	Immigrated 1640. (1, fol. 27; 5,

fol. 64).

Richardson, William	4	140	Transported 1655. Servant.
Richardson, William	16	505	" 1671.
Richardson, William	18	160	" 1674.
Richardson, William	19	615	Married Eliz., Ex'x of Richard

Talbott, of Anne Arundel Co. prior to 1677.

Richbell, John	6	293	Transported 1664.
Richee, Alice	8	502	" 1665. Wife of William.
Richee, Eve	8	502	" 1665. Daughter of

William.

Richee, William	9	310-311	Living in Talbot Co. 1664. Evi-

dently from Gloucester Co., Virginia.

Richee, William	8	502	Immigrated 1665.
Richeene, John	11	374	Transported 1668.
Richeson, Frances	10	391	" prior to 1666, when

she appears as the 2nd wife of Jno. Newman. Servant.

Richeson, John	9	39	Transported 1651.
Richeson, Mark	6	119	" 1653.
Richeson, Thomas	6	88	" 1654.
Richins, John	15	503	Immigrated 1678. Of Dorset Co.
Richman, John	7	462	Transported 1664.
Richman, Margaret	4	568	" 1660.
Richmond, Daniel	15	560	" 1678.
Richmond, George	15	452	Immigrated 1678.
Richway, Elizabeth	18	84	Transported 1674.
Rickard, Elizabeth	Q	67	Immigrated 1650. Wife of Nicholas.
Rickard, Nicholas	Q	67	" 1645.
Rickett, William	ABH	424	" 1655.
Ricketts, James	12	584	Transported 1670. Servant. (17, 609).

389

NAME	Liber	Folio	REMARKS
Ricketts, Miles	ABH	61	Transported 1640. Servant. (See Richards). (1, fol. 27).
Ricketts, Thomas	15	431	Transported 1677.
Rickin, Margaret	5	484	" 1661.
Rickots, Ann	17	330	" 1672.
Ricks, John	9	28	" 1664.
Ricks, John	16	72	Immigrated 1670. Of Anne Arundel County.
Ricle, William	9	249	Immigrated 1665, with wife.
Ricout, Joseph	15	504	Transported 1678.
Ricrafs, Martin	13	122	" 1668.
Riddall, Robert	8	130	" 1664.
Riden, Charles	8	131	" 1664.
Rider, Eleanor	9	54	" 1665.
Rider, Elizabeth	12	496	" 1670.
Rider, Henry	16	113	Immigrated 1671. Of St. Mary's Co.
Rider, John	5	93	Transported 1661 by Wm. Burges.
Rider, Joseph	18	24	" 1674.
Rider, Richard	5	127	" 1662.
Rider, Richard	10	433	" 1666.
Rider, William	17	377	" 1669.
Ridge, Elizabeth	8	88	" 1665.
Ridge, Jona.	6	136	" 1656.
Ridgell, Richard	9	33	" 1660-5.
Ridgeley, Henry	7	461	Immigrated about 1659, and married Eliz. Howard.
Ridgely, Martha	16	400	Service 1671. Wife of Robt. of St. Mary's Co.
Ridgely, Robert	14	441	Patent for 500 acres called "Timberly".
Ridgely, Robert	WC2	255,340	Rights 1680. Of St. Mary's Co. (WC2, fol. 359, 377).
Ridgely, Robert	16	594	Clerk, residing in City of St. Mary's. Grant from Lord B. of "Gallowes Greene". Site for offices. (20, fol. 269).
Ridgely, William	16	553	Immigrated 1672. Of Anne Arundel County.
Ridger, John	7	639	Service 1665.
Ridgill, Richard	12	554	Transported 1670.
Ridgley, John	WC2	206	" 1680. Servant.
Ridgway, Edward	WC2	130	" 1679. Servant. (40 years old).
Ridgway, William	18	84	Transported 1674.
Ridley, Thomas	17	395	" 1672.
Ridwell, Jane	9	33	" 1660-5.
Rievs, William	13	114	" 1669.
Rigan (Rygan), James	WC2	23	" 1679.
Riganet, Christopher	7	496	Warrant for 1000 acres, 1664, provided he make remainder of his rights appear and transport his family.
Rigby, Catherine	4	53	Transported 1659. Wife of James.
Rigby, Constance	6	127	" 1660.
Rigby, James	4	53	Service 1659.

NAME	Liber	Folio	REMARKS
Rigby, John	15	527	Transported 1678.
Rigby, John	WC2	111	" 1680.
Rigby, Mary	9	329	" 1665.
Rigby, Peter	18	137	" 1674.
Rigby, Robert	12	379	" 1669.
Riggen, Teage	17	383	Immigrated 1672.
Riggs, Francis	7	24	Witness to assignment by Francis Armstrong, 9th Apl. 1663.
Riggs, Jane	10	433	Transported 1667.
Right, Edward	WC2	167,169	" 1680.
Right, John	15	531	Service 1678. Of Somerset Co. Planter.
Right, Lettis	WC2	415	Transported 1666-80. Servant.
Right, Mary	5	256	" 1663.
Right, Nathaniel	16	447	" 1671.
Right, Robert	6	347	" 1663. (16, fol. 281).
Right, William	7	562	" 1662.
Rights, Susan	9	330	" 1665.
Rigsbie, Robert	15	416	" 1677.
Rilye, Timothy	WC2	381	" 1675-80. Servant.
Rine, Richard	WC2	89	" 1676. Servant.
Rinward, Miles	ABH	1	Servant 1646.
Rindall, Mary	18	313	Transported 1675.
Ring, Ann	15	505	" 1678.
Ringold, James	19	599	Established a town in Kent Co. near Grey's Inn Creek, 1675.
Rinthell, William	7	343	Transported 1664.
Riper, James	16	411	" 1671.
Ripley, John	10	466	Immigrated 1667.
Rirles, Mathew	12	415	Transported 1669.
Ris, Walter	15	501	" 1678.
Risall, Edmond	6	293	" 1664.
Risbrooke, Susan	6	17	" 1663.
Risby, Paul	18	334	" 1675.
Rishford, Mark	15	407	" 1676.
Rite, Christopher	5	191	Service 1662. (See Wright).
Rite, Edmond	ABH	331	Immigrated 1646. (2, fol. 567).
River, John	7	498	Transported 1660.
River, Mary	6	127	" 1655.
Rivers, Christopher	4	584	Immigrated 1661.
Rivers, Edmond	4	584	Transported 1661.
Rivers, Isabell	4	584	" 1661. Wife of Christopher.
Rivers, Mary	4	584	Transported 1661.
Rivon, David	ABH	356	" 1651. Servant.
Rixon, John	16	536	Service 1671.
Roach, John	16	536	And Sarah, his wife. Service 1671. (15, fol. 432).
Roach, John	15	452	Transported 1678.
Roache, Edmond	15	348	" 1655. Servant.
Road, Walter	1	95	" 1635-40.

NAME	Liber	Folio	REMARKS
Roades, Abraham	5	251	Transported 1663. (17, fol. 584).
Roades, Frances	17	584	" 1673. Wife of Abraham.
Roadham, Matthew	1	19	Transported 1638.
Roads, Catherine	Q	70	" 1658.
Roads, John	6	107	" 1663.
Roafee, Mary	WC2	23	" 1679. Servant.
Roagues, Ann	8	486	" 1664.
Robards, Elizabeth	15	601	Service 1676. Wife of Thomas.
Robards, Thomas	15	601	" 1676.
Robbison, Peter	11	537	Transported 1668.
Robenson, Francis	12	281	" 1668.
Robenson, Thomas	12	459	" 1669.
Robert, the Welch Boy	15	322	" 1675.
Robert, Thomas	7	567	" 1657. Servant.
Roberts, Ann	10	341	" 1666. Daughter of Peter.
Roberts, Ann	18	291	Transported 1674.
Roberts, Ann	15	566	" 1678.
Roberts, Daniel	17	376	" 1672.
Roberts, Dorothy	5	256	" 1663.
Roberts, Edmund	11	144	Immigrated 1667.
Roberts, Edward	5	305	Transported 1663.
Roberts, Edward	15	376	" 1676.
Roberts, Eli	15	505	" 1678.
Roberts, Elias	WC2	57	" 1678.
Roberts, Elizabeth	8	484	" 1664.
Roberts, Ellias	15	553	" 1678.
Roberts, George	9	334	" 1666.
Roberts, Gilbert	7	464	" 1663.
Roberts, Grace	11	378,548	" 1668.
Roberts, Griffin	15	540	" 1676.
Roberts, Henry	15	397	" 1676.
Roberts, Henry	15	501	" 1678.
Roberts, Hugh	11	546	" 1668.
Roberts, Isaac	8	484	" 1665.
Roberts, James	8	484	" 1664.
Roberts, James	15	422	Service 1677.
Roberts, Jane	18	77	Transported 1674. (15, fol. 428).
Roberts, Jasper	17	603	Immigrated 1671.
Roberts, Joane	5	516	Transported 1663.
Roberts, John	7	560	" 1665. (8, fol. 42).
Roberts, John	11	171-172	Service 1667. Of Somerset Co. (15, fol. 362).
Roberts, John	15	370	Transported 1676.
Roberts, John	15	455	" 1678.
Roberts, Joseph	6	299	" 1661.
Roberts, Margaret	4	530	" 1659. (5, fol. 64, 66).
Roberts, Margaret	17	402	" 1652.
Roberts, Mary	15	434	Service 1677. Wife of John of St. Mary's County.

NAME	Liber	Folio	REMARKS
Roberts, Mary	WC2	50,51	Transported 1674. (15, fol. 572).
Roberts, Maudlin	12	516	" 1669. Servant.
Roberts, Peter	10	341	Immigrated 1666, with wife. Of St. Mary's County.
Roberts, Peter	17	330	Transported 1672.
Roberts, Phobby	16	395	Immigrated 1671, with Grace, his wife. Of St. Mary's Co.
Roberts, Richard	12	415	Transported 1669.
Roberts, Richard	12	554	" 1670.
Roberts, Roger	WC2	16	" 1677.
Roberts, Roger	12	280,284	" 1668. Servant.
Roberts, Roger	17	411	" 1673. (18, fol. 80).
Roberts, Roger	15	574	" 1678.
Roberts, Stanhyre	ABH	46	Immigrated 1645.
Roberts, Stanop (Stanhop)	3	22	" about 1645.
Roberts, Thomas	5	529	Transported 1661.
Roberts, Thomas	8	484	" 1665. (11, fol. 312).
Roberts, Thomas	11	167	" 1667.
Roberts, Thomas	15	413	Immigrated 1677.
Roberts, Thomas	17	510	Transported 1667.
Roberts, William	8	484	" 1665.
Roberts, William	10	558	" 1665.
Roberts, William	9	448	" 1666. Servant.
Roberts, William	15	167	" 1673.
Roberts, William	15	380	" 1676.
Roberts, William	15	443,454	" 1677.
Roberts, William	15	531	" 1678.
Robertson, Francis	7	427	" 1664. Servant.
Robertson, Francis	17	33	Immigrated from Virginia 1672, with wife and daughter. Of Somerset County.
Robertson, James	4	21	Transported 1659.
Robertson, John	15	429	" 1674.
Robertson, John	WC2	146,162	" 1680.
Robertson, Richard	15	569	" 1678.
Robertson, Roger	15	555	" 1675. Servant.
Robertson, Stephen	15	314	" 1675.
Robes, Mr. John	5	73	Immigrated 1662, with John, his son.
Robeson, James	18	35	Transported 1673.
Robeson, Robert	WC2	65	" 1679.
Robins, Alice	10	291	" 1666.
Robins, Elizabeth	ABH	40	" 1649. (2, fol. 614).
Robins, George	18	93	Immigrated 1674. Of Talbot Co.
Robins, John, Gent.	15	372	Of Northampton, Virginia, acquires land in Maryland, 1675.
Robins, John	17	59,74	Immigrated 1672.
Robins, John	15	532,570	" from Virginia to Somerset Co., 1678. Of Virginia. Cordwainer.
Robins, Judith	15	540	Transported 1677.
Robins, Katherine	15	532	" 1678. Wife of John.
Robins, Margaret	17	508	Immigrated 1671. Wife of George.

NAME	Liber	Folio	REMARKS
Robins, Mary	10	291	Transported 1666.
Robins, Mary	15	532,570	" 1678. Daughter of John.
Robins, Robert	2	604	Immigrated 1648 with wife and child.
Robins, Robert	ABH	36	Immigrated 1649 with wife and child.
Robins, Samuel	12	216	Transported 1667.
Robins, Sarah	15	532,570	" 1678. Daughter of John.
Robins, Thomas	11	348	Transported 1668.
Robinson, Alice	9	369	" 1665.
Robinson, Alice	10	563	" 1667.
Robinson, Andrew	5	93	" 1661. (9, fol. 448).
Robinson, Andrew	WC2	406	" 1680.
Robinson, Ann	13	65	" 1670. Servant.
Robinson, Ann	18	167	" 1674.
Robinson, Barbareth	16	174	" 1671. Wife of James.
Robinson, Bridgett	15	318	" 1675. Daughter of Mary.
Robinson, Christopher	18	166	Transported 1674.
Robinson, Edward	1	21	Rights 1642.
Robinson, Mr. Edward	ABH	58	His assignee, Arthur Penruddock demands land on Conditions &c.
Robinson, Elin	15	540	Transported 1676.
Robinson, Elizabeth	Q	67	Servant 1658. (4, fol. 63).
Robinson, Elizabeth	7	87	Transported 1660.
Robinson, Elizabeth	15	356	" 1675.
Robinson, Elizabeth	15	453	" 1675-7.
Robinson, Frances	16	174	" 1671. Daughter of James.
Robinson, Francis	12	514	Service 1668.
Robinson, George	15	501	Transported 1678.
Robinson, Henry	1	166	" 1650. Servant.
Robinson, Henry	Q	199	Immigrated 1658. Married Dorothy Leaster.
Robinson, James	ABH	200	Transported 1651. Servant.
Robinson, James	Q	62	Immigrated 1658.
Robinson, James	10	312	Transported 1664.
Robinson, James	8	484	" 1665. (9, fol. 54).
Robinson, James	10	563	" 1667. (11, fol. 196).
Robinson, James	16	174	Immigrated 1671 with his wife, Barbareth and daughter, Frances. Of Somerset County.
Robinson, Joane	16	79,630	Transported 1670.
Robinson, John	1	110,130	" 1633. Carpenter.
Robinson, John	3	77	" 1635. Servant.
Robinson, John	ABH	50	" July 1635. Servant.
Robinson, John	ABH	94	" 1633. Servant.
Robinson, John	ABH	37,64	Servant 1638.
Robinson, John	1	18,33, 171	Transported 1638. (2, fol. 605).

NAME	Liber	Folio	REMARKS
Robinson, John	ABH	103	Immigrated 1641. Carpenter.
Robinson, John	6	14	Transported 1663.
Robinson, John	7	560	" 1665.
Robinson, John	12	488	Service 1670. Of Charles Co.
Robinson, John	16	123	" 1671. Of St. Mary's Co.
Robinson, John	16	393	Transported 1671. (18, fol. 24).
Robinson, John	18	331	" 1674. (15, fol. 301).
Robinson, John	15	407	Immigrated 1676.
Robinson, John	15	416,507	Transported 1677.
Robinson, John	WC2	124	" 1679. Son of Elizabeth Portwood.
Robinson, Jone	9	448	Transported 1666. Servant.
Robinson, Josling	15	446	" 1677.
Robinson, Margaret	18	137	" 1674.
Robinson, Martha	8	486,499	" 1664.
Robinson, Mary	8	486,499	" 1664.
Robinson, Mary	WC2	167,169	" 1679.
Robinson, Mary Paramore	15	318	Claims land for transporting her children.
Robinson, Mathew	5	415	Transported 1658.
Robinson, Oliver	6	83	" 1656-63.
Robinson, Patrick	9	449	" 1666.
Robinson, Rebecca	7	79	" 1663.
Robinson, Rebecca	18	177	" 1674.
Robinson, Rebecca	WC2	308	" 1678.
Robinson, Richard	ABH	269	" 1650. Servant. (1, fol. 166). From Va. ?)
Robinson, Richard	13	66	Transported 1669. Servant.
Robinson, Richard	16	94	" 1670. (15, fol. 310).
Robinson, Richard	15	318	" 1675. Son of Mary.
Robinson, Robert	8	202	" 1665. (17, fol. 557).
Robinson, Robert	15	362	" 1676.
Robinson, Robert	15	442	" 1677.
Robinson, Robert	WC2	327	Service 1680. Of Dorchester Co.
Robinson, Samuel	6	124	Transported 1663.
Robinson, Sarah	ABH	324	" 1652. Servant.
Robinson, Thomas	ABH	249	Immigrated 1653.
Robinson, Thomas	5	81	Transported 1659.
Robinson, Thomas	15	318	" 1675. Son of Mary.
Robinson, Thomas	15	505	" 1678.
Robinson, William	Q	204	" 1658.
Robinson, William	5	241	" 1662.
Robinson, William	8	486	Immigrated 1664.
Robinson, William	7	612	Transported 1665.
Robinson, William	9	105	" 1665.
Robinson, William	16	629	" 1672.
Robinson, William	18	121	" 1674.
Robinson, William	15	318	" 1675. Son of Mary.
Robison, John	WC2	206	" 1680. Servant.
Robison, Joseph	WC2	120	" 1680.

NAME	Liber	Folio	REMARKS
Robison, Mary	WC2	120	Transported 1680.
Robison, Penelope	WC2	77,80	" 1679. Servant.
Robison, Thomas	WC2	206	" 1680. Servant.
Robnet, Francis	ABH	66	" 1633. (See Rabnet).
Robotham, John	WC2	309	" 1678.
Robotham, William	15	167	" 1673.
Robothom, George	16	431	Immigrated 1671. Of Calvert Co.
Robson, Anne	WC2	167,169	Transported 1679.
Robson, Charles	WC2	208	Son of William. Of Dorchester Co.
Robson, George	16	70	Transported 1668.
Robson, William	5	234	Service 1662.
Roch, Peter	12	285	Transported 1668. Servant.
Roche, Edmond	15	348	" 1655. Servant.
Rochester, Richard	17	469	" 1673.
Rochford, Ann	15	446	" 1677.
Rock, David	15	553	" 1678.
Rock, Joseph	2	570-571	Immigrated 1649. (ABH, fol. 34).
Rocke, John	4	580	Transported 1661.
Rockwood, Francis	16	65	" 1670.
Rockwood, John	ABH	245	" 1642.
Rockwood, Thomas	ABH	245	" 1642.
Rodam, Mathew	ABH	61	" 1633-41.
Rodam, Matthew	1	27	" 1633-41.
Rodes, Francis	15	565	" 1679.
Rodgers, Charles	20	185	" 1679.
Rodgers, Thomas	15	514	" 1677.
Rodman, Mary	15	433	" 1677.
Rodway, John	12	551	Immigrated 1670. Of St. Mary's Co.
Roe, Ann	WC2	42	Transported 1679. Daughter of George.
Roe, Edmond	5	217	Transported 1663.
Roe, Edward	9	35,333	" 1664. Builds house for travellers in Oxford in Tredhaven Creek, 1674. (18, fol. 167).
Roe, Elizabeth	9	333	Transported 1666.
Roe, Elizabeth	WC2	42	" 1679. Daughter of George.
Roe, George	4	198,206	Transported 1659.
Roe, George	WC2	42	Immigrated 1679 with wife and 3 children. Of Dorchester Co.
Roe, Isabella	Q	32	Transported 1653-8.
Roe, John	WC2	42	" 1679. Son of George.
Roe, John P.	4	63	Immigrated 1638. (See Pow).
Roe, Judith	WC2	42	Transported 1679. Wife of George.
Roe, Mark	7	87	" 1657.
Roe, Mary	9	333	" 1666.
Roe, Peter	7	87	" 1657.
Roe, Richard	ABH	23	Servant 1649.
Roe, Richard	2	511	Transported 1649. Servant.
Roe, William	Q	208	" 1658.
Roe, William	16	78	" 1670.
Roebuck, Robert	18	95	" 1674.

NAME	Liber	Folio	REMARKS
Rogall, Edmund	9	50	Transported 1665.
Roger, John	5	482	" 1662.
Rogers, Mr. ---	1	20,37, 166	" 1633-4.
Rogers, Mr. ---	ABH	66	Immigrated 1634.
Rogers, Ann	4	565	Transported 1661.
Rogers, Charles	WC2	86-87	" 1679.
Rogers, Cicily	12	372	" 1669.
Rogers, Daniel	10	286,417	" 1666.
Rogers, David	15	570	Service 1670.
Rogers, Edward	Q	347	Gift from Lord B. 1658.
Rogers, Elizabeth	17	470	Immigrated 1673, with 3 sons.
Rogers, Francis	17	470	Transported 1673. Son of Eliz.
Rogers, Hannah	4	54	" 1659.
Rogers, Henry	16	522	" 1672.
Rogers, Henry	15	526	Immigrated 1678.
Rogers, Jace	15	526	Transported 1678. Daughter of Henry.
Rogers, James	5	607	Transported 1658-63. (7, fol. 154).
Rogers, Jane	7	639	" 1665. (9, fol. 48).
Rogers, Jane	15	526	" 1678. Wife of Henry.
Rogers, John	17	470	" 1673. Son of Elizabeth.
Rogers, John	18	138	Immigrated 1674. Of Dorset Co.
Rogers, John	17	449	Transported prior to 1672.
Rogers, John	15	553	" 1678.
Rogers, John	20	2	" prior to 1678.
Rogers, Joseph	18	137	" 1674.
Rogers, Joyce	18	313	" 1675.
Rogers, Mary	15	430	" 1677.
Rogers, Mary	WC2	16,170	" 1679. Servant.
Rogers, Peter	7	465	" 1660.
Rogers, Robert	7	569	" 1663-4.
Rogers, Sarah	5	515	" 1661.
Rogers, Sarah	9	271	" 1665.
Rogers, Thomas	17	470	" 1673. Son of Elizabeth.
Rogers, Thomas	15	533	" 1678.
Rogers, William	4	204	" 1649.
Rogers, William	WC2	58	" 1676.
Roles, Joseph	15	505	" 1678.
Rolls, Matt.	15	359	" 1676.
Rolls, Robert	9	175	Immigrated 1665. Of Choptank River in Talbot Co.
Roman, Susan	13	116	Transported 1671.
Ronan, Morrich	WC2	380	" 1675-80. Servant.
Ronayne, Joan	WC2	128	" 1679.
Rooan, William	15	565	" 1679. (See Rovan).
Rood, Robert	15	506	His widow married Michael Miller prior to 1678.
Roode, John	18	339	Service 1675. Of St. Mary's Co.
Rooe, Richard	2	571	Transported 1649. Servant.
Rooke, John	9	105	" 1665.

NAME	Liber	Folio	REMARKS
Rooker, Edward	17	77	Immigrated 1672. Of St. Mary's Co.
Rookes, Charles	12	270	Service 1668.
Roosey, David	11	225	Immigrated 1667, with wife, of Talbot Co.
Roosey, Elizabeth	11	225	Transported 1667. Daughter of David.
Ropeman, Joseph	9	333	Transported 1666. Servant.
Roper, Edward	9	333	" 1666.
Roper, Mary	6	80	" 1660.
Roper, Mary	15	376	" 1676.
Roper, Susan	6	85	" 1653.
Roper, Thomas	ABH	174	" 1650. Servant.
Roper, Thomas	6	80	" 1660.
Roperton, Richard	12	554	" 1670.
Rorety, Edmond	WC2	10	" 1679.
Rosbridge, William	18	329	" 1675.
Rosdon, Susanna	16	411	" 1671.
Rose, Daniel	5	2	" 1661.
Rose, Elizabeth	5	416	" 1663.
Rose, Elizabeth	15	322	" 1674.
Rose, Jane	15	430	" 1677.
Rose, John	12	190	" 1668. Servant.
Rose, Paul	7	508	" 1664.
Rose, Robert	12	459	" 1669.
Rose, Walter	18	291	" 1674.
Rosebrooke, Susanna	8	131	" 1664. Servant.
Rosen, Susan	12	314	" 1669.
Roser, Benjamin	15	481	Letter to Gov. Notley, Oct. 23, 1677.
Rosester, Sible	4	585	Transported 1661.
Roseter, Edward	15	395	" 1677.
Rosewell, William	9	54	Immigrated 1665.
Rosier, William	6	137	Transported 1655.
Rositer, Francis	17	469	" 1673.
Ross, John	12	271	" 1668. Servant.
Ross, John	15	362	" 1676.
Rosse, Cornelia	15	367	" 1676. Daughter of John.
Rosse, Elizabeth	15	367	Transported 1676. Wife of John.
Rosse, George	17	479	" 1673.
Rosse, John	15	367	Immigrated 1676. Of Dorchester Co.
Rosse, John	15	367	Transported 1676. Son of John.
Rosse, John	15	442	" 1677.
Rosse, Olive	15	367	" 1676. Daughter of John.
Rosse, Ruben	15	367	Transported 1676. Son of John.
Rosse, Samuel	15	367	" 1676. Son of John.
Rossel, Philip	15	507	Service 1678.
Rossell, George	6	132	Transported 1659.
Rosser, Hugh	9	321	" 1665.
Rossiter, Mary	17	495	" 1673.
Rossle, John	12	391	" 1669.

NAME	Liber	Folio	REMARKS
Roster, Elizabeth	15	557	Transported 1678.
Rotherne, Patrick	WC2	318	Service 1680.
Rothery, Matthew	15	429	Transported 1674.
Rothwell, Jane	7	567	" 1657. Servant.
Rothwell, William	WC2	352,412	" 1680.
Rothwell, William	WC2	412	" 1681.
Roules, Walter	12	551	Immigrated 1670. Of St. Mary's Co.
Rouls, Stephen	15	416	Transported 1677.
Roult, John	15	574	" 1678.
Round, James	15	414	Immigrated 1677.
Rouney, Thomas	1	19	Transported 1637. Servant. (See Rowney).
Rountwaile, Thomas	15	544	Transported 1677.
Rousby, Christopher	11	436	Immigrated 1668. Of Calvert Co.
Rousby, John	19	603	And Barbara, his wife, daughter of Henry Morgan, living 1677.
Rousby, William	WC2	22,122	Transported 1679.
Rouse, Gregory	4	12	" 1655. Servant.
Rouse, Matthew	4	555	" 1661.
Rousy, John	15	531	Immigrated 1678. Planter.
Rousy, John, Jr.	15	531	Transported 1678.
Rousy, Mary	15	531	" 1678. Wife of John.
Routly, John	15	433	" 1677.
Rovan, William	15	565	" 1679.
Row, Isaac	9	105	" 1665.
Row, Thomas	16	165	Immigrated 1670, with Ann, his wife, and Philip, his nephew. Of Somerset Co.
Rowark, Cornelius	18	152	Transported 1674.
Rowbottom, Edmond	5	221	" 1662. Servant. (8, fol. 130).
Rowcastle, Charles	WC2	167,169	Transported 1680.
Rowe, Alice	WC2	380	" 1675-80. Servant.
Rowe, Daniel	WC2	380	" 1675-80. Servant.
Rowe, George	8	501	" 1665.
Rowe, Thomas	17	501	" 1673.
Rowe, William	4	555	" 1661.
Rowell, William	10	305	" 1666. Servant.
Rowght, William	6	59	" 1663.
Rowland, Eleanor	5	489	" 1655.
Rowland, Eleanor	8	502	" 1665.
Rowland, Elizabeth	9	386	" 1666.
Rowland, John	4	140	" 1656. Servant.
Rowland, John	6	294	" 1664.
Rowland, Luke	WC2	201	" 1680. Servant.
Rowles, Christopher	6	84	" 1649.
Rowles, John	5	306	" 1663.
Rowles, John	11	344	" 1668.
Rowley, Christopher	6	84	" 1656.
Rowlings, Mary	15	454	" Oct. 1677.
Rowlinson, William	15	454	" Oct. 1677.
Rowney, Thomas	ABH	37,44,64	" 1637. Servant.

NAME	Liber	Folio	REMARKS
Rowney, Thomas	1	33,171	Transported 1637. Servant. (See Rouney).
Rows, Ann	17	531	Transported 1673.
Rowse, Abraham	7	560	Immigrated 1665.
Rowse, Abraham	15	452	Transported 1677.
Rouse, Alice	7	567	" 1657. Servant.
Rowse, Bridget	18	91	Immigrated 1658. Wife of Gregory.
Rowse, Christopher	9	105	" 1665.
Rowse, Gregory	18	91	Service 1674.
Rowse, John	7	605	Transported 1665.
Rowse, Nath.	Q	208	" 1658.
Rowse, Robert	5	529	" 1651.
Rowth, Gremel	Q	32	" 1653-8.
Roy, Christian	17	571	" 1673.
Royall, Edmund	17	630	And Isabell, his wife. Service 1673.
Royall, Elizabeth	WC2	308	Transported 1678.
Royall, Martha	16	464	Wife of Thomas of Talbot Co. Service 1667.
Royally, Ann	15	353	Transported 1674. (18, fol. 280).
Royland, John	6	47	" 1663.
Royland, William	18	177	" 1674.
Roylands, William	WC2	308	" 1678.
Royle, Henry	WC2	23	" 1679. Servant.
Royle, John	12	282	" 1668.
Royle, John	WC2	23	" 1679. Servant.
Royle, Margaret	12	281,514	" 1668.
Royston, James	15	516	" 1678.
Royston, James	WC2	135	" 1679. Servant.
Royston, John	15	454	" Oct. 1677.
Royston, Mary	18	3	" 1674.
Royston, Richard	10	507	Immigrated 1667.
Royston, Robert	6	80	Transported 1662.
Rozer, Benjamin	5	307	Immigrated 1663.
Rozer, Benjamin	12	215	Transported 1668-9.
Rozer, Col. Benjamin	WC2	130-131	Rights 1679.
Ruckstone, Alice	8	483	Transported 1665 from Virginia.
Ruckstone, Nicholas	8	483	" 1665 from Virginia.
Rudd, John	16	71	" 1670.
Rudd, Nathaniel	5	85	" 1661.
Rudde, Margaret	11	541	" 1668.
Rudden, Garrett	4	554	Immigrated with three sons 1661.
Rudden, Mary	4	554	Transported 1661. Wife of Garrett.
Rude, Nicholas	8	483	" from Virginia 1665.
Rue, James	16	393	" 1671.
Rugg, Elizabeth	15	396	" 1675.
Rugg, Furbur	WC2	253,398	" 1680.
Rugg, John	15	322	" 1675.
Ruggles, Mary	18	77	" 1674.
Rugmore, Mary	18	174	" 1674.
Rumbald, Moses	7	464	" 1655.
Rumfie, Elizabeth	7	464	" 1660.

NAME	Liber	Folio	REMARKS
Rumley, Mark	6	266	Transported 1662.
Rumney, Mark	17	363	" 1672.
Rumsey, Thomas	12	504	Service 1669.
Rumsey, William	WC2	167,169	Transported 1679.
Rundy, Nicholas	4	137	" 1659.
Rusell, Edward	11	344	" 1668.
Rushby, Alice	WC2	183	" 1680.
Rushell, Michael	16	435	" 1671.
Russ, Alester	4	140	" 1651. Servant.
Russ, James	15	452,531	" 1677.
Russ, Thomas	16	282	Service 1671. Of Calvert Co.
Russam, Edward	15	416	Transported 1677.
Russell, Abraham	6	299	" 1664.
Russell, Ann	5	208	" 1662. Daughter of Nicholas.
Russell, Christopher	2	254	Immigrated 1647.
Russell, Christopher	ABH	5,203	" 1652.
Russell, Daniel	7	569	Transported 1663-4.
Russell, Edward	5	81	" 1659.
Russell, Edward	4	589	" 1661.
Russell, Edward	11	465	" 1668. (11, fol. 524).
Russell, Edward	12	478	" 1670. (13, fol. 112; 15, fol. 309).
Russell, Fran.	15	540	Transported 1677.
Russell, Gerret	15	553	" 1678.
Russell, Godfry	15	449	" 1677.
Russell, John	Q	62	" 1658. (4, fol. 55).
Russell, John	4	609	" 1661. (7, fol. 554).
Russell, John	12	194	" 1668. Servant.
Russell, John	WC2	112	" 1679. (20, fol. 185).
Russell, Joyce	Q	29	Servant 1658.
Russell, Margaret	11	162	Transported 1667.
Russell, Nicholas	ABH	60,66	" 1637. (1, fol. 25,38,39).
Russell, Nicholas	5	208	Immigrated 1662.
Russell, Phebe	16	505	Transported 1665.
Russell, Richard	Q	73	" 1658.
Russell, Richard	4	56	" 1659. Servant.
Russell, Richard	9	330	" 1665.
Russell, Richard	15	362	" 1676.
Russell, Richard	15	442	" 1677.
Russell, Thomas	17	445,567	Service 1673. Of Worcester Co.
Russell, Vaughan	17	553	Immigrated from Virginia 1665. Of Baltimore Co.
Russell, William	5	3	Transported 1661.
Russell, William	6	86	" 1662.
Russell, William	6	106	" 1663.
Russell, William	12	491	Immigrated 1670. Of Anne Arundel County.
Russten, Christopher	10	116	Transported 1666, with wife.
Rust, Henry	5	59	" 1662.
Ruterford, Gaven	16	79	" 1670. (See Rutherford).

NAME	Liber	Folio	REMARKS
Ruth, Ann	15	567	Transported 1678.
Ruthbane, William	15	362	" 1676.
Rutherford, Gaven	16	79	" 1670.
Ruthland, Margaret	6	105	" 1654.
Ruthy, Daniel	15	429	" 1674.
Rutland, Margaret	6	105	" 1654.
Rutledge, John	1	132	Immigrated 1640.
Rutlidge, Edward	12	589	Transported 1670.
Rutlidge, John	ABH	104	Immigrated 1640.
Rutter, Elizabeth	12	285	Transported 1668. Servant.
Rutter, Richard	15	448	" 1678.
Rutter, Thomas	4	59	" 1652-9.
Rutter, William	17	448	" 1673.
Rutter, William	WC2	411	" 1681.
Ruttland, Esther	4	11	" 1659. Servant.
Rutton, John	8	501	" 1665.
Ruxton, Nicholas	17	552	Immigrated 1664 from Virginia, with Alice, his wife.
Ryal, Thomas	12	376,385	Service 1669. Of Talbot Co.
Ryan, Elizabeth	WC2	82	Transported 1679.
Ryan, John	15	446	" 1677.
Ryan, John	WC2	120	" 1680.
Ryan, Mary	15	553	" 1678.
Ryan, Pat.	15	553	" 1678.
Ryan, Patrick	WC2	57	" 1678.
Ryce, John	Q	428	" 1657.
Rycraft, John	5	257	" 1663.
Ryder, Charles	Q	71	" 1652-3.
Ryder, Honor	WC2	132	" 1680. Servant.
Rye, John	16	466	Immigrated Mar. 10, 1668, with Ann, his wife. Of Kent Co.
Rye, John	20	184	Transported from Ireland 1678.
Ryell, Elizabeth	18	177	" 1674.
Ryell, Thomas	8	89	" 1665.
Ryely, Thomas	17	15	" 1673.
Ryen, Lawrence	18	137	" 1674.
Ryland, John	7	461	" 1664.
Ryland, William	WC2	52	Service 1679. Of St. Mary's Co.
Ryley, Dina	6	263	Transported 1662.
Ryley, Richard	11	581	" 1668.
Ryley, Thomas	9	270	" 1665.
Ryly, Thomas	7	150	" 1664.
Ryman, William	15	574	" 1668-79.
Rynolds, Hannah	7	150	Immigrated 1664.
Rynolds, John	7	150	Transported 1664. Son of Hannah.
Rynolds, Thomas	7	150	" 1664. Son of Hannah.
Ryten, Thomas	11	581	Immigrated 1667.
Sabbell, Richard	3	23	Transported before 1648.
Sabell, Richard	ABH	47	" prior to 1648. Servant.
Saben, Robert	Q	71	" 1652-3.
Saborham, Henry	15	455	" 1678.

NAME	Liber	Folio	REMARKS
Sackleton, Usle	16	435	Transported 1671.
Sacknew, Charles	11	344	" 1668.
Sacrey, Robert	5	242	" 1662.
Sacye, William	17	421	Immigrated 1663. Of Kent Co.
Sadd, Edward	5	93	Transported 1661.
Sadey, Will.	15	430	" 1677.
Sadgate, Anthony	6	290	" 1663.
Sadler, Charles	12	474	" 1670.
Sadler, Dorothy	5	409	Widow of Giles. Married Hugh
Stanley, Gent., prior to 1663.			
Sadler, Dorothy	9	54	Transported 1665.
Sadler, Eleanor	8	503	" 1665.
Sadler, Elizabeth	4	5	" 1659. Servant.
Sadler, Giles	4	2	Immigrated prior to June 1658. (12, fol. 591).
Sadler, Henry	5	339	Transported 1663.
Sadler, John	6	97	" 1657.
Sadler, John	15	530	" 1678.
Sadler, Peter	WC2	406	" 1677. (15, fol. 454).
Sadler, Richard	9	269	" 1665.
Sage, George	15	428	" 1677.
Sagor, Peter	6	96	Immigrated 1656.
Sailes, Abraham	17	533	Service 1673. Of Charles Co.
Saindge, William	17	503	Transported 1668.
Sainsbery, Ann	17	417	" 1673.
Saint, Richard	17	545	" 1673.
Saint George, William	WC2	167,169	" 1679.
Sakell, Ann	16	630	" 1670.
Sakit, Ann	16	79	" 1670.
Salah, Mary	16	503	" 1671.
Salberry, Samuel	4	137	" 1657. Servant.
Salby, Nicholas	11	564	Service 1668.
Sale, Edward	15	446	Transported 1677.
Sales, Roger	15	376	" 1676.
Salesbury, John	5	192	Immigrated 1662, with wife.
Salisberry, Thomas	6	19	Transported 1660-3.
Salisbury, Andrew	WC2	411	" 1681.
Salisbury, Joan	WC2	411	" 1681.
Salisbury, John	15	397	" 1676.
Salisbury, John	WC2	411	Immigrated 1681.
Salisbury, Mary	15	516	Transported 1678.
Salisbury, Nicholas	9	69	" 1660-5.
Salisbury, Pettigrew	WC2	411	" 1681.
Salisbury, Thomas	5	466	" 1661.
Salisbury, William	16	339	Immigrated 1671, with Sarah, his wife. Of Baltimore Co.
Salkeld, William	5	488	Transported 1651-62.
Sallaway, Andrew	9	399	Immigrated prior to 1666.
Sallenge, John	8	129	Transported 1665. Servant.
Sallenger, Sarah	15	377	" 1676.
Sallisbury, Samuel	4	550	" 1661.

NAME	Liber	Folio	REMARKS
Salloway, Ann	7	567	Transported 1665.
Salloway, John	7	464	" 1662.
Sally, John	17	610	" 1673.
Salmon, Edward	8	478	" 1665. (15, fol. 404).
Salmon, Francis	5	488	" 1651-2.
Salmon, Mary	10	117	" 1666.
Salmon, Ralph	6	79	Immigrated 1655.
Salmon, Stephen	ABH	9,41	" 1646. (ABH, fol. 35, 94; 2, fol. 423).
Salmon, Stephen	2	572,624	Service 1649.
Salmore, Thomas	10	598	Immigrated 1667.
Salsbury, George	17	596	Transported 1673.
Salsbury, John	17	596	" 1673.
Salt, Mary	15	566	" 1678.
Saltarsh, Rebecca	17	488	" 1667.
Salter, Jacob	18	117	" 1674.
Salter, John	4	62	Married the widow of Francis Lumbard prior to 1659.
Salter, John	5	413	Immigrated 1663.
Salter, Richard	2	529	Transported 1644. Servant.
Salter, Richard	ABH	27	Servant 1644.
Salter, Thomas	WC2	112	Transported 1680.
Salts, Mark	12	194	" 1668. Servant.
Salvage, James	Q	69	" 1654.
Salvar, Henry	6	131	" 1661.
Salway, Anthony	Q	70	Immigrated 1657.
Sames, John	12	460	Transported 1669.
Samford, William	Q	33	" 1655.
Sammes, Margaret	ABH	348	" 1652-3. Servant.
Sample, William	ABH	383	Immigrated Feb. 1653.
Sampson, Edward	16	170	Transported 1671.
Sampson, Francis	9	272	" 1665.
Sampson, Henry	7	88	" 1657.
Sampson, Jane	15	450,507	" 1678.
Sampson, John	ABH	338	" 1650. Servant.
Sampson, John	12	413	" 1669.
Sampson, Robert	5	482,536	" 1662. (11, fol. 144-5).
Sampson, Thomas	4	67,70	Service 1659. (4, fol. 549).
Sampson, Thomas	6	48	Transported 1663. Servant.
Sampson, Thomas	11	110	Of St. Mary's Co. Mariner. Immigrated 1667.
Sampson, Thomas	10	600	Transported 1667.
Sampson, William	6	127	" 1655.
Sams, Margaret	Q	70	" 1652. Married Jno. Askew prior to 1659. (4, fol. 60).
Samuell, Elizabeth	17	495	Transported 1673. Daughter of Richard.
Samuell, Mary	17	495	Transported 1673. Wife of Richard.
Samuell, Richard	17	495	Immigrated 1673. Of Somerset Co.
Samuell, Robert	17	495	Transported 1673. Son of Richard.
Samwyes, Jonathan	5	245	" 1662. Servant.

NAME	Liber	Folio	REMARKS
Sandall, Peter	6	128	Transported 1651.
Sandall, Samuel	6	96	" 1658.
Sandbanke, Thomas	15	454	" 1677.
Sandbroke, Mary	11	374	" 1668.
Sandcroft, Edward	12	507	" 1669. Servant.
Sanderlin, Patrick	15	544	" 1674.
Sanders, Ann	ABH	249	" May 1651. Daughter
of Sarah, wife of Jno. Covett.			
Sanders, Ann	6	123	Transported 1663.
Sanders, Caleb	12	209	" 1668.
Sanders, James	5	367	" 1649.
Sanders, Jane	15	567	" 1678.
Sanders, John	6	299	" 1662.
Sanders, Joseph	15	505	" 1678.
Sanders, Margaret	WC2	158	" 1680.
Sanders, Mary	15	354	" 1676.
Sanders, Mary	WC2	72	" 1679.
Sanders, Mathew	5	305	" 1663. (6, fol. 299).
Sanders, Richard	9	48	" 1665.
Sanders, Robert	5	367	" 1649.
Sanders, Thomas	4	556	" 1661.
Sanders, Thomas	5	411	" 1663.
Sanderson, Ann	16	437	" 1671.
Sanderson, Anna	12	505	Service 1669.
Sanderson, Hester	15	322	Transported 1675.
Sanderson, John	11	581	" 1668.
Sanderson, John	13	113	" 1670.
Sanderson, Martha	15	442	" 1677.
Sanderson, William	13	114	" 1669.
Sandford, Alice	7	81	" 1663.
Sandford, Ann	15	442	" 1677.
Sandford, Augustine	18	24	" 1674.
Sandford, James	15	450,507	" 1677.
Sandford, John	9	332	Mate of the ship, "Golden Wheat
Sheaf", which made a voyage to Maryland with immigrants, 1664.			
Sandford, Robert	7	612	Transported 1665.
Sandlett, Henry	6	97	" 1654.
Sandome, William	5	126	Immigrated 1660.
Sandon, Richard	15	405	Service 1676.
Sandown, William	4	5	Transported 1659. Servant.
Sandowne, Richard	16	71	" 1670.
Sandry, Francis	9	476	" 1666.
Sands, Robert	WC2	395	" 1680. Servant.
Sandwell, Jonathan	7	464	" 1659.
Sandy, Elizabeth	15	322	" 1675.
Sandy, Mary	15	322	" 1675.
Sanebury, Richard	WC2	406	" 1680.
Sanefort, George	15	455	" 1678.
Sanes, Francis	WC2	406	" 1678.
Sanfford, Mary	12	209	" 1668.
Sanford, William	17	425	Immigrated 1673. Of Dorchester Co.

NAME	Liber	Folio	REMARKS
Sangester, Henry	15	455	Transported 1678.
Sanghier, George	2	456	Immigrated 1647 with wife and 3 children.
Sangster, James	WC2	318	Immigrated 1680.
Sanner, John	WC2	276	Service 1680. Of St. Mary's Co.
Sansbury, John	17	503	Transported 1672.
Sansbury, John	17	417	" 1673. (18, fol. 36).
Sanson, Jane	20	185	" 1679.
Sant, Miles	11	348	" 1668.
Sapford, William	15	438	Service 1677. Of Dorset Co.
Sapple, Garrett	17	347	" 1672. Of Dorset Co.
Sargeson, William	16	21,437	Transported 1671.
Sarsemnet, Henry	18	128	" 1674.
Sasegar, Susanna	18	84	" 1674.
Sash, William	15	439	" 1677.
Saughier, George	ABH	14	Immigrated 1647 with wife and 3 children. (Q, fol. 69).
Saule, Jonathan	17	363	Transported 1672.
Saunders, Abraham	6	121	" 1657.
Saunders, Ann	Q	427	Servant 1658.
Saunders, Ann	7	581	Transported 1665.
Saunders, Ann	8	502	" 1665. Servant.
Saunders, Caleb	12	501	" 1669.
Saunders, Ebednezer	18	36	" 1673.
Saunders, Elizabeth	12	459	" 1669.
Saunders, Elizabeth	18	94	" 1674.
Saunders, Elizabeth	15	331	" 1675.
Saunders, Francis	11	318	" 1668.
Saunders, Mr. John	ABH	65	Immigrated 1633.
Saunders, John	7	528	Transported 1664. (11, fol. 87).
Saunders, Margaret	19	258	" 1663.
Saunders, Mary	11	318	" 1668.
Saunders, Mathew	7	372	" 1664.
Saunders, Philip	15	505	" 1678.
Saunders, Richard	15	319	Immigrated 1675.
Saunders, Robert	5	488	Transported 1659.
Saunders, Robert	8	128	" 1664. Servant. Of Baltimore Co.
Saunders, Robert	10	599	Transported 1667.
Saunders, Thomas	11	316	" several persons into Maryland 1668. Of the City of Bristol.
Saunders, Thomas	15	370	Transported 1676.
Saunders, William	19	258	" 1663.
Saunders, William	9	305	" 1665.
Saunderson, Ann	11	465	" 1668.
Saunderson, John	16	394	" 1671.
Saundry, Francis	16	405	Service 1671. Of Anne Arundel Co.
Sauraft, Thomas	20	185	Transported 1679.
Savadge, Elizabeth	5	537	" 1660. (7, fol. 371).
Savadge, Margaret	WC2	395	" 1680. Servant.
Savadge, Peter	8	478	" 1665.

NAME	Liber	Folio	REMARKS
Savage, Edward, Gent.	12	267	Of Dorchester Co. Service to Hon. C. Calvert, Esq. 1669.
Savage, Elizabeth	5	467	Transported 1660.
Savage, John	8	130	" 1664.
Savage, John	16	394	" 1671.
Savage, John	WC2	120	" 1680.
Savage, Mary	15	413	" 1676.
Savage, Will	15	565	" 1679.
Savage, William	17	66	Immigrated 1672.
Savage, William	15	430	Transported 1677.
Savedge, Rowland	18	37	" 1673.
Saven, Elizabeth	WC2	73	" 1665.
Saven, Susanna	18	94,160	" 1674.
Savery, Nicholas	16	432	" 1671.
Savon, John	7	427	" 1664. Son of William.
Savon, William	7	427	Immigrated 1664, with wife.
Savory, Fridishwith	Q	33	Transported 1658.
Savoy, Isaac	17	566	Immigrated 1673. Of Worcester Co.
Savoy, Martha	17	566	Transported 1673. Wife of Isaac.
Saw, Adam	9	104	" 1665.
Sawayn, John	15	300	" 1675.
Sawcer, Benjamin	18	107	Immigrated 1666. (See Sawser).
Sawcer, Benjamin	16	369	" 1671. Of Dorchester Co. (18, fol. 118).
Sawder, Peter	15	601	Transported 1678.
Sawser, Ann	15	531,570	Service 1678. Wife of Benjamin.
Sawser, Benjamin	15	531,570	Immigrated 1678. Of Somerset Co. (See Sawcer).
Sawyer, Agatha	18	160	Transported 1674.
Sawyer, John Anderson	5	126	Immigrated 1660. (See Anderson).
Sawyer, Peter	16	112	Transported 1671.
Saxon, Anne	WC2	213	Service 1680. Wife of John.
Saxon, John	WC2	213	Rights 1680.
Saxtone, William	9	99	Transported 1665.
Sayer, Cornelius	15	438	" 1677.
Sayer, Capt. Peter	WC2	252,253, 377,388	Rights 1679. Of Talbot Co.
Sayle, Clement	5	345	Transported 1662.
Sayle, Jane	5	345	" 1662.
Saylee, Abraham	11	378	" 1668.
Sayse, John	15	354	" 1676.
Saywells, Thomas	10	4, 5	" 1665.
Scadding, Damoras	WC2	114	" 1680. Servant.
Scaddon, Damas	WC2	398	" 1680.
Scadgell, Nathaniel	15	353	" 1674.
Scales, Samuel	12	333	" 1669.
Scampe, Susannah	WC2	380	" 1675-80. Servant.
Scamroe, Alexander	18	80	" 1674.
Scarborough, Charles	19	604	Of Accomack, Virginia. Married daughter of Richard Bennett, of Virginia, prior to 1677.
Scarborough, Dennis	WC2	320	Transported 1680. Son of Mathew.

NAME	Liber	Folio	REMARKS
Scarborough, Hannah	WC2	320	Transported 1680. Wife of Mathew.
Scarborough, Hannah	WC2	320	" 1680. Daughter of Mathew.
Scarborough, Mathew	17	388	Transported from Virginia 1672.
Scarborough, Mathew	WC2	260,261	Immigrated 1680 with wife, two children and 17 servants. (WC2, fol. 320, 348).
Scarburgh, Alice	12	343	Transported 1669.
Scarlet, Samuel	16	411,513	" 1671.
Scidmore, Abraham	15	517	" 1678.
Scoffin, Alice	16	395	" 1671.
Scofield, Matthew	11	441	" 1668.
Scoles, Henry	9	105	" 1665.
Scollar, Henry	9	45	" 1665.
Scolthorp, Jon.	15	505	" 1678.
Scory, Grace	WC2	50-51	" 1674.
Scot, Richard	16	411	" 1671.
Scot, Robert	17	614	Immigrated 1673. Of Calvert Co.
Scot, Thomas	16	404	Of Baltimore Co. Aged 28 years in 1671. (17, fol. 545).
Scot, William	17	36	Service 1672. Of Somerset Co. Tailor.
Scotcher, Rose	4	53	Transported 1659.
Scotchman, Francis	5	188	" 1658. Servant. (6, fol. 14).
Scotsford, Richard	1	128	Transported 1637-40.
Scott, Andrew	ABH	141	" 1651.
Scott, Cuthbert	WC2	99	Immigrated 1679. Of St. Mary's Co.
Scott, Elizabeth	9	334	Transported from New Foundland 1665.
Scott, Elizabeth	10	264	Transported 1666. Wife of John.
Scott, Elizabeth	10	264	" 1666. Daughter of John.
Scott, James	4	14	" 1652. Servant.
Scott, James	WC2	31	" 1679.
Scott, Jane	6	239	" 1663.
Scott, Jane	9	250	" 1665.
Scott, John, the	5	367	" 1649. (ABH, fol. 151).
Scott, John	Q	239	" 1651-2.
Scott, John	4	63	" 1652-9.
Scott, John	6	235	" 1663.
Scott, John	10	264,391	Immigrated 1666.
Scott, John	10	264,391	Transported 1666. Son of John.
Scott, John	11	569	" 1668.
Scott, John	15	318,437	" 1674.
Scott, John	15	446	" 1677.
Scott, John	WC2	398	" 1680.
Scott, Jone	9	270	" 1665. Married Thomas Wright.
Scott, Margaret	Q	70	Servant 1658.
Scott, Michael	1	88	Transported prior to 1640.
Scott, Michael	ABH	87	" 1640. Servant.
Scott, Richard	WC2	125	Service 1679. Of St. Mary's Co.

NAME	Liber	Folio	REMARKS
Scott, Robert	WC2	21	Transported 1679.
Scott, Roger	Q	183	Immigrated 1658.
Scott, Samuel	Q	284	" 1658.
Scott, Samuel	10	277	Transported 1666.
Scott, Sarah	ABH	371	" 1651. Wife of William.
Scott, Thomas	7	506	" 1664.
Scott, Thomas	16	79	" 1670.
Scott, Thomas	16	129	" 1671.
Scott, Thomas	18	137,291	" 1674.
Scott, William	ABH	45	Servant 1650.
Scott, William	ABH	371	Immigrated 1651. Mariner.
Scott, William	5	489	Transported 1659.
Scott, William	15	443	" 1677.
Scott, William	WC2	201	" 1680. Servant.
Scovell, George	3	116	" prior to 1650. Servant.
Scovell, George	ABH	56,246	" 1650. Servant.
Scovell, Samuel	ABH	61	" 1633-41.
Scovell, Samuel	1	19,27	" 1638.
Scowerfield, Ann	16	513	" 1672.
Scowler, William	10	390	" 1666.
Screen, William	18	291	" 1674.
Screwes, John	7	505	" 1664.
Screwes, Jonas	15	425	" 1677.
Screwton, Ann	15	553	" 1678.
Screwton, Mary	15	553	" 1678.
Screwton, Thomas	15	553	" 1678.
Scriven, Arthur	15	517	" 1678.
Scriven, William	15	444	" 1677.
Scrivener, Edward	6	293	" 1664. (4, fol. 550).
Scrivener, Richard	15	574	" 1678.
Scull, Cornelius	16	537	" 1671.
Sculle, William	10	117	" 1666.
Seaborn, Bridgett	Q	208	" prior to 1654 and married John Greenwell.
Seabourne, Thomas	12	216	Transported 1668.
Seabrett, Thomas	15	509	" 1677.
Seadden, Benjamin	10	433	" 1667.
Seagerr, James	12	209,315	" 1666.
Seagrrave, Joseph	17	454	" 1672.
Seakey, John	15	600	" 1678.
Seal, Emanuel	15	347	" 1676.
Seale, Edward	10	412	" 1665.
Seale, Edward	WC2	106	" 1679.
Seale, John	15	356	" 1675.
Seale, William	17	490	" from "Southward of Va." 1665.
Sealus, Mary	12	342	Service 1669.
Sealus, Stephen	11	334	Of Limboe River on the E. Shore. Service 1668.
Seaman, John	9	216	Transported 1665.
Seaman, William	9	216	" 1665.

NAME	Liber	Folio	REMARKS
Seamar, William	15	443	Transported 1667.
Seamer, Thomas	3	173	Immigrated 1655.
Seamour, John	Q	323	Transported 1655-8.
Seamour, Thomas	Q	370	Immigrated 1654 with his wife, Ann.
Seanline, Katherine	15	438	Transported Oct. 1677.
Searchwell, Thomas	Q	317	Immigrated 1658.
Seare, Daniel	15	519	Transported 1674.
Seare, Francis	12	322	" 1669.
Seare, Rachel	9	33	" 1660-5.
Seares, James	5	79	" 1662. Servant.
Seares, Johana	12	489	" 1670.
Searle, Dorothy	15	454	" 1677.
Searle, James	5	248	" 1663.
Searle, John	17	408	" 1673.
Searle, Richard	6	123	" 1663.
Searne, William	17	478	Immigrated 1673. Of Dorchester County.
Sears, William	7	130	Formerly servant to Mr. Wm. Parker, married prior to 1663, Elizabeth Lovell.
Seaton, Samuel	11	441	Transported 1668.
Seavere, Charles	7	536	" 1664.
Seaverne, Collet	17	33	" from Virginia 1672.
Seawall, Samuel	16	131	Immigrated 1671. Of Dorchester Co.
Seaward, Elizabeth	12	341	Transported 1668.
Seaward, James	18	31	" 1674.
Seaward, Josias	11	579	Immigrated 1668. Of St. Mary's Co.
Seaward, Josias	WC2	76	Rights 1679. Of Somerset Co.
Seaward, Thomas	16	100	Transported 1667.
Sebastian, Anthony	4	59	" 1649-52.
Sebastian, Stephen	15	307	" 1675.
Seble, Henry	6	84,119	" 1654.
Sectman, William	16	409	" from Virginia 1671.
Sedgrave, Robert	ABH	66	" 1637. (1, fol. 20, 25, 38, 39).
Sedwicks, Thomas	16	37	Service 1670. Of Calvert Co.
See, Thomas	15	531	Transported 1678.
Seeld, Hannah	9	321	" 1665.
Seeling, Ann	6	293	" 1664.
Seeling, Ann	12	471	" 1670. Wife of George.
Seeling, George	12	471	Immigrated 1670. Of St. Leonard's Creek. (6, fol. 293).
Seely, ---	Q	28	Transported 1653.
Seemell, Samuel	Q	18	" 1651.
Seemer, Ann	15	318	" 1674.
Seemons, John	9	270	" 1665. Servant.
Seeny, Sarah	15	446	" 1677.
Seeres, William	5	259	" 1656.
Seers, Francis	15	381	Service 1675. Of Dorchester Co.
Seeth, Susanna	5	373	Transported 1663.
Segar, Edmond	16	72	" 1670.
Sehea, Thomas	15	543	" 1678.

NAME	Liber	Folio	REMARKS
Seircen, William	15	318	Transported 1674.
Selby, Daniel, Gent.	14	334	Immigrated 1674. Of Virginia.
Patent to land in Maryland, 1671. (18, fol. 38).			
Selby, Edward	Q	71	Married Eleanor Matthews, 1658.
Selby, George	7	87	Transported 1657. Servant.
Selby, James	12	375	Service 1669.
Selby, John	6	142	Transported 1658.
Selby, John	7	536	" 1663.
Selby, Katherine	ABH	151	" 1649-50. Servant.
Selby, Richard	18	279	" 1675.
Selby, William	4	190	" 1659.
Sellame, Herman	10	352	" 1666.
Sellby, James	9	386	" 1666.
Sellers, Roger	7	513	" 1663.
Selling, Charles	5	489	" 1662.
Selling, Dorothy	8	502	" 1665.
Sellman, John	15	301	Service 1675. Of Anne Arundel Co.
Selman, Henry	17	585	Transported 1673.
Selman, William	12	216	" 1666 by Capt. Burges.
Selmon, John	6	63	" 1658-63.
Selvey, Thomas	15	310	Petition 1675. (See Selvy).
Selvy, Andrew	18	39	Transported 1674. Servant.
Selvy, Elizabeth	18	39	" 1674. Daughter of Thomas.
Selvy, Grace	18	39	Transported 1674. Daughter of Thomas.
Selvy, Mary	18	39	Transported 1674. Wife of Thomas.
Selvy, Thomas	18	39	Immigrated 1674.
Selvy, Thomas	18	39	Transported 1674. Son of Thomas.
Selway, Mr. ---	Q	71	Married Martha Wells 1652-8.
Semarr, Jane	15	454	Transported 1677.
Semer, Edward	9	269	" 1665.
Semster, William	9	38	" 1665.
Sene, Daniel	10	575	" 1667.
Sennet, Montague	16	414	" 1671.
Sennett, Jane	15	430	" 1677.
Senstone, James	5	125	" 1662.
Seny, Sarah	15	446	" 1677.
Serceck, Paul	9	216	" 1665.
Sergant, William	9	322	Immigrated to Choptank River 1665. Of Virginia.
Sergeant, Joseph	7	498	Transported 1664.
Serjeant, John	5	531	" 1662. Service 1667. (16, fol. 533).
Serjeant, Seth	WC2	358-359	Immigrated 1680. Of St. Mary's Co.
Serle, Robert	1	17,19	Transported 1637. Aged 12 years.
Serle, Robert	ABH	150	" 1637. Servant.
Serle, Susanna	10	4	" 1665.
Sermon, Edward	5	209	Immigrated 1662.
Seroby, Eleanor	7	84	Transported 1649.
Seroby, John	7	84	Immigrated 1649.

NAME	Liber	Folio	REMARKS
Seroby, Timothy	7	84	Transported 1649.
Servant, John	15	366	" 1676.
Servant, Ruth	15	396	" 1676.
Sessions, Elizabeth	15	297	" 1675.
Seth, Jacob	15	518	Service 1673.
Seth, Margaret	15	518	" 1675. Wife of Jacob.
Seth, William	18	17	Transported 1669.
Setle, John	18	72	Immigrated 1674. Of St. Mary's Co.
Seton, Samuel	11	337	Transported 1668.
Seuthern, Edward	5	209	Immigrated 1662.
Seuthern, Mary	5	209	Transported 1662. Wife of Edward.
Sevaly, Robert	Q	69	" 1649. Servant.
Seveeteld, Thomas	5	120	" 1661. (See Sweetelad).
Severne, Amy	5	89	" 1661.
Seviniord, John	6	121	" 1663. (See Swiniord).
Sewall, Ann	16	358	" 1671.
Sewall, Elizabeth	5	251	" 1663. Daughter of Henry.
Sewall, Francis	8	130	Transported 1665.
Sewall, George	16	358	" 1671.
Sewall, Henry, Esq.	4	615	Of London. Special Warrant for 2,000 acres, Sept. 12, 1661, &c. (See Sewell).
Sewall, Henry	5	490	Service 1662. (9, fol. 448).
Sewall, Henry	6	294	Immigrated 1664. Merchant.
Sewall, Mr. Henry	6	42	"My Secretary", order from Lord B. respecting estate of "Mattaponia", Aug. 14, 1663.
Sewall, Jane	5	251	Transported 1663. Wife of Henry. (See Sewell, Henry).
Sewall, Jane	15	523	Widow. Immigrated with daughter Mary, prior to 1678, when she appears as the wife of Stephen Bond.
Sewall, Mary	17	531	Transported 1673.
Sewall, Mary, Jr.	16	358	" 1671.
Sewall, Mary, Sr.	16	358	" 1671.
Sewall, Nicholas	5	251	" 1663. Son of Henry.
Sewall, Richard	4	5	" 1659. Servant.
Sewall, Thomas	11	236	Service 1667. Of St. Mary's Co.
Sewall, Thomas	17	382	" 1672.
Sewall, Ursula	16	452	Transported 1678.
Seward, George	17	452	Immigrated 1673 with Mary, his wife, and Ann and Mary, his daughters. Of Dorchester Co.
Seward, James	6	83	Transported 1656.
Seward, Mary	6	83	" 1656.
Sewdum, John	11	582	" 1668.
Sewell, Francis	4	551	" 1661.
Sewell, Henry, Esq.	5	251	Immigrated 1663. (See Sewall).
Sewell, Jeremiah	18	84	Transported 1674.
Sewell, John	ABH	140	" 1651.
Sewell, Mary	18	37	" 1673. Daughter of Jane Bond, wife of Stephen Bond.
Sewen, Thomas	9	48	Transported 1665.
Sewer, John	4	565	" 1661.

NAME	Liber	Folio	REMARKS
Sewett, John	18	84	Transported 1674.
Sewope, George	5	246	" 1656.
Sexby, Richard	16	452	" 1667.
Sexomd, Edmund	10	352	" 1666.
Sexton, Darby	17	490	" from "Southward of Va.", 1665.
Sexton, Jeremiah	7	84	Immigrated 1660.
Sexton, Patrick	WC2	184	Transported 1680. Servant.
Sexton, Richard	15	500,558	" 1676-7.
Sexton, Richard	WC2	399	" 1677.
Sexton, Thomas	15	500,558	" 1676-7.
Sexton, Thomas	WC2	399	" 1677.
Sexton, Thomas, Jr.	15	500,558	" 1676-7.
Sexty, William	11	463	" 1668.
Sexway, George	16	110	" 1671.
Sexway, Roberty	16	110	" 1671.
Seyborn, Mrs. Winifred	ABH	6,67	Immigrated 1638, and afterwards married Thos. Green, Esq., and later, Mr. Robt. Ceart.
Seyborne, Mrs. Winifred	2	346	Immigrated 1638. Wife of Thomas Greene.
Seycroft, Edward	17	479	Immigrated 1673. Of St. Mary's Co.
Seygoe, John	11	216	Service 1667. Of Charles Co.
Seymor, Ann	17	495	Transported 1673.
Seymor, Owen	ABH	9	Immigrated prior to 1648.
Shackerly, John	4	554	Transported 1661.
Shackerly, Phillis	17	601	Widow of Wm. Hampton, living 1673.
Shacklady, James	5	259	Transported 1655. (6, fol. 293; 7, fol. 561).
Shackland, Mathew	WC2	168-169	Transported 1680.
Shacklary, John	9	487	Immigrated 1665.
Shackney, John	18	110	Service 1674. Of Charles Co.
Shackues, John	16	85	Transported 1670.
Shacock, Roger	9	488	Immigrated 1664. (17, fol. 422).
Shacroft, Richard	12	551	Transported 1670.
Shaddock, Ellin	WC2	309	" 1678.
Shadock, John	15	422	Service 1677.
Shadwell, Christopher	12	477	Transported 1670.
Shadwell, John	8	129	" 1664.
Shadwell, Michael	8	129	" 1664. Servant.
Shafts, Catherine	4	555	" 1661.
Shafts, John	15	167	" 1673.
Shakelton, William	18	102	Service 1674.
Shakeshaft, Edmund	18	135	Transported 1674.
Shale, Joshua	5	466	" 1662.
Shall, John	4	64	" 1659. Son of Peter.
Shall, Maria	4	64	" 1659. Daughter of Peter.
Shall, Peter	4	64	Immigrated 1659 with "Breta Andrews", his wife.
Shallaton, John	WC2	106	Transported 1679.

NAME	Liber	Folio	REMARKS
Shan, William	4	57	Service 1659.
Shanck, John	15	370	Transported 1676.
Shancks, Thomas	WC2	23,400	Immigrated 1679. Of Somerset Co.
Shanke, John	16	93	Transported 1670. '
Shanks, Abigail	ABH	232	" 1650 by Robt. Brooke, Esq. Wife of John.
Shanks, John	ABH	78,101	Transported 1637-40. Servant. (ABH, fol. 15).
Shanks, John	1	63,128	Transported 1640.
Shanks, John	2	457	Service about 1648.
Shanks, John	ABH	167,230	" 1651-2.
Shapgood, Jonas	17	602	" 1673.
Shapgood, Susanna	17	602	" 1673. (als. Butcher).
Shapleigh, Philip	16	129,316	Deputy Surveyor for Somerset Co. 1671. Age 27. (See Shapley).
Shapley, John	12	601	Transported 1669.
Shapley, Philip	11	171	Immigrated 1667. Of Calvert Co. (See Shapleigh).
Share, William	18	285	Transported 1674.
Sharlin, Roger	17	551	Service 1673. Of St. Mary's Co.
Sharp, John	15	435	Transported 1677.
Sharp, Peter	Q	28	Immigrated 1650.
Sharp, Robert	ABH	9	" 1646.
Sharp, Susan	11	374	Transported 1668.
Sharp, William	ABH	376	" 1654. Servant.
Sharpe, Eleanor	17	572	" 1672.
Sharpe, John	15	358	" 1675.
Sharpe, Katherine	17	531	" 1673.
Sharpe, Mary	15	448	" 1677.
Sharpe, Nathaniel	4	216	" 1659.
Sharpe, Peter	9	86	Of the E. Shore. Quaker. Living 1665.
Sharpe, Robert	2	425	Immigrated 1646.
Sharpe, Robert	17	37	Transported 1672.
Sharpe, Sarah	6	290	" 1663. (9, fol. 270).
Sharpe, Susan	15	565	" 1679.
Shartell, Oliver	WC2	106	" 1679.
Shatton, Mrs. ---	ABH	36	Returned to England prior to 1649. (See Stratton).
Shaw, Amelia	Q	69	Transported 1657.
Shaw, Christopher	13	17	" 1668.
Shaw, Cisty	15	499	" 1677.
Shaw, Elizabeth	15	429	" 1674.
Shaw, George	5	221,307	" 1662. Servant.
Shaw, Jarvis	16	110	" 1671.
Shaw, John	Q	72	Immigrated 1658.
Shaw, John	15	397	Transported 1676.
Shaw, John	15	598	" 1678-9.
Shaw, John	WC2	410	Service 1681. Of St. Mary's Co.
Shaw, Margery	12	189	Transported 1668.
Shaw, Margaret	15	530	" 1678.

NAME	Liber	Folio	REMARKS
Shaw, Mary	12	190	Transported 1668.
Shaw, Mathew	18	152	" 1674.
Shaw, Nicholas	15	337	Immigrated 1675.
Shaw, Ralph	6	209	Transported 1663.
Shaw, Samuell	WC2	21-22, 122	" 1679.
Shaw, Thomas	15	358	" 1675.
Shawe, Joseph	WC2	206	" 1679. Servant.
Shea, Daniel	15	553	" 1678.
Shea, Jone	15	553	" 1678.
Shea, Nicholas	15	553	" 1678.
Shea, Thomas	15	553	" 1678.
Sheale, Robert	1	166	" 1650. Servant.
Sheapheard, Nicholas	18	136	Service 1675. Of Anne Arundel Co.
Sheapheard, William	18	337	Transported 1675.
Sheares, Elizabeth	12	190	" 1668. Servant.
Sheares, Joseph	6	294	" 1664.
Shearly, Hannah	17	463	" 1673.
Sheediman, Jeremiah	9	39	" 1657.
Sheehane, Cornelius	WC2	129	" 1679.
Sheele, Cap.	WC2	187	" 1678.
Sheely, Daniel	WC2	355	Service 1680. Of Somerset Co.
Sheely, Ellinor	WC2	355	" 1680. Of Somerset Co. Wife of Daniel.
Sheep, Launcelot	ABH	48	Transported 1646.
Sheercliff, John	1	18	" 1638.
Sheers, Elizabeth	Q	68	" 1641.
Sheffell, Samuel	15	454	" 1677.
Sheffield, Francis	17	590	Service 1673. Of Charles Co.
Shefield, Mary	5	305	Transported 1663.
Shehawne, Thomas	20	184	" from Ireland 1678.
Shehee, Roger	11	329	Immigrated from Virginia to St. Mary's Co. 1668.
Shehey, David	15	567	Transported 1679.
Shelleck, William	12	205	" 1667.
Shelletto, Thomas	17	585	" 1673.
Shelley, Edward	ABH	6	" 1640-8.
Shellgar, Martin	6	217	" 1663.
Shellits, Thomas	16	12	Immigrated 1670. Of Somerset Co.
Shelly, Edward	2	327	Transported 1640-8.
Shelly, Mathew	4	59	" 1649-52.
Shelly, Susannah	WC2	320	" 1680. Servant.
Shelton, Anthony	WC2	79,99	" 1679.
Shelton, Thomas	5	2	" 1661.
Shelton, Thomas	10	598	" 1667.
Shelvers, John	18	294	" 1675.
Shenston, George	5	167	" 1660.
Shepard, Francis	WC2	328,329	Service 1680.
Shepard, Hannah	WC2	328	" 1680. Wife of Francis.
Shepard, Mary	11	344	Transported 1668.
Shepard, Richard	15	430	" 1677.

NAME	Liber	Folio	REMARKS
Shepard, William	15	301	Transported 1675.
Shepeard, Joseph	10	433	" 1667.
Shepeard, George	18	160	" 1674.
Shepherd, James	17	51	" 1672.
Shepherd, Mary	ABH	9	Servant 1640.
Shepherd, Mary	2	425	Transported 1640. Servant.
Shepherd, Mary	7	462	" 1660. Wife of Arthur Delahay.
Shepherd, Sarah	6	299	Transported 1661.
Shepherd, William	ABH	9	" 1640.
Shepherd, William	2	425	" 1640. Servant.
Shepley, Adam	15	300	Service 1675. Of Anne Arundel Co.
Shepley, Honor	16	94	Transported 1670.
Shepman, Bridget	15	544	" 1676.
Sheppard, Charles	12	506	Service 1669. Of Baltimore Co.
Sheppard, Eleanor	12	375	Transported 1669. Wife of John.
Sheppard, Henry	16	100	" 1668.
Sheppard, Isaac	17	395	" 1672.
Sheppard, John	5	341	" 1659.
Sheppard, John	9	489	Immigrated 1665.
Sheppard, John	12	375	" 1669. Of St. Mary's County.
Sheppard, Lewis	16	170	Transported 1675.
Sheppard, Sarah	9	433	" 1663.
Sheppard, Stephen	18	84	" 1674.
Sheppard, Thomas	16	11	" 1670.
Sheppard, William	16	41	" 1670.
Shepway, John	7	80	Immigrated 1664. Of the E. Shore.
Sherbone, Mr. Thomas	12	386	Transported 1669.
Sherbrooke, Elizabeth	WC2	380	" 1675-80. Servant.
Sheregood, Mary	WC2	167,169	" 1679.
Sherford, William	12	403	" 1669.
Sherica, Thomas	15	391	Service 1676. Of Calvert Co.
Sherin, John	5	466	Transported 1661.
Shering, Abraham	18	117	" 1674.
Sherington, Richard	10	466	Service 1667.
Sherland, William	ABH	339	Transported 1653. Servant.
Sherly, James	10	600	" 1667.
Sherly, Joseph	WC2	79,140, 141,142	Service 1679. Of Somerset Co.
Sherly, Mary	15	320	Transported 1674.
Sherly (Sherley), Robert	1	20,37, 38,166	" 1633.
Sherman, John	10	342	" 1666. (12, fol. 315).
Sherrif, Alexander	8	202	" 1664.
Sherriff, William	7	507	" 1659.
Sherrill, Samuel	6	295	" 1664.
Sherry, Roger	16	507	" 1671.
Shert, William	10	406	Immigrated 1666 with wife.
Shertcliffe, Anne	4	29	Transported 1657. Daughter of John.
Shertcliffe, John	2	418,425	Immigrated 1646.

NAME	Liber	Folio	REMARKS
Shertcliffe, Mary	4	29	Transported 1657. Daughter of John.
Shervington, Richard	Q	453	" 1658.
Sherwood, Edward	4	576	" 1661.
Sherwood, Francis	6	268	" 1662.
Sherwood, Hugh	7	370	Immigrated 1661. (8, fol. 202).
Sherwood, James	5	238	Transported 1662.
Shesley, Daniel	18	36	" 1673.
Shew, Andrew	ABH	274	" 1651-2. Servant.
Shewbrook, John	20	185	" 1679.
Shewbrooke, Dorothy	15	443	" 1677.
Shewell, Jonathan	15	501	" 1678. Son of Samuel. (17, fol. 34).
Shewell, Mary	15	501	Transported 1678. Wife of Samuel. (17, fol. 34).
Shewell, Mary	15	501	Transported 1678. Daughter of Samuel. (17, fol. 34).
Shewell, Samuel	15	501	Immigrated prior to 1678. (17, fol. 34).
Shewes, Edward	15	300	Service 1675. Of Anne Arundel Co.
Shewleman, Katharine	15	563	Transported 1678.
Shield, Daniel	15	449	Immigrated 1677. Of Somerset Co.
Shield, Eleanor	15	449	Transported 1677. Wife of Daniel.
Shield, George	6	142	" 1660.
Shield, William	15	397	" 1676.
Shiell, Thomas	11	313	Immigrated 1668. Of Somerset Co.
Shielle, George	16	94	Transported 1670.
Shiggle, Mark	6	127	" 1662.
Shingins, Elizabeth	15	553	" 1678.
Shingleton, Edmond	6	97	" 1658.
Shingler, John	9	448	" 1666.
Shingles, John	9	334	" 1666.
Shinson, Mary	WC2	167,169	" 1679.
Shinson, Thomas	15	376	" 1676.
Ship, William	ABH	37	Servant 1637.
Ship, William	7	499	Transported 1660.
Shipleigh, Adam	13	17	" 1668.
Shiply, Daniel	10	392	Service 1666.
Shippard, Abigail	13	111	Transported 1668.
Shippy, Richard	12	194	" 1668. Servant.
Shipsey, Thomas	7	499	" 1660.
Shircliffe, John	ABH	150	Married Ann Goldsborough prior to 1651, died prior to 1667. Daughters married. (10, fol. 474, 477).
Shirley, Francis	ABH	244	Transported 1637.
Shirt, Michael	ABH	142	" 1651.
Shirt, William	ABH	142	" 1651.
Shirtcliffe, John	ABH	8	Immigrated 1646.
Shittleworth, Thomas	6	267	Transported 1662.
Shivers, Thomas	5	307	" 1663.
Shoakley, Richard	16	174	" 1671.
Shoar, Thomas	13	112	" 1668.
Shoare, Katherine	WC2	46	Service 1679. Wife of Thomas.

NAME	Liber	Folio	REMARKS
Shoare, Thomas	WC2	46	Service 1679. Of St. Mary's Co.
Shoares, Thomas	13	113	Transported 1671.
Shoares, William	6	31	" 1663.
Shoemaker, Joseph	4	576	" 1661.
Shoolevant, Derby	11	378	" 1668.
Shoolevant, James	11	378	" 1668.
Shoolevant, Julian	11	378	" 1668.
Shore, Edmund	15	505	" 1678.
Short, Alice	18	137	" 1674.
Short, Clare	5	466	" 1659.
Short, Elizabeth	Q	239	" 1651-2.
Short, Henry	16	507	" 1671.
Short, John	9	322	" 1666.
Short, Robert	1	88-89	Petition to confirm title to land granted by Capt. William Clayborne, 1640.
Short, Robert	WC2	217	Transported 1680.
Shortwell, Oliver	15	446	" 1677.
Shott, Stephen	WC2	318,400	Immigrated 1680.
Shovell, Andrew	ABH	229	Transported 1651. Servant.
Shovell, Elizabeth	16	439	" 1671.
Showemaker, John	WC2	309	" 1678.
Shreusbery, Henry	17	517	" 1673.
Shriefe, William	5	167	" 1662.
Shrigley, Deborah	13	116	" 1671.
Shrigley, Samuel	WC2	199	" 1680.
Shrill, Mary	9	262	" 1665.
Shrives, William	15	259	" 1675.
Shropshire, Thomas	Q	323	" 1650 with wife and one child.
Shrubb, Thomas	6	130	Transported 1654.
Shulavane, Jane	16	435	" 1671.
Shuler, John	9	54	" 1665.
Shulevan, Ann	17	572	" 1672.
Shulevan, John	17	572	" 1672.
Shulivane, Frances	16	464	Service 1669. Wife of Patrick.
Shulivane, Jone	16	435	Transported 1671.
Shullavane, Gelline	15	438	" 1677.
Shullworth, Vincent	17	356	" 1672.
Shurry, Peter	15	433	" 1677.
Shutt, Jean	WC2	206	" 1680. Servant.
Shutt, William	16	482	" 1670-1.
Shuttleworth, Mary	18	36	" 1673. Wife of Vincent.
Shuttleworth, Thomas	WC2	265	Immigrated 1661. Service 1680. Of Charles Co.
Shuttling, John	10	291	Transported 1666.
Shuttwell, Thomas	17	475	" 1673.
Shyn, Jerman	17	448	" 1673.
Sibbe, Henry	6	122	" 1655.
Sibrey, Jonathan	9	269	Immigrated 1665.
Sickamore, John	4	550	Transported 1661. (5, fol. 243).
Sicks, John	5	220	Immigrated 1662.

NAME	Liber	Folio	REMARKS
Sicks, Sibilla	5	220	Transported 1662. Wife of John.
Sidall, Elizabeth	15	504	" 1678.
Sidebottom, Robert	16	482	" 1670-1.
Sideman, Thomas	9	386	" 1666.
Sides, Peter	10	392	Immigrated 1661.
Sidgett, John	15	520	Transported 1677.
Sidie, Thomas	17	487	" 1667.
Sidney, Elizabeth	5	359	" 1663.
Sidney, Samuel	17	543	Service 1673. Of Dorset Co.
Sidre, John	11	318	Transported 1668.
Sidron, James	15	560	" 1678.
Sidwell, Roger	11	4	Immigrated from Virginia 1667. Of Baltimore County.
Sields, Peter	6	239	Transported 1663.
Sifrason, Mark	Q	63	Immigrated 1658.
Sight, Frances	6	159	Transported 1663.
Signey, Samuel	WC2	46-47	Immigrated 1673.
Sigsworth, Thomas	18	137	Transported 1674.
Sikes, John	9	222	" 1665.
Sille, Axell	Q	63	Immigrated 1650. (See Stille).
Silly, Barbara	6	133	Transported 1655.
Silly, Obadiah	15	370	" 1676.
Silly, William	15	564	" 1679.
Silson, Edward	15	416	" 1677.
Silver, Nicholas	15	317	Immigrated 1674. Of Virginia.
Silverside, Henry	17	411	Transported 1673.
Silversides, Francis	17	479	" 1673.
Silvester, James	15	570	Service 1673.
Sim, Alexander	18	152	Transported 1674.
Simbarb, Anne	11	308	" 1665.
Simcots, Thomas	17	463	" 1673.
Simeox, Thomas	5	247	" 1659.
Simes, Robert	11	581	" 1668.
Simeton, Alexander	18	167	" 1674.
Simm, Marmaduke	12	204	Married Fortune, widow of Bulmer Metford, prior to 1669. (9, fol. 326).
Simme, Richard	10	600	Immigrated 1667.
Simmonds, Ann	5	249	Transported 1663.
Simmonds, Mary	5	307	" 1663.
Simmonds, Thomas	5	248	" 1663.
Simmons, Alice	9	330	" 1665.
Simmons, John	17	383	Immigrated from Virginia 1672.
Simmons, Mary	9	330	Transported 1665.
Simmons, Robert	5	128	" 1662.
Simmons, Thomas	5	209	" 1639.
Simmons, Thomas	6	94	" 1661.
Simms, Mrs. Ann	9	336	" 1663.
Simms, Ant.	15	565	" 1679.
Simms, Francis	9	336	Immigrated 1663.
Simms, Francis	12	381	Transported 1669.
Simon, Humphrey	15	446	" 1677.

NAME	Liber	Folio	REMARKS
Simon, Thomas	ABH	212	Transported 1642. Servant.
Simond, Mary	15	405	Service 1676.
Simonds, George	Q	71	Transported 1652.
Simonds, John	15	454	" 1677.
Simonds, Thomas	3	63	" about 1640. Servant.
Simonds, Thomas	6	27	Service 1663.
Simonds, William	17	76,354	Transported 1671. (16, fol. 432).
Simons, Andrew	15	553	" 1678.
Simons, Barbary	15	356	" 1675.
Simons, Elizabeth	15	359	" 1676.
Simons, Henry	Q	71	" 1652-3.
Simons, Isaac	15	356	" 1676.
Simons, John	17	415	" 1669.
Simons, John	15	557	Immigrated 1675. Of Somerset Co.
Simons, Mary	4	576	Transported 1661.
Simons, Mary	15	416	" 1677.
Simons, Owen	15	439	" 1677.
Simons, Roger	15	454	" 1677.
Simons, Thomas	ABH	212	" 1642. Servant.
Simons, Thomas	15	500	" 1676-7.
Simons, Thomas	WC2	399	" 1677.
Simpcocks, Alexander	ABH	269	" 1651. Servant.
Simpkin, Robert	2	524	Immigrated 1647.
Simple, Will.	15	553	Transported 1678.
Simpson, Alexander	5	306	Immigrated 1663.
Simpson, Anslow	ABH	26	" 1646.
Simpson, Anslowe	2	517	" 1646. Deceased about 1649.
Simpson, Benjamin	WC2	120	Transported 1680.
Simpson, Edward	9	436	" 1666.
Simpson, Edward	WC2	396	Immigrated 1680. Of Talbot Co.
Simpson, Elizabeth	9	54	Transported 1665.
Simpson, Francis	5	530	" 1660.
Simpson, George	5	85	" 1661.
Simpson, George	15	397	" 1676.
Simpson, Henry	6	95	" 1650.
Simpson, Henry	7	464	" 1655.
Simpson, Jeremiah	15	508	Service 1667. Of Calvert Co. (11, fol. 379).
Simpson, Jeremiah	18	329	Transported 1675.
Simpson, Jerome	11	465	" 1668.
Simpson, John	17	567	" from Virginia 1673.
Simpson, John	15	398	" 1676.
Simpson, Margery	4	66	" 1658.
Simpson, Margery	9	54	" 1665.
Simpson, Mary	WC2	396	" 1680.
Simpson, Paul	ABH	161	Mariner. Living 1647.
Simpson, Robert	ABH	65	Transported 1633. (1, fol. 19, 37, 38, 166).
Simpson, Robert	ABH	26	Immigrated 1647.
Simpson, Robert	15	559	Transported 1679.

NAME	Liber	Folio	REMARKS
Simpson, Sarah	9	35	Transported 1664.
Simpson, Stephen	9	271	Service 1665.
Simpson, Thomas	Q	28	Servant 1649-50.
Simpson, Thomas	ABH	186	Transported 1651.
Simpson, Thomas	17	411	" 1673.
Simpson, William	Q	28	Servant 1649-50.
Simpson, William	8	478,483	Transported 1665.
Simpson, William	15	437	" 1674.
Simpstone, Thomas	13	65	" 1668. Servant.
Sims, Eleanor	15	565	" 1679 with her child.
Sims, John	12	416	" 1669.
Sims, Samuel	17	38	Immigrated from Virginia 1672. Of Somerset Co.
Simson, Alexander	16	79	Transported 1670.
Simson, Grace	WC2	133	" 1680.
Simson, John	18	137	" 1674.
Simson, John	15	453	" 1676.
Simson, Richard	13	122	" 1668.
Simson, Samuel	17	475	" 1673.
Simson, William	16	70	" 1668.
Sincklare, James	9	271	" 1665. Son of Joseph.
Sincklare, Joseph	9	271	Immigrated 1665.
Sinckleare, William	ABH	245	Transported 1651.
Sinckler, John	5	188	" 1655 with wife.
Sincklow, Jane	5	189,242	" 1655. Wife of John.
Sincklow, John	5	189,242	Immigrated 1655.
Sincleer, Agnus	18	152	Transported 1674.
Sindmore, Barnaby	11	581	" 1668.
Sineall, Ric.	15	565	" 1679.
Sines, Philip	16	411	" 1671.
Singleton, James	9	104	Immigrated 1665.
Singleton, John	5	238	" 1662.
Singleton, John	16	354,393	Transported 1671.
Singleton, Richard	5	610	Immigrated 1654. (17,fol. 608).
Singleton, William	5	238	Transported 1662.
Singleton, William	18	160	" 1674.
Sinhouse, John	17	383	Immigrated 1672 with Jane, his wife, and Mary, his daughter.
Sinke, Margaret	9	38	Transported 1665.
Sinkefield, Hugh	15	390	" 1676.
Sinkhorne, Jonathan	6	93	" 1661. (See Linkhorne).
Sinkler, George	16	99	" 1670.
Sinner, Charles	13	114	" 1671.
Sinnett, Alice	15	446	" 1677.
Sinnster, Thomas	WC2	73	" 1665.
Sipsey, John	15	393	" 1671.
Sisell, John	8	88	" 1665.
Sissell, Thomas	15	353	" 1675.
Sisson, Frances	5	484	" 1659. Wife of John.
Sisson, James	5	623	" 1661. Son of Jane, wife of John Delahay.

NAME	Liber	Folio	REMARKS
Sisson, Joane	5	516	Transported 1660. Daughter of John.
Sisson, John	5	484,516	Immigrated 1659.
Sivethall, Dorothy	5	241	Transported 1662. (See Swethall).
Sivett, William	ABH	348	" 1652. Servant.
Sixbee, Richard	16	42	" 1667.
Sixtey, William	11	344	" 1668.
Skale, John	6	159	" 1652.
Skale, Mary	6	159	" 1652.
Skandlin, Eleanor	16	435	" 1671.
Skate, William	ABH	151	" 1641. Servant.
Skearne, Luke	17	407	" 1673.
Skellen, Elizabeth	12	190	" 1668.
Skellton, Israel	17	411	" 1673.
Skelton, Henry	16	411	" 1671.
Skelton, Richard	9	38	" 1665.
Skelton, William	15	357	" 1676.
Skelton, William	15	598	" 1678-9.
Skerfe, John	9	479	" 1665. Servant.
Skidmore, Henry	16	168	" 1670.
Skidmore, Mary	Q	74	Immigrated 1658. Wife of Edward.
Skidmore, Thomas	16	168	Transported 1670.
Skiffe, John	WC2	168-169	" 1680.
Skillington, Mary	6	71	" 1663. Wife of Thomas.
Skillington, Thomas	Q	32	Servant Feb. 1652.
Skillington, Thomas	6	71	Immigrated 1663. Quaker.
Skillinson, Mary	6	90	Transported 1660.
Skillinson, Thomas	6	90	" 1653.
Skillinton, Thomas	3	173	" 1655.
Skink, Henry	ABH	102	" 1641. Servant.
Skinner, Ann	12	378	" 1669. Wife of Andrew.
Skinner, August	11	168	" 1667.
Skinner, Elizabeth	12	351	Immigrated from Virginia 1669. Wife of Thomas of Dorset Co.
Skinner, Jane	Q	239	Transported 1651-2.
Skinner, John	12	351	" 1669. Son of Thomas.
Skinner, John	17	407	" 1673.
Skinner, Peter	WC2	406	" 1679.
Skinner, Richard	WC2	16	" 1677.
Skinner, Thomas	6	294	" 1664.
Skinner, Thomas	12	215	" 1668-9.
Skinner, Walter	8	483	" from Virginia 1665.
Skip, Martin	7	462	" 1664.
Skipper, William	6	117	" 1663.
Skipton, George	10	558	" 1665.
Skipworth, Samuel	9	448	" 1666.
Skipworth, William	6	17	" 1663.
Skitters, John	6	90	" 1656.
Skott, John	17	572	" 1672.
Skrine, Roger	15	502	Service 1678.
Slade, Charles	ABH	165	Transported 1649. Servant.

NAME	Liber	Folio	REMARKS
Slade, Edward	WC2	89,92	Service 1679. Of Calvert Co.
Slade, Joseph	11	465	Transported 1668.
Slade, Margaret	4	550	" 1660.
Slaid, Mary	6	85	" 1662.
Slaid, Nathan	6	129	" 1660.
Slate, Edward	WC2	41	" 1679.
Slateny, Thomas	15	438	" 1677.
Slater, Bartholomew	1	19,125	" 1637.
Slater, Bartholomew	ABH	100	" 1641. Servant. Service 1670. (16,fol.78).
Slater, Bartholomew	16	78	Transported 1670. Son of Bartholomew.
Slater, Eleanor	16	78	Transported 1670. Daughter of Bartholomew.
Slater, Jane	16	78	Transported 1670. Wife of Bartholomew.
Slater, John	17	73	Service 1663.
Slater, John	18	84	Transported 1674.
Slater, John	15	394,450	" 1677.
Slater, John	15	507	" 1678.
Slater, Robert	17	469	" 1671.
Slatery, Philip	15	553	" 1678.
Slaughter, Bartholomew	3	63	" prior to 1648. Servant. (ABH,fol.50).
Slaughter, John	15	527	Transported 1678.
Slaughter, Joseph	15	362	" 1676.
Slaughter, Richard	5	484	" 1661.
Slaughter, Thomas	17	395	" 1672.
Slaughter, William	5	307	" 1663.
Slayd, William	5	514	" 1649. Servant.
Slaymaker, Elizabeth	15	454	" 1677.
Slayter, John	WC2	394	" 1680. Servant.
Slea, Edward	15	560	" 1678.
Slead, Francis	15	313	" 1675.
Sled, Edward	15	560	" 1678.
Sleep, Lancelot	ABH	6	" 1640-8.
Sleepe, Lancelot	2	327	" 1640-8 by Ralphe Beane.
Sleepe, Lancelot	2	254	Transported 1646 by John Medley. Servant. (3,fol.24).
Sleeppy, Richard afterwards married Mary Mills.	9	52	Immigrated prior to 1665 and
Sleford, Hannah	16	482	Transported 1670-1.
Sletle, John	17	572	" 1672.
Slick, Christopher	15	454	" 1677.
Slidge, Elizabeth	9	21	" 1665.
Slingesby, John	3	22	Immigrated about 1646.
Slingsby, John	ABH	46	" 1646.
Slingsby, Elizabeth	17	395	Transported 1672.
Slipne, Richard	4	10	" 1658. Servant.
Sloane, John	18	152	" 1674.

NAME	Liber	Folio	REMARKS
Slocer, John	18	126	Transported 1674.
Slock, Robert	Q	33	" 1658.
Sloman, Elizabeth	WC2	16	" 1679.
Sloop, Henry	9	39	" 1651.
Sloper, Ann	17	64	Immigrated 1659. Wife of Christ. of Talbot Co.
Sloper, Christopher	17	64	Service 1672.
Sluter, John	4	551	Transported 1661.
Sly, Charles	7	461	" 1664.
Sly, Jane	15	517	" 1678.
Sly, John	12	393	" 1669.
Slye, Robert	Q	208	Immigrated prior to 1658. (4, fol. 549).
Slyth, Eleanor	15	565	Transported 1679.
Smale, Edward	WC2	16	" 1679.
Smale, Mary	WC2	50-51	" 1674.
Small, ---	1	27	" 1633-41.
Small, Edward & John	14	332	Of Virginia. Gents. Conditional Patent of land in Md. 1670.
Small, Elizabeth	15	353	Transported 1675. (17, fol. 440).
Small, Elizabeth	WC2	168-169	" 1680.
Smallard, Ann	5	514	" 1656.
Smallpiece, John	16	117	Immigrated 1671. St. Mary's Co.
Smallwood, Hester	9	432	Transported 1650.
Smallwood, James	9	432	Immigrated 1664.
Smart, Elizabeth	Q	18	Transported 1656.
Smart, John	Q	19	" 1656.
Smeate, Rebecca	WC2	168-169	" 1680.
Smedley, John	Q	449	" 1658.
Smiddock, Mary	7	491	" 1664.
Smith, Abraham	17	567	" 1673.
Smith, Alce	7	78	" 1654. Servant.
Smith, Alexander	5	180	Immigrated 1651.
Smith, Alexander	Q	431	Transported 1658.
Smith, Alice	WC2	138	" 1674.
Smith, Alice	15	417	" 1677. Wife of Thomas.
Smith, Allen	16	437	" 1671.
Smith, Ann	3	25-26	" 1648. Servant.
Smith, Ann	ABH	48	" 1648, by Dr. Jno. Wade, whose mistress she afterwards became. See his Will. Servant.
Smith, Ann	5	59	Transported 1660.
Smith, Ann	10	412	" 1666. Wife of George.
Smith, Ann	4	581	" 1661.
Smith, Ann	12	498	" 1670. (13, fol. 112).
Smith, Ann	16	36	" 1670.
Smith, Ann	16	393	" 1671.
Smith, Ann	17	475	" 1673.
Smith, Ann	18	84,166	" 1674.
Smith, Ann	15	429	" 1677.
Smith, Ann	15	537	" 1679.
Smith, Ann	20	185	" 1679.

NAME	Liber	Folio	REMARKS
Smith, Anne	17	377	Transported 1669.
Smith, Anne	WC2	320	" 1680. Servant.
Smith, Anthony	20	185	" 1679.
Smith, Baker	6	347	" 1663.
Smith, Catherine	ABH	86	A minor, heiress of Henry Crawley
of the Isle of Kent, dec'd. 1640.			
Smith, Charles	4	591	Transported 1661.
Smith, Charles	5	305	" 1663.
Smith, Charles	16	393,432	" 1671.
Smith, Charles	18	84	" 1674. (15, fol. 441).
Smith, Charles	WC2	253	" 1679.
Smith, Daniel	4	14	" 1652. Servant. (12, fol. 241).
Smith, David	8	478	Transported 1665.
Smith, Edmond	ABH	337	Service 1653.
Smith, Edmond	10	229	Transported 1665. Servant.
Smith, Edmond	18	137	" 1674.
Smith, Edward	ABH	60	" 1642. Servant. (1, fol. 25).
Smith, Edward	ABH	10	Immigrated 1646. (2, fol. 425).
Smith, Edward	2	423	Transported about 1648. Servant.
Smith, Edward	Q	58	" 1658.
Smith, Edward	13	114	" 1669.
Smith, Edward	12	498	" 1670.
Smith, Edward	17	29	Immigrated 1672, from Virginia,
with wife and five children. Of Somerset Co.			
Smith, Edward	17	510	Transported 1673.
Smith, Edward	18	331	" 1674. (15, fol. 310).
Smith, Edward	15	356	Service 1676. Of Talbot Co.
Smith, Edward	15	530,532	Transported 1678.
Smith, Eleanor	5	188	" Aug. 1651. Wife of Richard.
Smith, Eleanor	11	540	Transported 1668.
Smith, Eleanor	15	376	" 1676.
Smith, Elizabeth	5	87	" 1661.
Smith, Elizabeth	7	371	" 1662.
Smith, Elizabeth	8	88,478	" 1665. (7, fol. 568).
Smith, Elizabeth	WC2	138	" 1674. (18, fol. 152).
Smith, Elizabeth	WC2	380	" 1675-80. Servant.
Smith, Elizabeth	15	441	Service 1677. Wife of George.
Smith, Elizabeth	20	185	Transported 1679.
Smith, Elizabeth	WC2	170	" 1679. Servant.
Smith, Elizabeth	WC2	318	Service 1680.
Smith, Elizabeth, Jr.	15	444	Transported 1677.
Smith, Elizabeth, Sr.	15	444	" 1677.
Smith, Emperour	4	2	Immigrated 1653.
Smith, Ester	WC2	399	Transported 1677.
Smith, Francis	Q	69	" 1656.
Smith, Francis	6	106	" 1659.
Smith, Francis	5	87	" 1661.
Smith, Francis	12	393	" 1669.

NAME	Liber	Folio	REMARKS
Smith, Francis	15	454	Transported 1677.
Smith, George	5	412	" 1658-63.
Smith, George	10	412	Immigrated 1666.
Smith, George	4	581	Transported 1661.
Smith, George	7	82	" 1663.
Smith, George	9	448	" 1666.
Smith, George	15	390	" 1676.
Smith, George	WC2	318	" 1680.
Smith, Gerard	16	85	" 1670.
Smith, Hannah	10	397	" 1666. Wife of John.
Smith, Hannah	9	33	" 1660. Wife of Peter.
Smith, Hannah	10	397	" 1666. Daughter of John. (15, fol. 402).
Smith, Henrick	17	567	Transported 1673.
Smith, Henry	ABH	78	" 1635-40.
Smith, Henry	1	62,128	" 1637-40.
Smith, Henry	ABH	101	" 1637-40. Servant.
Smith, Henry	5	118	" 1658.
Smith, Henry	5	416	" 1663.
Smith, Henry	17	47	Immigrated 1672 with Sarah, his wife. Of St. Mary's Co.
Smith, Henry	15	438,442	Transported 1677.
Smith, Henry	WC2	21	" 1679.
Smith, Henry	WC2	253,398	" 1680.
Smith, Henry, Jr.	16	40	" 1670.
Smith, Henry, Sr.	16	40	Immigrated 1670. Of Somerset Co.
Smith, Herbert	ABH	85	Transported 1636. Servant. "Massacred by Indians on Poplar Island".
Smith, Hester	15	500	Transported 1676-7.
Smith, Isabell	13	113	" 1670.
Smith, Isabella	11	230	" 1667.
Smith, James	9	33	" 1660. Son of Peter.
Smith, James	4	589	Immigrated 1661 with wife and two children.
Smith, James	5	88	Transported 1661.
Smith, James	10	433	" 1667.
Smith, James	17	350	" 1671.
Smith, James	WC2	308	" 1678.
Smith, James	17	595	Service 1673. Of Talbot Co.
Smith, James	15	427	Transported 1677.
Smith, James	15	565	" 1679.
Smith, James	WC2	402	" 1680.
Smith, Jane	19	258	" 1663.
Smith, Jane	17	356	" 1672.
Smith, Jane	WC2	130	" 1679. Servant.
Smith, Jasper	18	174	" 1674.
Smith, Jean	10	325	" 1666.
Smith (als. Brettam), John	ABH	66	" 1637. (1, fol. 38-39).
Smith, John	1	20	" 1637.
Smith, John	6	120	" 1653.

NAME	Liber	Folio	REMARKS
Smith, John	1	86	Petition to confirm title to land, 1640.
Smith, John	Q	431	Transported 1658.
Smith, John	Q	67	Immigrated prior to 1658.
Smith, John	5	514	Transported 1659. Servant.
Smith, John	5	516	" 1659.
Smith, John	5	59	" 1660. Son of Ann.
Smith, John	5	535	" 1660.
Smith, John	4	581	Immigrated 1661.
Smith, John	5	208	Transported 1661.
Smith, John	5	12	" 1662. (5, fol. 531).
Smith, John	7	86	" 1663. (5, fol. 358).
Smith, John	8	128	" 1664. Servant. Of Baltimore Co.
Smith, John	7	554	Service 1665.
Smith, John	10	397	Immigrated 1666. Of Calvert Co.
Smith, John	10	600	" 1667.
Smith, John	12	189	Service 1668.
Smith, John	11	348,462	Transported 1668. (11, fol. 344, 374).
Smith, John	12	209,358	" 1668. (12, fol. 203).
Smith, John	11	316	" from London 1668. Servant.
Smith, John	16	40	Transported 1670. (12, fol. 475).
Smith, John	13	113	" 1670.
Smith, John	17	411,463	" 1673.
Smith, John	15	429	" 1674.
Smith, John	18	72,84	Service 1674. Of St. Mary's Co.
Smith, John	18	335	Transported 1675.
Smith, John	15	500	" 1676-7.
Smith, John	WC2	399	" 1677.
Smith, John	15	417	" 1677. Son of Thomas.
Smith, John	15	558	" 1677, with Mary, his wife.
Smith, John	15	455,531	Transported 1678.
Smith, John	15	565	" 1679. (WC2, fol. 112).
Smith, John	WC2	76	Immigrated 1679 from Virginia with wife, Martha. Of Somerset Co.
Smith, John	WC2	321	Rights 1680.
Smith, John, Jr.	4	581	Transported 1661.
Smith, Jonah	16	307	" 1671. Wife of Henry, Gent. Of Somerset Co.
Smith, Jone	15	566	Transported 1678.
Smith, Joseph	13	64	" 1668.
Smith, Joseph	17	456	" 1670.
Smith, Joseph	16	393	" 1671.
Smith, Joseph	WC2	138	" 1674.
Smith, Joseph	18	329	" 1675.
Smith, Joseph	15	455	" 1678.
Smith, Josias	ABH	199	Immigrated 1651.
Smith, Joyce	16	85	Transported 1670.
Smith, Julian	18	162	Service 1674. Wife of Henry.

NAME	Liber	Folio	REMARKS
Smith, Katharine	WC2	381	Transported 1675-80. Servant.
Smith, Katherine	1	85-86	Petition to confirm title to land by her guardian, William Brainthwaite, 1640.
Smith, Katherine	9	36	Transported 1665. Wife of William.
Smith, Katherine	11	465	" 1668. Wife of William.
Smith, Margaret	9	156	" 1661.
Smith, Margaret	Q	67	Immigrated prior to 1658. Wife of John, and widow of Francis Hunt.
Smith, Margery	16	40	Transported 1670.
Smith, Marmaduke	15	369	Immigrated March 1675.
Smith, Martha	17	382	Service 1672. Wife of George.
Smith, Martha	WC2	76	Transported 1679. Wife of John.
Smith, Mary	5	259	" 1656.
Smith, Mary	6	121	" 1657.
Smith, Mary	4	73	" 1657-9.
Smith, Mary	5	2	" 1661.
Smith, Mary	6	268	" 1662.
Smith, Mary	6	90	" 1663. Wife of William.
Smith, Mary	9	38,45	" 1665.
Smith, Mary	12	194	" 1668. Servant.
Smith, Mary	12	243	" 1669.
Smith, Mary	16	132	" 1671.
Smith, Mary	18	37	" 1673.
Smith, Mary	WC2	138	" 1674.
Smith, Mary	17	635	" 1674 by Jos. S., of Liverpool.
Smith, Mary	15	259	Transported 1675.
Smith, Mary	15	359,369	" 1676.
Smith, Mary	19	382	About to marry Garret Vanswer-ingen, Gent. of St. Mary's City, Oct. 5, 1676.
Smith, Mary	WC2	406	Transported 1677. (15, fol. 454).
Smith, Mary	15	560	" 1678 by Capt. Francis Partis.
Smith, Mary	15	569	Transported 1678 by William Burges.
Smith, Mary	20	48	Widow of Lieut. Wm. Married Danl. Jenifer, Gent., prior to 1678.
Smith, Mary	WC2	321	Service 1680. Wife of John.
Smith, Mather	ABH	82,202	Transported 1651. Servant.
Smith, Mathew	6	82	" 1658.
Smith, Mathew	7	529	" 1664. (17, fol. 416).
Smith, Mathias	18	33	Service 1674. Of Kent Co.
Smith, Matthew	4	13	Transported 1653. Servant. Married Eliz., widow of Rich. Manship, 1658.
Smith, Nath.	WC2	138,317	Transported 1674.
Smith, Nathan	5	90	Immigrated 1661.
Smith, Nathan	5	411	Transported 1663. (6, fol. 214).
Smith, Nathaniel	12	215	" 1668-9.
Smith, Nathaniel	16	170	" 1671.
Smith, Nicholas	ABH	12	Servant 1648.
Smith, Nicholas	9	325	Transported 1666.

NAME	Liber	Folio	REMARKS
Smith, Nicholas	15	427	Immigrated 1672.
Smith, Nicholas	17	444,477	Transported 1673.
Smith, Nicholas	WC2	412	" 1681.
Smith, Nicolas	2	439	" 1648.
Smith, Nixon	13	112	" 1670.
Smith, Peter	9	33	Immigrated 1660. Of Herring Creek, St. Mary's Co.
Smith, Peter	9	33	Transported 1660. Son of Peter.
Smith, Peter	7	524	" 1664.
Smith, Philip	16	307	" 1671. Of Virginia. Servant.
Smith, Philip	32	121	
Smith, Ralph	8	502	Transported 1665.
Smith, Ralph	16	411	" 1671.
Smith, Randall	6	87	" 1650.
Smith, Randolph	6	266	" 1662.
Smith, Rebecca	Q	435	" 1658.
Smith, Rebecca	4	581	" 1661. Wife of John.
Smith, Rebecca	15	514	" 1677.
Smith, Richard	ABH	61,86	" 1633-41. (1, fol. 27).
Smith, Richard	1	87	" 1640. Servant.
Smith, Richard	ABH	23	Immigrated 1644. (2, fol. 509, 541).
Smith, Richard, Gent.	5	188	" Feb. 1649.
Smith, Richard	5	87	Transported 1649-62.
Smith, Richard	5	516	" 1650.
Smith, Richard	5	63,73	" 1660.
Smith, Richard	6	293	" 1664.
Smith, Richard	11	168,170	Service 1667. Of Anne Arundel Co.
Smith, Richard	16	507	Transported 1671.
Smith, Richard	17	572	" 1672.
Smith, Richard	18	306	" 1675.
Smith, Richard	20	285	Married Eliz., sister to Chas. Brooke of Calvert Co., prior to 1679.
Smith, Richard, Jr.	15	444	Transported 1677.
Smith, Richard, Sr.	15	444	" 1677.
Smith, Robert	ABH	37	" 1633-4. Married Rose Gilbert. (4, fol. 193).
Smith, Robert	1	82	Transported 1636. Servant.
Smith, Robert	9	33	" 1660. Son of Peter.
Smith, Robert	1	133-134	License to marry Rose Gilbert, Nov. 23, 1638.
Smith, Robert	2	606	Service to Lord Baltimore, 1649.
Smith, Robert	7	513	Transported 1663. (5, fol. 417).
Smith, Robert	18	318	" 1667. Service 1673.
Smith, Robert	16	340	Service 1671. Of Calvert Co.
Smith, Robert	17	40	Transported 1672.
Smith, Robert	17	608	" 1673.
Smith, Robert	15	433	Immigrated 1677.
Smith, Robert	15	530	Transported 1678.
Smith, Roger	7	567	" 1657. Servant.
Smith, Rose	2	606	" prior to 1649. Widow

NAME	Liber	Folio	REMARKS
of Richard Gilbert. Married Robert Smith by 1649.			
Smith, Samuel	Q	208	Transported 1658.
Smith, Samuel	4	555	" 1661. (12, fol. 319, 320).
Smith, Samuel	WC2	201	Transported 1680. Servant.
Smith, Sarah	4	11	" 1659.
Smith, Sarah	16	505	" 1671.
Smith, Susan	6	210	" 1663.
Smith, Thomas	ABH	66	" 1633. (1, fol. 38).
Smith, Thomas	6	63	" 1658-63.
Smith, Thomas	4	204	" 1659.
Smith, Thomas	7	498	" 1660.
Smith, Thomas	5	84	" 1661.
Smith, Thomas	5	124	" 1662.
Smith, Thomas	6	347	" 1663.
Smith, Thomas	8	259	" 1665.
Smith, Thomas	17	68	" 1672.
Smith, Thomas	17	451,475	" 1673.
Smith, Thomas	15	359	" 1676.
Smith, Thomas	15	417	Immigrated 1677. Of St. Mary's Co.
Smith, Thomas	WC2	308,309	Transported 1678.
Smith, Thomas	20	184	" from Ireland 1678.
Smith, Thomas	WC2	21-22, 122	" 1679.
Smith, Thomas	WC2	325	Service 1680. Of St. Mary's Co.
Smith, Thomas	WC2	306	Immigrated 1680. Of Talbot Co.
Smith, Thomas Oliver	1	27	Transported 1633-41.
Smith, Thomas Oliver	ABH	61	" 1641.
Smith, Thomas, Jr.	16	38	" 1670.
Smith, Thomas, Sr.	16	38	" 1670.
Smith, Walter	ABH	5	Immigrated 1647.
Smith, Walter	2	284	Rights 1648.
Smith, Mr. William	ABH	6	Immigrated 1633.
Smith, William	ABH	67	" 1633. (1, fol. 17, 41-42; 2, fol. 346).
Smith, William	ABH	85	Transported 1636. Servant. (1, fol. 82).
Smith, William	Q	18,28	Transported 1651.
Smith, William	Q	69	" 1657
Smith, William	4	204,216	" 1659.
Smith, William	5	307	" 1660.
Smith, William	8	39	" 1662.
Smith, William	5	221,235	Immigrated 1662.
Smith, William	6	90	" 1663.
Smith, William	9	36	" 1665.
Smith, William	9	325	Transported 1666. (10, fol. 392).
Smith, William	11	465	Immigrated 1668. Of Calvert Co.
Smith, William	12	514	Transported 1668. Servant.
Smith, William	12	478	" 1670.
Smith, William	17	411,510	" 1673.
Smith, William	15	322	" 1675.

NAME	Liber	Folio	REMARKS
Smith, William	15	376,540	Transported 1676.
Smith, William	WC2	254	" 1680 by Mathew Nicklus.
Smith, William	WC2	320	Transported 1680 by Mathew Scarborough. Servant.
Smith, William	WC2	201	Transported 1680 by Thomas Barker. Servant.
Smith, Lieut. William	17	579	Died prior to 1673, leaving widow, Mary. Her sister Hannah married Vincent Atcheson.
Smith, Mr. Zephaniah	ABH	35	Immigrated 1649.
Smith, Zephaniah	2	575	" 1649 with 5 servants.
Smithe, John	20	185	Transported 1679.
Smithee, George	6	263	" 1662. Service 1671. (16, fol. 315).
Smithlaw, Thomas	15	322	Transported 1674.
Smithson, Alexander	8	501	" 1665.
Smithson, Hannah	17	61	" 1672.
Smithson, John	2	514	Immigrated 1635. Dec'd prior to 1649.
Smithson, John	ABH	24	Immigrated 1635. Widow married Jno. Norman.
Smithson, John	15	394	Immigrated 1677. Of London. Merchant.
Smithson, Mary	4	11	Transported 1659. Servant.
Smithson, William	WC2	5,40, 343	Immigrated 1679. Of Dorchester Co.
Smiton, Mary	9	449	Transported 1666. Daughter of William.
Smiton, Sarah	9	449	Transported 1666. Wife of William.
Smiton, William	9	449	Immigrated 1666. Of Monokin.
Smoote, Ales	ABH	230	Transported 1646. Daughter of William.
Smoote, Alice	7	577	Transported 1665.
Smoote, Ann	ABH	230	" 1646. Daughter of William.
Smoote, Elizabeth	ABH	230	Transported 1646. Daughter of William.
Smoote, Grace	ABH	230	Transported 1646. Wife of William. Was first married to ----- Wood.
Smoote, Grace	7	577	Transported 1665.
Smoote, James	WC2	135	" 1679. Servant.
Smoote, Richard	ABH	230	" 1646. Son of William.
Smoote, Richard	17	517	And Elizabeth, his wife. Service prior to 1673.
Smoote, Thomas	ABH	230	Transported 1646. Son of William.
Smoote, William	ABH	230	Immigrated 1646.
Smoote, William	ABH	1,41	" 1646 with wife and two children. (2, fol. 210).
Smoote, William	2	617	Rights 1646.
Smoote, William	7	577	Immigrated 1665.
Smoote, William	14	352,353	Eldest son and heir of Thomas, 1671.

NAME	Liber	Folio	REMARKS
Smout, James	15		Transported 1675.
Smullan, William	WC2	120	" 1680.
Smyth, James	WC2	129	" 1679.
Snaggs, William	5	532	Service 1660.
Snaggs, William	10	352	Transported 1666.
Snead, Sarah	17	463	" 1673.
Snell, Roger	11	545	" 1661. Service 1668. (5, fol. 56).
Snell, Thomas	15	538	Immigrated 1676.
Snelling, Samuel	8	484	Transported 1665.
Snipe, William	1	171	" about 1637. Servant.
(See Knipe, Snype).	(2, fol. 605; 3, fol. 17).		
Snipe, William	ABH	44,246	Transported 1638. Servant.
Snodell, Henry	12	190	" 1668.
Snole, Elizabeth	10	204	" 1666.
Snook, John	16	507	" 1671.
Snossell, Christopher	7	91	" 1664.
Snoswell, Christopher	18	38	" 1673.
Snow, Abell	ABH	93,94	Of Cresitors Office, Chancery Lane, London. Living 1640.
Snow, Ann	12	550	Transported 1670.
Snow, Valentine	6	95	" 1659.
Snow, William	12	517	" 1670.
Snowden, Isaac	15	442	" 1677.
Snowden, John	18	126	" 1674.
Snowden, Richard	4	68	" 1658.
Snowe, Thomas	5	514	" 1653. Servant.
Snowell, Hannah	16	168	" 1671.
Snowkes, Thomas	4	64	Service 1659.
Snype, William	1	19	Transported 1637. Servant. (See Knipe, Snipe).
Snow, Justinian	1	55-60	Immigrated prior to 1639. Dec'd. brother of Abel Snow.
Snow, Marmaduke	1	19	Immigrated 1638.
Soaker, Thomas	7	507	Transported from Virginia 1664.
Soales, John	7	466	Immigrated 1664.
Sockes, John	9	157	Transported 1665.
Soden, Isaac	15	449	" 1677.
Softly, George	16	411	" 1671.
Solby, George	12	382	Service 1669. Of St. Mary's Co.
Soleawan, Daniel	WC2	184	Transported 1680. Servant.
Solleis, Samuel	12	615	Service 1670.
Solley, Benjamin	16	43	Immigrated 1670. Of Charles Co.
Solley, Edward	16	43	Transported 1670.
Solley, Gilbert	11	582	" 1668.
Solley, Lydia	16	43	" 1670. Wife of Benjamin.
Solman, Stephen	16	43	Transported 1670.
Solman, Thomas	12	611	Immigrated 1670. Of St. Mary's Co.
Solmons, Ralph	5	489	Transported 1655.
Somerfort, Jeremy	6	211	" 1662.

NAME	Liber	Folio	REMARKS
Somers, Benjamin	15	319	And wife. Service 1675.
Somers, Thomas	11	229	Transported 1667.
Somerscales, Jonas	18	291	" 1674.
Somersett, William	11	526	" 1668. Servant.
Somkins, Michael	11	104	" 1667.
Sommers, John	WC2	173-174	Service 1680. Of Calvert Co.
Sommerson, John	9	451	Transported 1666.
Somner, Ralph	5	491	" 1662.
Sonnick, John	9	216	" 1665.
Sopdale, Henry	16	394	" 1671.
Soper, John	15	338	" 1676.
Sorens, William	17	29	" from Virginia 1672.
Sorrell, Ann	5	66	" 1662 by Robt. Somel.
Sorrell, Mary	ABH	23	Servant 1648.
Sorrell, Richard	15	322	Transported 1674.
Sorrell, Thomas	5	267	" 1663.
Sorrell, Thomas	7	553	" 1664.
Sorrell, Thomas	12	205,373	" 1667.
Sorry, Nicholas	4	139	" 1650. Servant.
Sotanstale, Tobias	WC2	23	" 1679. Servant.
Souch, William	17	440	" 1673.
Soulby, Anne	WC2	415	" 1680. Servant.
Sourton, Francis, Gent.	15	337	Immigrated 1675. Of St. Mary's Co.
Sousa, Matthias	1	19,37,38	Transported 1633. A Molato. (See Zause).
South, Abraham	4	565	Transported 1660.
South, Elias	5	319	" 1663.
South, Elizabeth	15	505	" 1678.
South, John	6	48	" 1663.
South, Mr. Thomas	ABH	307	Immigrated 1649.
South, William	12	584	Transported 1670.
Southerd, Thomas	9	386	" 1666.
Southerine, Edward	8	204	Immigrated 1665.
Southerine, Mary	8	204	Transported 1665. Wife of Edward.
Southerly, William	6	211	Immigrated 1663.
Southern, Henry	18	329	Transported 1675.
Southern, Thomas	4	5	" 1659. Servant.
Southern, Valentine	4	5	" 1659. Servant.
Southerne, Anne	15	400,430	" 1677. Wife of Richard.
Southerne, Bridg.	15	540	" 1677.
Southerne, Elizabeth	15	400	" 1677. Daughter of Richard.
Southerne, John	15	400	Transported 1677. Son of Richard.
Southerne, Richard	15	400	Immigrated 1677. Of Calvert Co.
Southerne, Richard	15	533	Transported 1678.
Southersby, Bridgett	15	557	" 1678.
Southersby, William	Q	29	" 1658.
Southin, George	16	170	" 1671.
Southy, John	17	388	Immigrated 1666. Of Dorchester Co.
Sowden, William	15	567	Transported 1678.
Sowder, Mary	15	567	" 1679. (See Louder).

NAME	Liber	Folio	REMARKS
Sowell, Thomas	9	17	Transported 1664.
Sower, John	4	538	" 1659. Servant.
Sowerbutts, Richard	15	598	" 1678-9.
Sowerbutts, Richard	WC2	211	" 1679. Servant.
Spalding, Christian	10	475	" 1667.
Spalding, Katherine	18	101	Service 1674. Wife of Thomas.
Spalding, Thomas	10	500	Service 1667.
Spall, George	6	239	Transported 1663.
Sparke, Mary	12	413	" 1669.
Sparke, Mary	15	380	" 1676.
Sparke, Matt	15	397	" 1676.
Sparke, Walter	6	80	" 1659.
Sparke, William	6	90	" 1662.
Sparkes, Hester	18	106	" 1674.
Sparkes, Mary	11	348	" 1668.
Sparkes, Richard	17	477	Service 1673. Of St. Mary's Co.
Sparkes, Thomas	13	114,122	Transported 1669.
Sparks, William	6	71	" 1663. (18, fol. 6).
Sparman, Francis	15	454	" 1677.
Sparnon, Joseph	12	415	" 1669.
Sparrow, Catherine	6	97	" 1657.
Sparrow, Elizabeth	6	10	" 1663.
Sparrow, Lydia	5	240	" 1662. (6, fol. 215).
Sparrow, Thomas	5	243	" 1662.
Sparrow, William	7	463-464	" 1654.
Sparry, Edward	WC2	395	" 1680. Servant.
Spatt, John	4	616	" 1660. (See Spratt).
Spaulding, Thomas	4	29	" 1657. Servant.
Speak, Mr. Thomas	ABH	237	Immigrated 1639.
Speake, Jane	16	482	Transported 1670-1.
Speake, Thomas	16	281	Service 1670.
Speare, Robert, Jr.	16	100	Transported 1667.
Speare, Robert, Sr.	16	100	" 1667.
Spearman, Hannah	12	498	" 1670.
Spearman, John	16	85	" 1670.
Speed, Alexander	9	399	" 1666.
Speed, Roger	6	89	" 1663.
Speer, John	9	25	" 1665.
Spell, Joseph	9	55	" 1665.
Speltburg, Margaret	18	137	" 1674.
Spence, Ann	11	499	" 1667. Wife of David.
Spence, David	11	499	Immigrated from Virginia 1667. (15, fol. 449).
Spence, David	9	99	Immigrated 1665.
Spence, John	10	407	Service 1666.
Spencer, Ann	16	522	Transported 1672.
Spencer, Dorcas	9	399	" 1666.
Spencer, Francis	7	578	Immigrated 1665.
Spencer, James	WC2	18	Transported 1648.
Spencer, John	5	361	" 1663.
Spencer, John	9	271	" 1665.

NAME	Liber	Folio	REMARKS
Spencer, Mary	6	117	Transported 1663.
Spencer, Mary	9	270	" 1665.
Spencer, Mathew	15	428	" 1677.
Spencer, Robert	15	505	" 1678.
Spencer, Susan	7	578	" 1665. Wife of Francis.
Spencer, Walter	9	24,325	" 1665.
Spencer, William	5	359	" 1663.
Sperforth, John	6	239	" 1663.
Spicer, Alexander	15	527	" 1678.
Spicer, George	15	516	" 1678.
Spicer, Margaret	15	413	Service 1677. Wife of John.
Spicer, Samuel	12	211	Transported 1668.
Spicer, William	12	269	" 1669. Servant.
Spicket, John	16	132	" 1671.
Spike, George	6	137	" 1661.
Spille, Margaretta	20	185	" 1679.
Spillinson, Thomas	6	90	" 1653. (See Skillinson).
Spillman, Francis	18	293	" 1674.
Spinal, Thomas	7	569	" 1663-4.
Spink, Henry	ABH	32	Service 1649.
Spink, Henry	1	130	Transported 1641. Servant.
Spink, Margaret	11	162	" 1667. Wife of Thom.
Spink, Thom	11	162	Immigrated 1667. Of St. Mary's Co. Carpenter.
Spinke, Eleanor	12	550	Service 1670. Wife of Henry.
Spinke, William	16	432	Transported 1671.
Spinloe, Andrew	8	498	" 1665.
Spinner, Richard	4	560	" 1661.
Spira, Ralph	15	560	" 1678.
Spire, Alice	WC2	310	" 1680.
Spite, William	6	93	" 1661.
Spittle, Elizabeth	5	306	" 1663.
Sponner, Ales	2	511	" about 1649.
Spooner, Alice	4	58	" 1659.
Spooner, Charles	12	190	" 1668.
Spooner, William	15	454	" 1677.
Spore, George	17	486	" 1667.
Spottswood, Alexander	ABH	269	" from Virginia 1650, by Gov. Stone.
Spragg, William	15	523	Service 1678. Of St. Mary's Co.
Spragge, Mary	5	181	Transported 1661.
Spratt, George	15	453	" 1675-7.
Spratt, John	4	616	" 1660.
Spratt, Mary	15	357	" 1676.
Sprey, Christopher	17	606	Service 1673. Of St. Mary's Co.
Sprigg, Thomas	5	182	Uncle of Thos. Stone, 1662.
Sprignall, Arthur	8	129	Transported 1664. Servant.
Spring, Margaret	15	394	" 1677.
Spring, Mary	4	56	" 1659. Servant.
Spring, Rose	ABH	269	" 1651. Servant.
Spring, William	WC2	114,115	Immigrated from Virginia 1679.

NAME	Liber	Folio	REMARKS
			Of Kent County.
Springer, Daniel	10	305	Transported 1666. Servant.
Springer, George	WC2	402	" 1680.
Sprint, Mary	10	526	" 1667.
Spruce, George	4	22	" 1659. Servant.
Spruce, John	10	246,247	Immigrated 1662.
Spry, Aba	15	443	Transported 1670.
Spry, Christopher	18	338	Service 1675. Of St. Mary's Co. (12, fol. 473).
Sprye, Oliver	Q	64	Letter referring to his son, Godfred, May 23, 1658.
Spryer, Thomas	WC2	114	Transported 1680. Servant.
Spur, Elizabeth	15	397	" 1676.
Spurdance, John	Q	69	Service 1658.
Spurnegay, Philip	9	262	Transported 1665.
Spurr, Philip	ABH	45,66	" 1636. Servant.
Spurr, Phillip	1	20,25,38	" 1637.
Spurr, Robert	WC2	380	" 1675-80. Servant.
Spurrer, Tripas	15	356	" 1675.
Spurway, William	15	369	" 1676.
Spuzre, Philip	ABH	60	" 1637.
Squiborne, Ab.	15	443	" 1672.
Squier, William	9	55	" 1665.
Squire, Edith	12	194	" 1668. Servant.
Squire, Elizabeth	15	436	" 1677.
Squire, John	4	4	" 1658.
Squire, Jonathan	16	393	" 1671. Nephew and heir of Jno. Morecroft of St. Mary's Co. (15, fol. 1; 19, fol. 409).
Squire, Margaret	6	290	Transported 1663.
Squire, William	Q	441	" 1651.
Squire, William	7	81	" 1654.
Squire, William	3	174	" 1656.
Squire, William	9	354	" 1662.
Squires, Elizabeth	18	82	" 1674. Daughter of John.
Squires, Ethelia	18	82	Transported 1674. Wife of John.
Squires, John	18	82	Immigrated 1674. Of Somerset Co.
Squires, Mary	18	82	Transported 1674. Daughter of John.
Squofield, Robert	17	451	Transported 1673.
Squyre, William	5	319	" 1663.
Stabond, John	15	390	" 1676.
Stacey, Edward	15	539	" 1678.
Stacey, John	12	554	" 1670.
Stacey, Sarah	5	307	" 1661.
Stacey, William	9	3	Immigrated 1665.
Stack, James	WC2	380	Transported 1675-80. Servant.
Stackey, William	15	429	" 1674.
Stacy, Martha	6	622	" 1661.
Stacy, Mary	15	317	" 1674. Wife of Simon.
Stacy, Sarah	9	59	" 1662.

NAME	Liber	Folio	REMARKS
Stacy, Simon	15	317	Immigrated 1674. Of Calvert Co.
Stacy, Richard	4	560	Transported 1661.
Stacy, Richard	15	332	" 1663.
Stacy, William	5	80	" 1661, with wife. (9, fol. 268).
Stafford, John	6	95	Transported 1669.
Stafford, William	17	440	" 1673.
Stafford, William	15	565	" 1679.
Staford, Ann	11	318	" 1668.
Staggrave, Edward	9	325	" 1666.
Stagwell, Edward	12	358	" 1668.
Staines, Joseph	6	80	" 1659.
Stainley, Mary	5	491	" 1658. Wife of William.
Stallins, Richard	Q	70	" 1657.
Stallins, William	15	433	" 1677.
Stamer, Grace	15	558	" 1679.
Stamford, Ann	15	362	" 1676.
Stamford, John	WC2	22,122	" 1679. (See Stanford).
Stamp, Ann	6	294	" 1664.
Stamp, Mary	6	294	" 1664.
Stanbank, Thomas	WC2	406	" 1677.
Stanberry, Daniel	WC2	380	" 1675-80. Servant.
Stanbricks, Thomas	15	300	" 1675.
Stanbridge, Rebecca	6	290	" 1663.
Stanbridge, Thomas	5	85	" 1661. (7, fol. 578).
Stanbriggs, Thomas	18	160	" 1674.
Stanbrook, Mary	12	209,314	" 1669. Servant.
Standell, Elizabeth	18	335	" 1675.
Standforth, Augustine	WC2	77	Service 1679. Of Somerset Co.
Standidge, Prudence	16	86	Transported 1670.
Standell, Elizabeth	18	335	" 1675.
Standish, Alexander	12	594	" 1670.
Standish, John	Q	203	Servant 1658.
Standish, John	6	263	Transported 1661.
Standish, Thomas	Q	453	" 1658.
Standley, Peter	5	63	" 1660.
Standley, Robert	5	80	Immigrated from Virginia 1661, with wife.
Standley, Robert	17	382	Transported from Virginia 1672.
Standsted, Sarah	9	356	" 1666.
Stanesby, William	17	636	Immigrated 1674. Of Calvert Co.
Staney, Ann	17	495	" 1673. Of Somerset Co.
Stanford, ---	6	126	Transported 1660.
Stanford, Augustine	15	318	" 1674.
Stanford, John	15	454,455	" 1678.
Stanford, John	WC2	21-22	" 1679.
Stanford, Richard	2	581	" 1648. Servant.
Stanford, Richard	ABH	36	Servant 1649.
Stanhope, Jasper	6	87	Transported 1661.
Stanley, Adam	Q	30	Immigrated 1658.
Stanley, Frances	15	552	Transported 1679. Wife of James.

NAME	Liber	Folio	REMARKS
Stanley, George	10	598	Immigrated 1667.
Stanley, Hugh, Gent.	5	409	Married Dorothy, widow of Giles
Sadler, prior to 1663. (9, fol. 92).			
Stanley, James	15	552	Of Cecil Co. Immigrated 1679.
Stanley, John	15	343	Service 1666. Of St. Clements Bay.
Stanley, John	10	573	Transported 1667. Son of William.
Stanley, John	15	377	Service 1676. Of St. Mary's Co.
Stanley, John	15	552	Transported 1679. Son of James.
Stanley, John, Gent.	19	294	Commission as Deputy Surveyor of Talbot Co. 1676.
Stanley, Mary	10	573	Transported 1667. Wife of William.
Stanley, Mary	16	79	" 1670.
Stanley, Thomas	6	119	" 1656.
Stanley, Thomas	7	484	" 1664.
Stanley, Thomas	10	573	" 1667. Son of William.
Stanley, Thomas	17	36	" 1672.
Stanley, William	4	531	" 1658.
Stanley, William	4	576	" 1661.
Stanley, William	10	572,573	Immigrated from Virginia 1667.
Of Swan Island, Talbot Co. (15, fol. 389).			
Stanley, William	11	171	Immigrated 1667. Of Calvert Co.
Stanley, William	10	573	Transported 1667. Son of William. (15, fol. 389).
Stanly, George	12	209	Transported 1668.
Stanly, William	Q	70	" 1658.
Stannaway, Joseph	11	171	" 1667.
Stannee, Margaret	12	403	" 1669.
Stansbey, John	Q	443	" 1658.
Stansby, Joanna	18	84	" 1674.
Stanton, Gillion	15	397	" 1677.
Stanton, William	16	510	" 1672.
Stanward, Nicholas	15	559	" 1679.
Stany, Richard	7	86	" 1659.
Staple, Isaac	15	443	" 1670.
Staple, Joane	6	120	" 1655.
Staple, John	16	508	" 1670.
Staple, Sarah	5	467	" 1659.
Stapledonn, John	WC2	380	" 1675-80. Servant.
Stapleford, Robert	6	90	" 1661.
Staplefort, Raymond	6	22	Immigrated 1660-3. Married
widow of Thos. May, prior to 1666. (9, fol. 355).			
Staples, Henry	WC2	173-174	Immigrated 1680. Of Kent Co. Chyrurgion.
Staples, John	WC2	112	Transported 1679.
Stapleton, Ann	18	160	" 1674.
Stapleton, Bryant	7	464	" 1659.
Stapley, John	15	504	" 1678.
Stardy, William	15	359	" 1676.
Stares, Edward	15	551	" 1679.
Starkes, William	12	333	" 1668.
Starkley, Alice	7	85	" 1661.

NAME	Liber	Folio	REMARKS
Starlin, Alice	16	537	Transported 1671. Wife of John.
Starlin, John	16	537	Immigrated 1671.
Starrs, Bennett	7	63	Transported 1659.
Start, James	9	323	" 1666.
Start, Philadelphia	5	410	" 1663.
Start, William	15	386	" 1676.
Startop, Stephen	5	488	" 1651-62.
State, Edward	15	418	" 1677.
State, John	6	210	" 1663.
Statham, Thomas	1	19,37,166	" 1633.
Stathen, Hugh	16	41	" 1670.
Stavely, John	16	432	" 1671.
Stavely, Nicholas	16	432	" 1671.
Stavis, John	WC2	106	" 1679.
Staynes, John	15	598	Immigrated 1668. Of Calvert Co.
Staynestreet, Thomas	5	307	Transported 1663.
Stead, Ann	9	262	" 1665.
Steade, John	WC2	165	" 1680.
Steakely, John	7	463	" 1657.
Steale, John	WC2	217	" 1680.
Stebens, Grace	11	344	" 1668.
Stedams, Amey	10	600	Immigrated 1667.
Steed, Elizabeth	17	440	Transported 1673.
Steed, John	9	271	Immigrated 1665.
Steed, John	WC2	113	Transported 1680.
Steed, John	17	440	" 1673.
Steed, John, Jr.	17	440	" 1673.
Steed, Robert	17	416	" 1673.
Steed, Thomas	5	201	Immigrated 1661.
Steede, Ann	5	393	Transported 1663.
Steel, Matthew	15	313	" 1675.
Steele, Alice	WC2	399	" 1677.
Steele, John	12	205	" 1667.
Steele, William	WC2	38	" 1679.
Steevens, Christopher	4	11	" 1659. Servant.
Steevens, David	4	140	" 1651. Servant.
Steevens, Edward	WC2	110	" 1676. Servant.
Steevens, John	4	565	" 1661.
Steevens, Katherine	4	576	" 1661.
Steevens, Lawrence	Q	69	" 1656.
Stelarbe, Thomas	7	569	" 1633-4.
Stell, Alice	15	500	" 1676-7.
Stell, Richard	12	459	" 1669.
Stelle, James	WC2	24,106	" 1678.
Stennett, William	4	590	" 1661.
Stent, Thomas	1	98	Immigrated 1636.
Stente, Thomas	ABH	90	" 1636.
Stephand, John	ABH	63	Transported 1638. Servant.
Stephen, John	2	604	" about 1638. Servant.
Stephen, John	ABH	50	" 1648. Servant.
Stephens, Charles	5	359	" 1663.

NAME	Liber	Folio	REMARKS
Stephens, Charles	15	600	Transported 1678.
Stephens, David	ABH	313	" 1652. Servant.
Stephens, Edmond	WC2	406	" 1676.
Stephens, Joane	5	228	" 1662.
Stephens (Stephans), John	1	25,31	" 1638. Servant.
Stephens, John	ABH	60	" 1641.
Stephens, John	ABH	141	" 1651. Son of William.
Stephens, John	ABH	201	" 1650.
Stephens, John	4	538	" 1659. Servant.
Stephens, Lewis	7	492	" 1664.
Stephens, Magdalen	ABH	141	" 1651. Wife of William.
Stephens, Richard	4	53	" 1659.
Stephens, Richard	10	213	" 1665.
Stephens, Sibill	12	333	" 1668.
Stephens, Simon	4	57,58	" 1659.
Stephens, Simon	WC2	395	" 1680. Servant.
Stephens, Thomas	WC2	23	" 1679. Servant.
Stephens, William	ABH	141	Immigrated 1651. Of Patuxent River.
Stephens, William, Jr.	ABH	141	Transported 1651. Son of William.
Stephenson, Christopher	ABH	396	" 1654. Son of William.
Stephenson, Connaul	5	245	" 1662.
Stephenson, Elizabeth	16	45	" 1668.
Stephenson, Frances	ABH	396	" 1654. Daughter of William.
Stephenson, George	18	331	Transported 1674.
Stephenson, James	5	607	" 1658-63.
Stephenson, John	5	607	" 1658-63.
Stephenson, Mary	ABH	396	" 1654. Daughter of William.
Stephenson, Nicholas	8	498	Transported 1665.
Stephenson, Stephen	9	105	" 1665.
Stephenson, William	ABH	396	Immigrated "from the Tertudos" 1654, with wife.
Stepley, Daniel	5	489	Transported 1661.
Stepps, Ann	18	83	Service 1674. Of Calvert Co.
Steptoe, Kingsmale	15	548,597	Immigrated 1679. Of St. Mary's Co.
Steptoe, Penelope	15	597	Service 1679. Wife of Kingsmale of St. Mary's Co.
Sterlin, James	15	501	Transported 1678.
Sterling, Ann	9	333	" 1666.
Sterling, Thomas	6	63	" 1663.
Sterlings, George	15	540	" 1676.
Sterman, John	12	194	" 1668. Servant.
Sternber, Tobias	6	82,84	" 1658.
Sternbergse, Detmorus	6	82,84	" 1658.
Sternbergse, Renscoe	6	82,84	" 1658. Wife of Detmorus.
Sterne, Thomas	7	84	Transported 1663. Servant.
Sterton, George	9	329	" 1665.

NAME	Liber	Folio	REMARKS
Steven, John	3	63	Transported prior to 1648. Servant.
Stevens, Ann	ABH	49	" by Rev. Wm. Wilkinson, 1650. Servant.
Stevens, Anne	3	62	Transported 1650. Servant.
Stevens, Barnaby	8	88	" 1665.
Stevens, Charles	5	485	Living 1662. Son of Chas., who died 1658.
Stevens, Charles	9	448	Immigrated prior to 1666. Of Anne Arundel Co. Widow married Jno. Havard. (10, fol. 499).
Stevens, Charles, Jr.	9	448	Transported 1666. Son of Charles.
Stevens, Edward	11	5	" 1667. Son of William.
Stevens, Edward	15	370	" 1676.
Stevens, Eliza.	12	484	" 1670. Daughter of John.
Stevens, Elizabeth	9	217	Transported 1665. Wife of William. (11, fol. 5).
Stevens, Elizabeth	9	448	Transported 1666. Daughter of Charles.
Stevens, Elizabeth	16	297	Transported 1671.
Stevens, Frances	11	499	" 1667. Wife of Richard.
Stevens, Francis	10	117	" 1666.
Stevens, Giles	16	508	Immigrated 1670.
Stevens, Griffith	11	552	Transported 1668. (15, fol. 600).
Stevens, Jane	15	167	" 1673.
Stevens, John	10	117	" 1666.
Stevens, John	12	190	" 1668. Servant.
Stevens, John	12	484	Immigrated 1670.
Stevens, Joshua	6	120	Transported 1651.
Stevens, Jude	12	484	" 1670. Daughter of John.
Stevens, Lettis	16	394	Transported 1671.
Stevens, Lewis	17	421	Service 1672.
Stevens, Mary	7	576	Transported 1665.
Stevens, Mary	12	584	" 1670.
Stevens, Mary	17	608	" 1673.
Stevens, Matt.	15	443	" 1677.
Stevens, Michall (?)	16	466	" Jan. 1669. Daughter of Richard, of Talbot County.
Stevens, Patrick	9	157	Transported 1665.
Stevens, Rebecca	Q	197	" 1658.
Stevens, Rebecca	15	167	" 1673.
Stevens, Richard	16	466	Immigrated 1660. Of Talbot Co.
Stevens, Richard	9	54,222	Transported 1665.
Stevens, Richard	11	499	Immigrated from Virginia 1667.
Stevens, Richard	15	390	Transported 1676.
Stevens, Richard	15	433	" 1677.
Stevens, Richard	15	567	" 1678.
Stevens, Robert, Jr.	9	326	" 1665.
Stevens, Sarah	9	448	" 1666. Daughter of Charles.
Stevens, Seaboarne	11	5	Transported 1667. Son of William.

NAME	Liber	Folio	REMARKS
Stevens, Simon	10	391	Service 1666.
Stevens, Simon	WC2	288	Transported 1680.
Stevens, Susan	9	448	" 1666. Wife of Charles. Married Jno. Howard.
Stevens, Susan	9	448	Transported 1666. Daughter of Charles.
Stevens, Thomas	7	85	Immigrated 1662.
Stevens, Thomas	12	351	Transported 1669.
Stevens, Thomas	15	338	" 1676.
Stevens, William	ABH	336	" his kinswoman, Cath. Ware, 1652.
Stevens, William	6	22	Transported 1663.
Stevens, William	8	88	Immigrated 1665. (9, fol. 217).
Stevens, William	11	5	" 1667. Of Talbot Co.
Stevens, William	16	78	Transported 1670.
Stevens, William	15	430	" 1677.
Stevens, William	15	505	" 1678.
Stevens, Col. William	WC2	399	Special Warrant for 10,000 acres.
Stevenson, Danning	15	317	Transported 1674.
Stevenson, Edward	16	394	" 1671.
Stevenson, Edward	15	563	Immigrated 1678.
Stevenson, Elizabeth	8	483	Transported from Virginia 1665.
Stevenson, Henry	WC2	13-14	Son-in-law Thos. Phillips, 1679.
Stevenson, Katherine	8	483	Transported from Virginia 1665.
Stevenson, Martha	10	568	" 1667. Servant.
Stevenson, Mary	8	498	" 1665.
Stevenson, Mary	15	569	" 1678.
Stevenson, Mathias	12	217	" 1669. Service 1673. (17, fol. 513).
Stevenson, Oliver	11	581	Transported 1668.
Stevenson, Percy	15	412	" 1677.
Stevenson, Philip	8	483	" from Virginia 1665.
Stevenson, Sarah	8	483	" from Virginia 1665.
Stevenson, Thomas	8	483	" from Virginia 1665.
Stevenson, Thomas	WC2	13	Son-in-law Thos. Phillips 1679.
Steward, Charles	1	87	Transported 1640.
Steward, Charles	ABH	86	" 1640. Servant.
Steward, Charles	ABH	376	Immigrated prior to 1651.
Steward, David	7	135	Transported 1664.
Steward, David	11	526	" 1668.
Steward, Elizabeth	15	454	" 1677.
Steward, Elizabeth	WC2	16	" 1679. Wife of William.
Steward, Francis	12	516	" 1669.
Steward, George	16	411	" 1671.
Steward, Henry	17	475	" 1673.
Steward, John	ABH	140	" 1651.
Steward, John	6	83	" 1653.
Steward, John	8	44	" 1665.
Steward, John	12	345,382	Immigrated 1669. Of St. Mary's Co.
Steward, John	16	88	Transported 1670.
Steward, John	17	571	" 1673. (16, fol. 174).

NAME	Liber	Folio	REMARKS
Steward, John	18	15	Transported 1673.
Steward, John	20	185	" 1679.
Steward, Margaret	ABH	335,352	" 1653. Wife of Charles.
Steward, Margaret	15	397	" 1676.
Steward, Margaret, Jr.	11	581	" 1668.
Steward, Margaret, Sr.	11	581	" 1668.
Steward, Mary	4	190	" 1659.
Steward, William	WC2	16	Immigrated 1679.
Stewart, Charles	Q	68	" 1658.
Stewart, David	5	87	Transported 1649.
Stibbs, William	5	414	Service 1663.
Stickle, George	6	126	Transported 1657.
Stiffe, Richard	15	530	" 1678.
Stiffe, Richard	WC2	402	" 1680.
Stiler, Robert	6	266	" 1661.
Stiles, Elizabeth	Q	30	" 1658.
Stiles, Henry	15	551	" 1679.
Stiles, Mary	ABH	198	" 1647. Wife of William.
Stiles, Mary	12	459	" 1669.
Stiles, Mary	15	398	" 1676.
Stiles, Nathaniel	ABH	140	Immigrated 1651. Of Patuxent River.
Stiles, Robert	Q	239	Transported 1651.
Stiles, Robert	ABH	140	" 1651.
Stiles, William	1	19	" 1637.
Stiles, William	ABH	150	" 1639.
Stiles, William	ABH	4,100	" 1641. Servant. (1, fol. 125).
Stiles, William	2	249	Service 1646.
Stiles, William	15	455	Transported 1678.
Still, Thomas	15	340	Freedom 1668. Of Cecil Co.
Still, William	16	635	Immigrated with Ann, his wife, 1667. Of Talbot Co.
Stille, Axell	Q	63	Immigrated 1650.
Stille, Oxell	5	341	Living 1662.
Stills, Robert	7	505	Transported 1664.
Stilos, Mary	15	453	" 1676.
Stilton, Chr.	15	416	" 1677.
Stinchcomb, Nathaniel	5	607	Immigrated 1663.
Stinson, John	5	487	Transported 1659.
Stinson, John	18	152	" 1674. (15, fol. 431).
Stinson, William	11	168	" 1667.
Stinton, George	15	413	" 1677.
Stinton, Richard	7	560	" 1665.
Stoakes, Amy	12	378,584	" 1669.
Stoakes, Elizabeth	7	154	" 1660. Wife of William.
Stoakes, Elizabeth	7	154	" 1660. Daughter of William.
Stoakes, John	7	154	Transported 1660. Son of William.
Stoakes, Margaret	12	391	" 1669.
Stoakes, William	7	154	Immigrated 1660.
Stoakes, William	7	154	Transported 1660. Son of William.

NAME	Liber	Folio	REMARKS
Stoakley, John	15	358	Transported 1675.
Stock, Garrett	18	27	Immigrated 1674.
Stock, John	15	362	" 1676. Of Talbot Co.
Stockbridge, James	18	331	Transported 1674.
Stockdale, Francis	4	11	" 1659. Servant.
Stockden, William	ABH	141	Immigrated 1651.
Stockely, William	ABH	246	Transported years before 1652.
Stocker, Alice	WC2	381	" 1675-80. Servant.
Stocker, Andrew	10	434	" 1667.
Stocker, Edward	6	133	" 1654.
Stocker, Robert	6	62	" 1663.
Stockett, Francis	Q	62	Immigrated 1658.
Stockett, Henry	Q	62	Transported 1658. Brother to Francis.
Stockett, Col. Lewis	10	264	Demands land in 1666 for transporting himself.
Stockett, Thomas	Q	62	Transported 1658. Brother to Francis.
Stockhouse, Hannah	12	604	Transported 1670.
Stockin, Eleanor	15	564	" 1679.
Stockley, Ann	Q	219	" 1653.
Stockley, Anthony	5	411	" 1663.
Stockley, Elizabeth	7	530	Immigrated 1664.
Stockley, Michael, Gent.	16	431	" Dec. 1671. Of Kent Co
Stockwell, John	5	466	Transported 1662. (6, fol. 7).
Stofield, James	12	194	" 1668.
Stogden, Robert	18	291	" 1674.
Stoght, Roger	11	441	" 1668.
Stoke, John	9	48	" 1665. Service 1668. (11, fol. 530).
Stoke, John	12	403	Transported 1669.
Stokefield, John	WC2	2	" 1679.
Stokeley, Woodman	3	170	Rights 1655.
Stokes, Anne	WC2	206	Service 1680. Wife of Peter.
Stokes, Francis	15	454	Transported 1677.
Stokes, John	17	332	" 1666.
Stokes, Peter	15	450	Service 1677. Of Dorchester Co.
Stokes, Peter	WC2	206-207	Rights for wife's service, 1680.
Of Dorchester Co.	(WC2, fol. 313, 355, 376).		
Stokey, Elizabeth	WC2	65	Transported 1679. Servant.
Stokeley, America	Q	219	Immigrated 1652. Wife of Woodman.
Stokley, James	Q	219	Immigrated 1652. Son of Woodman.
Stokley, Woodman	Q	219	" 1652. (See abstracts of Test. Proc. for Will).
Stone, Ann	17	547	Transported 1673.
Stone, Daniel	WC2	101	" 1679.
Stone, Elizabeth	ABH	150	" 1649-50. Daughter of William.
Stone, Elizabeth	7	372,469	Transported 1664.
Stone, Francis	6	85	" 1654.

NAME	Liber	Folio	REMARKS
Stone, Francis	1	150	License to marry Deborah Paulus, June 28, 1642.
Stone, Hugh	9	250	Transported 1665. Son of Katherine.
Stone, Hugh	WC2	19	Service 1679. Of Calvert Co.
Stone, Isaac	15	563	Service 1677.
Stone, John	ABH	150	Transported 1649-50. Son of William.
Stone, John	8	502	" 1665.
Stone, Jane	15	397	" 1676.
Stone, John	WC2	415	" 1666-80. Servant.
Stone, John	15	455	" 1678.
Stone, John	WC2	7, 8	Service 1679. Of Calvert Co.
Stone, Katherine, Jr.	9	250	Transported 1665. Daughter of Katherine.
Stone, Katherine, Sr.	9	250	Transported 1665.
Stone, Margaret	5	243	" 1662.
Stone, Mary	8	30	" 1665.
Stone, Mathusalem	17	608	" 1673.
Stone, Mrs.	ABH	150	" 1649-50. Wife of William. Servant.
Stone, Philip	16	39	Transported 1670.
Stone, Richard	ABH	150	" 1649-50. Son of William.
Stone, Richard	5	71	" 1661.
Stone, Richard	15	438	" 1677.
Stone, Robert	15	428	" 1677.
Stone, Sarah	WC2	71, 242	" 1677.
Stone, Thomas	ABH	150	" 1649-50. Son of William.
Stone, Thomas	5	182	Nephew of Thos. Sprigg, 1662.
Stone, Thomas	18	128	Transported 1674.
Stone, Thomas	15	369	" 1676.
Stone, William, Esq.	ABH	150	Immigrated 1648.
Stone, William	15	356	Transported 1676.
Stone, William	15	446	" 1677.
Stoneman, Elizabeth	WC2	170	" 1679. Servant.
Stoner, Robert	4	63	" 1658.
Stonestreet, Thomas	5	221	" 1662. Servant. Service, with Eliz., his wife, 1668. (11, fol. 544).
Stonge, Margaret	10	259	Transported 1666.
Stooke, John	11	246	Service 1667. Of St. Mary's Co.
Stoole, Edward	6	127	Transported 1663.
Stooper, Henry	ABH	241	" 1649. Servant. Gift from Lord. B. (Q, fol. 370).
Stopherd, William	17	635	Transported 1674.
Stopper, Christopher	Q	69	" 1655.
Storey, John	12	209	" 1668.
Storey, Jonas	6	293	" 1664.
Storey, Robert	18	331	" 1674.
Storry, John	15	530	" 1678.
Story, Elizabeth	7	527	" 1664.
Story, Francis	16	480	" Jan. 1671.
Story, John	15	544	" 1674.

NAME	Liber	Folio	REMARKS
Story, John	WC2	402	Transported 1680.
Story, Joseph	18	160	" 1674.
Story, Robert	18	306	" 1675.
Story, Thomas	13	1	" 1669. Servant.
Stout, Mary	15	429	" 1677.
Stout, Roger	11	337	" 1668.
Stout, Stephen	17	51	" 1672.
Stoward, John	15	454	" 1677.
Stowe, James	5	182	" 1662.
Stower, Francis	1	25,31	" 1638. Servant.
Stower, Francis	ABH	60	" 1641.
Stower, Robert	Q	67	Servant 1658.
Strabett, Servia	8	89	Transported 1665.
Strach, William	15	369	" 1676.
Stradling, Margaret	7	567	" 1665.
Straham, James	5	411	" 1663.
Strand, Abraham	10	598	" 1667.
Strand, Joane	17	443	Immigrated from Virginia 1669,
and married Thos. King of Balto. Co., prior to 1673.			
Strand, William	20	185	Transported 1679.
Strange, Ellenor	12	472	" 1670.
Strange, Richard	15	530	" 1678.
Stratford, Joseph	7	80	" 1664. (15, fol. 441).
Stratford, Richard	ABH	101	" 1637-40. Servant.
Stratford, William	12	271	" 1668. Servant.
Stratham, Thomas	ABH	65	" 1633.
Straton, Thomas	15	449	" 1677.
Stratton, John	16	521	Immigrated 1672. Of Dorset Co.
Strawhan, Adam	17	474	Transported 1672.
Strawhan, Mary	17	474	" 1672.
Strawhen, David	WC2	321	Immigrated 1680 with wife.
Strawhen, Elizabeth	WC2	321	Transported 1680. Wife of David.
Street, Edward	12	216	" 1668.
Street, Francis	9	488	" 1664. (7, fol. 530).
Street, Francis	17	422	" 1672.
Street, John	17	567	" from Virginia 1673.
Street, John	18	173,291	" 1674.
Street, John	15	433	" 1677.
Street, Thomas	17	463	" 1673.
Street, Thomas	15	552	" 1679.
Street, William	11	344	" 1668. (17, fol. 376).
Streete, Ann	15	449	" 1677.
Strem, Jane	WC2	415	" 1666-80. Servant.
Strength, Mary	10	558	" 1665. (9, fol. 343).
Strickland, Mathew	WC2	170	" 1680. Servant.
Strickley, William	16	411	" 1671.
Striford, William	15	443	" 1674.
Stringe, Katherine	9	476	" 1666.
Stringer, John	9	437	" 1664.
Stringer, John	17	635	" 1674.
Stringley, Mary	16	630	" 1670.

NAME	Liber	Folio	REMARKS
Strong, Elizabeth	14	40	Immigrated 1651, and married Chas. James prior to 1670. Daughter and heiress of Leonard Strong.
Strong, George	Q	74	Transported 1650.
Strong, George	6	87	" 1653. (16, fol. 293).
Strong, Hannah	6	87	" 1656.
Strong, Capt. James	WC2	415-416	Rights 1666-80. Commander of ship "Assistance".
Strong, John	17	417	Transported 1673.
Strong, Michael	15	451	" 1678.
Strong, Richard	7	469	" from Virginia 1664.
Strong, Robert	6	94	" 1661.
Strong, Thomas	15	313	" 1675.
Stronge, John	13	1	" 1669. Servant.
Strood, George	15	318	" 1674.
Strother, Isabella	WC2	412	" 1681.
Stroud, James	6	219	Immigrated 1663.
Stroud, Mary	6	219	Transported 1663. Daughter of James.
Stroud, Rebecca	6	219	Transported 1663. Wife of James.
Stroud, Samuel	12	472	" 1670.
Stroy, Dorothy	7	567	" 1657. Servant.
Stroy, Leonard	15	300	" 1675.
Strutty, Thomas	15	397	" 1676.
Stuard, Jane	18	306	" 1675.
Stuart, Jen.	4	139	" 1650. Servant.
Stubbs, Henry	5	413	" 1660.
Stubbs, Joseph	WC2	198,200	Service 1680.
Stubeard, John	15	430	Transported 1677.
Stuberfield, Ann	20	185	" 1679.
Stuble, Hendrick	6	128	" 1653.
Stuckett, Elizabeth	8	130	" 1665. Servant.
Studd, Thomas	9	308	Immigrated 1666.
Studham, Ann	18	177	Transported 1674.
Studham, Anne	WC2	308	" 1678.
Stukeley, Francis	6	134	" 1657.
Sturd, John	15	443	" 1667.
Sturdham, Michael	18	306	" 1675.
Sturdivant, William	16	470	Immigrated June 16, 1669.
Sturdivant, Richard	17	76	Transported 1671.
Sturdy, George	18	306	" 1675.
Sturges, Abraham	17	469	" 1673.
Sturges, George	15	526	Immigrated 1678.
Sturges, Jane	17	469	Transported 1673.
Sturkey, John	15	443	" 1670.
Sturkey, Richard	15	443	" 1670.
Sturley, Edward	12	601	" 1669.
Sturly, Mary	15	567	" 1679.
Sturman, Ann	ABH	50	" 1640. Daughter of Thomas.
Sturman, Anne	3	63	Transported about 1640. Daughter of Thomas.

NAME	Liber	Folio	REMARKS
Sturman, Elizabeth	ABH	50	Transported 1640. Daughter of Thomas.
Sturman, Elizabeth	3	63	Transported about 1640. Daughter of Thomas.
Sturman, John	3	63	Transported about 1640. Son of Thomas.
Sturman, John	ABH	50	Transported 1640. Son of Thomas.
Sturman, Mrs. John	3	63	" 1648. Daughter-in-law of Thomas Sturman.
Sturman, Thomas	3	63	Immigrated about 1640 with wife, 3 children and 2 servants.
Sturman, Thomas	ABH	50	Immigrated 1640 with wife.
Sturmy, George	17	76	Transported 1671.
Stwett, William	7	526	" 1664.
Styles, Ann	17	487	Service 1673. Wife of Samuel.
Styles, Samuel	17	487	Transported 1663.
Stylman, Elias	4	216	" 1659.
Suasdell, Christopher	16	437	" 1671.
Subberwater, George	13	122	" 1668.
Succer, John	4	533	" 1659.
Suce, Robert	15	442	" 1677.
Sucker, John	ABH	230	Immigrated 1651.
Sucksmith, James	18	137	Transported 1674.
Sudberry, Henry	5	257	" 1663. Son of Peter.
Sudberry, James	5	257	" 1663. Son of Peter.
Sudberry, John	5	257	" 1663. Son of Peter.
Sudberry, Margaret	5	257	" 1663. Wife of Peter.
Sudberry, Peter	5	257	Immigrated prior to 1663.
Sudberry, Peter	5	257	Transported 1663. Son of Peter.
Sudberry, Richard	5	257	" 1663. Son of Peter.
Sudberry, William	5	257	" 1663. Son of Peter.
Sudbery, George	11	348	" 1668.
Sudden, Elizabeth	16	537	" from Virginia 1671.
Sudman, Ann	6	347	" 1663.
Sudman, Edward	6	347	" 1663.
Suds, Robert	8	478	" 1665.
Sudsdell, Christopher	16	625	" 1663.
Sudward, Elizabeth	Q	73	Immigrated 1658. Daughter of James.
Sudward, James	Q	73	Immigrated 1658.
Sudward, Mary	Q	73	Transported 1658. Wife of James.
Suell, Margaret	18	77	" 1674.
Suellock, William	12	465	" from Virginia 1669. Servant.
Sueton, John	16	437	Transported 1671. (14, fol. 443).
Sugar, Jane	5	404	" 1660. Servant.
Suitt, John	15	540	" 1676.
Sulevant, Ann	WC2	14	Service 1679. Wife of Dennis.
Sulevant, Dennis	WC2	14	Service 1667. Of St. Mary's Co.
Sulivan, Margaret	15	553	" 1678.
Sulivan, Mary	15	553	" 1678.

NAME	Liber	Folio	REMARKS
Sulivant, Ann	15	563	Service 1679. Wife of Dennis.
Sullen, Herman	5	513	Transported 1656.
Sullevan, Darby	WC2	128	" 1679.
Sullevan, Gilliam	9	48	" 1665.
Sullevan, Patrick	16	21	Service 1667.
Sulliman, Robert	4	556	Transported 1661.
Sulling, Richard	9	25	" 1665.
Sullivan, Jeremy	16	11	Immigrated 1670. Of Anne Arundel County.
Sullivant, James	WC2	339,340, 341	Service 1680. Of Dorchester Co.
Sumerfield, Jiles	15	416	Transported 1677.
Sumerfoott, Alce	7	471	" 1664.
Sumerfoott, Jeffry	7	471	" 1664. (12, fol. 360).
Sumers, Thomas	WC2	73	" 1678.
Summer, John	16	394	" 1671.
Summer, Robert	9	304	" 1665.
Summer, Robert	WC2	16	" 1677.
Summer, Robert	15	574	" 1678.
Summers, Ann	18	24	" 1674.
Summers, John	18	287	Service 1674. Of Kent Co.
Summers, Mary	15	422	Transported 1669.
Summers, Oliver	18	280	" 1675.
Summers, Roger	8	478	" 1665. (9, fol. 304).
Summers, Thomas	15	340	And Eleanor, his wife. Service 1676.
Sumner, Benjamin	4	580	Transported 1661.
Sumner, David	15	527	" 1678.
Sumner, John	5	417	" 1663.
Sumner, Thomas	WC2	53	" 1677. (15, fol. 445).
Sumons, Thomas	15	544	" 1676.
Sunderland, John	17	396	" 1669.
Sunderson, William	13	122	" 1669.
Sundes, John	18	166	" 1674.
Sundley, Henry	12	415	" 1669.
Suptoe, Kingsmale	15	548	Immigrated 1679. Of St. Mary's Co. (See Steptoe).
Surd, Richard	17	330	Transported 1672.
Surfect, William	4	14	" 1649. Servant.
Surrey, Thomas	16	411	" 1671.
Suton, William	11	441	" 1668.
Sutte, Edward	Q	18	" 1657.
Sutten, William	7	87	" 1658.
Sutton, Francis	ABH	78,101	" 1640. (1, fol. 63, 128).
Sutton, George	18	80	" 1674.
Sutton, John	Q	239	" 1652-3.
Sutton, John	Q	62	" 1654-7.
Sutton, John	16	170	" 1671. (17, fol. 456).
Sutton, John	15	376	" 1676.
Sutton, Philip	17	74,607	" 1671.
Sutton, Robert	15	509	" 1674.
Sutton, Jeremiah	6	81	" 1651.

NAME	Liber	Folio	REMARKS
Sutton, William	6	134	Transported 1663.
Sutton, William	11	337	" 1668. (12,fol.379,415).
Swaine, Ann	12	590	" 1670.
Swaine (Swayne), Elizabeth	WC2	58	Service 1677. Wife of John.
Swaine, James	6	85	Transported 1657.
Swaine, John	9	54	" 1665.
Swaine (Swayne), John	WC2	58	Husband of Elizabeth 1677. Of Talbot Co. (WC2, fol. 180,182,203,208,320).
Swaine, John	WC2	320	Transported 1680. Servant.
Swaine, Mary	WC2	320	" 1680. Servant.
Swallow, John	15	397	" 1676.
Swallow, John	WC2	130	" 1679. Servant. 18 years old.
Swallwell, John	12	415	Transported 1669.
Swan, Edward	7	489	Immigrated 1662.
Swan, Henry	12	372,416	Transported 1669.
Swan, John	15	445	" 1677. (WC2,fol.53).
Swan, Loar	10	259	" 1660. Wife of Mark. Servant.
Swan, Mark	10	259	Transported 1660. Servant. (5,fol. 489).
Swan, Violetta	6	106	Transported 1657. (7,fol.561).
Swane, George	15	353	" 1675.
Swane, John	15	430	" 1677.
Swann, Anthony	18	167	" 1674.
Swann, Margaret	18	167	" 1674.
Swann, Michael	18	166	" 1674.
Swann, Samuel	16	411	" 1671.
Swanson, Dr. James	8	204	Immigrated 1665.
Swanson, John	18	137	Transported 1674.
Swanson, John	15	530	" 1678.
Swanston, Edward	18	29	Service 1674.
Swanston, Francis	12	591	Of Calvert Co. Chirurgeon. (See Swinstone).
Swanston, Isabella	17	39	Immigrated 1672. Wife of Francis of Calvert Co.
Swarbrooke, Dorothy	5	93	Transported 1661.
Swayne, John	17	605	Immigrated 1668.
Swayne, William	5	416	Transported prior to 1663.
Sweatman, Jefery	15	537	" 1678.
Sweatnam, Edward	WC2	133	Rights 1680. Of Kent Co.
Sweatnam, John	15	413	Transported 1677.
Sweatnam (Sweatman), John	15	425	" 1677. Son of Richard.
Sweatnam (Sweatman), Mary	15	425	" 1677. Wife of Richard.
Sweatnam (Sweatman), Richard	15	425	Immigrated 1677. Of St. Mary's Co.
Sweatnum, William	15	330	Service 1675.
Sweeny, Girlugh	15	599	Transported 1678.

NAME	Liber	Folio	REMARKS
Sweetman, William	11	338	Transported 1668.
Sweeton, Ann	13	65	" 1670. Servant.
Swenroy, Darby	15	527	" 1678.
Swethall, Dorothy	5	241	" 1662.
Swetnam, Edward	16	112	" 1671.
Swetnam, Edward	17	611	Of Baltimore Co. Service 1673.
Swickin, Samson	16	432	Transported 1671.
Swift, Ralph	12	413	" 1669.
Swinbarne, Jane	18	15	" 1673.
Swinbarne, Margaret	11	581	" 1668.
Swindon, Edward	6	78	" 1662. Servant.
Swindon, Joseph	7	463	" 1660.
Swine, Sarah	WC2	106	" 1679.
Swiney, Briant	WC2	187	" 1678.
Swiney, Mary	WC2	187	" 1678.
Swinfar, John	15	535	" 1678.
Swinfield, John	9	400	" 1666.
Swinfield, Mary	18	84	" 1674.
Swinfield, Phebe	15	322	" 1675.
Swiniord, John	6	121	" 1663.
Swinston, Emanuel	15	397	" 1676.
Swinstone, Francis	12	591	Of Calvert Co. Chirurgeon. Married widow of Giles Sadler prior to 1670. (See Swanston).
Swish, John	13	122	Transported 1668.
Swithingham, Thomas	15	436	" 1677.
Sworton, John	12	190	" 1668.
Swotnam, William	18	336	Service 1675. Of St. Mary's Co.
Swyny, Edmond	WC2	10,17	Transported 1679.
Sykes, John	17	608	" 1673.
Sylvester, John	Q	359	" 1651-8.
Sylvester, John	12	584	" 1670.
Symes, Ann	8	130	" 1664. Daughter of Mr. Symes.
Symmons, John	18	295	Transported 1669. Of Talbot Co.
Symonds, Andrew	WC2	56	" 1678.
Symonds, Elizabeth	5	466	" 1662. (6, fol. 7).
Symonds, Lawrence	6	218	Immigrated 1663, with his son-in-law, Anthony Alexander.
Symonds, Mary	5	367	Transported 1649.
Symonds, Robert	16	396	" 1671.
Symonds, Thomas	Q	443	" 1658.
Symons, George	3	24	" 1650. Servant.
Symons, Joane	4	137	" 1659. Servant.
Symons, Katherine	15	503	" 1678.
Symons, Saunder	5	530	" 1661.
Symons, Thomas	ABH	151	" 1640. Servant.
Symons, Thomas	12	285	" 1667.
Symot, Dorothy	15	553	" 1678.
Sympson, Elizabeth	5	70	" 1662. Wife of Thomas.
Synes, John	5	248	" 1663.
Synnet, Mary	18	137	" 1674.

NAME	Liber	Folio	REMARKS
Synnot, Dorothy	WC2	56	Transported 1679.
Syse, Edmond	17	332	" 1666.
Syse, Edmond	16	119	Immigrated 1671. Of St. Mary's County.
Tabett, William	20	185	Transported 1679.
Tabley, Winifrett	10	558	" 1667. Servant.
Tabor, James	17	469	" 1673.
Tacker, Seaborne	16	482	" 1671.
Tackett, Thomas	4	625	" 1661.
Tackwood, Samuel	16	393	" 1671.
Taggert, Thomas	18	152	" 1674.
Taillor, Alice	15	537	" 1679.
Taillor, Henry	15	566	" 1678.
Taillor, Nich.	15	430	" 1677.
Taillor, Thomas	15	540	" 1677.
Taillor, Timothy	15	416	" 1677.
Tailor, George	1	18	" 1637. Aged 15 years.
Tailor, Henry	1	73	" 1634.
Taine, Mary	17	552	" from New York 1672.
Takeman, William	18	166	" 1674.
Talbot, George	18	117	" 1674.
Talbot, Mary	18	310	Service 1675. Of St. Mary's Co.
Talbot, Richard	19	615	Of Anne Arundel Co. Died prior to 1677, leaving son, Edward and widow, Eliz., who married Wm. Richardson.
Talbot, Richard	17	595	Service 1673. Of St. Mary's Co.
Talbot, William	17	493	Immigrated from Virginia 1671.
Talbot, William, Esq.	16	79	Nephew of Charles Lord Baltimore 1670.
Talbot, Wm., Hon. Sir	13	82	Baronet and Principal Secy. of Md. 1671. (16, fol. 112).
Talbott, Albrett	5	416	Transported 1663.
Talbott, Edward	5	361	Son of Richard, dec'd. 1663.
Talbott, George	WC2	356	Special Warrant for 4,000 acres from Lord Baltimore, 1680.
Talbott, Henry	6	81	Transported 1660.
Talbott, John	5	361	Son of Richard 1663.
Talbott, Mary	7	464	Transported 1655.
Talbott, Richard	4	66	Assignment of land from his father-in-law, Maj. Richard Ewen, 1659.
Talbott, Richard	15	565	Transported 1679.
Talbott, William	4	63	" 1646.
Talle, Anthony	7	493	Immigrated 1662.
Talle, Elizabeth	7	493	Transported 1663. Wife of Anthony.
Talle, Philip	7	493	" 1663. Son of Anthony.
Talle, Rebecca	8	477	" 1665.
Talley, Thomas	4	140	" 1654. Servant.
Tallington, Mary	18	94	" 1674.
Tallis, Richard	17	397	Of Talbot Co. Service 1672.
Tallor, Dorothy	15	360	Transported 1676.
Tally, Peter	15	451	" 1678.
Tame, Gabriel	6	87	" 1661.

NAME	Liber	Folio	REMARKS
Tamen, John	9	44	Transported 1651.
Tamer, John	12	548	" 1670.
Tammison, Stephen	1	110	" 1633.
Tanner, John	16	507	" 1671.
Tanner, John	WC2	170	Rights 1680.
Tanner, Sarah	15	353	Transported 1674. (18, fol. 280).
Tannor, William	5	515	" 1661. Servant.
Tansell, Francis	9	333	" 1666.
Tansey, Alexander	WC2	406	" 1680.
Tant, John	15	536	" 1678.
Tant, Thomas	Q	30	" 1656.
Tantle, Joane	Q	239	" 1651-2.
Tapito, Alice	15	567	" 1678.
Tapley, Christopher	12	283	Immigrated 1668.
Tapper, John	6	183,290	Transported 1663.
Tapper, John	12	271	Immigrated 1668.
Tapper, Lewis	17	9	Service 1672. Of St. Mary's Co.
Tapscoate, George	12	491	Transported 1670.
Tapscott, George	10	286,417	" 1666.
Tarbie, Thomas	10	609	" Elizth. Labs, whom he married prior to 1667.
Tarkim, James	16	437	Transported 1671.
Tarkington, John	18	387	Immigrated with wife and three children. Of Cecil Co.
Tarkington, John, Jr.	18	387	Transported 1668. Son of John.
Tarkington, Prudence	18	387	" 1668. Wife of John.
Tarkington, Samuel	18	387	" 1668. Son of John.
Tarkington, William	18	387	" 1668. Son of John.
Tarleton, Alice	18	137	" 1674.
Tarleton, James	16	121	" 1671.
Tarling, Andrew	15	504	" 1678.
Tarneck, John	18	152	" 1674.
Tarrandall, Richard	9	489	" 1665. Servant.
Tarver, William	3	62	Immigrated 1650.
Tasker, John	18	331	Transported 1674.
Tasker, Thomas	17	538	Of Calvert Co. Service 1673.
Tassell, William	18	9	Service 1673. Of Kent Co.
Tate, John	7	527	Transported 1664.
Tate, John	15	358	" 1675.
Tatnell, Hannah	17	411	" 1673. (18, fol. 285).
Tattersall, Mary	2	508-509	" 1648.
Tattersall, William	2	508-509	" 1648.
Taunt, John	17	612	Service 1672. Of St. Mary's Co.
Taver, Elizabeth	9	38	Transported 1665.
Tawney, Mary	16	124	" 1671. Wife of Michael of Calvert Co.
Tawney, Michael	7	639	Service 1665.
Taxton, Robert	15	515	Transported 1678.
Taylard, William	WC2	358	Immigrated 1680. Of St. Mary's Co.
Tayler, Ann	7	371	Transported 1663.
Tayler, Bryan	5	411	" 1663.

NAME	Liber	Folio	REMARKS
Tayler, Jasper	6	305	Transported 1664.
Tayler, John	12	217	" 1669.
Tayler, John	15	531	Service 1678. Carpenter.
Tayler, Richard	9	27	Immigrated prior to 1665.
Tayler, Thomas	9	47	Transported 1665.
Taylor, Abraham	11	337,441	" 1668.
Taylor, Alice	6	62,80	" 1663.
Taylor, Amy	9	79	" 1665.
Taylor, Angis	11	572	Immigrated 1668.
Taylor, Ann	ABH	150	Transported 1648. Servant.
Taylor, Ann	18	177	" 1674.
Taylor, Ann	15	357,369	" 1676.
Taylor, Anne	9	297	" 1665.
Taylor, Anne	WC2	308,309	" 1678.
Taylor, Anthony	6	123	" 1663.
Taylor, Anthony	8	486	" 1664.
Taylor, Arthur	4	219	" 1659. Son of John.
Taylor, Barnett	11	441	" 1668.
Taylor, Bennett	11	337	" 1668.
Taylor, Dorothy	Q	4	Servant 1656.
Taylor, Edmond	5	59,306	Transported 1662.
Taylor, Edward	11	436	" 1668.
Taylor, Edward	17	608	" 1673.
Taylor, Eleanor	15	501	" 1678.
Taylor, Elizabeth	ABH	229	" 1640. Wife of John.
Married Wm. Wilkes prior to 1655. (ABH, fol. 427).			
Taylor, Elizabeth	6	239	Transported 1663.
Taylor, Elizabeth	9	297	" 1665.
Taylor, Elizabeth	15	354	" 1676.
Taylor, Elizabeth	17	531	Service 1673. Wife of Edward of Dorset Co.
Taylor, Ellen	16	630	Transported 1670.
Taylor, Ellen	17	376	" 1672. Wife of George of Charles Co.
Taylor, Fran.	15	454	Transported 1677.
Taylor, Francis	5	223	" 1662.
Taylor, Francis	15	540	" 1676.
Taylor, George	ABH	244	" 1639.
Taylor, George	9	431	Immigrated 1661.
Taylor, George	7	474	Transported 1664.
Taylor, George	12	356	" 1669.
Taylor, George	8	477	Immigrated 1665.
Taylor, Grace	11	108	Transported 1667. Daughter of Henry.
Taylor, Henry	ABH	82	Transported 1634. Servant.
Taylor, Henry	11	108	Service 1667. Of St. Mary's Co. Tailor.
Taylor, Henry	17	417	Transported 1673.
Taylor, Henry	WC2	130	" 1679. Servant.
Taylor, James	5	248	" 1663.
Taylor, Jane	18	306	" 1675.

NAME	Liber	Folio	REMARKS
Taylor, Jeremy	7	371	Transported 1663-4.
Taylor, Joel	9	99	" 1665. Service 1670. (16, fol. 167).
Taylor, John	ABH	7,101	Transported 1637-40. Servant.
Taylor, John	2	347	" 1639. Servant.
Taylor, John	1	63,128	" 1640. (ABH, fol. 78).
Taylor, John	6	121	Immigrated 1650. (ABH, fol. 165).
Taylor, John	ABH	140,427	Transported 1651.
Taylor, John	Q	239	Immigrated 1651.
Taylor, John	5	532	" 1659. (4, fol. 219).
Taylor, John	5	413	" 1663.
Taylor, John	7	474	Transported 1664. Son of Thomas.
Taylor, John	9	332	" 1666.
Taylor, John	11	337	" 1667.
Taylor, John	11	348,440	" 1668.
Taylor, John	16	513	Service 1672. Of Calvert Co.
Taylor, John	18	39	Transported 1674.
Taylor, John	15	454	" 1677.
Taylor, John	WC2	77,80	Immigrated from Virginia 1679. Of Somerset Co.
Taylor, John	WC2	16	Transported 1679 by Capt. John Elly.
Taylor, John	WC2	167,169	" 1679 by Samuel Groome.
Taylor, John	WC2	120	" 1679 by Thomas Pemberton.
Taylor, Joseph	9	454	Transported 1666. (11, fol. 166; 16, fol. 308; 12, fol. 190, 415, 416, 511).
Taylor, Joyce	WC2	352	Transported 1680.
Taylor, Margaret	5	532	" 1659. Wife of John.
Taylor, Martha	12	474	" 1670.
Taylor, Marthay	WC2	381	" 1675-80. Servant.
Taylor, Mary	ABH	37,63	Servant 1637.
Taylor, Mary	1	18,31	Transported 1638. Servant. (2, fol. 605).
Taylor, Mary	ABH	141	Immigrated 1651. Wife of Robert.
Taylor, Mary	4	219	Transported 1659. Daughter of John.
Taylor, Mary	10	583	" 1667. Wife of Robert.
Taylor, Mary	11	108	" 1667. Wife of Henry.
Taylor, Mary	17	571	" 1673.
Taylor, Mary	18	334	" 1675.
Taylor, Michael	WC2	33	" 1679.
Taylor, Priscilla	15	398,453	" 1676.
Taylor, Prudence	18	22	Service 1673. Wife of Robert of Kent County.
Taylor, Richard	9	343	Transported 1666.
Taylor, Richard	16	135,532	" 1668-70.
Taylor, Richard	17	451	" 1672.
Taylor, Richard	15	353,401	" 1676. Service 1677.
Taylor, Robert	ABH	141,313	Immigrated 1651. Of Patuxent River.
Taylor, Robert	4	219	Transported 1659. Son of John.
Taylor, Robert	10	583	Immigrated 1667.
Taylor, Robert	11	374	Transported 1668.

NAME	Liber	Folio	REMARKS
Taylor, Robert	11	337,441	Transported 1668.
Taylor, Robert	12	382	" 1669. (17, fol. 355).
Taylor, Robert	17	575	Immigrated 1673. Of St. Mary's Co.
Taylor, Robert	18	174	Transported 1674.
Taylor, Robert	15	411	" 1677.
Taylor, Robin	ABH	374	" under 1st Conditions.
Taylor, Samuel	ABH	313	" 1652. Son of Robert.
Taylor, Samuel	Q	449	" 1658.
Taylor, Sarah	ABH	165	Immigrated 1650. Wife of John.
Taylor, Sarah	Q	68	Servant 1653-8.
Taylor, Sarah	8	502	Transported 1665.
Taylor, Sarah	9	343	" 1666.
Taylor, Sarah	12	278	" 1668.
Taylor, Susan	9	431	" 1666. Wife of George.
Taylor, Swithen	15	455	" 1678.
Taylor, Thomas	ABH	427	Son of John. Living 1655.
Taylor, Thomas	Q	70	Immigrated 1658.
Taylor, Thomas	4	565	Demands land due his mother 1661, 400 acres.
Taylor, Thomas	5	88	Transported 1661.
Taylor, Thomas	6	263	" 1663.
Taylor, Thomas	16	431	Service 1669. Of Kent Co.
Taylor, Thomas	16	121,168	Transported 1671.
Taylor, Thomas	18	135	Immigrated 1674 with wife and daughter. Of Dorset Co.
Taylor, Thomas	18	137,291	Transported 1674.
Taylor, Thomas	15	259	" 1675.
Taylor, Thomas	WC2	110	" 1676. Servant.
Taylor, Thomas	WC2	108,167	" 1679.
Taylor, Thomas, Gent.	11	339	Immigrated 1668. Of Calvert Co.
Taylor, William, the	5	207	Transported 1662.
Taylor, William	5	252	" 1663. (9, fol. 336).
Taylor, William	10	556	" 1664-5.
Taylor, William	9	157	" 1665. (11, fol. 169).
Taylor, William	11	374,572	" 1668.
Taylor, William	15	330	" 1675.
Taylor, William	WC2	254	" 1680.
Taylour, Ellen	16	79	" 1670.
Taylour, George	12	478	" 1670.
Taylour, Jeremiah	16	140	Service 1671.
Taylour, John	13	116	Transported 1671.
Taylour, Lawrence	13	65	" 1668. Servant.
Taylour, Lidia	16	406	" 1671.
Taylour, Robert	12	551	Immigrated 1670. Of Calvert Co.
Taylour, Thomas	12	381,416	Transported 1669. (17, fol. 72).
Taylour, Thomas	16	168	" 1671. Son-in-law of Jno. James.
Taylour, William	12	415	Transported 1669.
Taylour, William	16	41	" 1670.
Tayor, Edward	Q	71	" 1652-3.
Teag, Sheily	11	378	" 1668.

NAME	Liber	Folio	REMARKS
Teage, Edward	15	319	Transported 1675.
Teage, Elizabeth	12	589	" 1670.
Teagle, Nathaniel	17	553	Service 1673.
Teague, Gabriel	WC2	17	Immigrated 1679.
Teake, George	9	25	Transported 1665.
Teare, Reynold	11	572	" 1668.
Teasman, William	4	21,140	" 1657.
Teckerell, Thomas	12	213	" 1668.
Ted, Thomas	1	31	" 1638. Servant. (See Tidd). (2,fol. 604).
Tedder, Ellinor	WC2	415	Transported 1666-80. Servant.
Tedley, Thomas	5	530	" 1662.
Tegger, James	4	59	" 1659.
Teirwell, Nath.	15	443	" 1671.
Tembel, Margaret	5	304	" 1662. Servant.
Temperly, William	9	104	" 1665.
Tempest, Mary	12	393	" 1669.
Temple, Ann	18	95	" 1674.
Temple, Richard	6	131	" 1654.
Templer, Mary	15	397	" 1676.
Templer, Ruth	15	569	" 1678.
Tenand, Richard	5	467	" 1658.
Tenant, Edward	Q	66	" 1653.
Tench, Ester	15	559	" 1679.
Tench, Francis	12	413	" 1669.
Tench, Jane	12	413	" 1669.
Tench, Jane	15	530	" 1678.
Tench, John	12	412,413	Immigrated 1669. Of Talbot Co. Mariner.
Tench, Thomas	WC2	381	Rights 1680.
Tenchall, Andrew	15	337	Immigrated 1667. Of Calvert Co.
Tendall, Robert	18	160	Transported 1674.
Tendergrass, James	15	527	" 1678.
Tenings, William	15	317	" 1674. Of Virginia.
Tennant, John	16	170	" 1671.
Tenney, Mary	12	471	" 1649. Wife of Thomas.
Tenney, Sarah	12	471	" 1649, and married Robt. Davadge of Anne Arundel Co., 1669. Daughter of Thomas.
Tenney, Thomas	12	471	Immigrated 1649.
Tenson, Isaac	11	436	Transported 1668.
Tenson, Mary	9	386	" 1666.
Tent, Mabella	15	369	" 1676.
Teppett, John	17	411	" 1673.
Terboe, John	ABH	5	Immigrated 1646.
Terras, Robert	8	129	Transported 1664. Servant. Of Baltimore Co.
Terratt, William	18	102	Transported 1674, with Ann.
Terre, Betty	WC2	415	" 1666-80. Servant.
Terre, Christian	8	131	" 1664. Servant.
Terrell, John	4	576	" 1661.
Terrett, Nicholas	10	395	" 1666. (18,fol. 314).

NAME	Liber	Folio	REMARKS
Terrick, John	Q	31	Transported 1658.
Terricker, Thomas	16	437	" 1671.
Terrissell, Alexander	5	207	" 1662.
Terry, Michael	9	38	" 1665.
Terry, Richard	18	174	" 1674.
Terry, Thomas	5	409	" 1661.
Terson, Andreas	4	552	Immigrated 1661.
Terson, Ann	4	552	Transported 1661. Daughter of Andreas.
Terson, Katherine	4	552	Transported 1661. Wife of Andreas.
Tescott, Daniel	7	471	" 1664.
Tetersell, Edmond	ABH	60	" 1637.
Tetersell, Edward	1	25,38,39	" 1637.
Tethmare, Judith	15	453	" 1676.
Tett, John	4	140	" 1654. Servant.
Tettershall, William	4	618	Married a Lewger prior to 1661.
Teuckesbury, William	16	458	Transported 1672.
Tew, John	9	216	" 1665.
Texell, John	15	453	" 1675-7.
Thacke, James	7	496	" 1664.
Thacker, Mordant	WC2	86-87	" 1679.
Thacker, Thomas	17	597	Immigrated 1673. Of Dorset Co.
Thacker, Thomas	15	500,558	Transported 1676-7.
Thacker, Thomas	WC2	399	" 1677.
Thadlett, John	18	17	" 1674. Son of Mary, wife of Dr. Jno. Higgs.
Thatcher, John	15	536	Immigrated 1678.
Thatcher, Mary	15	567	Transported 1678.
Thellwall, Mary	10	267	" prior to 1666. Wife of William.
Thellwall, William	10	267	Transported prior to 1666.
Theobalds, Elizabeth	5	306	" 1663. Daughter of Clement.
Theobalds, Mary	5	306	Transported 1663. Wife of Clement.
Theobalds, Penelope	5	306	" 1663. Daughter of Clement.
Theobalds, Thomas	5	306	Transported 1663. Son of Clement.
Thexton, Thomas	17	419	Service 1672.
Thickpenny, Henry	ABH	313	Transported 1652. Servant.
Thimbleby, John	3	25	Service prior to 1650.
Thimbly, John	ABH	48	" 1650.
Thinn, Walter	12	576	Transported 1670.
Thocold, Timothy	15	455	" 1678.
Tholerby, Thomas	5	87	" 1649-62.
Thomas, Alexander	18	36	" 1673, with Rice. Service 1675. (15, fol. 319).
Thomas, Alice	WC2	254	Transported 1680. (WC2, fol. 340-1).
Thomas, Andrew	8	484	" 1665.
Thomas, Ann	9	327	" 1666. Wife of Tristam.
Thomas, Ann	16	399	" 1668.
Thomas, Ann	17	424	" 1673.

NAME	Liber	Folio	REMARKS
Thomas, Anne	WC2	259	Transported 1680 by Hugh Thomas.
Thomas, Anne	WC2	288	" 1680 by William Morgan.
Thomas, Arthur	12	372	Transported 1669.
Thomas, Benjamin	12	194	" 1668. Servant.
Thomas, Benjamin	13	112	" 1669.
Thomas, Caleb	5	416,537	" 1651. Son of Philip.
Thomas, Charles	4	576	" 1661. (16, fol. 405).
Thomas, Christopher	1	87	" 1640.
Thomas, Christopher	ABH	86	" 1640. Servant.
Thomas, Christopher	7	471	Immigrated 1664 with wife and two children.
Thomas, Christopher	8	483	Transported 1665.
Thomas, Christopher	9	327	" 1666. Son of Tristam.
Thomas, Christopher	12	333	" 1668.
Thomas, Davey	16	85	" 1670.
Thomas, David	17	349	" 1662.
Thomas, David	16	41	" 1670.
Thomas, Dorothy	16	129	" 1671.
Thomas, Edward	5	491	" 1661.
Thomas, Edward	17	488	" 1662.
Thomas, Edward	11	344	" 1668.
Thomas, Edward	15	446	" 1677.
Thomas, Elizabeth	ABH	202	" 1651. Wife of Thomas.
Thomas, Elizabeth	5	416,537	" 1651. Daughter of Philip.
Thomas, Elizabeth	15	443	Transported 1670.
Thomas, Ellis	WC2	309	" 1678.
Thomas, Ellis	WC2	67	Service 1679. Of St. Mary's Co.
Thomas, Evan	10	433	Transported 1667. (12, fol. 194).
Thomas, Evan	16	86	" 1670. (17, fol. 68).
Thomas, Frances	12	242	" 1669. Wife of William.
Thomas, George	17	417	" 1673.
Thomas, Halett	9	24	" 1665.
Thomas, Henry	9	38,100	" 1665.
Thomas, Hugh	4	555	" 1661.
Thomas, Hugh	WC2	259,260	Rights 1680. Of Charles Co.
Thomas, James	ABH	202	Transported 1651. Son of Thomas.
Thomas, James	7	528	" 1664.
Thomas, James	WC2	213-214	" 1671-73.
Thomas, John	16	532	" 1668-70.
Thomas, John	5	20	" 1663.
Thomas, John	9	54	" 1665.
Thomas, John	9	99	" 1665.
Thomas, John	9	326	" 1666.
Thomas, John	10	498	" 1667.
Thomas, John	12	194	" 1668. Servant.
Thomas, John	16	393	" 1671. (18, fol. 30).
Thomas, John	12	242	" 1669. Son of William.
Thomas, John	15	371	Service 1676. Of St. Mary's Co.
Thomas, John	15	446	Transported 1678. Son of Philip.

NAME	Liber	Folio	REMARKS
Thomas, John	WC2	406	Transported 1680.
Thomas, Jone	18	17	" 1669.
Thomas, Katherine	10	443	" 1667.
Thomas, Margaret	11	338	" 1668.
Thomas, Margaret	16	409	" from Virginia 1671.
Thomas, Mary	4	625	" 1658-61.
Thomas, Mary	9	478	" 1665. Servant.
Thomas, Mary	12	242	" 1669. Daughter of William.
Thomas, Mary	12	554	Transported 1670.
Thomas, Mary	15	446	" 1678. Wife of Philip.
Thomas, Mary	WC2	308	" 1678.
Thomas, Nicholas	15	446	" 1678. Son of Philip.
Thomas, Owen	12	618	" 1670.
Thomas, Owen	17	363	" 1672.
Thomas, Philip	5	416,537	Immigrated 1651.
Thomas, Philip	5	416,537	Transported 1651. Son of Philip.
Thomas, Philip	12	194	" 1668. Servant.
Thomas, Philip	15	446	Immigrated 1678. Of St. Mary's Co.
Thomas, Rice	17	417	Transported 1673.
Thomas, Rice	WC2	304,307	Service 1680. Of Calvert Co.
Thomas, Richard	11	378	Transported 1668. (13, fol. 114).
Thomas, Richard	WC2	308	" 1678. (15, fol. 504).
Thomas, Robert	Q	208	Immigrated 1658.
Thomas, Robert	12	356	Transported 1669.
Thomas, Robert	12	554	" 1670.
Thomas, Robert	15	380	" 1676.
Thomas, Rose	18	137	" 1674.
Thomas, Sarah	5	416,537	" 1651. Wife of Philip.
Thomas, Sarah	4	416,537	" 1651. Daughter of Philip.
Thomas, Sarah	15	533	Transported 1678.
Thomas, Sarah	WC2	16	" 1679. Daughter of Mary Carter.
Thomas, Susan	15	446	Transported 1678. Daughter of Philip.
Thomas, Susanna	WC2	66	Immigrated 1669. Wife of William.
Thomas, Susanna	12	478	Transported 1670.
Thomas, Thomas	ABH	37,82	Servant 1634.
Thomas, Thomas	1	73	Transported 1635. (2, fol. 606).
Thomas, Thomas	ABH	202	Immigrated 1651.
Thomas, Thomas	6	83	Transported 1653.
Thomas, Thomas	9	327	" 1666. Son of Tristam.
Thomas, Tristam	9	327	" 1666.
Thomas, Tristam	9	327	" 1666. Son of Tristam.
Thomas, Walter	10	503	" 1665. Servant. (16, fol. 301).
Thomas, Welthean	11	344	Transported 1668.
Thomas, William	5	66	" 1662.
Thomas, William	7	469	Immigrated from Virginia to the Eastern Shore 1664.

NAME	Liber	Folio	REMARKS
Thomas, William	12	242	Immigrated from Virginia 1669.
Thomas, William	WC2	66	Rights 1669. Of Charles Co.
Thomas, William	15	337	Transported 1676.
Thomas, William	15	413	" 1677.
Thomas, William	15	446	" 1678. Son of Philip.
Thomas, William	WC2	254	" 1680. (WC2, fol. 340-1).
Thomas, William	WC2	288	" 1680. (WC2, fol. 306).
Thomas, Zachariah	16	503	" 1671.
Thompkins, Isaac	12	215	" 1668-9.
Thompkins, Sarah	12	242	" from Virginia 1669.
Thompson, Alexander	Q	65	Immigrated 1658.
Thompson, And.	15	559	Transported 1679.
Thompson, Ann	Q	18	" 1657.
Thompson, Ann	6	89	" 1663.
Thompson, Ann	15	300	" 1675.
Thompson, Ann	15	559	" 1679.
Thompson, Anne	WC2	308	" 1678.
Thompson, Anthony	12	618	" 1670. (17, fol. 57).
Thompson, Arthur	5	63	" 1660.
Thompson, Arthur	6	89	" 1663.
Thompson, Arthur	WC2	330,358	Immigrated 1680.
Thompson, Catherine	13	1	Transported 1669.
Thompson, Edward	10	558	" 1667. Servant.
Thompson, Elizabeth	4	30,533	" 1659. Servant.
Thompson, Elizabeth	4	622	" 1661.
Thompson, Elizabeth	16	116	" 1671. (18, fol. 164).
Thompson, Elizabeth	18	306	" 1675.
Thompson, Elizabeth	15	598	" 1678-9.
Thompson, Frances	Q	201	Immigrated 1656. Daughter of James.
Thompson, Francis	6	293	Transported 1664.
Thompson, Giles	ABH	162	" 1651. Servant.
Thompson, Godfrey	11	582	" 1668.
Thompson, Henry	Q	239	" 1652-3.
Thompson, Henry	9	334,448	" 1666. (16, fol. 419).
Thompson, Henry	15	560	" 1678.
Thompson, James, Rev.	6	89	"Clark". Immigrated 1663.
Thompson, James	Q	201	Immigrated 1656.
Thompson, James	10	571	Transported 1667 on the "Adventure". Servant.
Thompson, James	16	79	Transported 1670.
Thompson, James	15	258	Deputy Surveyor, Calvert and St. Mary's Counties, Nov. 20, 1674.
Thompson, James	18	167	Transported 1674.
Thompson, Jane	Q	201	Immigrated 1656. Wife of James.
Thompson, Jeane	12	213	Transported 1668.
Thompson, Jeffrey	18	152	" 1674.
Thompson, John	1	82	" 1636. Servant.
Thompson, John	ABH	85	" 1636-7. Servant. Massacred by Indians on Poplar Island.
Thompson, John	16	399	Transported 1668.

NAME	Liber	Folio	REMARKS
Thompson, John	17	457	Transported 1669.
Thompson, John	16	39	" 1670.
Thompson, John	16	399	" 1671.
Thompson, John	WC2	331	" 1676.
Thompson, John	WC2	406	" 1677. (15, fol. 454).
Thompson, John	15	559	" 1679.
Thompson, Joseph	16	537	" 1671.
Thompson, Joseph	11	372	" 1668.
Thompson, Joseph	16	41	Service 1670.
Thompson, Margaret	12	591	Transported 1668.
Thompson, Marmaduke	17	610	" 1673.
Thompson, Mary	12	190	" 1668.
Thompson, Mary	18	291	" 1674.
Thompson, Mary	15	530	" 1678.
Thompson, Richard	ABH	65	" 1633. (1, fol. 37-38).
Thompson, Richard	ABH	85	Immigrated 1636. Of the Isle of Kent.
Thompson, Richard	1	82-84	Immigrated 1636 with wife, child and servants. Of Isle of Kent.
Thompson, Richard	1	148	License to marry Ursula Bish, June 24, 1641. Of Isle of Kent.
Thompson, Richard	16	135	Transported 1671.
Thompson, Richard	15	558	" 1677 with Eleanor, his wife.
Thompson, Robert	ABH	35	Servant 1649.
Thompson, Robert	17	26	Immigrated 1672. Of Charles Co.
Thompson, Robert	WC2	254	Transported 1680.
Thompson, Sarah	Q	65	Immigrated 1658. Wife of Alexander.
Thompson, Thomas	18	80	Transported 1674.
Thompson, Thomas	11	582	" 1668. (16, fol. 532).
Thompson, William	ABH	5	And Wife, 1646.
Thompson, William	ABH	179	Transported 1650. Servant.
Thompson, William	Q	58,71	" 1652-3.
Thompson, William	6	123	" 1663.
Thompson, William	9	305	" 1665.
Thompson, William	13	66	" 1669. Servant.
Thompson, William	16	116	" 1671.
Thompson, William	16	536	Immigrated from Virginia 1671.
Thompson, William	16	537	Transported from Virginia 1671.
Thompson, William	17	40,349	Immigrated 1672. Of Dorset Co.
Thompson, William	17	424	Transported 1673.
Thompson, William	15	357	" 1676.
Thompson, Zachary	WC2	309	" 1678.
Thomson, Anthony	17	363	" 1672.
Thomson, Daniel	WC2	213-214	" 1671-3.
Thomson, Edward	17	572	" 1672.
Thomson, Elizabeth	WC2	211	" 1679. Servant.
Thomson, Francis	15	567	" 1678.
Thomson, George	5	214	Demands 1000 acres by Special Warrant Oct. 6, 1662. (See Tomson).

NAME	Liber	Folio	REMARKS
Thomson, William	7	498	Transported 1660.
Thomsone, William	7	474	" 1664.
Thorington, Ann	4	188	" 1659.
Thorman, William	4	198	" 1659.
Thorn, Ann	ABH	415	" 1653-4.
Thornbery, Samuel	11	167	Service 1667. Of Anne Arundel Co.
Thornborough, Rowland	6	26	Transported 1660-3.
Thorndon, Mary	Q	74	Servant 1658.
Thorne, John	11	337,441	Transported 1668.
Thorne, Joseph	17	395	" 1672.
Thorne, Mary	15	445	" 1678.
Thorne, Parly	WC2	187	" 1678.
Thorne, Thomas	12	343	" 1669.
Thorne, William, Capt.	6	19,135	Immigrated 1663.
Thorne, Winifred	6	19,135	Transported 1663. Wife of Capt. William.
Thornerly, Henry	WC2	211	Transported 1679. Servant.
Thorneton, Ginett	WC2	199	" 1680.
Thornhill, Robert	18	84	" 1674.
Thornley, Henry	15	598	" 1678-9.
Thornton, Edward	17	67	Service 1672.
Thornton, Eleanor	12	341	Transported 1668.
Thornton, James	1	20	" 1633.
Thornton, James	ABH	66	" 1635. (1, fol. 37-38).
Thornton, John	15	396	Immigrated 1676.
Thornton, John	15	439	" 1677. Of Anne Arundel County.
Thornton, John	WC2	167,169	Transported 1679.
Thornton, Richard	12	281	Service 1668.
Thornton, Thomas	16	411	Transported 1671.
Thororson, Andrew	4	64	Immigrated 1659.
Thoroughgood, Ann	17	488	Transported 1664.
Thoroughgood, Frances	7	490	" 1664. Wife of Thomas. (12, fol. 343).
Thorowgood, Cyprian	3	106	Special grant of 300 acres by Lord Baltimore, 1637.
Thorowgood, Cyprian	1	125	Immigrated 1641.
Thorowgood, John	11	348	Transported 1668.
Thorowgood, Steven	16	126	Service 1671.
Thorowgood, Thomas	7	490	Transported 1674. (12, fol. 343).
Thorowgood, William	16	126	Service 1671.
Thorowgood, William	17	40	Immigrated 1672. (See Throrowgood).
Thorpe, John	WC2	415	Transported 1666-80. Servant.
Thorpe, John	15	370	" 1676.
Thorpe, Thomas	17	463	" 1673.
Thorpe, Thomas	15	378	Immigrated 1676.
Thorsbey, Bridgett	4	186	Transported 1639, by John Nevell, her husband.
Thory, Henry	13	122	Transported 1670.
Threende, Philip	4	214	" 1650-9.

NAME	Liber	Folio	REMARKS
Threft, James	WC2	368	Transported 1680.
Thresher, Peter	10	272	" 1666.
Threskill, Daniel	15	438	" 1677.
Thretfull, Stephen	7	84	" 1660.
Thrift, John	9	34	" 1665.
Thrile, George	15	406	Service 1676.
Thromwell, Andrew	ABH	313	Transported 1652. Servant.
Throrowgood, Cyprian	ABH	56,100	Immigrated 1641. Grant of 300
acres for good services in the business of Pocomoke, May 22, 1637.			
Throughton, Mary	12	561	Immigrated 1638. Widow. Of St. Mary's County.
Throughton, Mrs. Mary	1	18,65-68	Immigrated 1638. Widow.
Througood, Simpkin	2	579	Special Grant from Lord Baltimore about 1649.
Thruacts, Francis	ABH	99	Transported 1638. Servant.
Thrumball, Samuel	WC2	318,400	Immigrated 1680.
Thrumbell, Michael	15	391	Transported 1676.
Thrumble, James	12	459	" 1669.
Thureld, George	12	498	" 1670.
Thurman, Roger	15	451	" 1678.
Thurmerston, John	Q	427	" 1658.
Thurrell, Richard	4	555	Immigrated 1661.
Thurston, Gilbert	10	2	Transported 1663.
Thurston, Mary	15	534	" 1674.
Thurston, Thomas	19	258	Immigrated 1663 with wife and
two daughters. Of Baltimore County.			
Thwaits, Francis	1	123	Transported 1638. Servant.
Thwaytes, Francis	1	18	" 1638.
Thymble, John	2	254	Service 1633-46.
Thynn, Walter	12	344	" 1669. Of St. Mary's Co.
Tibbells, John	4	616	Transported 1660.
Tibbet, James	16	435	" 1671.
Tibbetts, Thomas	15	557	" 1675. Servant.
Tibbin, William	8	30	" 1665.
Tibbot, John	18	80	" 1670.
Tibbotts, Catherine	4	530	" 1654. Wife of Clement.
Tibbotts, Catherine	4	530	Transported 1654. Daughter of Clement.
Tibbotts, Clement	4	530	Immigrated March 1654.
Tichbourne, Mary	6	122	Transported 1654.
Ticlecampe, Ments	17	492	Immigrated from Delaware 1665.
Tidd, Thomas	1	25	Transported before 1641. (See Ted).
Tidd, Thomas	ABH	60	" 1641.
Tidder, Edward	5	308	" 1662.
Tidgson, Francis	11	440	" 1668.
Tier, Ann	15	525	" 1678. Wife of Thomas.
Tier, James	15	525	" 1678. Son of Thomas.
Tier, Thomas	15	525	Immigrated 1678. Planter.
Tier, Thomas	15	525	Transported 1678. Son of Thomas.

NAME	Liber	Folio	REMARKS
Tigg, John	16	302	Transported 1671.
Tignie, Richard	17	475	" 1673.
Tike, Jeremy	8	381	" 1665.
Tilbey, John	17	608	" 1673.
Tilding, Charles	15	413	Immigrated 1677.
Tile, John	15	390	Transported 1676.
Tiler, Alice	7	536	" 1663.
Tilesby, Thomas	6	17	" 1663.
Tilghman, Elizabeth	10	433	" 1667 by Dr. Richard T.
Tilghman, Jane	10	204	" 1666.
Tilghman, Jean	10	342	" 1666.
Tilghman, Richard	Q	465	Citizen and Surgeon of London,

undertakes to immigrate 1657. Special Warrant from Lord Baltimore,
1658. (4, fol. 20).

Tilghman, Samuel	Q	460	Of London. Mariner, undertakes

to immigrate 1657. Special Warrant from Lord Baltimore 1657. (4,
fol. 19). Com'r. of "Constant Friendship". (11, fol. 675).

Tillard, John	7	561	Immigrated from Virginia 1665.
Tilleson, James	12	463	Transported 1669.
Tillett, Thomas	18	291	" 1674.
Tillett, Thomas	WC2	109,111	Service 1679.
Tilley, Anne	WC2	171	Transported 1679.
Tillison, John	13	122	" 1670.
Tillman, Gideon	17	444	Service 1673.
Tills, John	11	265	Transported 1667.
Tillsey, William	11	515	Immigrated from Virginia 1668.
Tillsley, Thomas	17	51	Service 1672. Of Calvert Co.
Tilly, Elizabeth	15	347	Transported 1676.
Tilly, John	7	79	" 1663.
Tilsley, Thomas	1	171	" about 1639.
Tilson, John	16	428	" 1670.
Tilton, Humphrey	18	152	" 1674.
Timm, Thomas	WC2	21	" 1679.
Timmins, Priscilla	WC2	346-347	Immigrated 1680.
Timmins, William	WC2	346-347	" 1680. (See Tinnings).
Timms, William	11	168	" 1667. Of Anne Arundel County.
Timperson, Anthony	13	122	Transported 1668.
Tims, William	18	309	Immigrated from London 1666.
Tinch, Elizabeth	15	439	Transported 1677.
Tindall, Thomas	13	1	" 1669. Servant.
Tine, John	9	216	" 1665.
Tingle, John	12	576	" 1670. (17, fol. 574).
Tingles, Hugh	12	334	" 1668.
Tinkeay, Thomas	WC2	206	" 1679. Servant.
Tinnings, Priscilla	WC2	318	" 1680. Wife of William.
Tinnings, William	WC2	318	Immigrated 1680 with wife. (See Timmins).
Tinsley, Seth	Q	18,48	Immigrated 1656.
Tinsley, Thomas	7	79	Transported 1664.
Tinsond, Thomas	15	531	" 1678.

NAME	Liber	Folio	REMARKS
Tipent, Sarah	12	194	Transported 1668.
Tippett, Philip	WC2	412	" 1681.
Tipping, William	17	58	Immigrated 1664, with wife. (17, fol. 355).
Tipple, James	6	86	Transported 1660.
Tipps, Francis	ABH	40	" 1650.
Tipton, Edward	11	379	" 1668.
Tipton, Edward	WC2	123	Service 1674.
Tire, Mary	6	63	Transported 1658-63.
Tirer, James	6	94	" 1662.
Tirwhit, Benjamin	16	37	" 1670.
Tisen, William	12	190	" 1668. Servant.
Titcomb, William	11	337	" 1668.
Titmarsh, Jane	5	128	" 1662. Wife of John.
Titmarsh, John	5	128	Immigrated 1662.
Titmarsh, John	Q	33	Transported 1653-8.
Titon, Peter	6	393	" 1664.
Titton, Thomas	18	329	" 1675.
Tizard, John	16	166	Immigrated 1670, with Barbara, his wife. Of Somerset County.
Toale, Joan	7	471	Transported 1664.
Toate, Frances	16	70	" 1670.
Toate, Robert	16	70	" 1670.
Toband, Robert	6	17	" 1663.
Tobby, John	ABH	48	" 1648. Servant.
Tobert, John	WC2	16	" 1677.
Tobert, John	15	574	" 1678.
Tobin, Richard	4	338	" 1659. Servant.
Tockley, Mary	15	435	" 1676.
Tod, Alexander	4	434	" 1666.
Tod, Elizabeth	9	269	" 1665.
Tod, Thomas	ABH	63	" 1638. Servant.
Tod, Thomas	16	630	" 1670.
Todd, Ann	12	202	" 1669. Wife of Capt. Thomas.
Todd, Ann	12	202	Transported 1669. Daughter of Capt. Thomas.
Todd, Cornelius	6	129	Transported 1654.
Todd, David	4	137	" 1659.
Todd, Francis	6	87	Immigrated 1658.
Todd, Francis	12	202	Transported 1669. Son of Thomas.
Todd, Francis	13	122	" 1670.
Todd, Jane	18	160	" 1674.
Todd, Johannah	12	202	" 1669. Daughter of Thomas.
Todd, John	12	202	Transported 1669. Son of Thomas.
Todd, John	15	544	" 1674.
Todd, Richard	16	394	" 1671.
Todd, Robert	9	269	" 1665.
Todd, Robert	12	202	" 1669. Son of Capt. Thomas.

NAME	Liber	Folio	REMARKS
Todd, Thomas, Capt.	12	202	Immigrated 1669.
Todd, Thomas	16	79	Transported 1670.
Todd, Thomas	15	448	Immigrated 1678.
Todvane, Nicholas	15	318	Transported 1675.
Toe, John	16	395	" 1671.
Tofte, Thomas	15	500	" 1675.
Toiser, Joseph	WC2	398	" 1680. (See Tozer).
Tokey, Mary	15	514	" 1677.
Toldersby, Thomas	18	309	Service 1666.
Tole, Frances	16	43	Transported 1670.
Tole, Henry	16	366	Immigrated 1671. Of Baltimore Co.
Tole, Robert	16	43	Transported 1670.
Tole, Roger	16	46	Service 1670. Of Dorset Co.
Tolesberry, Thomas	11	169	Immigrated 1667.
Tollard, William	9	25	Transported 1665.
Tollingsayne, Ann	10	4	" 1666.
Tollison, Brunell	11	537	" 1668.
Tolson, Thomas	7	526	Of London. Merchant. Special
Warrant for 1,000 acres, 1664.			
Tomblin, Edward	15	406	Service 1676.
Tomblings, Francis	7	463	Transported 1661.
Tomes, John	9	69	" 1660-5.
Tomkins, Ann	17	57	Service 1672.
Tomkins, Francis	11	344	Transported 1668.
Tomkins, Jone	15	567	" 1679.
Tomkins, Joseph	15	359	" 1676.
Tomkins, Sarah	11	344	" 1668.
Tomkinson, John	ABH	378	Immigrated 1651 with wife.
Tomlin, Joseph	7	639	Transported 1665.
Tomline, Edward	17	415	" 1669.
Tomling, Christopher	12	194	" 1668. Servant.
Tomlins, Thomas	17	411	" 1673.
Tomlinson, John	10	277	" 1666.
Tomlinson, Thomas	WC2	21	" 1679.
Tommes, Arthur	12	416	" 1669.
Tomms, William	9	49-50	Immigrated 1665.
Tompkins, Ann	11	344	Transported 1668.
Tompkins, Benjamin	15	436	" 1677.
Tompkins, William	11	167	" 1667.
Tompkins, William	16	165	" 1670.
Tompson, Alice	10	559	" 1667. Daughter of Peter.
Tompson, Ann	15	429	Transported 1674.
Tompson, Ann	10	434,567	" 1667.
Tompson, Bernard	10	567	Immigrated from James River, Va. Of Anne Arundel Co.
Tompson, Clare	10	434	Transported 1667.
Tompson, Elizabeth	10	567	" 1667. Daughter of Bernard.
Tompson, Francis	15	501	Transported 1678.
Tompson, George	10	559	" 1667. Son of Peter.

NAME	Liber	Folio	REMARKS
Tompson, Jane	10	559	Transported 1667. Wife of Peter.
Tompson, Joyce	10	567	" 1667. Wife of Bernard.
Tompson, Mary	15	439	Transported 1666.
Tompson, Mathew	15	511	" 1676.
Tompson, Michael	15	385	Immigrated 1676. Of St. Mary's Co.
Tompson, Patrick	11	436	Transported 1668.
Tompson, Peter	10	559	Immigrated 1667 from Northumberland Co., Virginia. Of Marrow Creek, Baltimore County.
Tompson, Robert	2	575	Transported 1649. Servant.
Tompson, William	1	124	Special Grant from Lord Baltimore, 1641.
Tompson, William	16	507	Transported 1671.
Toms, John	15	369	" 1676.
Toms, William	17	454	" 1672.
Tomson, George	5	214	Demands 1000 acres by Special Warrant, Oct. 6, 1662.
Tomson, John	18	329	Transported 1675.
Tomson, William	8	129	Immigrated 1664. (9, fol. 489).
Tomson, John	1	20	Transported 1633.
Tonend, John	9	38	" 1665.
Tongue, Friendship	ABH	165	Immigrated 1649.
Tongue, Thomas	3	24	Transported 1650. Servant.
Tonkey, Vene	10	565	" 1667.
Toogood, Mary	ABH	47	" 1649. Servant. (Q, fol. 9, 18, 19; 3, fol. 24).
Toones, Gilbert	8	501	Transported 1665.
Tootle, Andrew	6	14	" 1663.
Topley, Martha	16	168	" 1670.
Topliffe, Henry	5	87	" 1649-62.
Topping, Henry	1	171	" about 1639.
Topping, John	WC2	199	" 1680.
Torlin, Andrew	12	269	" 1669. Servant.
Torningham, Eleanor	4	79	" 1654 and married Jos. Edlowe prior to 1659.
Tory, Hugh	5	259	Transported 1657.
Tosall, John	15	370	" 1676.
Totman, William	17	547	" 1673.
Tottenham, Bridget	WC2	330	Service 1673.
Tottenham, William	WC2	330,358	" 1673.
Tottersall, Mary	ABH	23	Transported 1648.
Tottersall, William	ABH	23	" 1648.
Tottersill, Edward	ABH	66	" 1637.
Touchester, Mary	15	549	" 1678.
Tough, Katherine	18	167	" 1674.
Toule, William	18	331	" 1674.
Toulson, Brindell	15	434	Service 1677.
Toulson, Mary	15	314	Transported 1675.
Toulson, William	9	459	Of Anne Arundel Co. Father-in-law of Thos. Francis, of said county, 1666.
Toulson, William	15	317	Transported 1674.

NAME	Liber	Folio	REMARKS
Toulson, William	15	205	Of Baltimore Co., Gent. Toleches-ter, 1673.
Tousa, Mathias	ABH	65	Transported 1633. A "Molatto".
Tousing, Christopher	17	463	" 1673.
Tovey, Elizabeth	15	565	" 1679. Wife of Samuel, of Kent County.
Tovey, Elizabeth	WC2	194	Transported 1680. Wife of Samuel.
Tovey, Elizabeth	WC2	194	" 1680. Daughter of Samuel.
Tovey, Henry	WC2	415	Transported 1666-80. Servant.
Tovey, Henry	WC2	194	Rights for wife, two children and one other person. Of Kent Co.
Tovey, Samuel	15	337,565	Immigrated 1675. Of Kent Co. Transported wife and two children 1679.
Tovey, Samuel, Jr.	WC2	194	Transported 1680.
Tovey, Thomas	16	39	Service 1670. Of Calvert Co.
Tovy, John	ABH	24	Servant 1648.
Tovy, John	3	25	Transported 1648. (2, fol. 512).
Tovye, Henry	17	396	" 1669.
Tow, William	17	474	" 1672.
Tower, Francis	ABH	63	" 1638. Servant.
Towers, Deborah	ABH	150	" 1639. Servant.
Towers, Francis	2	604	" about 1638. Servant.
Towers, John	4	585	" 1661.
Towers, Jonathan	9	489	Immigrated 1665. (10, fol. 504).
Towers, Katherine	10	504	Service 1666. Wife of Jonathan.
Towers, Thomas	18	84	Transported 1674.
Towes, Robert	9	38	" 1665.
Towes, Robert, Jr.	9	38	" 1665.
Towhill, Edmond	4	68	Immigrated prior to 1651.
Towle, Elizabeth	WC2	213	Service 1680. Wife of Roger.
Towle, Roger	16	437	Transported 1671.
Towle, Roger	WC2	213	Rights 1680. Of St. Mary's Co.
Towley, Barbary	11	339	Transported 1667.
Towley, Richard	11	339	" 1668.
Town, Thomas	9	216	" 1665.
Towne, John	15	430	" 1677.
Townhill, Thomas	8	381	" 1665.
Townly, Edmond	5	182	" 1662.
Townsend, Barbary	11	344	" 1668.
Townsend, Elizabeth	10	437	" 1667.
Townsend, John	10	437	Immigrated 1667.
Townsend, John	16	393	Transported 1671.
Townsend, John	15	318	" 1675.
Townsend, Margaret	11	344	" 1668.
Townsend, Richard	11	344	" 1668.
Townsend, Richard	18	35	Immigrated 1672.
Townsend, William	15	403	Transported 1676.
Towrey, Thomas	6	62	" 1663.
Towse, Elizabeth	5	417	" 1663. Daughter of Robert.

NAME	Liber	Folio	REMARKS
Towse, Elizabeth	5	417	Transported 1663. Wife of Robert.
Towse, Mary	5	417	" 1663. Daughter of Robert.
Towse, Robert	5	417	Immigrated 1663.
Towse, Robert	5	417	Transported 1663. Son of Robert.
Toyld, Thomas	9	54	" 1665.
Toyley, Alexander	4	580	" 1661.
Toyley, John	4	580	" 1661.
Tozer, Henry	WC2	381	" 1675-80. Servant.
Tozer, Joseph	WC2	253	" 1680. (See Toiser).
Tracy, Alice	16	358	" 1671.
Tracy, Ann	16	358	" 1671.
Tracy, Samuel	16	60	Immigrated 1670. Of Baltimore Co.
Tracy, Teague	15	537	Transported 1679.
Tracy, Timothy	17	595	Service 1673. Of St. Mary's Co.
Traherne, Anne	10	583	Transported from Virginia 1667.
Traherne, George	17	503	" 1669.
Traherne, George	16	303	" from Virginia 1671. Of Somerset Co.
Traherne, Margaret	9	304	Transported 1665.
Trapenny, Henry	ABH	141	" 1651.
Trauton, Mary	ABH	57	Demands land 1643, due by Special Grant from his Lordship, dated London, Aug. 1638. (See Troughton).
Travers, Elizabeth	9	333	Transported 1665.
Travers, William	9	333	" 1665.
Traverse, James	WC2	211	" 1679. Servant.
Traverse, William	12	333	Immigrated 1669. Of Charles Co.
Traverse, William	17	422	Transported 1672.
Traviss, James	15	598	" 1678-9.
Trayman, William	5	243	" 1662.
Treagoe (Trego), William, Sr.	WC2	72	Marriner 1679. Of the City of Bristol. Rights 1679. (WC2, fol. 213-214).
Treane, Thomas	15	362	Transported 1676.
Trebitt, Richard	4	66	" 1658.
Tredwell, William	17	615	Service 1673. Of St. Mary's Co.
Tren, Henry	17	451	Transported 1671. (15, fol. 344).
Trepp, Henry	9	26	Married widow of Michael Brooke prior to 1665.
Treshy, James	WC2	182	Transported 1680.
Trevellion, John	7	560	" 1665.
Trevent, Robert	17	417	" 1673.
Treverse, Walter	6	107	" 1661.
Trevor, Morris	15	565	" 1679.
Trewe, Richard	ABH	230	Immigrated 1648.
Treyman, Thomas	4	551	Transported 1661.
Tricle, Ann	15	454	" 1677.
Trigge, Alice	8	3	Service 1665.
Triggs, Joane	1	18	Transported 1637.
Triggs, William	1	18	" 1637. A boy.
Trippe, Henry	6	255	Immigrated 1663.

NAME	Liber	Folio	REMARKS
Trippes, Francis	2	615	Transported 1649.
Trippett, John	4	10	" 1658. Servant.
Trippos, Anna	Q	74	Immigrated 1650. Wife of Francis.
Trippos, Francis	Q	74	" 1650.
Tripshaw, John	WC2	321	" 1680. Bricklayer.
Troaton, Ann	17	567	Transported 1673 from Virginia.
Troce, Alice	15	500	" 1676-7.
Troce, Alice	WC2	399	" 1677.
Tromelly, John	18	329	" 1675.
Trood, Thomas	15	395	" 1677.
Troope, Edward	6	96	" 1660.
Troope, Elizabeth	9	32	" 1660.
Troope, Elizabeth	8	30	" 1665.
Troope, Lieut. Robert	4	584	Immigrated 1651. Special Warrant from Lord Baltimore for his services at Severn.
Trott, Andrew	ABH	313	Transported 1652. Servant.
Trotter, Elizabeth	18	306	" 1675.
Trotter, Mary	15	430	" 1677.
Troughton, Mary	ABH	79	Immigrated 1638. Widow. (See Trauton).
Troughton (Treuton), Mary	1	21	Special Warrant for 2000 acres granted by Lord Baltimore 1638. (See Throughton).
Troute, Thomas	19	258	Transported 1663.
Trowse, Thomas	6	235	" 1663.
Truce, John	6	159	" 1652.
Truckle, Elizabeth	6	128	" 1654.
True, William	16	414	Immigrated 1665. Of Kent Co.
True, William	18	20	Service 1674. Of Dorset Co.
Trueman, Ann	17	454	Transported 1672. Wife of James.
Trueman, Ann	17	454	" 1672. Daughter of James.
Trueman, Mr. James	17	454	Immigrated 1672.
Trueman, Martha	17	454	Transported 1672. Daughter of James.
Trueman, Mary	17	454	Transported 1672. Daughter of James.
Trueman, Robert	13	122	Transported 1668.
Trulock, Constant	15	338	" 1676. Wife of Henry.
Trulock, Henry	15	338	Immigrated 1676. Of Calvert Co.
Trulock, Joseph	15	338	Transported 1676. Son of Henry.
Truman, Alice	9	272	" 1665.
Truman, Henry	15	534	" 1677.
Truman, Nathaniel	9	462	Immigrated 1665.
Truman, Stephen	15	167	Transported 1673.
Truman, Suffiah	7	464	" 1660.
Truman, Thomas, Esq.	10	13	Of Calvert Co. Brother of Nath'l. Truman of Calvert County, Gent. 1666.
Trumble, Mica.	15	307,379	Transported 1675.
Trump, John	12	517	" 1670.
Trumpetter, Thomas	ABH	349	Immigrated 1653.

NAME	Liber	Folio	REMARKS
Trunch, Ann	16	79,630	Transported 1670.
Truste, Gabriel	9	326	" 1666.
Trymary, Thomas	16	507	" 1671.
Tuan, Mark	5	90	" 1653-61.
Tubb, Elizabeth	12	498	" 1670.
Tubb, William	15	167	" 1673.
Tubbman, Richard	12	624	Service 1670. Of Dorset Co.
Tubbs, Isaac	9	308	Transported 1666.
Tubbs, Isabell	9	308	" 1666.
Tubbs, Richard	4	616	" 1660.
Tuberville, Gilbert	18	130	Immigrated 1675 and assigns rights. Of St. Mary's Co.
Tubs, Richard	15	551	Transported 1679.
Tuck, Daniel	15	337	" 1676.
Tucker, Ann	12	497	" 1670. (15, fol. 296).
Tucker, Aymye	Q	204	Immigrated 1658. Wife of John.
Tucker, Elizabeth	11	167	Transported 1667.
Tucker, Grace	18	84	" 1674.
Tucker, Jacob	6	120	" 1650.
Tucker, John	Q	204	Immigrated 1658.
Tucker, John	Q	204,316	" 1658. Son of John.
Tucker, John	16	60	Transported 1670.
Tucker, John	15	398,453	" 1676.
Tucker, John	WC2	327	Service 1680. Of Somerset Co.
Tucker, Richard	11	167	Transported 1667.
Tucker, Richard	15	318	" 1674. (18,fol.24).
Tucker, Richard	15	388	" 1675.
Tucker, Sarah	15	550	" 1679.
Tucker, Thomas	18	17	" 1669.
Tucker, Thomas	16	540	" 1671.
Tucker, Walter	5	307	" 1664. (9,fol.92).
Tucker, Walter	15	338	" 1676.
Tuckwett, Thomas	15	443	" 1674.
Tudor, Owen	15	454	" 1677.
Tudson, John	ABH	201	" 1650-1.
Tue, John	ABH	66,212	" 1637. (ABH,fol. 60; 1,fol.17,20,25,38,39).
Tue, John	4	610	Transported 1661.
Tue, Restituta	ABH	244	" 1636.
Tue, Restituta	1	138	License to marry John (Hallowes) Hellis, June 1,1639.
Tuffen, John	WC2	73	Transported 1678.
Tuinsad, Aron	WC2	23	" 1679. Servant.
Tulchstone, Richard	WC2	87	" 1679.
Tule, Mary	6	210	" 1663.
Tulford, Humphrey	ABH	64	" 1637. Servant.
Tull, Richard	17	382	Immigrated 1672.
Tull, Thomas	17	382	" 1672.
Tullentire, Mary	18	160	Transported 1674.
Tulley, Stephen	6	27	" 1663.
Tulley, Thomas	9	38	" 1661.

NAME	Liber	Folio	REMARKS
Tully, Anne	WC2	16	Transported 1679.
Tully, Charles	WC2	65	" 1679.
Tully, Joane	5	120	" 1661.
Tully, John	15	531	" 1678.
Tully, Stephen	WC2	2-3	Special Warrant for 900 acres from Lord Baltimore, 1678.
Tully, Thomas	16	109	Transported 1665.
Tully, Thomas	16	109	" 1671.
Tully, Walter	15	378	Service 1676.
Tuly, Capt. John	5	195	Special Warrant 1662.
Tuman, William	15	516	Transported 1678.
Tumbleson, Henry	15	411	" 1677.
Tunck, William	11	548	Service 1668. Of St. Mary's Co.
Tunhill, William	ABH	239	Transported 1651. Servant.
Tunk, William	12	355	Service 1669. Of St. Mary's Co.
Tunnell, Thomas	ABH	55	Transported 1649.
Tunnet, Thomas	3	104	" 1650. Servant.
Tunny, Jane	15	307	" 1675.
Tunstead, Robert	Q	48	Immigrated 1656.
Turberfield, Richard	15	433	Transported 1677.
Turberville, William	5	257	Immigrated 1659.
Turbutt, Michael	WC2	184,195	" 1680.
Turfery, Thomas	15	454	Transported 1677.
Turfey, Thomas	WC2	406	" 1677.
Turkin, Frances	WC2	146,162	" 1680.
Turley, Edward	18	126	" 1674.
Turley, John	15	397	" 1676.
Turling, Andrew	16	112	" 1671.
Turloe, William	15	397	" 1676.
Turby, Benjamin	9	489	Immigrated 1665.
Turner, Abraham	16	354	Transported 1671.
Turner, Arthur	ABH	371	Immigrated 1639.
Turner, Borham	10	469	Transported 1667. (17, fol. 66).
Turner, Cicily	15	167	" 1673.
Turner, Daniel	15	353	" 1675.
Turner, David	17	492	Immigrated from New York 1671, with Ann, his wife, and Constance, his daughter.
Turner, Dor.	15	567	Transported 1679.
Turner, Edward	ABH	55	" Aug. 1649. Servant. (Q, fol. 10, 19).
Turner, Edward	3	104	Transported 1650. Servant.
Turner, Edward	ABH	323	" 1652-3. Son of William.
Turner, Elizabeth	12	271	" 1668.
Turner, Elizabeth	15	319,420	Service 1675. Wife of Richard.
Turner, Elizabeth	15	567	Transported 1678.
Turner, Emma	4	530	Sister to Jno. Longsworth, living 1659.
Turner, George	11	162	Transported 1667.
Turner, George	12	356	" 1669.
Turner, George	17	567	" 1673 from Virginia.
Turner, Grace	17	510	" 1673 from Virginia.

NAME	Liber	Folio	REMARKS
Turner, Henry	16	341	Immigrated 1671. Of Dorset Co.
Turner, Henry	15	167	Transported 1673.
Turner, James	7	464	" 1661.
Turner, John	ABH	315	Immigrated 1651.
Turner, John	ABH	323	Transported 1652-3. Son of William.
Turner, John	4	140	" 1652. Servant.
Turner, John	ABH	356	" 1653. Servant.
Turner, John	4	530	" 1659.
Turner, John	7	82	" 1662.
Turner, John	5	412	Immigrated 1663.
Turner, John	6	123	Transported 1663.
Turner, John	6	296	" 1664.
Turner, John	9	38	" 1665.
Turner, John	12	205	" 1667.
Turner, John	17	518	Immigrated 1673, with wife and son. Of Dorset County.
Turner, John	15	552	Transported 1679.
Turner, Judith	8	88	" 1665. Daughter of Thos. Mattingly.
Turner, Margaret	5	2	Transported 1661. Wife of Arthur.
Turner, Mary	ABH	371	Immigrated 1639. Wife of Arthur.
Turner, Mary	11	337,487	Transported 1668.
Turner, Mary	16	358	" 1671.
Turner, Mary	17	552	" from Delaware 1673.
Turner, Mary	15	313	" 1675.
Turner, Mary	WC2	309	" 1678.
Turner, Matthew	15	436	" 1677.
Turner, Miles	WC2	308	" 1678.
Turner, Richard	5	306	" 1663. Servant.
Turner, Richard	16	538	Immigrated from Virginia 1672.
Turner, Richard	15	319,420	" 1675.
Turner, Robert	7	86	" 1663.
Turner, Robert	6	293	Transported 1664.
Turner, Thomas	6	82	Immigrated 1653.
Turner, Thomas	Q	28	Transported 1655.
Turner, Thomas	Q	201,203	Immigrated 1658.
Turner, Thomas	16	170	Transported 1671.
Turner, Thomas	15	167	" 1673.
Turner, Walter	9	24,325	" 1665.
Turner, William	ABH	323	Immigrated 1652-3, with wife.
Turner, William	ABH	323	Transported 1652-3. Son of William.
Turner, William	11	339	" 1668.
Turner, William	12	472	" 1670.
Turner, William	17	40	" 1672.
Turner, William	15	539	" 1678.
Turner, William	WC2	5	Of Calvert Co. Petition for 300 acres due to his sister's son, William Clifton, deceased 1679.
Turner, William	WC2	48	Transported 1679.
Turnerup, Edward	18	17	" 1669.
Turney, Richard	4	5	Immigrated 1659.
Turnor, Arthur	3	63	" 1649 with wife and

NAME	Liber	Folio	REMARKS
			servant.
Turnor, Thomas	WC2	217,330	Transported 1680.
Turpen, William	5	85	" 1661.
Turpinn, William	16	303	Service 1671.
Turrendall, Richard	10	600	Immigrated 1667.
Turtaine, Paul	7	371	Transported 1659.
Turtle, James	7	87	" 1660.
Turvile, Arcadia	15	413	" 1677. Daughter of William.
Turvile, Margery	15	413	Transported 1677. Wife of William.
Turvile, Robert	WC2	127	" 1679.
Turvile, William	15	413	" 1677. Son of William.
Turvile, William	15	413	Immigrated 1677.
Turvill, William	12	479	Service 1670.
Tusen, Sarah	10	352	Transported 1666.
Tutall, John	WC2	21	" 1679.
Tuthill, Jane	15	322	" 1675.
Tutt, Robert	ABH	174	" 1649. Servant.
Tuttle, Peter	WC2	352	" 1680.
Tuxton, Robert	15	428	" 1677.
Tweelve, George	15	449	Immigrated 1677. Son of Robert.
Tweelve, Margaret	15	449	" 1677. Wife of Robert.
Tweelve, Robert	15	449	" 1677. Of Somerset Co.
Tweelve, Robert	15	449	" 1677. Son of Robert.
Twesh, Henry	20	185	Transported 1679.
Twider, Robert	5	339	" 1663.
Twidley, Roger	13	65	" 1668. Servant.
Twiford, Ann	5	12	" 1662.
Twiford, George	WC2	276	Service 1680. Of St. Mary's Co.
Twigg, Charles	6	170	Transported 1655.
Twigg, Francis	6	127	" 1655.
Twiggs, John	5	307	" 1663.
Twiner, Arthur	ABH	50	Immigrated 1649, with wife.
Twist, Hugh	18	334	Transported 1675, with Charles.
Twixtborough, Robert	6	133	" 1650.
Twyford, Francis	17	531	Immigrated 1673. Of Dorset Co.
Twyner, Thomas	10	520	Transported 1667.
Tydings, Richard	4	68	Service 1659.
Tydings, Richard	10	600	" 1667.
Tyfe, Alexander	Q	388	Servant 1658.
Tyle, Joane	5	415	Transported 1662.
Tyler, Edward	5	516	" 1657.
Tyler, Francis	WC2	50,98	" 1679.
Tyler, Robert	5	87	" 1649.
Tyler, Robert	5	487	Service 1662.
Tymbelin, Henry	5	529	Transported 1661.
Tyme, Abram	17	451	" 1671.
Tyrling, John	WC2	412	Immigrated 1681. Of St. Mary's Co.
Tyson, Thomas	5	467	Transported 1661. (6, fol. 19).
Tyson, Thomas	18	291	" 1674.
Tyson, William	12	271	" 1668. Servant.

NAME	Liber	Folio	REMARKS
Ubanck, Richard	15	358	Transported 1675.
Ubanck, Thomas	15	358	" 1675.
Udell, Christopher	15	515	" 1678.
Uentson, Herrigue	12	473	" 1670.
Uige, Jane	7	471	" 1664.
Underhill, Edward	7	90	" 1661.
Underhill, Elizabeth	7	90	Immigrated 1661.
Underwood, An'o.	15	567	Transported 1678.
Underwood, Edward	WC2	16	" 1677.
Underwood, Edward	15	574	" 1678.
Underwood, Elizabeth	5	514	" 1650. Wife of Thomas.
Underwood, Henry	WC2	168-169	" 1680.
Underwood, John	12	404	" 1669.
Underwood, Katherine	10	259	" 1666.
Underwood, Peter	17	572	Service 1673. Of Dorset Co. Left two daughters. Widow married James prior to 1676. (19, fol. 590).
Underwood Rachel	13	114	Transported 1671.
Underwood, Rowland	5	73	" 1660-1.
Underwood, Thomas	5	514	Immigrated 1650.
Underwood, Thomas	15	566	Transported 1678.
Underwood, Thomas	WC2	130	" 1679. Servant.
Underwood, William	15	559	" 1679.
Unketell, Jonathan	8	41	Immigrated 1665.
Upe, Richard	ABH	60	Transported 1637.
Upley, John	5	466	" 1662.
Upperdine, James	15	337	" 1676.
Upton, Grace	17	552	" 1671.
Upton, Mary	WC2	114	" 1680. Servant.
Upton, Matthew	15	337	" 1676.
Upton, Nathaniel	17	603	And Eliz., his wife. Service 1673.
Ursley, Elizabeth	13	65	Transported 1668. Servant.
Uty, Amy	12	355	Service 1669.
Utye, George	Q	234	Brother to Nath. 1658.
Uxgale, Richard	5	126	Immigrated 1660, with wife.
Vahon, Thomas	16	507	Transported 1671.
Valings, Thomas	WC2	106	" 1679.
Valle, Elizabeth	20	185	" 1679.
Vallen, Peter	15	527	" 1678.
Vallenson, Elizabeth	20	185	" 1679.
Vallett, William	16	165	" 1670.
Valley, Elizabeth	7	580	" 1665. Wife of Thomas.
Valley, Elizabeth	7	580	" 1665. Daughter of Thomas.
Valley, John	7	580	Transported 1665. Son of Thomas.
Valley, Margaret	7	580	" 1665. Daughter of Thomas.
Valley, Rachel	7	580	Transported 1665. Daughter of Thomas.
Valley, Thomas	7	580	Immigrated 1665. Of the Eastern Shore.
Valley, Thomas	15	533	Transported 1678.

NAME	Liber	Folio	REMARKS
Vallon, Nicholas	WC2	32	Transported prior to 1679.
Valvar, Anthony	WC2	402	" 1680.
Vandan, Francis	ABH	45,198	And wife. Service 1650.
Vandan, Francis	3	20	Service 1650. Married servant of Thomas Greene, Esq.
Vandrell, Mary	18	291	Transported 1674.
Van Einders, Francis	ABH	60,244	" 1635. Servant.
van Eynden, Francis	1	26	" 1635.
Vanhack, John	ABH	201	" 1650. Son of Katherine, wife of George Mee.
Van Hesse, Margaret	5	223	Transported 1662.
Van Heyst, Abraham	12	243	" 1669. Son of Mrs. Rynier.
Van Heyst, John	12	243	Transported 1669. Son of Mrs. Rynier.
Van Heyst, Mrs. Rynier	12	243	Transported 1669.
Vansweeringen, Mary	WC2	341	Immigrated 1680. Wife of Garrett.
Vansweringen, Garrett	19	381	Of St. Mary's Co. Ante nuptial settlement on Mary Smith, of said county. Spinster, Oct. 5, 1676.
Van Veman, William	10	598	Immigrated 1667.
Varby, Anne	WC2	253	Transported 1679.
Varby, Anne, Jr.	WC2	253	" 1679.
Varby, Elizabeth	WC2	253	" 1679.
Varely, Christopher	15	553	" 1678.
Varely, Christopher, Jr.	15	553	" 1678.
Varely, Elizabeth	15	553	" 1678.
Varely, James	15	553	" 1678.
Varely, Jenett	15	553	" 1678.
Varely, John	15	553	" 1678.
Varely, Mary	15	553	" 1678.
Varhoofe, Anthony	17	567	" 1673.
Varley, James	17	544	And his two wives. Service 1673.
Varlow, James	Q	32	Transported 1653-8.
Varrin, Edward	Q	197	" 1658.
Vas, Sarah	16	537	" from Virginia 1671.
Vaughan, Anne	5	305	" 1663.
Vaughan, Bruton	12	403	" 1669. (18, fol. 28).
Vaughan, David	15	565	" 1679.
Vaughan, Ellen	6	105	" 1662.
Vaughan, Elizabeth	Q	115	" 1655.
Vaughan, John	5	268,536	" 1663. (19, fol. 258).
Vaughan, John	16	553	Immigrated 1671.
Vaughan, John	15	523	" 1678.
Vaughan, Morgan	9	157	Transported 1665.
Vaughan, Rice	12	212	" 1668, with wife and two children.
Vaughan, Richard	ABH	35	Servant 1649.
Vaughan, Richard	2	575	Transported 1649. Servant.
Vaughan, Richard	5	308	" 1663.
Vaughan, Robert	ABH	90,130	Service 1640. (1, fol. 99).
Vaughan, Capt. Robert	2	567	Rights 1649.

NAME	Liber	Folio	REMARKS
Vaughan, Ruth	15	344,395	Service 1675. Wife of Thos. of St. Mary's Co.
Vaughan, Thomas	6	36,37	Immigrated 1663. (15, fol. 441).
Vaughan, William	16	536	" 1671 from Virginia. Of Somerset Co.
Vaukes, David	13	111	Transported 1668. (18, fol. 318).
Vaune, William	WC2	415	" 1666-80. Servant.
Vaux, Leonard	Q	29	" 1658.
Veale, Eleanor	6	26	" 1660-3.
Veale, Elizabeth	WC2	86-87	" 1679.
Veapon, Thomas	13	66	" 1669. Servant.
Vear, Job	15	454	" 1677.
Vecher, John	5	208	" 1662.
Veenson, Floores	10	598	" 1667.
Veez, Cornelius	17	567	" 1673.
Veich, James	ABH	142	Immigrated 1651. Patuxent River.
Veitch, James	Q	107	Married Mary Gakerlin prior to 1658.
Vellett, Sarah	18	387	Transported 1668.
Vellia, Francis	4	555	" 1661.
Venables, John	5	245	" 1662.
Venables, Mary	15	433	" 1677.
Venn, John	17	633	Immigrated 1674. Of St. Mary's Co.
Venner, John	WC2	380	Transported 1675-80. Servant.
Venson, Nathaniel	18	37	" 1673.
Verborgh, Hindrick	WC2	50-51, 56	" 5 servants in 1674.
Verity, John	15	357	" 1676.
Verlow, James	Q	203	" 1658.
Vernall, Robert	WC2	167,169	" 1679.
Vernon, Daniel	18	310	Immigrated 1675.
Versey, Francis	9	336	Transported 1666.
Versey, Sezer	11	438	" 1668. Servant.
Very, Margaret	15	540	" 1676.
Vesey, Margaret	12	278	" 1668.
Viall, John	15	453	" 1676.
Vicaris, John	12	497	Immigrated 1670. Of Somerset Co.
Vicars, Isaac	WC2	309	Transported 1678.
Viccaris, John	9	386	Immigrated 1666.
Viccars, Edward	12	404	Transported 1669.
Viccary, John	15	322	" 1675.
Viccary, Joshua	17	451	" 1671.
Viccary, Mary	15	322	" 1675.
Vicearis, Thomas	17	44	Service 1672. Of Dorset Co.
Vickers, Francis	15	509	Transported 1677.
Vickers, John	18	329	" 1675.
Vicks, David	11	344,465	" 1668.
Vigers, Thomas	8	130	" 1665.
Villaine, John	ABH	10	Immigrated 1646. (2, fol. 427).
Villers, Oliver	18	94	Transported 1674.
Vince, Mary	9	216	" 1665.

NAME	Liber	Folio	REMARKS
Vincent, Charles	6	183,290	Transported 1663. (12, fol. 513).
Vincent, Dorothy	13	66	" 1669. Servant.
Vincent, Elizabeth	15	567	" 1678.
Vincent, Francis	8	495	" 1665.
Vincent, Francis, Gent.	16	357	" 1671. Of St. Mary's Co.
Vincent, Henry	9	333	" 1665.
Vincent, Hon.	9	35	" 1664.
Vincent, Joane	11	36,338	" 1668.
Vincent, John	16	135	" 1671.
Vincent, Mary	8	495	" 1665.
Vine, Mary	7	475	" 1663.
Vine, Elizabeth	7	577	" 1665.
Viner, Henry	5	249	" 1663.
Viner, John	15	564	Immigrated 1678.
Viners, Nathaniel	15	376	Transported 1676.
Vines, Elizabeth	12	548	" 1670.
Vines, Samuel	6	123	" 1663.
Vines, Samuel	9	92	" 1665.
Vines, William	16	12	" 1670.
Vines, William	WC2	77	Service 1679.
Viney, John	10	206,394	Immigrated 1666. Of Talbot Co.
Vinson, Mary	15	422	Transported 1664.
Vinson, Susanna	15	422	" 1664.
Vintin, John	WC2	319	Service 1680.
Virginia	ABH	61	1641.
Visaite, Peter	17	486	Transported 1667.
Vissard, John	9	92	" 1665.
Vissarde, Henry	5	241	Immigrated 1662.
Vitty, Eleanor	16	537	Transported from Virginia 1671.
Vivin, Ralph	18	80	" 1674.
Vizerd, Henry	4	610	" 1661.
Voe, William	15	446	" 1677.
Vointebolonie, Jarvis	12	415	" 1669.
Volley, Cornelius	6	17	" 1663.
Vos, Cornelius	7	464	" 1661.
Vowell, John	12	601	" 1670.
Vowell, John	WC2	123	Service 1674.
Vreison, John	17	590	" 1673. Of Charles Co.
Vyall, John	15	398	Transported 1676.
Vye, Ann	11	548	Service 1668.
Wackham, John	15	322	Transported 1675.
Waddall, James	16	115	" 1671.
Waddall, Roger	13	114	" 1669.
Wadding, William	4	176	" 1659.
Waddington, Jacob	10	324	" 1666.
Waddle, George	6	170	" 1654.
Waddle, Thomas	12	624	Service 1670.
Waddle, William	5	514	Transported 1662.
Waddy, Elizabeth	10	429	" 1664.
Waddy, Jane	9	250	" 1665. Wife of Thomas.
Waddy, Thomas	9	250	Immigrated 1665.

NAME	Liber	Folio	REMARKS
Waddylove, Amy	4	4	Transported 1659. Wife of Nicholas.
Waddylove, Comfort	4	4	" 1659. Daughter of Nicholas.
Waddylove, Nicholas	4	4	Immigrated 1659. Widow married Thos. Fowkes. Brought 4 daughters and 13 servants. (10, fol. 463).
Waddylove, Patience	4	4	Transported 1659. Daughter of Nicholas.
Waddylove, Temperance	4	4	Transported 1659. Daughter of Nicholas.
Wade, Andrew	6	142	Transported 1657.
Wade, Edward	4	72	" 1658.
Wade, Edward	16	308	" 1671.
Wade, Jane	15	301	Service 1675. Of Anne Arundel Co.
Wade, Jeremiah	6	120	Transported 1653.
Wade, Mr. John	ABH	49,166	Immigrated 1648. Chirurgeon.
Wade, John	3	25-26	" 1648. Chirurgeon.
Wade, John	11	338	Transported 1668.
Wade, Margaret	15	567	" 1679.
Wade, Mary	16	482	" 1670-1.
Wade, Robert	6	48	" 1662.
Wade, Robert	11	104,170	" 1667.
Wade, Thomas	5	259	" 1655.
Wade, Zachary	2	575	" 1641. Servant.
Wading, John	WC2	309	" 1680.
Wadson, Abraham	5	64	" 1662.
Wadson, Elizabeth	5	87	" 1649-62.
Wadson, Sarah	Q	239	" 1651.
Wadson, William	5	88	" 1661.
Wadson, William	15	404	" 1676.
Wadsworth, Eleanor	9	399	" 1666. Daughter-in-law of Maximillian Hooper.
Wagent, Katherine	15	527	Transported 1678.
Waghop, Archibald	5	306	Immigrated 1663.
Waghop, John	Q	189	Service 1658. Married widow of John Goss.
Waghop, John	5	516	Immigrated 1659.
Wagstaffe, Francis	7	464	Transported 1660.
Wagstaffe, Mary	17	584	" 1673.
Wahar, Richard	9	156	" 1663.
Waid, Richard	15	300	Service 1675. Of Anne Arundel Co.
Wainwright, Josias	17	632	Transported 1673.
Wake, William	8	501	" 1665.
Wakefield, Elizabeth	18	160	" 1674.
Wakefield, Hester	10	637	" 1677. Wife of Thomas.
Wakefield, John	ABH	141,204	" 1651.
Wakefield, John	16	341	" 1671.
Wakefield, Nicholas	16	358	" 1671. (15, fol. 377).
Wakefield, Pars.	15	454	" Oct. 1677.
Wakefield, Thomas	10	637	Immigrated to Charles Co. 1667. Of Virginia.
Wakefield, Thomas	15	376	Transported 1676.

NAME	Liber	Folio	REMARKS
Wakefield, William	15	599	Transported 1678.
Wakeings, Isaac	WC2	110	" 1676. Servant.
Wakelin, Henry	6	125	" 1659.
Wakenn, George	12	194	" 1668. Servant.
Waker, Mary	7	576	" 1665.
Waker, Richard	5	188	" 1660.
Waker, William	6	18	" 1662.
Wald, Edward	16	165	Immigrated 1670. Of Somerset Co.
Wald, Elizabeth	16	165	" 1670. Wife of Edward.
Walder, Edward	8	129	Transported 1664. Servant.
Wale, Margaret	6	85	" 1654.
Waler, Alice	7	562	" 1665. Wife of John.
Waler, John	7	562	Immigrated 1665.
Waler, Majoe	7	562	Transported 1665. Daughter of John.
Waler, William	7	562	Transported 1665. Son of John.
Walford, Elizabeth	12	190	" 1668.
Walgrove, Mr. William	12	385	" 1669.
Walker, Alice	10	407	Service 1666. Wife of Daniel.
Walker, Ann	15	424	Transported 1677.
Walker, Benjamin	12	497	" 1670. Son of Daniel.
Walker, Catherine	6	136-137	" 1658.
Walker, Daniel	5	514	" 1657. Servant. (18, fol. 8).
Walker, Daniel	12	497	Immigrated 1670. Of Somerset Co.
Walker, Earskin	17	463	Transported 1673.
Walker, Elizabeth	16	112	" 1671.
Walker, Francis	9	35	" 1664.
Walker, Francis	18	283	" 1674.
Walker, George	9	400	" 1666.
Walker, Hannah	WC2	112	" 1679.
Walker, Henry	9	400	" 1666.
Walker, James	2	457	Service about 1645.
Walker, James	3	23	Transported before 1648.
Walker, James	ABH	15,47	Service 1648.
Walker, James	Q	2	Immigrated 1657.
Walker, James	10	498	Transported 1667.
Walker, James	18	291	" 1674.
Walker, John	1	19	" 1638.
Walker, John	Q	70	" 1658.
Walker, John	10	343	" 1665.
Walker, John	9	332	" 1666.
Walker, John	13	114	" 1671.
Walker, John	12	498	" 1670.
Walker, John	16	167	Service 1670. Of Somerset Co.
Walker, John	18	10	And Frances, his wife. Service 1673.
Walker, John	18	152	Transported 1674.
Walker, John	15	454	" 1677.
Walker, John	WC2	319	Immigrated 1680.
Walker, John	WC2	319	Transported 1680. Servant.

NAME	Liber	Folio	REMARKS
Walker, Joseph	6	80	Transported 1659.
Walker, Katherine	18	137	" 1674.
Walker, Mager	15	430	" 1677.
Walker, Margery	15	414	" 1677.
Walker, Mary	19	503	" 1676.
Walker, Mary	15	424	" 1677.
Walker, Patience	WC2	66	" 1679.
Walker, Peter	11	517	" 1668. Servant.
Walker, Richard	ABH	78,101	" 1637-40. Servant.
Walker, Richard	1	63,128	" 1640.
Walker, Richard	18	94	" 1674.
Walker, Robert	12	189	" 1668.
Walker, Robert	18	287	" 1674.
Walker, Simon	19	503	" 1676.
Walker, Simon	15	424	" 1677.
Walker, Thomas	8	202	" 1665. (11, fol. 235).
Walker, Thomas	10	465	Immigrated 1667.
Walker, Thomas	16	133	Transported 1671. (15, fol. 362).
Walker, Thomas	WC2	309	" 1678. (15, fol. 553).
Walker, Thomas	WC2	49,119	Service 1679. Of Calvert Co. (WC2, fol. 164, 309, 390, 391).
Walker, Thomas	WC2	390-391	Married Sarah Osbourne. Of Dorchester Co.
Walker, William	6	106	Transported 1662.
Walker, William	12	576	" 1670.
Walkerton, Joanna	17	488	" 1665.
Walkin, Abraham	5	339	" 1663.
Walkins, Evan	ABH	98	" 1633. Servant.
Walkins, John	5	253	" 1663.
Wall, Alice	18	301	" 1675. Daughter of Thomas.
Wall, Alice	15	499	Transported 1677.
Wall, Andrew	4	610	" 1661.
Wall, Joane	17	578	" 1673.
Wall, John	6	10	" 1663.
Wall, John	15	433	" 1677.
Wall, Lawrence	12	190	" 1668.
Wall, Peirce	WC2	287	" 1680.
Wall, Richard	15	443	" 1670.
Wall, Thomas	18	301	Service 1675. Of Dorchester Co. And Alice, his wife.
Wallas, Joseph	16	411	Transported 1671.
Wallbie, John	10	312	" 1664.
Wallby, John	9	191	" 1665. Servant.
Walle, Isabell	9	280	" 1665.
Waller, Christopher	12	404	" 1669.
Waller, John	ABH	348	" prior to 1652. Servant.
Waller, William	15	451	" 1678.
Walley, Amphillis	15	371	" 1675.
Walley, Catherine	13	112	" 1670.
Walley, Elizabeth	8	19	" 1665. Wife of Thomas.

NAME	Liber	Folio	REMARKS
Walley, John	8	19	Transported 1665. Son of Thomas.
Walley, Margaret	8	19	" 1665. Daughter of Thomas.
Walley, Rachel	8	19	Transported 1665. Daughter of Thomas.
Walley, Thomas	WC2	17,99	Transported 1679. Servant.
Wallingford, Thomas	16	71	" 1670.
Wallis, Abraham	6	36	" 1663. (8, fol. 410).
Wallis, Alexander	18	152	" 1674.
Wallis, Annis	ABH	356	" 1648. Servant.
Wallis, Catherine	5	56	" 1660.
Wallis, Christopher	6	294	" 1664.
Wallis, Hugh	18	167	" 1674.
Wallis, Joane	18	137	" 1674.
Wallis, Joane	WC2	301,302	Service 1680.
Wallis, Katherine	5	253	Transported 1663.
Wallis, Mary	18	137	" 1674.
Wallis, Richard	15	353	" 1676.
Wallis, Richard	15	446	" 1677.
Wallis, Thomas	16	507	" 1672.
Wallis, William	11	581	" 1668.
Wallis, William	18	152	" 1674.
Walls, John	15	445	" 1678.
Wallston, John	18	305	Immigrated 1675. Of Baltimore Co.
Wallton, Thomas	5	66	Transported 1662.
Wally, Piers	WC2	128	" 1679.
Wally, Thomas	8	19	Immigrated 1665. (See Valley).
Walmer, William	15	543	" 1673.
Walmesley, Mary	Q	453	Transported 1658.
Walraven, Mathias, G.V.A.	17	573	Immigrated 1673. Of St. Mary's Co.
Walson, William	15	390	Transported 1675.
Walstore, William	11	264	Immigrated 1667. Of St. Mary's Co.
Walter, Anne	WC2	118	Transported 1679. Daughter of Thomas.
Walter, Christopher	4	29	Transported 1659. Servant.
Walter, Emanuel	13	114	" 1671.
Walter, John	2	347	" 1642. Servant.
Walter, Richard	15	370	" 1676.
Walter, Roger	ABH	60	" 1635. (1, fol. 26).
Walter, Samuel	18	178	Service 1674. Of Charles Co.
Walter, Thomas	18	128	Transported 1674.
Walter, Thomas, Jr.	WC2	118	" 1679.
Walter, Thomas, Sr.	WC2	118	Immigrated 1679 with wife and two children. Of Somerset County.
Walter, William	17	383	Transported 1672.
Walterlin, Walter	1	26	" 1635.
Walterlin, Walter	ABH	37,60	" 1635-41. Servant.
Walters, Andrew	6	172	" 1663.
Walters, Diana	14	347	" 1671.
Walters, Hester	14	347	" 1671.

NAME	Liber	Folio	REMARKS
Walters, Humphrey	4	551	Transported 1661.
Walters, James	15	445	" 1678.
Walters, John	9	460	" 1662.
Walters, John	12	190	" 1668.
Walters, John	14	347	Immigrated 1671. Of Charles Co.
Walters, Peter	6	129	Transported 1651.
Walters, Phoebe	14	347	" 1671.
Walters, Thomas	15	446	" 1677.
Walters, William	5	74	Of Accomack, Virginia. Acquired land in Maryland, 1662.
Walterworth, Ann	15	378	Transported 1674.
Waltham, John	ABH	6	Immigrated 1647.
Walton, Eleanor	4	555	Transported 1661. Wife of John.
Walton, Francis	ABH	151	" 1649-50. Servant. (Q, fol. 259).
Walton, Jane	4	555	Transported 1661.
Walton, John	5	305	Immigrated 1649.
Walton, John	WC2	21	Transported 1679.
Walton, John	ABH	377	" 1653. Servant.
Walton, John	4	555	Immigrated 1661.
Walton, John	16	85	Transported 1670.
Walton, Rebecca	15	318	" 1675. Wife of William.
Walton, Roger	17	416	" 1673.
Walton, Thomas	Q	183,208	" 1655.
Walton, Thomas	5	123	" 1662.
Walton, William	15	318	Immigrated from Virginia 1675.
Waltonne, Mary	12	215	Transported 1668-9.
Wamsley, John	12	280	" 1668. Servant.
Wamsley, Thomas	10	598	Immigrated 1667.
Wancklen, John	9	100	Transported 1665.
Wanckling, Jane	7	83	" 1664.
Wanfield, Elizabeth	5	207	" 1662.
Wanham, Giles	9	313	" 1665.
Wanis, Thomas	7	154	" 1663.
Wanlas, James	15	442	" 1677.
Wanles, Richard	9	451	" 1666.
Waples, Frances	15	532	" 1678. Wife of Peter.
Waples, Peter	15	532	Immigrated from Virginia 1678. Of Somerset Co. Cordwainer.
Wapshot, Jane	18	174	Transported 1674.
Wapshott, Thomas	17	600	Immigrated 1672, with Jane, his wife.
War, Thomas	2	340	Immigrated 1648 with wife and two children.
Warbrooke, John	WC2	309	Transported 1678.
Warburton, Cassandra	17	411	" 1673. (18, fol. 285).
Warburton, Mary	15	446	" 1677.
Ward, Alicia	Q	69	" 1658.
Ward, Andrew	11	525	Immigrated 1668.
Ward, Ann	5	218	Transported 1662.
Ward, Ann	15	317	" 1674.

NAME	Liber	Folio	REMARKS
Ward, Anne	WC2	213-214	Transported 1671-3.
Ward, Edmond	ABH	244	" 1641.
Ward, Edward	5	404	" 1659.
Ward, Edward	5	393	" 1663. (12, fol. 222).
Ward, Elizabeth	Q	359	Widow of Thos., and wife of Deliverance Lovely, 1658.
Ward, Elizabeth	8	484	Transported 1665.
Ward, Elizabeth	5	218	" 1662.
Ward, Elizabeth	16	165	" 1670.
Ward, Esame	8	484	" 1665.
Ward, Hannah	5	123	" 1662.
Ward, Henry	8	484	Immigrated 1665.
Ward, Henry	18	334	Transported 1675.
Ward, Isabella	8	484	" 1665.
Ward, Jo.	2	345	Immigrated 1646.
Ward, John	ABH	66	Transported 1633. (1, fol. 38).
Ward, John	ABH	6,48	Immigrated 1646.
Ward, John	3	25	" 1647.
Ward, John	5	252	Transported 1648.
Ward, John	ABH	150	Immigrated 1651.
Ward, John	11	338	Transported 1668. (12, fol. 341).
Ward, John	12	215	" 1668-9.
Ward, John	WC2	124	" 1673. Servant.
Ward, John	15	438	" 1677.
Ward, John	WC2	201	" 1680. Servant.
Ward, Joshua	4	216	" 1659.
Ward, Joyce	18	279	" 1675.
Ward, Lawrence	ABH	251	Immigrated 1651.
Ward, Margaret	11	525	Transported 1668. Wife of Andrew.
Ward, Margaret	16	79,630	" 1670.
Ward, Margaret	18	39	Service 1674. Wife of Cornelius.
Ward, Mary	16	79	Transported 1670.
Ward, Mary, 2nd	16	79	" 1670.
Ward, Mr. Matthew, Gent.	16	356-358	Of St. Mary's Co. Atty. of Prov. Court Commn. to take probate of rights in Talbot, Kent and Baltimore Counties, 1671.
Ward, Nathaniel	6	122	Transported 1661.
Ward, Richard	15	353	" 1676.
Ward, Richard	15	440	Immigrated 1677.
Ward, Robert	7	491	Transported 1663.
Ward, Robert	16	79,170	" 1670.
Ward, Thomas	ABH	241	Immigrated 1649. Surgeon. (Q, fol. 359).
Ward, Thomas	5	306	Transported 1663.
Ward, Thomas	11	379	" 1668.
Ward, Thomas	17	416,608	" 1673.
Ward, Valentine	12	209	" 1668.
Ward, William	ABH	202	" 1650-1. Servant.
Ward, William	10	276	Immigrated from Virginia 1666.
Ward, William	15	344	Transported from Virginia 1675 with Sarah, his wife. (15, fol. 405).

NAME	Liber	Folio	REMARKS
Ward, William	WC2	309	Transported 1680.
Warde, Alexander	15	530	" 1678.
Warde, Christiana	18	316	" 1674. Daughter of Thomas.
Warde, Cornelius	15	407	Immigrated 1676.
Warde, Cornelius	WC2	98	" 1679 with wife.
Warde, John	17	469	Transported 1673.
Warde, John	18	174	" 1674.
Warde, Margaret	19	258	" 1663.
Warde, Margaret	15	407	" 1676.
Warde, Margaret	WC2	98	" 1679. Wife of Cornelius.
Warde, Mary	18	173	Transported 1674.
Warde, Mathew	17	59	Of Talbot Co. Gent. Aged 35 years in 1672.
Warde, Rebecca	18	316	Transported 1674. Wife of Thomas.
Warde, Richard	15	376	" 1676.
Warde, Samuel	15	430,431	" 1677.
Warde, Thomas	18	316	Service 1674. Of St. Mary's Co.
Warden, John	7	372	Transported 1664.
Warder, John	17	497	And Margery. Service 1671.
Warder, Thomas	ABH	59	Transported 1641.
Wardner, Andrew	7	87	His widow married Rich. Gaines prior to 1664.
Wardner, Christopher	12	189	Transported 1668.
Wardner, Sarah	11	237	" 1667. Wife of Thomas.
Wardner, Thomas	11	237	Immigrated 1667. Of St. Mary's Co.
Ware, Catherine	ABH	336	Transported March 1652. Kinswoman of Wm. Stevens.
Ware, Cornelius	5	73,255	Transported 1661.
Ware, Elizabeth	8	460	" 1662.
Ware, Ellen	16	507	" 1671.
Ware, Emanuel	16	394	" 1671.
Ware, Michael	16	393	" 1671.
Ware, Richard	ABH	15,180	Immigrated 1645. (2, fol. 458).
Warfield, Elizabeth	18	94	Transported 1674.
Warfield, Richard	18	165	Service 1660. Of Anne Arundel Co.
Warfield, Richard	5	484	Transported 1662.
Warfrey, Lewis	5	246	" 1663.
Warham, John	17	449	" 1672.
Warin, Thomas	5	417	" 1663.
Waring, Francis	8	87	" 1665. Servant.
Waring, Thomas	WC2	106	" 1679.
Warley, Matthew	15	397	" 1676.
Warner, Andrew	ABH	201	Immigrated 1650-1.
Warner, Ann	15	560	Transported 1678.
Warner, George	20	284	Of Cecil Co. Married Eliz., daughter of Godfrey Bailey, prior to 1679.
Warner, Henry	16	174	Transported 1672.
Warner, Isabella	ABH	201	" 1651. Daughter of Andrew.

NAME	Liber	Folio	REMARKS
Warner, John	4	68	Transported 1659.
Warner, John	16	83	" 1670.
Warner, Mary	ABH	201	" 1651. Wife of Andrew.
Warner, Mary	11	509	" 1668. Daughter of William.
Warner, Mary	16	507	Transported 1671.
Warner, Ruth	11	509	" 1668. Wife of William.
Warner, Ruth	11	509	" 1668. Daughter of William.
Warner, Samuel	15	517	Transported 1678.
Warner, William	11	509	Immigrated from Virginia to St. Mary's Co. 1668.
Warpe, John	6	80	Transported 1657.
Warr, Bernard	15	443	" 1677.
Warr, Thomas	ABH	6	Immigrated 1648, with wife and two children.
Warrall, Francis	WC2	254	Transported 1680.
Warre, John	17	596	" 1673.
Warren, Fran.	15	359	" 1676.
Warren, Henry, Esq.	5	308	Immigrated 1661.
Warren, Humphrey	5	235-236	" 1662. Merchant.
Warren, Humphrey	5	235-236	Transported 1662. Son of Humphrey. (9, fol. 309).
Warren, Humphrey	WC2	81	Son and heir of Humphrey 1679. Of Charles Co.
Warren, James	9	334	Transported 1666.
Warren, John	ABH	37,64	Servant 1638.
Warren, John	1	33,171	Transported 1638. Servant. (2, fol. 605).
Warren, John	2	512	Immigrated 1646 with wife.
Warren, John	ABH	24	Transported 1646 with wife.
Warren, John	ABH	133	And wife. Servants 1650.
Warren, Lawrence	16	507	Transported 1671.
Warren, Mary	18	318	" 1675.
Warren, Mary	15	531	" 1678.
Warren, Patrick	15	527	" 1678.
Warren, Richard	15	318	Immigrated from Virginia 1674.
Warren, Thomas	5	305	Transported 1663. (6, fol. 7).
Warren, Valentine	6	106	" 1660.
Warren, William	ABH	25,35	Servant 1648.
Warren, William	2	516,575	Transported 1648. Servant.
Warren, William	ABH	49	" 1650. Servant. (3, fol. 62).
Warren, William	4	17	Immigrated 1659.
Warren, William	6	134	Transported 1657.
Warren, William	16	414	" 1671.
Warrenton, Elizabeth	10	499	" 1667.
Warrfield, Elizabeth	5	207	" 1662.
Warrick, John	12	617	" 1670.
Warrin, Ann	17	614	" 1673.
Warring, John	12	459	" 1669.

NAME	Liber	Folio	REMARKS
Warring, Sampson	12	200	Aged 50 years in 1668.
Warring, Sarah	Q	32	Transported 1653-8 (?) Wife of Sampson.
Warring, Thomas	11	228	Service 1667. Of St. Mary's Co.
Warringer, Margaret	7	483	Transported 1664.
Warry, Robert	16	100	" 1667.
Warthy, Ambrose	17	571	" 1673.
Warwick, Henry	6	131	" 1657.
Warwick, Jane	15	553	" 1678.
Warwick, Jeane	WC2	56	" 1679.
Warwick, William	18	137	" 1674.
Wasbe, John	12	285	" 1668. Servant.
Washford, Ann	10	573	" 1667.
Wason, Philip	11	4	" 1667. Servant.
Wasse, James	18	302	Citizen and Chirurgeon of London, acquires Radcliffe Manor in Maryland, 1674.
Wasse, James	15	358	Transported 1675.
Wasse, John	11	374	" 1668.
Wassey, Christopher	5	253	" 1663.
Wasy, John	12	209	" 1668.
Water, Joseph	ABH	229	" 1652. Servant.
Watercase, Theodorick	13	116	" 1671.
Waterhouse, Anna	5	55	" 1661.
Waterhouse, John	17	40,411	" 1673.
Waterhouse, John	18	279	" 1675.
Waterland, Michael	9	155	" 1665.
Waterling, Walter	ABH	244	" 1635.
Waterling, Walter	2	606	Service 1649.
Waterman, Ellen	9	52	Transported 1659. Wife of Nicholas.
Waterman, Nicholas	ABH	348	" 1652. Servant.
Waterman, Nicholas	9	52	Immigrated 1659. Of Anne Arundel County.
Waters, Alexander	10	311	Of Kent Co. Married Margaret, daughter of Andrew Hanson, prior to 1666.
Waters, Alexander	WC2	153,154, 155	Service prior to 1669. Of Kent Co.
Waters, Ann	WC2	50,98	Transported 1679.
Waters, Christopher	17	485	" 1666.
Waters, Edward	5	260	" 1660.
Waters, Edward	12	381,416	" 1669.
Waters, Francis	8	501	" 1665.
Waters, Francis	15	407	Immigrated 1676.
Waters, George	ABH	49	Transported 1649. Servant.
Waters, George	18	306	" 1675.
Waters, Griffith	18	149	" 1669.
Waters, Hannah	16	118	" 1671.
Waters, John	12	269	" 1668.
Waters, John	12	217	" 1669.
Waters, Jonathan	7	464	" 1660.
Waters, Judith	15	430	" 1677.
Waters, Mary	5	89	" 1661.

NAME	Liber	Folio	REMARKS
Waters, Mary	10	559	Transported 1667. Daughter of Richard.
Waters, Mary	10	559	Transported 1667. Wife of Richard.
Waters, Mary	WC2	406	" 1680.
Waters, Richard	10	559	" 1667. Son of Richard.
Waters, Richard	10	559	Immigrated from York in Va. 1667. Of Talbot Co. Cooper.
Waters, Sampson	18	35	Immigrated 1672. Mariner.
Waters, Thomas	ABH	49	Transported 1649. Servant. (3, fol. 62).
Waters, Thomas	5	255	Immigrated 1663.
Waters, Thomas	10	179,180	" 1666. Of St. Mary's Co. Drummer.
Waters, Thomas	10	559	Transported 1667. Son of Richard.
Waters, Thomas	17	463	" 1673.
Waters, Thomas	ABH	36	" 1640.
Waters, Walter	2	604	" about 1640.
Waters, William	5	221	Cousin to Capt. Miles Cooke, 1662.
Waterson, Robert	12	386	Immigrated from Virginia 1669.
Waterton, Michael	9	304	Transported 1665.
Wath, Mary	15	430	" 1674.
Wathen, John	18	16	Service 1674.
Wathen, William	11	338	Of Bristol. Master of the ship "Providence", proves rights to 400 acres, 1668.
Watkins, Ann	10	541	Transported 1667.
Watkins, Evan	1	121	" 1633.
Watkins, Francis	16	175	" 1671.
Watkins, Francis	WC2	150	Immigrated 1680. Of Baltimore Co.
Watkins, Henry	18	291	Transported 1674.
Watkins, James	8	130	" 1664.
Watkins, James	8	501	" 1665.
Watkins, John	Q	70	Son-in-law of Mr. Edward Lloyd, 1658.
Watkins, John	8	40	Transported 1665. Servant.
Watkins, John	15	445	" 1678.
Watkins, Lydia	WC2	334	Widow of Thomas, 1680.
Watkins, Mary	10	541	Transported 1667.
Watkins, Sybell	12	373	" 1669.
Watkins, Thomas	10	1	" 1666.
Watkins, Thomas	19	609	Of Anne Arundel Co. Married Eliz., daughter of Henry Cattline, prior to 1677.
Watkins, Thomas	15	455	Transported 1678.
Watkins, Thomas	16	393	" 1671.
Watkins, Thomas	WC2	411	" 1681.
Watkins, William	16	531	Service 1672. Of Dorset Co.
Watkins, Zachariah	10	541	Transported 1667.
Watkinson, Cornelius	13	66	Immigrated 1670. Of Charles Co.
Watkinson, Cornelius, Jr.	13	66	Transported 1670.
Watkinson, Jane	13	66	" 1670. Wife of Cornelius.
Watlow, Elizabeth	15	430	Transported 1677.

NAME	Liber	Folio	REMARKS
Watmere, John	20	2	Transported 1678.
Watson, Abraham	5	65	Immigrated 1661.
Watson, Andrew	ABH	377,378	" 1650.
Watson, Anthony	13	1	Transported 1669. Servant.
Watson, Elizabeth	17	597	Service 1673. Wife of Thos., of Talbot Co.
Watson, George	17	33	Service 1672. Of Somerset Co.
Watson, Henry	13	1	Transported 1669. Servant.
Watson, James	17	440	" 1673.
Watson, Jane	16	461	Service 1672. Wife of John.
Watson, Jane	18	152	Transported 1674.
Watson, Jane	WC2	17,99	" 1679. Wife of Peter.
Watson, John	12	269	" 1669. Servant.
Watson, John	15	559	" 1679.
Watson, John	WC2	17,96,99	" 1679. Son of Peter.
Watson, John	18	331	" 1674.
Watson, John	15	530	" 1678.
Watson, Margaret	18	84	" 1674.
Watson, Mary	18	37	" 1673.
Watson, Mary	WC2	17,99	" 1679. Daughter of Peter.
Watson, Onin	9	216	Transported 1665.
Watson, Peter	WC2	17,99	Immigrated 1679 with wife and three children. Of Somerset County.
Watson, Peter, Jr.	WC2	17,99	Transported 1679.
Watson, Rebecca	5	253	" 1663. Wife of William.
Watson, Richard	ABH	229,347	" 1651. Servant.
Watson, Richard	11	337	" 1668. Servant.
Watson, Sarah	ABH	140	" 1651.
Watson, Thomas	Q	68	Servant 1653-8.
Watson, Thomas	8	478	Transported 1665.
Watson, Thomas	17	376	" 1672.
Watson, William	7	639	Service 1665.
Watson, William	18	335	Immigrated 1675. Of Dorset Co.
Watterman, Nicholas	9	476	" 1665, with wife.
Watters, Christopher	WC2	65	Transported 1679.
Watters, Thomas	18	174	" 1674.
Wattkin, James	9	313	" 1665.
Wattkins, Ann	4	30	" 1659. Servant.
Wattkins, Thomas	5	359	" 1663.
Wattkins, Walter	6	172	" 1663.
Watton, Anthony	15	375	Immigrated 1676. Of Talbot Co.
Watton, William	15	360	Transported 1676.
Watts, Alexander	ABH	150	" 1648. Servant.
Watts, Ann	7	560	" 1665.
Watts, Ann	9	34	" 1665. Wife of George.
Watts, Ann	10	570	" 1666. Daughter of George, of Talbot Co.
Watts, Ann	15	430	Transported 1677.
Watts, Christopher	11	581	" 1668.
Watts, Dorothy	15	566	" 1679.

NAME	Liber	Folio	REMARKS
Watts, Edward	5	482	Transported 1662.
Watts, Eleanor	5	129	" 1662. (10, fol. 325).
Watts, Eleanor	16	115	" 1671.
Watts, Elizabeth	9	92	" 1665.
Watts, Francis	4	66	" 1651.
Watts, Gabriell	6	166	" 1660.
Watts, George	3	63	" about 1640. Servant.
Watts, George	9	343	" 1663.
Watts, George	9	34	Immigrated 1665.
Watts, George	9	34	Transported 1665. Son of George.
Watts, George	9	431	Immigrated from Virginia 1666.
Watts, George	10	563	Transported 1667.
Watts, George	17	572	" 1672. (18, fol. 338).
Watts, Joane	5	467	" 1663.
Watts, John	Q	68	" 1657.
Watts, John	5	242	Immigrated 1662.
Watts, John	9	155	Service 1663. Of the Isle of Kent.
Watts, John	9	34	Transported 1665. Son of George.
Watts, John	12	190	" 1668. Servant.
Watts, John	12	351	" 1669.
Watts, John	16	339	" 1671.
Watts, Joyce	9	431	" 1666. Wife of George.
Watts, Katherine	11	378	" 1668.
Watts, Margarett	1	166	" 1650. Servant.
Watts, Mary	10	570	" 1666. Daughter of George.
Watts, Mary	15	314	Transported 1675.
Watts, Mary	15	397	" 1676.
Watts, Hindell	15	567	" 1679.
Watts, Peter	7	528	Immigrated 1664.
Watts, Peter	15	512	Transported 1678.
Watts, William	5	320	Immigrated 1646.
Watts, William	ABH	150	Transported 1648. Servant.
Watts, William	2	425	" 1648.
Watts, William	9	34	" 1665. Son of George.
Wattson, Alexander	4	11	" 1659. Servant.
Wattson, David	15	454	" 1677.
Wattson, Elizabeth	6	94	" 1656.
Wattson, Elizabeth	4	59	" 1657.
Wattson, Elizabeth	6	290	" 1663.
Wattson, John	9	100	" 1665.
Wattson, John	11	581	" 1668.
Wattson, Katherine	6	267	" 1649. Wife of Richard.
Wattson, Katherine	11	541	" 1668.
Wattson, Mens	4	68	" 1649.
Wattson, Robert	9	386	" 1666.
Wattson, Thomas	9	304	" 1665.
Wattson, William	4	538	" 1659.
Wattson, William	15	541	Service 1678. Of Dorset Co. And Frances, his wife.
Waye, Richard	5	248	Transported 1663.

NAME	Liber	Folio	REMARKS
Wayham, John	5	203	Transported 1662.
Wayman, Leonard	15	301	Service 1675. Of Anne Arundel Co.
Wayman, Miles	15	362	Transported 1676.
Wayncote, John	15	557	" 1676. Servant.
Wayte, James	17	440	" 1673.
Wayte, John	17	440	" 1673.
Waytes, Robert	15	369	" 1676.
Weade, Richard	12	403	" 1669.
Weatherborne, William	15	390	" 1676.
Weatherer, Gabriell	16	407	" 1671.
Weaver, Adam	17	575	Service 1673. Of Calvert Co.
Webb, Alice	6	132	Transported 1657.
Webb, Anne	WC2	253	" 1680.
Webb, Anthony	10	434	" 1667.
Webb, Arthur	1	18	" 1637.
Webb, Benjamin	15	376	" 1676.
Webb, Christopher	6	142	" 1654.
Webb, Deborah	5	253	" 1663.
Webb, Edmond	17	54	Service 1672.
Webb, Eleanor	8	502	Transported 1665.
Webb, Elizabeth	15	451	" 1678. Daughter of William.
Webb, Elizabeth	15	569	Transported 1679.
Webb, Emera	WC2	146,162	" 1680.
Webb, Francis	15	436	" 1677.
Webb, George	6	85	" 1655.
Webb, Hannah	15	451	" 1678. Wife of William.
Webb, John	ABH	141	Immigrated 1651. Of Patuxent River.
Webb, John	15	435	Transported 1677.
Webb, John	20	45	Married Susanna, widow of Thos. Webb, John Barbary, Calvert Co., prior to 1678.
Webb, John	WC2	8	Immigrated 1679. Of Calvert Co.
Webb, Jone	8	88	Transported 1665.
Webb, Mary	5	89	" 1661.
Webb, Mary	6	90	" 1661.
Webb, Mary	6	71	" 1663.
Webb, Mary	15	532	Service 1678. Wife of Richard, of Somerset Co. Planter.
Webb, Mary	15	451	Transported 1678. Daughter of William.
Webb, Michael	7	639	Transported 1665.
Webb, Peter	6	85	" 1658.
Webb, Richard	Q	29	Servant 1658.
Webb, Richard	6	160	Immigrated 1661.
Webb, Richard	16	309,507	" from Virginia 1671. Of Somerset Co.
Webb, Richard	15	381	Service 1675. Of Charles Co.
Webb, Richard	WC2	406	Transported 1677. (15, fol. 454).
Webb, Robert	4	198	" 1659. (6, fol. 63).
Webb, Robert	8	501	" 1665. (9, fol. 189).

NAME	Liber	Folio	REMARKS
Webb, Roger	ABH	349	Transported 1641. Servant.
Webb, Roger	4	79	" 1654. Servant.
Webb, Stephen	9	400	" 1666.
Webb, Thomas	9	105	" 1665.
Webb, Thomas	15	451	" 1678. Son of William.
Webb, William	7	560	" 1665.
Webb, William	15	418	Immigrated 1673, with Ann, his wife. (18, fol. 36).
Webb, William	18	33	Transported 1674.
Webb, William	18	335	" 1675.
Webb, William	15	451	Immigrated 1678.
Webber, John	16	41	Transported 1670.
Webbor, Humphrey	6	170	" 1663.
Webscum, John	5	489	" 1653.
Webster, Dorothy	17	605	Service 1673. Wife of John.
Webster, Edward	WC2	24,106	Transported 1678. Servant.
Webster, George	6	159	" 1657.
Webster, John	5	90	" 1653-61.
Webster, John	7	84	" 1663. (11, fol. 500).
Webster, John	11	582	" 1668. (12, fol. 194).
Webster, John	17	24	Service 1672.
Webster, Jolling	9	326	Transported 1665.
Webster, Joshua	8	478	" 1665.
Webster, Mark	6	126	" 1649.
Webster, Nicholas	7	484	" 1664.
Webster, Peter	6	81	" 1659.
Webster, Thomas	17	40	" 1672.
Weddill, Roger	17	418	And Christian, his wife. Service 1673.
Wedge, Jane	18	84	Transported 1674.
Wedge, John	5	488	" 1651-62. (16, fol. 127).
Wedge, Robert	17	551	" 1673.
Wedy, Mary	17	463	" 1673.
Weeb, Thomas	12	403	" 1669.
Weeb, William	16	372,393	" 1671.
Weecomb, Samuel	15	447	" 1677.
Weedingham, Anne	WC2	77	Servant 1679.
Weedon, James	10	213	Transported 1665.
Weedon, Ruth	10	213	" 1665.
Weeke, John	17	454	Service 1672.
Weeke, Thomas	12	351	Transported 1669.
Weekes, John	15	443	" 1677.
Weekes, Martin	WC2	217	" 1680.
Weekes, Richard	15	565	" 1679.
Weekes, William	Q	430	" 1658.
Weeks, Henry	7	86	" 1663.
Weeks, Joseph	ABH	164	Immigrated 1651.
Weeks, Margaret	6	89	Transported 1663.
Weel, Thomas	12	403	" 1669. (See Weeb).
Weeldin, Henry	11	440	" 1668.
Weight, Jonathan	18	84	" 1674.

NAME	Liber	Folio	REMARKS
Weikes, Martha	12	500	Transported 1670.
Weirlock, Thomas	15	553	" 1678.
Welborne, Robert	5	516	" 1662.
Welborne, Samuel	7	463	" 1659.
Welch, Anthony	6	37	" 1663.
Welch, Bernard	6	118	" 1657.
Welch, Daniel	6	89	" 1663.
Welch, Dankum	16	85	" 1670.
Welch, Edward	15	380,381	" 1676.
Welch, James	WC2	89	" 1676. Servant.
Welch, John	11	379	" 1668.
Welch, John	17	408	" 1673.
Welch, John	16	370	" 1671.
Welch, John	WC2	21,45	" 1679.
Welch, Jone	15	381	" 1676.
Welch, Jone	15	438	" 1677.
Welch, Morris	11	378	" 1668.
Welch, Richard	15	322	" 1674.
Welch, Robert	5	257	" 1655.
Welch, Thomas	15	397	" 1675.
Welch, Thomas	12	278	" 1669.
Welde, Anthony	7	507	" 1664.
Welden, John	12	209,315	" 1666.
Weldon, Henry	11	337	" 1667.
Weldon, Hugh	11	337	" 1668. (11,fol. 487).
Wellberks, Richard	10	598	" 1667.
Weller, William	6	263	" 1662.
Wellin, Thomas	9	48	" 1665.
Wellings, Joseph	15	429	" 1674.
Wellman, Henry	15	370	" 1676.
Wellman, Michael	WC2	106	" 1679.
Wells, Amy	5	249	" 1663.
Wells, Ann	ABH	347	" 1652-3. Daughter of Richard.
Wells, Anna	Q	71	Immigrated 1652-3.
Wells, Barbara	6	107	Transported 1669.
Wells, Bartholomew	7	577	" 1665.
Wells, Bartholomey	5	12	" 1662.
Wells, Benjamin	Q	71	Immigrated 1652-3.
Wells, Benjamin	ABH	347	Transported 1652. Son of Richard.
Wells, Chris	4	14	" 1653. Servant.
Wells, Edward	5	247	" 1651. Child of Robt. Kingsberry.
Wells, Eleanor	7	614	Transported 1665.
Wells, Eleanor	16	435	" 1671.
Wells, Elizabeth	5	247	" 1651. Child of Robt. Kingsberry.
Wells, Elizabeth	Q	71	Immigrated 1652-3.
Wells, Elizabeth	ABH	347	Transported 1652. Daughter of Richard.
Wells, Elizabeth	5	342	Transported 1661-2.

NAME	Liber	Folio	REMARKS
Wells, Elizabeth	7	519	Transported 1664.
Wells, Elizabeth	10	407	" 1666. Servant.
Wells, Elizabeth	18	166	" 1674.
Wells, Elizabeth	15	429	" 1677.
Wells, Ellen	10	4	" 1665.
Wells, Frances	ABH	347	" 1652-3. Wife of Richard.
Wells, Frances	ABH	347	Transported 1652-3. Daughter of Richard.
Wells, Francis	Q	71	Immigrated 1652-3.
Wells, Francis	12	391	Transported 1669. (15, fol. 523).
Wells, Francis, Jr.	Q	71	Immigrated 1652-3.
Wells, George	Q	71	" 1652-3.
Wells, George	ABH	347	Transported 1652-3. Son of Richard.
Wells, Grace	ABH	35	Transported 1649. Servant. (2, fol. 575).
Wells, Henry	11	374	Transported 1668.
Wells, James	11	582	" 1668.
Wells, John	Q	71	Immigrated 1652-3.
Wells, John	ABH	347	Transported 1652-3. Son of Richard.
Wells, John	8	486	Transported 1664.
Wells, John	10	4	" 1665.
Wells, John	15	433,441	Service 1677.
Wells, Margaret	7	82	Transported 1662.
Wells, Margaret	9	304	" 1665.
Wells, Martha	Q	71	Immigrated 1652-3. Married Mr. Selway.
Wells, Martha	WC2	187-188	Relict of John. Of Kent Co.
Wells, Mary	Q	71	Immigrated 1652-3.
Wells, Mary	ABH	347	Transported 1652-3. Daughter of Richard.
Wells, Nicholas	WC2	309	Transported 1678.
Wells, Ralph	5	410	" 1663. (18, fol. 115).
Wells, Mr. Richard	Q	71	Immigrated 1652-3.
Wells, Richard	ABH	347	" 1652-3.
Wells, Richard	ABH	347	Transported 1652-3. Son of Richard.
Wells, Richard	12	415	Transported 1669. (13, fol. 56, 57).
Wells, Richard, Jr.	Q	71	Immigrated 1652-3.
Wells, Robert	ABH	347	Transported 1652-3. Son of Richard.
Wells, Robert	Q	71	Immigrated 1652-3.
Wells, Swithen	WC2	160	" 1680. Of Cecil Co.
Wells, Thomas	WC2	50, 57	Transported 1679.
Wells, Toby	16	400	Immigrated 1658. Of Kent Co. - 1671.
Wells, Toby	4	53	Transported 1659.
Wells, William	ABH	245	" 1651.
Wells, William	Q	71	Immigrated 1652-3.

NAME	Liber	Folio	REMARKS
Wells, William	ABH	347	Transported 1652-3. Son of Richard.
Wells, Zerobabell	5	342	" 1661-2.
Welsh, Elish	WC2	57	" 1678.
Welsh, Ellis	15	554	" 1678.
Welsh, James	WC2	89	" 1676. Servant.
Welsh, John	17	517	" 1673.
Welsh, John	WC2	287	" 1680.
Welsh, Jone	15	553	" 1678.
Welsh, Margaret	15	446	" 1677.
Welsh, Philip	15	553	" 1678.
Welsh, Thomas	13	122	" 1668.
Welsh, Thomas	15	443	" 1670.
Welsh, Thomas	15	553	" 1678.
Welsh, Walter	12	473	" 1668.
Welsh, William	15	553	" 1678.
Welshman, Charles, a	ABH	60,66	" 1637.
Welson, Peter	9	38	" 1665.
Welt, George	6	128	" 1657.
Welt, James	6	166	" 1655.
Wenam, William	11	551	Of Calvert Co., and Alice, his wife. Service 1668.
Wennam, Rice	12	314	Transported 1669.
Went, Christian	12	373	" 1669.
Wentham, William	ABH	205	" 1648. Servant.
Wenton, Edward	9	216	" 1665.
Wenton, Peter	8	502	" 1665.
Werat, William	16	308	" 1671.
Werlidge, Stephen	Q	18	" 1658.
Werters, Christian	8	129	" 1664. Servant.
Wesby, Jane	4	30	" 1659. Servant.
Wesseluz, Tennis	Q	323	" 1652.
Wesson, Thomas	10	598	" 1667.
West, Ann	12	271	" 1668. Servant.
West, Edward	5	106	Immigrated 1658.
West, Edward	8	88	Transported 1665. (9, fol. 432).
West, Edward	10	475	Immigrated 1667.
West, Elizabeth	5	416	Transported 1663.
West, Elizabeth	17	348	" 1667.
West, Elizabeth	17	363	" 1672.
West, Elizabeth	12	618	" 1670. Wife of William.
West, Francis	6	10	" 1663.
West, Hannah	5	416	" 1663.
West, Henry	10	1,2	" 1666.
West, Henry	17	440	" 1673.
West, Henry	18	39	" 1674.
West, Henry	15	397	" 1677.
West, Jane	18	331	" 1674.
West, John	7	88	" 1649.
West, John	6	128	" 1653.
West, John	7	464	" 1655.
West, John	18	280	" 1675.

NAME	Liber	Folio	REMARKS
West, Jone	15	443	Transported 1672.
West, Margaret	20	184	" from Ireland 1678.
West, Mary	12	618	" 1670. Daughter of William.
West, Mary	17	363	Transported 1672.
West, Mary	15	436	" 1677.
West, Peter	10	193,407	" 1666. Servant.
West, Phillip	1	19	" 1638.
West, Ralph	6	86	" 1658.
West, Richard	ABH	48,411	" 1648.
West, Richard	3	24	" 1648. Servant.
West, Richard	13	112	" 1669.
West, Robert	15	452	" 1677.
West, Rose	5	416	" 1663.
West, Simon	18	296	" 1674.
West, Thomas	12	415	" 1669.
West, William	12	413	" 1669.
West, William	12	618	" 1670. Son of William.
West, William	12	618	Immigrated 1670. Of St. Mary's Co.
West, William, Jr.	17	363	Transported 1672.
West, William, Sr.	17	363	" 1672.
Westbe, Edward	ABH	151	" 1640. Servant.
Westbery, William	11	168	" 1667. Of Anne Arundel Co.
Westby, Barbara	6	80	Transported 1656.
Westcoate, Thomas	17	363	" 1672.
Westerband, Abraham	10	573	Service 1666.
Westerby, Francis	18	166	Transported 1674.
Westerland, Abraham	5	123	" 1662.
Westernall, Peirce	5	367	" 1663.
Westford, John	10	305	Immigrated 1666. Of Anne Arundel County.
Westlake, John	7	80	Immigrated 1664, with wife and son.
Westlake, Magdalen	7	80	Transported 1664. Wife of John.
Westley, Elizabeth	5	367	" 1663.
Westome, John	10	4	" 1666.
Weston, John	17	463	" 1673. (15, fol. 343).
Weston, Thomas	ABH	58	Immigrated 1640. (10, fol. 392).
Westoras, James	6	130	Transported 1658.
Westrope, Elizabeth	13	65	" 1668. Servant.
Wetbridge, Grace	6	165	" 1653.
Wetherby, James	15	353	" 1675.
Wetherell, Ann	15	300	" 1663.
Wetherell, Thomas	ABH	159	Immigrated 1648.
Wetherell, Thomas	Q	348	Gift from Lord B. 1658.
Wetherly, James	15	302	Of Virginia. Immigrated 1671, married Ann, widow of Richard Ackworth prior to 1677. (15, fol. 398).
Wetherly, Susan	16	435	Transported 1671.
Weyman, Thomas	15	430	" 1677.
Weymouth, Jane	WC2	380	" 1675-80. Servant.
Weymouth, John	WC2	184	" 1680. Servant.

NAME	Liber	Folio	REMARKS
Whack, Mary	15	414	Transported 1677.
Whaley, Anthony	8	89	" 1665.
Whaley, John	10	406	Service 1666.
Whaley, John	8	483	Transported from Virginia 1665.
Whaley, John	18	137	" 1674.
Whaley, Peter	8	89	Immigrated 1665.
Whalley, George	12	194	Transported 1668.
Whalley, James	Q	453	" 1658.
Wharf, Leby	6	48	" 1663. Servant. (17, fol. 490.
Wharle, Steven	6	134	Transported 1662.
Whart, Susan	6	85	" 1662.
Wharton, Alice	11	337,441	" 1668.
Wharton, Eleanor	16	85	" 1670.
Wharton, Elizabeth	15	157	Wife of Dr. Jesse Wharton. Patent for "Barbadoes", 1,000 acres in Charles Co. 1673.
Wharton, George	7	567	Transported 1657. Servant.
Wharton, Henry	6	27	Service 1663.
Wharton, Henry	15	359	Transported 1676.
Wharton, Jane	8	478	" 1665.
Wharton, Jesse	16	85	Immigrated 1670.
Wharton, John	6	170	Transported 1657.
Wharton, Margaret	11	187	" 1667. Wife of Thomas.
Wharton, Mary	12	575	" 1670.
Wharton, Mary	16	482	" 1670-1.
Wharton, Mary	17	608	" 1673.
Wharton, Ralph	17	487	" 1667.
Wharton, Richard	18	36	Service 1673.
Wharton, Thomas	11	187	Immigrated 1667. Of Charles Co.
Whasfield, Robert	11	307	Transported 1668. Servant.
Whealane, Joane	WC2	87	" 1679.
Wheateley, William	2	222	Immigrated 1643.
Wheatley, John	2	250	" 1641 with wife and son.
Wheatley, John	ABH	4	" 1661, with wife and son.
Wheatley, John	17	572	Service 1673. Of Dorset Co.
Wheatley, Joseph	15	430	Transported 1677.
Wheatley, Mary	15	370	" 1676.
Wheatley, William	ABH	2	Immigrated 1643.
Wheatley, William	WC2	120	Transported 1680.
Wheatly, John	ABH	244	" 1641 with wife and son.
Wheatly, John	5	339	" 1663.
Wheatly, Mary	6	87	" 1659.
Wheeler, Anne	Q	63	Immigrated 1658. Daughter of John.
Wheeler, Catherine	Q	63	" 1658. Wife of John.
Wheeler, Cezar	10	489	Transported 1667. Servant.
Wheeler, Charles	17	448	" 1673.
Wheeler, Edward	15	452	" 1678.
Wheeler, Elizabeth	17	67,454	Service 1672. Wife of Samuel.
Wheeler, George	6	86	Transported 1652.
Wheeler, George	16	400	" 1671.
Wheeler, John	5	90	" 1653-61.

NAME	Liber	Folio	REMARKS
Wheeler, John	Q	63	Immigrated 1658.
Wheeler, John	5	515	Transported 1661. Servant.
Wheeler, John	9	34	Immigrated 1665.
Wheeler, John	15	314	Transported 1675.
Wheeler, John, Jr.	Q	63	Immigrated 1658. Son of John.
Wheeler, Richard	12	584	Transported 1670.
Wheeler, Richard	WC2	168-169	" 1680.
Wheeler, Samuel	Q	63	Immigrated 1658. Son of John.
Wheeler, Samuel	17	67,454	" June 1672.
Wheeler, Thomas	17	382	" from Virginia 1672.
Wheeler, William	15	544	Transported 1676.
Wheeler, William	WC2	147	" 1680.
Wheelewright, Stephen	WC2	183-184, 195	" 1680.
Wheelock, Edward	15	301	Of Anne Arundel Co., and wife. Service 1675.
Wheemyard, Thomas	4	59	Transported 1652-9.
Whelan, Patrick	WC2	57	" 1678. (15, fol. 553).
Whelbes, John	18	329	" 1675.
Whener, Ann	15	369	" 1676.
Whestler, James	6	131	" 1649.
Whetstone, John	12	576	" 1670.
Whetstone, Stephen	10	406	Immigrated 1666.
Whett, Ralph	7	472	Transported 1664.
Whettingham, William	18	329	" 1675.
Whettston, Stephen	4	58	" 1649.
Whibrow, John	18	115	" 1674.
Whickacker, Henry	15	322	" 1674.
Whickham, John	12	271	" 1668.
Whiett, Mary	15	509	" 1677.
Whiett, Richard	9	321	" 1666.
Whilington, Francis	15	454	" 1677. (See Whitington).
Whilington, James	15	454	" 1677. (See Whittington).
Whimley, Thomas	16	79	" 1670.
Whinfield, John	Q	29	Immigrated 1658.
Whirch, Richard	17	417	Transported 1673.
Whitacher, John	12	190	" 1668. Servant.
Whitacre, John	15	397	" 1676.
Whitaker, Elizabeth	17	469	" 1668.
Whitaker, Elizabeth	WC2	308	" 1678.
Whitaker, John	15	534	" 1677.
Whitburne, Hannah	17	462	" 1673.
Whitby, Elizabeth	17	76	" 1672.
Whitby, Francis	6	80	" 1660.
White, Ambrose, Jr.	15	533	" 1678.
White, Ambrose, Sr.	15	533	Immigrated 1678. Of Somerset Co.
White, Mr. Andrew	ABH	65	" 1633.
White, Mr. Andrew	1	19,37,166	Transported 1633.
White, Ann	16	77	" 1670.
White, Ann	15	330,358	" 1675.
White, Ann	WC2	158	" 1680.

NAME	Liber	Folio	REMARKS
White, Catherine	5	393	Transported 1663.
White, Christopher	7	62	" 1664.
White, Christopher	12	317	" 1669.
White, Comfort	15	533	" 1678.
White, Dennis	4	555	" 1661.
White, Dorothy	WC2	108	" 1679.
White, Elizabeth	15	563	" 1678.
White, Elizabeth	WC2	321	" 1680. Daughter of John.
White, Frances	ABH	59	Immigrated 1641. (1, fol. 24).
White, Frances	18	25	" from Virginia 1666.
Wife of Jos. of Baltimore County.			
White, George	ABH	60, 66	Transported 1637. (1, fol. 17, 20, 25, 38).
White, Grace	15	533	Transported 1678.
White, Gratiana	WC2	321	" 1680. Daughter of John.
White, Gustavus	18	33	Transported 1674.
White, Guy	6	299	" 1648. Servant.
White, Henry	4	338	" 1659.
White, Henry	16	73	Immigrated 1670. Of Anne Arundel County.
White, Hester	17	608	Transported 1673.
White, Hierome	5	257	Immigrated 1663.
White, Hugh	6	106	Transported 1655.
White, Hugh	7	561	" 1665.
White, James	4	58	Immigrated 1659.
White, James	6	47	Transported 1663.
White, Jane	18	15	" 1673.
White, Jane	18	306	" 1675.
White, Jane	15	527	" 1678.
White, Jerome, Esq.	5	421	Surveyor General. Special Grant from Lord B. 1662. (5, fol. 428-429; 12, fol. 558).
White, Johanna	WC2	318	Transported 1680.
White, John	4	5	" 1659. Servant.
White, John	5	63	" 1660.
White, John	6	107	" 1663. (18, fol. 309).
White, John	10	169	Immigrated 1667.
White, John	11	344	Transported 1668.
White, John	18	17	" 1669.
White, John	12	498	" 1670. (16, fol. 508).
White, John	16	537	Immigrated from Virginia 1671.
White, John	15	436	Transported 1677.
White, John, Gent.	15	567	Of Somerset Co. Living 1679.
White, John	WC2	321	Immigrated 1680 with wife and four daughters.
White, Katherine	9	47	Transported 1665. Servant.
White, Margaret	WC2	106	" 1679.
White, Martha	17	615	" 1673.
White, Mary	15	446	" 1677.
White, Mary	ABH	150	" 1637. Servant.

NAME	Liber	Folio	REMARKS
Afterwards married Wm. Edwins.			
White, Mary	Q	29	Transported 1658.
White, Mary	10	342	" 1660.
White, Mary	5	307	" 1663. (5, fol. 606).
White, Mary	7	568	" 1665.
White, Mary	10	433	" 1666.
White, Mary	15	544	" 1676.
White, Mary	WC2	321	" 1680. Wife of John.
White, Mary, Jr.	WC2	321	" 1680. Daughter of John.
White, Nicholas	ABH	374	Transported 1st Condition. Servant.
White, Nicholas	17	40	" 1672.
White, Nicholas	15	397	" 1676.
White, Phineas	6	28	" 1663. Servant.
White, Phineas	9	516	" 1666.
White, Rachel	5	606	" 1663.
White, Ralph	5	90	" 1653-61.
White, Ralph	8	131	" 1664.
White, Rebecca	8	88	" 1665.
White, Richard	Q	70	" 1657.
White, Richard	5	513	" 1660.
White, Richard	8	88	Immigrated 1665.
White, Richard	WC2	253	Rights 1680.
White, Richard (Rowland)	WC2	167,169	Transported 1680.
White, Robert	9	488	" 1665.
White, Robert	12	205	" 1667.
White, Robert	15	358	" 1675.
White, Rowland	9	24	" 1665.
White, Samuel	12	216	" 1668.
White, Samuel	17	396	" 1671.
White, Samuel	16	635	" 1672.
White, Sarah	6	123	" 1663.
White, Stephen	5	488	" 1659.
White, Stephen	10	599	" 1667.
White, Susan	6	83	" 1655.
White, Susannah	WC2	108,321	Daughter of John.
White, Susannah	WC2	321	Transported 1680. Daughter of John.
White, Thomas	1	62	" 1635-6.
White, Thomas	ABH	35,78	" 1635-40.
White, Thomas	1	18	" 1637.
White, Thomas	1	128	" 1637-40.
White, Thomas	2	580	Service about 1640.
White, Thomas	6	217	Transported 1663.
White, Thomas	9	48,54	" 1665.
White, Thomas	11	104	" 1667.
White, Thomas	18	158	Service 1674. Of St. Mary's Co.
White, Thomas	WC2	21-22	Transported 1679. (WC2, fol. 122).
White, Thomas	WC2	129	" 1679.
White, Walter	WC2	89	" 1676. Servant.
White, William	ABH	6	Immigrated 1646.

NAME	Liber	Folio	REMARKS
White, William	4	20	Transported 1658.
White, William	9	437	" 1664.
White, William	8	88	" 1665.
White, William	13	1	" 1669. Servant.
White, William	18	94	" 1674.
White, William	15	508	Service 1678. Of Calvert Co.
Whiteall, Simon	11	344	Transported 1668.
Whitecraft, Ruth	18	291	" 1674.
Whitefield, Fasey	17	54	Service 1672.
Whitehall, Charles	16	406	Transported 1671.
Whitehall, Symon	16	462	Service 1670.
Whitehart, Richard	16	507	Transported 1671.
Whitehead, Elizabeth	Q	431	" 1651.
Whitehead, John	5	412	" 1645.
Whitehead, John	WC2	45	" 1679.
Whitehead, Mary	1	17,19	" 1637. Servant.
Whitehead, Mary	15	598	" 1678-9.
Whitehead, Mary	WC2	211	" 1679. Servant.
Whitehead, Robert	13	116	" 1671.
Whitehead, Silence	15	376	" 1676.
Whitehead, Simon	17	76	" 1671.
Whitehead, William	6	63	" 1658-63.
Whitehouse, William	17	451	" 1673.
Whitemore, Clanne	9	304	" 1665.
Whiteroe, Samuel	12	477	" 1670.
Whitewell, Simon	13	111	" 1667.
Whitey, Arthur	15	369	" 1676.
Whitfall, Fran.	15	369	" 1676.
Whitfell, Susanna	16	393	" 1671.
Whitfield, Thomas	4	580	" 1661. Wm. immigrated 1668. (12, fol. 283).
Whitford, John	5	125	Transported 1662.
Whiting, Clement	5	214	" 1659.
Whiting, John	9	104	" 1665. (17, fol. 554).
Whitington, Francis	15	454	" 1677.
Whitle, Jane	WC2	38	" 1679.
Whitle, William	2	345	Immigrated 1646.
Whitler, Richard	WC2	73	Transported 1678.
Whitley, John	18	94	" 1674.
Whitlock, Aaron	16	95	" 1665 with Eliz., his daughter.
Whitman, Stephen	7	484	Transported 1664.
Whitmore, Edward	16	482	" 1671.
Whiton, Clomer	9	38	" 1665.
Whitrow, Robert	17	451	" 1671.
Whittacker, Margaret	18	177	" 1674.
Whitte, John	10	569	" 1665-6. Servant.
Whitter, James	17	596	" 1673.
Whittey, James	16	86	" 1670.
Whittington, Andrew	16	308	Immigrated with Ursula, his wife, 1671. Of Somerset Co.

NAME	Liber	Folio	REMARKS
Whittington, Francis	16	37	Transported 1670.
Whittington, James	15	454	" 1677.
Whittington, John	6	127	" 1654.
Whittington, John	6	117	" 1662.
Whittington, William	16	37	" 1670.
Whittle, George	Q	203	Immigrated 1658.
Whittle, Magdalen	Q	19	Transported 1646. (ABH, fol. 244).
Whittle, Margaret	7	530	" 1664.
Whittle, Nicholas	4	53	" 1659.
Whittle, Susan	4	137	Immigrated 1657 with two daughters named Williams.
Whittle, William	ABH	200	Immigrated 1646.
Whittlock, David	5	383	Transported 1663.
Whittly, Alice	10	291	" 1666.
Whittman, Mary	15	567	" 1678.
Whittmarsh, Richard	9	55	Immigrated 1665.
Whitton, Richard	8	130,502	Transported 1665. (12, fol. 281).
Whitton, Thomas	17	348	Service 1672. Of St. Mary's Co. and wife.
Whittop, Thomas	17	445	Immigrated 1673. Of Somerset Co.
Whitty, Edward	Q	48	Servant 1658.
Whitty, Elizabeth	9	216	Transported 1665. Wife of Richard.
Whitty, Richard	9	216	Immigrated 1665.
Whord, Anthony	5	267	Transported 1663.
Whort, Susan	6	85	" 1662. (See Whart).
Whorton, Thomas	WC2	23	" 1679. Servant.
Whyborow, John	17	411	" 1673.
Whyting, John	5	267	" 1663.
Wibb, Elizabeth	15	569	" 1678.
Wickam, Ann	ABH	340	" 1652. Servant.
Wickcliff, David	1	19	" 1638.
Wicker, Margaret	4	533	" 1659.
Wickers, Thomas	6	172	" 1663.
Wickes, William	ABH	269	" 1650. Servant.
Wickeslow, Nicholas	WC2	253	" 1680.
Wickett, Joseph	10	390	" 1666.
Wickham, John	12	500	Service 1669.
Wickliffe, David	ABH	91	Immigrated 1636.
Wickliffe, Jane	ABH	49	Widow of David. Married to Henry Brooks by 1650. (3, fol. 62).
Wicks, John	12	190	Transported 1668.
Wicks, Joseph	Q	66	Immigrated 1650.
Wicks, Mary	Q	66	" 1656. Wife of Joseph.
Wicks, Richard	4	198	Transported 1659. Servant.
Wicks, Richard	4	486	Immigrated 1664.
Widiaker, William	11	581	Transported 1668.
Widmore, Elizabeth	15	544	" 1676.
Widmott, John	5	89	" 1661.
Wier, John	17	440	" 1668.
Wigens, John	7	77	" 1664. Servant.
Wiggin, Ann	ABH	244	" 1637.

NAME	Liber	Folio	REMARKS
Wiggin, William	11	162	Transported 1667.
Wiggins, James	17	635	" 1671.
Wiggins, John	9	35	" 1664.
Wiggins, William	18	177	" 1674.
Wiggins, William	WC2	308	" 1678.
Wiggons, Charles	17	443	" 1673.
Wiginna, Jane	7	529	" 1664.
Wigley, John	12	604	" 1670.
Wigley, Thomas	17	599	Service 1673. Of Kent Co.
Wignell, Jane	4	196	Transported 1659. Wife of Wm.
Wignell, William	4	196	Immigrated 1659.
Wignes, James	16	170	Transported 1671.
Wilbanck, Cornelius	12	333	" 1669. Son of Helmanus Frederick.
Wilbanck, Helmanus Frederick	12	333	Immigrated 1669.
Wilbanck, John	18	291	Transported 1674.
Wilbanck, Johnaken C.	12	333	" 1669. Wife of Helmanus Frederick.
Wilbe, Thomas	16	411	Transported 1671.
Wilby, Nicholas	15	560	" 1678.
Wilcock, John	10	407	" 1666.
Wilcock, Thomas	15	377	Service 1676.
Wilcocks, Anthony	4	206	Transported 1658.
Wilcockse, Richard	17	553	" 1667.
Wilcox, Elizabeth	18	339	" 1675. Wife of John.
Wilcox, John	18	339	Immigrated 1675. Of St. Mary's Co.
Wild, Christopher	6	170	Transported 1655.
Wild, Daniel	WC2	158	" 1680.
Wild, John	10	598	" 1667.
Wild, Sarah	15	519	" 1678.
Wild, Thomas	18	331	" 1674.
Wildblod, Joseph	17	608	" 1673.
Wildblood, Joseph	WC2	410	Service 1681. Of St. Mary's Co.
Wilde, Abraham	16	43	Transported 1670.
Wilde, Sarah	WC2	1	" 1679.
Wilden, Robert	8	87	" 1665. Servant.
Wilder, Edward	15	346	Immigrated 1669.
Wilder, Solomon	6	130	Transported 1660.
Wildey, Edward	15	423	" 1677.
Wildgoose, Alice	15	413	" 1677.
Wildgoose, Deborah	15	413	" 1677.
Wildgoose, Elizabeth	15	413	" 1677.
Wildgoose, James	17	411	" 1673. (18, fol. 115).
Wildgoose, Richard	15	413	" 1677.
Wildgos, Robert	WC2	341-342	Immigrated from Virginia 1679. Of St. Mary's Co.
Wilding, Hugh	15	300	Service 1675. Of Anne Arundel Co.
Wildman, William	12	242	Transported from Virginia 1669.
Wildswith, John	11	374	" 1668.
Wildswith, Thomas	12	604	" 1670.

NAME	Liber	Folio	REMARKS
Wiley, Ann	18	331	Transported 1674.
Wilford, William	12	393	" 1669.
Wilkenson, John	12	459	" 1669.
Wilkenson, Lance	16	411	" 1671.
Wilkerton, Thomas	17	475	" 1673.
Wilkes, John	7	469	" 1664.
Wilkes, William	ABH	151	" 1649-50. Servant.
Wilkes, William	ABH	427	Of St. Mary's Co. Married Eliz., widow of Jno. Tayler of Poplar Hill prior to 1655.
Wilkes, William	18	311	Transported 1675.
Wilkeson, Edward	18	306	" 1675.
Wilkeson, Margaret	18	306	" 1675.
Wilkeson, Richard	18	152	" 1674.
Wilkins, James	WC2	276	Service 1680. Of St. Mary's Co.
Wilkins, Mary	15	397	Transported 1676.
Wilkins, Michael	WC2	282-283	Rights 1680. Commander of ship "John and Thomas".
Wilkinson, Alice	6	210	Transported 1663.
Wilkinson, Elizabeth	3	62	" 1650. Daughter of William.
Wilkinson, Elizabeth	ABH	49	Transported 1650. Daughter of Rev. Wm.
Wilkinson, Henry	15	500,501	Transported 1678.
Wilkinson, Isabella	17	395	" 1672.
Wilkinson, James	7	130	" 1656-63.
Wilkinson, John	4	14	" 1655. Servant.
Wilkinson, John	Q	70	" 1658.
Wilkinson, John	6	96	" 1660.
Wilkinson, John	7	468	Immigrated prior to 1664.
Wilkinson, John	8	478	Transported 1665. (9, fol. 313).
Wilkinson, John	18	15	" 1673.
Wilkinson, John	15	598	" 1678-9.
Wilkinson, John	WC2	211	" 1679. Servant.
Wilkinson, Jone	9	326	" 1666.
Wilkinson, Margaret	11	436	" 1668.
Wilkinson, Mary	ABH	49	" 1650. Daughter of Rev. Wm. (3, fol. 62).
Wilkinson, Mary	6	94	Transported 1662.
Wilkinson, Mary	5	339	" 1663. (9, fol. 282).
Wilkinson, Mary	10	117	" 1666.
Wilkinson, Mary	15	359	" 1676.
Wilkinson, Peter	11	436	" 1668.
Wilkinson, Rebecca	ABH	49	" 1650. Daughter of Rev. Wm. (3, fol. 62).
Wilkinson, Robert	6	117	Transported 1654.
Wilkinson, Thomas	4	5	" 1652-9.
Wilkinson, Thomas	17	538	Service 1673.
Wilkinson, Thomas	WC2	146,162	Transported 1680 by Joseph Eaton.
Wilkinson, Thomas	WC2	158	" 1680 by Richard Lamb.
Wilkinson, William	5	253	Immigrated 1663. (6, fol. 125).

NAME	Liber	Folio	REMARKS
Wilkinson, Mr. Wm.	ABH	49	Clerk. Immigrated with wife and children 1650. Afterwards rector of Poplar Hill Church. Special Warrant for 1000 acres on Eastern Shore. (4, fol. 5).
Wilkinson, William	3	62	Immigrated 1650 with wife, daughters and servants.
Wilkinson, William	9	282	Transported 1663.
Wilkinson, William	11	263	Immigrated 1667. Of St. Mary's Co.
Wilkinson, William	12	314	Transported 1669.
Wilkinson, William	15	314	" 1675.
Wilkinson, William	15	366	" 1676.
Wilkinson, William, Jr.	17	363	" 1672.
Wilkinson, William, Sr.	17	363	" 1672.
Willafore, John	16	507	" 1671.
Willan, Elizabeth	4	12	" 1659. Wife of Richard.
Willan, Lucie	15	451	" 1678. Daughter of Robert.
Willan, Mary	15	451	Transported 1678. Wife of Robert.
Willan, Richard	3	21	Immigrated 1638 and immigrated again 1646 to assist Leonard Calvert in regaining the Province.
Willan, Robert	4	550	Transported 1661.
Willan, Robert	15	451	Immigrated 1678.
Willard, George	ABH	242	" Jan. 1652.
Willard, Samuel	ABH	242	Transported Jan. 1652. Son of George.
Willboe, Mathew	7	81	Transported 1662-3.
Willby, Marmaduke	6	133	" 1659.
Willcock, Edward	6	79	" 1663.
Willcocks, John	9	157	" 1665.
Willcocks, Mathew	20	185	" 1679.
Wille, Thomas	16	513	" 1672.
Willen, Andrew	15	433	" 1677.
Willen, Thomas	12	190	" 1668. Servant.
Willers, Susan	6	347	" 1663.
Willersly, Philip	15	550	" 1679.
Willes, John	12	190	" 1668. Servant.
Willes, Thomas	12	589	" 1670.
Willett, John	11	318	" 1668.
Willett, Jone	15	430	" 1677.
Willett, Mary	15	517	" 1678.
Willett, William	15	359	" 1676.
Williams, Abigail	12	269	" 1668. Daughter of Elizabeth.
Williams, Abigail	17	486	Transported 1667.
Williams, Abigail, Jr.	9	304	" 1665.
Williams, Abigail, Sr.	9	304	" 1665.
Williams, Alexander	6	235	" 1663.
Williams, Alexander	17	382	Immigrated 1672 from Virginia with wife and daughter.
Williams, Alexander	WC2	15	Transported his servant Mary Cryps, 1679.
Williams, Alice	15	451,601	Transported 1678.

NAME	Liber	Folio	REMARKS
Williams, Andrew	8	501	Transported 1665.
Williams, Ann	ABH	165	" 1649. Wife of Edward.
Williams, Ann	7	565	" 1665. Wife of Edward.
Williams, Ann	9	204	" 1665.
Williams, Ann	15	397	" 1676.
Williams, Ann	WC2	18	Service 1679. Of St. Mary's Co.
Williams, Anthony	7	567	Transported 1665.
Williams, Baraat	15	504	" 1678.
Williams, Blanch	5	68	" 1662. (6, fol. 15).
Williams, Blanch	10	308	" 1663. Servant.
Williams, Blanch	18	9	" 1673.
Williams, Catherine	6	15	" 1661.
Williams, Charles	17	30	" 1672 from Virginia.
Williams, David	7	82	" 1662.
Williams, David	6	123	" 1663.
Williams, David	9	270	" 1665.
Williams, David	10	433	" 1667. (17, fol. 382,545).
Williams, David	15	566	" 1678.
Williams, David	WC2	254	" 1680. (WC2, fol. 340-1).
Williams, David	WC2	395	" 1680. Servant.
Williams, Deborah	6	88	" 1661.
Williams, Dorothy	6	85	" 1660.
Williams, Dorothy	9	304	" 1665.
Williams, Dorothy	9	321	" 1666. Wife of Morgan.
Williams, Dorothy	10	434	" 1667.
Williams, Edward	ABH	89	" 1635.
Williams, Edward	1	95	" 1635-40.
Williams, Edward	2	426	" 1644. Servant.
Williams, Edward	ABH	10	Servant 1644.
Williams, Edward	ABH	165	Service 1651.
Williams, Edward	7	565	Immigrated 1665 with wife and 2 sons and daughter.
Williams, Edward	9	304	Transported 1665.
Williams, Edward	11	4	" 1667. Servant.
Williams, Edward	12	359	" 1669. Servant.
Williams, Edward	17	40	Immigrated 1672. Of Talbot Co.
Williams, Edward	WC2	141-142	Service 1675. Of Somerset Co.
Williams, Edward	15	380	Transported 1676.
Williams, Edward	WC2	319	Service 1680.
Williams, Edward, Jr.	7	565	Transported 1665. Son of Edward.
Williams, Eleanor	1	166	" 1650. Servant.
Williams, Elizabeth	4	137	" 1657. Daughter of Susan Whittle.
Williams, Elizabeth	4	172	Transported 1659. Wife of John.
Williams, Elizabeth	6	235	" 1663.
Williams, Elizabeth	11	373	" 1668. Wife of John.
Williams, Elizabeth	17	486	" 1667.
Williams, Elizabeth	12	269,280	Immigrated 1668 with her children.
Williams, Elizabeth	16	407	Transported 1671.
Williams, Elizabeth	15	318	" 1674. (18, fol. 174).
Williams, Elizabeth	18	313	" 1675.

NAME	Liber	Folio	REMARKS
Williams, Elizabeth	WC2	288	Transported 1680.
Williams, Eunice	5	411	" 1663.
Williams, Evan	15	319	Service 1675.
Williams, Francis	9	488	Transported 1665. Servant. (17, fol. 512).
Williams, George	9	304	Transported 1665.
Williams, George	11	465	" 1668.
Williams, Harman	10	600	" 1667.
Williams, Henry	10	117	" 1666.
Williams, Henry	11	1	Immigrated 1667.
Williams, Henry	13	112	Transported 1669.
Williams, Henry	18	311	" 1675.
Williams, Henry	15	537	" 1679.
Williams, Hester	17	572	" 1672.
Williams, Hopkin	18	39	" 1674.
Williams, Hugh	9	487	Immigrated 1664.
Williams, Hugh	16	60	Transported 1670.
Williams, Hugh	15	380,503	" 1676.
Williams, Hugh	WC2	395	" 1680. Servant.
Williams, Humphrey	6	290	" 1664.
Williams, Humphrey	15	443	" 1669.
Williams, Jacob	15	347	" 1676.
Williams, James	5	201	" 1661.
Williams, James	5	243	" 1662.
Williams, James	7	565	" 1665. Son of Edward.
Williams, James	15	397	" 1676.
Williams, James	15	455	" 1678.
Williams, Jane	4	13	" 1656. Servant.
Williams, Jane	16	522	" 1672.
Williams, Jane	15	380	" 1676.
Williams, John	ABH	27	Servant 1640.
Williams, John	2	529	Transported 1640. Servant.
Williams, John	Q	323	" 1655.
Williams, John	4	172	" 1659. Son of John.
Williams, John	4	172	Immigrated 1659.
Williams, John	5	81	Transported 1661. (7, fol. 154).
Williams, John	5	530	" 1662. (6, fol. 81).
Williams, John	6	82,106	" 1663. (6, fol. 235).
Williams, John	7	471	Of Va. Acquired land in Md. 1664.
Williams, John	7	559	Transported 1664.
Williams, John	9	49,105	Immigrated 1665.
Williams, John	10	277	Transported 1666.
Williams, John	10	489	" 1667. Servant.
Williams, John	11	373	Immigrated 1668.
Williams, John	11	373	Transported 1668. Son of John.
Williams, John	11	379	" 1668.
Williams, John	12	403	" 1669.
Williams, John	14	421-423	Of Somerset Co. Original title to land from Virginia.
Williams, John	17	399	Service 1672. Of St. Mary's Co.
Williams, John	15	353	Transported 1674.

NAME	Liber	Folio	REMARKS
Williams, John	15	370,500	Transported 1676. (15, fol. 397).
Williams, John	15	379	" 1676.
Williams, John	WC2	161	" 1680 by Ellis Humphrys.
Williams, John	WC2	288	" 1680.
Williams, John	WC2	255,340	" 1680 by Robert Ridgely.
Williams, Jonathan	5	411	Transported 1663.
Williams, Jone	5	411	" 1663.
Williams, Jone	9	233	" 1665.
Williams, Jone	15	380	" 1676.
Williams, Joseph	15	391	Service 1668. Of Calvert Co.
Williams, Joyce	5	491	Transported 1662.
Williams, Katherine	6	293	" 1664.
Williams, Lazara	5	127	" 1662.
Williams, Lewis	5	411	" 1663.
Williams, Lewis	16	503	" 1671.
Williams, Lewis	15	449,534	" 1677. Servant.
Williams, Lodwick	12	284	Service 1668.
Williams, Lydia	12	576	Transported 1670.
Williams, Mandlin	5	411	" 1663.
Williams, Margaret	9	157	" 1665. (17, fol. 399).
Williams, Margery	15	353	" 1674.
Williams, Mary	Q	323	" 1655-8.
Williams, Mary	6	31	" 1663.
Williams, Mary	8	486,495	" 1665.
Williams, Mary	9	49	" 1665. Wife of John.
Williams, Mary	9	269	" 1665.
Williams, Mary	11	373	" 1668. Daughter of John.
Williams, Mary	12	472,496	" 1670.
Williams, Mary	13	116	" 1671. (15, fol. 432).
Williams, Mary	17	452	" 1671.
Williams, Mary	15	353	" 1674.
Williams, Mary	18	166	" 1674.
Williams, Mary	15	540	" 1677.
Williams, Maudlin	5	411	" 1663.
Williams, Michael	4	580	" 1661.
Williams, Michael	5	209	" 1662. Orphan.
Williams, Morgan	4	64	Immigrated 1652.
Williams, Morgan	9	353	Transported 1666.
Williams, Morgan	12	241	" 1669.
Williams, Morgan	16	12	" 1670. (18, fol. 48).
Williams, Nathaniel	WC2	187	" 1678.
Williams, Nicholas	Q	68	Servant 1653-8.
Williams, Oliver	9	49	Transported 1665. Daughter of John.
Williams, Owen	12	504	Immigrated 1669.
Williams, Owen	15	380	Transported 1676.
Williams, Owen	WC2	395	" 1680. Servant.
Williams, Paul	15	544	" 1676.
Williams, Peter	11	537	" 1668.
Williams, Phebe	11	1	" 1667. Wife of Henry.
Williams, Rachel	15	507	Service prior to 1677, when she

NAME	Liber	Folio	REMARKS
appears as the wife of Sam. Woollson.			
Williams, Ralph, Jr.	5	411	Transported 1663.
Williams, Ralph, Sr.	5	411	Immigrated 1663.
Williams, Rebecca	Q	71	Transported 1658.
Williams, Richard	ABH	82	" 1634. Servant.
Williams, Richard	1	25,73	" 1634. Servant.
Williams, Richard	11	379	" 1668.
Williams, Richard	16	394	" 1671.
Williams, Richard	17	408,547	" 1673.
Williams, Richard	WC2	380	" 1675-80. Servant.
Williams, Richard	15	359	" 1676.
Williams, Richard	15	454	" 1677.
Williams, Richard	WC2	327	Service 1680. Of Dorchester Co.
Williams, Robert	17	572	Transported 1672.
Williams, Robert	18	174	" 1674.
Williams, Robert	WC2	381	" 1675-80. Servant.
Williams, Roger	5	417	" 1663.
Williams, Roger	11	229	" 1667.
Williams, Roger	12	204	" 1669.
Williams, Roger	15	544	" 1676.
Williams, Rowland	17	486	Immigrated 1667. Of Baltimore Co.
Williams, Rowland	12	594	Transported 1670.
Williams, Rowland	18	106	" 1674.
Williams, Samuel	12	496	" 1670. (17, fol. 590).
Williams, Samuel	15	397	" 1676.
Williams, Sarah	4	64	" 1652. Wife of Morgan.
Williams, Sarah	4	64	" 1652. Daughter of Morgan.
Williams, Sarah	4	580	Transported 1661.
Williams, Seth	6	235	" 1663.
Williams, Simon	6	216	" 1663.
Williams, Sisley	18	313	" 1675.
Williams, Stephen	15	443	" 1672.
Williams, Susan	4	137	" 1657. Daughter of Susan Whittle.
Williams, Susan	4	550	Transported 1661.
Williams, Susanna	6	124	" 1663.
Williams, Susanna	18	77	" 1674.
Williams, Thomas	ABH	64	" 1637. Servant. (1, fol. 19, 33, 171).
Williams, Thomas	ABH	246	Transported years prior to 1652.
Williams, Thomas	4	580	" 1661.
Williams, Thomas	5	123	" 1662.
Williams, Thomas	5	255	" 1663.
Williams, Thomas	6	235	Immigrated 1663.
Williams, Thomas	9	304	Transported 1665.
Williams, Thomas	12	333	" 1668.
Williams, Thomas	12	217,372	" 1669.
Williams, Thomas	12	404	" 1669.
Williams, Thomas	15	438,514	" 1677. (15, fol. 523).
Williams, Thomas	WC2	254	" 1680. (WC2, fol. 340-1).

NAME	Liber	Folio	REMARKS
Williams, Thomas	WC2	201	Transported 1680. Servant.
Williams, Thomas, Jr.	6	235	" 1663.
Williams, William	5	90	" 1656.
Williams, William	Q	435	" 1658.
Williams, William	4	10,22	" 1658. Servant.
Williams, William	4	551	" 1661.
Williams, William	6	16	Immigrated 1663.
Williams, William	6	235	Transported 1663. (16, fol. 536).
Williams, William	18	296	" 1674.
Williams, William	15	397	" 1676.
Williams, William	WC2	108	" 1679.
Williams, Yarrow	9	45	" 1665.
Williamson, Ann	18	137	" 1674.
Williamson, Christ	18	177	" 1674.
Williamson, Christo-pher	WC2	308	" 1678.
Williamson, Christo-pher	WC2	281	Service 1680. Of St. Mary's Co.
Williamson, David	11	312	Immigrated 1665.
Williamson, Elizabeth	1	166	Transported 1650. Servant.
Williamson, Elizabeth	WC2	113,165	" 1680.
Williamson, Francis	10	600	" 1667.
Williamson, George	15	429	" 1674.
Williamson, John	4	4	" 1658.
Williamson, Margery	15	362	" 1676.
Williamson, Martha	1	17,19	" 1637. Servant.
Williamson, Samuel	18	14	" 1674.
Williamson, Thomas	Q	431	" 1658.
Williamson, Thomas	11	581	" 1668.
Williamson, Thomas	15	359	" 1676.
Williamson, William	1	19	" 1638.
Williamson, William	5	247	" 1662.
Williamson, Yanses	11	537	" 1668.
Williford, Thomasin	15	390	" 1675.
Willis	1	19	" 1638.
Willis, Charles	15	431	" 1677.
Willis, Edward	5	530	" 1656.
Willis, Francis	ABH	24	" 1649. Servant. (2, fol. 512).
Willis, Jane	9	94	Transported 1665. Servant.
Willis, John	11	436	" 1668.
Willis, Mary	WC2	58	" 1678.
Willis, Thomas	ABH	6	" 1633. Servant.
Willis, Thomas	2	346	" 1634. Servant.
Willis, Thomas	13	56	" 1670.
Willis, Thomas	18	37	Immigrated 1673.
Willis, Thomas	WC2	320	Transported 1680. Servant.
Willivs, Mary	15	397	" 1676. (See Wilkins).
Willkinson, Jone	9	326	" 1666.
Willkinson, William	8	30	" 1665.
Willman, Ann	12	385	" 1669.

NAME	Liber	Folio	REMARKS
Willmore, Charles	15	347	Transported 1676.
Willmer (Wilmore), Simon	WC2	107	Immigrated 1679. Of Calvert Co. (WC2, fol. 208, 316).
Willmott, Francis	6	95	Transported 1657.
Willmott, Robert	15	455	" 1678.
Willoby, John	15	369	" 1676.
Willonghby, Elizabeth	12	477,591	" 1669. Servant.
Willoughby, Elizabeth	15	382	" 1673.
Willoughby, Thomas	5	513,514	" 1661.
Willoughby, Thomas	8	478	" 1665.
Willoughby, William	17	585	Immigrated 1673 with Hannah, his wife. Of Dorset Co.
Willoughby, William	WC2	147	Rights 1680. Of Dorchester Co.
Willowby, Anne	5	253	Transported 1663.
Willowby, William	9	332	" 1666.
Willox, Roger	17	407	" 1673.
Wills, John	7	506	" 1662.
Wills, Mary	6	125	" 1663.
Wills, Thomas	ABH	67	" 1634. Servant. (1, fol. 17, 41).
Wills, Thomas	16	110	Transported 1671.
Willson, Alice	15	566	" 1678.
Willson, Andrew	15	511	Service 1678.
Willson, Ann	4	140	Transported 1657. Servant.
Willson, Ann	15	446	" 1677.
Willson, Anthony	6	90	" 1659.
Willson, Edward	15	455	" 1678.
Willson, Faith	Q	71	" 1652-3.
Willson, George	8	484	" 1665.
Willson, Henry	4	140	" 1658. Servant.
Willson, Henry	5	2	" 1661.
Willson, Jane	WC2	398	" 1680 by Col. William Colebourne.
Willson, John	4	591	Transported 1657.
Willson, John	4	625	" 1658.
Willson, John	5	417	" 1663.
Willson, John	10	417	" 1666.
Willson, John	15	544	" 1674.
Willson, Joseph	WC2	65	" 1679.
Willson, Mary	5	245	" 1662.
Willson, Mary	9	157	" 1665.
Willson, Mary	10	362	Immigrated 1665. Wife of Thomas.
Willson, Mary	15	322	Transported 1673.
Willson, Patrick	15	318	Service 1674.
Willson, Robert	5	2	Transported 1661.
Willson, Robert	15	452	" 1677.
Willson, Robert	WC2	282	" 1680.
Willson, Simon	WC2	415	" 1666-80. Servant.
Willson, Thomas	10	262	Immigrated 1665. Of Talbot Co.
Willson, Thomas	10	262	Transported 1665. Son of Thomas.

NAME	Liber	Folio	REMARKS
Willson, Thomas	11	581	Transported 1668.
Willson, Thomas	15	433	" 1677.
Willson, Thomas	20	185	" 1679.
Willson, William	4	214	Immigrated 1659. (5, fol. 414).
Willson, William	8	478	Transported 1665.
Willson, William	9	157,373	" 1665.
Willson, William	15	566	" 1678.
Willy, Humphrey	12	209,314	" 1668.
Willymote, John	15	376	" 1676.
Wilson, Alexander	16	405	Service 1671. Of St. Mary's Co.
Wilson, Andrew	ABH	205	Servant 1651.
Wilson, Andrew	7	454	Transported 1664.
Wilson, Ann	18	329	" 1675.
Wilson, Ann	15	369	" 1676.
Wilson, Anne	WC2	112	" 1679.
Wilson, Charles	WC2	168-169	" 1680.
Wilson, Cobrey	15	442	" 1677.
Wilson, Edward	7	530	" 1664.
Wilson, Edward	12	554	" 1670.
Wilson, Edward	WC2	167,169	" 1679.
Wilson, Elizabeth	12	190	" 1668.
Wilson, Elizabeth	11	176	" 1667. Daughter of Matthew.
Wilson, Elizabeth	11	176	Transported 1667. Wife of Matthew.
Wilson, George	12	403	" 1669.
Wilson, George	16	168	Immigrated 1670 with wife and five children. Of Somerset Co.
Wilson, George	WC2	21-22	Transported 1679. (WC2, fol. 122).
Wilson, Giles	17	516	Service 1673. Of St. Mary's Co.
Wilson, Grace	12	383	Transported 1669.
Wilson, James	ABH	140,254	" 1651. (ABH, fol. 315).
Wilson, James	15	362	" 1676.
Wilson, James	17	445,567	" from Virginia 1673. (15, fol. 339).
Wilson, James	15	417,514	Transported 1677.
Wilson, Jane	WC2	158	" 1680 by Richard Lamb.
Wilson, John	12	194,242	" 1668. Servant.
Wilson, John	16	412	" 1669.
Wilson, John	16	405	" 1671. (17, fol. 574).
Wilson, John	18	291	" 1674.
Wilson, John	15	512	" 1678.
Wilson, John	15	532	Immigrated 1678. Of Baltimore Co.
Wilson, Jonathan	17	40	Transported 1672.
Wilson, Katherine	18	166	" 1674.
Wilson, Lawrence	18	331	" 1674.
Wilson, Margaret	17	356	" 1672.
Wilson, Mary	ABH	141	" 1651.
Wilson, Mary	18	174	" 1674.
Wilson, Mathew	16	537	Immigrated 1671 with wife.
Wilson, Mathew, Jr.	16	537	Transported 1671.
Wilson, Nicholas	17	463	" 1673.

NAME	Liber	Folio	REMARKS
Wilson, Richard	15	353	Transported 1674.
Wilson, Richard	15	540	" 1676.
Wilson, Robert	17	531	Immigrated 1673 with wife and five children. Of Somerset County.
Wilson, Samuel	16	458	Transported 1672.
Wilson, Thomas	18	15	" 1673.
Wilson, Thomas	18	167	" 1674. (18, fol. 331):
Wilson, Thomas	15	422	Service 1677.
Wilson, William	Q	73	Transported 1658.
Wilson, William	9	44	" 1663.
Wilson, William	13	65	" 1668. Servant. (12, fol. 386).
Wilson, William	12	404	Transported 1669.
Wilson, William	12	582	Immigrated from Virginia 1670. Of St. Mary's Co.
Wilson, William	18	167	Transported 1674.
Wilson, William	WC2	70	Service 1679. Of Kent Co. (WC2, fol. 151, 155).
Wilson, William	WC2	396	Transported 1680.
Wilton, Mr. Richard	ABH	46	Immigrated 1638. Returned to England and came to Md. again in 1646 with Leonard Calvert.
Wiltshire, Mary	WC2	253	Transported 1680.
Winall, John	9	44,374	" 1652.
Winbridge, John	15	514	" 1677.
Winches, George	2	425	" 1640.
Winches, George	ABH	10	" 1641.
Winckles, Edward	7	150	" 1663. (16, fol. 472).
Winckles, Edward	10	390	Immigrated 1666.
Winckly, Ann	11	462	Transported 1668.
Wincler, Bridget	9	450	" 1666.
Wincor, Jane	18	137	" 1674.
Wind, Daniel	10	350	" 1666.
Wind, John	10	507	" 1667. Servant.
Windall, Richard	12	358	" 1668.
Windall, William	15	445	" 1678.
Windall, William	WC2	255,340	" 1680.
Winder, Bridgett	8	486	" 1664.
Winder, John	9	450	Immigrated 1666.
Winder, Susan	8	486	Transported 1664.
Winder, Susanna	9	450	" 1666.
Winder, Thomas	18	24	" 1674.
Winder, Thomas	15	449	" 1677. Son of John of Somerset Co. Gent.
Windlas, Timothy	8	131	Transported 1664.
Windle, Thomas	WC2	66	" 1669.
Windleigh, James	15	449	" 1677.
Windoe, John	Q	58	" 1646.
Windoes, Joseph	10	499	" 1667.
Window, Elizabeth	WC2	277-278	" 1680.
Window, Thomas	11	344	" 1668. (17, fol. 356, 522).
Window, Thomas	WC2	277-278	Rights 1680.

NAME	Liber	Folio	REMARKS
Window, William	WC2	277-278	Transported 1680.
Windsor, Alexander	18	387	Service 1675. Of St. Mary's Co.
Windsor, Joane	17	440	Transported 1673.
Windwright, Martha	Q	71	" 1652-3.
Wine, Ann	WC2	35-36	" 1679.
Wine, John	WC2	35-36	" 1679.
Wine, Thomas	18	296	" 1674.
Wine, Thomas	15	574	" 1678.
Winfield, Thomas	6	81	" 1659.
Wingfield, Jane	15	332	" 1675.
Wingood, Thomas	9	321	" 1666.
Wingot, Thomas	16	308	Immigrated from Virginia 1671, with Eliz., his wife.
Winkfield, Sarah	18	291	Transported 1674.
Winley, Edward	8	478	" 1665.
Winlock, Charles	18	293	" 1674. Son of Edward.
Winlock, Edward	18	293	" 1674.
Winlock, Ruth	18	293	" 1674. Wife of Edward.
Winn, Margaret	18	293	" 1674.
Winn, Michael	5	123	" 1662.
Winn, Sarah	WC2	363	" 1680.
Winne, Ann	WC2	17	" 1679.
Winne, John	5	245	" 1663.
Winne, John	WC2	17	" 1679.
Winne, Leonard	6	294	" 1664.
Winnett, Thomas	11	167	Service 1667. Of Anne Arundel Co.
Winnington, Richard	6	210	Transported 1663.
Winslow, Anne	WC2	322	" 1680. Daughter of William.
Winslow, Anthony	18	152	Transported 1674.
Winslow, Elizabeth	18	152	" 1674.
Winslow, James	18	152	" 1674.
Winslow, Mary	WC2	322	" 1680. Wife of William.
Winslow, Samuel	7	154	Immigrated 1663.
Winslow, William	18	152	Transported 1674.
Winslow, William	WC2	322	Immigrated 1680 with wife and two children.
Winslow, William, Jr.	WC2	322	Transported 1680. Son of William.
Winsmore, Ann	16	522	" 1672. Wife of Robert.
Winsmore, Ann	16	522	" 1672. Daughter of Robert.
Winsmore, Elizabeth	16	522	Transported 1672. Daughter of Robert.
Winsmore, John	16	522	Transported 1672. Son of Robert.
Winsmore, John	17	33	Immigrated 1672. Of Somerset Co.
Winsmore, Judith	16	522	Transported 1672. Daughter of Robert.
Winsmore, Robert	16	522	Immigrated 1672. Of Dorset Co.
Winsmore, Robert	16	522	Transported 1672. Son of Robert.
Winson, Richard	15	544	" 1676.
Winsor, Alexander	18	177	" 1674.

NAME	Liber	Folio	REMARKS
Winsor, Alexander	WC2	308	Transported 1678.
Winsor, Jane	16	412	" 1671.
Winsor, Jarvis	WC2	259,260	Immigrated 1679.
Winsor, Thomas	13	112	Transported 1670.
Wint, Christian	7	138	" 1664.
Winter, Abigail	7	576	" 1665.
Winter, John	15	560	" 1678.
Winter, John	WC2	253,398	" 1680.
Winter, Mary	7	567	" 1657. Servant.
Winter, Robert	11	374	" 1668.
Winters, Joseph	13	1	" 1669. Servant.
Winterton, George	5	122	" 1660. Servant.
Wintle, Susanna	18	279	" 1675.
Winton, Charles	18	291	" 1674.
Wintour, Mr. Edward	ABH	66	Immigrated 1633.
Wintour, Mr. Frederick	ABH	66	" 1633.
Wintour, Robert	1	18	" 1637.
Winwright, Ann	15	436	Transported 1677.
Wisdale, Margery	5	246	" 1657 by Philip Calvert, Esq.
Wisdom, Henry	17	440	Transported 1673.
Wisdon, Henry	15	534	" 1677.
Wise, Christopher	8	410	" 1665.
Wise, Mary	13	65	" 1668.
Wise, Mary	15	318	" 1675.
Wise, William	15	370	" 1676.
Wiselack, Abraham	6	159	" 1652.
Wiseman, Elizabeth	15	504	" 1678.
Wiseman, John	10	507	" 1667. Servant.
Wiseman, John	17	440	" 1673.
Wiseman, John	WC2	108	" 1679.
Wiseman, Richard	15	359	" 1676.
Wiseman, Thomas	4	5	" 1652-9.
Wiseman, William	6	294	" 1664.
Witham, John	ABH	142	Immigrated 1651. Patuxent River.
Wither, Jane	20	185	Transported 1679.
Witherell, Giles	4	533	" 1659. (5, fol. 556).
Witherly, James	16	79	" 1670.
Withers, Hercules	15	376	" 1676.
Withers, James	9	436,437	Immigrated from Virginia 1666.
Withers, Margaret	18	137	Transported 1674.
Withers, Ruth	9	436,437	" 1666. Wife of James.
Withnell, John	8	483	" from Virginia 1665.
Withrington, Elizabeth	15	530	" 1678.
Witt, Moses	6	10	" 1663.
Wittaker, George	ABH	372	Service 1654.
Witte, Ralph	12	270	" 1668.
Witter, Thomas	17	26	Immigrated 1672. Of Charles Co.
Witty, Humphrey	11	374	Transported 1668.
Wockes, Elizabeth	12	576	" 1670.
Wolebancke, Elizabeth	18	137	" 1674.

NAME	Liber	Folio	REMARKS
Wolfe, George	4	48	Transported 1659. Servant.
Wolfe, Oliver	20	185	" 1679.
Wolfe, Will.	1	88	" prior to 1640.
Wolfe, William	ABH	87	" 1640. Servant.
Wollahan, Morris	WC2	287	" 1680.
Wollamson, Peter	11	537	" 1668.
Wollidge, Samuel	WC2	415	" 1666-80. Servant.
Wolmley, John	11	581	" 1668.
Wolseley, Mrs. Mary	15	371	Immigrated 1675.
Wolseley, Mrs. Winifred	15	371	" 1675.
Wolsey, John	9	322	Transported 1666.
Wolson, John	5	120	" 1661.
Wolston, John	16	452	" 1671.
Wolston, Thomas	16	304	Immigrated from Virginia 1671. Of Somerset Co.
Wolton, William	9	69	Transported 1660-5.
Wolverston, Walter	WC2	281	Service 1680.
Wood, Ann, Jr.	15	332	Transported 1675.
Wood, Ann, Sr.	15	332	" 1675.
Wood, Avery	10	309	Immigrated from Gloucester Co., Virginia 1665. Of Anne Arundel County.
Wood, Avery	10	309	Transported 1665. Son of Avery.
Wood, Benjamin	11	490	" 1668.
Wood, Edward	WC2	18	" 1648.
Wood, Edward	ABH	202	" 1650-1. Servant.
Wood, Edward	4	23	Immigrated 1654.
Wood, Edward	5	339	Transported 1663.
Wood, Edward	7	343	And Mary, his wife, of Calvert Co. 1663. (16, fol. 316).
Wood, Edward	7	471	Transported 1664.
Wood, Edward	18	332	" 1674.
Wood, Eleanor	Q	197	" 1658.
Wood, Eleanor	7	568	" 1665.
Wood, Eleanor	13	66	" 1669. Servant.
Wood, Elizabeth	ABH	230	" 1646. Daughter of Grace, wife of Wm. Smoote.
Wood, Elizabeth	5	211	Transported 1662.
Wood, Florence	8	131	" 1664.
Wood, Francis	11	569	" 1668.
Wood, Henry	ABH	44	" many years prior to 1650.
Wood, Henry	3	17	Transported prior to 1650.
Wood, Henry	6	128	" 1657.
Wood, James	15	534	" 1677.
Wood, Jane	15	517	" 1678.
Wood, John	10	309	" 1665. Son of John.
Wood, John	16	170	" 1671.
Wood, John	18	329,335	" 1675.
Wood, John	15	430	" 1677.
Wood, John	15	501	" 1678.
Wood, John	WC2	395	" 1680. Servant.

NAME	Liber	Folio	REMARKS
Wood, Mary	10	309	Transported 1665. Wife of Avery.
Wood, Matthew	6	48	" 1663. (12, fol. 283).
Wood, Mathew	15	322	" 1675.
Wood, Richard	4	69	" 1650.
Wood, Richard	5	610	" 1659-63.
Wood, Richard	4	616	" 1660.
Wood, Samuel	15	430	" 1677.
Wood, Sarah	15	454	" 1677.
Wood, Silvenas	8	89	" 1665.
Wood, Simon	8	131	" 1664.
Wood, Thomas	9	270	" 1660.
Wood, Thomas	13	17	" 1668.
Wood, Thomas	17	411	" 1673.
Wood, Thomas	WC2	217	" 1680.
Wood, Walter	9	325	" 1666.
Wood, William	ABH	179	" 1650. Servant.
Wood, William	11	168	Service 1667. Of Anne Arundel Co.
Wood, William	15	397	Transported 1676.
Wood, William	15	455,525	" 1678.
Wood, William	WC2	12	Service 1679. Of Somerset Co.
Woodall, James	15	514	Transported 1677.
Woodard, John	9	334	" 1666.
Woodard, John	17	463	" 1673.
Woodard, Joseph	10	265	" 1666. Of St. Mary's Co.
Woodard, Thomas	17	463	" 1673.
Woodart, Ann	17	26	" 1672.
Woodberry, Hugh	12	374	Of New England. Mariner. Acquires rights to lands in Maryland 1669.
Woodcock, Margaret	15	332	Transported 1668.
Woodcock, Margaret	13	79	" 1670.
Woode, Thomas	16	393	" 1671.
Woode, Walter	4	555	" 1661.
Wooden, Mary	6	153	" 1663.
Wooderd, Isabell	Q	68	" 1658.
Woodfall, Thomas	9	38	" 1665.
Woodford, Lucrecia	15	428	" 1677.
Woodford, Lucy	15	322	" 1675.
Woodgate, William	16	165	Immigrated 1670. Of Somerset Co.
Woodgreen, Edmond	5	607	Transported 1658.
Woodhered, John	WC2	259	" 1680.
Woodhouse, John	16	88	" 1670.
Woodhouse, Rose	5	249	" 1663.
Wooding, Robert	WC2	167,169	" 1679.
Woodland, Ann	15	319	" 1675. Wife of William.
Woodland, Ann	WC2	36	" 1679. Wife of William.
Woodland, Ann	WC2	36	" 1679. Daughter of William.
Woodland, Joseph	WC2	320	Transported 1680.
Woodland, Richard	15	319	" 1675. Son of William.
Woodland, Richard	WC2	36	" 1679. Son of William.
Woodland, William	15	319	Immigrated 1675. Tailor.

NAME	Liber	Folio	REMARKS
Woodland, William	WC2	36	Immigrated 1679 with wife and 2 children. Of Somerset Co.
Woodlow, John	5	257	Transported 1663.
Woodman, Thomas	17	608	" 1673.
Woodnat, Ann	ABH	230	" 1650. Servant.
Woodnett, Lawrence	WC2	256	" 1680.
Woodrofe, Christopher	WC2	199	" 1680.
Woodrof, Walter	Q	208	" 1658.
Woodrofe, Christopher	WC2	199	" 1680.
Woodrofe, Francis	Q	203	" 1658.
Woodroffe, William	Q	202,430	" 1658. (ABH, fol. 403).
Woodrow, Cornelius	7	88	" 1650.
Woodrowe, Christopher	5	90	" 1661.
Woods, Martha	18	176	" 1674.
Woods, Martha	15	429	Service 1677. Wife of Nicholas.
Woods, Mathias	16	38	Transported 1670. Of Dorset Co.
Woods, Mathias	18	319	Service 1675. Of St. Mary's Co.
Woodstock, Sarah	12	498	Transported 1670.
Woodunt, Lawrence	16	395	" 1671.
Woodward, Elizabeth	Q	72	" 1658.
Woodward, James	15	540	" 1677.
Woodward, John	17	61	" 1672. (15, fol. 433).
Woodward, John	15	565	" 1679.
Woodward, John	WC2	253	" 1680.
Woodward, Ralph	WC2	415	" 1666-80. Servant.
Woodward, William	15	446	" 1677.
Woodware, Martha	17	635	" 1674.
Woodyard, Alice	6	63	" 1658-63.
Woolcock, Mary	9	35	" 1664.
Woolcott, John	5	467	Immigrated 1649.
Wooldridge, Edward	17	443	Transported 1662.
Wooldridge, Nicholas	6	133	" 1651.
Wooldye, Richard	11	552	" 1668.
Wooley, Thomas	12	189	" 1668.
Woolford, Mary	6	134	" 1663.
Woolford, Mary, 2nd	6	134	" 1663.
Woolford, Roger	5	210	Immigrated 1662.
Woolford, Roger	6	134	" 1663.
Woolfry, Lucy	18	174	Transported 1674.
Woolgast, Cornelius	17	567	" 1673. Son of Otta.
Woolgast, Elizabeth	17	567	" 1673. Wife of Otta.
Woolgast, Otta	17	567	Immigrated 1673.
Woolhouse, Frances	2	567	Transported 1640. Servant.
Woolhouse, Francis	ABH	33	Servant 1640.
Woolhouse, William	5	530	Transported 1660.
Woolistone, Thomas	15	371	Immigrated 1676.
Woollbeck, John	7	464	Transported 1653.
Woollen, Edmond	18	35	Immigrated 1672.
Woollis, John	18	84	Transported 1674.
Woolman, Eleanor	18	160	" 1674.
Woolman, Richard	4	58	Immigrated 1649.

NAME	Liber	Folio	REMARKS
Woolson, Borry	11	537	Transported 1668.
Wooltey, Miles	12	194	" 1668. Servant.
Woolthwith, Henry	ABH	175	Immigrated 1649.
Woord, Thomas	15	501	Transported 1678.
Woosin, Ralph	15	354	" 1676.
Wooter, John	16	308	Immigrated from Virginia 1671. Of Somerset Co.
Wooters, John	17	503	Transported 1668.
Wooters, Richard	17	503	" 1672.
Wooters, Richard	18	36	" 1673. Son of John.
Wootes, John	15	424	Service 1677. Of Cecil County.
Wooton, John	16	297	Transported 1671.
Wooton, Mary	16	297	" 1671.
Wooton, Thomas	12	351	Immigrated from Virginia 1669. Of Dorset Co.
Word, Elizabeth	6	154	Transported 1663.
Word, Ralph	6	81	" 1661.
Wordsworth, Ann	Q	200	Immigrated Feb. 1657. Daughter of Richard.
Wordsworth, Joan	Q	200	Immigrated Feb. 1657. Wife of Richard.
Wordsworth, Mary	Q	200	Immigrated Feb. 1657. Daughter of Richard.
Wordsworth, Richard	Q	200	Immigrated from Accomack, Va., 1657.
Wordsworth, Richard	Q	200	Immigrated 1657. Son of Richard.
Workman, Anthony	12	194	Transported 1668. Servant. (13, fol. 112; 17, fol. 548).
Worland, John	17	348	Immigrated 1662. Of Charles Co.
Wormley, Ralph	7	569	Transported 1663-4.
Worpted, Richard	Q	67	Servant 1658.
Worrall, John	18	177	Transported 1674.
Worrell, John	4	56	" 1659.
Worrell, William	Q	71	" 1658.
Worrillow, William	17	356	Immigrated 1672. Of Somerset Co. Carpenter.
Worship, Walter	4	4	Immigrated 1658.
Worslake, John	5	210	" 1662.
Worslake, John	5	210	Transported 1662. Son of John.
Worslake, Magdalen	5	210	" 1662. Wife of John.
Worth, Anne	WC2	357,377	" 1680. Daughter of John.
Worth, Charles	11	236	Service 1667. Of St. Mary's Co.
Worth, Christopher	WC2	357,377	Transported 1680. Son of John.
Worth, John	WC2	357	Immigrated 1680 with wife and two children. Of Kent Co. (WC2, fol. 376-377, 414).
Worth, Joice	WC2	357	Transported 1680. Wife of John. (WC2, fol. 376-377).
Worthelen, Samuel	20	185	Transported 1679.
Worthington, William	7	526	" 1664.
Wortley, John	1	19	" 1638.

NAME	Liber	Folio	REMARKS
Wortley, John	ABH	72	Immigrated 1639. (1, fol. 50).
Worton, John	12	314	Transported 1669.
Worts, William	6	264	Immigrated 1659.
Woster, Timothy	4	216	Transported 1659.
Wotes, Jane	7	80	" 1664.
Wotts, John	18	116	" 1674.
Wouldhave, William	WC2	17,99	Immigrated 1679 with wife.
Woulfe, Nicholas	15	439	Transported 1677.
Wrath, James	8	128	" 1664. Servant. Of Baltimore Co.
Wrath, Parnall	9	25	Transported 1665. (10, 1667).
Wray, John	7	638	" 1665.
Wray, Roger	7	492	" 1664.
Wreath, James	10	598	Immigrated 1667.
Wreath, Mary	10	598	Transported 1667.
Wren, James	6	105	" 1659.
Wren, Peter	6	132	" 1657.
Wrench, Bartholomew	ABH	24	Servant 1645.
Wrench, Bartholomew	2	513	Transported 1645. Servant.
Wreneson, James	6	79	" 1663.
Wrest, Melleson	6	136	" 1658.
Wreston, Wadeing	8	503	" 1665.
Wright, Ann	ABH	141	Immigrated 1651. Wife of Ishmael.
Wright, Ann	ABH	229	Transported 1650. Servant.
Wright, Ann	15	357	" 1676.
Wright, Anthony	WC2	406	" 1677. (15, fol. 454).
Wright, Arthur	ABH	141,204	Immigrated 1651.
Wright, Arthur	3	174	Rights 1656.
Wright, Avelin	ABH	201	Transported 1650-1. Servant. (9, fol. 234).
Wright, Mrs. Barbara	16	129	Transported 1671.
Wright, Chr.	15	430	" 1677.
Wright, Christopher	5	188	" 1656. Servant.
Wright, Edmond	ABH	26	Immigrated 1646.
Wright, Edmund	2	523	" 1646.
Wright, Edward	WC2	321	" 1680.
Wright, Elizabeth	16	411	Transported 1671.
Wright, Ellen	17	330	" 1672.
Wright, Ellener	WC2	68	" 1679.
Wright, Francis	4	72	Immigrated 1659.
Wright, George	9	229	" 1665.
Wright, Henry	Q	208	Transported 1655.
Wright, Isaac	5	413	" 1662. (17, fol. 349).
Wright, Ishmael	ABH	141	Immigrated 1651. Of Patuxent River. (Q, fol. 440).
Wright, Ishmael	ABH	141	Transported 1651. Son of Ishmael.
Wright, James	8	39	" 1657.
Wright, James	15	396	" 1677.
Wright, John	ABH	161	Immigrated 1650.
Wright, John	4	139	Transported 1650.
Wright, John	4	174	Immigrated 1659.

NAME	Liber	Folio	REMARKS
Wright, John	4	568	Transported 1660.
Wright, John	7	85	" 1660.
Wright, John	6	27	" 1663.
Wright, John	9	386	" 1666.
Wright, John	10	217	Son of Ishmael, Sr., living 1666.
Wright, John	11	170,265	Married widow of Philip Conner
prior to 1667. (11, fol. 264; 12, fol. 221).			
Wright, John	11	549	Service 1668. Of Charles Co.
Wright, John	16	411,536	Transported 1671. (16, fol. 507).
Wright, John	17	52,454	" 1672.
Wright, John	15	409	Service 1677. Of Somerset Co.
Wright, John	WC2	12	Service 1679. Of Somerset Co.
Wright, John	WC2	206	Transported 1679. Servant.
Wright, Jone	17	424	" 1673.
Wright, Katherine	Q	441	" 1651. Wife of Arthur.
Wright, Luke	WC2	308	" 1678.
Wright, Mary	5	267	" 1663.
Wright, Mary	9	229	" 1665. Wife of George.
Wright, Mary	10	433	" 1667.
Wright, Mary	12	373	" 1669.
Wright, Mitchell	11	104	" 1667.
Wright, Nathaniel	17	611	" 1673.
Wright, Nathaniel	WC2	182	Service 1680.
Wright, Peter	7	81	Transported 1658.
Wright, Peter	4	16	" 1659. Servant.
Wright, Prudence	17	415	" 1669.
Wright, Richard	ABH	78,101	" 1637-40. Servant.
Wright, Richard	1	63,128	" 1640.
Wright, Richard	12	271	" 1668.
Wright, Richard	13	114	" 1671.
Wright, Richard	17	567	" from Virginia 1673.
Wright, Richard	15	567	" 1679.
Wright, Robert	10	523	" 1667.
Wright, Robert	15	430	" 1677.
Wright, Samuel	12	498	" 1670.
Wright, Solomon	17	611	" 1673.
Wright, Susan	5	514	" 1659.
Wright, Susan	5	413	" 1663.
Wright, Susanna	5	419	" 1659.
Wright, Thomas	ABH	101	" 1637-40. Servant.
Wright, Thomas	ABH	201	" 1650-1. Servant.
Wright, Thomas	9	234	" 1652. Servant.
Wright, Thomas	7	79	" 1664. (9, fol. 270).
Wright, Thomas	16	437	" 1671.
Wright, William	ABH	100	Immigrated 1641. (1, fol. 125).
Wright, William	ABH	25,163	" 1644. (2, fol. 514).
Wright, William	16	432	Transported 1671. (17, fol. 382).
Wrinch, William	15	525	" 1678.
Write, Ralph	12	415	" 1669.
Writt, Edward	15	453	" 1675-7.
Wroughton, Allina	17	547	" 1673. Daughter of Wm.

NAME	Liber	Folio	REMARKS
Wroughton, Diana	17	547	Transported 1673. Daughter of William.
Wroughton, Elizabeth	17	547	Transported 1673. Daughter of William.
Wroughton, Johanna	17	547	Transported 1673. Wife of William.
Wroughton, Thomas	17	547	" 1673. Son of William.
Wroughton, William	17	547	Immigrated 1673. Of Dorset Co:
Wyat, Richard	18	117	Transported 1674.
Wyat, Timothy	12	205	" 1667.
Wyatt, John	15	516	" 1676.
Wyatt, Nicholas	7	507	" 1664.
Wyatt, William	16	507	" 1671.
Wyatt, William	18	31,160	" 1674.
Wyatt, William	15	454	" 1677.
Wye, Elizabeth	18	94	" 1674.
Wym, Leonard	10	335	" 1666.
Wyne, Francis	4	584	" 1660. Servant.
Wyne, Francis	WC2	100-101	Rights 1679. of Charles Co.
Wynegood, Thomas	6	48	Transported 1661.
Wynlie, Richard	4	576	" 1661.
Wynn, James	9	222	" 1665.
Wynn, Lovey	9	222	" 1665.
Wynn, Richard	15	362	" 1676.
Wynn, Robert	17	575	Immigrated 1673 with Isabell, his wife. Of Calvert Co.
Wynn, Stephen	12	205	Transported 1667. Servant.
Wynn, Thomas	7	553	Immigrated 1665.
Wynn, Thomas	15	362	Transported 1676.
Wynn, Thomas	18	293	" 1674, with Ann, his wife.
Wynne, John	16	96	Service 1670. Of St. Mary's Co.
Wynne, Thomas, Gent.	5	304	Immigrated 1662.
Yableson, Matthew	15	560	Transported 1678.
Yableson, Nath.	15	560	" 1678.
Yalkley, Susan	15	514	" 1677.
Yallop, Giles	15	449	Immigrated 1677. Of Somerset Co. Merchant.
Yards, George	15	390	Transported 1676.
Yarrett, James	8	486	" 1664.
Yarwood, Elizabeth	12	391	" 1669.
Yate, George	12	558	Cousin to Jerome White 1670. (5, fol. 428, 429). Deputy Surveyor, Balto. Co. 1672. (15, fol. 183; 19, fol. 270).
Yate, George	WC2	144	Commission as Deputy Surveyor of Anne Arundel County, 1680. (WC2, fol. 155-156).
Yate, John	18	128	Transported 1674.
Yateman, Elizabeth	18	291	" 1674.
Yates, Francis	8	202	" 1664.
Yates, Henry	18	329	" 1675.
Yates, Humphrey	16	121	" 1671. (17, fol. 81).
Yates, John	17	575	Service 1673. Of St. Mary's Co.
Yates, John	WC2	167,169	Transported 1680.

NAME	Liber	Folio	REMARKS
Yates, Ralph	8	502	Transported 1665.
Yates, Richard	5	188	" 1662, with wife.
Yates, William	12	216	" 1668.
Yaule, Thomas	17	543	Service 1673. Of Talbot Co.
Yeamans, William	9	344	Transported 1665.
Yeates, Francis	5	531	" 1662.
Yeatman, Erasmus	7	429	Immigrated 1651.
Yembarer, Ann	7	466	Transported 1664. Servant.
Yeomans, William	10	572	" 1667.
Yerenson, Gilbert	8	129	" 1664.
Yerrell, George	15	501	" 1678.
Yewell, John	15	500	" 1678.
Yewell, Thomas	1	80-82	Service with Capt. William Clayborne, 1640. Of Isle of Kent.
Yewmersome, Mary	WC2	58	Transported 1678.
Yoare, James	18	137	" 1674.
Yoasley, Thomas	15	369	" 1676.
Yolden, William	18	38	" 1673.
Yore, James	WC2	95,96,97	Service 1679.
York, Ann	12	378	Transported 1669.
York, Peter	9	216	" 1665.
York, Thomas	ABH	244	" 1636. Killed at Nanticoke.
York, Thomas	11	348	Transported 1668.
Yorke, Ann	17	396	" 1669.
Yorke, William	4	554	" 1661.
Yorpe, John	18	174	" 1674.
Young, Alice	5	256	" 1663.
Young, Alice	9	33	" 1665.
Young, Ann	13	57	" 1670.
Young, Anthony	15	452	" 1677.
Young, Barbara	15	516	" 1676.
Young, Charles	9	321	" 1665.
Young, Charles	9	449	" 1666.
Young, Charles	17	475	" 1673.
Young, Daniel	7	520	" 1664.
Young, George	10	168	" 1660.
Young, George	7	563	" 1665.
Young, George	17	33	Immigrated 1672. Of Somerset Co.
Young, George	17	440	Transported 1673. (18, fol. 38).
Young, George	18	313	" 1675.
Young, Henrietta	13	57	" 1670.
Young, Honor	WC2	152	" from Virginia 1680. Servant.
Young, Jacob	Q	63	Immigrated 1658.
Young, Jacob	15	405	Transported 1676.
Young, James	10	429	" 1664.
Young, Jo.	18	331	" 1674.
Young, John	ABH	230	" 1651. Servant.
Young, John	15	539	" 1678.
Young, John	WC2	217	" 1680.

NAME	Liber	Folio	REMARKS
Young, Katherine	15	405	Transported 1676.
Young, Lance	15	516	" 1675.
Young, Lawrence	10	390,608	" 1667. Servant. (17, fol. 558).
Young, Lawrence	WC2	120	Transported 1680.
Young, Mary	15	558	" 1679.
Young, Michael	Q	29	" 1657. (17, fol. 67).
Young, Nicholas	Q	323	" 1655-8.
Young, Nicholas, Gent.	9	32	Immigrated 1656.
Young, Richard	15	534	Transported 1677.
Young, Theodorous	8	483	" from Virginia 1663.
Young, Theodorus	9	451	" 1666. (15, fol. 520).
Young, Thomas	7	520	" 1664.
Young, Thomas	18	294	" 1664. Service 1673. Of Talbot Co.
Young, Thomas	18	166	Transported 1674.
Young, Thomas	15	405	" 1676.
Young, William	7	563	" 1665. (8, fol. 484).
Young, William	11	378	" 1668.
Younge, James	8	129	" 1664. Servant.
Younger, Alexander	15	335	Immigrated 1675. Of Somerset Co.
Younger, Elizabeth	11	344	Transported 1668.
Younger, John	18	152	" 1674.
Younger, Mary	18	152	" 1674.
Youngman, John	12	205	" 1667.
Youngman, Samuel	6	93	" 1661.
Youngson, Christopher	11	537	" 1668.
Youson, Francis	4	616	" 1660.
Youth, William, a	5	358	" 1663.
Yowe, Stephen	4	130	Of Patuxent River. Aged 21 years in 1659.
Yowell, Thomas	ABH	84	Service 1640. Of the Isle of Kent.
Yuwell, Thomas	15	454	Transported 1677.
Zacharias, John	5	2	" 1661.
Zause, Mathias	1	166	" 1633 (See Sousa).

ADDENDA

NAME	Liber	Folio	REMARKS
Baker, John	WC2	320	Transported 1680.
Bissey, Richard	WC2	115	" 1680. (See also Byssy).
Boswell, John	WC2	33,134	Immigrated 1670 with wife Ann. Of Dorchester Co.
Boswell, Mary	WC2	33,134	Transported 1670. Wife of John.
Boswell, Robert	WC2	33	Immigrated 1677 with wife.
Brightet, Lawrence	WC2	406	Transported 1677.
Browning, John	WC2	73	" about 1665. Son of Thomas. Of Cecil Co.
Butler, James	WC2	158	Transported 1680.
Byssy, Richard	WC2	100	" 1680. (See also Bissey).
Chappell, Eleanor	WC2	319	Transported 1680. Wife of Thomas.
Chappell, Thomas	WC2	319	Immigrated 1680 with wife.
Jackston, Margaret	7	464	Transported 1655.
Kilson, Cuthbert	16	438	" 1671.
Klena, Andrewe	2	529	" 1644. Servant.
Morgan, Roger	ABH	60	" 1635.
Mulrean, Honor	WC2	129	" 1679.
Read, Ananias	1	73	" 1635.
Read, Thomas	3	171	Immigrated 1655 with wife and 3 children.
Richardson, Sarah	15	380	Transported 1676.
Robinson, James	12	269	" 1669. (15, fol. 404).
Weston, Thomas	1	22,23	Immigrated 1640 with 5 able men.